Space Law in the European Context

SPACE LAW IN THE EUROPEAN CONTEXT

NATIONAL ARCHITECTURE, LEGISLATION AND POLICY IN FRANCE

PHILIPPE CLERC

international publishing

Published, sold and distributed by Eleven International Publishing
P.O. Box 85576
2508 CG The Hague
The Netherlands
Tel.: +31 70 33 070 33
Fax: +31 70 33 070 30
email: sales@elevenpub.nl
www.elevenpub.com

Sold and distributed in USA and Canada
International Specialized Book Services
920 NE 58th Avenue, Suite 300
Portland, OR 97213-3786, USA
Tel.: +1 800 944 6190 (toll-free)
Fax: +1 503 280 8832
email: orders@isbs.com
www.isbs.com

Eleven International Publishing is an imprint of Boom uitgevers Den Haag.

ISBN 978-94-6236-797-5
ISBN 978-94-6274-876-7 (e-book)

© 2018 Philippe Clerc | Eleven International Publishing

This publication is protected by international copyright law.
All rights reserved. No part of this publication may be reproduced, stored in a retrieval system, or transmitted in any form or by any means, electronic, mechanical, photocopying, recording or otherwise, without the prior permission of the publisher.

Printed in The Netherlands

Preface

This book is timely, considering the rapid development of 'New Space' bringing more and more private actors into the arena, beyond the long-standing public actors. This requires a redesign of the legal framework regulating a wide range of activities in space, based on existing international treaties. This book is not a book of history, focused on the past: it is a book of anticipation, since the French National Space Law has been developed in anticipation of the development of private ventures, describing long-lasting principles. It is not a surprise that the first comprehensive National Space Law originated in France, under the leadership of CNES with its exceptional statute and role in Europe, that it stands at the origin of the first space entrepreneurs (Arianespace, Spot Image, etc.) and was drafted by people inventing the future every day – among them Philippe Clerc, the author of this book.

I have followed closely and carefully the design phase of this law when at ESA, in order to anticipate its consequences on ESA's activities and prospects. I have signed the agreement with CNES and the first implementing documents. Therefore, I can say that this law is not only a theory but has already accumulated practical experience and lessons learned. But even though I am familiar with this law, I have discovered a lot in reading this book which is providing in clear terms, the spirit and the content of the law. Still, there is a lot of work to do, considering the many ongoing developments everywhere in the world, not only in the United States, but also in Europe, requiring urgent reflections and actions. For the United States, the regulatory framework being developed is focused on serving U.S. national interests and striving to be the best jurisdiction in the world for attracting private investment and innovation; Europe should address a more universal approach to serve the future of Planet Earth.

This book will be an ideal reference for such reflections and actions by lawyers and much beyond, by space actors and others.

Jean-Jacques Dordain
Former Director General of the European Space Agency (2003-2015)
Paris, 8 January 2018

Foreword

It is my pleasure to introduce the book authored by Philippe Clerc, whose passion for the legal aspects of space activities is catching: as one of the fathers of CNES, the French Space Agency, in the early 1960s and after a lifelong involvement in the French space effort and its fruitful international cooperation, I find the work presented here, rich in lessons for a broad understanding of space law in France, policy and space architecture, especially with regard to what has become the institution and responsibilities of CNES.

In a step-by-step approach, the author reviews the 1961 CNES' Foundation Act up to its revision in 2008, therefore identifying law and regulation as assets for supporting national space policy ambitions and for reflecting the unique blend of French policy and programs. At the same time, they relate issues between scientific and technical research as well as between civilian defense priorities, privatization for market development, and the promotion of private initiatives. All these efforts centered around the office of the CNES are being balanced between strong national ambitions and the nation's role as a fervent advocate of European and international cooperation. From the legal point of view, this particular situation is due first and foremost to the exceptional legal status of CNES, conceived in 1961 as a public legal entity of an industrial and commercial nature – however with legal autonomy toward the State. Its extraordinary success rests on the flexibility of this status which permitted an unforeseen evolution. The incipient organization was supposed to be limited to an independent research department (*bureau d'études*) whose territory was nearly nonexistent: the development of the satellite launcher Diamant was entrusted to the organization devoted to the development of the military missiles called SEREB, and the launch operations to the Ministry of Defense on the Algerian site of Hammaguir. Even the satellites for the four so-called 'demonstration launches' of the Diamant rocket were to be built by SEREB. One wonders what was the domain of CNES in the mind of its political godfathers.

The small team in charge of the new (and minuscule) body, definitely unhappy with the idea of a '*bureau d'études*,' wanted to develop and run a full Agency, able to propose and manage all French space programs from beginning to end and, step by step, succeeded by acquiring the double capacity to propose and implement the French space program, both on launcher and orbital systems. CNES started to acquire know-how in satellite hardware by cooperating with NASA for the first French satellite FR-1, launched in 1965. Simultaneously, it built a telemetry-telecommand network of six stations all around the world, operational in 1965. In 1966, CNES convinced the government to build a full-fledged civilian launch site in Guiana for the future heir to the Diamant; at the same time, CNES created an internal Launch Division, as an obvious auxiliary to the Guiana Space Centre and conceived the follow-on Diamant B rocket, with a successfully first launch in 1970 in French Guiana. CNES positioned itself as the center of gravity of all French activities in space by adopting a doctrine of concentrating on the space matters in which nobody else was knowledgeable in the country, by importing and mastering the technology, then transferring the acquired technology to industry and to research centers. After having built the first French satellite, it transferred its expertise to the private industry for a first industrial satellite in 1972; after having developed the launcher Ariane as a prime contractor for the European Space Agency (ESA), it transferred the management of the whole program to Arianespace.

From the start, CNES adopted a three-pillared strategy:
- A national program including the launcher Diamant and the Guiana launch site, but also satellites as the Spot series and the Defense Helios and Syracuse programs,
- A bilateral cooperation with many partners, principally the United States, with successively FR-1, Eole, and Topex Poseidon, and the USSR (with the orbiting of French astronauts by Soyuz) but also with India, Israel, Japan, and China.
- A strong participation in the European Space Agencies: CNES was a major partner in the creation of the European Space Agencies ESRO, ELDO in 1962, and CETS in 1966. CNES also became in 1975 one of the main founders of the present ESA, built on the remnants of ESRO and ELDO. Therefore, CNES could also become a major player in outstanding European projects such as Ariane, Meteosat, and Galileo.

Legally endowed with a wide range of intervention resources, CNES used the flexible procurement tools provided by its law-facilitating agreements with the emerging space industry and the science community, for the support of its public program effort and private initiative development. Then, CNES succeeded in setting up operational bodies to forward the exploitation of its space-designed or developed projects, including the establishment of a commercial subsidiary or a start-up. This allowed for the establishment of an exemplary partnership framework with other public entities in the field of research, science, and space application. Last but not least, CNES has also been empowered to monitor international cooperation as well as dedicated European organizations with respect to French contributions to relevant space programs. CNES, for example, drafted together with Arianespace and insurance companies the first commercial space launch service contract which remains nowadays the international standard in this market. Also, the copyright clauses for the protection of access and enhancement of space remote sensing data and products were developed by CNES and its subsidiary Spot Image, before entering the market. All these organizations have become a forum for the generation of innovative legal instruments, and when necessary, for the support of their activity development. Such public effort has steadily been served by appropriate public budgets and labor resources secured in the long run, also at the level of the Law on Finance, where actions to be furthered are laid down in the so-called 'contract of objectives' and are agreed upon with the relevant supervisory ministries for a fixed period of five years. Due to this centralized organization, France acquired at the end of the 1960s the status of the third space power. By the development of a complete set of space tools, France was able to independently conceive, build, launch and operate satellites, complete with a major industry and its own launch base at the Guiana Space Centre. Thus, France was able to contribute substantially to the building of 'space Europe' and to participate in the most promising international projects.

As to space legislation, the 2008 French Space Operation Act had been designed to accompany the momentum of privatization of space activities which had started in France by the end of the 1990s in the wake of the privatization of Eutelsat and the opening of the Guiana Space Centre to non-European launchers. Its purpose is to set up predictable administrative and technical conditions under which a private operation on a space vehicle shall be authorized and controlled under French jurisdiction. This legislation has been maintained as consistent with the United Nations space treaties, the European Union general principles of law, as well as the national commitments of France toward ESA.

It is widely assumed today, following the conclusions of two triennial inventories made in 2013 and 2017 with all its stakeholders, that this new framework has met the joint challenge of ensuring safety of people and property, protecting public health as well as the earth and space environment, while contributing to the development of new space ventures and their economic spin-off. This achievement led the former Minister for Space Affairs, Genevieve Fioraso, to the statement in her report to the Prime Minister on the French spatial sector in 2016 that France has become a 'Space Law Power' of top class worldwide because, beyond the international recognition of its legal experts, French Space Laws as adopted in 2008 is now the second most applied in the world. French national space legislation has not only been an exemplary piece of innovative legislation in the field of high technology but it has also passed its test in practice. The role of CNES was also strengthened by the fact that it retained its full capacity as a space agency and technical center for the development and management of new space systems, for the operation of space vehicles of scientific and public interest, and for the support of innovation in general. In addition, as a repository of knowledge and skills on complex space system, CNES has been empowered with the responsibility of proposing and monitoring the relevant technical regulations on space system operations and is able to offer its support in the event of a setback or the necessity for emergency measures for safety.

Additional prospective surveys and hearings with academics and space stakeholders assume the robustness of this legal backbone to draft derivative regimes, *e.g.*, suborbital flights, innovative on-orbit services, manned occupation in outer space, and other space resources exploitation. All this led both legislations on CNES and space operations to be taken as a model by many countries in the development of their own space policy and law. Thus, the major contribution of this book is to explain in a well-documented but generally comprehensive way – also for non-legal experts – the interactive dynamics between the several texts forming national space law as a whole in accordance with other relevant legal instruments, namely the UN space treaties as well as other legislation relating to space applications, international agreements on space projects, as well as to ESA and EU instruments.

This book is further extended where necessary to other cross-sectorial legal issues applicable to space activities such as competition law, public procurement rules, public aids control, taxation law, data policy (free dissemination vs protection, liability for signals, interconnected objects, etc.), intellectual property, and new public-private transnational partnership models. This effort, sharing knowledge and experience on such complex legal issues, is supported by a 'system analysis approach' that is particularly helpful and accessible, especially for those who like myself are engineer minded! The book has been advantageously served by the rich experience of its author, who has acquired sound practical knowledge and vision in space legal issues by occupying over many years a great number of positions and responsibilities in CNES, Arianespace, and the French Space Ministry. He has held privileged positions for observing and interacting with all legal issues associated with the development and implementation of major space projects.

As a result, this comprehensive study on space architecture, law, and policy in France should be of assistance to all practitioners be it in the private or the public sector, for drafting or taking decisions on the matter of norms and agreements relating to space activities, such as contracts, partnerships, licensing, negotiations, as well as the adoption of laws and regulations, and furthermore for all of those – scholars or practitioners – who have to interpret or implement these instruments. It is also a valuable contribution for all those who are calling for the development of harmonized and enhanced space law, which should boost and secure the future of space adventure for the benefit of Europe and all countries worldwide.

Jacques-Emile Blamont
Paris, 9 January 2018

Table of Contents

Acknowledgment	xxxiii
Introduction	xxxvii
Part I The CNES Act from 1961 to Today	1
The Earliest Steps of the French National Space Policy and CNES	3

1 Statute and Mission — 7

- 1.1 Overall Original Mission under the 1961 Constitutive Act — 7
- 1.2 Expanded Mission Between 1961 and 2008 (FSOA) — 9
  - 1.2.1 Responsibility in Launcher Systems' Development — 11
  - 1.2.2 Building a Competitive Space Industry: CNES' Industrial Policy — 13
    - 1.2.2.1 Creation of a National Space Industry in the 1960s — 14
    - 1.2.2.2 Structural Adjustment Under New Framework of European and International Cooperation from the 1970s — 15
    - 1.2.2.3 Adaptation to the Operational and Commercial Use of Space by the End of 1970s and Privatization Process from 1990s to Nowadays — 16
    - 1.2.2.4 Abstract on CNES' Industrial Policy — 20
  - 1.2.3 Development and Management of Ground Facilities for Satellite and Launch Operations (Toulouse Space and Guiana Space Centres) — 21
  - 1.2.4 Shareholdings and Subsidiaries to Develop, Produce, and Market New Space Services — 23
  - 1.2.5 Public Interest Joint Organizations to Support Space-Related Research (GIP) — 27
  - 1.2.6 Participation, Along with the French Government, in the European Space Policy and Programs Governance (ESA and EU) — 28
  - 1.2.7 Responsibility in Defence' Space Segment Programs — 29
  - 1.2.8 Recurrent Space Operations — 30
  - 1.2.9 CNES as a Service Provider — 30

Table of Contents

	1.3	Synthesis of Chapter 1 on CNES' Statute and Mission before the Advent of FSOA	30

2 Governance and Management — 33

2.1 CNES' Administrative Authorities of Supervision – Space Policy Overall Organization and Functioning — 33
    2.1.1 CNES' Supervisory or Line Ministers (ministères de tutelle) — 35
        2.1.1.1 Overall Organization of the Government Supervision on Scientific and Technical Research and Space Policies — 35
        2.1.1.2 Supervision on Space Policy and CNES — 37
    2.1.2 Interministerial Committees on Space Policy — 42
        2.1.2.1 The Space Research Committee and the Space Council (1959-1976) — 42
        2.1.2.2 Committee on Space Applications (1976-1979) — 42
        2.1.2.3 The Space Committee (1989-1992) — 43
        2.1.2.4 The CoSpace (from 2013) — 44

2.2 CNES' Board of Directors and Executive Governance — 44
    2.2.1 Board of Directors' Competences — 45
    2.2.2 Committees Associated with the Board of Directors — 46
        2.2.2.1 The Board of Directors' Audit Committee — 46
        2.2.2.2 The Committee for Scientific Program (CPS) — 46
        2.2.2.3 Other Former Programs Committees — 47
    2.2.3 CNES' Chairman, Chief Executive Officer, Director-General and Deputy Director-General — 48
        2.2.3.1 Distribution of Powers Between the President and the Director-General since 1962 — 48
        2.2.3.2 The Current Powers of CNES' President, as Chief Executive Officer (CEO) — 50
    2.2.4 State Economic, Budgetary, and Financial Control: The General Controller — 51
    2.2.5 Public and Private Accountancy Rules: the Accounting Officer – the Statutory Auditors — 53
    2.2.6 Procurement Regulations: The Internal Procurement Commission — 54
    2.2.7 CNES' Staff Status — 55
    2.2.8 Synthesis on the Evolution of CNES' Governance Supervision — 56

3	**Resources and Associated Supervision and Audit**			**59**
	3.1	CNES' Budget Appropriation		59
	3.2	Auditing Bodies (ex-post control)		60
		3.2.1	The National Court of Auditors (Cour des Comptes)	60
		3.2.2	The High Council for the Evaluation of the Research and the Higher Education (HCERES)	60
		3.2.3	Other Specific High Level Assessment Missions or Appraisal Reports	61
4	**Mission's Conditions of Implementation: Space Research and Development Programs**			**63**
	4.1	French National Program and International Cooperation		64
		4.1.1	National Requirements	64
			4.1.1.1 General Regime for CNES' Program Authorization	65
			4.1.1.2 Specific Regime of Authorization on Space Operations and Space-Based Data (FSOA)	65
			4.1.1.3 Other Prior Authorizations: National Security, Frequency Spectrum, Network and Services and Competition Law Compliance	66
		4.1.2	CNES' International Cooperation Mechanisms	69
			4.1.2.1 Traditional Building Blocks of CNES' International Space Cooperation	71
			4.1.2.2 Other Forms of Arrangement	72
			4.1.2.3 Common Features on International Cooperation Instruments	73
		4.1.3	Implementation with Industry and Other Space Stakeholders	75
			4.1.3.1 CNES as Public Procurement Actor	76
			4.1.3.2 CNES' Partnership Policy	80
			4.1.3.3 CNES' Subsidiaries and Holdings	81
	4.2	CNES' Contribution to European Programs		82
	4.3	Interactions Issues between CNES' Missions		86
		4.3.1	The Issue of Potential Conflicts of Interests as Raised During FSOA's Law-Making Up Process	86
		4.3.2	Focus on Mission Entrusted to the CNES and Its President	88
		4.3.3	Impact on CNES' Staff Regime Regarding FSOA Officers	89
			4.3.3.1 FSOA Basic Controllers (FSOA Art. 28)	90
			4.3.3.2 Commissioned Officers (FSOA Art. 7)	90
			4.3.3.3 Sworn Officers (FSOA Art. 10)	91

	4.3.4	CNES' Traditional Activities as Technical Center and Space Operator Dealings with FSOA Delegated Activities	91
		4.3.4.1 CNES Activities as Space Program Agency	91
		4.3.4.2 CNES' Service Providing	92
	4.3.5	CNES' Stock Participations and Partnerships with Private Companies	93
	4.3.6	Conclusion	93

Part II The French Space Operations Act   95

5 Rational for Space Law-Making in France   99

5.1 The 1990s Telecommunication Liberalization Momentum Expanded to Satellites Information Services   101
    5.1.1 Privatization of Telecommunication Satellites Services   101
    5.1.2 Privatization of Earth Observation Satellites Services   103
5.2 Privatization of Launch Base and Launcher Services   110
    5.2.1 Agreements Between USA and Former USSR Countries Opening the Launch Services Market   111
    5.2.2 Agreements between the United States and China on the Commercialization of Launch Services   112
    5.2.3 Common Features of Bilateral Agreements on Launch Services Negotiated by the United States with China, Ukraine, and Russia   113
    5.2.4 Rules of the Road Discussions between the United States and Europe   114
    5.2.5 Cooperation between Europe and Russia for the Commercialization of Soyuz Launch Services   118

6 The Development Stages of Legislation on Space Operations, from the First Studies in 1999 to its Entry into Force in December 2010   123

6.1 Study Report 'The Legal Framework for Space Activities' from the Department of the Ministry in Charge of Space between 1999 and 2003   123
6.2 Referral to the Council of State by the Prime Minister in July 2004   126
6.3 The Study 'For a Legal Policy for Space Activities' Conducted by the Council of State between 2004 and 2006   126
6.4 Development of the Bill by the Ministries between February and April 2007   128

6.4.1		Addition of a Declaratory Regime for Operators of Space-Based Data	128
6.4.2		Explicit Exclusion of CNES from the Scope of the Law	129
6.4.3		Definition of the Regime of Investigation, Criminal Sanctions, and the Ascertainment of Offences	130
6.4.4		New Special Prerogatives for the State and CNES to Manage Emergencies	130

6.5 Legislative Scrutiny of the Law between July 2007 and May 2008 130
    6.5.1 First Reading at the Senate on 16 January 2008 130
        6.5.1.1 Implementation of a Licensing System Constituting Approval of Procedures and Systems 131
        6.5.1.2 Consultation with the Operator for Emergency Measures 131
        6.5.1.3 Restatement of the Powers of the President of CNES for Emergency Measures 131
        6.5.1.4 Referral to a Single Article on CNES Competences under FSOA 131
        6.5.1.5 Suppression of the Referral to an Overall Implementing Decree for the Law 132
        6.5.1.6 Recognition of the "Temporary Presence Exception" with Regard to Patent Infringement Seizure Actions 132
    6.5.2 First Reading at the National Assembly on 9 April 2008 132
        6.5.2.1 Introduction of an Orbital Control Phase for Space Objects 133
        6.5.2.2 Redrafting of the Definition of End of the Launch Phase 133
        6.5.2.3 Simplification of the Authorization Procedure for Operations 133
        6.5.2.4 Relaxing of Insurance Obligations 134
        6.5.2.5 Consolidation of the Liability Regime for Damage Caused to Third Parties 134
        6.5.2.6 Limitation on Recourse Action by the State (in Art. 14) 135
        6.5.2.7 Creation of a 'License Constituting Authorization' 136
        6.5.2.8 Strengthening CNES' Technical Compliance Mission as a Legal Entity 136
    6.5.3 Final Reading at the Senate on 22 May 2008 and Promulgation 136

	6.5.4	Finalization of Legislation on the State Guarantee in the Finance Act, following Validation by the European Union	137
		6.5.4.1 The State Guarantee under the European Commission's prior Opinion of 23 October 2007	137
		6.5.4.1.1 Singularity of the State Guarantee System for Space Damage	138
		6.5.4.1.2 Analysis of Compatibility	139
		6.5.4.2 The State Guarantee under Article 119 of the Finance Act of 30 December 2008	141
	6.5.5	Other Legislative Supplements Relating to the SOA: Amendment of the Insurance Code in 2011	144
6.6	Development of the Regulatory Mechanism: Implementing Decrees between 2008 and June 2009		144
	6.6.1	The Authorisation Decree of 2009 (D-A)	145
		6.6.1.1 Administrative and Financial Authorization Criteria	146
		6.6.1.2 The Concept of Technical Event	146
		6.6.1.3 A New Procedure for Pre-Certification of Procedures and Systems	147
		6.6.1.4 Various Clarifications Brought on some FSOA's Items	148
		6.6.1.5 Adjustments to the Obligation for the Operator to Take Out a Financial Guarantee or Insurance under Article 6 of the SOA	148
		6.6.1.6 Determination of the Date of Entry into Force of the Act	149
	6.6.2	The CNES' Decree of 2009 (CNES-D)	149
		6.6.2.1 Powers of the President of CNES at CSG	149
		6.6.2.2 Emergency Measures	153
		6.6.2.3 Maintenance of the Space Objects Register by CNES: CNES Decree and the August 2011 Registration Order	154
	6.6.3	The Space-Based Data Decree of 2009 (SBD-D) and Following Texts	155
	6.6.4	Development of Technical Regulations for Systems and Procedures (RT) and Operating Regulations for Installations at CSG (REI) – between 2008 and 2011	155

		6.6.4.1	The Order of 9 December 2010 Regulating the Operation of Installations at the Guiana Space Centre (REI-CSG)	156
		6.6.4.2	The Order on Technical Regulations of 31 March 2011 (TR or RT)	158
		6.6.4.3	Best Practice Guide (GBP)	161
		6.6.4.4	Common Features Between RT and REI-CSG	162
	6.7	Extension of Application of the SOA to ESA Activities, on a Negotiated Basis between 2009 and March 2013		163

7 The French Space Operations Act's Regimes — 167

- 7.1 Authorization and Control Regime for Space Operations — 168
  - 7.1.1 Architecture — 168
  - 7.1.2 Definition of Activities and Operators — 171
    - 7.1.2.1 Scope of the French Space Operation Act — 171
    - 7.1.2.2 Registration of Space Objects — 177
    - 7.1.2.3 FSOA's Exclusions or Exemptions — 181
  - 7.1.3 Authorization or License Application – Actors Concerned — 196
    - 7.1.3.1 Authorizations for a French Launch Operator or for any Person Providing a Launch Service in the French Territory — 197
    - 7.1.3.2 Authorizations for a French Satellite Operator — 198
    - 7.1.3.3 Disposals and Transfer of the Command of a Satellite in Orbit by or for a French Operator — 199
  - 7.1.4 Administrative and Technical Criteria — 200
    - 7.1.4.1 The Administrative Review — 200
    - 7.1.4.2 The Technical Review on Systems and Procedures Implemented in Space Operation — 201
    - 7.1.4.3 The Best Practice Guide — 208
  - 7.1.5 Licenses to Simplify the Authorization Processes — 209
    - 7.1.5.1 The 'Administrative' License Noting the Applicant's Moral, Financial, and Professional Guarantees — 209
    - 7.1.5.2 Operator License Noting the Technical Compliance of its Systems and Procedures — 210
    - 7.1.5.3 License Constituting Authorization — 210
  - 7.1.6 Procedure for Preliminary Certification to Accompany the Development of New Systems — 210
  - 7.1.7 Controlling the Preparation and the Implementation of a Space Operation after Its Authorization — 211

Table of Contents

		7.1.7.1	Obligations of the Authorization Holder	211
		7.1.7.2	Persons Empowered to Control Granted Authorizations	212
	7.1.8	Emergency Measures		212
	7.1.9	Penalties		213
		7.1.9.1	Withdrawal and Suspension of the Authorization (Administrative Sanctions)	213
		7.1.9.2	Fines (Criminal Sanction)	213
7.2	Operators Liability, Insurance, and State Guarantee for Damage Caused to Third Parties			214
	7.2.1	The Scope of Liability for Damage to Third Parties and Associated Insurance		214
	7.2.2	Governmental Guarantees (FSOA Art. 16 and 17)		215
	7.3	Legal Relationships between Private Stakeholders Participating in a Space Operation		217
7.4	Specific Rules for High-Resolution Space-based Data (FSOA Art. 23-25)			219
	7.4.1	Data concerned: High-Resolution Space-Based Data (SBD)		220
	7.4.2	The Entity Concerned: 'Primary Operator of Space-Based Data' (EPDOS)		221
	7.4.3	The Supervisory Authority: the SGDSN and the Interministerial Committee on Space-Based Data		222
	7.4.4	Restrictions on the Purchase and Dissemination of Data		222
	7.4.5	Regime for CNES' Earth-observation Activities		223
	7.4.6	Other Restrictions on SBD Dissemination		223
7.5	Other Procedures and Legislations to be Respected in France in order to Operate a Space Object or its Payload Services			224
	7.5.1	Authorization to Use the Frequency Spectrum		225
	7.5.2	Authorization for Satellite Telecommunication Network or Services Open to the Public		225
	7.5.3	Open Data Legislation		226
	7.5.4	Export Control Procedures		229
		7.5.4.1	For Dual-use Goods	229
		7.5.4.2	For Specifically Military Goods and Technologies	229
		7.5.4.3	Re-export of Imported Sensitive Goods	230
	7.5.5	Other Optional Procedures		231

8	Conclusion: Assessment and Perspectives for the French Space Operation Act	233
	8.1 Feedback from the Triennial Inventories of 2013 and 2017	233
	8.2 The 'Collective for Space Care' as an Ethical Spin-off of the FSOA	234
	8.3 Challenges with the New Space Economy at the Beginning of the Twenty-First Century	235
	8.4 Next Legal Challenges and Consequences on the FSOA	239

ANNEXES I - Original législation – French version	243
Annexe 1.1 – Loi relative au CNES codifiée au code de la recherche (Loi CNES)	245
Annexe 1.2 – Loi n°2008-518 du 3 juin 2008 relative aux opérations spatiales (LOS)	249
Annexe 1.3 – Décret n° 2009-643 du 9 juin 2009 relatif aux autorisations délivrées en application de la loi n° 2008-518 du 3 juin 2008 relative aux opérations spatiales (DA)	267
Annexe 1.4 – Décret n° 2009-644 du 9 juin 2009 modifiant le décret n° 84-510 du 28 juin 1984 relatif au Centre national d'études spatiales (D-CNES)	277
Annexe 1.4 (bis) – Arrêté du 12 août 2011 fixant la liste des informations nécessaires à l'identification d'un objet spatial en application du titre III du décret n° 84-510 du 28 juin 1984 relatif au Centre national d'études spatiales (AI)	283
Annexe 1.5 – Décret n° 2009-640 du 9 juin 2009 portant application des dispositions prévues au titre VII de la loi n° 2008-518 du 3 juin 2008 relative aux opérations spatiales (D-DOS)	285
Annexe 1.5 (bis) – Décret n° 2013-653 du 19 juillet 2013 modifiant le décret n° 2009-640 du 9 juin 2009 portant application des dispositions prévues au titre VII de la loi n° 2008-518 du 3 juin 2008 relative aux opérations spatiales (D-DOS)	289

Table of Contents

Annexe 1.5 (ter) – Décret n° 2013-654 du 19 juillet 2013 relatif à la surveillance de l'activité des exploitants primaires de données d'origine spatiale (DDOS-S)   293

Annexe 1.5 (quater) – Arrêté du 4 septembre 2013 relatif à la déclaration préalable d'activité effectuée par les exploitants primaires de données d'origine spatiale (A-DOS-D)   297

Annexe 1.6 – Arrêté du 31 mars 2011 relatif à la réglementation technique en application du décret n° 2009-643 du 9 juin 2009 relatif aux autorisations délivrées en application de la loi n° 2008-518 du 3 juin 2008 relative aux opérations spatiales (RT)   301

Annexe 1.6 (bis) – Arrêté du 11 juillet 2017 modifiant l'arrêté du 31 mars 2011 relatif à la réglementation technique (RT)   329

Annexe 1.7 – Arrêté du 9 décembre 2010 portant sur réglementation de l'exploitation des installations du centre spatial guyanais (REI-CSG)   337

ANNEXES II – "Original Legislation" English Version (non-official translation)   397

Annex 2.1 – CNES' constituent Act of 1961 as consolidated in the French Code of Research (CNES' Act)   399

Annex 2.2 – Space Operation Act of 3rd June, 2008 (FSOA 2008)   403

Annex 2.3 – Decree 2009-643 of 9th June, 2009 on authorization issued in accordance with SOA 2008 (Authorization Decree)   419

Annex 2.4 – Decree 2009-644 of 9th June, amending the 1984 CNES' Decree (CNES Decree)   429

Annex 2.5 – Decree 2009-640 of 9th June, 2009 on Space-Based Data (SBD Decree)   435

Annex 2.6 – Order of 31st March, 2011 on Technical Regulation (RT)   439

Annex 2.7 – Order of 9th December, 2010 regulating the operations on CSG facilities (REI)   467

ANNEX III – Comparison List of Usual Definitions	521
Comparison list of usual definitions and associated acronyms between RT-FSOA and IADC, UNGA and ISO Space Debris Mitigation Instruments	523
ANNEX IV – Concordance Table	533
ANNEXE V – Line Ministry for the Centre National d'Études Spatiales	579
Bibliography	587
About the Author	595

List of Acronyms

AD	Authorisation Decree: See DA
AECA	Arms Export Control Act (USA)
AERES	*Agence d'évaluation de la recherche et de l'enseignement supérieur* (2006) Agency for the evaluation of research and high education (superseded by HCERES below)
AGI	*Année géophysique internationale* International Geophysical Year (from June 1957 to December 1958)
ANFr	*Agence nationale des fréquences* French National Frequency Board
ATES	*Alcatel Thomson Espace and later Alcatel Espace*
ATV	Automatic Transfer Vehicle (an ESA contribution to the ISS program)
ASE (ESA)	*Agence Spatiale Européenne* European Space Agency
ARCEP	*Autorité de Régulation des Communications Electroniques et de la Poste* Regulation Authority on Electronic Communications and Post
ART	*Autorité de regulation des Telecommunications* (now renamed ARCEP) French Regulation Authority on Telecommunications, now renamed ARCEP
ASI	*Agenzia Spaziale Italiana* Italian Space Agency
ASL	Airbus Safran Launchers renamed in 2017 Ariane Group
BRGM	*Bureau des recherches géologiques et minières* Office for Geological and Mineral Research
CADA	*Commission d'accès aux documents administratifs* Commission on the Access to Administrative Documents
CAEPE	*Centre d'achèvement et d'essais des propulseurs et des engins* Centre for Completion and Testing of Thrusters and Engines
CAMR (WARC)	*Conférence administrative mondiale des radiocommunications* World Administrative Council for Radio Communications
CASDN	*Comité d'action scientifique de la Défense nationale* Scientific Action Committee for National Defence
CAO	Chief Authorising Officer (of all revenues and expenditures) *Ordonnateur principal (des recettes et des dépenses)*
CEA	*Commissariat à l'énergie atomique* Atomic Energy Commission
CECLES (ELDO)	*Centre européen pour la construction de lanceurs d'engins spatiaux* European Launcher Development Organization
CEL	*Centre d'essais des landes* Landes Test Centre
CEOS	Committee for Earth Observation Satellites

CEPA	*Centre d'étude des projectils autopropulsés*
	Centre for the Study of self-propelled projectiles
CEPT	*Conférence européenne des postes et télécommunications*
(ECPT)	European Conference for Post and Telecommunications
CERES (1)	*Centre d'essais et de recherches d'engins spéciaux*
	Test and Research Centre for Specialized Missiles
CERES (2)	*Comité d'Evaluation sur la Recherche et l'Exploration Spatiale (Cf. CPS)*
	Assessment Committee on Space Exploration Research a sub-committee of the below CPS
CERN	*Conseil européen pour la recherche nucléaire*
	European Council for Nuclear Research
CERS	*Centre européen pour la recherche spatiale*
(ESRO)	European Space Research Organization
CETS	*Conférence européenne des télécommunications par satellites*
	European Conference for Satellite Telecommunications
CEV	*Centre d'essais en vol*
	Flight Test Centre
CIEES	*Centre interarmées d'essais d'engins spéciaux*
	Joint Staff Centre for Special Missile Testing
CIBDU	*Commission Interministérielle des biens à double usage*
	Interdepartmental Committee on Dual Use Goods
CIRST	*Comité interministériel de la recherche scientifique et technique*
	Interdepartmental Committee on Scientific and Technical Research
CISG	*Communauté industrielle spatiale de Guyane*
	Space Industrial Community of French Guiana
CNER	*Comité national d'évaluation de la recherche scientifique*
	National Committee for Scientific Research Assessment
CNES	*Centre national d'études spatiales*
	National Centre for Space Studies
CNES-D	See D-CNES
CNET	*Centre national d'études des télécommunications*
	National Centre for the Study of Telecommunications
CNEXO	*Centre national pour l'exploitation des océans*
	National Centre for Ocean Exploitation
CNIL	*Commission nationale de l'informatique et des libertés*
	National Commission on Computer Technology (or Data Protection) and Freedom (or Liberties)
CNRS	*Centre national de la recherche scientifique*
	National Centre for Scientific Research

COCOM	Coordinating Committee for Multilateral Export Control
Comsat	*Communication satellite corporation*
COPERS	*Commission préparatoire européenne de recherches spatiales*
	European Preliminary Commission on Space Research
COSPAR	COmmittee on SPAce Research
COSPACE	*Comité de Concertation Etat Industrie sur l'Espace*
	State Industry Consultative Committee on Space
COPUOS	See CUPPEA
CISG	*Communauté industrielle spatiale de Guyane*
	Guiana Space Industry Community
CPCE	*Code des postes et des communications électroniques*
	French Electronic Communications and Postal Code
CPS	*Comité des programmes scientifiques (CNES)*
	Committee for Scientific Programmes (CNES)
CR (RC)	*Code de la Recherche*
	Code of Research (as to CNES' statute in particular under Art L331-1 to 8)
CRS	*Comité de recherches spatiales*
	Committee for Space Research
CSG	*Centre spatial Guianais (établissement du CNES en Guyane : base de lancement)*
	French Guiana Space Centre (the CNES' establishment of Guiana : launch range base)
CST	*Centre spatial de Toulouse (établissement du CNES à Tououse : systèmes orbitaux..)*
	Toulouse Space Centre (the CNES' establishment of Tpulouse : Orbital Systems…)
CUPEEA (COPUOS)	*Comité de l'ONU sur l'utilisation pacifique de l'Espace extra-atmosphérique (CUPEEA)*
	Committee on Peaceful Use of Outer Space (COPUOS)
DA – AD	*Décret d'application de la LOS (n°2009-643 du 9 juillet 2009)*
	Authorisation Decree. *i.e.*, the FSOA's application decree on authorization (n° 2009-643 of 9 July 2009)
DATAR	*Délégation à l'Aménagement du territoire et à l'action régionale*
	Delegation for Land Use and Regional Development
D-CNES	CNES' (Application) Decree, *i.e.*, the CNES' organization and functioning decree n° 84 510 of 28 June 1984 as modified by decree n° 2009-644 of 9 2009, following 2008 FSOA entry into force.
	Décret CNES ou décret d'application relatif au CNES

DEFA	*Direction des études et des fabrications d'armement*
	Armaments Studies and Construction Authority
DGA	*Délégation générale de l'armement*
	General Delegation for Armaments
DGAC	*Direction générale de l'aviation civile*
	General Directorate for Civil Avialtyion
DGI	*Direction Générale des Impôts*
	Tax General Directorate
DGRST	*Délégation générale à la recherche scientifique et technique rattachée au Premier ministre*
	General Delegation for Scientific and Technical Research
DGT	*Direction générale des Télécommunications*
	Telecommunications Government Office
DLA	*Direction des lanceurs (based in Paris Daumenil joint to ESA LD)*
DMA	*Délégation ministérielle pour l'Armement (DGA now)*
	Ministerial Delegation for Armaments
DTEn	*Direction technique des engins de la DMA*
	Technical and Industrial Directorate
DTI	*Direction technique et industrielle de l'aéronautique*
	Technical and Industrial Directorate *(from Air Force ministry)*
EAR	Export Administration Regulations (US legislation)
EADS	European Aeronautic Defense and Space (group) renamed Airbus (group) in January 2014, whose former space branch Astrium was renamed Airbus Defense and Space
EC *(CE)*	European Community
	Communauté européenne
EEC *(CEE)*	European Economic Community
	Communauté économique européenne
EGAS	European Guaranteed Access to Space (an ESA program concluded on March 2004)
EIG	see *GIE*
ELDO (CECLES)	European Launcher Development Organization *(or Centre européen pour la construction de lanceurs d'engins spatiaux – CECLES)*
ENSAE	Ecole Nationale Supérieure Aéronautique (now ISAE)
	Aeronautic High Level State School
ENAC	*Ecole nationale de l'aviation civile*
	Civil Aviation National School.
EOSAT	Earth Observation Satellite Company

EPA	*Etablissement public administratif*
	Public body of administrative nature
EPCU	*Ensemble de Préparation des Charges Utiles*
	Payload preparation complex
EPIC	*Etablissement public à caractère industriel et commercial*
	Public Body of an Industrial or Commercial Nature
EPRD	*Etat annuel de prévisions de recettes et de dépenses*
	Estimated expenditure and income statement
ESA *(ASE)*	European space Agency
	Agence Spatiale Européenne
ESRO (CERS)	European Space Research Organization
	Centre européen pour la recherche spatiale (CERS)
ETCA	*Études Techniques et Constructions Aérospatiales*
	a subsidiary of Thales Alenia Space located in Charleroi (Belgium)
Eutelsat	European Telecommunication Satellite Organization
EU *(UE)*	European Union *or Union européenne*
FA	Framework Agreement
FAA	Federal Aviation Administration (USA)
FCC	Federal Communications Commission (USA)
FSOA(LOS)	French Space Operation Act (on 3 June 2008)
	Loi sur les opérations spatiales
GATT	General Agreement on Tariffs and Trade
	Accord général sur les tarifs douaniers et le commerce
GATS	General Agreement on Trade in Services
	Accord général sur le commerce et les services (AGCS)
GBCP	*Gestion budgétaire et comptable publique (decree of 7 November 2012)*
	Regulations on public (or State) budget and accounting management.
FE	Fear event (in RT and REI-CSG)
	Evènement redouté (ER)
GEERS	*Groupe d'études européennes pour la recherche spatiale*
	European Study Group for Space Research
GEO	Geostationary Earth Orbit
GTO	Geostationary Transfer Orbit
GIE (EIG)	*Groupement d'intérêt public*
	Economic Interest Grouping
GIP (PIG)	*Groupement d'intérêt public*
	Public Interest Groupement
GIR SPOT	*Groupement interministériel restreint SPOT*
	Closed inter-departmental working group on SPOT

GWIC	Great Wall Industrial Corporation
HCERES	*Haut conseil de l'évaluation de la recherche et de l'enseignement supérieur (2013)*
	High council for the evaluation of the research and the higher education
IA	Implementation Arrangement (or Agreement)
ICAO	International Civil Aviation Organization
(OACI)	*Organisation de l'aviation civile internationale (OACI)*
IC	*Instructions de coordination (REI-CSG)*
	Coordination Instructions (REI-CSG)
ICPE	*Installations classées pour la protection de l'environnement*
	Classified Installations for Environnemental Protection
IFHE	*Institut français d'histoire de l'espace*
	French Space History Institute
IFP	*Institut français du pétrole*
	French Petroleum Institute
IFREMER	*Institut français de recherche pour l'exploitation de la mer*
	French Research Institute for Ocean Utilization
IGN	*Institut géographique national*
	National Geographical Institute
IGBP *(PIGB)*	International Geosphere-Biosphere Programme
	Programme International Biosphère-Geosphère
ILS	International Launch Services
INRA	*Institut national de recherche agronomique*
	National Agronomy Research Institute
INSEE	*Institut national de la statistique et des études économiques*
	National Institute of Statistics and Economical Studies
INSPIRE	(EU directive on) Spatial Data Infrastructure for the Purpose of Environmental Policy
	Infrastructure d'information géographique de l'Union Européenne
INTELSAT	International Telecommunications Satellite Consortium
IR	*Instructions réglementaires (REI-CSG)*
	Regulatory Instructions (REI-CSG)
ISS	International Space Station
ITAR	International Traffic in Arms Regulations (US legislation)
ITU *(UIT)*	International Telecommunication Union
	Union internationale des télécommunications (UIT)
ISAE	See ENSAE above
JORF	*Journal officiel de la République française,*
	The French official gazette

LEO	Low Earth Orbit	
LoA	Letter of Agreement	
	Lettre d'accord	
LoI	Letter of Intent	
	Lettre d'intention	
LOLF	*Loi organique sur les lois de finances*	
	Organic law on the finance laws *(1 August 2001)*	
LOS	*Loi sur les opérations spatiales*: see FSOA above	
LSI	*Loi sur la Société de l'Information (projet 2001)*	
	Law on Information Society	
LSF	*Loi de sécurité financière (1 August 2003)*	
	French Financial Security Act (1 August 2003)	
LRBA	*Laboratoire de recherches balistiques et aérodynamiques*	
	Ballistics and Aerodynamics Research Laboratory	
MEO	Medium Earth Orbit	
MMS	Matra-Marconi Space (become Airbus Defense and Space)	
MoU	Memorandum of Understanding	
	Mémoire d'entente ou protocole d'accord international	
MPTE	*Ministère des Postes, des Télécommunications et de l'Espace*	
	Ministry of Post, Telecommunications and Space	
MTCR	Missile Technology (Export) Control Regime	
(RTCM)	*Régime de contrôle de la technologie des missiles*	
NASA	National Aeronautics and Space Administration	
NATO	North Atlantic Treaty Organization	
(OTAN)	*Organisation du Traité de l'Atlantique Nord*	
NOAA	National Oceanic and Atmospheric Administration	
NSTP	National Space Transportation Policy (USA, 1994…)	
OECD	Organization for Economic Co-operation and Development	
(OCDE)	*Organisation pour la cooperation économique et le développement*	
OIV	*Opérateur d'importance vitale*	
	Vital Importance Operator	
OMC (WTO)	*Organisation mondiale du commerce*	
	World Trade Organisation	
ONERA	*Office national d'études et de recherches aérospatiales*	
	National Office for Aerospace Studies and Research	
OPECST	*Office Parlementaire d'Evaluation des Choix Scientifiques et Technologiques,*	
	Parliamentary Office for the Assessment of Scientific Choices	
ORFEO	Optical and Radar Federated Earth Observation	

OST	Outer Space Treaty (United Nation, 1967)
	Traité sur l'Espace Extra Atmosphérique (TEEA)
PAGSI	*Programme d'Action Gouvernementale pour la societé d'information*
	Governmental Action Programme on the Information Society
PCRD	*Programme cadre de recherche et de développement technologique (UE)*
(FTRP)	Framework Technology–Research-Development Program
PI	Prime Investigator
PIGB	*Programme international géosphère-biosphère* (IGPB in English)
PIP	Project Implementation Plan
PMRC	*Programme mondial de recherche sur le climat* (WCRP in English)
PRC	People's Republic of China
PSBDO	Primary Space-Based-Data Operator
(EPDOS)	Exploitant primaire de données d'origine spatiales
PSI	(the EU Directive on the re-use) of Public Sector Information
RAC	*Responsible d'avis de conformité*
	Responsible for Conformity Notice
RC *(CR)*	Research Code, see CR above
R&D	*Recherche et développement*
	Research and development
RFSA	Russian Federal Space Agency
	Also named Roscomos, Rosaviacosmos, RKA
RT	See TR / *RT* below
RTCM	*Régime de contrôle des technologies des missiles* (MTCR in English)
SAG	Space Advisory Group
	Groupe ad hoc 'Espace' à caractère consultatif, de la Commission européenne (années 90)
SBD	Space Based-Data (FSOA, Art. 23…)
	Données d'Origine Spatiale (DOS)
SBD-AD	Space Based-Data – Application Decree
SBD-MD	Space Based-Data – Monitoring Decree
SBD-PD-AO	Space Based-Data – Prior Declaration –Administrative Order
SBDU	*Services et biens à double usage*
	Dual Use Goods and Services
SEP	*Société européenne de propulsion*
	European Propulsion Company
SEPOR	*Service des programmes des organismes de recherche*
	Research Body Programmes Service
SEPR	*Société d'étude pour la propulsion à réaction*
	Jet Propulsion Studies Company

SEREB	*Société pour l'étude et la réalisation d'engins balistiques*
	Ballistic Missiles Research and Development Company
SERMIAT	*Société d'études et de réalisation de matériels et d'installations aéronautiques (implantation CSG)*
	Company for the Study and Construction of Aeronautic Equipment and Installations (CSG setting up)
SGDSN	*Secrétariat Général de la Défense et de la Sécurité Nationale*
	General Secretary for Defense and Security
SIMKO	*Société immobilière de Kourou (Guyane)*
	Kourou Real Estate Company (French Guiana)
SJT	*Société du Journal Téléphoné*
SNECMA	*Société nationale d'étude et de construction de moteurs d'aviation (Safran…)*
	National Company for the Construction of Aviation Engines
SNIAS	*Société nationale industrielle aérospatiale (Aérospatiale…)*
	National Company for Aerospace Industry
SNPE	*Société Nationale de Poudre et Explosifs*
SOPEMEA	*Société pour le perfectionnement des matériels et équipements aérospatiaux*
	Company for the Development of Aerospace Materials and Equipment
SOR-AO	Space Object Registration – Administrative Order
SPOT	*Satellite Probatoire d'Observation de la Terre*
START	Strategic Armament Reduction Talks
SYLDA	*Système de lancement double Ariane*
	Ariane Dual Launch System.
TAS	Thales Alenia Space
TFEU –	Treaty on the Functioning of European Union (TFEU, 2007)
TFUE	*Traité sur le fonctionnement de l'Union européenne (TFUE, 2007)*
TOSCA	Comité Terre, Océan, Surfaces Continentales Atmosphère (cf. CPS)
	The CPS sub-committee on Earth sciences, environment and climate
TR – *RT*	FSOA's Technical Regulation (2011)
	Réglementation Technique associée à la LOS
UE (EU)	*Union européenne*
	European Union
UEBS	*Union des employeurs de la base spatiale de Guyane*
	Union of Guiana Space Range Employers
UIT (ITU)	*Union internationale des télécommunications*
	International Telecommunication Union (ITU)
UN *(NU)*	United Nations
	Nations Unies
USC	United States Code

WCRP	World Climate Research Programme
(PMRC)	*Programme mondial de recherche sur le climat*
WMO	World Meteorological Organisation
	Organisation Mondiale de la Météorologie (OMM)
WTO	World Trade Organization, see OMC

Acknowledgment

I would like first to thank all those who have been encouraging me since the very beginning, at the end of the 1990s, to initiate the first studies in France on the evolution of its space law which is the main subject of the present work. I start with Jean-Yves Le Gall, at that time Director General of Arianespace and Starsem and now President of CNES, who always supported my efforts since my early prospective studies.

My appreciation goes to Pascal Colombani, Jacques Serris, and Arnaud Salomon respectively Director and Deputy Director for Technology, and Director of the Space Department at the Ministry of Research who allowed and promoted toward other ministers and their cabinets the setting up of the first thorough consultation on this issue under my coordination with officials, experts, and representatives of the space industry. This assessment led to the 2002 appraisal study about which I had the privilege to report for discussions at the High Level Symposium in March 2003, chaired by Claudie Haigneré, Minister of Research in charge of space affairs. I should not forget in my thanks the prominent contribution made by Bertrand Du Marais, State Councilor, to the whole legal assessment study, particularly with regard to the issue of Space Public Services.

In this respect, my sincere acknowledgment goes to all the experts, professors, students, and colleagues from space agencies, ministries, and industries in France and abroad who advocated and contributed actively between 1999 and 2003 to these task forces of prospective studies on a future French Space Law. I cannot cite them all here but let me mention a few of them. The Professors Philippe Achilleas, Mireille Couston, Armel Kerrest and Lucien Rapp. The legal practitioners Claude Dubreuil and Yan Aubin from Aerospatiale (Airbus D&S); Bernard Thery from ANFR; Paul Zermati from Arianespace; Alain Stevignon and Bradford Lee Smith from Alcatel (TAS); Alexandre de Fontmichel (Avocat), Michel de Guildenschmidt (Avocat), Peter Nesgos (Advocate, New York), Luc Dufresne from CNES; Bernard Schmidt Tedd from DLR; Christian Roisse from Eutelsat; Cecile Gaubert and Sophie Moysan from Marsh; Jacques Pelissier, Marie-Helene Montes, Ellen Verdure, Marie-Laure Mchanetski, and Thomas Lorne from the Ministry of Economy; Christine Brochet and Laure Tripier from the Ministry of Foreign Affairs; Stephane Dupont from Spot Image; Gilles Janvier, Didier Ardaine, and Michel Doubovick from Starsem; Martin J. Standford from Unidroit. The young promising lawyers Amine Laachani, Frédérique Lavina, Yolande Quelhas, and Caroline Videlier.

The distinguished experts Louis Laurent, Brigitte Vienne and Raymond Phan Van Phi from Arianespace; Franck Poirrier from EADS LV (Ariane Group); Dominique-Jean Rolfo and François Rancy from ANFR; Loic Taillanter, Michel Plazanet, and Dominique Mongin from ART (ARCEP); Fernand Alby, Henri Baccini, Daniel Hernandez, Guy Laslandes,

ACKNOWLEDGMENT

Roland Ivarnez, Didier Le Boulch, Bernard Mathieu, and Vincent Meens from CNES; Yves Blanc from Eutelsat SA; Pierre Lionnet from Eurospace; Isabelle Sourbes and Xavier Pasco from FRS; Dominisque Thebault from France Telecom; Stanislas Chapron from Marsh; Philippe Veyre and Charles Dupuy from Meteo France; Martine Kubler-Mamlouk and Pascal Chambon from the Ministry of Transports; Laurent Jacques and Olivier Tell from the Ministry of Justice; Anne-Marie Mainguy from Onera; Bruno Dejean from SGDSN; Philippe Munier and Prosper Izierte from Spot Image; Robert Blanc and Pierre Bescond from Satel Conseil; Pierre Latrille from WTO. I will not forget our deeply regretted fellows Françoise Bouzitat, Gabriel Lafferranderie, Hervé Loiseau, Jean-Claude Lumeaux, Laurence Ravillon, and Yolande Touré.

My thanks also go to Jacques Blot, Ambassador and State Councilor, for inviting me to contribute to the dedicated working group of its Report and Studies Section between 2004 and 2006 with Terry Olson, Julien Boucher, and Emmanuelle Cortot as rapporteurs. This enterprise led to the famous document 'for a legal policy on Space activities' proposing the first draft bill on space operation. Next my thanks are extended to those who supported the essential contribution of CNES to this legislative development from the beginning, in particular its President Alain Bensoussan between 1996 and 2002, Stephane Janichewski, as past Director for Strategy and Programs, and Elda Garrouste, CNES former Head of the Legal Department who championed this cause during all of her career. I would also like to offer my compliments to Julien Mariez, currently Head of Legal Corporate Service, who has assisted me since 2006 in this process. Finally, I would like to convey my utmost gratitude to Yannick d'Escatha, President of CNES between 2003 and 2012, who carried forward and defended this legislation project in order to maintain a key role for CNES between ministries and private actors. I am honored to have been so closely involved by him in this task.

I would like to thank a number of colleagues, among them legal and technical experts, who have supported and encouraged the writing of the present book. I wish to thank them cordially for their commitment, friendship, and cooperation. Simply to name them all would fail to indicate the degree to which I feel myself in their debt. I would however like to single out a few names. I owe appreciation to Caroline Aussilhou (Senior Expert Engineer, CNES Launcher Directorate) for giving valuable details on technical regulations; Christophe Bonnal (Senior Expert, CNES Launcher Directorate) for sharing his internationally recognized expertise in the field of space debris and providing valuable inspiration for possible legal solutions of this difficult issue; François Cahuzac (Senior Expert Engineer, CNES Launcher Directorate) for his insights into the drafting of the FSOA technical regulations in Chapter 7; Jean-Jacques Sussel (former Deputy General Director at CNES) for shedding light on the 1976-1979 Committee on Space Application; my assistant Corinne Dorel-Zucchi for the compilation and formal edition of all annexes; Caroline Dumas-Guillon (Legal Senior Expert, previously belonging to my team, now working at ESA) for her careful help in document research and her critical review; Christian Lardier (former Editor Manager of 'Air & Cosmos' Magazine) for his input with regard to the Russian launcher space policy in Chapter 6; Marie-Kerguelen Fuch, Clemence Lambrecht and Emilie Le Bert for the useful discussions and critical reading.

I owe a special thanks to Howard Nye (Senior Consultant and former ESA Senior Executive) who, as a native speaker, was meticulously reviewing my first texts in English of Chapter 5, thereby helping me to be more confident in further drafting my paper and Caroline Thro, 'precocious space lawyer' (and young trainee at ESA) for carefully reading Chapter 7 and exchange of views on Part I. I also wish to thank especially Marietta Benkö (Editor of the series 'Essential Air and Space Law') for having convinced me to accept and to carry out this project together with her sensitive guidance and her well-meant advice. I could not conclude without additional thanks and congratulations to Selma Hoedt (Publisher at Eleven International Publishing) for her patience, support and excellent work in the field of space law.

In conclusion, I offer my heartfelt thanks to Jean-Jacques Dordain, past Director General of ESA and Chancellor of the International Space University, for his sound interest in space legislation and its future developments and for caring about my book, especially for the great honor he awarded me by writing the Preface. Lastly, my foremost expectations were fulfilled as to the comprehension of the CNES study upon receiving the foreword from Professor Blamont. Indeed, Jacques-Emille Blamont was one of the most illustrious founding fathers of CNES and became in 1962 its first Scientific and Technical Director. For the past sixty years he has remained a world leader in the development of space science and exploration. I do not know how I can thank him for his unique testimony he gives us on the spirit of CNES and the earliest French contribution to mankind's conquest of space. Finally, I want to express my loving gratitude to Yolande, my wife, and my children Louise, Gabrielle, Zoé, Léonard, and Raphaël as their time was confiscated when writing this book.

Paris, 18 January 2018

Introduction

The French Space Agency, CNES for *Centre National d'Etudes Spatiales* or National Centre for Space Studies, was created 56 years ago, under the Presidency of General De Gaulle, to propose and implement an ambitious national space policy. CNES founding fathers were also those who supported, at the same time, the creation of these three European space organizations: the ELDO[1] and the ESRO,[2] the precursors of the present European Space Agency (ESA) on launcher and satellite development, and the CETS[3] on space telecommunications services. Their purpose, still applicable nowadays, is to provide France with an autonomous body to develop a strong domestic space capacity in the field of science, industry, and space applications together with initiating an ambitious cooperation policy with other space agencies at the international and European levels. Thus, the development of the French space capacity has been inseparably associated with an active policy of cooperation with other incumbent space powers such as the United States (since 1962) and Russia (since 1966 with USSR) as relayed in France with a constructive dialogue with existing public operators and research organizations, more particularly with the defense ones on behalf of first rocket projects.

The status, missions, and resources of the CNES were also significantly expanded from the beginnings by their legislative source, namely by its Constitutive Act of 19 December 1961 and the relating Programming Finance Act adopted by the same legislative assemblies. CNES authority on its side was strengthened by being placed by Act under the higher supervision of the Prime Minister. The creation of CNES boosted the French space program to the rank of third space power in 1965 with the first launch of a space object (A-1 named Asterix) with its Diamant-A rocket and the successful operations in orbit of the first French satellite FR1. These programs also contributed to organizing a strong space industry well-grounded to support European challenges and to competing on this promising strategic international market. The legal status of CNES remained unchanged for almost 50 years except for, on the one hand, an increased autonomy of functioning introduced by its application decrees as repealed in particular in 1976 and modified in 1979 and then reshaped in 1984 and, on the other, the additional missions gradually granted by government or

---

1 ELDO-CECLES on 29 March 1962 (European Launcher Development Organization, or *Centre européen pour la construction de lanceurs d'engins spatiaux*) was founded to develop and produce European launch vehicles. Its main programs were the Europa I and II three stage launchers.
2 ESRO-CERS on 24 June 1962 (European Space Research Organization *or Centre Européen pour la Recherche Spatiale*) was created to develop and build satellites for scientific and technical purposes.
3 ECST-CETS on 22 May 1963 (European Conference for Satellite Telecommunication or *Conférence européenne des télécommunications par satellites*) was set up to prepare negotiations with the United States and to prepare Europe's position on the international consortium Intelsat establishment.

resulting as a follow-up to its own achievement. Among its expanded competences, we may recall since 1965 the building, management, and safety authority of CNES at the Guiana launch base, since 1976 the capacity for it to develop commercial application systems or services (remote sensing, launch, telecommunication) with an autonomous capacity to create subsidiaries by the end of 1970s, in the wake of the Arianespace setting up model. In addition to its civil programs and pre-competitive effort on space application, CNES was entrusted in 1993 with a statutory competence on the national defense space program. However, its original procurement regime toward the space industry was gradually replaced by the ordinary law of public contracts, especially by 2007.[4]

The French Space Operation Act (FSOA) of 3 June 2008[5] provides France with a comprehensive national space legislation to facilitate the privatization of such activities in France in a safe way. This act also has a positive effect on competitiveness for enterprises operating under its jurisdiction, thanks to its appropriate system of liability, guarantee, and insurance associated with administrative and technical regulations compliance. On the other hand, this act did not lower CNES' competences as national technical center and space agency but instead empowered this agency with additional responsibilities in the regulatory domain, more specifically in designing and controlling the implementation of the French Technical Regulations on Space Operations and strengthening its responsibilities in launch safety and global management of the Guiana Space Centre. In this context, the present work aims to develop the role played by the law to the building up of the ambitious French Space Policy, closely linked to the setting up of an efficient European capacity, from the early 1960s, with the creation of CNES as the public space agency, and further with the FSOA of 3 June 2008 in accompanying the space sector privatization process.

Firstly, Part I, from Chapters 1 to 4, describes the French Space Policy & Program under CNES' design and implementation from 1961 to the present. It sets out CNES status, governance, and mission. It develops how its public interest space projects are authorized, financed, and controlled by the Government and Parliament and implemented in an international, European and national framework, especially in relation to the private industry.

Secondly, Part II details the legal background (Chapter 5), the building process (Chapter 6), and the current functioning (Chapter 7) of the FSOA of 2008 as a legal instrument designed to regulate and promote the private space entrepreneurship under its jurisdiction.

---

4 Following the application of Ordonnance n° 2005-649 du 6 June 2005 on contracts awarded by certain public or private entities not subject to the public procurement code.

5 'Loi n° 2008 -518 du 3 juin 2008 relatives aux opérations Spatiales' published in the French Official Gazette (JORF) on 4 June 2008. A nonofficial English translation of this Act can be found in Annex II.

The annexes of this book contain firstly the original legislation in French of the FSOA text and all its application decrees and orders (Annex I), secondly the available English translations of the same texts (Annex II), then as unpublished working documents: a comparison list of usual definitions (Annex III) and a table of concordance on different technical provisions between different FSOA texts and several international standards on space debris mitigation from IADC, UNGA, ISO (Annex IV) and, finally, the list of CNES Line Ministries from 1961 to 2017.

Part I
The CNES Act from 1961 to Today

The Earliest Steps of the French National Space Policy and CNES[1]

The launch of the Sputnik by the Soviet Union on 4 October 1957, the first artificial satellite to orbit the Earth, marks the beginning of the exploration of space. Such an extraordinary adventure of mankind, it immediately became a preferred civil area of competition between the United States and the former USSR in the existing context of the Cold War.

The return to power in May 1958 of General de Gaulle, who believed in a greater autonomy for France in relation to the two superpowers, the USA and the USSR, gave a new boost to scientific and technical research, especially in new strategic areas like space. Along with the USSR and the USA, the French government considered space as a vital concern and promoted a greater autonomy for France in high-level technological research to bring about the development of a national space policy.

The Interministerial Committee for Scientific and Technical Research (ICSTR) created on 28 November 1958,[2] pointed out the necessity to coordinate space activities among government administration departments because of the inter-disciplinary nature of space studies. This coordination effort was institutionalized by decree on 7 January 1959 with the creation of the Committee of Space Research (CSR), consisting of scientists, engineers, and representatives of the ministries concerned (Foreign Affairs, Armed Forces, Post and Telecommunications, Finance) under the chairmanship of the General Delegate on Scientific Research (Professor Pierre Auger) who reported to the Council President (Prime Minister

---

1   Some publications on CNES history:
  – C. Carlier, The First Thirty Years at CNES – The French Space Agency, edited by La Documentation Française/CNES, English edition, 1995. ISBN: 2-11-003368-1, Paragraph 1, CNES from its origin to 1992, p. 3-57.
  – P. Lelong, De Gaulle in his Century, Tome III, Moderniser la France – La recherche scientifique et technique (or 'Modernize France – Scientific and Technical Research'), Proceedings of the International days held in UNESCO, Paris, in 19-24 November 1990, organised by Charles de Gaulle's Institute, edited by La Documentation Française, Plon Collection Espoir: p. 677-681, 735-737, 742-744.
  – R. Aubinière & A. Lebeau, Le général Robert Aubinière, propos d'un des pères de la conquêtes spatiale (or 'The General Robert Aubinière, words from one of funding fathers of the French Space conquest,' edited by l'Harmathattan, 5-7, rue de l'Ecole polytechnique, 75005 Paris , 2008 2008, ISBN: 978-2-296-05193-5. Biography of Pierre Auger on foot note n° 73, p. 104.
  – P. Varnoteaux, (F), L'aventure spatiale française de 1945 à la naissance d'Ariane (or 'the French Space Adventure from 1945 to the birth of Ariane'), edited by Nouveau Monde Editions, 2015, 21, Square Etienne Saint-Charles, 75012 Paris, ISBN: 978-2-36942-157-3.
  – IFHE – CNES 3A. Proceedings of the Colloquium on the 50 years of CNES, hold on 9 February 2012 at CNES, Paris, 2 place Maurice Quentin, edited in December 2013 by IFHE-CNES.
2   Decree (décret) n° 58-1144 of 28 November 1958 (JORF 30 November) concerning scientific and technical research.

nowadays). The CSR mission was to propose to the government, and subsequently manage, a space research program. CSR's action, despite the quality of its membership, has been jeopardized by its lack of legal personality and associated proper budget. This committee proposed the first French space program (1961–1965) and the creation of CNES.

Then CNES, the French space agency, was created as a legal personality by Act of 19 December 1961 under Charles de Gaulle's presidency. Its aim was to design and implement the French government's space policy and it superseded the former committee (CSR).

The CNES Founding Fathers, in particular Professor Pierre Auger,[3] were also those who supported, at the same time, around 1962, the constitution of both European space organizations, the European Space Research Organisation (ESRO) and the European Launcher Development Organisation (ELDO), precursors of the present ESA organization. CNES by-laws were accordingly designed to endow France with an autonomous space capacity (launchers, satellites, instruments, telemetry, tracking network, scientific research, industry) serving a national independent policy in such a strategic emerging sector as well as to take part in international cooperation, either bilateral or European.

It thus shaped two driving factors that characterize the development of all space policy: *competition* and *cooperation*.[4] The competition driver derives from the high-level ambitions of the French space policy, in particular regarding autonomy as to strategic research and industry. Cooperation results from the genetic capacity of CNES to foster useful relationships with all other space partners.

CNES started its official activities on 1 March 1962, after the publication of its first Application Decree of 10 February 1962. This Decree, which regulates the CNES organization, including administrative and financial rules, was reviewed and superseded by the Decree of 27 January 1976, itself substantially modified in 1979, and afterwards superseded by the Decree of 28 June 1984, regularly reviewed since then, also known as the 'CNES 1984 Modified Decree.' This space agency promptly pushed France to the rank of third space power by achieving in 1965 the first launch of a space object (A-1) with the French Diamant rocket and operations in orbit of the first French satellite FR1 (Asterix). These

---

3 Professor Pierre Auger (14 May 1899 to 24 December 1993) was a famous physicist, discoverer of the "atomic auger electron effect". He was named President of the Committee of Space Research (CSR) established in 1959. He became the first President of CNES in 1962 and the first Director General of the European Space Research Organisation (ESRO) and was one of the forefathers (also with Edouardo Amadi) for the CERN, the European Organization for Nuclear Research created in 1954.

4 About this dualist approach *see* J.-J. Dordain, *Space is a Laboratory for Cooperation* (La Tribune 16 July 2016 n° 6005, www.latribune.fr/opinions/tribunes/l-espace-un-laboratoire-de-cooperation-586179.htm) where he recalls, with historical examples, the widely-held characteristic of Space activity's evolution being built *from competition to cooperation*.

The same approach is often highlighted by the Professor John M. Logsdon, in particular in its course 'Competition to Cooperation the Evolution of Global Space Activities' in the Space Policy Institute, Elliot School of International Affairs, The Washington University, Washington, DC, USA.

achievements yet relied on the implementation of its earliest partnerships, the first one with scientific and technical centers of the Ministry of Defence, the second with NASA, under the Framework Agreement signed on 21 March 1961.

No major change was made to the legislative status of CNES up to 2008 when France adopted legislation on space operations (FSOA) by a separate act on 3 June 2008, which entered into force on 10 December 2010. The CNES was empowered by this law with a full delegation as for the technical instruction of authorization applications (FSOA Art. 28g). The CNES president was entrusted with a special authority of 'administrative policing' on the general safety, security, and base management at the Guiana Space Center (GSC), and the European Launch Base for Ariane, Soyuz, and Vega.

In this context, Part I describes the institutional and legal framework of CNES, in particular its:
- Statute and Mission (Chapter 1);
- Governance and Management (Chapter 2);
- Resources and Associated Financial Supervision and Audit (Chapter 3);
- Mission's Conditions of Implementation (Chapter 4).

1 STATUTE AND MISSION

1.1 OVERALL ORIGINAL MISSION UNDER THE 1961 CONSTITUTIVE ACT

CNES' mission as defined by its Constitutive Act of 1961,[1] encompasses broadly:

- **Proposal of space development programs** for the government's final decision, namely a 'Research Program of National Interest,'[2] to be carried out by itself or another operational organization. The name 'Research Program of **National Interest**' also means **'general or public interest'** development program.[3] It basically consists of developing projects on space vehicles or instruments for scientific or any other governmental purposes.
- **Management and implementation of such programs,**[4] as contracting authority, or through cooperation or partnership, or through services provided by its technical centers' facilities or expertise; namely nowadays the Toulouse Space Centre (CST) for Orbital Systems, Science and Space Application, the Launcher Directorate for Launch Systems in Paris-Daumesnil and the launch range of Guiana Space Center in Kourou, French Guiana. As such, CNES was also empowered to implement its program by creation of dedicated public or private entities, or through financial participation agreements.
- **International space cooperation**[5] with other national space agencies. This competence is translated as follows:
  monitoring, in liaison with the Ministry of Foreign Affairs, issues relating to international cooperation in the space domain, and supervision of the implementation of that part of international programmes which France is in charge of.
  Basically, this provision constitutes the legal basis of the CNES permanent mandate (French representation) in decision-making in ESA's bodies (Council, Programme

---

1. CNES Constitutive Act, 19 December 1961 n° 1961-1382, Art. 2. This 1961 CNES' Act was codified by the Ordinance n° 2004-545 of 11 June 2004, into the French Research Code (here after RC), Art. L. 331-1 to L331-6, the whole being amended by Arts. 21 and 28 of French Space Operations Act June 3rd 2008 adding Art. L 331-7 and 8. **The current text of the CNES' Constitutive Act is reproduced in Annex I-1 with its English translation in Annex II-1.**
   CNES organization and functioning is at present regulated by the (amended) decree no. 84-510 of June 28th 1984, 'relating to the *Centre National d'Etudes Spatiales*,' available at www.legifrance.fr. This 1984 CNES' decree was amended in particular following FSOA issue by Decree n° 2009-644 issued on 9 June 2009, French Republic official Journal (*JORF*) 10 June 2009.
2. 1961's Act Art. 2.2 or RC: L.331-2 (b).
3. With regard in particular to FSOA's Art. 27 as to CNES exclusion to this act's authorization process.
4. 1961's Act Art. 2.3 or RC: L331-2 (c).
5. 1961's Act Art. 2.4 or RC: L 331-2 (d).

Boards, associated committees and working groups) or more recently within the European Union consultation processes. International cooperation therefore encompasses any kind of bilateral or multilateral international or European space cooperation, selective or permanent (*see* Chapter 4: §4.1.2 and §4.2).

- **Collection and publication of any information concerning space-related issues.**[6] This meant broadly that CNES shall be the state repository and disseminator of knowledge and expertise on space activities, be they of scientific, technic, economic, or political nature. This competence also paves the way for further CNES responsibilities on media production and communication, outreach programs, and promotion of space-based applications.

CNES has legal personality,[7] distinct from the one of the French State. That means that CNES disposes, under general authorization of its board, of an independent budget, can sue or be sued by third parties in courts, is solely responsible and liable in connection with its actions. In other words, despite its public statute and mission, the CNES is not a dismembering of the administration nor a branch of the government or a ministerial department like other space agencies in the world (NASA in particular).

Another asset resulting from its constitutive law is that CNES has been embodied as a State body of an **Industrial and Commercial nature** (*Etablissement à caractère industriel et commercial*, EPIC).[8] The advantages for CNES of an EPIC status, as regards to those of a traditional State administration or other public organizational status such as Public Administrative Organizations (*Etablissements publics à caractère administratif*, EPA)[9] mainly hinge on flexibility and autonomy of functioning.

This statutory attribution at the level of an act of parliament is an exceptional measure that deserves to be underlined, even for the time, since under the French Constitution,[10] the parliamentary process is only required for creating new categories of public bodies and not for their creation *per se*, in which case a specific decree suffices after the opinion of the Counsel of State. According to many testimonies from the time,[11] this legislative

---

6   Combination of (a) and (e) of RC: L331-2 (or of 1961's Act Art. 2.1 and 2.5): Collection of any information concerning space related issues (…) and publication, either directly or via subscriptions or granted subsidies, of scientific literature concerning space-related works.
7   1961's Act Art. 1. or RC: Art. L331-1.
8   Such EPIC status then was traditionally reserved to operational monopolistic public utilities such as EDF (*Electricité de France*), the monopolistic national electricity power supplier, or SNCF, the French railways state-owned company.
9   Such as METEO France, IGN (*Institut Géographique National*) the national geography agency, state museums, universities and high schools, official academies and agencies in France…
10   Art. 34 of the French Constitution: The law sets out the rules concerning: […] the creation of *categories* of public bodies.
11   *Cf.* Ibid. Carlier C. and Gilli C. in '30 premières années du CNES' ('First 30 years of CNES'), La documentation Française, Paris 1994. ISBN: 2-11-003368-1, p. 7-15.

recognition of CNES shows the great importance accorded by its founders, in particular, General de Gaulle, to the role of this body in implementing France's ambitions for the conquest of space.

Indeed, with such status, as discussed below in Chapter 2, CNES was given since its inception a large autonomy of governance with wide-ranging competences entrusted to its board of directors (§2.2.1); a strong executive management empowered by its president and director general (§2.2.3); an *ex-post* supervision by budget authorities on most of its decisions (§2.2.4 and §2.2.5); a trade and public regime of accountancy (§2.2.5); an autonomous procurement regime (§2.2.6); and a private staff regime, where CNES employees are not subject to the French civil-servant regime (§2.2.7).

However a singularity of CNES, as compared to other French EPIC or State-owned or -controlled economic operators, is that the latter are financed by their public mission's services turnover toward customers, while CNES' financial programs resources have always remained guaranteed by the national research budget, or by contracts or mandates financed by ministries or from other public agencies, including ESA. Thus, despite its commercial capacity as EPIC, CNES will never develop any 'commercial' permanent activity on its own. Basically, when raising such potential activities as to space operations or downstream applications, CNES would support their development and promotion into the marketplace through a concession framework agreement or a dedicated subsidiary, stock participation or *ad hoc* partnership (*see* §4.1.3.2 and §4.1.3.3).

1.2   EXPANDED MISSION BETWEEN 1961 AND 2008 (FSOA)

As indicated by professor Jacques Blamont,[12] one of the main CNES founding fathers,[13] such organization as designed by its Act of 19 December 1961 may be compared, in its earliest period to a 'design office' *(Bureau d'étude)*, without being vested with proper research and operation, production or management of large-scale facilities. Basically, CNES

---

12 In his foreword of this book and in the 'Proceedings of the Colloquium on the 50 years of CNES' organized by IFHE - CNES 3A, on 9 February 2012 at CNES, Paris, 2 place Maurice Quentin. Published under the aegis of IFHE in December 2013 (*see* footnote n° 6 above).

13 Jacques Blamont, born on 13 October 1926, graduated at the Ecole Normale Supérieure and received his D. Sc. from Paris University for his discovery of phase coherence in the multiple scattering of resonating light in excited atomic states under A. Kastler. He was elected professor at the University of Paris (1957) where he continued to teach to 1996. He is now emeritus professor, University of Paris VI. He created and directed the famous Aeronomy Division of CNRS (1958-1985) and was one of the few given the task of creating the French space agency CNES (1962) as scientific and technical director.
In this way, he is one of main actors of the French spatial program, in connection in particular with the NASA, the JPL, the space centers of the former Soviet Union and India. He played as scientific and technical director at CNES a major role in the development of the first French satellites, the creation of the launching site of Kourou in French Guiana (CSG) and the development of certain space probes thrown to explore the solar system. He is now in 2018 adviser to the President of CNES.

strengthened its position as the architect of space system projects and contracting authority: firstly in partnership with other French public research bodies having competences or experience in space-related projects, be they of civil or military status, and secondly through international cooperation, starting with NASA, which contributed to building up its expertise in satellite development (FR-1).

Then, CNES developed the necessary domestic capacity on space research and operation by federating or coordinating those of other national public bodies, among which were: CNRS (Division of Aeronomy[14]; SA, Spatial Astrophysics Institute; IAS, Meteorological Dynamics Laboratory; LMD, Space Astronomy Laboratory of Marseilles; LAS...); Observatoire de Paris[15] (Department of Space Research Paris Meudon Observatory; DESPA and its other affiliate laboratory or division...); CNET (Research Centre for Terrestrial and Planetary Environment Physics; CRPE); Météo France (Meteorological Dynamics Laboratory with CNRS; LMD); IGN (Space Geodesy Research Group; GRGS[16]...); CNEXO (now IFREMER); Ministry of Defence's related departments (DEFA, DMA, CEPA, LRBA, CASDN, CEV, CIEES, DTEn, DTI) or supervised bodies such as CEA (Astrophysics Department; Sap/CEA, Laboratory of Applied Biophysics; LPA...); ONERA (CERES[17]).

Then arose from the early 1960s between CNES and all these organizations an organized cooperation network though *mixed units or laboratories* or *long-run partnership framework*.[18] CNES also support the creation of a domestic space industry through a dedicated

---

14 The Division of Aeronomy (SA) was a French research laboratory of the CNRS (National Center for Scientific Research) specialized in the study of the ground atmosphere, the Sun, the telluric planets, the comets and the cosmological diffuse bottom. Created in 1958 and managed during almost 25 years by *Jacques Blamont*, it is the first French laboratory which dedicates itself to the scientific research since the space. It develops or contributes to the development of numerous instruments embarked aboard space probes, stratospheric balloons and space probes (Express Mars, Rosetta, sound Venera). The laboratory, implanted in Paris region to Verrières-le-Buisson and in the University Pierre et Marie Curie (Paris), merges at the beginning of 2009 with the Center of study of the ground and global environments (CETP) to form the LATMOS Laboratory (for *Laboratoire Atmosphères, Milieux, Observations Spatiales* or Atmospheres, Environment, Spatial Observations).

15 The *Observatoire de Paris* (Paris Observatory) is an astronomical observatory implanted on three sites: Paris, Meudon and Nancy.
The Paris Observatory arose from the project, in 1667, to create an astronomical observatory equipped with adequate instruments allowing to establish map for the navigation. Coming as a supplement to the Academy of Science established in 1666, it played a very important role in the western astronomy. It is there that took development in France the sciences as the geodesy, the mapping and the meteorology. It is the oldest observatory of the World still running.

16 The GRGS for Space Geodesy Research Group is an association of research teams from IGN, CNES, CERGA (Côte d'Azur Observatory) and the Bureau of Longitude (Bureau des Longitudes).
The Bureau des Longitudes on its side is a French scientific institution, founded by decree of 25 June 1795 under the impulse of Henri Grégoire, and charged with the improvement of nautical navigation, standardisation of time-keeping, geodesy and astronomical observation. During the 19th century, it was responsible for synchronizing clocks across the world, to cope with the naval mastery of England !

17 CERES for *Centre d'Essai et de Recherche d'Engins Spéciaux* or Test and Research Centre for Special Vehicles. CERES has a launching site located on the 'Iles du levant' near Hyeres South of France.

18 Ibid C. Carlier & M. Gilli *The First Thirty Years at CNES - The French Space Agency*, p. 184-186.

procurement policy (Industrial policy) directed to the existing French industry, whether military or civil, mainly from the aeronautics, missiles, nuclear, and electronics sectors. This policy was followed up later, from the late 1970s, by a 'subsidiary policy' to foster downstream the exploitation of its space projects in the marketplace. By this way CNES progressively expanded its scope of competence without formal legal changes in its constitutive act (1961) or organic decree. Notwithstanding these remarkable developments of responsibilities on which one may have questioned a tendency to over-centralize,[19] CNES, as a constant policy, always privileged cooperation and contract out for the development, operation, and commercialization of space systems, rather than carry out itself or soliciting specific enforceable orders from the government.

As another feature, also mentioned in the introduction of this book, CNES policy concentrated its efforts in space matters in which nobody else was knowledgeable, where its value addition is higher, and for the rests imported and mastered technology from others, then transferred the acquired technology and associated management skills to industry and to research centers, and so on.

These expended missions from 1961 to 2008 may be summarized as follows:

1.2.1   Responsibility in Launcher Systems' Development

Following the success of the maiden flight on 26 November 1965 of the first French launch vehicle Diamant A, initially developed under the aegis of the ministry of the Army (DMA[20]) and SEREB[21] being the prime contractor, CNES took the full responsibility in launcher's development programs on 30 June 1967 after a difficult agreement with the Ministry of Army, becoming *contracting and design authority* for the French Diamant-B's development project. CNES also took up the operational responsibility of launching vehicle from its new base of Kourou (Guiana Space Centre, CSG) starting in 1968 with the earliest French sounding rocket Veronique AGI, initially developed under the aegis of the LRBA from DMA (Ministerial Delegation for Armaments). CNES managed the *development and exploitation phases* of Diamant-B vehicle, which was successfully launched on 10 March 1970 inaugurating CSG as orbital vehicle launching base. After the successful launch on 27 September 1975 of the Aura research satellite of the French D-2 family, the Diamant-B upgraded BP4 program was closed by CNES in order to concentrate national resources

---

19 As commented by 1993 Gérard Longuet, Minister of Industry, Post ad Telecommunication and Export Trade, thus responsible for directing space policy in France, when prefacing the Carlier & Gilli, *The First Thirty Years at CNES – The French Space Agency*, p. IX.

20 *Délégation ministérielle pour l'armement*, or Ministerial Delegation for Armaments, now DGA for *Direction générale de l'armement* or General Delegation for Armaments

21 *Société pour l'étude et la réalisation d'engins balistiques* or Ballistic Missiles Research and Development Company.

on the new European launch vehicle *Ariane*. Indeed, as a result of the European 'L-IIIS Arrangement,' on 1 August 1973, CNES was delegated by ESA State members the responsibility of the development phase of the new launch vehicle Ariane. This delegation of duties to one national body was an exception for ESA (and ELDO) programs rules. According to contemporaries witnesses, such as Claude Carlier and Marcel Gilli,[22] the reason for this specific treatment was that CNES was the only European body with the necessary expertise[23] to determine the objectives of the program concerning technical matters, scheduling, costing management practices, and delegation of work to manufacturers. In addition, the financial risk for the other European member states was limited, since CNES accepted to absorb any extra cost and to provide its free workforce, in particular to avoid jeopardizing the geographical return for French industry. As part of this delegation, CNES was the sole *designing and contracting authority* toward the whole European industry in direct relationship between prime contractors and their subcontractors. On its side, Aerospatiale (merged into EADS in 2000 and since 2015 superseded by ASL-ArianeGroup) was delegated the role of final assembly with the responsibility of 'industrial architect.'

In March 2004, following the ESA conclusion of the recovery plan Ariane 5 ECA and the associate European Guaranteed Access to Space program (EGAS), EADS (now Ariane-Group) became the *Ariane's prime contractor* both for the ongoing production and for future developments. Nowadays, since the December 2014 ESA board's decision for the development of Ariane VI, the prime contractor and future commercial operator Ariane-Group has become the *design authority on the launcher system development*. On their side, ESA as *contracting authority* and CNES acting as the latter *technical expert*, both having collocated their launcher directorate on the same site of Paris-Daumesnil, retained the responsibility to specify and oversee the *high-level requirement of the system* under development.

CNES also retained its responsibility as prime contractor and *design authority of the related ground segment* (ELA 4) on the Guiana Space Centre.

Furthermore, about the future of launchers, CNES initiated the Prometheus' program of research and technology on reusable engine, currently carried out in partnership with ESA and ArianeGroup. CNES has also committed to develop a demonstrator of reusable launcher named 'Callisto'[24] under cooperation agreements, in particular with DLR (Germany) and potentially with JAXA (Japan).

---

22 *Ibid* Carlier & Gilli, *The First Thirty Years at CNES – The French Space Agency*, p. 41-42.
23 *I.e.*, CNES' system competence and design authority as successfully developed through Diamant-B the unique knowledge of interface ground-space interface, in particular with CSG facilities.
24 Pascal Tatiossian, Jean Desmariaux, Matthieu Garcia from CNES Launcher Directorate, CALLISTO Project – Reusable First Stage Rocket Demonstrator, 7th European conference for Aeronautics and Space (EUCASS), October 2017, 52 rue Jacques Hillairet 75612 Paris, France. DOI:10.13009 / EUCASS 2017-680.

1.2.2 Building a Competitive Space Industry: CNES' Industrial Policy

CNES from the beginnings stimulated French firms with the purpose of setting a strong and sustainable capacity able to implement the development and exploitation of its space systems program and to meet the political ambitions of the French government. The fundamental increment of space industry, by reference to the traditional one, relies on the fact that a space mission design is either seeking excellence in materials and service performances than responding to specific quality and reliability requirements to meet space environment constraints such as vacuum, radiation, celestial motion mechanisms, microgravity, thermic, remoteness from earth etc. An emerging space industry needs also, for being sustainable in the long run, to be assured in receiving further ordering from potential customers (government and/or market) to maintain its large-scale facilities, human resources, and expertise at the hedge of the technological state. At the time of creation of CNES no space industry really existed but its basement was already in place in the aeronautics and electronic sectors whether civil or military. Then CNES encouraged national industries to develop their skills of expertise toward space activities through a process that has been named 'industrial policy.'

This approach was implemented through the means of its flexible procurement instruments, in a coherent research and technology program with industry on critical subsystems and of course according the procurement needs of its main launcher and satellite systems development projects. The preference given to French-made, and later to European-made, components and systems should not be construed as the sign of a narrow protectionist attitude but as the objective of a balanced policy between the needs for quality and affordable materials and those of limiting import dependence toward sensible technologies controlled by foreign private monopolistic industries or government export control licenses. Thus, to avoid to restrict the domestic industries to the simple role of subcontractor, CNES soon encouraged the emergence of French prime contractors in critical construction and integration of space systems able to build facilities, expertise, and a strong network of industrial partners, first on satellites then on launcher systems.

Within this context, the French space industrial policy evolution can be divided up into the five following phases, each one addressing firstly launch industry and secondly satellite industry:
- The creation of a national space industry in the 1960s;
- Structural adjustment to European and international cooperation frameworks from the early 1970s;
- Adaptation to the operational and commercial use of space, by the end of 1970s;
- Privatization of space operators by the end of the 1990s;

- Emergence of 'New Space' industry from players of the new digital economy, from mid-2000s onwards.

The two latest phases on the list, about privatization and New Space, are further discussed in Part II, namely in Chapter 5 and in the conclusion of Chapter 7, as being part of the 2008 FSOA's law-making purpose and perspectives.

As a consequence, in this Part I, the phases of 'adaptation to the operational and commercial use of space by the end of 1970s' and 'the privatization process from 1990s' follow each other merged under a single heading. As part of CNES' responsibilities in its national space agency's mission, we may retain the following achievements:

1.2.2.1 Creation of a National Space Industry in the 1960s

With regard to the **launcher industry** the system and propulsion design and manufacturing, which were initially driven under the responsibility of the ministry of the Army (through the leadership of DMA and its research laboratory LRBA[25]) were first transferred to fully state owned limited companies such as:

- **SEREB** company, created on 17 July 1959 for the study and realization of ballistic missiles for the French nuclear strategic force, was under the Diamant programs, the prime manufacturer of the successful first French civil space launcher (Diamant A in 1965). In 1970, SEREB's merger with Nord Aviation and, Sud Aviation led to the creation of **SNIAS, later renamed Aerospatiale**.
- **SEPR**, the Jet Propulsion Studies Company (*société d'étude pour la propulsion à reaction*) led to the founding of **SEP**,[26] the European Propulsion Company (*Société européenne de Propulsion*) located in Vernon.

On the **satellite industry** side, the first line of technological satellite (D-1A) was fully awarded for manufacturing to the national industry, under the prime Contractorship (*maîtrise d'oeuvre*) of CNES. As early as 1969, CNES transferred this 'prime Contractorship' responsibility to **Matra** for the second satellite development program named D-2B. The 'Symphonie' joint geostationary telecommunications satellite project, agreed upon on 6 June 1967 between France and West Germany, gave rise to **CIFAS**,[27] the first Franco-

---

[25] LRBA for «*Laboratoire de recherches balistiques et aérodynamiques*» or Ballistic and Aerodynamics Research Laboratory located in the DMA's site of Vernon.

[26] SEP is the very early structure of Safran, the prime contractor on launcher propulsion, still located in Vernon, which merged in 2015 with Airbus Defense & Space to create Airbus Safran Launchers (ASL). The latter was
renamed ArianeGroup in May 2017 after taking over of the Arianespace control by acquiring the whole historical shareholding of CNES (see §1.2.3).

[27] CIFAS for *Consortium Industriel Franco-Allemand pour le satellite Symphonie*, Consortium of Franco-German Manufacturers for the Symphonie Satellite.

German consortium grouping together six manufacturers[28] and then establishing the basis for new industrial cooperation schemes at the European level.

1.2.2.2 Structural Adjustment Under New Framework of European and International Cooperation from the 1970s

Under the European *Ariane* **launcher** project decided in 1973, ESA members delegated prime Contractorship of the Ariane system to CNES for the whole program *development phase*; The latter convinced its partners to set up a completely dedicated European organization of more than 50 European companies. France contributing to 64% of financing to the project, four French companies were in charge of coordinating the main assemblies:

- **Aerospatiale-SNIAS** (formerly SEREB) the industrial architect (assembly and integration of the launch vehicle and also the prime contractor of the first and third stage).
- **SEP** prime contractor for all engines.
- **Matra** for the vehicle bay equipment.
- **Air Liquide** for the third stage fuel tanks using cryogenic propellants special technology.

On application satellites (telecommunications…), France's commitments to European programs, whether bilateral with Germany on 'Symphonie' or multilateral through **CERS/ESRO**[29] (as the predecessor of the European Space Agency on satellite development) led to a sharing of European manufacturers in line with the geographic return rules set up under these cooperative program organizations or agreements for the procurement sharing of the relevant system's development phase. Three European consortium or strategic alliance emerged, each with strong participation of the French industry:

- **COSMOS**: as a successor of the CIRAS-Symphony consortium, bringing together Aerospatiale-SNIAS (F), SAT (F), MBB (D), Siemens (D), Marconi/MSDS (GB), Selenia (I), ETCA (B).
- **MESH**: with Matra (F), VFM-ERNO (D), BAe (GB), Aeritalia (I), Saab (S), Fokker (NL), INTA (E).
- **STAR**: Thomson-CSF (F), SEP (F), Dornier (D), Bae (GB), Montedel (I), CGE-FIAR (I), Ericson (S), Fokker (NL), Contraves (CH).

---

28 CIFAS comprised the French companies SNIAS (Aerospatiale), SAT (*Société Anonyme de Télécommunications* or Telecommunication Public Limited Company) and Thomson-CSF, and on the German side AEG-Telefunken, Messerschmitt-Bölkow-Blohm (MBB).

29 Specifically, the fixed satellite telecom program adopted under the ageis of CERS-ESRO in 1973, with its first phase named OTS (Orbital Test Satellite), its second phase named MAROTS that became MARECS for Maritime applications, using OTS platform, and its third Phase named ECS or 3 Bis for operational satellite telecommunication services dedicated to the future European satellite operator, the Eutelsat organization promoted by Post and Telecommunications national operators and institutions.

Although these consortia on new satellite production were not formalized as limited company nor as permanent partnerships between their stakeholders, the experience gained through these flexible European cooperation schemes among industry paved the way for future integrations, as from the 1990s.

1.2.2.3 Adaptation to the Operational and Commercial Use of Space by the End of 1970s and Privatization Process from 1990s to Nowadays

On launcher, it became possible from 1977 to discuss about a *commercial future* of Ariane (i.e. in ESA language, its *'production phase'* or *'exploitation phase'*) taking into account the interest shown by several prospected customers, one of which was Intelsat.[30] In April 1978, before the end of the development phase, ESA ordered for manufacturing a batch of five 'promotional' launch vehicles in order to avoid the gap in production between development qualification launches and operational launches as to facilitate its commercialization. Following this commercialization approach, ESA also planned the building of satellite preparation facilities (EPCU[31]) on the Guiana launch base, as well as the development of equipment for the simultaneous launch of two geostationary satellites, named the SYLDA.[32] However, neither CNES, despite its EPIC status, nor ESA as intergovernmental organization with its privileges and immunities, seemed to be well adapted to produce and market launch vehicle services, as their main public statutory mission was promoting space research and technology development. Thus, on 2 May 1978, the CNES board agreed to the concept of a dedicated company to market Ariane launch services. This idea took shape with the publication of a document entitled *Production of the Ariane Launcher*, dated 30 August 1978,[33] which was adopted by the French government as base for negotiation with other European states. This document actually provided the baselines for the future 'Declaration Production of the Ariane Launcher,' a form of treaty among ESA's Participating Members, which entered into force on 14 April 1980, specifying the Ariane production scheme under the responsibility of a **Arianespace** company.[34]

Following the protocol agreement signed on 12 June 1979 at the Paris Air and Space Show between CNES and the main European manufacturers participating in the ESA-Ariane development program, *Arianespace* was set up on 26 March 1980, just after the ESA's decision to launch the production of a second 'promotion' batch of six launchers.

---

30 On 8th December 1978, the Intelsat organization chose Ariane to launch its satellite Intelsat V and signed a firm two option contract on 15 February 1979 few months before the launcher first flight that occurred on 24 December 1979.
31 EPCU for *Ensemble de préparation des charges utiles* or payload preparation complex.
32 SYLDA for *Système de lancement double Ariane* or Ariane Dual Launch System.
33 Carlier & Gilli, *The First Thirty Years at CNES – The French Space Agency*, p. 168.
34 The scheme set up pursuant to the Declaration by certain European governments on the Ariane launcher production phase, which entered into force originally on 14 April 1980 and has been renewed or extended until the end of 2008.

It is worth noting that the 1980 Ariane production framework set up pursuant to the Declaration by certain European governments on the Ariane launcher production phase, has been renewed and extended under the same feature until the end of 2020, by the 2007 Declaration[35] and expanded on 'the Launchers Exploitation Phase of Ariane, Vega, and Soyuz from the Guiana Space Centre.' The same steadiness applies to the composition of Arianespace shareholding from 1980 to the end of 2016, at the date of its taking over by ArianeGroup: except the CNES space agency's participation maintained at around 34% (blocking minority), the Arianespace shareholding reflected the level of participation of the European industry in the production work packages of the successive developed and exploited European launchers.

The launcher production or exploitation phase was organized under the responsibility of Arianespace, supported by CNES, which remained 'Design Authority' of the whole launcher system, under a procurement regime respecting broadly the work package apportionment defined by the ESA's development phase.

Getting back to the evolution of the launcher industry, Aerospatiale merged on 15 February 1999 its launcher activities with the Matra's remaining ones (Matra Hautes Technonolgies, MHT) to found a unique prime contractor on space launcher integration named 'Aerospatiale-Matra Strategic and Space Launchers' as part of the new space group 'Aerospatiale—Matra,' also extended to satellites.

This organization was more deeply modified from 2002, following the 2000 crisis in the Launcher sector,[36] in order to rationalize the production and further development under a unique European prime industrialist contractor, namely EADS Space Transportation, being the former prime 'launcher assembler' and 'launcher industrial architect.'

This consolidation was strengthened on January 2015, on the manufacturing side with the setting up of a joint enterprise, initially named **Airbus Safran Launchers (ASL)**,

---

35 Declaration published in the French official gazette by decree n° 2016-1778 of 19 December 2016, *JORF* n° 0296 du 21 December 2016.
36 This worldwide crisis was caused by the 'explosion of bubble internet' in the telecommunication and digital emerging industry. This crisis brought about bankruptcy of many ventures involved on LEO satellite constellations or the abandon of their second generation (Iridium, Globalstar) and those internet projects of SkyBridge (Alcatel, Space Loral), WEST (Matra…) or Teledesic (Microsoft). On the other hand, traditional national telecommunication operators (France telecom, British telecom Dutch Telecom…) froze their investment in the space sector, directly or via their shareholdings on international geostationary satellites organizations (Eutelsat, Inmarsat, Intelsat…), to concentrate their forces in the development terrestrial networks in particular on cellular telephone market (GSM).
These satellite market disarray affected drastically the demand toward launch service providers which had; on the contrary, anticipated a considerable increase of this market.
The resulting damage become even worse for Arianespace due to its dependence on international market (no domestic governmental Buy Act in Europe) and to the failure of Ariane V ECA maiden flight on December 2002 that seriously harmed, for the next few years, its position on the geostationary market.

merging the Airbus (formerly EADS) launcher branch and Safran space engine branch.[37] This integration between the launcher assembly prime contractor with the propulsion one was made with the objective of development and subsequent production of the Ariane 6 program, which was decided by ESA Member States at the Ministerial Conference in Luxembourg on 2 December 2014.

It appeared further necessary to adapt the governance system for the exploitation consistently with the greater responsibility given to the industry either on the Ariane VI launcher design phase or regarding its future economic balance during the commercialization phase to be entrusted to Arianespace SA. To that end, the French government and the Ariane stakeholders agreed that ASL took the full control of Arianespace (namely, 74% of its shareholding) by taking over CNES' historical shareholdings (of nearly 34%). The sale finalized at the end of 2016 was supported by an agreement passed between ASL, CNES, and the French government setting the associated commitments regarding the exploitation phase preparation. Airbus Safran Launchers (ASL) was renamed **ArianeGroup** as of 1 July 2017.

On satellite industry, from the end of 1970s, the integration process was shaped under the impulse of both ESA and CNES application and technological programs, the latter being also implemented into international or European bilateral cooperation. The industrialization and service commercialization of such agencies' developed systems[38] and their recurrent operational series were then driven by domestic market or export opportunities. The resulting alliances (*cf.* §1.2.2.2) :COSMOS (Aerospatiale), MESH (Matra), Star

---

37 Safran is a French group created in 2005 from a merger between SAGEM, a French company specialized in electronic equipment, and SNECMA for *société nationale d'étude et de construction de moteurs d'aviation*, a company specialized in air and spacecraft engines based on liquid propulsion. SNECMA itself took over on 1997 the space activity of SEP (for *Société Européenne de Propulsion*) created on 1971.
SAFRAN also contribute to ASL with its solid propellants branch (for booster's thrust), from Herakles its subsidiary initially named *SNECMA Propulsion Solide*, resulting from a former acquisition of the SNPE's company relevant asset.

38 Among these structuring programs toward industry and space commercialization **over the last 50 years** we may cite among other on ESA's side: ECS, ARTES, ERS, Envisat, Copernicus-Sentinel(s), Galileo, ATV, Columbus; and for CNES: Telecom and TDF families and Syracuse, Stentor, SPOT, Helios, Pleiades, CSO-Musis, Cosmo-skymed, Proteus and Myriad, Skybridge' partnership, Topex-Poseidon Jason, Athena-Fidus, Sycral, Microscope, Angels, or more recently from the French government, the 'Future Invetsment plan' (PIA) dedicated to space activities with initial supports on satellite electric propulsion (PPS 5000 of Safran), preliminary works on Ariane VI, Microcarb, Merlin.
The latest PIA, for 'Future Investment Program' (*Plan d'Investissement d'Avenir*), is a program initiated in 2010 by the French government to supports more broadly the innovative private initiative. This program renamed 'Investment plan' in 2017 establish a new bottom up mechanism allowing to finance innovative and exemplary projects proposed by industry that may include projects of Space systems and related services. CNES as a Space agency can be selected as facilitator and/or contract officer on behalf of the Government to support some PIA's projects

(Thomson-CSF), appeared poorly adapted to the development of the international market of telecommunication.

Two other organizations were created:
- **Eurosatellite** (Aerospatiale (F), MBB (D) and ETCA(B)) in 1977 for the development of Franco-German direct Broadcast satellite.
- **Satcom International** (Matra and Bae) in 1981 directed on the international satellite market.

This led in France to the formation of two *prime contractors*: **Matra** joined with the British industry and **Aerospatiale** joined with the German MBB (and with Ford Aerospace for non-European market. In 1983 Thomson-CSF ceded its space activities to Alcatel a major French group on transportation, energy, and telecommunication systems, which then become a specialist on *telecommunications payload*. The name of the new company was **Alcatel Thomson Espace** (ATES), quickly renamed **Alcatel Espace,** while keeping the same acronym **ATES**. As follow-up, there have been industrial and commercial agreements signed for export between Alcatel Espace and Aerospatiale in 1989, which was expanded to a consortium called the **Alliance** with the joining in 1990 of Alenia (Italy) and Daimler Chrysler Aerospace (DASA), from Germany. Later Alcatel Espace, Aerospatiale, DASA, and Alenia jointly took a 49% share in **Space system Loral** (the former space division of Ford Aerospace in the USA). On the other side, the group **Matra Marconi Space (MMS)** was integrated the same year as a merger of space activities of Matra (F) and Marconi Electronic Systems (GB).

In July 1998, Aerospatiale ceded its satellite branch (of Cannes) to **Alcatel Space**, which became the second European satellite prime contractor, along with Matra Marconi Space.

As a response, Aerospatiale and Matra Marconi Space merged on February 1999 all their space activities, specifically the former Aerospatiale's launcher branch and its remaining satellite equipment activities of *Les Mureaux*'s site and the Matra Marconi Space's satellite activities, mainly located in Toulouse (F) and Stevenage (GB), added to its launchers, namely on vehicle equipment bay. This gave rise to the first French-controlled integrated space group on launcher and satellite industry named **Aerospatiale-Matra.**

On 10 July 2000, this new Aerospatiale-Matra space group (F), DASA (D), and CASA (Construcciones Aeronáuticas Sociedad Anónima, from Spain) merged their space division to shape **European Aeronautic Defence and Space company (EADS)**, the European space group leader in launch and satellite activities[39] (nowadays named **Airbus Defence and Space**).

---

39 The EADS satellite branch was initially named **EADS-Astrium** (the space launcher branch being named initially EADS Launch Vehicle and then EADS Space Transportation in 2003). From 2006 to 2013 the name

Alcatel Space on its side merged later in July 2005 with the Italian Alenia Spazio (of Finmeccanica-Leonardo group) to become **Alcatel Alenia Space**. Then Alcatel (F) sold out its space branch to Thales (F) as a consequence of its merger with the US Lucent in April 2007. This gave rise to the new name of **Thales Alenia Space (TAS)**.

Thus satellite industry in France in 2018 remains stabilized around two prime industrial contractors of European scale, on the one hand **Airbus Defence and Space** (F, D, G-B, E) and on the other hand **Thales Alenia Space** (F, I, B).[40]

1.2.2.4   Abstract on CNES' Industrial Policy

To summarize this §1.2.2 on CNES' industrial policy, we may state that this ambitious policy was implemented since the earliest 1960s through its scientific and technological programs, by procurement on systems' development programs and further by the privatization of market-oriented projects' exploitation, in particular through shareholdings and concession or delegation agreements.

It contributed to the consolidation of space application and commercial-oriented skills within the French industry around a few champions. As from the 1970s, the latter expanded their expertise and shareholding at the European level and became competitive rooted players on the international marketplace. They are now listed as Airbus Defence and Space, Thales Alenia Space on space orbital systems and Ariane Group on launch and thrust systems. This industrial policy, as those of any other national or regional Space agencies, by nature was essentially focused on the development of Space industry as stemming from the aeronautics and electronics sectors, whether civil or military. This industrial policy thus relied upon existing procurement rules applicable to such public agency and their statutory capacity to create or foster new commercial ventures. To this extent, we may say that CNES was not served all that badly by its 1961 constitutive legal framework.

Nowadays, the new challenge for CNES toward industry, as for any other space agency in the world, is to have legal tools to support the later development through new forms of partnership, in compliance with existing international and European competition law or customs. This development supposed a balanced approach between the traditional space industry now fully privatized but still involved with general interest and strategic stakes and the 'new space' industry coming from the digital economy, with a long-standing experience of liberalization, competition, consumer market, and independence as to gov-

---

Astrium was extended to the whole EADS's activity on civil and military space systems and services. Then, on 2 January 2014, the whole EADS restructured group was renamed **Airbus** (taking the former name of the civil aviation branch) and its whole space branch was integrated to the renamed **Airbus Defence and Space** subsidiary.

40   Via its Belgium's subsidiary ETCA (acronym for *Études Techniques et Constructions Aérospatiales*) isun located in Charleroi (Belgium) taken over by Alcatel Space in 1989.

ernmental public contracting authorities. The issue of legal capacity as to support these private new ventures is developed in Chapter 4 and the conclusion of Part II in Chapter 8.

1.2.3 Development and Management of Ground Facilities for Satellite and Launch Operations (Toulouse Space and Guiana Space Centres)

Such a mission of CNES on developing and managing large-scale operational facilities was not provided for neither in its 1961 statute Act nor by most of its founding fathers.[41] A 'design office' was not designed to build and operate large facilities, especially a launch base. This responsibility, as in many other space-faring nation, was entrusted to defense authorities. In France, the first rocket launch site was located in Algeria's Sahara, in Hammaguir near Colomb-Béchar at 120 km. This launching base was under the responsibility of the CIEES (*Centre interarmées d'essais d'engins spéciaux*, or Joint Staff Centre for Special Missile Testing) managed from 1957 to 1962 by Robert Aubinière, an Air Force General, who afterwards became the first Director General of CNES. The 'Évian Agreement' signed on 18 March 1962 between France the Provisional Government of the Algerian Republic[42] ending the 1954-1962 Algerian War, paved the way for Algeria's independence from France. This agreement, however, authorized France to use these facilities until the first of July 1967. This relocation perspective prompts CNES leaders (Robert Aubinière, Jacques Blamont; Michel Bignier, Frederic d'Allest...) under the impetus of professor Auger, its founder president, to seek a new site that would satisfy the civil needs of both CNES and CERS-ELDO.[43] The selection process organized by CNES retained, in late 1963, the equatorial site of Guiana, among a short list of 14 locations of French overseas territories.

On 21 March of the same year, General de Gaulle made an official trip in Cayenne 1964, during which he upheld in a famous speech the international vocation of the future space launch base:

> we must achieve, you on the spot, and us in France with you, a great French undertaking in French Guiana, one that will be recognized throughout the part of the world where the '*Département*' (of the French Guiana) is situated. It must be seen and known everywhere. We have begun and we will continue...

---

41 *See*, J.-E. Blamont in the *Foreword* of this work and § 1.2, footnote 12.
42 The government-in-exile of FLN for *Front de Libération Nationale* or National Liberation Front.
43 On the choice of the Guiana Space Centre and its creation phase in the early sixties, *see*:
    - Carlier, *The First Thirty Years at CNES – The French Space Agency*, p. 279-285.
    - A. Lebeau and R. Aubinière, *Le général Robert Aubinière, propos d'un des pères de la conquête spatiale française* (The General Robert Aubinière, words from one of funding fathers of the French Space conquest, l'Harmathattan, 5-7, rue de l'École polytechnique, 75005 Paris , 2008 2008, ISBN: 978-2-296-05193-5, p. 149-160.

Thus CNES designed and built this international launch range base named Guiana Space Centre (CSG) between 1965 and 1968. The CSG became operational on 9 April 1968, with the launch of a Veronique sounding rocket. Its first orbital launch occurred on 10 March 1970 with Diamant B carrying the German satellite WIKA. The development and management of launch base, as to the CSG, was set up based on the main legal foundation of a decree of 21 May 1965,[44] and thereafter under the French government-ESA Agreement on CSG, signed on 5 May 1976, *i.e.*, a long time before the comprehensive national legal formalization of all these CNES' missions in Guiana through the FSOA of 2008 modifying the space agency 1961statutory act as developed in Part II.

The *Toulouse Space Centre (CST)* was created following a decision of an interministerial committee on 31 July 1963. The decision of land expropriation for public utility was taken by order of the minister of construction on 10 February 1965 (JORF 17 February).This location was, however, the result of a broader French policy of decentralization of space and aeronautics activities from Paris area to Toulouse dating back to 1955.[45] CNES was then required to join the newly inaugurated aerospace complex made with the *Ecole Nationale Supérieure Aéronautique* (ISAE now, or more familiarly 'Supaéro') and the *Ecole nationale de l'aviation civile* (ENAC), both as State aerospace high-level engineering schools.

The staff transfer from Bretigny Space Centre (near Paris in the south) was done in two phases. The first phase took place in three parts: the balloons activity in 1966,[46] the sounding rockets[47] in 1969, and the satellite development in 1971. The second phase was more ambitious, included the closing up of Bretigny Space Centre in 1974, Paris region initially retaining only the Head Office. Thus the relocation affected the ground support equipment, data processing and computing, and orbital maneuvers. The CST (for *Centre spatial de Toulouse* or Toulouse Space Centre) became the main technical center of CNES. Its workforce represents now about 70% of CNES' total workforce.[48] Today the activity of

---

44 Legal basis of the setting up of the CSG, under CNES responsibility, as published in the French Official Gazette (*JORF*): Decree n° 65-88 of 21 May 1965; *JORF* 25 May, p. 4267. Finance Modified Act of 1965 n° 65-1154 of 30 December 1965; *JORF* 31 December 1965, p. 11972. Decree of 25 July 1967 modifying the Decree n° 65-88 of 21 May 1965; *JORF* 2 August 1967, p. 7723.

45 Under the legal framework of the decree n° 55-873 on 30th June 1955 concerning the establishment of action plans regional and the decree n° 55-874 on the same date, 'on State financial guarantee and borrowing rate improved… in favor of the decentralization…'.
For a comprehensive biographical reference on the CST establishment, see the book published by CNES in October 1998 named *'Témoignage'* or 'Testimonials'', *1968-1998 Le Centre spatial de Toulouse a 30 ans* (or the *Toulouse Space Center is 30 years old*)".

46 The development activity for balloon was meanwhile removed from the Aeronomy Department of CNRS (*see above*, on Jacques Blamont). The operational and equipement centre was on its side located in Air-sur-Adour.

47 Incidentally, taking in consideration the subject of this book, we may retain that stratospheric balloon and sounding rocket activities of Toulouse, under French jurisdiction, are subject to air law and not to FSOA.

48 Repartition of CNES' workforce in 2017: total = 2434; Paris – 'les Halles' (head office) = 186; Paris-'Daumesnil' (DLA for launcher directorate) = 210; Toulouse (CST) = 1762; Kourou (CSG) = 276.

the CST includes satellite development projects, associated R&D program, ground network and orbital operations, and exploitation (as to mission payload: telemetry, processing of data, ...). It also includes stratospheric balloons activities whose assembly, integration and test (AIT) are run in other facilities located in Air sur Adour, near Pau.

The *launch Vehicle Directorate, or Direction des Lanceurs (Ariane) - DLA,* as such was created in 1973 to implement the ESA's Member States mandate on development management of Ariane. It was established in 1974 in Evry, in the south or Paris region, after a difficult negotiation with DATAR.[49] This launcher activity was not transferred to Toulouse as a result of a specific decision of an interministerial committee for national and regional development taken on 20 April 1972. The rationale for this was resulting from the necessary proximity toward the main launcher manufacturers and associated design offices around Paris (SEP in Vernon, Aerospatiale in Les Mureaux, Matra, in Velizy and ONERA in Chatillon...) and with ESA headquarters located in Paris.

A few decades later, following one of the eight conclusions of a report entitled 'A Stake for Space Policy: Ensuring an Autonomous and Sustainable Access to Space for Europe' submitted to the French prime minister François Fillon on May 2009,[50] it was decided that ESA would relocate CNES' launch vehicle directorate (DLA) in Paris to a new site close to the ESA launcher directorate. This 'colocation' of both launcher teams was made in the Paris-Daumesnil site in the early 2012 to be effective in view of the new Ariane VI development organization, as further decided on December 2014 among ESA Member States.

1.2.4 Shareholdings and Subsidiaries to Develop, Produce, and Market New Space Services

By the end of 1970s, as an extension of its earliest 'industrial policy,' as presented above, which mainly relied upon its development programs' procurement needs, CNES developed an active policy of creating subsidiaries. These holdings were settled as public or private bodies, with commercial or civil mission, or under a sustainable mix among these statuses. The purpose of this externalization or privatization policy is to anticipate the *operational phase* (or '*production phase*') of its *developed programs*, to prepare their commercialization, or to spin off its research and technology actions. Some of these shareholdings were pri-

---

49　DATAR for *Délégation à l'Aménagement du territoire et à l'action régionale or* Delegation for Land Use and Regional Development, is the ministry's department responsible for the French decentralization policy which has been very powerful during the sixties and seventies under de Gaulle and Pompidou presidency.

50　Report drafted by Bernard Bigot (Administrateur Général du CEA), Yannick d'Escatha (Président Directeur Général du CNES) and Laurent Collet-Billon (Délégué Général pour l'Armement) 'L'enjeu d'une politique spatiale: assurer durablement à l'Europe un accès autonome à l'espace' (A stake for space policy: ensuring an autonomous and sustainable access to space for europe), report submitted to the Prime Minister on 18 May 2009, and disclosed for public on 25 May 2009

marily activity-*promotion oriented*, such as Prospace, Scot Conseil, Sat-Control, and Dersi; others were more concerned with the marketing of new space-based services, data, or products such as Arianespace or Spot Image. Others were created or consolidated to have an operational role on behalf of public and private Space activities, such as Interspace, when that mission was not yet satisfactorily undertaken by the private sector.

CNES subsidiary effort basically remained focused on the *pre-competitive phase* and *space application*. The vocation of CNES cannot be to remain in the long run shareholder of a private company or to support a recurrent business. As far as the activity became mature or sustainable on the marketplace, the CNES withdrawal was negotiated with the other shareholders and stakeholders. This capacity of CNES of setting up and keeping shareholdings results from its 1961 Constitutive Act, as codified in CR Article L331-2 (c):

> CNES is entrusted to: (…) (c) to ensure implementation of such programs, either in laboratory and technical establishments created by itself, or by means or **research convention**[51] settled with other public or private organizations, **or financial shareholdings.**

It is also worth mentioning that any business creation as subsidiary of CNES was systematically associated with a *specific framework or concession agreement*[52] settling the terms and conditions of cooperation between the company and its public shareholder. Such agreements may be maintained as such or modified after the CNES withdrawal as shareholder, at least to keep an operational and legal link between CNES and the private actor on the exploitation concession of the public assets, be they tangible (satellites, ground facilities) or not (patents, know how…). For example, the withdrawal of CNES in Spot Image Shareholding in 2008 did not affect the '*delegation of public services*' granted to this company, after European competition, in compliance with the mandate given by the government on the *exploitation* of this program by decree of 2004.[53]

Naturally, such agreement shall be concluded or amended:
- in accordance with Article 228-35 of the French Code of Commerce, which regulates agreements between limited companies and their main shareholders (>10% of the voting), their members of the board and officers, and on the other hand,
- within the limit of legal capacity of CNES as public body, in particular with respect to global public aid legislation and competition law.

---

51 *I.e.*, through procurement, partnership or international cooperation agreements.
52 For further details on these framework or concession agreements between CNES and its subsidiary, *see below* in Part II, Chapter 5, §5.1.2, on Spot Image case and the evolution of this framework with Pleiade in 2004.
53 Arts. 1 and 2 of the Decree n° 2004-1395 on 20 December 2004, *JORF* 26 December 2004, p. 22002.

Basically for prior approval such agreement shall be submitted to both board of directors and, if legally required, to those of the competent competition authorities, the French *Autorité de la Concurrence* or the DG completion of the European Commission.

The major creations and/or stockholding of CNES are listed here by the chronological order of their creation:

- **Simko**: A private–public real estate company set up in 1968 to support the development of Kourou city in Guiana, following the implantation of the CSG Launch Base.
- **GDTA**: GIE for *groupement pour le développement de la télédétection aérospatiale* or 'Grouping for the Developpement of Aerospace Remote Sensing,' was founded in July 1973 by CNES and IGN. Its purpose was promotion, education, and training in remote sensing. It was deregistered in 2006.
- **Prospace:** Created in 1974, promotes commercially its members' space industry activities and products abroad, prospects market opportunities and markets their products whenever possible. It has been dissolved in December 2004.
- **Satel Conseil**: A joint venture founded in 1978 with France Telecom in the form of Economic Interest Grouping (EIG or *GIE for groupement d'intérêt économique*), for worldwide consultancy on space-based telecommunications systems and monitoring of such emerging world marketplace. CNES withdrew from this GIE in 2002 after its transformation into a limited company (*Société Anonyme*);
- **Arianespace** SA (now Arianespace SAS): The European launch service provider set up in 1980, responsible for the industrial production of launch vehicles and marketing of launch services, nowadays controlled by ArianeGroup since January 2017. The genesis of Arianespace establishment is detailed in §1.2.2.3;
- **Intespace** SA: Set up in 1983 to market to the industry space environment ground facility testing, nowadays controlled by Airbus Defence and Space.
- **Spot Image** SA: Set up in 1983, dedicated to the marketing for Space Remote Sensing data distribution, nowadays controlled exclusively by Airbus Defence and Space since July 2008.
- **Sat Control**: Created on 1985 in the form of EIG (*GIE*) with two major satellite prime contractor[54] to develop, produce, and market satellite control centers. CNES withdrew from this industrial task in 1989 with the conclusion of the development phase.
- **CLS** SA (for collecte localisation satellite, named initially CLS ARGOS): Set up in 1986, this company supplies satellite services on localization, positioning, collection of environmental data, observation of the oceans and the continental waters, and the surveillance of the ground and maritime activities. It is still under the control of CNES in 2017 (CNES 54%, Ardian 32%, and Ifremer 14%).

---

54 Respectively Aerospatiale (satellite branch) and Matra respectively seated in Cannes and Toulouse, now TAS and Airbus Defence and Space.

- **Novespace** SA: It was created in 1986 to design and conduct space technology transfer operations and to promote microgravity applications in space and then to organize parabolic flight on board zero-gravity aircrafts on which its activity focuses nowadays (Airbus A 310 since 2015).
- **Locstar** SA: It was created in 1988, to develop, produce and market a service of GEO satellite radiolocation systems. It was liquidated under amicable agreement in 1991, due to a lack of funding.
- **Medes-IMPS** (*médecine spatiale/ Institut de médecine et de physiologie spatiale*): A joint venture created in 1990 in the form of EIG with medicine faculty organizations and research centers. MEDES Conduct medical activities related to manned flights and provides operational medical support for resolving problems related to human life in space.
- **Dersi:** This was created in 1992 as a private limited company (SARL) held by CNES at 99.99% to further industrial cooperation between French firms and potential partners in Russia, following the dissolution of USSR. An office was opened in Moscow to that purpose. Dersi is now dissolved.
- **Starsem** SA: A joint European–Russian enterprise created in 1996 to commercialize the Russian Soyuz launch services from Baikonur. Starsem. It is headquartered in Évry, France (near Paris) and has the following shareholders: Russian Federal Space Agency (25%); 'TsSKB-Progress' Samara Space Center (25%), ArianeGroup (35%), Arianespace (15%). From 2011, Soyouz Rocket is also operated from CSG in French Guiana by Arianespace, one of its shareholders. CNES is not a shareholder but was involved in the funding of the company along with the Minister in charge of Space (F. Fillon); CNES is there as a 'censor' (without vote) on the Starsem Board.
- **Skybridge LP, via Telespace Participation SA**. Skybridge LP was a limited partnership set up by Alcatel and Loral and incorporated in the State of Delaware (U.S.A) in 1998[55] to develop and market the eponymous project consisting in a large constellation of 80 low-Earth-orbiting (LEO) satellite-based telecommunications systems providing global broadband access via local operators. The project was abandoned in 2002 following the burst of the internet bubble in 2001. CNES' shareholding in Skybridge LP was held by a fully controlled limited company, **Telespace Participation SA**, established for that purpose and nowadays still in activity.

Nowadays **Telespace Participation** only serves as the holding of CNES' shareholdings in limited companies (*Société anonyme, or SA*), namely CLS, Novespace and Argos. Originally

---

55 Alcatel (now TAS) was the General Partner of SkyBridge LP. The others, as Limited Partners included: Loral Space & Communications of the United States; Toshiba Corporation, Mitsubishi Electric Corporation and Sharp Corporation of Japan; SPAR Aerospace Limited of Canada; SRIW, a Belgian investment entity and Aerospatiale (satellites in Cannes, now TAS) and CNES of France. *See* Part II, §5.1.1.

Telespace Participation was submitted, by order of 3 April 1998 (JORF 5 April) to the regime of state control of state on public enterprises under the decree n° 53-707 of 9 August 1953. Telespace Participation was then obliged to apply for a special permission before any acquisition or disposal of shares; such authorization was to be granted in the form of a joint order signed by the ministers of economy, budget, and space. This formality was deleted by order of 14 April 2010 (JORF 24 April). Since that date, the authorization is formalized at the level of CNES board (*see* Art. 4.10 of the 1984 CNES decree). CNES holds 100% of Telespace Participation that has the capacity of investing or taking shares in start-up (*see* §4.1.3.3 and §4.3 last bullet).

1.2.5 Public Interest Joint Organizations to Support Space-Related Research (GIP)

In addition to the *historical scientific mix laboratories* and partnerships set up from the 1960s with major research public bodies,[56] CNES also expanded its sphere of intervention by supporting the creation of its significant participation in civil or nonprofit society, dedicated to space-related research and technology transfers between public partners and the industry. The major creations and/or participation of *Public Interest Group (GIP)*[57] public or semi-public bodies are listed here by the chronological order of their creation.

- **Cerfacs:** Set up in 1987 as a GIP and transformed into civil society in 1996. It is a research center on advanced calculation and new generations of scientific computers. It also develops research and assures trainings of European researchers and the engineers in scientific computation from industry and the public research bodies. A branch was created to contribute to the studies on the climate change.
- **Ultrasons:** Was created in 1990 by public–private partnership, with the objectives to continue fundamental ultrasound research, accelerate technology transfer to industry, and promote the spread of knowledge in that field. CNES left Ultrasons as soon as the GIP activity has reached its full maturity in 2000.
- **OST** (*Observatoire des Sciences et des Techniques*): This French Science and Technology observatory was also created in 1990 under the aegis of the ministry of research by representatives of public bodies to produce and publish science and technology indicators.
- **Institut Paul-Emille Victor (IPEV):** It was founded in 1992 under the name of French Institute for Polar Research and Technology *(Institut Français pour la Recherche et les*

---

56 *See* beginnings of this §1.2.
57 The Public Interest Grouping (GIP) is a legal public body which allows public and private partners to share expertise and assets for implementation of missions of general interest. This status was created, initially for research purpose only, by the Art. 21 of the Research Act n° 82-610 of 15 July 1982. It is now governed by Chapter II of the Act n° 2011-525 of 17 May 2011, *JORF* n° 0115 of 18 May 2011.

Technologies Polaires, IFRTP). Its function is to offer logistic support for its selected scientific and technological research programs in the French territories in the Antarctica (Terre Adelie base camp, Kergelen, Amsterdam, and Crozet) in the field of glaciology, atmospheric physics, and earth studies, and animal and plant biology.

- **Renater** (*Le Réseau National de télécommunications pour la Technologie, l'Enseignement et la Recherche*): It was created in 1993 as a dedicated network to accompany the internet development among French research and education community.
- **Medias-France:** It was set up in 1994 to deal with the themes related to the global change, to establish and maintain databases for the associated research, to exploit space-based Earth observation data and to provide elements of studies intended for the researchers. Medias was dissolved in 2009.
- **I-Space**: It is an association, created by CNES in 2001, in the aftermath of the initiative 'Space and Society' (1998–2002) promoted by the ministry of research and space to support development of space application toward public research organization and the marketplace. I-Space brought together a membership of nearly hundred members in business sectors and diversified fields of space utilizations, emerging or mature. I-Space absorbed the above GIE Prospace in 2004 to create the association named I-SPACE-PROSPACE, which closed its activity few years later.
- **Mercator ocean:** It was set up in 2002. Its purpose is to develop an operative system of oceanography based on existing satellite data and to facilitate its applications. Mercator participates in the GODAE project (Global Ocean Data Assimilation Experiment). In 2010, Mercator was transformed into a permanent civil society; meanwhile CNES was retiring from the enterprise. °

1.2.6 Participation, Along with the French Government, in the European Space Policy and Programs Governance (ESA and EU)

As an extension of its competence in international cooperation in association with the ministry for foreign affairs under its constitutive law, CNES as the national space agency always possessed an autonomous and permanent management delegation regarding the French contribution to the European space program through its participation in both ESRO and ELDO's boards. This delegation was extended to ESA Council and Program Boards since the founding of this organization in 1973, which became effective in 1975.[58]

---

58 The text of the ESA Convention elaborated by the VI° CSE on 31 July 1973 and 20 September 1973 (Ref. CSE CS(73)19, rev.7) was approved by the Conference of Plenipotentiaries held in Paris on 30 May 1975. The Convention was signed after this Conference by all Member States of the European Space Research Organisation and of the European Organisation for the Development and Construction of Space Vehicle Launchers (ESRO and ELDO) and opened for signature by the members States of the European Space Conference.

This responsibility goes hand in hand with its furthest contribution, as representing or accompanying the competent French ministries, at the European Union space-dedicated boards and committees since the Union involvement in space affairs policy and programs in the 1990s. EU Space competence was then formalized by the TFEU in 2007.[59] Relationship among CNES, the European Space Agency, and the European Union in regard to space programs are discussed in §4.2.

1.2.7 Responsibility in Defence' Space Segment Programs

The cooperation with the *Ministry of Defence*, put in a sleeping mode after the involvement of CNES in launcher development by 1965, was reinitiated in the 1980s with the Helios Program, a *Defence Earth observation satellite* utilizing the derived platform of the CNES' SPOT civil one. Following the lesson learned from first Gulf war in 1991, the French government decided to develop and strengthen a *coherent defense space policy*. In view of this, the 1984 CNES' decree was modified in 1993[60] to add the ministry of defense as co-responsible, along with the minister of research and the minister in charge of space affairs, for governmental space policy, in particular on CNES' supervision and funding. Then, CNES possesses a permanent delegation of responsibilities on defence programs on space segment in satellite platform or bus, in development or space operations, except as relates sensitive payload activities.

The European Space Agency functioned de facto from 31 May 1975. The ESA Convention entered into force on 30 October 1980. Date of deposit of instruments of ratification. A Cooperative Agreement between ESA and Canada as associated member entered into force on 1 January 1989.

59 Art. 4. "The Union shall share competence with the Member States in the following principal areas: (…) 3. In the areas of research, technological development and **Space**, the Union shall have competence to carry out activities, in particular to define and implement programmes; however, the exercise of that competence shall not result in Member States being prevented from exercising theirs."
Art. 189 (Title XIX):
1. To promote scientific and technical progress, industrial competitiveness and the implementation of its policies, the Union shall draw up a European space policy. To this end, it may promote joint initiatives, support research and technological development and coordinate the efforts needed for the exploration and exploitation of space.
2. To contribute to attaining the objectives referred to in paragraph 1, the European Parliament and the Council, acting in accordance with the ordinary legislative procedure, shall establish the necessary measures, which may take the form of a European space programme, excluding any harmonisation of the laws and regulations of the Member States.
3. The Union shall establish any appropriate relations with the European Space Agency.
4. This Article shall be without prejudice to the other provisions of this Title.
60 Decree n° 93-277 on 3 March 1993 (*JORF* 4 March) amending 1984 CNES' Decree n° 84-510 of 28 June 1984.

1.2.8   Recurrent Space Operations

CNES' responsibilities on 'operational' activities go in line with its development and research program mission's follow-on. Accordingly, CNES may retain the responsibility of operating its space systems, to complete their operational qualification or, since there is a deficiency or disinterest of public or private initiative, to carry out such operational activities. Thus, CNES has been authorized by its board of directors to undertake the following activities, without any other prior special formal statutory decision, neither by law nor by decree, under the sole basis of its 1961 Act' Article 2. 3 (or CR: L331-2 c):

- Government or private non-standard satellite in-orbit positioning and control service provider.
- Outer-stratosphere balloon launch and operation on behalf of scientific community, at a national scale or through international cooperation.

Conditions of implementation by CNES of such recurrent activities are developed in Chapter 4 and more specifically in its §4.3.

1.2.9   CNES as a Service Provider

This legal capacity of CNES to provide services on remunerated basis can be derives first from the industrial and commercial nature of its status as a public body (EPIC) and then from CR's Article L 331-2(c) of its codified act, as to its capacity to conclude any kind of agreement for the purpose of executing its activity program. In addition, Article L 331-4 of the Code of Research[61] governing its statute, expressly provides that, for the financing of its missions, CNES can receive 'fees for services rendered.' Basically service contracts performed by CNES, which were often inadequately named 'commercial contracts,' include the provision of infrastructure use, space operations on public vehicles, assistance, expertise, technology know-how or transfer, that services being invoiced on a non-profit or at a cost basis. The issue of avoiding potential conflict of interest with its other missions toward space industry is discussed in chapter 4.3, on interaction issues on CNES' different missions.

1.3   SYNTHESIS OF CHAPTER 1 ON CNES' STATUTE AND MISSION BEFORE THE ADVENT OF FSOA

As mentioned in the previous section, many additions to CNES' statutory missions and responsibilities were made implicitly or empirically between 1961 and 2008 with the advent

---

61   Also mentioned in the Art. 11 of the 1984 CNES's decree

of FSOA. However, the only explicit addition made as to its civil-based statute was the recognition of a competence on the national defence space program, formally introduced in 1993 in its 1984 decree, by empowering the ministry of defense as CNES' line ministry alongside the ministry of research responsible for the space policy governance. This allowed the freezing of a specific yearly financial contribution from this ministry (line 191 of the Yearly Finance Act) on behalf of CNES budget, without prejudice to case-by-case contracts awarded via its General Directorate for Armament (DGA) for services to be rendered on a specific project.

From this perspective, it is worth noting that the 2004 codification of CNES Constitutive Act of 1961 and its transfer by a legal ordinance to the Code of Research's provisions (in Arts. 331-1 to 6 of this code), was made without any change of its competence scope. Thus, the wording of 331-2 (a) to (e) remained strictly unchanged and even CNES' responsibilities as to the CSG were not referred to.

Among its extended competences, we may recall from 1965, the building, management, and safety authority of CNES at the Guiana launch base, from 1976 the capacity for it to develop commercial application systems or services (remote sensing, launch, telecommunication…) forwarded by an autonomous capacity to create subsidiaries in the form of a limited company from the end of 1970s in the wake of Arianespace setting up model. However, its original procurement regime[62] toward space industry gradually joined the ordinary law of public contracts especially by 2007, consistently with the submission of CNES to the ordinary rules of *public procurement*, first of all through the specific regime of the ordinance of 6 June 2005 applicable to EPIC bodies, then of those of 23 July 2015 concerning the whole public bodies and contracts. In this respect, legal incidences of FSOA on CNES' capacity and missions scope as a national agency are further developed in chapter 4, paragraph 4.3.

---

62 *See* chapter 4.1.3.1 below 'CNES as a Public Procurement Actor.'

2 GOVERNANCE AND MANAGEMENT

2.1 CNES' ADMINISTRATIVE AUTHORITIES OF SUPERVISION – SPACE POLICY OVERALL ORGANIZATION AND FUNCTIONING

CNES' Constitutive Act (1961's Act Art. 1 or CR Art. L 331-8) refers to a decree to facilitate the implementation of the rules of this Act. This decree relating to CNES has been revised in-depth many times, in 1962, 1976, 1979, and 1984 in the direction of more flexibility in the functioning and the management autonomy from the State, notably the 1979 one introducing the competence of its board on proposing the French Space policy and the 1984 one facilitating the creation of commercial subsidiaries. This decree, as in force, is the above-mentioned n°84-510 of 28 June 1984 relative to CNES as amended several times since.

This **application decree** (*décret application*) specifies in particular the competent ministries or administrative authorities of supervision (CNES' line ministries), the board of directors' competence and procedures, the executive powers of the Chairman (*Président* in French), and, if any, the ones of the Chief Executive Officer (in French, *Directeur général*), the conditions of delegation and more generally the administrative and financial functioning of the Centre. Up to now CNES had known three application decrees:
- its founding application decree of February 1962,[1]
- the decree of January 1976[2] amended twice in August 1977[3] and June 1979,[4]
- the current decree in force of June 1984[5] as modified seven times since then.

Indeed, the current 1984 CNES' decree has been modified on several occasions since its first version: in February 1989,[6] in March[7] and December 1993[8] (published in 1994), in

---

1 The 1962 CNES' Decree n° 62-153 of 10 February 1962, *JORF* 11 February, p. 1484-1485.
2 The 1976 CNES' Decree n° 76-104 of 27 January 1976, *JORF* of 1 February, p. 817-818.
3 The August 1977's Decree n° 77-977 of 22th August 1977 (JORF 30th Aug.) modifying the 1976 CNES' decree.
4 The June 1979's Decree n° 79-468 of 13 June 1979 (*JORF* 16 June 1979) modifying the 1976 CNES' decree
5 The 1984 CNES' Decree n° 84-510 of 28 June 1984, JORF of 29 June 1984, p. 2027
6 The February 1989s Decree n° 89-77 of 6 February 1989 (*JORF* 8 February) modifying the 1984 CNES' decree.
7 The March 1993s Decree n° 1993-277 of 3 March 1993 (*JORF* 4 march) modifying the 1984 CNES' decree.
8 The December 1993s Decree n°93-1441 of 27 December 1993 (*JORF* 4 January 2004) modifying the 1984 CNES' decree.

April 1996,[9] January 2005,[10] June 2009,[11] and November 2012[12] but neither abrogated nor fully replaced to date. This modifications mainly affected the composition of the supervising ministries and of the board (1989, 1993, 1996, 2005) especially in March 1993[13] as relates to the joint supervision of the ministry of defence, the competences of the board (2012), the powers of the *president* and of the (former) *director-general* (1996, 2005), the consequence of the French Space Operation Act (FSOA) regarding CNES and its president (in 2009) and the public budgetary and accountancy management (2012 /GBCP's decree).

Then, the CNES' application decree is completed by specific **administrative orders** (*arrêtés*) taken by the competent line ministries regarding the organization and functioning of: administration, financing, accounting, budget, and procurement. Included among these the Order of 20 July 1990[14] laying down the (financial) functioning procedures of CNES. Following the 2005[15] new regulation on public procurement, applying unequivocally to all 'EPIC' bodies, Article 9[16] of the above 1990s order was amended by the order of 4 July 2007, as to the membership and functioning rules of CNES' Procurement Commission (*Commission des Marchés*).[17] Henceforth CNES was subject to the public procurement rules with some exceptions, however, due to its statute of *public body of an industrial or commercial nature* (EPIC) or regarding the essence of space research activities (*see* §2.2.6

---

9   The April 1996s Decree n° 96-308 of 10 April 1996 (*JORF* 12 April) modifying the 1984 CNES' decree
10 The January 2005's Decree n° 2005-45 of 25 January 2005 (*JORF* 26 January) modifying the 1984 CNES' decree.
11 The June 2009's Decree n° 2009-644 of 9 June 2009 (*JORF* 10 June) modifying the 1984 CNES' decree (FSOA's decree on CNES).
12 The November 2012's Decree n° 2012-1247 of 7 November 2012 (*JORF* 10 November) modifying the 1984 CNES' decree /GBCP.
13 Decree n° 93-277 of 3 March 1993 modifying CNES' Decree n° 84-510 of 28 June, *JORF* n° 53 of 4 March 1993, p. 3388.
14 *JORF* n° 174 of 29 July 1990, p. 9147-9148.
15 Ordinance n° 2005-649 of 6 June 2005, *JORF* n°131 of 7 June 2005, p. 10014.
16 CNES's Procurement rules are set in the Art. 9 of this order of 20th July 1990. In its original version this article stipulated that **general terms and conditions for procurement**, funding, monitoring of contracts are determined by the CNES' Board of directors (this provision being consistently with the current version of 1984's CNES Decree in its Art. 4.7).
    It also recalls that **this rules are 'inspired' from State procurement regulations** (*i.e.*, from the French Public Procurement Code). Such provision was repealed by the Order of 4 July 2007 (*JORF* 7 July 2007, p. 12030) consistently with the submission of CNES to the ordinary rules of Public procurement firstly through the specific regime of the ordinance of n° 2005-649 of 6 June 2005, then of those of the 23 July 2015 ordinance on public markets (*JORF* n°0169 of 24 July 2015, p. 12602) and its application decree n° 2016-360 of 25 March 2016, (*JORF* n° 0074 of 27 March 2016) on public procurement (or *relatif aux marchés publics*).
17 The original Art. 9 Order of 20 July 1990 on CNES' financial functioning established a **procurement commission** (*Commission des marchés*) of which membership and functioning rules were determined by a dedicated ministry Order.
    This specific order was taken the same day on 20 July 1990 (*JORF* n° 174 of 29 July 1990, p. 9148-9149).
    It was repealed and superseded by ministry order 28 of June 2000 (*JORF* n°162 of 14 July 2000, p. 10869) which was itself definitely repealed by the order of 4 of July 2007 below.
    Henceforth this commission membership and functioning rules are determined only by CNES' board of director resolution.

and §4.1.3.1). Furthermore, on the budgetary, economic, financial, and accounting level, CNES was, since its establishment, subject to the general regime applicable to the state administration or to classical *public body of administrative nature* or EPA for *établissement public administratif* (see §2.2.4 and §2.2.5). This regime included in particular the former decree of 29 December 1962 on general regulation of the *public accountancy*,[18] the decree of 9 August 1953 modified on the control of the State over the national public enterprises and *certain bodies having an object of economic or social order*,[19] the latter being potentially applicable to CNES' majority shareholdings, and the decree of 26 May 1955 modified on the codification and adjustment of texts relative to the *economic and financial control of the State*.[20]

These general regulations over public budgetary, financial, and accounting were repealed or consolidated by the decree of 7 November 2012 (n° 2012-1246)[21] on the *public budget and accounting management* (GBCP's decree as usually named under its French acronym) in line with the previous reform of the organic legislation governing yearly finance acts made by the *LOLF* (*loi organique sur les lois de finances*) of 2001.[22]

The relevant provisions of GBCP decree n° 2012-1246 were incorporated by the decree n° 2012-1247, taken and published on the same date,[23] into the 1984 CNES' application decree.[24]

2.1.1 CNES' Supervisory or Line Ministers (ministères de tutelle)

2.1.1.1 Overall Organization of the Government Supervision on Scientific and Technical Research and Space Policies

Historically and basically, the supervision of the civil French space policy, and its associated program planning, felt under the competence of the minister responsible for governing

---

18 Decree n° 62-1587 *du 29 décembre 1962 portant règlement général sur la comptabilité publique JORF* 30th December 1962, p. 12828.
19 Decree n° 53-707 of 9 August 1953 modified, *relatif au contrôle de l'Etat sur les entreprises publiques nationales et certains organismes ayant un objet d'ordre économique ou social*.
20 Decree n° 55-733 of 26 May 1955 modified, *portant codification et aménagement des textes relatifs au contrôle économique et financier de l'État* (JORF 1 June 1955, p. 5547), previously modified by decree n° 2002-1502 of 18 December 2002, *JORF* 26 December 2002.
21 Decree n° 2012-1246 of 7 November 2012 *relatif à la gestion budgétaire et comptable publique (GBCP)* or 'on the public budget and accounting management', *JORF* n° 0262 of 10 November 2012, p. 17713.
22 *Loi organique n° 2001-692 du 1er août 2001 relative aux lois de finances* or « organic law on finance law », *JORF* n° 177 of 2 August 2001, p. 12480.
23 *Ibid* (footnote 12), Decree n° 2012-1247 of 7 November 2012, *portant adaptation de divers textes aux nouvelles règles de la gestion budgétaire et comptable publique* or 'adapting the different texts to the new regulations on budget and accounting management', *JORF* n° 0262 of 10 November 2012, p. 17731.
24 The provisions modified by the 2012 decree on the 1984 CNES' application decree are the later Arts. 3, 4 and 5 on the agency's Board competence and procedure and Art. 13 on its public accountancy regime or regarding the State's economic and financial verification mission.

the research policy as a whole, whether specified scientific, technic, technologic, industrial, or more recently by reference to new technologies or simply 'innovation.'

The return to power in May 1958 of General de Gaulle gave a new boost on the governance or scientific and technical research especially in new strategic areas like nuclear energy and space. This led to the adoption of the decree 58-1144 of 28 November 1958[25] concerning the scientific and technical research. The result was a high-level centralized organization under the authority of the prime minister based around:
- an executive board, the *Interministerial Committee on Scientific and Technical Research* (*Comité interministériel de la recherche scientifique et technique*, CIRST). This committee was composed of the prime minister, the minister of education, the minister of the army, the minister of finance and economic affairs, the minister of industry and commerce, the minister of agriculture, the minister of public health and population.
- an extensive consultative branch of this committee, the *Consultative Committee on Scientific and Technical Research* (CCRST) composed of qualified individuals.
- a *General delegate* (DGRST), reporting to the delegate ministry of research, acting as executive secretary of this committee and supervising the preparation and implementation of works.

As a result of this organizational scheme, the French policy on scientific and technical research was coordinated by the prime minister (basically delegating its powers to its minister or secretary of state, responsible for scientific and technic research and atomic energy[26]) and prepared and supervised on its implementation by the *general delegate* on scientific and technical research (DGRST), the latter being supported by teams of its eponymous Delegation (DGRST). This policy and associated programs projects, so prepared, were to be submitted for advisory opinion and final decision to the *consultative committee* and then to the *Interministerial Committee on Scientific and Technical Research*.

It is within this context that by decree of 7 January 1959, the *Space Research Committee* (SRC or CPS in French, the progenitor of CNES) was created in order to organize the French space research. This additional interministerial committee came under the direct authority of the prime minister (Michel Debré), assisted by its delegated minister responsible for scientific and technical research and atomic energy (Pierre Guillaumat), the latter being supported by the General delegate on scientific and technical research (Pierre Piganiol). The Committee as such was chaired by Professor Pierre Auger.[27]

---

25 *JORF* 30 November 1958, p. 10750-10751.
26 As provided for by the Art. 3 of the above 1958s decree
27 On Pierre Auger, *see* footnote n° 8 above in 'the Earliest Steps of the French National Space Policy and CNES'.

Coming back to the overall scientific and technical research policy, the above governance was maintained and expanded by decrees of August 1970[28] and October 1975,[29] in particular to consider industrial policy, while keeping the same structure and logic of functioning up to the end of 1970s. However, the role of the Interdepartmental Committee on Scientific and Technical Research will decrease in favor of some other interministerial structures not dedicated only to research, such as the higher Committee for Social and Economic Affairs created under the Raymond Barre government in 1976. With regard to CNES, it is worth noting that according to the wording of its founding Act of 1961 (Art. 2. 2°), among the center's main responsibilities was 'to prepare and put forward proposals to the Interministerial Committee on Scientific and Technical Research for development programmes of national interest in the field of space.' This reference at the level of the Act to this Interministerial Committee instead of 'government,' 'Prime minister,' or 'supervisory ministers of…' reflects the high value ascribed to such committee. This mention was superseded by the more generic one of 'administrative authority' not before 2004, on the occasion of the codification made of this act into Research code (CR, Art. L331-2 b).

2.1.1.2 Supervision on Space Policy and CNES

Scope of the ministerial supervision toward space policy and CNES
CNES nowadays has three line Ministers (Research, Space, and Defence) in addition of the minister of economy, finance, and budget's systematic supervision on any minister and state public body. The precedence on CNES supervision is attributed to the civil supervising ministers of research and space, both being merged since 1997 (*see* the following paragraph on the evolution of the ministerial supervision…). This competence is currently attributed, under decree of May 2017,[30] to the minister of higher education, research, and innovation. This line minister, with the support of its ministry and its department directorates, acts as the minister of coordination on space policy and CNES supervision toward the other supervisory ministers or of any other minister having interest in space policy and program. Such supervising ministries' representatives participate in the board of directors. They are responsible for the preparation and the execution of CNES' state *financial annual appropriation*, in relation to the *French parliament*, which votes the corresponding budget headings in the yearly finance act:

---

28 Decree n° 70-728 of 5 August 1970 (*JORF* 11 August) on the coordination of the scientific and technic research policy. This decree is completed by an order of 5 August 1970 (*JORF*, 11 August) on the organization of the General Directorate on scientific and technic research.
29 Decree n° 75-1002 of 29 October 1975 (*JORF* 31 October) on the coordination of the scientific and technic research policy.
30 Decree n° 2017-1083 of 24 May 2017, *relatif aux attributions du ministre de l'enseignement supérieur, de la recherche et de l'innovation or* « *on the powers of the ministry of high education, research and innovation* », *JORF* n° 0123 of 25 May 2017.

- The *ministry in charge of space affairs* (*i.e.*, ministry research and high education) is responsible for the civilian budget line numbered '193' under the organic law governing public finance acts (LOFT). As a matter of fact, this budget is shared, from many years, into similar proportion between the ESA budget and the CNES' program and activities budget, the latter including national program and international cooperation.
- The *ministry of defence* is responsible for an additional budget line for a program named *dual research* (N° 191 of LOLF).

Such supervisory ministries are also responsible for the CNES management overall control and monitoring. Since 1999,[31] a long-term contract is signed every 5 years between CNES and the French government, represented by the ministry of higher education and research, the ministry of defence, and the ministry of the budget, to give a vision for its missions and budgets for the same period of time, associated with indicators of performances. Prior to its each expiration term, this contract is renegotiated on the basis of the assessment made by the HCERES.[32]

Evolution of the ministerial supervision on space policy and CNES from 1961 to 2018
The government's supervisory authority over CNES was attributed at the later creation in 1961, directly to the prime ministry, at the upmost legal level of the CNES' founding Act (Art. 1) rather than through its application decree of February 1962. Some people saw this as a sign of precedence of CNES and space policy together over other public bodies and missions. In any case, under Georges Pompidou's presidency, the prime minister (Jacques Chaban-Delmas) decided to transfer by decree of July 1969[33] this supervision authority on CNES to the minister in charge of the industrial and scientific development (François Ortoli), the latter being henceforth full ministry on research, with an expanded competence on industry issues, and not any longer directly attached to the prime minister. This modification of the CNES Act, by a decree, was specially validated by decision from the Constitutional Court (*Conseil Constitutionnel*),[34] which has recalled that, 'notwithstanding of the provision of the 1961 'Act, the organization of the administration remains under the Government's responsibility and not of the Parliament' one.'

Since these decisions of 1969, the responsibility on space policy and consequently on CNES' supervision may be empowered, at the discretion of government changes, to any minister. This appointment shall be formalized through the relevant minister and ministry

---

31 Art. 1 of the Act n° 99-587 of 12 July 1999 on Innovation and Research (*JORF* 13 July 1999) completing the Art. 14 of the Act n° 82-610 of 15 July 1982 on the orientation and programming for research and technological development in France.
32 *See* HCERES, below in §3.2.
33 Decree n° 69-724 of 18 July 1969 concerning the attributions of the minister in charge of the industrial and scientific development, *JORF* 19th July 1969, p. 7313.
34 Decision referred to on 9 July 1969. Decision n° 69-56 L (*JORF* 13 July, p. 7162).

attribution's decree (*décret relatif aux attributions du ministre*) by the mention 'exerce la tutelle du CNES' or 'supervises or is the supervisory authority of CNES.' This mention may be completed by 'he or she is competent on space policy matters' or '*il est compétent en matière de politique de l'espace*'.[35] This ministerial attribution, however, was rarely transposed as such into the operative CNES' application decree, except in March 1993[36] for Defence and in January 2005 where the generic denomination of each supervising minister[37] was introduced. However, even on the silence of decrees, the ministry responsible for research was always associated with the supervision of CNES, as a consequence of its basic responsibility[38] in coordinating the overall planning of the national program on scientific, technique, or technological research (basic, applied, and developmental) or innovation policy.

In addition, and more broadly, the ministers of economy, finance, and budget hold a systematic monitoring power on the budgetary and accountancy management of any minister and state's public body as referred to in particular in the 2012 GBCP decree.[39] In case of joint supervision between two ministers, the supremacy goes, at least from an administrative point of view, to the one who hosts the CNES' *Commissioner of the Government* or *Commissaire du gouvernement*, whose role was mentioned in the CNES decree[40] since the 1976 one.

Having clarified this issue, the supervision authority after 1969 was subsequently given, under the presidency of Valery Giscard d'Estaing, in June 1974 to the minister responsible both for industry and for research, Michel d'Ornano, and then it was taken over again in April 1977 by the prime minister, Raymond Barre, jointly with the ministry of industry, commerce, and craft, René Monory, the latter being superseded in 1978 by the minister of industry, Andre Giraud. During this presidency of Giscard d'Estaing's, the supervision on CNES and French space policy was reorganized. The scope of the renewed CNES decree of 27 January 1976 was extended to the organization of the space policy, as named in its title. This coincided with the creation of the interdepartmental *Committee on Space*

---

35 For instance, Art. 2 first phrase of the decree 2002-959 of 4 July 2002 (*JORF* 5 July) on ...Research.
36 Decree n° 1993-277 of 3 March 1993/defence supervision.
37 Decree n° 2005-45 of 25 January 2005/supervising ministers (Research, Space, and Defence).
38 For instance, the scientific and technic planning Act n° 61-530 of 31 May 1961 (*JORF* 1 June), includes space research in its complementary a budget apportionment, in view of the CNES setting up.
    For its part, the general law n° 82-610 of 15 July 1982 on Technological Development and Research Planning (*JORF* 16 July) detailed, in its appended report, the long run planning on space application programs details in particular, Ariane 2, Ariane 3, Ariane 4, telecommunications satellites such as ECS and MARECS (ESA), Telecom 1, TDF1, remote sensing satellites Spot 1 and 2 , ERS1 (ESA)...
    The same applies to the general law n° 85-1376 of 23 December 1985 on technological development and research (*JORF* 27 December) in §4 of its appended report detailing and ambitious policy and program on 'space' technology and development.
39 *Ibid.* 2012 GBCP's Decree(s) n° 2012-1246/1247 of 7 November 2012, footnotes 12, 21, 23 in §2.1.
40 Since the decree of 1976 (27 January) Art. 9 (footnote 2 in §2.1). Now under, Art. 10 of the current 1984 modified decree of June 1984 (footnote 5 in §2.1).

Application (*see* §2.1.2.2). However, the interdepartmental supervisory organization upon CNES' governance shall be lowered during the ministerial mandate of Andre Giraud through the amendment of the 1976 CNES decree by the one of 13 June 1979 suppressing on the one hand the Committee on Space Application and on the second hand entrusting the CNES board of directors as a French government consultative body on space policy.

Under the first presidency of François Mitterrand, this main supervision authority was entrusted to a strong minister for research and technology, Jean-Pierre Chevènement,[41] in May 1981, then to the ministry for industry and research, Laurent Fabius, in July 1983. It is under Laurent Fabius supervisory mandate that the CNES decree of 1984, repealing the 1976 one, was thoroughly modified. A few months later, in August 1984, under the government of Laurent Fabius, CNES supervision was entrusted to the minister for research and technology, Hubert Curien, just former president of CNES (July 1976 to July 1984), along with the minister for industrial redeployment and foreign Trade, Edith Cresson. During the following period of '*political cohabitation*' (April 1986 to May 1988) between the President of the Republic François Mitterrand and the government of Prime Minister Jacques Chirac, the supervision of CNES was entrusted in April 1986 first to the minister delegate to the minister for national education responsible for research and higher education, Alain Devaquet replaced by Jacques Valade in February 1987, along with the minister for industry, post and telecommunications, and tourism, Alain Madelin.

Under the second presidency of François Mitterand, CNES' supervision was jointly assigned in May–June 1988 to the minister for research and technology,[42] Hubert Curien (second mandate), and to the minister of post, telecommunications, and space, Paul Quiles. The latter was superseded in June 1991 by the minister for infrastructure, housing, transport, and space attributed to the same Paul Quiles who personally maintained in this way its supervision on CNES and Space policy. Then, in April 1992, the minister for research and space, Hubert Curien (third mandate), became the sole space supervisory authority, by taking over the former related competences of the minister for infrastructure, housing, transport, and space. As from the decree n° 93-177 of 3 March 1993, CNES' supervision was shared with the minister for defence, Pierre Joxe.

However, the precedence on CNES' supervision remained to the relevant civil minister(s), consistently with the level of budgetary contribution from each of them (line 191/line 193 as to LOFT numbering). During this later period (May 1988 to end of March 1993) the supervising of CNES and space policy was deeply reorganized under the initiative of Paul

---

41 Jean-Pierre Chevenement was the initiator of the famous Act n° 82-610 of 15 July 1982 on the orientation and programming for research and technological development in France, that was repealed and codified by the ordonnance n° 2004-545 of 11 June 2004 as a part of the legislative book of the Research Code (CR).
42 Via the Minister of State, Minister of National Education, Research and Sports (Lionel Jospin)

Quiles, who was the first minister to associate the name 'space' to the full title of its ministry. Among his achievements the following two are noteworthy:

- First, the establishment an interdepartmental supervisory structure, over CNES' Board and officers, with the *Space Committee* or *Comité de l'espace* (*see* §2.1.2.3) by a special decree of 10 March 1989. It is worth noting that this space committee was neither incorporated nor referred to in the 1984 CNES decree thus in effect. The ministry of defence was positioned later in 1993[43] as co-chair of this Committee.
- Second, was the setting up of the *General Delegation for Space* or *Délégation Générale à l'espace* within the organization of the ministry of post, telecommunications, and space, by decree n° 90-1121 of 18 December 1990 (Arts. 1 and 5). This General Delegation's mission was to ensure the coherence of the French government policy on space matters and to assist directly the minister on CNES' supervision.

Then, from the second '*cohabitation period*' (April 1993 to May 1995) between the President of the Republic François Mitterrand and Prime Minister Jacques Chirac, the ministry's supervisory on CNES was empowered to the minister of industry, post and telecommunications, and export trade, Gérard Longuet, along with minister of higher education and research, François Fillon.

Next, under the presidency of Jacques Chirac, CNES' supervision was jointly attributed in May–June 1995 to the minister for information technology and the post office, renamed in November 1995 the minister delegate for the post office, telecommunications and *space*, François Fillon, and to the secretary of state for research, Elisabeth Dufourcq, superseded in November 1995 by François d'Aubert. As from the *cohabitation period* (June 1997 to May 2002) between the President of the Republic Jacques Chirac and the government of Lionel Jospin, the civil supervision of CNES returned the research minister, Claude Allegre (June 1997 to March 2000), replaced by Roger-Gérard Schwartzenberg (March 2000 to May 2002). Henceforth, since 1997 CNES civil supervision was exclusively and permanently assigned to the minister of research, irrespective to its denomination.

Then, during the second presidency of Jacques Chirac (May 2002 to 2007); the ministers supervising CNES were François Loos (May-June 2002); Claudie Haigneré (June 2002 to March 2004, formerly CNES' astronaut); François d'Aubert (March 2004 to May 2005); and François Goulard (May 2005 to May 2007). It is under the mandate of François d'Aubert, by decree of January 2005,[44] that the 1984 CNES' decree was formally modified in order to freeze, at the level of this text, the composition of the space agency's ministerial supervising. A new sentence was added at the beginning of its Article 1: "the CNES is subject to the supervision of the minister of defence, of the minister responsible of space

---

43 *See below* in §2.1.2.3, the decree n° 93-1212 of 3rd November 1993.
44 Ibid, footnote 10 in §2.1, decree n° 2005-45 of 25 January 2005, Art. 1 (*JORF* 26 January).

and of the ministry of research." Therefore, on the civil line, under such drafting of the CNES decree, the ministry of research is ensured to keep supervision over CNES in any case, either solely or jointly.

Then, under the presidency of Nicolas Sarkozy and François Fillon's government (May 2007 to May 2012), this responsibility was assigned to Valérie Pécresse (May 2007 to February 2011) and Laurent Wauquiez (February 2011 to May 2012).

Under the presidency of François Hollande (May 2012 to May 2017) it was assigned to Geneviève Fioraso (May 2012 to August 2014), Najat Wallaud-Belkacem (August 2014 to June 2015), and Thierry Mandon (June 2015 to May 2017).

Under the current presidency of Emanuel Macron and the government of Edouard Philippe, the ministry in charge of CNES supervision is Frédérique Vidal from May 2017.

2.1.2 Interministerial Committees on Space Policy

2.1.2.1 The Space Research Committee and the Space Council (1959-1976)

The Committee Space Research (*Comité de recherches spatiales*), the progenitor of CNES, survived to the later creation in 1961 renamed as Space Council (*Conseil de l'Espace*) in the form of an interdepartmental consultative body between the different ministries and departments concerned with space activities, under the authority of CNES' president. It shall be consulted before any board of directors' decision on programs. It was abolished as such by the 1976 CNES decree[45] (Art. 18) repealing the famous decree of 7 January 1959. The CRS is nowadays superseded by the Committee on Scientific Programs (CPS) acting as a Board's attached committee.[46] On its side, the Board of Directors, became a French government consultative body on space policy under the 1976 CNES decree (Art. 9).[47]

2.1.2.2 Committee on Space Applications (1976-1979)

The Committee on Space application, as a high-level interdepartmental body positioned above CNES' board of directors, was set up by the famous 1976 CNES decree, also organizing the *space research*. The purpose was to entrust CNES with an official competence in new space applications with operational, industrial and commercial vocation, in particular around the new program Spot on civil Earth observation. Its composition was defined in details in the decree (Art. 16[48]) and its members were appointed by order of the competent

---

45 *Ibid*, footnote 2 in §2.1, Decree n°76-104 of 27 January 1976 (*JORF* 1 February) superseding the 1962s one (62-153 of 10 February, p. 1062).
46 Art. 9 of the current CNES' application decree of 1984. As regard CPS, *see below* §2.2.2.2.
47 *Ibid*, footnote 2 in §2.1.
48 This composition was partly modified later by the decree n° 77-977 of 22 August 1977 (*JORF* 30 August). *Ibid*, footnote 3 in §2.1.

CNES' line ministers. This committee was dissolved by the decree of 1979[49] amending the 1976 CNES' decree on the initiative of its supervising minister, André Giraud, also in charge of the industry, in the purpose admitted to simplify the governance of such emerging CNES activities.[50] Indeed, it should be noted that the same decree of 1979 entrusted (through its Art. 4) the CNES board of directors as the minister's consultative body on the orientation projects of the French and on any matter of CNES' competence. Thus the suppression of this committee did not reduce this capacity for CNES of proposing or developing new Space application. On the contrary, CNES strengthened its autonomy in that field, thanks to the full support of the minister of industry and space, maybe at the expense of inter-department support, in particular regarding potential governmental user's programs.

2.1.2.3 The Space Committee (1989-1992)

This high-level body *(Comité de l'Espace)* was created by a specific decree of 1989[51] without any direct link with the one relating to CNES. It was composed of several top-level representatives from ministries. The Committee's mission was to prepare the government decisions relating to space policy, to examine the space programs' impact on the French and European industry, to prepare, notably on the CNES Director General report, the directions relative to the French position in the matter of international Space cooperation and, at last, to propose to the First Minister any action it thinks necessary. The committee Secretary was delegated to the General Delegation to Space (directorate of the Space Affairs Supervising Ministry), in connection with CNES. The committee composition has been modified first slightly in 1990 and more substantially in 1993[52] to place it in the co-chair of the ministry of defence in CNES supervision. Then, it was last referred to in the decree 95-760 of 1 June 1995 as to the attribution of the minister of technologies, information and post (François Fillon). From this time, the committee's activity appeared frozen without any official dissolution. Indeed, the Space committee's constitutive decree is still registered at the present date of 2018 in 'Legifrance,' the official gazette available on the online website. The so-called 'Bonnet' report[53] recommended at the beginning of 2003 to restart this organization. The French government then did not formally follow this suggestion.

---

49 Decree n° 79-468 of 13 June 1979 (*JORF*, amending the aforesaid CNES decree of 27 January 1976).
50 *See ibid.*, M. Gilli, *30 years of the CNES*, p. 49.
51 Decree n° 89-508 of 19 July juillet 1989 *portant création du comité de l'espace*, *JORF* of 21 July 1989, p. 9128.
52 Decree n° 90-1102 of 11 December 1990, *JORF* n° 288 of 12 December 1990, p. 15235. Decree n° 93-1212 of 3 November1993, *JORF* of 5 November 1993, p. 15329.
53 *See* Bibliography below: this report was ordered by the Space line ministries after the CNES' governance crisis of end 2002 and following the Ariane V ECA (V517) maiden failure.

2.1.2.4 The CoSpace (from 2013)

Following the mixed result of ESA Ministerial Council (20-21 November 2012) on the future Ariane (between Ariane V ME and Ariane VI), Genevieve Fioraso, the minister in charge of Space affairs, decided to create in September 2013 a high-level committee named *CoSpace* (for *State Industry Consultative Committee on Space*). The purpose outlined was to bring together representatives of competent ministry, space operators, space industry, scientific community, and space application users' communities in order to associate the latest to the design of new space policy and programs. This Committee is chaired by the minister in charge of space affairs. Ex-officio members of this consultation committee are:
- The various concerned ministries: ministry of foreign affairs, ministry of the economy and finance, ministry of the industrial recovery, the ministry of ecology, of the sustainable development and the energy, the ministry of the Defence/DGA.
- The CNES and the GIFAS (the professional society of the aeronautical and space French industries), which jointly act as the executive secretary of the committee.
- The Civil Aviation General Directorate (DGAC) and ONERA (the French Aerospace Lab).
- Representatives of the private sector: Prime Manufacturers (Airbus Defence and Space, Thales Alenia Space, ArianeGroup) and their equipment manufacturers (SMEs).
- Representatives of CNES' Committee for Scientific Program (CPS).
- Representatives of space operators (Arianespace, Eutelsat) and of space application users' communities (TBD).

We may say, as a matter of fact, that *CoSpace* has taken at its own the former role of the 1989 Space Committee being expanded to include representatives of industry and space applications users. However, on a legal point of view, without official mandate in the absence of binding decree, it may be considered that the durability or opposability of CoSpace' works would be affected by political changes.

2.2 CNES' BOARD OF DIRECTORS AND EXECUTIVE GOVERNANCE

According to its Constitutive Act (Art. L331-3), CNES is supervised by a board of directors including State representatives, persons chosen by the government with regard to their expertise in the CNES domain of activity, and staff representatives elected in the conditions provided by the 26 July 1983 n°83-675 Law, Chapter II, Title II, relating to the public sector democratization.

2.2.1 Board of Directors' Competences

The board of directors' competences have been changed on many occasions since 1962 on its list of domain and about the period of time allowed for opposition of CNES' line ministries. Its most noteworthy change in competence was made by CNES 1976 Decree as modified in 19 June 1979.[54] Thus the CNES board of directors gains the competence of proposing the Space Policy to the government through the addition of the following sentence, written just after the numbered list of attributions: "The board of directors shall be consulted by the Minister of industry[55] on the projects of orientation of the French space policy" (*Le conseil d'administration est consulté par le ministre de l'industrie sur les projets d'orientation de la politique spatiale française*). According to Article 4 of the current 1984 CNES' modified decree, the board of directors deliberates on the following subjects:

1° Activities and investments of CNES program;
2° Organization and functioning plan of CNES, the Committee of Scientific Programmes' internal regulation;
3° Budget appropriation (*i.e., the statement of receipts and expenditures, EPRD*) and, if necessary, amended statements during the year;
4° Annual activity report approval;
5° Approval of the financial account and of the results of the exercise appropriation;
6° Short-, medium-, and long-term loans approval;
7° General conditions of procurement for contracts, agreements, and public works contracts and the threshold from which such contracts must be submitted to it;
8° Conditions to prefinance expenditures before signing or executing a contract;
9° Approval of projects of sale and buying buildings, formation of mortgage or pledging;
10° Acquisition, extension, or stakes transfer;
11° Acceptance or refusal of donations;
12° Recruitment, employment, and payment scheme of the personnel;
13° Authorization to undertake, in order to implement the international relations of CNES program, negotiations to conclude international administrative agreements;
14° Legal actions and settlements included transaction.

The board of directors has a great autonomy of decision toward CNES' supervising administration. Indeed, the 1984 decree places the emphasis on an *expost* control rather than an *exante* control as to CNES' decisions. According to Article 5 of the same decree, all decisions of the board of directors are enforceable, unless possible opposition during a given period. The opposition period for the most important decisions (n° 6, 8,10 and 12)

---

54 Decree n° 79-468 of 13 June 1979 (*JORF* 16th June) modifying the CNES Decree n° 76-104 of 27 January 1976 in its Art. 4 antepenultimate sentence.
55 At that time, the CNES' line minister in charge of Space policy.

is of one-month delay by the major line ministries, and for the others of only 10 days, from the Government Commissioner (representing all the supervising ministry, attached to the Ministry in charge of Space Affairs), being given that opposition from the latter must be confirmed by major line ministries in a one-month period. In practice, to limit the duration of such periods of opposition, CNES invites few days after the board meeting decision the relevant representatives to notify expressly their non-opposition.

2.2.2 Committees Associated with the Board of Directors

2.2.2.1 The Board of Directors' Audit Committee

The board of directors' Audit committee has been instituted by the board of directors of 9 December 2006, pursuant CNES Decree 1984 modified Art. 4. Composed by three Board members, it is specially in charge of monitoring closely:
- Budget, statement of receipts and expenditures (or EPRD for *Etat prévisionnel des recettes et des dépenses*) and, if necessary, amended statements during the current year;
- Medium Term Plan of budget allocation (or PMT, for *Plan Moyen Terme*) at 5 years horizon;
- Formulation of the accounts and summary of the audit results achieved, definition of internal audits' programs;
- Selection procedure for CNES' Auditors;
- Any other mission entrusted by the board of directors.

2.2.2.2 The Committee for Scientific Program (CPS)

The CNES Scientific Programmes Committee (*CPS, Comité des programmes scientifiques*) is the eldest and highest consultative committee on Space programs of CNES. We may say regarding its scientific competence that this committee existed before the setting up of CNES, through the Committee of Space Research (CPS) created by the decree of 7 January 1959, and transformed into the *space council* following the CNES' decree adoption in February 1962 (*see* Art. 7 of this decree). It reappeared officially by minister Order of 1963[56] in the lower form of CNES' committee named *scientific committee* of which the members were named by CNES' president after hearing the opinion of its board. Its secretary was then provided by the CNES' Program Division, namely the scientific and technical directorate. This committee was surrounded by a *technical committee* and a *space program committee* created by ministerial order of the same day as mentioned in the following paragraph 'other former committees.'

---

56 Minister Order of 8 October 1963 (*JORF* 16 October 1963).

The *scientific council* (CS) was reshaped once by Minister Order 1970[57] and relabelled under its current name of *Committee for Scientific Programs*. Therefore, its composition was not any longer solely determined by the president of CNES, its vice-president being the director of the institute of astronomy and geophysics. Members of the board were then allowed to participate in this committee where two representatives of CNES' employees were also sitting. Then it was reformed and integrated directly in the CNES' decree, first by the January 1976 one and then by the June 1984 decree (Art. 9) and its subsequent modifications. Its members henceforth were appointed by formal Order taken by several CNES' line ministers and its mission is to 'assist' the board of directors. It reports on the scientific interest of the research programs suggested or proposed to CNES and the laboratories' capacities. It also gives recommendations (priorities, studies, etc.) on the CNES projects and scientific programs (planetary exploration, study of the Universe, basic physics and microgravity, scientific earth survey) and makes any helpful proposals concerning space research development in France.

The CPS is assisted by specialized working groups: namely the CERES (for *Comité d'Evaluation sur la Recherche et l'Exploration Spatiales*) on Univers, Exploration, Microgravity; and TOSCA (for *Terre, Océan, Surfaces continentales, Atmosphère*) on Earth Science, Environment, Climate, and the latter's sub-working groups. CNES provides the CPS' executive secretary.

2.2.2.3 Other Former Programs Committees

Prior to CNES 1976 decree, other committees were set up in order to assist CNES' board and executive management in preparing space programs or assessing their execution. Of these, mention may be made of the following ones established by specific orders:
- The *Technical Committee* (*comité technique*) created alongside the scientific Committee by another order of 8 October 1963 (JORF 16 October, p. 9252)
- The *Committee for Space Program* (*comité des programmes spatiaux*) created alongside the scientific and the technical committees by another order of 8 October 1963 (JORF 16 October, p. 9252)
- The *Permanent Commission of Space Education* (*commission permanente de l'enseignement spatial*), created by Order of 17 December 1963 (JORF 31 December).

Last but not least, CNES board created an internal *Committee for Applications Programs* (*comité pour les applications Spatiales*) on 13 April 1967 to propose missions for application satellites to be launched by the new French Diamant launcher family and the Europa family to be developed by ELDO (the parent of the current ESA organization in launcher development programs). This committee for application must not be confused with the

---

57 Minister Order of 16 July 1970 (*JORF* 15 September 1970).

1976 Application Council being positioned at inter-ministry level above CNES, but may be considered as the precursor to the latest committee with regard to the CNES' competence toward applications. The committee's function was to assist the Chairman, the Director General, and the CNES board in developing space applications and techniques. It was chaired by Marcel Boiteux, member of CNES board and assistant director of EDF, the French electricity operator.[58] The lifetime and the influence of such committees did not follow the one of the CPS above. The repeals of the technical, space programs and education committees were not formalized by any specific order. We may assume they were at least abrogated by the 'catch all' Art. 18 of the 1975 CNES decree repealing the 1962 CNES decree and all related texts.

2.2.3 CNES' Chairman, Chief Executive Officer, Director-General and Deputy Director-General

2.2.3.1 Distribution of Powers Between the President and the Director-General since 1962

CNES at its inception under its 1962 decree (Art. 2) was embodied with a bi-cephalous executive structure with:

- a *president* (P) or chairman of the board, without executive function, responsible for CNES' general policy and chosen as a high-level scientific person. The same decree provided the appointment from the board of a *vice-president*, empowered in case of absence or impediment of the president to carry out the function of chairman during board's meetings. This position was cancelled in the repealing of decree of 1976.
- a *director-general* (DG), or chief executive or managing director, with the qualification of engineer, who was delegated the implementation of the board's decisions, *i.e.*, the management of programs and activities on a daily basis. The director-general would be then in charge of staff and responsible for the agency's budget implementation and annual results.

The essence of this bi-cephalic governance system was to provide CNES with an efficient operational and technical management, ensured by its chief executive director-general, in a situation comparable to that of any private company, while guaranteeing that the scientific mission of CNES and other political considerations shall be monitored by the president.[59]

---

58 *See ibid* C. Carlier & M. Gilli, *The first thirty years at CNES*, edited by La Documentation Française, p. 27.
59 As referred to in this bibliography:
   - C. Carlier &M. Gilli, *The First Thirty Years at CNES – The French Space Agency*, p. 15.
   - A. Lebeau & R. Aubinière, 'The General Robert Aubinière, words from one of the founding fathers of the French Space conquest,' p. 114.

Since the 1962 CNES decree (Art. 2), the chairman was appointed at the higher level of the French Republic President in the form of a *minister council decree* (cabinet nomination) while the director-general (Art. 9) was appointed by the supervisory minister for CNES. The second CNES decree of 1976 (Art. 8) specified that the president shall be consulted on the choice of the DG before being proposed for appointment. By 1989[60] the director-general became similarly appointed in the form of a *minister council's decree*. As a matter of fact, following CNES social crisis by the end of 1996,[61] a new president (Alain Bensoussan) was named[62] but the vacant post of director-general remained unoccupied. Thus, the DG's executive powers were internally delegated to three specialized deputy managing directors.

Three month later, by decree of 10 April 1996,[63] the 1984 CNES decree (Art. 7) was amended to empower expressly the president with the former DG's competences of preparation and execution of the board's decision and the authority on staff. Meanwhile, the attributions of the DG (Art. 6) were reduced to the following: "The director-general carries out its functions under the authority of the president. He participates in the board's meetings without taking part in the votes." However, after a further three months, in July 1997, at the beginning of the political cohabitation Chirac-Jospin,[64] a director-general (Gérard Brachet) was appointed[65] and empowered with the necessary power on CNES' general management with direct authority on staff through a specific 'letter of mission' signed by the supervisory minister of research (Claude Allegre). However, the 1984 CNES modified decree remained unchanged in its 1996 amended version.

Then, the solution of a unique CEO[66] was retained again following another social crisis in the autumn of 2002. This crisis indeed led to the resignation of the director-general (G. Brachet on 19 September 2002) shortly followed by the president's one (A. Bensoussan on 30 January 2003). The choice for a 're-centralized' management was made taking into account the conclusions of the appraisal commission on space policy chaired by R-M. Bonnet.[67] Formally, the president's resignation of 30 January 2003 was specially declared

---

60   As a result of the general Decree n° 85-834 of 6 August 1985 (*JORF*, 7 August 1985, p. 9007) concerning the appointments of the managing positions in certain public institutions and national companies...
61   In the wake of a strong demonstration by the CNES' staff against the proposed French contribution to ESA for the ISS program during the ESA Ministerial Council of 18-20 October 1995 held in Toulouse, both president (A. Lebeau) and director-general (J.-D. Levi) were dismissed in the early 1996.
62   Decree of 31 January 1996 (*JORF* 6 February).
63   Decree 96-308 of 10 April 1996 (*JORF* 12 April).
64   June 1997 – May 2002: see §2.1.1.2 above.
65   Decree of 10 July 1997 (*JORF* 12 July).
66   Or *Président Directeur Général* (PDG) in French
67   R.-M. Bonnet, *Rapport de la commission de réflexion sur la politique spatiale (CRPS) – sans un CNES fort, pas d'Europe spatiale* (or 'Report of the appraisal commission on space policy – without a strong CNES, no Space Europe'), draft on 15 January 2003. Commission set up by letter of mission on 12 November 2002 at the request of both supervising ministers of the CNES, Michelle-Alliot Marie, Minister of Defence, Claudie Haigneré, minister delegate on the research and the new technologies, in charge of space policy. See also §2.1.2.3 on the Bonnet report regarding the Space Committee.

by a decree of 12 February[68] and soon a new president was appointed (Yannick d'Escatha) on 20 February.[69] The 1984 CNES decree was then amended a few years later by the 2005 decree abrogating all the content of its Article 8 on DG's attributions, but not the article's title, which remains reserved. Since 2005, a deputy director-general (DGD) or deputy CEO could be designated internally by the president, who would determine the scope of the delegated powers to this DGD.

2.2.3.2 The Current Powers of CNES' President, as Chief Executive Officer (CEO)

Under the current wording of the 1984 CNES decree (Art. 7),[70] the Chairman of the Board is to carry out the general management of the establishment. He represents the center in legal proceedings and all civil acts, in his dealings with third parties, and in the international relations. He ensures the preparation and the enforcement of the deliberations of the board. This decree specifies that "subject to the necessary approvals and within the framework of delegations granted by the board of directors, *the president is empowered* by in particular to":

- Conclude on behalf of the center any legal acts, agreements, or contracts;
- Implement any acquisitions, alienations, and value transfers as well as any purchases, sales, or rents of buildings;
- Implement any acquisition, deposit, or assignment of patent or of license;
- Represent the center in proceedings, enter into any transaction or international arbitrage;
- Take out any loans and pledge collateral or mortgage;
- Determine the use of liquid assets and the investment of the reserves.

Last but not least, the president has authority on the whole staff, concludes agreement of employment, recruits and dismisses the agents of any categories. As a result, the president is the *Chief Authorising Officer* (CAO)[71] of all revenues and expenditures. Formally, this means that the president is responsible and liable for the managing of budgetary funds and resources, for setting up advance funds, validate expenditures, and the checking of supporting document. Obviously, the president may delegate its *power* or its *signature*[72]

---

68 *JORF* n° 37, 13 February.
69 *JORF* n° 44, 20 February
70 Resulting from the January 2005's decree amending the 1984 CNES' one.
71 In French the *Ordonnateur Principal des recettes et des dépenses*.
72 According to the ordinary French administrative law:
   - the 'delegation of power' (or *délégation de pouvoir* in French) entails a full delegation (and discharge) of responsibility, for the purpose of accomplishing given tasks, the *delegate* receiving the liability burden.
   - the 'delegation of signature' (or *delegation de signature* in French) solely authorize the delegate to sign on behalf of the *principal* (or the *mandant* in French, i.e. the president), for the purpose of accomplishing given tasks, the later remaining responsible for the acts committed by the delegate in carrying out its mandate.

as CAO to *secondary* or other *authorizing officers*. Actually, the president of CNES, acting as CAO, delegates its responsibilities on CNES' daily management as follows:
- Delegation of power[73] in case of absence or impediment, and permanently as secondary authorizing officers to each director of establishment (Paris 'Head Office,' Paris 'launcher directorate,' Toulouse Space center and Kourou at the CSG launch range) as relates to security, logistics, health, discipline, and the overall administration.
- Delegation of signature, as CAO, for given operations to a large list of officers among CNES' managers and officers according to their hierarchical rank and to their respective specialization.

A separate regime of administrative delegations was set up from 2010 on matters related to the FSOA's implementation, in particular with regard to the safety and security authorities on activities to be carried out at the Guiana Space Center, where CNES' president has regulatory powers according to Article 21 of the FSOA.

2.2.4 State Economic, Budgetary, and Financial Control: The General Controller

The budgetary and financial control on CNES' daily management is exercised by a *General controller*[74] on behalf of the minister in charge of the budget.[75] The budgetary accounting for a public body like CNES[76] encompasses the accountancy of:
- *commitment appropriations* or *commitment authority* (or in French 'autorisations d'engagement', AE), in other words the financial capacity of contracting, in particular for launching or implementing space programs during the fiscal year[77];
- *payment appropriation* and *revenue,* or in French *crédits de paiement (CP)* and *crédits de recettes,* in other words the overall capacity of expense during the fiscal year.
- *employment authorization,* or in French *autorisations d'emplois,* in other words the allowed staff capacity.

Both delegations can be opposed to third parties.
73 *Ibid.*
74 Formerly named as 'State controller' or 'Economic and Financial Controller' for *Contrôleur économique et financier* or *Contrôleur d'Etat.*
75 Order of 12 February 2015 (*JORF* n° 0043 of 20 February, p. 3169) determining procedures for the exercise of budgetary and financial control on CNES taken in application of Arts. 220-228 of the aforesaid decree of n° 2012-1246 of 7 November 2012 and abrogating the former order of 5 June 2008 determining the special procedures for the economic and financial control of State on CNES.
76 Art. 204 of the aforesaid 2012 GBCP's decree.
77 Being understood that a multi-year commitment (*i.e.,* the signature of a contract) with industry on a space project development generates expenses during the current accounting year and/or beyond during the following one(s).

The above appropriations are themselves presented in the form of three envelopes: *staff* expenses, *functioning* expenses, and *investments* expenses. The budget scrutiny made by the general controller affects the *sustainability* and the regularity of the *budget planning* (*programmation budgétaire*) and running management with regard to the *commitments appropriations*. He also assesses the quality of the budgetary accounting. Basically, the *general controller* has his say on certain decisions or measures to be taken or implemented on behalf of CNES without prejudice, if any, of the final board or supervisory minister's competence on such decisions. To this extent, some CNES decisions having significant financial or economic consequences as listed in Article 7 of the CNES specific order of 2015,[78] in application of the aforesaid 2012 GBCP's decree, shall be submitted, by the relevant *authorizing officer*, to the *general controller* examination, in order to receive from the latter an *ex ante visa* (or *visa préalable*) or an *ex ante notice* (or *avis préalable*) as the case may be. The consequences of the general control assessment vary according to whether prior *visa* or prior *notice* is required:
- Where the *ex ante visa* is refused or withheld and the CAO maintains its proposal, the general controller refusal is referred to for decision to the higher supervising authority, i.e., the ministry in charge of the budget.
- Where the *ex ante notice*'s demand receives a negative response, the CAO may by means of reasoned and written decision, disregard under its own responsibility the general controller's refusal to endorse.

For example, according to Article 7 of the 2015 CNES order, the following are subject to the state general control's ex ante *visa*:
- general or category measures on recruitment, remuneration, or working time of employees having impact on the total payroll role of CNES;
- decisions on recruitment, remuneration, salary, and carrier development of executives;
- acquisitions and disposal of fixed assets (property ownership);
- leases other than state public domain land leases…

However, the following are to be submitted to the state general control's ex ante *notice*:
- framework procurement contracts with their associated policy rules;
- procurement contracts whose amount exceed a given threshold;
- transactions on litigation settlement before notification to third party for signature;
- staff recruitment contracts;
- penalties or indemnification for breach or resolution of contracts;
- loan, aids, and any shareholding transactions, when such operations were not approved before by the supervising authorities or the board of directors.

---

78   *Ibid.* Order of 12 February 2015.

Actually, in accordance with Article 10 of the 2015 CNES order, the general controller may, after discussion with the CAO, agree on a detailed list determining the operations to be submitted to its prior visa or notice, the respective threshold amount, the format of documents and justifications to be transmitted, as well as the periodicity and procedure of their transmission. Such an agreement was formalized in July 2015 by a joint decision signed by the general controller and CNES president. For the purpose of its mission, the general controller has an unlimited access to all documents relative to the enterprise's activity and management. He attends the board of directors meetings and the internal procurement commission without vote (CIM hereafter). The general controller is also entrusted with the mission of raising alarm toward the CNES' president as CAO and the minister supervising the State budget, for example in case of budgetary irregularity or financial risk in the execution of budget.

2.2.5 Public and Private Accountancy Rules: the Accounting Officer – the Statutory Auditors

Article 3 of December 1961 CNES' founding act indicated that the latter "ensures its financial management and presents its accountancy according to the *trade customs.*" However, a few months later, despite this mention of trade customs and its singular industrial and commercial nature, CNES was fully submitted to the general rules of public accountancy by the Order of 29 August 1963[79] on financial functioning procedure; this order itself refers to CNES' first application decree of 1962.[80] As a result, CNES was submitted to both *trade* and *public* rules of accountancy, the first one by act, the second by decree. This dual regime was endorsed, on the occasion of the formal codification of the 1961 founding act made on 2004, by a new wording of Article L331-5 of the Code of research. It was then specified that CNES "ensures its financial management and presents its accountancy following the regulations *relating to industrial and commercial public bodies* (EPIC) *having a public accountant.*"

It should be understood that *accountancy* does not mean only the passive bookkeeping, either by a trade or by a public standard, of financial and legal operations having an incidence on the balance sheet and statement of profit and loss. In public law,[81] *accountancy* also means *a prior systematic checking and formal validation*, made under the responsibility

---

79 See Art. 1, *JORF* 14 September 1963, p. 8316.
80 The later February 1962 CNES's decree (Art. 15) referring to the general regime of public accountancy which was reformed few months later by Decree n° 62-1587 of 29 December 1962 on public accounting general regulation, *JORF* 30 December 1962, p. 12828.
81 According to the regime nowadays consolidated by the aforesaid 2012 GBCP decree. The relevant provisions of the GBCP decree n° 2012-1246 of 7 November 2012 were introduced in the 1984 CNES' decree by the decree n° 2012-1247 (same date and same *JORF*).

of the *accounting officer (orAgent comptable)*, of any payment or billing proposed by the *authorising authority*. This formal *ex ante control* focuses on the regularity and the comprehensiveness of the supporting documents (invoice, contracts, quality of signatories, level of authorizing authority, but neither on the opportunity nor on the sustainability of the expense or the revenue as such.

Furthermore, in the application of the *financial security act* of 1 August 2003, CNES has been obliged, since 2006, as any private incorporated company, to draw up and publish consolidated accounts, for itself and its subsidiaries and stakes, with a management report and to make certified its accounts by *Statutory Auditors* or *'Commissaires aux Comptes'*.

2.2.6 Procurement Regulations: The Internal Procurement Commission

Since its 1962 decree and nowadays according to Article 4.7° of the 1984 decree, the CNES' board deliberates on *general conditions of procurement* for contracts, agreements, and public works contracts and the threshold from which such contracts must be submitted to it. As a result, a consultative *procurement commission* was set up to review the contract's proposal's prior acceptance either by the board or by the president, as the case may be.

The *procurement commission* statute is referred to in Article 9 of a ministerial order of 20 July 1990 dealing with the financial functioning procedures of CNES,[82] the latter forwarding to another interministerial order the task of determining the Commission's composition and functioning rules. This article 9, and its following application orders, were repealed by a ministerial order of 4 July 2007[83] transferring to the CNES' board the task of determining the composition and functioning rules and the powers of such commission, including its own submission thresholds. This commission became therefore a CNES internal consultative body.[84]

This reform of the internal procurement procedure was also a consequence of the application to the CNES as EPIC of the ordinary legal regime since the ordinance of n° 2005-649 of 6 June 2005. Indeed, before this 2005' ordinance, the general terms and conditions for procurement, funding, and monitoring of contracts were solely determined by the CNES' board of directors according to Article 4.7 of its 1984 decree. The only limit on the board's power of decision, under the original wording of Article 9 of the July 1990 order, whose wording had remained unchanged since the 1960s, was that such rules should

---

82 Order of 20 July 1990 on the CNES' *(financial) functioning procedures*, JORF n° 174 of 29 July 1990, p. 9147-9148. Not to be confused with its first application order, of the same day, determining the composition and the functioning rules of the *procurement commission* of CNES, published in the same JORF, p. 9148-9149. The later was abrogated by order of 28 June 2000 (JORF of 14 July, p. 10869) itself repealed by the aforesaid order of 4 July 2007. On this order of 1990 as to procurement commission, see also the beginning of §2.1.
83 JORF n° 163 of 17 July 2007.
84 Thus, its acronym became 'CIM' for *commission interne des marches* (Internal Procurement Commission)

be *inspired* from state procurement regulations, *i.e.*, from the *French Public Procurement Code*. It became then necessary to repeal this original provision of CNES' specific order, which had become inconsistent with the full application of the new regime of the 2005 ordinance. The new commission was then composed of six members, of which three were from CNES' staff appointed by the CNES' president. Three external members were appointed by the board of directors, under the CNES president's proposal, and no longer by order of the supervisory ministers as before. The general controller and the representative of the chief public accountant participate in the commission meetings without vote. The commission's opinion is rendered in the form of *prior notice*.[85] That means, in case of negative notice, that CNES president may disregard it under its own responsibility, by giving written reasons for its decision or, when applicable, by referring to the board of directors the commission's refusal to endorse the proposed contract. Implementation of CNES' procurement regime with industry and other space stakeholders is discussed in §4.1.3.1.

2.2.7 CNES' Staff Status

It is worth recalling here that one of the main reasons to provide CNES with an *EPIC* statute was to submit its staff to a private legal regime as to facilitate the process of recruiting high-potential individuals. This flexibility was of major interest to select, attract from the highest schools and universities, and further retain, CNES' engineers and scientists. This asset affected in particular the large range of staff to be sent on training mission at the NASA Goddard Space Flight Center (GSFC) for one year at least, in application of the 1961 bilateral agreement concerning the program FR-1 for the development of the first French satellite to be launched by a US launcher. CNES' employees thus were not subjected to a civil-servant regime for their recruitment, wages, and other benefits but to the Labor Code ordinary law (*see Code du travail, contrat de travail…*).

Nowadays, despite the increased administrative budgetary control on staff regime for any public body, private status of CNES' staff still facilitates recruitment, workforce management, pay increment, contributing to maintaining an attractiveness. As an illustration, as provided for by Article L611-7 of the Intellectual Property Code, CNES, like the industry, adopted a private regime of financial gratification for its employees' inventors of registered or exploited patents. CNES also set up a voluntary regime to facilitate incubation, spin-off, and start-up creations by its employees. This regime was *inspired* by the one provided for other public *administered research bodies* (such as CNRS…) set up by the *Allegre's Act* of 1999, July 12th. CNES' private staff status also have the advantage of enabling a *corporate*

---

85 Based on the same logic as those applicable on General controller's negative ex-ante notice (*see above* §2.2.4.4).

profit-sharing scheme based on its annual indicators of activity performance such as: completion of programs on due time and budget, functioning expenses reduction, increase of extra budgetary resources, number of successful launches, number of publications, number of patents registered...

However, as any staff working in a public organization or on behalf of a public mission, CNES' staff is subject to the common legal restrictions, with potentially associated criminal sanctions, on certain matters such as confidentiality, integrity, caution, deontology, and prevention of conflict of interests, corruption and bribery. These regulations are additional to those recently established toward the private sector on transparency to prevent corruption in economic affairs such as the so-called SAPIN's Act II.[86] In addition, due to CNES strategic mission as a Space agency and research center, its staff regime has been subjected to specific regulation on protection of national technology, export control, protection of its sensitive offices and premises....

Last but not least as a consequence of its FSOA new responsibilities, CNES has been required in 2009 by the government to guarantee, for itself and for its agents, that any data or information transmitted to it by operators or any private company for the needs of the authorization's application or monitoring process or for the needs of GSC' Regulations shall be kept confidential and strictly used for the purposes defined by such Space legislation. To this extent, in addition to the existing CNES staff regime on confidentiality, integrity, impartiality, ethics as inspired from civil servant staff regulations, a specific regime has been established with regard to CNES FSOA' officers. This regime is described in §4.3.3.

2.2.8 Synthesis on the Evolution of CNES' Governance Supervision

As a fore-conclusion on the CNES' governance supervision, we may retain that the traditional economic, financial, budgetary, and accounting state control has gradually been extended since 1961 to all the agency's management activities regarding space programs development, and notwithstanding its original industrial and commercial nature and the flexible statute designed by its founding act. On the other hand, one might also acknowledge that such state control rules have been drastically modernized along the same period in order to support the objectives of innovative public enterprises, in particular with the 1983 act on *democratization of public sector*, the 1982 and 1999 acts on research policy, the 2001 act governing *finance acts* (LOLF),[87] the 2003 *financial security act* (LSF),[88] the aforesaid

---

[86] In French: *Loi n° 2016-1691 du 9 décembre 2016 relative à la transparence, à la lutte contre la corruption et à la modernisation de la vie économique*, JORF n° 0287 of 10 December 2016.
[87] LOLF for *loi organique relative aux lois de finances* or 'Organic Law on Finance Laws', n° 2001-692 of 1 August 2001, JORF n° 177, 2 August 2001, p. 12480.
[88] LSF for *loi de sécurité financière* (or 'Financial Security Act') n° 2003-706 of 1 August 2003, JORF n° 177 of 2 August 2003, p. 13220.

ordinances of 2005 and 2015 on *public procurement* and the famous 2012 decree on *public budgetary accounting management* (GBCP).

Fortunately, both reverse curbs have converged on a right time for CNES, which in either way retained, even developed, its flexibility of functioning, its wide legal capacity and its financial strength. Indeed, as a matter of fact, the 1983 act on *democratization of public sector*, even storing definitively CNES and its majority shareholdings in the sphere of public enterprises, established institutions of personnel representatives (employee representative committee, or *comité d'entreprise*, employee representation at the CNES' board of directors with one-third of seats), which facilitated labour relations and helped to prevent social crises. It gave also the occasion to reform the CNES' functioning decree with the adoption of the June 1984 one that introduced many simplifications of management. Of which was the exemption of the administrative formality of a *prior specific order*[89] from supervising ministers before any acquisition and disposal of company's shares. Henceforth, all these decisions were just taken at the level of the board of directors (1984 decree, Art. 4.10). New legislations on *research policy* of 15 July 1982, 23 December 1985, and 12 July 1999, even rooting further CNES as a public research body despite its industrial and commercial nature, really contributed to reconciling both scientific and applicative or industrial research for the benefit of all space activities. These legislations set up many tools and incentives to facilitate transfers between the public scientific community and operational or market sectors, such as legal statutes for: GIP (group of public interest), spin-off, incubators, seed funding's instruments, compensations to inventor employees, creation of companies by public researchers…

The 2001's *LOFT on finance acts* confirmed, at the level of CNES, its existing *management framework model by objectives and performance indicators* as initiated since 2000, on a voluntary basis, with its first multi-year agreement conclude with the ministry of research in line with the *July 1999 Research Act* above. The *LSF of 2003 on financial security* brought CNES' financial and accounting management closer to the one of commercial companies providing it with a true *internal control system* (basically under the supervision of the board of directors' auditing committee), consolidating accounts with its majority shareholdings, and the control of external Auditors. The ordinances of July 2005 and July 2015 *on public procurement* enabled CNES to secure its tendering process, which had been developed empirically from the 1960s. The 2015 ordinance also formalized new procedures regarding R&D or pre-competitive activities, in particular the 'innovation partnerships' and the 'concession agreements' that CNES had experienced since the end of the 1990s but at that time without a clear established legal framework (*see, in particular*, in §4.1.3.2)

---

89 Under the ordinary regime of the Art. 2 of the Decree n° 53-707 of 9th August 1953 modified, « *relatif au contrôle de l'Etat sur les entreprises publiques nationales et certains organismes ayant un objet d'ordre économique ou social* » or « on state control of national public enterprises or certain public bodies of economic or social purpose »., *JORF* of 10 August 1953, p. 7051. See footnote 19 in §2.1.

More recently, the *2012 GBCP's decree* on public accounting and budgetary management gave a new impetus to the modernization and efficiency of its internal management and reporting system. All these regulations, rather than hindering CNES' functioning and missions contributed to strengthened them, while confirming solutions or procedures already anticipated by it or for which we may say that it was a precursor. To that extent, these external evolutions finally contributed to secure CNES' legitimacy and its trusting environment toward its various missions and programs.

3 Resources and Associated Supervision and Audit

3.1 CNES' Budget Appropriation

As provided by the Research Code's Article L331-1, CNES possess a financial autonomy. Article L331-4 on its part specifies how CNES can finance its missions. CNES has budget appropriations opened for Space research by the Finance Act (State Budget as authorized by the Parliament for the fiscal year), public or private subsidies, fees for services rendered, donations, financial profits and other benefits.

Basically, CNES resources come in majority from the civilian budget (on ministry of Research's proposal, namely at line 193 of the Finance Act), then from the ministry of Defence (line 191 of the Finance Act). The budget appropriation follows the *organic law* process relating to the *Finance laws* (for *loi organique relative aux lois de finances – LOLF*) as redrafted on 1 August 2001 to improve the efficiency of the public expenditures control. Actually, the budget for the following fiscal year is prepared between representatives from CNES and from its supervising ministers. The broad proposed appropriation as well as their associate objectives and performance expected and all the necessary information on the space program (line 193 and 191) are consolidated in the higher education and research minister's report annexed to the *draft finance act* (or the 'PLF' for *projet de loi de finance pour …*), as one of the so-called *yellow budgetary* (or *le jaune budgétaire*).[1]

The new *2001's organic law on public finance acts* (LOFT) reforming State budget process[2] organized a running by objectives of new public policies led to the setting up of appropriate efficiency indicators to measure these objectives' achievement. As a result, at the CNES level, a practice of five multi-year framework *contract of objectives* has been developed to aggregate CNES' programs and activities and their financial resources and staff appropriation and related expenditure payment plan, included the associated indicator of performance such as in respect of cost and delays, success of mission…[3]

Once voted and published in the finance act on each 31st December for execution in the coming year, CNES budget is adopted in a detailed form (EPRD) by the board (1984 CNES' decree Art. 4), under the control of the supervising ministers, in particular under

---

1 For 2018, *see* the following link: https://www.performance-publique.budget.gouv.fr/sites/performance_publique/files/farandole/ressources/2018/pap/pdf/jaunes/jaune2018_recherche.pdf.
2 LOLF, *see* footnote under §2.2.8 above.
3 *See below*, on the following section 3.2.2, the impact of HCERES' assessment report on the elaboration of each multi-year framework contract.

the one of the minister for budget, and then executed on behalf of CNES, under the authority of its president acting as *chief authorizing officer* (*ordonnateur principal*) and the daily monitoring or controls of the *general controller* (on budget) and of the *chief public accountant* (*agent comptable principal*).

3.2 Auditing Bodies (ex-post control)

3.2.1 The National Court of Auditors (Cour des Comptes)

By a special order of 3 April 1964,[4] CNES entered the list of public bodies subject to supervision of the national Court of Auditors (*Cour des comptes*). According to Article L 133-1 of the financial jurisdictions Code, the court may check and assess, over a given period of several years, the sincerity and reliability of CNES' accounts, including those of its shareholdings, such as Arianespace and Spot image formerly, and also the accounts of a given program, even those developed through a wider intergovernmental legal framework, provided that CNES made a significant contribution to the latter achievement (for instance: Ariane, Soyuz at CSG, Spot, Galileo). It is worth noting that the court's assessment also includes the examination of the advisability, or opportunity, of management decisions made on behalf of these programs or activities either from CNES' leaders or others. In this respect, lets recall that Auditors of the National Court should not be confused with the *Statutory Auditors* or '*Commissaires aux comptes*' responsible for certifying CNES annual accounts and financial statements as in all enterprise (see §2.2.5). The court's draft reports and its recommendations may, after discussion with CNES, be published in the form of official report. Such appraisal reports are generally largely covered by the media in France, like abroad.

3.2.2 The High Council for the Evaluation of the Research and the Higher Education (HCERES)

The *High Council for the evaluation of the research and the higher education* (or *Haut Conseil de l'évaluation de la recherche et de l'enseignement supérieur*, HCERES) is the French independent administrative authority competent in the field of public higher education and research. HCERES was set up by act of 2013,[5] abrogating the one of 2006[6]

---

[4] JORF 13 May 1964, p. 04048.
[5] Art. 90 of the Act n° 2013-660 of 22 July 2013 concerning the high education and research, *JORF* n° 0169 of 23 July 2013, p. 12235
[6] *Programme act for the research* n° 2006-450 of 18th April 2006, *JORF* n° 92 of 19 April 2006, p. 5820.

having created its progenitor, namely the *Agency of evaluation of the research and the higher education* (AERES). As a result, in accordance with the Research Code's Article L 114-3-1, CNES became subject successively to the assessment of the AERES and the HCERES.

Actually, this is a result of the incorporation made in 2004[7] of the 1961 CNES' statutory into the first codified Research Code (CR)'s legislative provisions, and more specifically under Articles L331-1 et seq. of the latter. It became then automatically registered as a *public research organization* and placed under the permanent and general supervisory authority of the minister for research, independently of the additional supervisory authority empowered specifically to the same minister on *space policy and CNES as space agency*.

This new evaluation procedure then has become anything but an additional formality since such evaluation from HCERES serves as a basis for the establishment of each multiyear *contract of objectives and performance.*[8]

3.2.3   Other Specific High Level Assessment Missions or Appraisal Reports

In addition to all these authorities, courts, councils, commissions, committees, and other bodies responsible either for *ex ante* or *ex post* permanent or punctual control, monitoring, auditing, or supervision of CNES activities as a public body, the French government or the French parliament has extensively favoured commissioning of high-level experts to get an independent view on space policy and programs and to evaluate CNES' governance performances and to propose necessary reforms. Among the most famous appraisal reports we may underline[9] since the end of the 1960s:

- J.-P. Causse, on the *preparation of the European space conference*, January 1968.
- P. Aigrain, *French Space Policy– report for the minister of scientific and industrial development*, March 1970.
- J.-P. Capron on French *Space Policy, report for the French minister of industry, commerce and small businesses*, October 1977.
- P. Sahut d'Izarn, Report for the Minister on *Space*, November 1986.
- F. Lepatre, on the *European space industry*, July 1988.

---

7   Ordinance n° 2004-545 of 11 June 2004 on the codification of the legislative part of the Research Code (CR), *JORF* n° 138 of 16 June 2004, p. 10719.
8   AERES, Self-evaluation report of 2010 from CNES to AERES, Paris, 15 July 2012. As a basis for the CNES' contract of objectives, on the period 2011-2015.
    HCERES, Assessment report on CNES by the High committee of assessment of research and science organizations, HCERES), January 2015. As a basis for the contract of objectives and performance – 'innovation and inspiration' on the period 2016-2020.
9   The list of which is given in this bibliography below.

- P. Loridant, on the *Orientation of the French and European Space policy*, OPECST, National Assembly, December 1991.
- CNER, *Assessment report on the French space program*, September1992.
- A. Paecht, *A new deal for military space*, report to the National Assembly's Finance Commission, January 1995.
- M. Carpentier, *the French space policy in the European and worldwide context* (CES), June 1997.
- H. Revol, *Space: a political and strategic ambition for Europe* (OPECST), May 2001.
- X. Pintat, *Space cooperation France-Russia* (Senate, April 2001).
- R.-M. Bonnet, *Report of the appraisal commission on space policy – without a strong CNES, no Space Europe*, January 2003.
- A. Pompidou, *Space policy on industrial research and development*, June 2004.
- J.-L. Pujet (edited by), report from the Academy of Science to the Ministry ot Research, 'French Space Research'. EDP sciences, March 2006.
- B. Bigot, Yannick d'Escatha and Laurent Collet-Billon, *a stake for space policy: ensuring an autonomous and sustainable access to space for the Europe* (May 2009).
- J.-L. Pujet, *Space sciences – adapting French research to space issues*. EDP sciences, Oct. 2010.
- E. Sartorius, CAP, *a space ambition for Europe* (October 2011)
- D. Lucas, Director of the Choiseul Institute, *which space policy for France – let us give more space to the industry* (July 2012).
- G. Fioraso, former minister for higher education and research, Report to the Prime minister – 'Open Space – openness as a response to the challenges of space sector', published on 26 July 2016,

Last but not least, the scientific output of such space programs is subject to frequent assessment by experts' commissions, ad hoc committees, peer review, CNES' Committee of Scientific Programs (CPS), ... and to the supervision of the ministry for research.

4 Mission's Conditions of Implementation: Space Research and Development Programs

Most of the space projects driven by CNES stem from commitments made under international cooperation, engaged by itself or under other diplomatic consideration by the French government, or within European institutions such as the European Space Agency or the European Union (UE). As developed by many experts or leaders on space policy and programs, such as Jean-Jacques Dordain or John Logdson,[1] the space effort for the last 60 years has been supported by states through the conjunction of two main drivers, which are apparently inconsistent with each other: 'cooperation and competition.' The spirit of cooperation was in the 'gene' of the 1967 UN Outer Space Treaty.[2] Furthermore, the UN General Assembly, in 1996, approved the 'Benefits Declaration,'[3] which promotes international cooperation by any means, while taking into particular account the needs of developing countries: their need for technical assistance for reaching their development goals on space capabilities, space science and technology, and their application.

On the other side, government's strategic interest, prestige race, economic policy and private initiative of the space industry, especially nowadays with the new space entrepreneurs, spur competition between each other. The technical and scientific level of complexity, the scope of financial burden required for investments in space projects lead first the governments, then more recently the private sector, or both jointly, to pool their efforts to achieve their common ambitions while reducing the risks and costs of each. CNES thus did not differ to this general two-headed nature of space agencies' mission, balancing between competition and cooperation, in other words in a dialectical relationship between:

---

1 See Chapter 1, footnote 4 here above in the 'earliest steps ....'.
2 Treaty on Principles Governing the Activities of States in the Exploration and Use of Outer Space, including the Moon and Other Celestial Bodies, of 27 January 1967.
Preambule: 'Desiring to contribute to broad *international cooperation* in the scientific as well as the legal aspects of the exploration and use of outer space for peaceful purposes, ... Believing that *such cooperation* will contribute to the development of mutual understanding and to the strengthening of friendly relations between States and peoples.'
Art. 1: [...] There shall be freedom of scientific investigation in outer space, including the Moon and other celestial bodies, and *States shall facilitate and encourage international cooperation* in such investigation.
3 The Declaration on International Cooperation in the Exploration and Use of Outer Space for the Benefit and in the Interest of All States, Taking into Particular Account the Needs of Developing Countries. General Assembly resolution 51/122 of 13 December 1996.

- A traditional *colbertist*[4] mission toward the domestic space sector in research and industry, in order to develop an autonomous and value-added national capacity on the benefit of developing economic growth and new applications of general interest, including security and environment.
- A *cooperative* mission, to further or enhance this current domestic capacity and share risks and management skills, especially for ambitious Space programs.

For these reasons, CNES, according to Article 2 of its 1961[5] constitutional Act, was empowered on the one hand to propose and implement research programs of *national interest* (in paragraph b and c), and on the other hand (the following paragraph d) to "monitor Space *international cooperation* related issues in relation with the Ministry of Foreign Affairs, and to ensure the implementation of international programs share allocated to CNES." In this respect, CNES' program and budgets were commonly separated into two parts: the national program, developed in §4.1, that is mostly, if not totally, implemented through international cooperation and the French (or CNES)'s contribution to the European space agency (ESA), generally representing half of its budget, as will be discussed in paragraph 4.2.

4.1 French National Program and International Cooperation

4.1.1 *National Requirements*

Any CNES' space project or activity has to be authorized with its given multiannual budget allocation by French governmental authorities, in compliance with the relevant finance Act enshrinement. As already mentioned herein, this governmental authorization is formalized through a decision made by the CNES' board of directors, the latter being effective except opposition offered by its line ministries within a given period (*see* §2.2.1 and below 4.1.1.1). Governmental decision on important space project may also be formalized by a specific interministerial decision released by the government through official press notice[6]

---

4   'Colbertism' is a concept of command economy developed in France in the 16th century by Jean-Baptiste Colbert, Minister of finance and General Controller of Finance of King Louis XIV. Such policy is traditionally implemented through public aids and subsidy to support exports, protectionism to control imports, and focussed public procurement toward potentially value added of domestic manufacturing industry.
5   Act n° 61-1382 of 19 December 1961, codified under the Research Code, in Art. L331-1 to L331-8.
6   For an example, Press notice from the Prime Minister' services, on October 4th, 1994, on the French spatial policy, announcing the decision to launch of following programs: SPOT 5 (civil Earth observation satellite) in synergy with the launch of second generation of the defence Earth observation satellite (Helios II) and Stentor a new generation telecommunication satellite demonstrator.

or published by decree in the official gazette.[7] In such circumstances, the board of directors shall deliberate on the implementation measures such as contracts and budget allocation. CNES is not subject to FSOA for its space operations and activities on space-based data (FSOA Art. 27) but has to respect certain procedures (*see below* 4.1.1.2). In addition, other national authorizations may be required as regards national security, frequency spectrum allocation, network and services and competition law compliance (*see below* 4.1.1.3).

4.1.1.1   General Regime for CNES' Program Authorization

As indicated above,[8] according to Article 4 of the current 1984 CNES decree, the administrative decision for any programs and activities belongs to its Board of Directors (*Conseil d'administration*), where all its line ministries (*ministères de tutelle*) sit.

More specifically, the board of directors deliberates on the program of activities and investments (4.1°), their budget appropriation (4.3°), and if necessary on authorization to undertake negotiations to conclude associated international administrative agreements (4. 13° and Art. 6). These board decisions are enforceable unless opposition notified by the *Government Commissioner* within a 10-day period, being given that such opposition to be effective shall be confirmed by major line ministries in a one-month period.

4.1.1.2   Specific Regime of Authorization on Space Operations and Space-Based Data (FSOA)

CNES is out of the scope of the FSOA administrative authorization process, for any of its Space Operation or other activity in relation with Earth observation satellites data receiving and programming (*SBD*), in application of its Article 27, provided that such activities fall under the scope of its 'public mission[9]... after approval by the administrative authority.' This 'public mission' refers to the CNES' main mission 'to prepare and put forward proposals to the administrative authority for programmes of national interest in the field of space.' As regards the FSOA administrative authorization, it is worth underlining that beyond the interministerial nature of any of these board decisions, such board includes the vote of the representative of supervisory ministry in charge of Space Affairs, which is as such the sole competent administrative department for any FSOA's authorizations. CNES' space operations or SBD activities are then prepared and carried out under the supervision of its president, in particular as regards the technical and safety compliance with the FSOA's Technical regulations and, as the case may be, with the CSG' facilities

---

7   For an example, the 2004 Pleiade's Decree n° 2004-1395 of 20 December 2004, namely the decree 'on the application of the Art. VIII of the agreement between the Government of French Republic and the Government of the Italian Republic concerning a cooperation on the Earth observation,' *JORF* n°300 of 26 December 2004.
8   In Chapter 2, §2.2.1.
9   Pursuant Art. L. 331-2 of the Research Code.

exploitation regulation (REI-CSG). Government administrative and financial of control and audit are carried out as described in this Part I in Chapters 2 and 3. This Article 27's FSOA exemption regime as to the *administrative procedure* affects the following situations where CNES acts as a *Space Operator* for a space vehicle under:
- a bilateral or multilateral international cooperation, where France is accordingly the Jurisdiction State, the Launching State and/or Registration State of the Space object under United Nation Space treaties (OST 1967[10], Art. VI, VII, and VIII, 1972 Liability Convention, 1975 Registration convention);
- a national partnership or contract with other public bodies (DGA for Defence ministry, public research organization CNRS-INSU, CEA, etc....).
- delegation of ESA, EU or their public partners.

As relates to launcher systems, it shall be underlined also that, on a strict legal point of view, CNES does not act any longer as a *Launch Operator* since the end of *Diamant-B* program with its last launch in September1975. Since the early beginnings of the Ariane program, this responsibility and the associated potential liability toward third parties belong to ESA with regard to the *systemdevelopment phase* up to the successful maiden qualifying flight, consistently with the provisions of the ESA–French Government Agreement on the CSG (since 1975). And then, along the *exploitation or production's phases* duration (since 1980), the space launch operation's responsibility and the associated potential liability toward third parties is entrusted to Arianespace company according to the relevant Declaration on production or exploitation[11] between the relevant participating ESA State Members. The same *declaration* also set up the associate allocation of third-party liability at the level of *launching state* between ESA' members and France, for each launch system *(i.e.; currently Ariane, Soyuz and Vega)* with regard to the UN 1972 Liability Convention and the indemnification burden to be left to Arianespace (*i.e.* currently the ceiling 60 million of Euros, see §7.2.2).

4.1.1.3 Other Prior Authorizations: National Security, Frequency Spectrum, Network and Services and Competition Law Compliance

In addition to the prior authorization to be granted by its board of directors to undertake any space project, CNES may require other specific governmental authorizations or licenses regarding national security, frequency spectrum use, network and services, and competition

---

10 Treaty on Principles Governing the Activities of States in the Exploration and Use of Outer Space (1967), including the Moon and Other Celestial Bodies, adopted by the General Assembly in its resolution 2222 (XXI), opened for signature on 27 January 1967, entered into force on 10 October 1967. The 1967 OST treaty
11 See 1.2.2.3., *Ibid* footnote 34 and 35.

compliance. These procedures for CNES are to be compared with the ordinary ones applicable for private operators.[12]

National security

CNES shall require a separate authorization from SGDSN,[13] the French national security board, prior to entering into any international cooperation. CNES may also require a specific assessment from the CIEEMG[14] for exporting or importing sensitive space vehicles or their components and associated services under the French Export Control's legislation. Furthermore, CNES shall also respect foreign Export Control regimes, such as the US International Traffic in Arms Regulations (ITAR) or Export Administration Regulations (EAR), that may regulate on their side import or transit on space-related articles and services. Such national and foreign legislations are indeed applicable for any space cooperation from the first preliminary discussions, by means of a dedicated Technical Assistance Agreement (TAA) and then for export, even temporary for the need of test or for launching purpose.

Frequency spectrum allocation for vehicle and payload telemetry

Any space vehicle, for the purpose of communicating with the Earth, has to have access to an appropriate bandwidth of the global radio-frequency spectrum. This right is to be assigned by the French government, namely the Ministry of Economy, Industry, and Digital, in accordance with the radio-communication rules of coordination defined within the framework of the International Telecommunication Union (ITU). Basically, the request for frequency allocation shall be made to the ANFr (the French National Frequencies Board), who checks conformity with the national Table of Frequency Band Allocations, declares the allocation to the IUT, and takes fees. Then the authorization decision of the Minister in charge of electronic communications is made after obtaining the opinion of the 'assigning authorities' for the frequencies concerned. It should be noted here that CNES is one of the 'assigning authorities' for certain frequency band related to Spacecraft command services or, by default, on unique space services such as exploration, observation, navigation, and meteorology from space according to the Order of 9 July 1987 (*JORF*, 1 August 1978, p. 8651). Thus for such space services systems, CNES remains its own 'assigning authority.' In this respect, CNES may be the assigning authority for its own

---

12 See §7.5.
13 For *Secrétariat Général de la Défense et de la Sécurité Nationale* or 'General Secretariat for Defence and Security,' a service attached to the Prime minister. A representative of SGDSN sits on CNES' Board on behalf of the Prime minister (Art. 1 of 1984 CNES' Decree).
14 *Commission interministérielle pour l'étude des exportations de matériels de guerre* (CIEEMG).

programs or activities of general interest, those of other public international organizations such as ESA and even EU,[15] or those of the private sector as to observation systems.

Network or services open to the public
Beyond the allocation of frequencies above, a specific authorisation may be necessary to operate a satellite telecommunication networks or to provide satellite telecommunications open to the public in France. As an illustration, for demonstrative or operational systems on *telecommunication services* such as *Locstar*, or *Stentor* in the 1990s CNES, was to obtain specific authorizations from the ministry or the competent regulation authority (ARCEP) as any other ordinary operator.[16]

Competition law compliance
Grounded in the principles of non-discrimination and free access to the market, the general World Trade Organization (WTO) and European Union (EU) Competition Law can also restrict drastically industry-government cooperation in the space sector, in particular:
- *Public procurement law*, affecting any kind of national space agencies contracts (purchase, partnership, concessions) to be awarded to domestic or foreign industry.
- *Public aid law* for any kind of State subsidies or support granted to the private sector, including privileges granted to the latter to access governmental facilities and services.

These legal requirements were not significant up to now toward traditional interventions of national agencies with their research and development (R&D) activities and space systems pre-competitive development programs due to the strategic character of such support to the industry. The question, however, is more likely to be raised in the context of *New Space* where projects are initiated and mainly financed by private entrepreneurs who intervened in a sector that has turned highly competitive such as the *Internet* sector and its *mobile applications*. As far as CNES is concerned, its general interest mission activities, on the scientific and technical field as stated in its founding act and supervised by its board and ministers' authorities, by nature remain limited to upstream research or to development activities of *pre-competitive* nature, in other words beneath the 'radar control' of public

---

15 ESA's satellites telemetry networks, telecommunication satellites demonstrators (ARTES), Ariane tracking stations… EU's Galileo navigation satellite bandwidth…
16 Order of 21 April 1994 of the ministry of industry, post office and telecommunication 'authorizing the exploitation of and independent telecommunication network by satellites' as to the creation of a Group of Closed Users or *Groupement fermé d'utilisateurs – (GFU)* associated with a project of space telecommunication demonstration, *JORF* n° 110 of 12 May 1994, p. 6948.
Decision of the French Regulation Authority of Telecommunications (*or Autorité de regulation des Telecommunications – ART*, now renamed 'ARCEP' for *Autorité de regulation des communications électroniques et de la poste* or 'Regulation Authority for Electronic Communications and Post office') concerning independents network; as to the creation of a Group of Closed Users for a broadcasting network among the space and education community

aid law. However, when applicable, in particular as relates to subsidiaries' operations, CNES shall seize the relevant competitions authorities, namely the French Authority of Competition or the EU's DG competition, prior to entering into any transaction falling under their competence such as shareholding acquisition or assignment, or concessions of public services…

4.1.2 CNES' International Cooperation Mechanisms

Traditionally Space cooperation agreements are generated by governments or their space agencies, on a bilateral or multilateral frame, in coherence with their own strategic interests in the domain of science, technology, public services, domestic industry, diplomacy, security, and defense. In France, such agreements are to be negotiated between the ministry of foreign affairs in connection with CNES[17] in accordance with the relevant regulations such as the Administrative Circular of 30 May 1997 on the 'Preparation and Conclusion of International Agreements.'[18] According to Article 53 of the French Constitution of 4 October 1958,[19] intergovernmental agreements committing the finance of French State or containing other substantial binding obligations or provisions that contradict common law (for example, as relates the IPR code, investments…) shall be ratified by Parliament. This ratification is a prerequisite for cooperation arrangement's entry into force, and such process may take several years and so being altered by political changes. Those ratification uncertainties or delays do not suit an efficient running of challenging space projects. This is one of the reasons why CNES was empowered through its founding Act[20] with a legal personality distinct from the one of the French State and a financial autonomy and legal capacity in order to propose, design, and then implement space activities under international cooperation, either for the purpose of its national program or for the ones driven at the European level of ESA.

Furthermore, at the level of its statutory decree,[21] CNES can be authorized by its board of directors "to undertake, for the implementation of its program of international relations, negotiations which can lead to the conclusion of International Administrative Arrangements" (*see* the Implementing Arrangements or MoU). On another note, CNES as many

---

17 CNES' Founding Act, CR L331-2 (d): "Among CNES responsibilities is to …develop international cooperation in the field of space in conjunction with the Ministry of Foreign Affairs and to ensure execution of France's contributions to international programmes."
18 *JORF* n° 0125 of 31 May 1997, p. 8415.
19 Current version of the text available on the Constitutional Council's web site at: www.conseil-constitutionnel.fr/…constitutionnel/francais/…constitution/…constitution…
20 1961 CNES' Act: Arts. 1, 2.2, 2.3, and 2.4 and then Code of Research: Arts. L331-1 and L331-2 (b), (c) and (e).
21 The 1984 CNES' modified decree in its Arts. 4-13 and 6.

other space agencies in the world, based its standard cooperation agreement on a principle of reciprocal 'best effort' obligations, without exchange of funds between parties, in order to also remain outside the scope of the French Constitution's Article 53. In any case, implementation of international projects shall respect the domestic rules on governmental authorizations, as indicated in §4.1, or towards private partners as discussed in §4.1.3, in particular with regard to public procurement law. CNES should also consider the financial autonomy and the legal capacity of the international partners with whom it cooperates:

- Some agencies are branches or administrative departments of their government with a strong delegated authority (NASA in the USA).
- Others like it have a full legal capacity, with own judicial personality distinct from that of the State, even if closely controlled by the latter.
- Others have an intermediate status (DLR in Germany, JAXA in Japan…).

All these discrepancies between space agencies statutes have to be duly taken into account while negotiating international cooperation agreements, in particular regarding the clauses of responsibility, management, liability, financing commitments, exchange of staff, confidentiality, waivers of claims, and termination and settlement of litigation. As an example, the intergovernmental cooperation framework between the United States and France, as initiated from 1961, extended in 1966[22] and later, had to be adapted in 2007[23] with regard to the cross-waiver of claim's clause, in order to integrate expressly CNES as the French Implementation Agency, given the fact that it has a judicial personality distinct from that of the French State. As a matter of fact, under the UN Space treaties, namely the 1972 UN convention on liability, for any damage to third parties resulting from their common cooperation, the relevant participating *launching states*, namely the French and U.S. governments, are solely potentially 'liable,' jointly and severally, for indemnification toward a third party (or the *state victim*) in connection with damage caused to the latter on ground or in air space. Thus, it was necessary regarding the application of such cross-waiver of claim to raise CNES at the level of the French State, consistently with the situation of NASA toward the U.S. government.

---

22   The first agreement was signed, before the CNES setting up, on 21 March 1961 by NASA and the French DGRST and Space Research Committee, represented respectively by High L. Dryden, Pierre Piganiol and Pierre Auger (the FR-1 agreement). This agreement was extended, for the purpose of FR-2 and Eole development, by exchange of letter, signed on 16 June 1966 and 17 June 1966; between the representatives of both governments confirming the agreement made initially by CNES and NASA. This exchange of letter was published on the French Gazette by the Decree n° 71-206 of 16 March 1966, *JORF* 20 March 1971.

23   Art. 9 A. (1) of the Agreement between the United States of America and France, signed at Paris on 23 January 2007.
     Agreement ratified by the Act n° 2008-133 of 13 February 2008, *JORF* n° 0039 of 15 February 2008, p. 2777.
     Published by Decree n° 2008-488 of 22 May 2008, *JORF* n° 121 of 25 May 2008.

4.1.2.1 Traditional Building Blocks of CNES' International Space Cooperation

The first step is to set up a 'framework agreement' at the state level, between the governments involved in close relations with their respective space agencies as 'implementing agencies.' Such umbrella agreements are generally prepared and implemented after their signature by such space agencies according to their own legal competence. Following steps on specific projects will be organized through 'implementation arrangement' between agencies. Cooperation can also be engaged or extended under alternative arrangements such as Letters of Intent (LoI), exchanges of Letter of Agreement (LoA), and Memorandum of Understanding (MoU).

All these agreements are built on common legal and contractual principles, which are broadly summarized as follows. Each Space agency is responsible for the implementation of its own work-package. Its achievement is managed in relation to its industry and/or the scientific community under contracts following its applicable procurement rules. These internal rules for CNES are developed in §4.1.3 and §4.3.

Framework agreements (FA)
Such higher level framework agreements shall define:
- *Fields of cooperation activities*, in identifying domains of mutual interest for developing programs or projects in cooperation, priority themes for which agencies intend to lead joint projects in a near future
- *Common terms and conditions*, which apply to any specific 'implementing agreement' for every future joint project in the absence of opposite clause. These include the following clauses: responsibilities, third party liability regime, exchange of staff, financial capacities, confidentiality, intellectual property, publication / communication, customs duties and taxes, export control, interpretation, dispute settlement and others legal clauses, etc.
- *Cooperation governance*, which is traditionally entrusted to an *Executive or Steering Committee* in charge of designing and reporting on the cooperation program and projects developed by the parties and proposing and approving any further domain of cooperation.

Framework agreements are concluded for a given duration, often with tacit renewal.

Implementing arrangements (IA)
In the second step, in explicit application of a framework agreement (FA), an *Implementation Arrangement* (IA)[24] is to be concluded to define the terms and conditions applicable to any specific project. IA resumes measures expressed in the framework agreement,

---

24 Called in France *Arrangement Administratif International* for 'International Administrative Arrangements.'

completes and modifies them whenever necessary, as long as it does not distort the essential principles. It contains a number of technical provisions related to project established:
- Precise description of the mission.
- Detailed definition of the technical responsibilities shared by parties, from the development to the end of exploitation of the Space system, with a reference to the 'Project Implementation Plan' (PIP) appended.
- Management of the project including settlement of dispute.
- Relation with third partners (other agencies involved, scientific community, users).
- Exchange of staffs.
- Intellectual property on developed systems.
- Confidentiality rules.
- Media policy.
- Customs and tax.
- Export control procedures in each country.
- Care of goods stored in the other party's facility (risks of loss, third party liability, maintenance costs).
- Registration of the Space vehicle (satellite, station…).
- Ownership on equipment (instruments *vs* satellites)
- Data policy on satellites measurements or images (right of access and use, price, IPR…).
- Third party liability for damage on the ground or Space.
- Recording of frequency band.
- Specific final and legal clauses: amendment, termination, notification, language, applicable law, court, dispute.

4.1.2.2 Other Forms of Arrangement

For more flexibility, the following formula, LoI, LoA and MoU, can be used among space agencies outside existing agreement above (FA or IP) or in addition to such agreements for specific or detachable projects. Attention should be paid to the fact that these types of instruments, in particular the 'memorandum of understanding' (MoU) can create confusion between parties of different law systems on the binding character of the signed commitment. An MoU may not always be considered as legally binding instruments but as 'gentleman's agreement' in some Anglo-Saxon countries. In France the international law approach is to recognize any commitment taken in the name of the government the value of an international agreement creating legal obligations. Parties shall therefore ensure that they are committed at the same level. For this purpose, the Administrative Circular of the General Secretary of Government of 1997[25] invites expressively French delegations to consider with precaution the negotiation of such form of agreement.

---

25   *See* footnote 18 above on 'Administrative Circular' of 30 May 1997.

The letter of intent (LoI)
The letter of Intent is a flexible and simple means to formalize the *kick-off* of discussions between agencies. It recalls a number of points already understood or agreed upon only informally. It formulates the parties' willingness to cooperate and the objectives to be discussed. As such it is the first written expression signed at the high level between the parties. LoI often contains precautionary measures on exchanges of information and confidentiality rules.

The letter of agreement (LoA)
The LoA stands for a cooperation agreement in the form of exchange of letters. LoA is often used within the framework of a cooperation program where one agency proposes to another to participate under conditions laid down in it. Such form is rather similar to an *adhesion contract*, given the fact that the response (acceptance), to form the agreement, is to be drafted strictly under the same words as those used in the first issued letter. However, basically agencies' teams have scrupulously negotiated the LoA's wording before forwarding it for the signature process toward their respective management.

The memorandum of understanding (MoU)
This type of arrangement is commonly used to cooperate on a particular project in a specific domain, outside or in the margin of any intergovernmental agreement or existing framework agreement between agencies. An MoU's content is generally more detailed as related to LoA and rather comparable to that of IA described above. However, MoU's legal enforceability is more questionable as mentioned above.

4.1.2.3 Common Features on International Cooperation Instruments
Irrespective of their various legal forms (FA, IA, LoI, LoA, MoU) as described above, all these arrangements broadly have a similar architecture and contains the same type clauses as described below:
- **Civil, scientific and/or technical main purpose** , but not exclusively for example the Russian-French 2003 cooperation agreement on Soyuz in Guiana, which has a rather *operational* and *commercial* scope. It also exists among Europe states *dual* or in *defense* cooperation's arrangements between ministries of defense and space agencies for the joint development of space systems such as, regarding CNES contributions, the earth observation satellites Pleiade, Helios, CSO Musis or the telecommunication system Athena-Fidus…
- **Best effort obligation** , as opposed to 'performance obligation' is established among states or between their respective agencies as a response of domestic budgetary proce-

dure (as an anticipation of the risk of credit freezing or cancellation) or to by-pass the obligation of parliament ratification required for any financially binding commitments.[26]

- **Full sovereignty of respective agencies on project achievement**. Each agency has to organize at its own expense in its own country or sphere of competence the implementation of its work package: *in house,* procurement to industry, partnership agreement (*see* §4.1.3 for CNES).
- **No exchange of funds**. In line with their 'best effort obligation' above, parties' commitments are only limited to the works of interface, coordination, and integration of their respective contributions. Thus, parties' contributions focus only on proper achievement of their technical work packages.
- **Monitoring and governance of interface coordination**. Falls within the competence of dedicate review and steering committee.
- **Prohibition or limitation of technology transfer**. It leads to very protective clauses of intellectual property, exchanges of knowledge limited to the strict needs of the cooperation such as interface knowledge as set in a dedicated appended 'Project Implementation Plan.' Thus, only with rare exception, technology transfer is generally speaking out of purpose of such international cooperation.
- **Confidentiality**. Toward third parties unless otherwise agreed.
- **Open data or non-discriminatory data policy**. For data obtained from Space instruments for any user due to the civil or scientific subject of most of space cooperation. However, it remains an exception in some scientific projects in favor of the selected *Prime Investigators* (PI) who may receive a limited exclusive period of use of data at the beginning of the mission in orbit, period generally associated with the calibration and validation process of data.
- **Absence of guarantee**. As a result of latent defect or willingness fault, in particular in case of failure during the launch or defective functioning in orbit. This clause is to be linked with the absence of exchange of fund and best effort obligation above.
- **Cross waivers of claims**. Between parties and their associates (Space agencies, scientific partners, subcontractors…). This exception to the common principle of enforceability of contracts, where each breach is to be potentially sanctioned by the judge, can be added to the other drastic limitation of parties' contractual responsibilities set in the above clauses of *no exchange of fund, best efforts* and *absence or limited guarantee*. It is worth underlining to this extent that such *waivers of claim' clauses* were also enshrined in FSOA's Article 21 toward the whole contracting parties associated with the same space operation.[27]

---

26 See French Constitution of 4 October 1958, Art. 53 above in footnote 19.
27 *See* Chapter 7, §7.3 'Legal Relationships between Private Stakeholders Participating to a Space Operation.'

4 Mission's Conditions of Implementation: Space Research and Development Programs

- **Settlement of dispute**. Decided as last resort exclusively by the parties, on the basis of the arrangement's terms and conditions. Basically, the competence of national courts and law has to be excluded for the interpretation of such arrangements.

4.1.3 Implementation with Industry and Other Space Stakeholders

The implementation of each work package of a space project either developed on a national scale or under international cooperation arrangement is to be managed at the level of the relevant space agencies involved. Thus, according to its legal capacities, CNES award contracts to the industry and to its scientific partners to satisfy its national or international commitments. For this purpose, purchase agreement or contract is the legal vehicle privileged by CNES because it allows a better monitoring of industry's performances and schedule. Originally procurement rules were quite flexible for national Space agencies' purchases as they were awarded to an emerging domestic industry. CNES under its earliest functioning rules[28] was strictly exempted from complying with the Public Procurement Code (or *Code des marchés publics*), being just invited to take into account such code principles in its contracts (*see* §2.2.6).

This period is now over. Public procurement regulation has been strengthened all over the world and is extended, besides governmental administrations, to all bodies even private ones entrusted with a public mission or largely financed or controlled by public sector. As a consequence, in Europe, following the European Union directive of 2004,[29] CNES has been subjected to the common regime of governmental procurement:
- First through the specific regime of the ordinance of n° 2005-649 of 6 June 2005 relative to contracts concluded by certain public or private persons not subjected to the state procurement code,

---

[28] Ministry Order *(arrêté)* on Financial Functioning of 29 August 1963 (*JORF* 14 September 1963) – Art. 8 "The general conditions of signing, financing and monitoring contracts are fixed by the Board of directors. They are inspired by the State procurement regulation." This sentence also appeared in the Order of 20 July 1990 concerning the operating procedures of the CNES until its modification by the Art. 5 of the Order of 4 July 2007 (*JORF* 17 July 2007).

[29] Directive 2004/18/EC of the European Parliament and of the Council of 31 March 2004 on the coordination of procedures for the award of public works contracts, public supply contracts and public service contracts. Art. 5 of this directive named "Conditions relating to agreements concluded within the World Trade Organisation" recalls the predominance of rules from such international organisation, in particular the "most favoured nation clause" brought forward by the Agreement on Government Procurement (AGP), concluded in the framework of the Uruguay Round multilateral negotiations.

- Then following the transposition of the 2014 EU directive,[30] under the ordinance of 23 July 2015, which consolidated all French public market rules under a uniform state procurement code.

Originally, such classical formalized procedures for standard governmental purchase were not designed to facilitate innovative solutions, in particular on behalf of space projects. Indeed, pursuant to such public procurement process, the contracting authorities, among which space agencies, are strictly required to fix in advance toward industry, in the contract notice published in the official gazette, their system or *mission requirements* as well as their *contractual terms and conditions*. As a result, such regulation prohibits any *post offer negotiation* between the *contracting authority* and the tenderers as *economic operators*. Fortunately, all over the world, regulations have evolved in the past years toward new competitive and cooperative procedures supporting innovation between public and private sector that may also benefit to space projects and CNES procurement policy. These procurement procedures are developed below in*§4.1.3.1*. CNES also retains the capacity to enter into partnership agreement with industry. This capacity may be utilized in particular to support pre-competitive space system developments that are designed and promoted initially by industry. This capacity is developed in §4.1.3.2. In addition, CNES may also, as indicated above in §1.2.4, sponsor or set up new subsidiaries, take shareholding in innovative start-up, awarding to the latter IPR transfers or concession of public services or delegation.[31] This capacity is discussed §4.1.3.3.

4.1.3.1   CNES as Public Procurement Actor

CNES, under its essential law codified in the code of the research, "can ensure the execution of its programs by means of research convention with other public or private bodies" (L331-2 c). Basically, the term 'convention' refers to any form of agreement from cooperation memorandum of understanding under best effort rules to procurement contracts with performance obligation (or *obligation de résultat*). It is worth recalling that, rather than public aids or grants support, contract is the legal vehicle privileged by CNES; as *contracting authority* (or *donneur d'ordre or maître d'ouvrage*) to manage its mission toward industry, because contracting allows a better monitoring on the contractor's performances and schedule on a given space project. As already specified herein, the general conditions of signing of contracts, agreements, and markets, as well as the threshold above which these markets must be submitted to the board of directors' examination, are defined by

---

30 Directive 2014/24/EU of the European Parliament and of the Council of 26 February 2014 on public procurement and repealing Directive 2004/18/EC. *Official Journal of the European Union (OJEU)* 28 March 2014.

31 In this regard, on the example of the Pleiades' delegation of public services from 2004 decrees, *see* §5.1.2 'Privatization of Earth observation satellite services'.

the latest. But from 2005, following the related 2004 EU's directive, the conditions of procurement by CNES are subject to the ordinary French rules of public procurement.

Call for competition

Beyond classical procedures of open public tender existing in Europe, mention is to be made of the effort of flexibility engaged under the aforementioned 2014 Directive,[32] as to allow constructive public-private negotiations in a competitive process of contract award, according to the following procedures:

Competitive procedure with negotiation (Directive 2014, Art. 29), which allows discussions with any candidates in order to clarify requirement and to improve *tenderers'* proposals up to their *Best And Final Offer (the BAFO)* submitted for the *contracting authority's* final selection.

Competitive dialogue (Directive 2014, Art. 30), where the contracting authority shall open, with the participants selected, a dialogue the aim of which shall be to identify and define the means best suited to satisfying its needs. Then, the contracting authority may discuss all aspects of the procurement with the chosen participants during this dialogue. In other words, it becomes possible to renegotiate the technical and contractual requirement originally set in by the contracting authority, to have a better idea on strengths and weaknesses of potential solutions, provided that such authority ensures equality of treatment among all participants. To that end, contracting authority shall not provide information in a discriminatory manner, which may give some participants an advantage over others.

Innovation partnership (Directive 2014, Art. 31), forwards the dialogue mechanism above in order to support R&D activities though partnership between the contracting authority (CNES) and *economic operator(s)*, namely space industrialists in our view herein. In the procurement documents, the contracting authority shall identify broadly the need for an innovative product, service, or work that cannot be met by purchasing products, services, or works already available on the market. The innovation partnership shall aim at the development of an *innovative* product, service or works and the *subsequent purchase* of the resulting supplies, services or works, provided that they correspond to the *performance levels* and *maximum costs agreed* between the contracting authorities and the participants. It indicates which elements of this description define the minimum requirements to be met by all tenders, provided that the minimum requirements and the award criteria shall not be subject to negotiations. The information provided shall be sufficiently precise to enable *economic operators* to identify the nature and scope of the required solution and decide whether to request to participate in the procedure. Then the contracting authority may decide to set up the innovation partnership with one partner or with several partners conducting separate research and development activities. In any case, the contracting

---

32 *See* preceding footnote, transposed in France by the aforesaid ordinance of 23 July 2015.

authority shall ensure that the structure of the partnership and, in particular, the duration and value of the different phases reflect the degree of innovation of the proposed solution and the sequence of the research and innovation activities required for the development of an innovative solution not yet available on the market. The estimated value of supplies, services or works shall not be disproportionate in relation to the investment required for their development.

Regardless of the use of such formal procedure as above, which are specially designed for negotiation between public and private sector, a space agency such as CNES as an ordinary Contracting Authority can always exempt itself from application of such ordinary framework for governmental purchase based on the exceptions expressly provided for in the latter. In particular, under 2014 EU directive, Contracting Authority shall not be required to follow a formal open competitive process in the following cases:

- *Single economic operator* (Directive 2014, Art. 32). Direct or restricted consultation remain possible where the works, supplies, or services can be supplied only by a particular *economic operator* for technical reasons or for protection of exclusive rights, including intellectual property rights;
- *Award organized pursuant to international rules* (Directive 2014, Art. 9). This faculty can be used in execution of an international cooperation agreement rules or in application of specific international organization rules such as the one on European Space Agency for example.
- *Service contracts awarded on the basis of an exclusive right* (Directive 2014, Art. 11). The directive shall not apply to public service contracts awarded by a contracting authority to another contracting authority or to an association of contracting authorities on the basis of an exclusive right that they enjoy pursuant to a law, regulation, or published administrative provision, which is compatible with the TFEU. This exemption may be utilized concretely toward a company already entrusted with a *concession of public service* (ex: for Earth Observation data distribution).
- *Public contracts between entities within the public sector*: the *In House* exception (Directive 2014, Art. 12). A public contract awarded by a contracting authority to a legal person governed by private or public law and controlled by the contracting authority or authorities. This faculty may be used toward space agencies' branches or subsidies.
- *Research and development services* (Directive 2014, Art. 14). This regime addresses more specifically the interest of space agencies provided that both of the following conditions are fulfilled: (a) the benefits do not accrue exclusively to the contracting authority for its use in the conduct of its own affairs (*i.e.*, IPR ownership is not fully transferred to the contracting authority); and (b) the service provided is not wholly

remunerated by the contracting authority (*i.e.*, are also financed by the economic operator).
- **Procurement involving national defence or security aspects** (Directive 2014, Arts. 15 and 16). This exemption, besides defence systems and their sensitive technology, may be used also in civil defense projects (*i.e.*, Pleiade dual Earth observation satellites in Europe…) or in procurement of civil technology involving military export control.

Despite such enhancements options or exemption faculties that benefit to cooperation with or among the private sector, we may assess that the traditional top-down procurement procedures that are used by all space agencies acting as contracting authorities remain, as things stand, inadequate to support the projects that have been previously designed and financed by the private sector; in other words, to accompany private *bottom-up space projects* supported by the *new space* players (*see* Part II, Chapter 8). It is in this sense that CNES introduced since the end of the 1990's a 'partnership policy' toward space industry to support the development of private or market oriented systems (see §4.1.3.2).

Execution terms and conditions of CNES' procurement contracts
Contracts concluded by space agencies contain some characteristics that are connected to their missions or to their public statutes or to existing common practices within the space sector regarding contracts (*see* in Part II, Chapter 7, §7.1.2.3 about the FSOA's regime on waiver of claim). In French law, a public service contract or a public procurement is a contract concluded by at least a public person, and that is a matter of an administrative court *(Tribunal Administratif and Conseil d'Etat)*. It can be qualified as such by the law, or by the jurisprudence if it deals with the execution of a public service or contains 'exorbitant clause(s)' as relates to the common law, giving unilateral powers to the public body. Among such 'exorbitant clauses' in favour of the public person we shall retain: the power of direction or control of the contract, which can be translated in particular by the emission of *work order notice* (or *lettre valant ordre de service*); the power of control of the execution of the contract; the power of penalty in case of fault; the power of modification for motive of general interest, in respect for the financial balance of the contract; the power of termination on the grounds of the public interest, for compensation of its contractor. These powers are justified by the necessary requirements arising from their missions of general interest, to the continuity of public service or in their sovereign or discretionary powers.

So CNES shall ensure, toward its own supervising authorities and for the general satisfaction of industry or user's needs, a fair balance between interests of the public person and of the contractor such as the principle of continuity of the public service, its adaptability, the transparency, and the non-discrimination. For example, to reconcile the balance in the economy and the continuity of the service, the public contracts in the space domain recognize the *hardship* theory of the *lack of foresight*, which is much more favourable to the provider of services than the *force majeure* provision as contained in the classical contracts under private or commercial law. In case of *unforeseen and additional constraints* (in French *sujétions imprévues*) such as climatic, geological hazards, or of *important economic hazards* such as sharp price rise on raw materials or consequences of bankruptcy of a partner likely to upset the economy of the contract, the contract holder may obtain a corresponding revision of the conditions of the contract or lifting of the penalties in case of delay or of partial nonfulfillment.

4.1.3.2 CNES' Partnership Policy

Beyond its traditional procurement top-down intervention or its shareholding policy, CNES, introduced from 1997 an intermediate Public Private Partnership policy following a vast dialogue on the subject with its stakeholders, namely communities of: the science, the industry, European organization (ASE and EU), the defence, and the downstream space application sector. This reflection generated the edition of a first reference guide drawing the outlines of a programmatic and legal approach more particularly suited to the agency-industry relationship. Such relationship approach was then contrasting from the traditional client/supplier relationship, where the agency remains the design authority specifying in details its technical requirements, while the industry acts only as an implementer. It also diverged with the CNES' subsidiary policy as inaugurated in the 1980s for its business-oriented application projects.

As an example of first contemporary applications, we may mention that in 1997 the partnership on the joint development of a generic mini platform named 'Proteus' with Aerospatiale (now Thales Alenia Space being its satellite branch), the partnership and joint-venture 'Skybridge' with Alcatel Space (now Thales Alenia Space) for the design and the industrialisation of a large constellation of internet service satellites and a few years later 'Pleiade' the first partnership on dual Earth-observation satellite development and data policy associating defence and civil ministries in Europe and Spot Image (now Airbus Defence & Space). This movement was extended toward the research and scientific community (CNRS-INSU, ONERA, CEA) with which a standardized multi-year framework agreement's policy was inaugurated. This guide of partnership was only disseminating within the targeted industrialists concerned, *i.e.*, among the membership of GIFAS. It remains, however, a didactic frame for the design of balanced models of public-private cooperation for innovative projects that have become familiar today for the whole space sector. Indeed, this partnership pattern is rather similar to the 'Innovation Partnership'[33] model generalized a few years later by the 2014 UE Public Procurement Directive's Article 31 as a new dialogue mechanism to support R&D activities though partnership between

---

33   *Ibid* §4.1.3.1.

contracting authorities and economic operator. However, CNES partnership model can be concluded on a non-exchange of fund basis, contrary to a procurement agreement.

More broadly, these partnerships may also be compared with the ones of NASA as allowed by its updated constitutive act that provides this agency with the authority to enter into a wide range of 'other transactions', commonly referred to as Space Act Agreements (SAAs). Such agreements which are, as the case may be, categorized as *Reimbursable, Non-reimbursable, Funded or International*, are legally enforceable with diverse groups of people and organizations, both in the private and public sector, foreign partners included. One of the most famous application of this space agreement policy is the Commercial Orbital Transportation Services (COTS), a program launched by NASA to coordinate the delivery of crew and cargo to the International Space Station by private companies. The program was announced on 18 January 2006 and successfully flew all cargo demonstration flights by September 2013. It also contributes to the successful development of Space X company lead by Elon Musk, and to that of the latter launcher Falcon 9 and its derivatives. As already mentioned herein, these new patterns of partnership remain to be developed and harmonized to facilitate cooperation on common international standards between space agencies and private sector to build innovative and ambitious future space systems, in a fair competitive environment, in the so called context of New Space.

4.1.3.3 CNES' Subsidiaries and Holdings

This issue was largely developed first under the history of *Arianespace*'s creation, in §1.2.2.3 on *adaptation to the operational use of space from the end* 1970s, then on §1.2.4 on *shareholdings and subsidiaries to develop, produce and market new space services*. We just recall hereunder that:

- CNES' capacity to undertake commercial activities remains limited to the necessary transition period before the transfer of the activities to the private sector, as a kind of incubation process, or when a default of a private offer or capacity occurs.
- Such pre-competitive activities operated by private subsidiaries, namely space operations or downstream applications, are always carried out through a concession *framework agreement* (or *concession of public services*) granted in parallel to the relevant stock company, with regard to the technology or developed space systems or facilities transferred by the space agency to this private operator.
- CNES may be required by its supervising authorities to assign its shareholdings as soon as the market allows.
- The FSOA's entry into force does not prevent as such CNES from creating new private subsidiaries (*see* the end of §4.3.5).

4.2 CNES' Contribution to European Programs

Since the early beginnings in the 1960s, as it was designing guidelines for its national space policy, CNES was either firmly involved in the establishment of a European space organization framework. This effort was concretized first in 1962 by the creation of both European Launcher Development Organisation (ELDO) on 29 March and the European Space Research Organisation (ESRO) on 14 June. After the dissolution of ELDO following the launchers Europa's failures, the European Space Conference (ESC) meeting in Brussels in 1973 decides on the famous 'package deal' of three new programs: L3S (Ariane), Spacelab (module of Space station), and MAROTS (Satcom) and the creation of the European Space Agency (ESA), for which the founding Convention was signed on 30 May 1975. Nowadays with the success of its achievements, ESA has become one of the major space players in the world and remains a unique model of permanent organization creating and managing space international cooperation.

The European Union on its side, which was, after being established in 1958, thriving in the so-called European Economic Community (EEC), has expanded progressively its competence in the space domain:
- First, the Single European Act of February 1986 included a competence in Research and Technological Development fields that was open to space projects; This program is still implemented nowadays through multiannual *RDT Framework Programs*, its current 8th version is named 'Horizon 2020.'
- Second, the EU have started from the 1990s to position itself on the one hand as a *'proxy' of users of Space application* and, on the other through its regulatory authority or under its executive powers on sectorial policies in the fields of agriculture, environment, transport, and telecommunications.

This led EU to support, altogether with ESA, the Global Monitoring Environment and Security initiative in Earth Observation (GMES, later renamed *Copernicus*), or the European Navigation Satellite Positioning Systems *EGNOS and Galileo*. It also led on the regulatory side, from 1994, to the *liberalization of satellite telecommunications*, which brought about the abolition of the monopoly of national historical telecommunications operators such as French Telecom, British Telecom, and Deutch Telecom. This implied privatization of the latest common monopolistic international satellite organizations, such as Eutelsat, Inmarsat, Intelsat... (*see* Part II, §5.1.1).

Other regulatory initiatives of European Commission have indirectly shaped the legal regime of *space applications*, in particular as relates Earth observation from Space. Among these normative initiatives are the Directive of 11 March 1996 on the *legal protection of* databases,[34] the *INSPIRE Directive* establishing an infrastructure for spatial information in Europe to support environmental policies, entered into force on May 2007,[35] the directive on the re-use of Public sector information of 1993 known as the PSI Directive[36] and the 1995 data protection directive[37] (officially Directive 95/46/EC on the protection of individuals with regard to the processing of personal data) repealed by the expanded General Regulation on Personal Data (RGPD) of 2016, enforceable from 25 May 2018.[38] National transposition of these European legislation on the opening-up of space based-data is discussed in §7.5.3.

Also should be mentioned the aborted project of directive on the dissemination of Earth observation *high resolutions satellite data* (HRSD) for commercial purposes.[39] The goal of this directive proposal was to define and control high resolutions satellite data (HRSD) as a distinct category of data requiring a differentiated regulatory regime when it is disseminated for commercial purposes due to the higher potential risk that its unauthorized handling can entail. Given that foreign policy and national security and defence remain sovereign competences of the EU State members, the EU legislative competence on this field was justified on the legal basis of the Article 114 of TFEU. This provision can be used to contribute, on behalf of the European *internal market*, to the removal of appreciable distortions of competition which are likely to arise from the diverse *national rules*. Due to a lack of support, the Commission withdrew its proposal on 1 July 2015, few months following the inception of College of Commissioners chaired by Jean-Claude Juncker.

Last but not least, Article 4.3 the Lisbon Treaty (2007) on the Functioning of the European Union (TFUE) entrusted EU with a capacity in *space policy and programs* as a specific 'shared competence' with its Member States (MS). It is worth noting that this new European *shared competence* as relates to *research, technological development (RTD) and*

---

34 Directive 96/9/EC of 11 March 1996 on the legal protection of databases published in the Official Journal of the European Communities on 27 March 1996 (L 77/20).
35 Directive 2007/2/EC of 14 March 2007 establishing an Infrastructure for Spatial Information in the European Community (INSPIRE) published in the Official Journal of the European Union on 25 April 2007 (L 108/1).
36 Directive 2003/98/EC of 17 November 2003 on the re-use of public sector information, Official Journal L 345, 31 December 2003, pp. 90-96, entered into force on 31 December 2003, revised by Directive 2013/37/EU of 26 June 2013, official journal 17 June 2013, (L 175/1), entered into force on 17 July 2013.
37 Directive 95/46/EC of 24 October 1995 on the protection of individuals with regard to the processing of personal data and on the free movement of such data, Official Journal L 281, 23 November 1995, pp. 31-50.
38 Regulation (EU) 2016/679 of 27 April 2016 on the protection of natural persons with regard to the processing of personal data and on the free movement of such data (General Data Protection Regulation or GDPR), Official Journal of the European Union, 4 May 2016, L 119/1, repealing directive 95/46/EC of 24 October 1995. *See* §7.4.6.
39 Proposal for a directive published by the European Commission on 17 June 2014, COM (2014) 344.

space's policies differs from the one in other sectors under Article 4 of the TFEU,[40] insofar as EU countries for the first ones retain their full competence, either on their own or through ESA framework, to manage programs, legislate and adopt legally binding international agreement on RTD and space, even where EU has already exercised its competence. In this respect, Article 189 of the same treaty allows EU to design and implement a European space program and calls for the development of *appropriate relationship with ESA*.

However, this Article 189 deprives the EU of a legal capacity to *harmonize the national space legislations of the European countries*, in particular those derived from *space treaties*. These distinct European organizations in terms of status, competence, and membership design together dedicated cooperation framework for the purposes of programs like *Galileo (positioning) and Copernicus (observation) programs*, both for the development and exploitation phase.

Basically, ESA and EU competences are rather complementary on the benefit of Space activities, thus without prejudice to their Member States' competence, which remain intact. In addition, such organizations have in common to maintain a stable and predictable governance regime of cooperation for Space projects between European partners, on a voluntary basis (ESA optional program and potentially UE through its TFUE Arts. 184 and 185) or mandatory basis (UE RDT&S programs and ESA scientific program). In this respect, we may underline in the following development the main features and the complementarity between the respective status and missions of such European organizations.

The European Space Agency is a permanent cooperative organization with judicial personality specialized in space programs. As a consequence, each ESA program decision taken by Member States Board in the framework of ESA Council and formalized as a 'Program Declaration' is legally equivalent to an international Treaty signed by the same state parties, without any formality of ratification. ESA in itself has the capacity to enter into specific international arrangements of any form of cooperation agreements or contracts. For example, ESA represents and supersedes the European partners in the International Space Station MoU signed in 1998 with NASA. ESA can also cooperate with national Space agencies of its Member States on its own programs; for instance, in hosting in its European platform scientific instrument achieved at a national level. ESA may also delegate operational tasks to national space agencies, in particular to CNES for the management of the Guiana Space Centre or for ATV or Galileo's satellites in-orbit manoeuvres ... ESA is then a flexible and efficient organization to initiate and run ambitious cooperation for developing innovative or prototypes systems in relation with space industry.

---

40 *I.e.*, Internal market, social policy, but only for aspects specifically defined in the Treaty, economic, social and territorial cohesion (regional policy), agriculture and fisheries (except conservation of marine biological resources), environment, consumer protection, transport, trans-European networks, energy, area of freedom, security and justice, shared safety concerns in public health matters, limited to the aspects defined in the TFEU.

Last but not least, from the point of view of the ministries of finance and economy, the 'geographical return principle' characterizing ESA rules of contract award, namely by a just apportionment of contracts in favour of a domestic industry proportional to the corresponding member state's budget allocation to the ESA program, remains a secure guarantee of good use of national budget. The advantages of such guaranteed return toward domestic economy growth may balance the drawback of scattering the work package among European industry and, as a result, impairing the later competitiveness in the international market. At all events, the money invested in *ESA's optional programs* development basically remains in the running domestic economy, less the operations cost internal to ESA. Moreover, from a macroeconomic point of view, the return on public investment may be leveraged on *gross domestic product* (GDP) if the recurrent operational systems maintain for decades the same geographical industrial return, as it happens in the non-reusable launcher exploitation phase.

Finally, from ESA's statute results the same virtuous dialectic rule as mentioned for CNES about the 'competition-cooperation' *tandem*. On one hand ESA is fully invested by its establishing of convention in a cooperation mission within its member's states, or toward its member's states and third countries, and, on the other hand, it preserves national interests and competition within the European industry as a result of the geographical return on procurements.

The European Union provides on its side the necessary regulatory framework and a political and integrated dimension to the European space efforts. EU's legal framework is well appropriated to the assessment of needs of the user communities and consequently to design new Space application programs consistently with European policies in environment, transport, agriculture, common infrastructures, and of course, research (RDT)… In other words, the EU competence on Space activities is more focused on spacecraft's payload capacity of services onto the Earth, than space vehicle's operations as such.

EU's Commission is also contemplating funding recurrent investments on *essential European facilities* and their associated operating costs. This covers integrated programs forwarded to ground solutions such as Copernicus Galileo or the ongoing initiatives with ESA or some member's states on Space Situation Awareness (SSA). SSA is generally understood as covering three main areas, namely Space Surveillance and Tracking (SST), Space Weather Monitoring and Forecasting and Near-Earth Objects. The SST is a European integrated project for monitoring space traffic and preventing collisions. It has been subject to a specific EU decision on May 2014.[41]

---

41 Decision N° 541/2014/EU of the European Parliament and of the Council of 16 April 2014 establishing a Framework for Space Surveillance and Tracking Support, Official Journal of the European Union of 27 May 2014, L 158/227.

The concept of *essential European facilities* would be also appropriate potentially to justify a contribution on investment and maintenance costs for the Guiana Space Centre, the European Spaceport. EU obviously has also its legitimate say on global governance of European programs on the long run altogether with proposition and implementation of its associated regulations. It has to be underlined finally that besides the traditional top-down approach of its RDT Framework mechanism under TFEU's Article 182, other legal instruments such as Articles 184 and 185 would allow the European Union to participate in cooperation arrangement of European interests initiated by Member States in a way that can be likened to ESA regime for optional programs or scientific ESA project open to voluntary national contributions. However, such legal vehicles for research cooperation with Member States have not been experimented for space projects.

In any case as to France, according to its statutory law, CNES participates in the monitoring of both of these European organizations jointly with other French ministries or by mandate French state.

Finally, with regard to the procurement procedures applicable to the space in Europe, we may retain another example of paradoxical European treatment, toward national space agencies. Indeed, CNES, as any other European civil public body or national agency, is required to open its procurement without discrimination to all the European industry in application of the aforesaid EU's directive on procurement; meanwhile, an equivalent contribution to a European project under the umbrella of ESA shall ensure a legal guarantee of 'geographical return' on behalf of national industry.

4.3 Interactions Issues between CNES' Missions

4.3.1 *The Issue of Potential Conflicts of Interests as Raised During FSOA's Law-Making Up Process*

It is to be underlined that through FSOA the French government delegated to CNES and its president the whole of its technical responsibility for authorizing and monitoring space operations under its jurisdiction. This delegation scheme was originally proposed in April 2006 by the Council of State *(Conseil d'Etat)* itself in its preliminary study report entitled 'A Legal Policy for Space Activities.'[42] In its report (*see* its p. 77 and 78), the Council of State assumes that it is not necessary to create an independent authority to regulate the space sector, as previously done in other economic sectors, such as telecommunications and energy. It suggests that the future SOA's implementation's decree appoints the *ministry of space affairs* as the *administrative authority* in charge of delivering authorization.

---

42   See below §6.3.

Meanwhile, it recommends, due to CNES' unique technical expertise, especially in the launcher area, and the lack of resources and means of the ministry of space affairs in such technical fields, to delegate to CNES the assessment of compliance of the space systems and procedures with the *technical regulations*.

It is to be underlined that the *Council of State* while making this recommendation especially points out the risk of 'conflict of interests' between new CNES' SOA missions and its previous missions (under RC Art. L 331.2…), in particular as *contracting authority*, *space operator* of private satellite for *on-orbit* positioning and manoeuvres, and as *shareholder* of Arianespace SA and Spot Image SA in particular. It does not retain, however, any legal impediment, provided that CNES separates its activities into two different sectors (SOA and non-SOA activities), ends any supply of commercial services and transfers its shareholdings in business companies to another governmental agency, the State Participation Agency (APE, *Agence des Participations de l'Etat*). Such legal opinion from the Council of State, under its *Study and Report Section*, and endorsed by its *Plenary Assembly*, was very comforting during the following SOA's law-making process, given the fact that despite its *legal advisory and assessment role on regulatory matters* on behalf of the government, the Council of State acts as well finally as the *French supreme administrative court*.

On its side, Claudie Haigneré the minister for space affairs, in its signed preface of the 2002 preliminary report drafted by her space department (*Space law Evolution in France*) and while opening the following colloquium of 13 March 2003,[43] urged to strengthen the role of CNES under the future space legislation, by entrusting it with a technical authority in certifying, controlling, and holding registries of space activities… The content of this 2002 ministerial report also assesses the risk of conflict of interests and proposed remedies (*see* p. 42–45).

During the law-making process, the Henri Revol's report on behalf of the *Senate's Economics Affairs Commission* (report n° 161, p. 42 and 43)[44] also recommended to legitimize such CNES technical authority for FSOA's purposes and, noting possible conflicts of interests, calls for an unquestionable disengagement of CNES from any activity and stock holding incompatible with the exercise of its new legal responsibilities. A special annex to this report (Annex II, in p. 93–95) makes a comprehensive inventory of CNES' current interests in competitive activities, distinguishing on the one hand CNES commercials activities with a description of its situation and remedies already taken or to be taken and, on the other hand, CNES shareholding situation and remedies taken or to be taken. The text suggests that CNES abandon any in-orbit services for private companies and commercial satellites and to withdraw from Arianespace and Spot Image stock.

---

43   *See below* §6.1.
44   *See below* §6.5.1. Senate: Henri Revol's report, on behalf of the Economics Affairs Commission, 15 January 2008, n° 161 et n° 328 (2007-2008).

Last but not least, the European Commission, in assessing with the French government in April 2007, the conformity of the State Liability Ceiling under the European Union public aid legislation on the basis of EC Treaty Article 88 §3[45] takes note of "measures undertaken by French authorities in order to prevent any conflict of interest between CNES technical control of space operations and its commercial activities directly or by means of its participations." Mention was made there that the governance of CNES guarantees sufficient independence through the traditional framework convention between ESA and Arianespace since 1980, as renewed in compliance with the 2007 Intergovernmental Launcher Declaration on European Launchers exploitation[46].

4.3.2 Focus on Mission Entrusted to the CNES and Its President

CNES' situation regarding FSOA's provisions is largely discussed in Part II.[47] As regards the issue developed in this §4.3, we may recall the following about FSOA's missions entrusted to the CNES as legal body and to the CNES' president personally.

First, *CNES' mission* under FSOA focuses on the assessment of technical compliance of space operations regarding the technical regulations and on registration of French space objects as set forth in Article 28 and translated into Article L. 331-2 (f), (g), and (h) of the Code of Research, namely:

f) To assist the Government in the *definition of the technical regulations* relating to space operations;

g) To certify, by delegation of the minister in charge of space, that the systems and procedures implemented by the space operators *comply with the technical regulation* mentioned in paragraph f);

h) To hold the *register of the space objects* on behalf of the Government.

Second, the *CNES' president authority* under FSOA is legally qualified as an 'administrative police mission.' This means a power to enforce regulations on safety to prevent any breaches, as opposed to the 'judicial police,' whose purpose is to stop and punish any infringement. Such president competences are set forth in Article 21 and translated into Article L. 331-6 of the Code of Research as follows:

- As to the Guiana Space Centre's safety: CNES' president exercises on behalf of French government the 'Special Exploitation Police' on facilities of the Guiana Space Centre. As such, it is in charge of a *general mission of safeguard* consisting of controlling the technical risks related to the preparation and carrying out of the launches from the

---

45 *See below* §6.5.4.1.
46 *See* §1.2.2.3 on Ariane Declaration, *footnotes* 31 and 32.
47 *See below* §6.4, §6.5.2, §6.6.2, §7.1.2.1, §7.1.6, §7.1.7, §7.1.8.

Guiana Space Centre in order to ensure the protection of persons, property, public health, and the environment, on the ground and during the flight, and set out to this end the specific regulations applicable.

In addition, CNES' president, under the authority of the government representative in French Guiana, has a *coordinating power* on the implementation by companies and other entities settled in GSC of measures taken in order to ensure the *security of the facilities* and of the activities undertaken therein, and check that those companies and agencies fulfil their obligations in this respect.

Basically, CNES' president has delegated the almost all of his 'administrative police competence' (*i.e.*, a *preventive police*) to the *director of the CSG* and to the latter delegates, who maintain a fulltime presence on that site. CNES' president has just retained the power to enact and update the core regulation on the operations on CSG facilities (REI-CSG).[48]

As to *emergency measures* more broadly (rescue, removal of command...), the CNES' president authority under FSOA Article 21 III was translated into CR Article L. 331-7. Thus, the president may take for any space operation, by delegation of the minister in charge of space affairs, the necessary measures to ensure the safety of persons and property, as well as the protection of public health and the environment.

4.3.3 Impact on CNES' Staff Regime Regarding FSOA Officers

As a consequence of its FSOA new responsibilities, CNES has been required during 2009 by its supervision ministry of research, the latter acting as FSOA's administrative authority, to ensure that its staff regulation guarantees that any data or information transmitted to it from operators or any private company for the needs of the authorization's application or monitoring process or for the needs of CSG Regulations shall be kept confidential and strictly used for the purposes defined by such space legislation. This confidentiality obligation shall therefore apply either toward:
- Any third party, to any data received, technical or not, and not only to that information marked 'proprietary information,' from any form or support of communication oral or written. For example, the dissemination of an information about a minor failure in a system, even not sensitive on a technological or safety point of view, may have considerable consequences on the value of the relevant space operators stock quotation and business and shall be prohibited.

---

48 *See* this Annex 1.7 and 2.7: Order of 9th December, 2010

- Any other CNES activities or staff, in particular as to staff involved in missions and systems development projects, upstream technical or technological research, in other words regarding any activities performed under CR Article L 331-2 a to e. The aim of this measure is to avoid that controller's assessment may be influenced by its colleagues being involved with industry in the design of the same systems.

As a result, only three categories of personnel are involved in FSOA's activities and the Guiana Space Center' special Police regime. All this staff is subject to a specific regime as refers to hierarchy, confidentiality, and deontology rules:

4.3.3.1 FSOA Basic Controllers (FSOA Art. 28)

CNES FSOA' *controllers* shall check and assess that systems and procedures implemented by the operator comply with the FSOA's Technical Regulation. They intervene during the authorization application process or after, during the preparation phase of the space operation or its carrying out. Controllers are appointed by CNES' president for a given period of time. This staff, assigned on FSOA' technical compliance responsibilities are not working in any other conflictual fields of activities for the duration of their controller's mandate. Controllers shall subscribe specific deontology and confidentiality commitments. Controllers' mission is to assess the conformity of space systems and procedures as to the technical regulations and as such CNES' controllers are not supposed to provide any technical advice or support to the operator as applicant for authorization. Transition measures of assistance and training have, however, been implemented toward Arianespace to facilitate the full acquisition of its competence. This transitory period is now over.

4.3.3.2 Commissioned Officers (FSOA Art. 7)

The *commissioned officers* are empowered by the Space Affairs' Minister of an *administrative police* mission to proceed to the necessary controls, only after the granting of the authorization, during the preparation and implementation phases of the space operation, in order to ascertain that the special requirements mentioned under FSOA's Article 5 in the authorization are fulfilled. As part of their assignment, commissioned officers shall have access at any time to the buildings, premises, and facilities where space operations are conducted and to the space object itself. They can ask for any document or useful item, irrespective of their medium. They can make copies and gather any necessary information and justification, in situ or upon notification. The *operator* is informed at the latest when the controlling operations begin that he may attend the operations and be assisted by any person of his choice, or that he can be represented for that purpose. The Commissioned Officers are bound by professional confidentiality under the conditions and penalties set out by Articles 226-13 and 226-14 of the Penal Code. They are appointed and dismissed by the ministry in charge of space affairs, the FSOA's administrative authority, under proposition of CNES' president (FSOA Article 7 I. 1° and 2009 FSOA's Authorization Decree Arts. 19, 21, 22, and 23).

4.3.3.3 Sworn Officers (FSOA Art. 10)

Sworn officers are *commissioned officers* with *judicial police powers*. In addition to their ability to have access at any time to the buildings, premises, and facilities where space operations are conducted and to the space object, *sworn officers* are authorized, in accordance with the *Code of Criminal Procedure*, to investigate and record any breaches to FSOA' requirements, in particular facts that give rise to a fine of €200,000, pursuant to its Article 12 or, pursuant to Article 10, entails a withdrawing or a suspension of the granted authorization. Sworn officers record these breaches in reports that are considered authentic unless the contrary is proved. Such reports are sent to *head of the prosecution department* (or the *Procureur de la République*), the latest deciding either to suit or not the infringer. Sworn officers take an oath, after endorsement by the Head of the Prosecution Department, at the *court of first instance of general jurisdiction* (or the *tribunal de grande instance*, TGI) under FSOA's Authorization Decree Art. 19, 21, 22, and 23.

4.3.4 *CNES' Traditional Activities as Technical Center and Space Operator Dealings with FSOA Delegated Activities*

CNES' missions under FSOA dealing with the *compliance assessment* of private applicant systems with the *technical regulations* shall be exercised in an independent, objective, and impartial way, without interference from any relationship and interest, in particular with regard to CNES ability to deliver services, expertise or concludes other arrangements with the private sector. A survey was made in 2009 by CNES of its business interests in relation to private operators applicant for authorization, in order to assess the potential risk of conflicts of interests and to propose remedies as the case may be. The following two fields of activity have been found in this survey to have been affected:

4.3.4.1 CNES Activities as Space Program Agency

As a procurement agency for the needs of its development space programs (new launcher satellite assets or services purchase, R&D contracts award), CNES is subjected to the ordinary public procurement rules. Such rules as mentioned in §2.2.6 and §4.1.3.1 were derived from EU directives on public procurement. It is so required basically that contract award respects the principles of freedom of access to procurement, equal treatment of candidates, and transparency of procedures. These principles call for prior definition of the procuring entity's needs, compliance with the publication and competition requirements, and selection of the economically most advantageous tender. On this basis, the risks of conflicts of interests is diverted for such procuring mission and thus the CNES' capacity as a space program agency (under CR Art. L331-2 b to d) shall not be impaired as a result of FSOA.

4.3.4.2 CNES' Service Providing

In accordance with its unchanged codified statutory Act (namely under CR Art. L331-2 c and L331-4), as a natural extension of its main mission on space project development, CNES is allowed to supply services, grant access to its facilities, and give expertise support to private companies. This faculty may be used by all its technical centers of Toulouse (Satellites, Science, Space Applications), Paris-Dausmenil (launcher development programs), or Kourou (launch range base). These services shall be provided on a non-discriminatory basis and at a reasonable cost (between the real cost and the market price), provided that this activity does not jeopardize its main mission of developing its space program and international cooperation according to its unchanged codified statutory Act (CR Art. L331-2 a to e). As a consequence, the following activities for CNES shall not be affected by FSOA implementation:

- In-orbit operation for governmental entities (including ESA, EUMETSAT, inter-governmental or agency cooperation);
- Marginal utilization of testing facilities, computing facilities, station network (2 GHz)etc.;
- Payload preparation facilities (EPCU), physics and chemical measures laboratories managed by CNES at GSG etc.

On the other hand, CNES ended any questionable supply activity, such as:
- In-orbit operation for private entities, French or not (Eutelsat, SES Astra, ...), even more for foreign governments, if awarded in an international or competitive call for tender directed to the open market;
- Any contract of supply as sub-contractor on behalf of a prime manufacturer or a company operating a market oriented space system (satellite, launcher or other) potentially subject to FSOA's authorization or control regime. As a result, CNES terminated its contracts on quality support, computing services (trajectory optimization…) for Arianespace, the *launch operator* under FSOA. The same applies toward European competitors of the above-mentioned French manufacturers or operators in order to avoid any interference in the European market competition.

4.3.5 CNES' Stock Participations and Partnerships with Private Companies

The authorities consulted during FSOA's law-making process,[49] *i.e.*, the Council of State, National Assembly, Senate, French government, European Commission… unanimously underlined that CNES should abandon, when feasible, its shareholdings in Arianespace SA and Spot Image SA. CNES sold in July 2008 the whole of its stockholding in Spot Image SA to Astrium SAS, an EADS subsidiary in satellite sector, now renamed Airbus Defence & Space. For Arianespace SA, the transfer was achieved by the end of 2016 on behalf of Ariane Group, a joint enterprise set up one year before between Airbus Defence and Space and Safran (the aerospace engine manufacturer) following the reorganization of the European launcher sector governance accompanying the development of Ariane VI system.[50]

It remains, however, legally possible for CNES, under its unchanged codified statutory act,[51] to set up new subsidiaries or to hold stakes in private company, start up, pre-seeding funds, or other new venture shareholding, provided that financial commitments, market impact, or project development step does not exceed legal thresholds of control or satisfy requirements from either French and European relevant authorities (*i.e.*, the French Competition Authority or *Autorité de la concurrence* and the EU Commission's DG completion).

4.3.6 Conclusion

As a conclusion on the issue of avoiding potential conflict of interests toward private operators, being or likely to be, subject to the FSOA's authorization and control regime, it may be assumed that none of the assessments and audits made by external or internal authorities, before and after FSOA entered into force, has shown any critical restriction. Such appraisal, on the contrary, have contributed to identifying, for existing but also future services, a set of prior acceptance criteria and pricing policy consistently with legal doctrine and *case law* on the French *public services* as well as the European law. These requirements may be summarized as follows: continuity of service, transparency, non-discrimination, predefined pricing policy based on real costs, no subordination links with a private company, activities in close relation with a public investment or facility, services being as a natural extension of a CNES traditional mission or expertise, without jeopardizing the latter, prohibition of commercial and competitive activities. Basically, the respect of the above requirements allowed CNES to hold off risks of conflict of interests between its

---

49 *See above* §4.3.1 and below in Part II, §6.1 to §6.5.
50 *See above* §1.2.2.
51 *See above* §1.2.4 and §4.3.5.

FSOA's responsibilities and its activities in selling services. Moreover, such conditions contribute to maintain the capacity of CNES as a strong contracting space agency and enable it to focus on its core missions toward the private sector as a public organization supporting innovation, upstream technical research and competitiveness of this industry consistently with its legal mission, especially under CR Art. L331-2 b to d.

Part II
The French Space Operations Act

The French Space Operations Act (FSOA) as a necessary link between the French government responsibilities under the public international space law and the aspirations of industry and private operators

In Part I we reviewed CNES law to examine how space programs of 'general interest' undertaken in France are regulated in the framework of this national space agency. Such legal framework firstly includes its own scientific or technical spacecraft and demonstrator's projects for future applications, including those of potential commercial purpose ultimately. It includes secondly, under specific delegation or partnership with the concerned public organization, operations on public service satellites in the following domain of application: Earth observation, Navigation, Meteorology and Defense. CNES' regulatory regime can be also extended to international or European governmental projects under dedicated agreement, as has been made with the European Space Agency (ESA) or bilateral cooperation (*e.g.* SPOT, Pleiade, etc.), provided that the relevant space objects are operated or designed to be operated or used from the French territory or by a French national.

However, outside the cases outlined below, CNES was never allowed to operate any spacecraft with a profit-making objective or in competition with other operators in an established market. Such activities are incompatible with its space agency mission of supporting space industry competitiveness and could raise today conflicts of interest as related to its empowered mission of technical control, on behalf of the Government, of any commercial systems to be operated under French jurisdiction.

Thus, the purpose of Part II is to review the legal regime applicable to private space activities undertaken under French jurisdiction or French launching state liability. Obviously, the lack of a national legislative framework before 2008 does not suggest that there was a legal vacuum in France to regulate the authorization, supervision, and responsibility for launch operations or the control of space vehicles.

Previously, the legal relationship between the French government and the operators concerned was conventional or contractual, administrative, or capital-intensive when specific international commitments did not directly apply, such as those generated in the wake of the ESA launcher programs or through dedicated international cooperative organizations such as Eutelsat established in Paris. This *empirical model* has remained suitable for projects being originally designed, managed, and financed by CNES and other governmental agencies or organized under specific public-private partnership. However, it has been proven inadequate throughout the 1990s to regulate the emergence of new systems exclusively designed and financed by the private sector or for any space operations on spacecraft not being designed, developed, or integrated in France. Thus, the main motivation for the legislative approach foreseen in the early 2000s was to allow a smooth privatization of space operations in the context of the proposed opening of the Guiana Space Centre to launchers other than Ariane, the emergence of new private investors with the first telecommunications constellations, and the transformation of the Eutelsat intergovernmental organization, the incumbent European operator, into a limited company with its headquarters in France.

The basic purpose of FSOA was to introduce a *unified governmental control and licensing system* based *on predetermined and objective criteria*, essentially technical, whose sole purpose was to ensure the safety of private space operations in the most general sense. The content of the Act was therefore based essentially on a codification of the international legal and treaty obligations between France, the UN, and the ESA.

Specifically, the aim was to set the generic conditions according to which the French government could authorize and control the space operations under its jurisdiction or its international responsibility as a launch State, in accordance with the major UN international treaties on space, in particular:

- The Treaty on Principles Governing the Activities of States in the Exploration and Use of Outer Space, including the Moon and other celestial bodies, of 27 January 1967, referred to as the Space Treaty (Articles VI and VII).
- The Convention on International Liability for Damage Caused by Space Objects, signed on 29 March 1972 (third-party damage).
- The Convention of 14 January 1975 on the Registration of Objects Launched into Outer Space.

The law also had to take into account the European commitments previously made by the French government with the ESA since 1975, especially with the agreements on the Guiana Space Centre for the Ariane launch complexes, and those undertaken with European states for the operation of these launchers in the industrial and commercial phases. Finally, the law integrated various commercial and technical uses well established within the space community between industry, operators, space agencies and their relationships with customers, users, banks and insurers, supervisory authorities or shareholders.

In this context, Part II analyses the development and the implementation of the 2008 French Space operation legislation:

- The privatization of space activities throughout the 1990s and the reasons why it became advisable to elaborate a dedicated law are discussed in Chapter 5, "Rational for Space Law-Making in France";
- The process of law making is outlined in Chapter 6, "The Development Stages of Legislation on Space Operations", from the first studies in 1999 to its entry into force in December 2010;
- The functioning of the law is developed in Chapter 7, "The French Space Operation Act's Regimes";
- The conclusion in Chapter 8 provides "Assessment and Perspective on the French Space Operation Act".

5 Rational for Space Law-Making in France

Questioning the opportunity to enact national legislation for space activities in France resulted in the first wave of large-scale privatization that emerged at the end of the 1980s in the worldwide satellite applications sectors of telecommunications and Earth observation and in the launch service market. With regard to satellite services, as shown in greater detail in §5.1 below, this phenomenon was mainly driven by factors external to the space sector with the advent of the information society and new Internet applications. Firstly, this led to a scission in 1990[1] at the state-controlled level in France, between the regulatory authority, assigned to the newly created Regulatory Directorate of the Ministry of Post, Telecommunication and Space, and France Telecom,[2] the operator of services (telephony, data flow) which had retained its monopoly. At the same time, France Telecom, which was originally organized as a branch of the State administration,[3] had acquired legal personality through the new statute of 'Public Operator.' Secondly, France Telecom became a private stock company in 1996[4] and its share capital was progressively opened to the public[5] while its monopolistic activities were progressively opened up to competition leading to the abolition of its monopoly in the fixed-line telephony on 1 January 1998. This privatization was ancillary to the transformation of the International Governmental Organizations (IGO) in the space telecommunication sector, namely Intelsat, Eutelsat, and Inmarsat, into private companies under relevant national legislations. At the time of this transformation, France Telecom was acting as 'Signatory' for France in all these

---

1 Act n°90-568 of 2 July 1990 (*JORF* n° 157 du 8 July 1990, p. 8069) on the organization of the French Postal Service and France Telecom and the Decree n° 90-1121 of 18 December 1990 organizing the central administration of the Ministry of Post, Telecommunication and Space, applicable the first of January 1991. The first one creates the new statute of 'Public Operator' for France, the second one split the administrative organization of the former Directorate-General of Telecommunication of the line ministry into several branches, among which the Regulatory Directorate and the General Directorate of Space affairs.
2 Named Orange since 2013.
3 This decision had a collateral effect of restricting the financial maneuverability of the Ministry of Post, Telecommunication and Space which was deprived of an important autonomous source of income from the telephony and postal monopoly that was organized under the special regime of Finance Act 30 June 1923 on 'Annex Budget of PTT.' This will therefore incidentally affect the availability for budget allocation to CNES through this ministry which was standing for 80% of its budgetary resources, the remainder being allocated by the Ministry for Research.
4 Since 31 December 1996, France Telecom became a *société anonyme* (SA) (stock corporation or limited company), under the Act n° 96-660 of 26 July 1996, and its application decree n°96-1174 of 27 December 1996.
5 At the end of December 2016, the State participation in Orange remains at 13.45% via the APE (*Agence des Participations de l'Etat*), the government participation agency: www.economie.gouv.fr/agence-participations-etat/Les-participations-publiques, 'Portefeuille de participations cotées de l'Etat le 30 décembre 2016.'

organizations[6] and as such was the sole operator of the current satellite capacity allocated to this country.

This privatization also brought about a split between the relevant regulatory authorities namely ARCEP (originally named ART set up on 5 January 1997, following the mission of Regulatory Directorate of the line Ministry created in July 1990) for telecom services,[7] CSA[8] for Council Superior of Audiovisual (originally the High Authority for Audiovisual Communication) for television broadcasting and ANFR for the overall management of the radio frequency spectrum assigned to France within the framework of the International Telecommunication Union (ITU).

This worldwide privatization of existing state-owned utilities of geostationary satellites was taking place concurrently with the development of challenging new systems based on fleets of low Earth satellites, promoted by U.S. companies from the telecommunication and the space equipment industry, acting independently and in competition with such historical operators. The fact that such private systems were using hundreds of satellites in low earth orbit (LEO) for global coverage, instead of the few geostationary systems belonging to the historical operators, generated an explosion in demand for launch services, exceeding the current Western governmental capacity.

Faced with this change of scale in the demand stood the phenomenal capacity of Russian launchers. Other emerging space powers such as Japan, India, and China also began to position themselves in this market. However, these latter initiatives remain scattered as a result of other government program priorities and are jeopardized by export rules on satellite components, like the ITAR legislation in the United States, restricting the launch of Western satellites in non-NATO countries. The collapse of the USSR economy following its breakup in the early 1990s precipitated the worldwide commercialization of its launch services industry, made possible by earlier bilateral agreements between the U.S. government and Russian industry. This resulted in the first wave of global privatization, as detailed in §5.2 below, that then raised the issue of the adaption of the national legal regime on space activities.

---

6   *See in particular* Arts. X and V (a) of the original convention establishing the European Telecommunication Satellite Organization EUTELSAT that entered into force on 1 September 1985. www.eutelsatigo.int/en/institutional-texts/.
7   Originally named ART (*Autorité de régulation des télécommunications* or 'regulation authority on telecommunication')-set up on 5 January 1997. The mission and statute of ARCEP (*Autorité de Régulation des Communication Electroniques et de la Poste* or 'regulation authority on electronic communications and post') are set in the *code des postes et des communications électroniques (CPCE)* the French Post and Electronic Communications Code, in particular: art. L. 36-5 et seq. and art. L. 130 et seq.
8   The CSA for 'Conseil supérieur de l'audiovisuel' the Higher Audiovisual Council, has been created by act N° 89-25 du 17 January 1989 modifying the Act N° 86-1067 du 30 September 1986 Law on Freedom of Communication 1986, *JORF* n° 15 du 18 January 1989, p. 728-733, NOR MCCX8800132LL 1. It superseded the *Commission nationale de la communication et des libertés (CNCL, 1986-1989)*, which itself has replaced the *Haute autorité de la communication audiovisuelle* (1982-1986).

5.1 THE 1990S TELECOMMUNICATION LIBERALIZATION MOMENTUM EXPANDED TO SATELLITES INFORMATION SERVICES

5.1.1 Privatization of Telecommunication Satellites Services

Following a worldwide trend triggered in the United States in the 1980s, European directives[9] of 1994 extended the liberalization implemented in 1990 in the markets for telecommunications services[10] to satellites. This brought about in particular the abolition of the exclusive rights of domestic or state-owned operators such as French Telecom, British Telecom, Deutsche Telekom, etc. followed by the privatization of their common-owned monopolistic international satellite organizations such as Inmarsat, Intelsat, and more specifically Eutelsat, the European intergovernmental organization established in Paris. The French administration was particularly affected by the privatization of the intergovernmental organization Eutelsat, finalized in 2001, as its headquarters had been registered in Paris since its creation in 1977. This privatization process had to be implemented by the conversion of signatory rights of such national stakeholders based on system capacity (i.e., from the transponders) into shares of the new Eutelsat-incorporated company, a classical 'société anonyme', to be registered under French law.

Meanwhile, Prime Minister Lionel Jospin, as announced in his 'Hourtin' speech of 25 August 1997, launched a vast action program for the country's entry into the 'Knowledge Society' and Internet named PAGSI.[11] This initiative raised many legal questions related to the digitalization and globalization of telecommunications technologies, beyond the traditional concerns of Space Law, such as personal data protection, database protection, broadcasting licenses, freedom of information, support to domestic industry competitiveness vs. competition law, consumer protection, protection of author rights, threat to security and defense, and organization of exchanges between administrations and the citizens. All these matters were to be addressed in an omnibus bill named 'Act on the Information Society' (*Loi sur la Société de l'Information – LSI*) whose final project, as adopted by the Government on 6 June 2001 and transmitted to the Parliament[12] was abandoned at the end of the legislature session in May 2002.

This is the context in which the Ministry of Telecommunication launched an interministerial task force in 1998 specialized in satellites services on the telecommunication side

---

9   Commission Directive 94/46/EC of 13 October 1994 amending Directive 88/301/EEC and Directive 90/388/EEC in particular with regard to satellite communications, OJ L 268 of 19 October 1994.
10 Commission Directive 90/388/EEC of 28 June 1990 on competition in the markets for telecommunications services, OJ L 192 of 24 September 1990.
11 PAGSI for *Programme d'action gouvernementale pour la société de l'information*.
12 National Assembly, 11th Legislature session, LSI draft n° 3143 registered by the NA's Speaker on 14 June 2001.

of the said LSI project. This led a few years later, in 2004, to the bill of modernization of the digital economy, integrating a new specific regime on the satellite systems (title IV and art L 32 of the Code of the P&T) relating to assignment of frequencies and authorization of services. However, such discussions did not address any space law provisions stemming from the 1967 United Nation Outer Space Treaty's (OST) related to government authorization and control of satellites or to launch operations!

At the same time, the U.S. Space Industry had already anticipated this liberalization process. To deal with the challenge of monopolistic geostationary systems owned and operated by the historical national telecommunication operators and their international extensions, Intelsat, Inmarsat, Eutelsat, and Intersputnik, the manufacturing industry in satellite and telecommunication equipment promoted the development of new LEO constellations of satellites to offer global services in mobile telephony and data. Such projects were impressive in terms of the cost and number of satellites. As a matter of fact, the Iridium constellation presented in June 1990 by Motorola totalled 77 satellites, the Globalstar one, sponsored in March 1991 by Loral and Qualcom consisted of 48 satellites, and the project Teledesic, sponsored by Microsoft in 1993, was originally designed for 840 satellites. In response, in 1996, Alcatel and Alenia in Europe associated with Loral in the United States, promoted the Skybridge constellation of 80 satellites for data services. These initiatives directly sponsored by the space industry and financial markets led to the privatization of the aforementioned intergovernmental organizations responsible for satellites telecommunications services. These constellations also provoked a peak in the demand for launch services which traditional actors, busy with government or commercial geostationary needs, were not in a capacity to fulfil. This was another influence of privatization on the launch services industry, as developed in §5.2 below.

In Europe and more particularly in France, the Globalstar and Skybridge constellations projects benefitted from substantial sponsorship from industry (Aerospatiale Alcatel Alenia and DASA) as well as government support for frequency allocation and export credit. Space agencies had not been excluded: in order to develop generic technology for Skybridge's needs, CNES inaugurated a new private-public partnership framework in 1997[13] with Alcatel Space (now TAS) that broke with its traditional procurement policy. CNES also set up a holding company 'Telespace Participation' to enable its participation as 'Limited Partner' in the newly created project's company, Skybridge Limited Partnership (LP) registered in Delaware (United States).[14]

---

13   See above Part I, §4.1.3.2, 'CNES' Partnership Policy'.
14   As a matter of fact, nowadays the CNES' Skybridge participation is over, but Telespace Participation still owned by CNES at 100% continues its activities in 2017 in shareholding its current subsidiaries (CLS, NOVESPACE, etc.) and more recently as a possible vector of Seed Funding for innovative Start Up on Space systems or applications. See above Part I, §1.2.4 and §4.1.3.3 on CNES' policy on subsidiaries and holdings.

Despite the contribution of European stakeholders from the public and private sectors, none of these new ventures and space systems chose registration or jurisdiction either in France, or in other European country. This raised questions about the suitability and attractiveness of the old continent's legislations to support such business opportunities.

5.1.2 Privatization of Earth Observation Satellites Services

The first example of privatization in the sector of satellite observation occurred in the beginning of 1980s in order to manage distribution of governmental optical satellite data from Spot 1 (France) and Landsat 4 and 5 (U.S.A.) through private companies: Spot Image SA, incorporated in 1983, and EOSAT[15] selected in 1985. The privatization of earth observation satellite systems was to follow later in the 1990s in the wake of the U.S. government's new Landsat policy. The U.S. government adopted a new legislation in remote sensing of 1992,[16] repealing the Land Remote-Sensing Commercialization Act of 1984, in order to end the Landsat concession contract as granted to EOSAT. This act was followed by President Clinton's directives of 1994 and 1995, firstly to introduce a convergence between satellite meteorology and remote sensing's legal and administrative regimes, secondly to accelerate the development of domestic private high resolution satellites either by relaxing resolution security and defense constraints for civil purposes and promoting a new 'anchor tenancy policy' to allow governmental agencies to procure future data at the early stage of development of new private systems (Earthwatch, Space Imaging, Orbview, etc.).

This new private capacity encouraged by the U.S. government allowed public agencies to purchase directly from private companies, in advance and for a significant part, services or data from systems not yet manufactured or developed. This capacity was particularly helpful to encourage the private sector to invest in new commercial systems, it being understood further that income would be also largely guaranteed by additional governmental needs, and marginally by a new private emerging demand. Such a new policy also promoted an open dissemination data policy for governmental satellites such as Landsat, limiting or denying application of copyright protection for such public data.

---

15 EOSAT for *Earth Observation Satellite Company* a joint venture between Hughes Aircraft et RCA selected by the National Oceanic and Atmospheric Administration (NOAA) after a call for tender in 1985, following a decision of President Ronald Regan taken in 1984.
16 The Landsat remote sensing Act passed by Congress on 11 February 1992. President Clinton's Directives of 10 March 1994 approving new private high-resolution systems and two directives in May 1995, the first to merge civil and defense meteorological programs and the second to confirm the LandSat strategy to open a free dissemination of such civil data.

In Europe, many questions arose about the ad hoc public-private model of delegation granted in France by CNES to Spot Image SA, its subsidiary specially created[17] in 1983 for the commercialization of SPOT satellite's multiuser optical data. Issues raised mainly affected competition law, public aids, IPR regime, public data policy, freedom of information rules, security regulation, and privacy. Basically, the continuity of exclusive commercial rights granted by CNES to Spot Image was questionable as the world remote sensing market became more mature and competitive, and taking into account the U.S. government's 1992 decision to revert its similar 1984 exclusive scheme, by cancelling the contract granted to EOSAT for the commercialization of Landsat data.

More broadly, the French government hesitated between following its original voluntary commercialization approach with 'for-fee' data (through Spot Image company) and the opportunity of opening a free dissemination policy on public data. On the one hand, the commercialization approach was encouraged by a 1994[18] Prime Minister circular on the dissemination of public data, driven by the necessity for public agencies like CNES, Météo-France, and IGN to finance their observing instruments and related maintenance. On the other hand, the French administration was being urged by directives adopted[19] or envisaged by the European Union (EU) or by the recommendations of the Green Paper of the European Commission on Public-Sector Information in the Information Society, to allow free access to any civil and public source of its data, in conjunction with pressures of the space application industry and users.

This trend, external to the space remote sensing community, mainly affected data in the field of mapping, geography, environment, and digital data. It was relayed in France

---

17 In association with IGN, the National Geographic Institute and Matra Marconi Space (now Airbus Defence and Space), the latest being once the exclusive manufacturer of the same satellite family.

18 *Circulaire du 14 février 1994 relative à la diffusion des données publiques* or Circular on 'public data dissemination'), *JORF* n°42 du 19 février 1994; This circular was elaborated after consultation by a dedicated task force of the Prime Minister's office named OJTI (for *observatoire juridique des technologies de l'information or Legal Observatory for Information Technology*) to which Philippe Clerc, the present author was associated as CNES representative.

19 Directive 96/9/EC of the European Parliament and of the Council of 11 March 1996 on the legal protection of databases; The concern has raised on what could potentially restrict the effectiveness of such 'sui generis' or copyright protection on behalf of governmental administration or agencies on data produced in execution of their official mission. This question appeared in the light of the ongoing contemporaneous consultations on other projects of directives such as the PSI and the INSPIRE ones designed to force national administrations to open their huge deposits of data.

The Directive PSI (Public Sector Information) on the reuse of public sector information will be adopted on 17 November 2003 (Directive 2003/98 CE) and amended in 2013. The Inspire Directive (for Infrastructure for Spatial Information in Europe) will enter into force on 15 May 2007 (directive 2007/2/CE of 14 March 2007). It aims to support the community environmental policies, and policies or activities which may have an impact on the environment. It facilitates production and exchange of necessary data for the European policies on environment.

through many high-level governmental reports,[20] calling for a harmonization of data dissemination among the various relevant state agencies, having as a primary mission the collection and dissemination of public data (Météo-France, IGN, INSEE, the national statistical institute; *Journal officiel,* the French Republic gazette publishing acts and regulation, etc.).

CNES however had remained out of scope of the provisions of such reports owing to its status as a space agency: its constitutive mission was to develop innovative space systems and not to distribute data to the general public. Moreover, most of the CNES data, excluding that of the Spot satellites, originated from scientific satellites or experimental satellites, sponsored through dedicated programs and partners, that had not been designed (and financed) to deliver data on a standard and continuous basis. But CNES data could also be regarded as public when considering the governmental origin of its judicial identity and budget. This approach was shared by the scientific community supporting global research programs on Earth climate and environment, in particular under the auspices of the CEOS (Committee on Earth Observation System) in forcing national space agencies to freely disseminate data in support of the IPGB needs (International Program on Geosphere and Biosphere).

The incertitude regarding CNES data status also resulted from several reversals of French jurisprudence, in particular in the so-called 'Météo-France-SJT'[21] case in the context of decisions on whether or not to grant free access to high-value–added meteorological data generated by the public sector for public use (Météo-France) to the private sector (SJT) for commercial use. As a matter of fact, the related data were originally dedicated to the safety purposes of airports authority as regulated by governmental authorities under the aviation national code. Another subsequent issue was the potential extension of the well-established World Meteorological Organization (WMO) principle of free exchange from the national organizations' restricted community to the private sector.

---

20   The Berthier (CNIG president) Report 1998 on Public Mapping Data Access and Pricing, the 'Mandelkern' Report 1999 on Public Data Distribution with the Digital Revolution – Public report to the Prime minister and *Commissariat Général du Plan* – authors Mandelkern (Dieudonné) and Marais (Bertrand Du) from the French Council of State – edited by la Documentation française: www.ladocfrancaise.gouv.fr. or www.cnig.fr. The 'Lengagne' Report of 1999 on Geographical Information – Evolution and Consequences for the IGN Geographical Agency. Public Report to the Prime minister – author Lengagne (Guy), Deputy Mayor of Boulogne sur Mer – edited by *la Documentation française*: www.ladocfrancaise.gouv.fr. or www.cnig.fr.

21   *Société du journal téléphoné(S.J.T.)* against *Direction de la Météorologie nationale (D.M.N.).* Decision of *Cour de Cassation* (the French supreme court) – *Chambre Commerciale,* 12 December 1995 n° 93-1380. Bull. 1995 IV n°301 P. 276. See also previous decision of the French Authority of Competition (*Conseil de la concurrence*) n° 95-D-58 on 12 September 1995 following execution of a decision from the Paris' Court of Appeal of Paris on 18 March 1993 against the *Conseil de la concurrence's* decision n° 92-D-35 on 13 May 1992.

The occurrence of this litigation, that finally ended with the lifting of the penalty of Météo-France as decided by the competition authority, led the Ministry of Space to set up a dedicated task force, early in 1994, chaired by Marc Gillet from Météo-France seconded by representatives of the space department (Gilles Someria) and CNES (Philippe Clerc)[22] with the mission to propose an adequate data policy for Earth observation from space. The conclusion of such an appraisal report published in 1995[23] remained steady in confirming the existing empiric separation of data policy regimes into three categories, according to the mission assigned to the space systems and the status of their relevant sponsors.

- The first data policy stated by this report affected *experimental projects and onboard instruments designed for research*. This policy was derived from the well-established regime applicable to scientific space instruments. The dissemination had to be free, or at a marginal cost; however, access to data could be restricted in favor of a category of users, namely the Principal Investigators (PI), if selected according to an independent procedure under specific requirements defined by the sponsors of the projects, the related space agency, or scientific community.
- The second data policy encompassed all *space systems developed by a structured and closed community* of user to satisfy its own needs of general interest (i.e., meteorology and defense). These systems were designed and financed by entities already aware or their own requirements, sometimes reduced to a single organization (Eumetsat, Météo-France). This community was deemed to define its own data policy, including data pricing, according to its objectives and missions. Beyond its own needs, this community could marginally open its data to support scientific or environmental needs, in particular under the framework of global programs, but without modifying either its principal mission, status, or its economic balance. However, as such, commercial activity for this data to the general public or open private sector was not directly taken into consideration by these report recommendations.
- The third category, residually brought together *multiuser systems public or private operational or nearly operational*, whose data were deemed to be disseminated on a nondiscriminatory and financial basis. It was duly specified that *financial basis* did not necessarily mean *commercial basis*, the price may include only the marginal cost to satisfy the user request. The Spot system was classified in that category, thus exceeding its original prototype nature since the 1980s.[24]

---

22 The present writer.
23 Inter-ministry report named in French, *Politique de diffusion des données d'observation de la Terre à partir de l'Espace* was published in April 1995 by the Delegation of Communication of the MIPTCE, the Ministry of Post, Telecommunication Foreign Commerce that was also responsible for space activities.
24 Originally the acronym of SPOT was *satellite probatoire pour l'observation de la Terre* which meant literally speaking 'probationary satellite for Earth observation.'

This three-block data policy regime has proven to be fit for purpose, and is still relevant today in allowing each category, be they public or private, to protect investments in space projects and corresponding data rights primarily for their relevant sponsors. However, this policy remained questionable from the point of view of users that could feel being discriminated, in terms of access price or rights of use, as for the satisfaction of their needs on similar or substitutable data, for depending on each (discretionary) satellite data policy, even for those sponsored by the French public sector in France. In particular, institutional or scientific users were complaining of paying full commercial price on Spot data, based on the non-discrimination principle, despite the fact that the satellite was developed and operated exclusively from CNES' public budget resources, such budget originating from the Research ministry apportionment (see §3.1, the '193 line'). Users were also concerned about copyright restriction of use attached to such data given that they were only interested by the free-information content derived from such data. On the other hand, potential private competitors of Spot Image Company, that would decide to fund entirely their own commercial system, may challenge in court the support granted by CNES as unlawful or claim an equivalent treatment.

To meet these risks and demands, CNES decided in 1994 on a voluntary basis to launch the ISIS program[25] to set up a *two-tiered* pricing policy similar to that of Landsat in the United States. Consequently, users eligible for ISIS support could receive Spot data for their own use at a reduced price, close to its marginal cost, directly from Spot Image Company (now entirely controlled by Airbus Defense and Space group), subject to CNES decision under the ISIS program, subsiding the difference between such reduced price and the Spot commercial price. This privileged access for non-commercial users nevertheless remained limited by ISIS program budget allocation and exclusive eligible scientific criteria and was not regulated by any supervisory legal framework.

This regulatory gap was later filled by the successor to the Spot system, namely Pleiade. This Earth observation constellation was the optical component of a dual-civil Franco-Italian cooperation[26] named ORFEO (Optical and Radar Federated Earth Observation), the radar component being to be brought by Italy with its Skymed program. In application of the Franco-Italian agreement and other cooperation agreements passed by France for Pleiade with European sponsors,[27] the French government decided for the first time to

---

25 ISIS is the acronym of *Incitation à l'utilisation Scientifique des Images SPOT* for Incentive for Scientific use of Spot Imaging.
26 Formalized under the Agreement of Turin, a treaty signed on 29 January 2001 between the French and Italian governments. This agreement was published in *JORF* by the decree n° 2004-1167 of 26 October 2004, namely "on the publication of the Agreement between the Government of the French Republic and the Government of the Italian Republic concerning a cooperation on the observation of the Earth, signed in Turin on January 29th, 2001." *JORF* n° 257 of 4 November 2004, p.18626.
27 Space agencies: France, Sweden, Belgium, Spain, and Austria. Ministry of Defense: France, Spain, and Italy.

specify in the form of a dedicated decree,[28] the competence of CNES for the exploitation phase of a project beyond its development phase under the responsibility of such space agency. In application of this decree, CNES could delegate exclusive rights for commercialization of Pleiade civil data to Spot Image, in addition to that of the former Spot satellites, but this time after an open competition process and through a formal public service delegation as called for under European law.

The importance of such a decision, that was vested under the form of a special decree, should be underlined, because it represents a major turning point with regard to the legal capacity of CNES to drive its Earth observation exploitation programs, and more broadly with regard to its legitimacy to manage any operational application programs of general public interest. Basically, since the origin of the CNES in 1961, this management capacity on satellite operations and its payload and payload was considered obvious in the right continuity of its development mission. As a matter of fact, decisions on exploitation scheme and data policy of space system, be they public use or market oriented, were taken in line with relevant international and national project cooperative agreements as negotiated by CNES with other sponsors before engaging the development phase. The responsibility of the same agency was being fully implied in the management of the exploitation phase, at least for the French contribution. In this respect, CNES was deemed to have full autonomy pursuant to its own internal governance and through its own various contractual tools as provided for by its constitutive law,[29] including the capacity of founding dedicated commercial subsidiary. Indeed, such responsibility has been entrusted to CNES president competence under the supervision of the Board of directors controlled by ministry representatives of the French government. Thus, with regard to CNES' constitutive Act, as raised in Part I above, the Pleiade's 2004 decree has constituted a precedent on CNES' governance and mission capacity. Notwithstanding its competence in the Space program development phase, CNES shall henceforth require a dedicated decree in order to manage the exploitation phase of operational and multiuser Earth observation programs. This formality consequently will affect the data policy design process for future CNES' projects.

To summarize, and getting back to the end of the 1990s, it meant that the exploitation of a legal framework of a *public-civil Earth observation system* – including those delegated to private companies – had been put or was to be on a satisfactory regulation track, without the need for a dedicated law process involving Parliament.

---

28 The 2004 'Pleiade's decree' n° 2004-1395 of 20th December 2004, namely the decree "on the application of the Art. VIII of the agreement between the Government of French Republic and the Government of the Italian Republic concerning a cooperation on the Earth observation." *JORF* n°300 of 26th December 2004.

29 CNES Founding Act, 19 December 1961 n° 1961-1382, as codified by Legal Ordinance of 11 June 1 2004 n° 2004-545, into the French Code of Research, Arts. L. 331-2- C): "To achieve these programs execution either in laboratories and technical establishments set up by itself, or via any research agreements signed with other public or private entities, or through financial participation" (the later allowing capital participation to commercial venture).

This was not the case of the *dissemination security control regime* for such data as being set up within the "GIR SPOT". In anticipation of the exploitation of Spot 1 satellite, the French government had created in July 1982 a dedicated interministerial group named GIR SPOT in order to control dissemination, including from archives, of data of a resolution quality higher than 20 meters (from multispectral sensors) or higher than 10 meters (from panchromatic sensors), from foreign territories or to foreign customers as well as international agreements with countries intending to procure Spot data receiving station.

Following its internal rules established in September 1984, the GIR SPOT was composed of representatives of departments of the Ministry of Foreign Affairs, (the Presidency and the Secretary), the General Secretary on Defense and National Security (SGDN) attached to the Prime ministry, the Minister of Defense, the Home Secretary, the Ministry for Space Affairs and CNES. It was functioning on the basis of meetings at least every 6 months, excepting emergency procedures, and its decisions were taken by consensus. Possible restrictions were the subject of confidential governmental notification to Spot Image as related to data dissemination or to the relevant receiving station prime contractor exporter.

The GIR SPOT regime has given rise to legal questions among the SPOT stakeholders community when a potential competition was emerging between this Spot system and other private systems. These doubts concerned the informal setting of GIR SPOT as well as its control regime based on CNES-Spot Image historical relationship, either on contract or on shareholding. Among the highlighted risk was the possibility of a penalty imposed to Spot Image by Competition authorities for 'refusal of sale' to a customer or consumer as a result of a GIR SPOT decision, the latter not being formally recognized even under French law and regulation. Another risk under Company law rested upon the shoulders of the management and Directors of Spot Image Company, included CNES representatives, in accepting restrictions to the primary commercial interest of the company, the said *affectio societatis*, without being entitled to invoke any legal source or formal governmental decision. Another concern was the fact that Earth observation information products from Space, unlike receiving stations and their equipment as physical goods or assets, by their intangible and civil essence could not be *ex ante* classified legally speaking as weapons or associated technology subject to existing domestic export control regimes.

By the end of the 1990s, these questions affecting the evolution of the GIR SPOT regime data dissemination regime lead the Secretary-General on Security and Defense (SGDSN) together with the Foreign Affairs ministry to raise the matter with all the involved national departments, included CNES. The outcome of these discussions was included in the 2006 Council of State working group report.[30] These recommendations were followed by the government in 2007 while preparing the FSOA' bill (*See* §6.4.1).

---

30 Annexe 5, p. 147 of the appraisal study, as of 6 April 2006, 'A Legal Policy for Space Activities' (*Pour une politique juridique des activités spatiales*), Council of State's Reports and Studies Section of the (*Section du*

5.2 Privatization of Launch Base and Launcher Services

This privatization of the launch services sector started in the early years by the setting up in 1980 of the Arianespace Company, founded as a limited company (*société anonyme*) under French legislation, to commercialize the European Ariane launch services.

By the end of the 1980s, Arianespace had taken over with its Ariane launcher more than fifty percent of the worldwide market share. Faced with this Ariane domination in this emerging commercial market, the United States announced in 1988 a new space policy[31] that included a new Commercial Space Initiative to encourage U.S. commercial satellite launches to be privatized and limit NASA's involvement in commercial space operations.

The most decisive factor of privatization followed a few years later with the dissolution of the USSR regime, after the opening up of the Berlin Wall in October 1989, as a result of bilateral governmental agreements between the United States and the former Soviet Union.

Of note is that the Russian space industry, in order to maintain its capacity, had a vital need for both foreign currency and market opportunities. On the U.S. side, government was worried about the possible 'proliferation' of Russian launcher high-level technology in countries it has labelled as 'rogue states', namely North Korea, Cuba, Iraq, Iran, and Libya. The U.S. government was also concerned by the dominance of the European launcher Ariane in the growing international market of satellite launch services that could not face the Space shuttle[32] or the current U.S. civil domestic non-reusable launcher capacity whose development had been jeopardized in the 1970s, while the U.S. government policy was supporting exclusively the Shuttle program. Thus, the U.S. government was in a position to allow unilaterally Russian launcher services to enter in the market in a manner that will support its new diplomacy consistent with its commercial interests on such a worldwide market and subject to the setting up of appropriate export control agreements.

Rapport et des Etudes du Conseil d'Etat) – edited by La Documentation Française, Paris 2006, ISBN: 2-11-006205-3. *See* §6.3.

31 'Presidential Directive on National Space Policy,' 11 February 1988.

32 The Space Shuttle services were restricted, under the 1988 amendments of 1984 Commercial Space Launch Act (still codified at 49 U.S.C. §70101…) only for institutional needs (science, international cooperation, space station servicing and defense) as a consequence of the tragic accident of the vessel Challenger in 1986. The U.S. government then decided that all commercial launches would be handed over to the private sector.

5.2.1 Agreements Between USA and Former USSR Countries Opening the Launch Services Market

First, in the beginnings of 1990's START (Strategic Armaments Reduction Talks)[33] had decided on the withdrawal of about 2000 ballistic missiles. Rather than destroying physically these weapons, it was accepted to use these military missiles for civil and commercial purposes. It is within this context that the medium-range missile SS 19 was reconverted to give rise to a small (non-reusable) launcher, adapted to LEO satellites, to be commercialized by a dedicated company Eurockot Launch Services GmbH[34].

Then, in the fall of 1992, discussions between the U.S. and Russian governments gave rise to specific bilateral trade agreements that allowed the export of U.S. satellites and components, under derogation of classical ITAR[35] rules, to be launched by Russian launch systems, under contracts with Russian-American dedicated joint ventures, in particular on Proton under contract with ILS[36] and with Zenit under contract with Sea Launch consortium. Such agreements were also designed, in the eyes of the U.S. government, to prevent unfair competition, in particular the risk of dumping toward western services.

The agreement on Proton launch services was signed in 1993,[37] after Russia agreed to abide by the terms of the MTCR. The agreement contained in its first version an allowed quota by the United States of eight commercial launch service contracts with Proton, to be signed before 31 December 2000. Prior to Russia's first launch of a U.S.-built satellite, a Technology Safeguard Agreement among the United States, Russia, and Kazakhstan (where the launch site is located) was signed in January 1999. A similar agreement for launches from Russia's Plesetsk, Svobodny, and Kapustin Yar launch sites was signed in January 2000. A similar agreement was signed between the United States and Ukraine in February 1996 to allow commercialization by the Sea Launch joint venture[38] of services of its vehicle Zenit-3SL, consisting of a Ukrainian two-stage Zenit rocket with a Russian third stage. This vehicle was designed to be launched from a mobile ocean oil rig named Ocean

---

33 The first signed in July 1991 and the second signed in January 1993.
34 Eurockot, registered in Germany in 1995, is jointly owned by Airbus Defense and Space GmbH, which holds 51%, and by Khrunichev State Research and Production Space Center, which holds 49 percent. Eurockot launches from dedicated launch facilities at the Plesetsk Cosmodrome in northern Russia.
35 The International Traffic in Arms Regulations (ITAR) as governed now by 22 U.S.C. 2778 of the Arms Export Control Act.
36 ILS International Launch Services, Inc. (ILS). The American-Russian joint venture founded in 1995 between Lockheed Martin (LM), Khrunichev, and Energia with exclusive rights to the worldwide sale of commercial Proton rocket launch services from the Baikonur Cosmodrome in Kazakhstan and the U.S. Atlas launchers.
37 In its first version, on 2 September 1993 between the U.S. Vice President Al Gore and the Russian Prime Minister Victor Chernomyrdin. See L. Christian and B. Stephan, *les deux vies de Soyouz* (translated in English as: *The Soyuz Launch Vehicle: The Two Lives of an Engineering Triumph*) p. 250. © Editions Edite, 2010 Paris, ISBN 978-2-846-08266-2.
38 Of four companies from Norway (Kvaerner), Russia (Energomash), Ukraine (Yuzhnoye), and the United States (Boeing), the latter managing the consortium.

Odyssey being built by Kvaerner (Norway). This platform usually moored in Long Beach (Los Angeles, USA) is shipped for each operation, with the Sea Launch Commander center ship, on its launch site in the higher international sea near the equatorial Pacific Ocean.

5.2.2 Agreements between the United States and China on the Commercialization of Launch Services

In another direction, the U.S. government, urged by its domestic satellite industry, has engaged a dialogue policy to open the satellite launching services market to China's capacity based on the Long March vehicles as commercialized by Great Wall industrial Corporation (GWIC).[39] In December 1988, the United States Trade Representative agreed with China on a set of three agreements that entered into force in 1989 governing respectively: safeguard satellite technology transfer, third-party liability, and fair trade practices.[40] With regard to their dual-use related technologies, export of satellites[41] to be launched in China requires prior authorization of the U.S. government. Such approval remains subject to consultation under the western multilateral non-legally binding framework of the COCOM (Coordinating Committee for Multilateral export control) before its replacement in 1996, by the 1994 Wassenaar Agreement.[42] Actually, the implementation of these 1989 U.S.-P.R.C. agreements was jeopardized firstly by human rights concerns in the U.S. public view following China's brutal June crackdown in Tiananmen Square, few months after the signature of such agreements; secondly by the ambiguous export control policy of China toward the Missile Technology Control Regime,[43] despite its positive pledges in

---

39 Memorandum of Agreement Between the Government of the United States of America and the Government of the People's Republic of China Regarding Trade in Commercial Launch Services, 13 March 1995.
40 The three 1989 agreements between the United States and China on launching services were:
    - The Memorandum of Agreement on Satellite Technology Safeguards, 17 December 1988, U.S.-P.R.C., State Dept. 89-114 (enforced 16 March 1989).
    - The Memorandum of Agreement on (*third party*) Liability for Satellite Launches, 17 December 1988, U.S.-P.R.C., State Dept. 89-115 (enforced 16 March 1989).
    - The Memorandum of Agreement Regarding International Trade in Commercial Launch Services, 26 January 1989, United States-P.R.C., State Dept. 89-116 (enforced 16 March 1989).
41 Namely, the U.S. government approval for any U.S. satellite or any foreign satellite (re-export) using U.S. sensitive technology to be launched from China.
42 The Wassenaar Arrangement for Export Controls for Conventional Arms and Dual-Use Goods and Technologies, 1 August 1996 (listing dual-use goods which include missile-related technologies).
43 The Missile Technology Control Regime (MTCR) effects on its side transfer of technology (exports) on launcher vehicle and associated services because of their similarities with those of Missiles. MTCR was established in April 1987 by the G7 (Western) countries (Canada, France, Germany, Italy, Japan, Great Britain, and the United States) in order to curb the spread of unmanned delivery systems (missiles) for nuclear weapons. It was agreed in July 1992 to expand its scope to include nonproliferation of unmanned aerial vehicles (UAVs) for all weapons of mass destruction. Prohibited materials are divided into two categories, which are outlined in the MTCR Equipment, Software, and Technology Annex. Membership has grown to 35 nations, including Russia (1995) and India (2016).

1991 and 1994, that led to increased U.S export sanctions in April 1991 and August 1993; thirdly, because of technical problems affecting reliability and finally competitiveness of its launching services, more specifically after the failure of Long March 3B on 15 February 1996, striking a village and causing a large number of fatalities in a village near the Xichang launch. In this context, the second agreement with China in March 1995[44] designed to implement the 1994 pro-trade Bill Clinton policy[45] did not make it possible to overcome these problems.

5.2.3 Common Features of Bilateral Agreements on Launch Services Negotiated by the United States with China, Ukraine, and Russia

All these 1990s trade agreements on satellites launch services set up by the United States with China, Ukraine, and Russia can be analyzed, from an external and European point of view, as follows:

- The achievement of a coherent open policy toward nonmarket economies of satellite launch services driven by the U.S. government without formal consultation with western allies, neither within the Alliance (North Atlantic Treaty Organization – NATO) nor within the Organisation for Economic Co-operation and Development (OECD).
- A bilateral approach to trade agreements negotiation driven outside the traditional framework of specialized multilateral agreements on Trade, such as General Agreement on Tariffs and Trade (GATT) as completed on services (GATS) at approximately the same time under the aegis of the Uruguay Round Agreements signed in Marrakesh on 14 April 1994, which also established the World Trade Organization (WTO).
- A promotion of the U.S. domestic space industry interests wisely balanced between the satellite sector demand on the one hand, being favoured with the opening of low price launch services from nonmarket economies and the launch services providers on the other, whose market position in the United States was safeguarded, even increased, thanks to a strengthened anchor tenancy procurement policy[46] and, inciden-

---

The People's Republic of China is not a member of the MTCR, even though it has agreed to abide by the original 1987 Guidelines and Annex. Although it has verbally pledged that it would adhere to the MTCR in November 1991, reiterated this engagement in the October 1994 US-China joint statement and formally applied in 2004, China was not accepted to join the MTCR, because of concerns about its export control practices. As a matter of fact, China has been criticized, rightly or wrongly, for having supplied ballistic missiles and technology to Pakistan, North Korea, Iran, and Syria.

44 Memorandum of Agreement Between the Government of the United States of America and the Government of the People's Republic of China Regarding Trade in Commercial Launch Services, 13 March 1995. *See* H. Meijer, *Trading with the Enemy: The Making of US Export Control Policy Toward the People's Republic of China*, Oxford University Press, 2016, p. 218, ISBN 0190277696, 9780190277697, footnote n° 85.
45 National Space Transportation Policy, NSTC-4, 5 August 1994.
46 Buy American legal instruments on launch services set up following Clinton's National Space Transportation Policy (NSTP) of 5 August 1994.

tally, the opportunity to compete with the European Ariane services in operating cheap and reliable launchers through exclusive joint ventures set up in application of such bilateral trade agreements (ILS[47] with Lockheed Martin and Sea Launch[48] with Boeing).
- The efficiency of the U.S. government's extra-territorial law enforcing provisions of such bilateral trade agreements:
  - The most well-known instrument applicable to the space industry stems from the U.S. Export Law[49] (ITAR and EAR Regimes) that allows the U.S. administration to control the export or the reexport of any U.S. satellite or U.S.-sensitive component to be launched outside its territory.
  - As another famous coercive instrument, the discretionary authority given to the President, named 'special 301',[50] to take all appropriate action, including retaliation, to obtain the removal of any act, policy, or practice of a foreign government that violates an international trade agreement or is unjustified, unreasonable, or discriminatory, and that burdens or restricts U.S. commerce.

As a result, such U.S. policy based on bilateral governmental trade agreements,[51] especially the outcome from the ones with the former USSR potentially affected Ariane's overseas market development from the end of the 1990s, given the fact that the U.S. launcher industry outlet was already secured in its domestic huge governmental market and could increase its commercial market share against Ariane thanks to participation in Sea Launch and ILS joint ventures.

5.2.4 Rules of the Road Discussions between the United States and Europe

In this context, talks among western countries or open economies on launch services trade occurred in 1990 on 'the rules of the road' negotiations between the United States and

---

47 International Launch Services (ILS), the American-Russian joint venture between Lockheed Martin (LM), Khrunichev, and Energia, with exclusive rights to the worldwide sale of commercial Proton rocket launch services from the Baikonur Cosmodrome in Kazakhstan ILS also co-marketed nonmilitary launches on the U.S. Atlas expendable launch vehicles.

48 See Launch was established in 1995 as a consortium of four companies from Norway, Russia, Ukraine, and the United States, managed by Boeing to commercialize the Ukrainian-Russian launch services of Zenit-3SL from a mobile maritime launch platform. The first rocket was launched in March 1999.

49 The cornerstone of this U.S. Export Control Law is the Arms Export Control Act (AECA). The Department of State (the US Foreign Affairs Ministry) implements this statute by the International Traffic in Arms Regulations (ITAR). The regulation of the export or reexport of U.S.-origin *dual-use* goods, software, and technology is implemented by the Department of Commerce that implements this authority through the Export Administration Regulations (EAR).

50 Section 301 of the U.S. Trade Act of 1974 as amended in 1979 (Pub.L. 93–618, 19 U.S.C. §2411).

51 For an in-depth study about all this U.S. bilateral trade agreement on launch services, *see* J.L. Reed, 'The Commercial Space Launch Market and Bilateral Trade Agreements in Space Launch Services.' *American University International Law Review* 13, no. 1 (1999): 157-217.

Europe. Their outcomes were not so successful. Despite the secrecy surrounding such negotiations, obvious reasons can be raised to explain the failure to reach an agreement[52]:
- The litigation context within which were processed negotiations starting under the serious threat of U.S. unilateral sanctions under the 'super 301' against the ESA Member States participating in the Ariane production program as a result of the claim from 'Transpace Carriers Inc.'[53]
- The dominant position of Ariane with fifty percent of the commercial market rapidly acquired in the 1980s to the detriment of the United States, hardening concessions on both sides.
- European concerns faced with the policy claimed by the U.S. government (reaffirmed in 1994 under NSTP) to prohibit U.S. agencies to procure foreign launch services in particular from Ariane for internal use in line with the Buy American Act.
- Last but not least, from a legal and institutional point of view, the absence on the European side of a principal interlocutor fully entitled to negotiate such Launch Service Trade agreements with the U.S. government:
  - The ESA, as an intergovernmental space agency, was not entrusted with a proper competence on trade issues within the framework of its constitutive convention of 30 May 1975. Such competence on the Ariane commercial phase, to date, has been regulated by a specific mandate given by the participating State of the Ariane

---

52 As quoted in the preceding footnote, J.L. Reed, at 53, note 335, see (1) C. Garcia, 'Heaven or Hell: The Future of The United States Launch Services Industry,' 7 *Harv. J.L. & Tech.* (1994) Garcia, p. 366 'stating that the reasons why there was a failure to reach an agreement in the *Rules of The Road* talks are unknown because the negotiations were secret'; (2) D.P. Radzanowski & M.S. Smith, 'Space Launch Vehicles: Government Requirements and Commercial Competition,' 14 *Cong. Res. Service*, 1997, arguing that Europe's protection of the market share and unwillingness of the United States to allow Europe to launch U.S. government satellites contributed to the failure to establish a fair agreement in the *Rules of the Road* talks.

53 On 25 May 1984 Transpace Carriers Inc., a private U.S. company to which NASA has licensed commercialization of non-reusable rockets THOR DELTA filed a petition to the Office of U.S. Trade Representative (OUSTR) against the ESA State Members accused of subsiding the Arianespace launch services private company to the prejudice of TCI and other U.S. private launch service providers.
The main arguments put forward by TCI were firstly the dual pricing system on Ariane services during the 'promotion phase program' in which ESA States members accepted higher prices for their institutional missions and thus resulted in lower price (dumping) for other foreign customers; secondly the existence of ESA State Members' subsidies on fixed operating cost of the Guiana Space Center, the European launching base used by Ariane.
After inquiry on that case completed by the OUSTR, the President R. Reagan decided on 11 July 1985 to close the case without any sanction, asking further the US trade representative on 15 August 1985 to engage consultation with foreign officials concerning trade in commercial launch services and related goods, consultation which actually includes the European one, in the foregoing 'Rules of road' discussions. The reason for rejecting TCI claim was that it had appeared along the inquiry, that TCI was obliquely denouncing unfair competition of the current NASA Space Shuttle commercial services toward classical non-reusable launches licensed to US private sector (Statement made by Gary C. Huston, President of Pacific Launch Systems, according to Space Business, 16 July 1984). Thus comparison on respective governmental supports on Ariane and the Space Shuttle has clearly turned to direct concerns on the U.S. exploitation model.

development program in the so-called Ariane Production Declaration.[54] As a consequence, ESA in itself has no counterpart to propose in bilateral negotiations without prior special consent of its Member States. Furthermore, the European governments individually or grouped within the ESA, be they were politically willing[55] to negotiate bilateral trade agreement, or restrict foreign access to their domestic market, should reckon with the EU rules and policies on trade.

- The EU, at that time the European Economic Community (EEC), held a legal capacity to negotiate such trade agreements,[56] but its capacity was restricted to the trade of 'goods.' The EU competence on 'services' had been toughly discussed with its Members States during the Uruguay round negotiation.[57] This question was laboriously settled by the European Court of Justice in its advisory opinion 1/94[58] and a subsequent revision of the EU Treaty[59] both resulting in a complex mixed competence between EU and Member States as set up nowadays in article 204-7 of the TFUE. Furthermore, the EU competence on space policy was not to be recognized before 2007 with the Lisbon Treaty on the Functioning of the European Union (TFEU)[60] and this competence shall remain nonexclusive, firstly as it does not

---

54 Declaration by certain European Governments on the Production Phase of Ariane (Ariane Production Declaration) entered into force on 14 April 1980, see §1.2.2.3 (footnote 34).
55 Actually, there is no unconditional declared willingness among European States in setting common legally binding rules on launch service procurements within Europe or through international agreements. Each national policy fluctuates in accordance with the degree of its domestic industrial participation in the Ariane program or, inversely, with the importance of lobbies of its satellite industry in favor of cheap launch services.
56 Under the contemporary wording of Art. 113 of the Treaty of Rome, signed on 25 March 1957.
57 The Uruguay Round was the 8th round of multilateral trade negotiations conducted within the framework of the General Agreement on Tariffs and Trade (GATT), spanning from 1986 to 1994. This Round led to extend GATT trade rules to areas previously exempted, in particular 'trade in services.' The Marrakesh Agreement, signed in Marrakesh, Morocco, by 124 nations on 15 April 1994, achieved the outcomes of the 12-year-long Uruguay Round and established the World Trade Organization (WTO), which officially came into being on 1 January 1995.
58 Opinion of the Court of 15 November 1994 – Competence of the Community to conclude international agreements concerning services and the protection of intellectual property – Art. 228 (6) of the EC Treaty. Opinion 1/94. European Court reports 1994, p. I-05267
59 The Treaty of Nice, signed on 26 February 2001, came into force on 1 February 2003. *See* Art. 133 confirming advisoryopinion1/94, Lisbon 2007 on mixed competence.
The Treaty of Lisbon (initially known as the Reform Treaty which nowadays forms the constitutional basis of the European Union [EU]). The Treaty of Lisbon was signed by the EU member states on 13 December 2007, and entered into force on 1 December 2009. It amends the Maastricht Treaty (1993), known in updated form as the Treaty on European Union (2007) or TEU, and the Treaty of Rome (1957) or TEEC then TEC, known in updated form as the Treaty on the Functioning of the European Union (2007) or TFEU. The exclusive competence of EU is set up in Art. 3.2 and 216.1 of TFEU "The Union shall also have exclusive competence for the conclusion of an international agreement when its conclusion is provided for in a legislative act of the Union or is necessary to enable the Union to exercise its internal competence, or in so far as its conclusion may affect common rules or alter their scope."
60 Art. 4.3 on the Functioning of the European Union (TFUE): "In the areas of research, technological development and space, the Union shall have competence to carry out activities, in particular to define and

prevent Member States from exercising theirs (art 4.3 TFEU) and secondly as it requires the Union to establish any appropriate relations with the ESA (art 189.3).

Basically, the unique commitment on Ariane Preference procurement among European governments was the aforementioned intergovernmental treaty named 'Declaration by certain European Governments on the Production Phase of Ariane' (Ariane Production Declaration) entered into force on 14 April 1980.[61] This was worded as follows in Article 1.4 (b) and (c):

- b) The Participant [i.e. governments parties to the Declaration- P. Clerc] agree to take into account the Ariane launcher when defining and executing their national programmes and to grant preference to its utilisation except where such use compared to the use of other launchers or space transport facilities available at the envisaged time is unreasonably disadvantageous with regard to cost, reliability or mission compatibility.
- c) The Participant will endeavour to support the use of the Ariane launcher within the framework of the international programmes in which they participate and shall consult together to that end.

This commitment was reaffirmed and strengthened in the 2007s 'Launcher Exploitation Declaration' for all launchers operated from the European spaceport of the Guiana Space Centre.[62] Such a renewed treaty is applicable until the end of 2020, but this 'preference'

---

implement programmes; however, the exercise of that competence shall not result in Member States being prevented from exercising theirs."
Art 189 (TFUE):
1. To promote scientific and technical progress, industrial competitiveness, and the implementation of its policies, the Union shall draw up a European space policy. To this end, it may promote joint initiatives, support research, and technological development, and coordinate the efforts needed for the exploration and exploitation of space.
2. To contribute to attaining the objectives referred to in paragraph 1, the European Parliament and the Council, acting in accordance with the ordinary legislative procedure, shall establish the necessary measures, which may take the form of a European space programme, excluding any harmonisation of the laws and regulations of the Member States.
3. The Union shall establish any appropriate relations with the European Space Agency.
[…]

61 Art. 1(4)(b) and (c)
62 Declaration by certain European Governments on the Launchers Exploitation Phase of Ariane, Vega, and Soyuz from the Guiana Space Centre finalized on 30 March 2007 (Text ratified in France and published by Decree n° 2016-1778 of 19 December 2016; JORF (official gazette) n° 0296 of 21 December 2016):
Paragraph 8 The Parties hereto will take the ESA-developed launchers and the Soyuz launcher operated from the CSG into account when defining and executing their national programmes as well as the European and other international programmes in which they are involved, **except** where such use compared to the use of other launchers or space transport means available at the envisaged time presents an unreasonable disadvantage with regard to cost, reliability, or mission suitability.
Preference to their utilisation shall be granted by the Parties in the following order of priority:
- ESA developed launchers,

provision remains a voluntary guidance being neither unconditional nor legally binding contrary to its equivalent provision in the U.S. law.

With such an uncertain background, Europe failed to set up a binding uniform legal regime and to reach an agreement with the United States on launch services trade.

5.2.5 Cooperation between Europe and Russia for the Commercialization of Soyuz Launch Services

So the European response to face competition with such nonmarket launchers services supported by the U.S. company, namely with Proton and Sea Launch, was essentially based on a similar agreement with Russia regarding the Soyuz launcher. In the wake of the new agreement between the French and Russian governments on space cooperation signed in Paris on 26 November 1996,[63] Arianespace and Aerospatiale (now joined within *Ariane-Group*) created a joint venture named Starsem and registered in France[64] with the Russian Federal Space Agency and 'TsSKB-Progress' Samara Space Center with the purpose to commercialize the three-stage Soyuz launcher services as operated from Baikonur Space Center. Upgrades made to the ground payload facilities in Baikonur and the Soyuz launcher, especially with the addition of a new restartable upper stage 'Ikar,' quickly improved by 'Fregat,' as well as the Arianespace's expertise on the market and financial guarantee will soon propel Starsem to the top of the worldwide commercial launch operator in the promising market of LEO satellite constellations.[65]

Both parties were interested in furthering their commercial partnership by operating launches Soyuz from the Guiana Space Center, the European Spaceport.[66] Russia, on its

---

- the Soyuz launcher operated from the CSG when comparing the options to launch missions by non-ESA-developed launchers,
- other launchers.

Paragraph 9:

The Parties hereto agree to support collectively the setting up of a framework governing the procurement of launch services for European institutional programs and ensuring a level playing field for Europe on the worldwide market for launch services.

63 Published by Decree n° 98-825 of 9 September 1998 in JORF n°214 on 16 September 1998, p. 14125.
64 As a Limited Company (*Société Anonyme* – S.A.). Starsem shareholding has been distributed as follows: Russian Federal Space Agency (25%), 'TsSKB-Progress' Samara Space Center (25%), Aerospatiale (Airbus D&S) (35%), Arianespace (15%).
65 During the year 1999, less than 3 years after its creation, Starsem will succeed to launch 24 satellites of the Globalstar constellation in 6 launches.
66 "European" spaceport as a result of the 5 May 1976 Agreement between the French government and the European Agency on the Guiana Space Center (CSG) regularly renewed to date. Since the subsequent agreement, signed on 11 April 2002, the French government decided to submit it to the Parliament for ratification to secure its legal enforceability. See JORF n°0265 of 14 November 2008, p. 17386 *Décret n° 2008-1160 du 12 novembre 2008 portant publication de l'accord entre le Gouvernement de la République française et l'Agence spatiale européenne relatif aux ensembles de lancement et aux installations associées de l'Agence au Centre spatial guyanais*. LOI n° 2015-1705 du 21 décembre 2015 autorisant l'approbation de

side, contemplated to reduce its dependency on the Baikonur Launch Space, because of its location. This base first has passed under the foreign territory of Kazakhstan which requires appropriate international agreements and a permanent dialogue with this country in particular on safety aspects of launches. Secondly, as a matter of fact, the northern latitude of this base is not adapted to the launch of geostationary (GEO) satellites that represent the major part of the commercial market that the Russian industry needs to conquer. Europe, as it has been recalled *supra,* needed to maintain the Arianespace competitiveness on this Low Earth Orbit (LEO) market of constellation with a reliable, flexible, and affordable launcher to supersede the medium class launcher Ariane IV, whose production was to cease with the ramp up of heavy launcher Ariane V exploitation as well as to deal with the new competition of Proton and Sea Launch on its favourite market of geostationary satellites, where Soyuz can board small-medium satellites that can be match properly within the dual-launch capacity of Ariane V. European governments were also concerned to maintain an independent affordable access to space for their satellites of sovereignty (observation, navigation, meteorology, etc.), mostly non-geostationary that could better be launched from a Western country's launch pad like the CSG, to prevent the risk of technology evasion or to comply with export control restrictions such as the ITAR ones.

These political and economic considerations by the end of the 1990s urged the parties represented by their national agencies, the Russian Federal Space Agency (RFSA, previously Rosviacosmos and now Roscosmos) and CNES, in association with ESA, to enter into proximity talks on opening the CSG to the Russian launcher Soyuz. The prospect of the opening of CSG's facilities was raising many complex issues, among them: technical compatibility, safety of flights, ground coordination, export rules, security, acceptance by the ESA Member States and the Ariane industrial community, Arianespace exclusivity of exploitation, socioeconomic consequences in Guiana, financing of works on the base and launcher upgrading, relevant commitments to agree with Russia, ESA, and other international partners, adaption of the role of CNES and of the French national legislation, etc.

The treatment of these matters will be organized under the umbrella of two framework agreements that will be negotiated in parallel by CNES, on behalf of the French Ministry in charge of Space affairs, with ESA and the Russian Federal Space Agency between 1999 and 2004.

The first agreement, signed on 7 November 2003, sets out the general cooperation framework between the governments of France and Russia *i.e.* state and national space agency's responsibilities and liabilities, security and safety, customs, technology safeguards, personnel's status, Arianespace rights and duties as exclusive launch service operator, etc.

---

l'accord entre le Gouvernement de la République française et l'Agence spatiale européenne relatif au Centre spatial guyanais et aux prestations associées, signé à Paris le 18 décembre 2008. JORF of 22 December 2015, texte: 0296.4, p. 23684 (Accord).

The second agreement between the French government and ESA, signed on 21 March 2005,[67] was designed to adapt existing agreements on management of CSG and ESA facilities. ESA on its side has signed with the Russian Federal Space Agency on 19 January 2005 an agreement on long-term cooperation and partnership in the field of the development, implementation, and use of launchers.[68] The above agreements, like in any traditional space cooperation partnership concluded at the level of governments and space agencies, did not provide for any exchange of funds. For this purpose, a program was launched for subscription in March 2004 as a formal *optional program* of this European agency.[69]

The program cost as agreed by the ESA Council at the ministerial level on 15 December 2004 and January 2005, estimated at 344 million Euros (M€), was broken down between the Russian suppliers (M€ 121) to be funded by Arianespace, through a loan to be agreed with the European Bank of Investment, and the European suppliers (M€ 223) to be funded by the relevant Participating Member States according to the accepted geographical return rules.[70]

The European Commission chaired by Romano Prodi, which supported the project by its Research Commissioner Philippe Busquin, contemplated whether to make a financial contribution of up to 10% of the project cost[71] but the succeeding college chaired by Manuel Barosso reconsidered this proposal, invoking the lack of legal instrument to support such investment as long as the future Constitutional treaty,[72] assigning a Space competence to the EU, had not yet been adopted.

---

67   Published by Decree n° 2009-426 of 16 April 2009, following Parliament ratification, on *JORF* n°0092 of 19 April 2009, p. 6742 as *décret portant publication de l'accord entre le Gouvernement de la République française et l'Agence spatiale européenne relatif à l'Ensemble de lancement Soyouz (ELS) au Centre spatial guyanais (CSG) et lié à la mise en œuvre du programme facultatif de l'Agence spatiale européenne intitulé 'Soyouz au CSG' et à l'exploitation de Soyouz à partir du CSG (ensemble deux annexes), signé à Paris le 21 mars 2005.*
68   This agreement forms a part of the intergovernmental framework agreement between ESA and the Government of the Russian Federation on Cooperation and Partnership in the Exploration and Use of Outer Space for Peaceful Purposes, signed by the Russian Minister of Foreign Affairs and ESA's Director General in Paris on 11 February 2003.
69   The first decision of ESA Council on 13 June 2002 (in Montreal, Canada) affirmed the 'principle of opening' the Guiana Space Centre (CSG) to the Soyuz launcher. The launch of the program will be decided in February 2004 (Declaration on the Soyuz at the CSG Programme).
70   The project was then financed up to 91%: 63.13% for France, 8.71% for Italy, 6.53% for Belgium, 3.26% for Spain, 2.72% for Switzerland, 5.65% for Germany and 1% for Austria. The description of the programs was provided in 'Project Proposal of Program on the Exploitation of Soyuz in CSG,' ESA/PB-ARIANE (2003)29, 4 April, 2003, p. 5.
71   White Paper dated 11 November 2003 on Space Policy 'Space: A New European Frontier for an Expanding Union.'
72   The Treaty establishing a constitution for Europe (so-called handled with Rome II or handled with Rome of 2004, sometimes abbreviated TECE or TCE), signed in Rome on 29 October 2004 has proposed to attribute to EU a competence in Space Policy and Program. This treaty could not be ratified because it was rejected, in particular, by the French referendum held on 29 May 2005. The EU institutional competence

Funding and implementation provisions of this program were settled separately between stakeholders through a developed set of agreements signed from 21 March 2005.[73]

Beyond the above international and national contractual framework governing the programmatic and financial conditions of installation of Soyuz launching facilities at CSG, it became necessary to complete the domestic regulatory framework firstly to specify the mission delegated to CNES on safety and security at the CSG, and secondly to determine the necessary measures allowed by the relevant French authorities and CNES in the interests of state security and for the respect of penal and policy laws and regulation (including the capacity to destroy the launcher with its payload in flight to prevent risks for populations).

Traditionally, CSG governmental agreement had simply provided, without any national legislative or regulatory reference, that "ESA *takes note* that CNES has been entrusted [by the French Government], of a *safety (or safeguarding) mission* at the CSG consisting in managing the technical risks, on ground and in flight, associated with preparation and conduct so as to protect person and property and the environment against damage of all kinds in accordance with the French laws and regulation in force and with French international obligation."[74] As a matter of fact, these regulatory, policy, and judiciary competences,

---

on Space policy will be set up latter by the Lisbon Treaty as mentioned supra (TFEU art 4.3 and 189) signed on 13 December 2007, effective on 1 December 2009.

73 Main agreements on Soyuz at CSG program signed in 2005 were:
- The specific Rider 5.3 signed on 21 March 2005 between the Agency and Arianespace to their 2004 Framework Convention on the Ariane launcher production phase signed on 3 April 2004, named Rider 5.3 'on the exploitation of the Soyuz launcher' from the CSG (ESA/C(2005)18). Such Framework Convention can be presented as the 'concession agreement' between ESA and Arianespace on ESA Launcher program exploitation phase, namely Ariane before 2004. This Convention is now entitled the 'Arrangement.' The said Rider 5.3 governed both the development and exploitation phase of this Soyuz ESA program, in particular counterparts for Arianespace subscription of M€ 121.
- The agreement between the French Government and ESA on the Soyuz Launch Site signed on 21 March 2005 (the 'ELS Agreement') that was ratified by the French Parliament and published by decree n° 2010-375 of 12 April 2010, *JORF* n° 0088 15 April 2010, p. 7034.
- The Loan agreement, also signed on 21 March 2005, between the European Bank of Investment and Arianespace with a special guarantee from the French government granted by the Finance Act provision voted on 10 December 2004.
- The order contract on the equipment to be supplied by the Russian industry signed on 11 April 2005, between Arianespace and Roscosmos, the value of which includes works on the launching facilities and upgrading of the Soyuz launcher (version 2.1b).
- Program Development contract on 19 July 2005 between ESA and CNES assigning to the latest the project management authority of ground works carried out on the CSG launch base, namely the procurement coordination of works between the European industry and the Russian industry. The associated prime contracts were awarded to Vinci for the European works and to Arianespace for the management of services to be delivered by the Russian industry.
74 Reference to the responsibility on Safety and Security at the CSG delegated by the French government to CNES is formalized through Arts. 3-2 and 5 of the agreements with ESA on the Guiana Space Centre ('the CSG Agreement') and the Agency's launch sites and associated facilities at the CSG (the 'ELA Agreement') both signed on 11 April 2002, and on the Soyuz Launch Site signed on 21 March 2005 (the 'ELS Agreement').

recognized on behalf of the French government and delegated to CNES through the successive agreements with ESA on the CSG, were not formally transposed into French national laws and regulations, especially as related to safety missions assigned to CNES, the latter being a public legal entity different from the French State. In this context of privatization and opening the CSG to other launchers than the European Ariane, it therefore became essential to translate the rights and obligations recognized to CNES under the CSG agreements into domestic legislation.

This meant firstly on a constitutional ground to submit the latest agreements to the French Parliament for ratification to give them an enforceable legislative value,[75] secondly to integrate this agreement provisions in a more comprehensive and developed domestic legislation, including the necessary associated regulatory framework for decisions to be taken as the case may be at the level of the government[76] or by the CNES as an independent legal body entrusted with a public mission at CSG.

The problem of the national enforceable value of the CSG European intergovernmental agreements was settled since those agreed on 11 April 2002 were to be ratified, however belatedly, on 2008 for the 'ELA Agreement'[77] and on 2010 for the 'CSG Agreement.'[78]

Thus the issue of an appropriate *implementing legislation and regulation on the whole space operations* remained to be addressed in greater detail by the French Ministry of Research in charge of the space policy.

In March 1999, the Space Department of this Ministry undertook a study as a basis for further reflection on this matter. Rather than carrying out this survey internally or within a limited circle with CNES and consultants, the department proposed to organize a large consultation among the whole space community and experts. The kick-off meeting of this project was held on 19 May 1999. This consultation process continued into 2010 with the completion of all the 2008 Space Act implementation regulations detailed in Chapter 6.

    In the agreement currently in force signed on 18 December 2008, the same provisions are provided in Arts. 3-3 and 5. [Addition by author.]

75 Under Art. 53 of the French Republic Constitution of 4 October 1958, translated as follows: 'Peace treaties, commercial treaties, treaties or agreements relative to the international organization, *treaties which lay out State finances, those which modify provisions of a legislative nature*, and those which relate to the status of persons… may not be approved and ratified except by virtue of a law. They shall only take effect once they have been ratified or approved.'

76 Art. 37 of the French Republic Constitution of 4 October 1958: Matters other than those coming under the scope of statute law (*author's note*: matters listed before in Art. 34) shall be matters for regulation (under competence of the Government, the executive power).

77 As published by decree n° 2008-1160 of 12 November 2008 – *JORF* n° 0265 of 14 November 2008, p. 17386.

78 Decree n° 2010-375 of 12 April 2010 – *JORF* n°0088 of 15 April 2010, p. 7034.

6 The Development Stages of Legislation on Space Operations, from the First Studies in 1999 to its Entry into Force in December 2010

6.1 Study Report 'The Legal Framework for Space Activities' from the Department of the Ministry in Charge of Space between 1999 and 2003

As stated above, it was primarily the prospect of establishing Soyuz in French Guiana that led the minister in charge of space to reflect on the advisability of adopting national space legislation. At the end of 1998, this ministry urged the *Centre national d'études spatiales* (CNES) to study the legal consequences, under national law, of such establishment for the Guiana Space Centre (hereinafter CSG) in relation to the European Space Agency (ESA), Arianespace, and industry operators present at the space base. Potential issues included whether CSG belongs to the public or private domain of the French State.

CNES replied by means of a study report conducted, at its request, by Mr. Edouard Philippe[1] who was at the time Auditor of the Council of State. This non-public report concluded, that at the level of principles, such an opening to Soyuz fell under a sovereign decision by France, without the need for prior approval from ESA. It recommended negotiating appropriate agreements with ESA and the Russian partners to tackle issues such as coordination, liability, and financing. It considered that, in these conditions, national legislation was not an essential prerequisite to such establishment except, at a minimal level, to clarify CNES' status regarding its own 1984 decree.[2]

On this basis, the ministry's department[3] proposed to organize a broader preliminary reflection. Indeed, in order to negotiate such agreements with ESA and the Russians from a position of strength, it seemed prudent to have as a basis a preexisting national doctrine

---

[1] Edouard Philippe is the French Prime Minister at the date of writing this book (JORF n° 0115 *du 16 mai 201, 7, Décret du 15 mai 2017 portant nomination du Premier ministre*).
[2] *Ibid*. Part 1, §2.1. *Cf.* Decree n° 84-510 of 28 June 1984 on the *Centre national d'études spatiales*.
[3] At this stage, the issue had only been dealt with by CNES and the administrative departments of the ministry of research and space, namely its Department of Space. The minister and his office, who had been informed of and who supported the exploratory approach, only become directly involved during preparation for the 2003 conference and, of course, to drive the process leading to the bill itself.

that was coherent and consensual, governing the authorization and monitoring of all launching activities from French soil.

The traditional and pragmatic solution of negotiating international agreements on a case-by-case basis (ESA and Russian government) also had its limitations, in particular, because of the need to subsequently ratify these same agreements, through the legislative route by the Parliament. Furthermore, going through this legislative route now seemed inevitable to amend CNES' constituent act regarding its responsibilities at CSG.[4] In view of this, it was advisable for the Ministry of Space to be prepared for a parliamentary debate on the completeness of these issues, if only to anticipate any broadening, beyond the CNES context, toward a space bill being urged by the wide-ranging privatization movement of space launch and telecommunications services.

The ministry then planned to organize a high-level symposium bringing together public and private decision makers, on a national and European level and the parliamentarians concerned to debate the appropriateness and conditions of such legislation. To do so, it firstly wanted to have an overview of the issue that would be as comprehensive and consensual as possible. This need led it to organize a broad consultation of stakeholders and practitioners in the space sector and legal experts.

This reflection took place between May 1999 and mid-2002, steered by the Department of Space of this ministry, in close consultation with CNES, centered around several working groups bringing together lawyers, spatial economy experts and management, universities and various public authorities, ministries and European bodies concerned. Each group submitted a report on its own study theme, namely: launch services, Earth observation from space, spatial telecommunications (including satellite navigation) and the crosscutting theme of ownership of and security interests in space objects.[5] The summary report was

---

[4] Indeed, the CNES' constituent act of 19 December 1961 did not mention the responsibilities of CNES at CSG, the French and European launch base located in Kourou in French Guiana, on which construction began only a few years later in 1964 and which entered into service in 1968.

[5] The creation of this group responded to an initiative undertaken at the same time by the UNIDROIT office in Rome to draw up an international agreement to govern this subject of security interests (guarantees, pledges) on space vehicles and their payloads. On the French side, the aim was to facilitate participation in UNIDROIT's works and to anticipate any future amendments that would have to be made nationally to our property law. UNIDROIT's initiative resulted in the adoption of the Protocol on matters specific to space assets in the convention on international interests in mobile equipment, in Berlin on 9 March 2012. Space legislation adopted in France in 2008 made a connection to this international security and guarantee regime, by making provisions in its registration regime for the obligation to disclose the name of the owner and any security interests in a space object in orbit (Art. 14-5 of Decree n° 2009-644 of 9 June 2009 amending Decree n° 84-510 of 28 June 1984 on the *Centre national d'études spatiales* (CNES), Art. 1 §4 of the order of 12 August 2011 by the minister in charge of space laying down the list of information required to identify a space object pursuant to title III of Decree n° 84-510 of 28 June 1984 above).

drawn up by the ministry's Department of Space[6] under the supervision of a reviewing committee composed of qualified professionals. At the end of 2002, the first edition of the report was submitted to Ms. Claudie Haigneré, Minister of Research in charge of space affairs, who authorized its publication.[7] It was on the basis of this preliminary work that the minister decided to organize a high-level symposium, in association with CNES with the support of ESA and the sponsorship of GIFAS, Arianespace, EADS, and Marsh SA, in Paris on 13 March 2003 in the premises belonging to the French National Assembly. This symposium was an opportunity to validate the main proposals of the report, which can be summarized as follows:

- Establish an authorization or licensing system for space operations (launch, monitoring of space vehicles in orbit) in coherence with other national[8] or European[9] standards and authorities and, of course, with the United Nations' international framework (space law treaties and principles).
- Prepare a proposal for fair sharing of liability in respect of losses caused to third parties between the State and private space operators on the basis of an upper limit of €60M set for the Arianespace launches.
- Adapt private law (property law, intellectual property, securities, guarantees, liability disclaimers, waivers of recourse, etc.) to current space community and market usage.
- Secure new legal instruments to promote partnerships between space agencies and the private sector to develop new space applications (public and private partnerships, public service concessions, joint laboratories, etc.).
- Strengthen the role of CNES as an authority and independent technical expert, without undermining its role as a space agency supporting future public interest programs, in particular, for science or industry, and clarify, if necessary, its relationships with its business subsidiaries operating in a competitive market.
- Prolong this reflection in a European framework, bringing together the ESA and the European Union to harmonize various national laws and practices.
- Put forward a proposal to the Prime Minister to prolong this approach to begin preparatory work for changes to legislation in these fields.

---

6   The preparation of this report and the overall management of working groups were given to Philippe Clerc, this author.

7   Ministère Délégué à la Recherche et aux Nouvelles Technologies, *Evolution du droit de l'espace* (*Developments in space law*), www.ladocumentationfrancaise.fr/var/storage/rapports-publics/034000134.pdf

8   *I.e.*, mainly ANFR (French frequency agency) for frequency attribution, ARCEP (French electronic communications and postal regulation authority) for telecommunications services, CSA (French broadcasting authority) for satellite television, and SGDSN (French Secretariat-General for Defence and National Security) for sensitive data exportation or disclosure.

9   In particular, all commitments undertaken in the framework of ESA (see §5.2, footnote n°54 and 62 on Ariane Declaration and footnote N° 66 on CSG agreements, etc.) and the implementation of European Union regulations and directives on services, markets, public funding, and competition (see § 4.2, §6.5.4.1, §7.5.3, etc.).

6.2 Referral to the Council of State by the Prime Minister in July 2004

These recommendations were followed up by a referral letter sent by the Prime Minister, Jean-Pierre Rafarin, to the Vice-President of the Council of State on 27 July 2004.[10] In view of privatization of the major European players established in France (Eutelsat, Arianespace, Aerospatiale/Matra EADS, Spot Image, etc.), this letter highlighted the need to assess and, if necessary, strengthen the legal framework applicable to space activities, in particular, liability for launches at CSG. It also pointed out that, as a result of this privatization, transposition of international space law (Outer Space Treaty of 1967, 1972 convention on liability, conventions between the State and ESA) could take place outside the conventional existing framework between CNES, ESA, Arianespace, and the existing satellite operators. It thus proposed to examine setting up a general regime for launch authorization, registration, and monitoring in the area of launches and satellites. It also called for a review of private law (property, securities, intellectual property, civil and contractual liability, insurance) to encourage the use of French law in international contracts and collaborations involving the space industry in France. Finally, it urged the Council of State to include European aspects in its assessment so that, following its adjustment, the national framework could become a benchmark for any future European legislation.

This referral was unprecedented in that, for the first time, in the name of the government, *i.e.*, those holding political power, the desire was expressed to develop legislation dedicated to the development of space activities in France, for which the Council of State was given an unequivocal mandate to propose draft legislation.

6.3 The Study 'For a Legal Policy for Space Activities' Conducted by the Council of State between 2004 and 2006

The study was assigned to the Reports and Studies section of the Council of State under the chairmanship of Jacques Blot, State Councilor in extraordinary service and former Ambassador. Jacques Blot organized his work with the support of a study group, having as rapporteurs Terry Olson, Julien Boucher, and Emmanuelle Cortot, and bringing together representatives from relevant public bodies (ministries, CNES), universities, and Arianespace. The group organized hearings of many prominent figures from the national and

---

10 Letter in Annex 1 (p. 133 and 134) in the final report *of the Council of State (from its Section Reports and Studies) named:* 'For a Legal Policy for Space Activities' (hereinafter CS Report 2006), a study adopted by the General Assembly of the Council of State on 6 April 2006, published by *La Documentation Française*, 29-31 quai Voltaire, www.ladocumentationfrancaise.fr, ISBN 2-11-0062005-3.

European space sector.[11] It also used, as a basis, the results of consultations conducted under the auspices of the Ministry of Research between 1999 and 2003.[12] His report, adopted by the General Assembly of the Council of State on 6 April 2006, was divided into two parts – observations and detailed proposals – with, in Annex 4, the first version of the draft legislation which was used as a basis for developing the French Space Operation Act (SOA) that we are concerned with here.[13]

The fact that the first draft legislation developed was so simple, short (7 pages in all), and consensual helped reassure the most anxious economic players and promote the interests of a legislative approach, which was unprecedented in the space sector since its growth from the 1960s onward.

The mission of CNES was also strengthened by this draft which confirmed, by way of new administrative policing powers, its security and safeguarding mission for all activities relating to launches from the CSG base, as was already recognized but with the deficiencies that we highlighted above, regarding agreements between the French government and ESA concerning this space base. CNES was also given new technical authority to develop and follow-up the authorization and monitoring process for space operations in general.

With support from CNES, the Council of State organized a high-level symposium bringing together ministers, members of Parliament, and key decision makers from the space sector under the title of its report 'For a legal policy for space activities' on 31 January 2007 at *Cité des Sciences et de l'Industrie* in Paris. The success of this gathering prompted the government to commence interministerial consultations prior to introducing a bill before Parliament. These consultations started in February 2007 under the auspices of Mr. François Goulard, Minister of Research in charge of Space Policy.

At the same time, reflection was instigated in France to establish the foundations for a new space policy and on governance of the space sector in Europe following a report submitted, in February 2007, in the name of the Parliamentary Office for the Assessment of Scientific Choices (OPECST)[14], by Senator Henri Revol[15] and MP Christian Cabal, both members of the Parliamentary Group for Space.[16] This report recommended *a sweeping law on space programming*, like the one for Defense, to give greater long-term intelligibility to the objectives and financing of space policy in France. Even if this concomitant parlia-

---

11 The composition of the study group and the list of the prominent figures consulted is in Annexes 2 and 3 (p. 135-138) of the CS' Report 2006 mentioned above.
12 *Cf.* CS Report 2006, p. 9 citing the report by the Minister of Research from November 2002 and the symposium proceedings of 3 March 2003.
13 *Cf.* CS Report 2006, p. 139.
14 OPECST for Office Parlementaire d'Evaluation des Choix Scientifiques et Technologiques, set up by Act n°83-609 of 8 July 1983 (JORF 9 July).
15 A few months later, Henri Revol became the rapporteur of the bill on space operations on behalf of the Senate.
16 *Cf.* www.gpespace.fr.

mentary initiative highlighting space challenges for France and Europe had not been acted upon, it brought additional political impetus to the government-driven initiative to secure the legal framework of space operations within the national jurisdiction.

6.4 Development of the Bill by the Ministries between February and April 2007

The preparatory work at the interministerial level, conducted in close collaboration with CNES and its legal department, contributed to introducing the following amendments to the draft legislation resulting from the Council of State's studies:

6.4.1 Addition of a Declaratory Regime for Operators of Space-Based Data

When the first discussions about the desirability of a Space law were undertaken, the only French civilian systems (SPOT 1 to 5 and soon the Pleiades dual system) were developed and operated by CNES on behalf of the State, and their data were marketed since 1986 by a commercial company called Spot Image, controlled by CNES as the majority shareholder in accordance with a specific framework agreement that today would be equated to a *public service delegation*. In order to preserve France's national defense and security interests and respect its international commitments, the control of the dissemination of data and the export of data from receiving stations was then entrusted to a special interdepartmental group called GIR SPOT, which operates in a strictly confidential and informal setting (*see* §5.1.2).

The emergence of international or national competition backed by private investors, the expected privatization of the Spot Image company (achieved in 2008 by integrating it with EADS, currently the Airbus Defence and Space group), and the difficulties for the commercial company to refuse sales without being able to assert legal restrictions, led to a reappraisal of the empirical rules which had been built up with the SPOT network (*ibid* §5.1.2).

As a result, in accordance with the recommendations of the report of the Council of State working group and from a restricted dedicated interdepartmental group convened by the SGDSN, the government used the opportunity of the Space operations bill to add a chapter on access control or dissemination of Space-based Earth observation data, data designated by the term 'Space-based data' (SBD). This SBD chapter was an express exemption to the main scope of the FSOA concerning operations on Space Objects[17] "to the exclusion of the consequences arising from the use of the signal transmitted by this

---

17 Namely, the launch, control, or return to Earth of space vehicles or objects.

Object" for users (FSOA Art. 1.1°). It established for this activity a *declaratory* administrative system of rules and not a prior authorization system as for Space operations, meaning that any primary operator of Space-based data needs only to declare its activity to the government beforehand.

The SBD-operator is the one who, in France, programs the taking of pictures from the satellite or receives data directly from the satellite. It is also therefore the one who ensures the first archival storage of the data and their first distribution to the users or customers. The French government having received notification from the SBD-operator can then, at any time, prescribe the necessary measures to restrict its activity to safeguard the fundamental interests of the nation (national defence, foreign policy, and international commitments). These decisions are confidential by nature and targeted in order not to unduly penalize the marketing and future exploitation of the data for civilian purposes. These decisions and the reasons for them are not supposed to be published as referring to secrecy defence measures.

6.4.2 Explicit Exclusion of CNES from the Scope of the Law

This exclusion is due to its role as a public body, being a separate legal entity from the State, and to its public interest mission. Indeed, this exclusion was justified by the fact that this body, with regard to its own space operations, was already responsible for the technical compliance monitoring process, following the same conditions as proposed by this bill[18] and by the fact that the prior *administrative* assessment regarding the same operations was already made by the government during the examination of decisions on corresponding programs submitted to its Board of Directors, the latter being predominantly composed of members appointed by the State (§4.1.1.2).

Another reason for this exclusion was to avoid any risk of *conflict of interest*, by limiting CNES' operational missions to programs of public interest or in the service of the State; in other words, this provision excludes business or competitive services where its involvement would be incompatible with its new sovereign prerogatives to monitor and police[19] private players operating in these markets. Follow-up measures taken by CNES to prevent conflict of interest are developed in §4.3.

---

18 Under Art. 28 (final version) of the SOA supplementing Art. L331-2 §f and g of its constitutive act and written into the Research Code.
19 Arts. 21 and 28 of the SOA (final numbering).

6.4.3 Definition of the Regime of Investigation, Criminal Sanctions, and the Ascertainment of Offences

The inter-ministries work contributed to complete the draft of the Council of State left in blank on the following issues: administrative and criminal sanctions and the status of officers entrusted with monitoring the authorization application, preparation and implementation process under FSOA, included their inquiries powers.

6.4.4 New Special Prerogatives for the State and CNES to Manage Emergencies[20]

Ministries meetings also empowered the *administrative authority* and *CNES President* under delegation, to make the appropriate decisions in case of *emergency* under article 8. After parliamentary debates focused on the delegations of CNES and its president on this matter, the powers of the latter were specified in the second paragraph of Art. 21.[21]

The bill was then deliberated at one of the last Councils of Ministers of Dominique Villepin's government, at the end of Jacques Chirac's presidential term in April 2007.

The bill was thus ready to be sent for examination by Parliament but in an uncertain timing and political context since the National Assembly was nearing the end of its term in June and the presidential elections were to take place in May. This situation undoubtedly explains the fact that it was sent to the Senate for its first reading.

6.5 LEGISLATIVE SCRUTINY OF THE LAW BETWEEN JULY 2007 AND MAY 2008

6.5.1 First Reading at the Senate on 16 January 2008

The introduction of the text through the Senate was advantageous for the rest of the debates because, on the one hand, the Senate is traditionally more inclined to attentively examine the legal quality of texts and, on the other hand, it was already understood that the new National Assembly college to be elected in June shortly after the election of the new French President would be primarily committed to adopting the first political measures of the future presidential or parliamentary majority.

---

20 Under Arts. 8 and 21 (final version) of the SOA supplementing Art. L331 (§7) of its constitutive act and written into the Research Code.
21 *Ibid* Senate report n°161, P. 50-51; National Assembly Report n°775, P. 35-36 and 49.

Hearings began in the Senate in the summer of 2007 and took place in a calm atmosphere under the leadership of Senator Henri Revol, rapporteur of the bill. On the government side, the bill was led by Mrs. Valérie Pecresse, Minister of Research and Space Policy.

The main amendments adopted by the Senate at its 16 January 2008 sitting[22] concerned:

6.5.1.1 Implementation of a Licensing System Constituting Approval of Procedures and Systems

This license proposed in addition to the license already in place for approval of *operators* as such, is to be used for *recurrent systems* in order to simplify the burden of application process and CNES' technical monitoring on each operation, at least with regards to the generic and common area of the file (SOA Art. 4 paragraph, 2nd sentence).

6.5.1.2 Consultation with the Operator for Emergency Measures

Senate introduced a systematic obligation for the administrative authority or CNES to consult the operator before making any decision for *emergency reason* (Article 8,) except in the case of immediate danger.

6.5.1.3 Restatement of the Powers of the President of CNES for Emergency Measures

The President of CNES have therefore the legal capacity to take the initiative and to decide on these measures, instead of only being able to obtain delegation of authority from the minister on a case-by-case basis.

6.5.1.4 Referral to a Single Article on CNES Competences under FSOA

The new competences of CNES under FSOA which were scattered among many articles in the government's bill following the Counsel of State's draft (4.2, 5, 8, 12 etc.) have been aggregated by Senate into the article 28 of the final version of the SOA supplementing CNES' constitutive act, as codified in the CR, in its Art. L331-2 paras. f, g, and h.

The following CNES competences are concerned:
- Assisting the State in defining technical regulations for space operations (Art 28 f);
- Verifying, at the "request" *of the minister in charge of space*[23], that systems and procedures implemented by space operators are compliant with the technical regulations mentioned above (Art 28 g);

---

22 Bill n° 297 (2006-2007). Report by Mr Henri Revol, on behalf of the Committee on Economic Affairs, n° 161 (2007-2008). Debate and adoption on 16 January 2008 (TA n° 50).

23 It should be underlined that it is the first and only article, in the SOA text, where is specified the "minister in charge of space", with reference to CNES' Act and technical regulation compliance. The other articles of the SOA retain the generic term of "administrative authority" given that it is of competence of the French government to appoint, through an application decree, the relevant ministry(ies) empowered with such authority (*see* §6.6.1, §6.6.3 and §7.4.3).

- Maintaining a register of space objects, on behalf of the State (Art 28 h).

6.5.1.5 Suppression of the Referral to an Overall Implementing Decree for the Law

The wording of Article 28 (old numbering of the government's bill) proposing a 'catch all' application decree was abolished by the Senate. Henceforth, each article of the bill can thus specify, where necessary, the provisions to be developed by decree.

6.5.1.6 Recognition of the "Temporary Presence Exception" with Regard to Patent Infringement Seizure Actions

In order to be able to apply the "reciprocity principle" of the "temporary presence" stipulated in the article 5ter of the Agreement of Paris of 1883 on Patent protection, to protect from seizures the French satellites intended to be launched abroad, the Senate introduce an amendment adding the case of the space object to the list of items for which the French code of the intellectual property plans this exception. This exception plans that the monopoly of the patent does not apply to any foreign space vehicle, or satellite susceptible to contain foreign patented technology, which pass "in transit" in a "temporary way" on the French territory (CSG) to be launched. This recognition aims to secure the competitiveness of Ariane and Arianespace toward their foreign customers while reducing by reciprocity the insecurity of the manufacturers of European satellites intended to be launched in other countries where the domestic law also recognizes this exception, like in the legislation of U.S.A.

6.5.2 First Reading at the National Assembly on 9 April 2008

The text thus adopted was referred to the National Assembly.[24] The rapporteur of the text at this assembly, Pierre Lasbordes, organized a new consultation with industry players, space operators, and insurers, without any representative of the government or public sector aside from the presence of legal experts from CNES, who could continue to monitor the works.[25] The consensual proposals made by this working group helped increase the value of this law in the eyes of these economic players.

The substantial amendments resulting from its examination by the Assembly were as follows:

---

[24] Bill adopted by the Senate, n° 614. Report by Mr Pierre Lasbordes, on behalf of the Committee on Economic Affairs, n° 775. Debate and adoption on 9 April 2008 (TA n° 120).
[25] List of the members of the working group mentioned on p. 89 of this National Assembly's report.

6.5.2.1 Introduction of an Orbital Control Phase for Space Objects

This 'phase of command' follows the 'launch phase' to better define the authorization, monitoring, and liability regime applicable to satellite operations (Art. 1-5°). The *phase of command* starts at the moment when the object to be put in outer space is separated from its launch vehicle and ending when the first of the following events occurs:
- when the final manoeuvres for de-orbiting and the passivation activities have been completed;
- when the operator has lost control over the space object;
- the return to Earth or the full disintegration of the space object into the atmosphere;

6.5.2.2 Redrafting of the Definition of End of the Launch Phase

Henceforth, the 'launch phase' ends 'upon *separation* of the launcher from the object intended to be placed in orbit in outer space', whatsoever the reason of such separation This wording has been based on that used in contracts for space launch services in current usage, in particular, that of Arianespace. The original version proposed by the Council of State's draft stated, "when the object intended to be placed in outer space *can only move using its own resources*", in other words, is in a position to be operated independently by the satellite operator that procured the launch. However the indication of a transfer of responsibility between the launch phase and the orbital control phase relating to the separation of objects can always be specified on a case-by-case basis in the corresponding authorizations,[26] in particular, to ensure for instance that the satellite operator does not appear to be liable for a satellite that was badly positioned or rendered inoperable during the launch phase, not of his doing.

6.5.2.3 Simplification of the Authorization Procedure for Operations

Basically this simplification affects launch operations, conducted abroad for the benefit of a French party in order to allow a total or partial exemption from French technical compliance inspections (Art. 4-4). In addition to arguments of a technical nature regarding the foreign country's organization, as already recognized under the Council of State's draft, justifying exemption from the French Technical Regulation's compliance inspections, it became henceforth possible to invoke the existence of national and international *legal commitments* from the foreign country concerned, of a *private nature* (contracts, insurance) or *governmental nature*[27] to hold the French State harmless from potential third-party claims.

---

26 *Cf.* "subject to any provisions contained in the authorization issued under this law."
27 These governmental commitments may include: national legislation's specific provisions, liability ceilings, guarantees expressly granted to the launch State having jurisdiction on the satellite to be operated on orbit....

6.5.2.4 Relaxing of Insurance Obligations

The amendment made in article 13 allows the operator to be its own insurer as it is customary for leading operators operating a fleet of geostationary satellites (Eutelsat in particular).

6.5.2.5 Consolidation of the Liability Regime for Damage Caused to Third Parties[28]

The liability regime was firstly redrafted by explicitly adopting the breakdown of the 1972 United Nations Convention depending on the area where the damage is suffered. Accordingly, the operator's liability is:

(i) <u>Strict</u> or *objective* or *for damage caused by things*: meaning that the victim is not obliged to provide proof of fault on the part of the operator(s) concerned for damage caused, during the operational phase, on the ground and in the airspace.

(ii) on the basis of *proven fault* of the operator for damage caused in orbit.

The provision specifying that 'this liability can only be limited or excluded by proof of the fault of the victim'[29] was however maintained as a common factor in the two liability regimes (i and ii). This keeping may seem odd with regard to French civil law in terms of *no-fault liability* (or *damage caused by things* or *strict liability* (i)), according to which, in bodily injury, the liability of the *custodian of the thing* is not reduced by the victim being at fault.[30] Such limitation due to the possible fault of the victim can also, by analogy with the United Nations Convention of 29 March 1972, give rise to questions with regard to the international 'absolute' or 'objective' liability regime for damage caused by space objects on the ground or in the airspace (i), given that the international regime excludes any discussion that could limit the victim's rights to compensation. On the other hand, this provision of the law provides a valuable insight into the regime of liability for fault (ii) in orbit

---

28   Amendment of Article 13, initially numbered 12 in the Council of State's draft legislation.
29   It should be noted here that the initial drafting of this Art. 13, resulting from the Council of State's working group on liability for damage on the ground and in the airspace was transposed word for word from that applicable to aircraft under Art. L6131-2 of the new Transport Code (at the time, Art. L141-2 of the Civil Aviation Code) which states: "The operator of an aircraft is strictly liable for damage caused by the progression of the aircraft or any objects that detach from it, to individuals and property located on the ground. Such liability may only be limited or excluded by proof that the victim was at fault." This wording was proposed by Terry Olson (Council of State), rapporteur of the Council of State's working group and prominent expert in air law. Council of State study report of 6 April 2006, mentioned above, p. 105.
    However, the liability regime for damage caused in outer space, for its part, had not been specified in the draft legislation proposed by the Council of State, perhaps because this concept of fault in space remains poorly defined by international law.
30   Under the current Art. 1242 of the Civil Code (1984 para. 1 in the old numbering) on so-called 'liability for damage caused by things' that one has in one's custody, as interpreted in 1930 by the famous 'Jand'heur' case law (Court of Cassation, joined chambers, public hearing of Thursday 13 February 1930, published in the *bulletin* [official gazette] and on the Legifrance website).

between an operator liable for damage caused by its debris and an operator that is the victim, possibly at fault for not managing to avoid it.[31]

Operators' liability was limited in time for a maximum period of one year (last paragraph of Art. 13) to avoid 'infinite' exposure of their liability which could not be insured in the market or which would be inconsistent with the limited life span of any (legal or natural) private person. This one-year limit begins at the end of nominally planned operations as set out in the authorization, or in the case of unintentional failure[32] at the time of such an event. If no damage is caused during this one-year period, the operator is discharged from all liability toward third parties, which is then taken over in total by the State with regard to compensation due to any victims. For details on FSOA liability regime, see below §7.2.

6.5.2.6 Limitation on Recourse Action by the State (in Art. 14)[33]

The possible recourse action of the state against the authorized operator liable for damage after the launch phase is capped to the same upper limit of basically 60 million euros (as in Art. 17) when France, as the launch State, has directly compensated the State representing the rights of the victim pursuant to the United Nations Convention of 29 March 1972 on international liability for damage caused by space objects. It should be noted that this limitation on recourse action by the State can result in different financial consequences for a French satellite operator who is liable for *damage due to its fault in orbit (hypothesis (ii) above under article 13)* depending on whether the victim uses the channel of France's international liability as the launch State pursuant to the 1972 convention or directly sues this operator before a national court. In the first case, compensation by the operator will be capped at the upper limit of recourse action under Article 14 (*i.e.*, the 60M € amount); in the second case, compensation can be unlimited since this *sued operator* cannot invoke the State guarantee provided for in Article 15, which only applies to damage caused during the launch phase or on the ground or in the airspace after this phase (in other words, the Art. 15 State guarantee shall not apply to damage occurred in orbit after the launch phase). Moreover, recourse action by the State is excluded in the case of actions not caused by the operator targeting State interests (terrorism, actions prejudicial to the security of the State, etc.). Here also, this limitation aims to have the State cover risks that private operators or insurers cannot legally or economically cover.

---

31 For instance, [addition of Philippe Clerc] this case may notably correspond to a situation identical to that where the American operator of the Iridium constellation, on 10 February 2009, did not manage to avoid the collision between its Iridium-33 satellite and the decommissioned Russian military telecommunications satellite in a state of debris, despite the technical and information resources at its disposal.
32 Or a 'risk item' within the meaning of the technical regulations: non-activation of the satellite, failure to separate, loss of control, collision, etc.
33 To the same upper limit as that set out in the finance act (of 31 December 2008) in application of Art. 17 (or 16) of the SOA, i.e., to 60 million euros.

6.5.2.7 Creation of a 'License Constituting Authorization'[34]

This license is especially intended for satellite operators who, like Eutelsat, operate a homogeneous fleet of satellites in geostationary orbit. This system reverses the burden of proof in favor of the operator. Any authorization applied under this license is deemed acquired for the total duration of the latter (up to ten years) and cannot be revoked unless there are events, whether unforeseen, new, technical, or otherwise, that are liable to challenge tacit authorization. Under these conditions, the operator is obliged to inform the administrative authority of the conditions of its future operation just one month before its initiation.[35]

6.5.2.8 Strengthening CNES' Technical Compliance Mission as a Legal Entity[36]

Following a proposal of MP Chantal Berthelot, the National Assembly modified SOA article 28 supplementing CR article L331-2 (g) on CNES mission by stipulating that it exercises its technical compliance verification of the systems and the procedures *by delegation*, and not *on request*, of the minister in charge of space.

6.5.3 Final Reading at the Senate on 22 May 2008 and Promulgation

The text, as amended by the National Assembly at its 9 April 2008 sitting, was approved without amendments by the Senate at its second reading on 22 May 2008.[37]

The SOA was thus promulgated by the French President, Nicolas Sarkozy on 3 June 2008 and published in the *Journal Officiel* (official gazette) on 4 June 2008.

---

34 Article Art. 4, last sentence of paragraph 2; in addition to the 'operator' licence proposed in the Council of State's draft legislation and the 'procedures and systems' licence introduced by the Senate.
35 Art. 10 of the Authorisation Decree (DA) of 10 June 2009.
36 It should be noted that the competences of the President of CNES are already the subject of an article on its own (Art. 21 of the final numbering) in respect of the special police for operations at CSG and emergency measures under Art. 8 (final numbering).
37 Bill n° 272 (2007-2008). Report of 14 May 2008 by Mr H. Revol, on behalf of the Committee on Economic Affairs, n° 328 (2007-2008). Debate and adoption on 22 May 2008 (TA n° 97).

6.5.4 Finalization of Legislation on the State Guarantee in the Finance Act, following Validation by the European Union

6.5.4.1 The State Guarantee under the European Commission's prior Opinion of 23 October 2007[38]

As a prerequisite for putting in place such legislation, it was necessary to obtain a formal positive opinion from the European Commission on the compatibility of the State guarantee above with treaty rules with regard to its 'State Aid' regime.[39] Prohibited State Aid means aid granted to a company by the State using public resources, conferring a selective advantage and affecting trade between Member States and competition. The envisaged State guarantee of up to 70 million euros to the sole benefit of space operators, in particular on behalf of companies taking place in the very competitive telecommunications sector, had been identified, following the study conducted by the Council of State, as being liable to affect trade between Member States or to distort competition[40].

The question remaining was whether this aid could nevertheless be considered as compatible with the internal market within the meaning of the exception provided for in paragraph 3 of the same article, in particular its §c. Indeed, this provision permits validation of aid intended to "facilitate the development of certain activities or certain economic areas, where such aid does not adversely affect trading conditions to an extent contrary to the common interest."

At this time in mid-2007, the Commission did not have shared competence for the space field, because the draft treaty establishing a Constitution for Europe, establishing such competence was rejected by the French referendum of 29 May 2005. This competence was introduced by the Lisbon Treaty, which was signed on 13 December 2007 and entered into force in December 2007. In any case, this issue of competence with respect to space remains of secondary importance with regard to the validity of this guarantee because the Union's competition law is autonomous and takes precedence over that of Member States and public economic policies, starting with those driven by the Commission (transport, energy, telecommunications, etc.).

The exemption procedure was instigated by the French government in a letter dated 27 April 2007, just after validation of the bill by the government (see §6.4 above).

After one or two additional written requests and replies, interspersed by a meeting in Brussels on 11 July 2007 with representatives of the ministry in charge of space and CNES,

---

[38] Brussels, 23 October 2007, C (2007) 5093 final, State Aid N 208/2007 – France, State Guarantee for damage caused to third parties in the context of space operations.

[39] Rules set out by Arts. 87 et seq. of the European Community Treaty (ECT) and by Arts. 61 et seq. of the Agreement on the European Economic Area (EEA), now Arts. 107 et seq. of the Treaty on the Functioning of the European Union (TFEU).

[40] *Ibid* report of the Council of State, §2.2.1.3.4, pp. 49-51.

the Commission issued a favorable opinion by decision of 23 October 2007 signed by European Commissioner Neelie Kroes. This decision concluded that "the aid is designed to achieve goals of Community interest and does not impact on trading conditions to an extent contrary to the common interest."

It is interesting to develop the reasoning used for validating this *state aid* because this decision represented the first formal opinion of the European Commission on the state of competition in the launching services sector. Due to the details of its rationale, this opinion therefore constituted a valuable precedent for examining the compliance of any aid granted by Member States of the ESA to the operator Arianespace or to European industry for the operation of European launch services.

Firstly, the Commission noted the international legal context and the European context, as forged by ESA, which already governed its activities in France, in particular, in the area of launches, the famous CSG agreements and the Declaration of certain European governments (from ESA) on the operation phase of Ariane, Vega, and Soyuz launchers at the Guiana Space Centre. It noted that developments in the sector, in particular, the privatization of Eutelsat, the opening up of CSG to launchers other than Ariane, the unique exposure of France in terms of international liability and the limited capacity of the insurance market, justified the development of legislation to clarify each party's liability and secure the rights of the private sector to also avoid the risks of recourse between these players that would jeopardize their development. The opinion described the SOA and its authorization and obligatory insurance regimes, and the capped liability of operators. It noted that *the unlimited occurrence over time* of space damage caused by an operation and, consequently, the liability of the private actors concerned, *justifies the absence of a time limitation to the State guarantee.*

The Commission then analyzed the aid. After recognizing its existence and the legality of the application, since it was declared prior to its adoption and implementation,[41] it assessed its compatibility with the treaty. In this respect, it had to ensure, on the one hand, that this aid would *contribute to an aim of Community interest* and, on the other, that it would not have a *disproportionate adverse effect on trade and competition in the common market.*

6.5.4.1.1 Singularity of the State Guarantee System for Space Damage
It firstly noted that there are no European block exemption regulations that apply to this type of guarantee. It noted, in this respect, that its Communication of 11 March 2000 on the compatibility of State aid in the form of guarantees,[42] setting up a regime having its

---

41 Art. 88 §3 of the ECT, now Art. 108 §3 of the TFEU.
42 JORF (official gazette) n° C 071 of 11 March 2000, p. 14-18; JORF (official gazette) n° 0224 of 25 September 2016 text n° 4.

own ramification in the export of space systems,[43] was only covering guarantees in relation to transactions between a *creditor* and a *debtor,* or coverage of the risk of *bankruptcy* or *insolvency*. The guarantee envisaged by the SOA bill, for its part, covered the risk of *damage to third parties*. The Commission noted that the guarantee in the French bill did not interfere in the relationship between operators and their insurance companies and did not have the purpose of alleviating debtor insolvency. This operator-insurance problem results from the obligation to take out insurance under Article 6 of the SOA that applies below the amount where the State guarantee is activated.

The Commission thus concluded that the guarantee envisaged by the SOA for space damage came under a totally autonomous regime. It noted, in this respect, that the latter resulted from the *United Nations Convention of 29 March 1972 on international liability for damage caused by space objects*. Indeed, this international convention places the burden for unlimited, joint, and several compensation exclusively on the launch State(s) concerned to victims on the ground or in the airspace, leaving it up to the former state(s) to firstly define the conditions of any possible recourse between themselves,[44] then, according to their national legislation, the conditions of their recourse (cf. recourse action below) against the operators concerned, whether governmental or otherwise in their jurisdiction and under their control.[45]

6.5.4.1.2 Analysis of Compatibility

The Commission considered that the aims of the guarantee serve Community interests in terms of their concern with protecting individuals and property and the economic development of the space sector in Europe, in the context of privatization. It highlighted the risks for the safety of individuals and property, which are high, though with low probability of occurrence. It also noted that the launch phase of a space object is all the riskier due to its low level of reversibility. In this respect, it considered that such activities are more like nuclear activities than air activities. It endorsed the argument regarding the need for this guarantee to promote the development of private activities, whose significant economic stakes is highlighted in its own political communications on space.[46] It also recognized the

---

43 Regime known as COFACE in France governed by decree, currently by Decree n° 2016-1245 of 22 September 2016 on the provision of a State guarantee for acquisition transactions, by French companies, of civil spaceships or spacecraft produced in France. This legislation results from Art. 11 of the OECD Understanding on officially supported export credits of 1 October 2013, made applicable in the European Union by regulation EU n° 1233/2011 of the European Parliament and the Council of 16 November 2011, on the application of certain guidelines on officially supported export credits and repealing the decisions of the Council 2001/76/EC and 2001/77/EC.
44 According to Art. IV 2 of the aforementioned 1972 convention on liability.
45 According to Arts. VI and VIII of the UN's Outer Space Treaty of 1967.
46 The Commission referred to its own Communication to the Council and the European Parliament on European space policy dated 26 April 2007, COM (2007) 212 final – not published in the *Journal officiel* (official gazette).

importance of the resulting advantages for the institutional needs of States[47] and autonomous European access to space, particularly within the framework of the ESA, to the extent that the purchase cost of these governmental systems could be considerably reduced by lowering of fixed costs resulting from the commercial development of the latter in the market due to increased productivity.[48] More generally, such an increase in productivity contributes to greater reliability and, consequently, better performance of these systems. The purpose scheme of the aid still had to be examined according to the usual methodology to verify (i) whether it was based on an appropriate legal instrument, (ii) whether it was necessary and proportional, and (iii) that its effect on trade and competition would be limited.

(i) *Concerning the appropriateness of the legal instrument* the Commission noted that space legislation adopted or in the process of being adopted by other European states included provisions similar to the measure proposed. In addition, it took into account the fact that the United States, the leading space power in the world, put in place a guarantee system similar to the French mechanism.

(ii) The Commission *also justified the need (ii)* for aid with regard to France's exposure to international liability at CSG as the launch State, and also with regard to the limited capacity of the insurance market to cover such risks. It acknowledged the appropriateness of the mechanism used, which channels liability toward the operator, limiting its amount and duration, while at the same time protecting industry players through legal recognition and automatic application of exclusion clauses. It noted that this mechanism is inseparable from the State's prior authorization and monitoring regime which limits technical risks with the sole public interest aim of the safety of individuals and property. Incidentally, the Commission highlighted with satisfaction the measures envisaged by the French government to disengage CNES from its interests in commercial companies to avoid *conflicts of interest* regarding its mission to monitor technical compliance for the government by processing applications and verifying proper fulfillment of authorizations arising within the private sector. Concerning *proportionality*, the Commission noted the limits set for application of the guarantee, in particular, the exclusion relating to intentional fault (or even, serious failure to comply with the specifications of the authorization under the finance act 2008) and the exclusion concerning damage caused in orbit. It reiterated that the guarantee only covers space damage that is, by its nature, exceptional and unquantifiable and which would not be insurable by a private operator without such a guarantee. It also highlighted again that this state aid is capped (guarantee or recourse action) in a transparent manner (finance act) at an amount coherent with international and European

---

47 That is for defence satellites or civil public-service satellites such as meteorology, Earth observation, etc.
48 *Cf.* last three paragraphs of §3.4.1, p. 8 of opinion EC n° 208/2007.

standards (Declaration of operation of ESA launchers). It also noted that the systematic use of exclusion clauses is only the formalization of current usage in business contracts.

(iii) Finally, it concluded that there would be a *limited impact on trade* since the guarantee is provided not only to French operators or operators working in France but also to all authorized operators carrying out their activities in the European Economic Area (EEA). It also noted that share ownership of the leading French operators, Ariane and Eutelsat, is broadly spread across various European Union Member States and ESA and that the aid would benefit the whole European space sector.

The European Commission also noted that, aside from the blocking minority of CNES, the governance of Arianespace[49] is primarily based, on the one hand, on the decisions of its other shareholders, who are also industrial suppliers for Ariane and Vega launchers and, on the other hand, and above all, on the rights and obligations set down by ESA under the Arrangement entered into with this company, which granted it exclusive operation of its launchers and facilities at CSG. This arrangement itself results from the aforementioned declaration of certain European governments on the operation phase of Ariane, Vega, and Soyuz launchers at the Guiana Space Centre. Taking into account this European, intergovernmental, and industrial governance of the company Arianespace was therefore an argument that played down the impact of CNES' interest in its capital.

6.5.4.2 The State Guarantee under Article 119 of the Finance Act of 30 December 2008[50]

Beyond the compliance with the European Union law, the liability regime and liability guarantee laid down by the SOA could not be complete without determining, for each authorization, the range within which the upper limit for recourse action by the State could be fixed according to the case, or above which the guarantee provided by the State applies. Pursuant to the organic law of 2001 (LOFT),[51] the SOA[52] explicitly refers to a finance act to define the financial conditions and limits of this guarantee or of this capped recourse action. These measures apply, in fact, to state guarantees for the debts of third parties (in

---

49 That is 34% of its voting rights, via its interest in the Holding Arianespace Participation SA, which at the time held almost 95% of the capital of Arianespace SA. On 31 December 2016, CNES transferred the totality of its interest to the joint venture Airbus Safran Launchers (ASL).
50 JORF (official gazette) n° 0304 of 31 December 2008, p. 20518, Art. 119.
51 *Cf.* 5° and 6° of II of Art. 34. Organic law n° 2001-692 of 1 August 2001 on finance legislation (known as 'LOLF'). "In the second part, the finance act for the year: … 5° Authorises the provision of guarantees by the State and sets out their regime; 6° Authorises the State to assume the debts of third parties and to give any other undertakings corresponding to a unilateral acknowledgement of debt, and sets out the regime for such debt assumption or undertakings."
52 *Cf.* Arts. 16 and 17 of the SOA.

French: *'caution'*). This situation for State accounts could also be compared to an off-balance sheet commitment in business accounting (in French: *'engagement hors bilan'*).

The finance act relating to the SOA is the act that was promulgated on 30 December 2008. In its Article 119, it caps support to the benefit of the operator at an amount between 50 and 70 million euros. In actual practice, however, the amount of 60 million euros is the specified amount. For each authorized operation, it is therefore the same amount within this range that applies:
- at the upper limit of the recourse action (SOA, Art. 14) when the latter asks to be reimbursed by the operator for compensation it had to pay to a victim in its capacity as the launch State[53];
- at the threshold amount from which the State guarantee (SOA, Art. 15) can apply in favor of an operator who had to directly compensate a victim.

The rationale behind this provision is that, for any damage caused by a space object to a third party on the Earth ground or in the airspace, the State must guarantee that a duly authorized space operator who did not commit any intentional fault in carrying out its operations should, in the end, never have to bear more than the predefined amount of between 50 and 70 million euros in compensation to the victim; regardless of the proceedings used by this victim to obtain damages. It is also this same upper limit that is used as a basis for the obligation on the space operator to take out insurance or dispose of an equivalent financial guarantee to cover the amount that is not covered by the State (SOA, Art 6).

In these conditions, if we add the insurance or financial guarantee taken out by the operator, below the upper limit of between 50 and 70 million euros (60 million euros by hypothesis) fixed in each authorization, to the guarantee provided by the state above this upper limit, we obtain a guarantee of total solvency for compensation of any victim on the ground or in the airspace of a space object operated under an SOA authorization.

This range is also consistent with the maximum amount of 60 million euros that, since 1980, the launch operator Arianespace must reimburse to France in the event that the latter pays compensation for damage caused by Ariane (or since October 2011 by Soyuz) launches from CSG, under the relevant 'Declaration' applying to the production or the exploitation phase of European launchers signed by the ESA Member States concerned.[54]

That being said, aside from defining a simple financial range, the finance act of 2008 discreetly introduced a special exception similar to the notion of 'gross negligence' by

---

53 United Nations Convention of 27 March 1972 on international liability for damage caused by space objects.
54 Nowadays, under Art. III-1-h of the Declaration by some European governments on the operational phase of Ariane, Vega, and Soyuz launchers at the Guiana Space Centre (CSG), adopted in Paris on 30 March 2007. Text ratified in France and published by Decree n° 2016-1778 of 19 December 2016; *JORF* (official gazette) n° 0296 of 21 December 2016.

stating that "this guarantee applies, except ... *serious failure to comply with the specifications of the authorization.*" This restriction and the potential resulting sanction considerably strengthened the operator's obligation to comply with the 'specifications' issued in the interests of safety of individuals and property under Article 5 of the SOA, in particular, those laid down by CNES upon each authorization in application of the technical specifications. Moreover, the *finance act* reaffirmed that the state is authorized to guarantee compensation of damage caused to third parties in the context of an authorized space operation conducted in France and also from another country in the EEA. This extension permits coverage of the activities of a French company conducting its space activities from another European state. This unilateral extension of the French guarantee to the benefit of activities carried out in the jurisdiction of other European states provides a benefit to the latter as *launching state*[55] by lightening their compensation burden in the case of damage caused to third parties. This decision to unilaterally provide a French State guarantee to the benefit of other European states is a direct result of the preparatory work conducted under the auspices of the Council of State between 2004 and 2006. This position is fully justified in the final report by this council,[56] following a comparative study of American and Australian law.[57] Unlike the latter legislations which cover, without limitation, damage caused by their nationals during authorized operations abroad, this body recommended not to extend the national guarantee to French nationals conducting operations abroad, at least, not outside the EEA. The main idea of this solution was to secure the activities of large European groups like EADS (today known as Airbus Defence and Space) and Alcatel (today known as Thales Alenia Space), and Eutelsat, having their main center of activities in France but whose activities could be shared between the various branches or technical sites of the group within the European Economic Area, for example, for satellite positioning or other critical maneuvers on satellites. It was also important to reassure France's European partners from the ESA and to convince the European Commission that the State guarantee planned for French space operators could not be interpreted as protectionism aiming to only promote activities conducted from national soil. This recommendation proved useful, as we saw above (§6.5.4.1), in obtaining validation of this planned public guarantee from the European Commission's Directorate-General for

---

55   For instance, a French operator can thus invoke the French State guarantee for damage caused by satellites launched or operated by itself under a foreign European jurisdiction, and liability regimes for damage to third parties (UN Convention 1972) or registration (UN Convention 1975).
56   *Cf.* §2.2.1.3.2 'conditions for granting the guarantee,' p. 95 and 97 of the CS Report 2006 mentioned above in §1.3. It should be noted that the Chairman of the working group, Jacques Blot, had consulted high-level representatives of the European Commission: J. Barrot, European Commissioner and Paul Wissenberg, Director of 'aerospace industry, safety, defence and equipment' (*cf.* p. 138 of the report).
57   Respectively the US Commercial Space Launch Act, Section 70113, (a) (1) and (e) (2) – Section 70104, (a) – Section70112, (a) (1) (B) and the Space Activities Bill (Australia) 1998, Part 4, Division 2, §69.

Competition with regard to provisions in European treaties governing state aid for companies.

6.5.5 Other Legislative Supplements Relating to the SOA: Amendment of the Insurance Code in 2011

By Ordinance-law of 15 July 2011,[58] a new chapter VI 'Civil Liability Insurance Relating to a Space Operation' was added to the legislative section of the Insurance Code to take into account the specificity of this insurance contract in relation to this 2008 space operations act, in particular, the recourse action by the State provided for in the latter act's Article 14.

6.6 DEVELOPMENT OF THE REGULATORY MECHANISM: IMPLEMENTING DECREES BETWEEN 2008 AND JUNE 2009

Development of the implementing decrees was also carried out in close consultation with the players concerned (CNES, operators, industry, insurers, etc.) under the leadership of the ministry of research in charge of space affairs and the departments of this ministry.

These consultations also allowed for useful discussions on the interpretation of the new law and preparation of a consensual doctrine on sensitive issues, including the notion of *independent operator*, the *succession of operators on orbit*, interrelationships between proper observance of technical regulations (RT) and application of the liability and State guarantee regime under the SOA, possible overlaps between launch procedures and systems in the RT and the *provisions of the regulations concerning CSG installations (REI)*[59] which apply to the launch campaign proper. These issues are developed in further detail below in the examination of the corresponding regimes.

---

58 Art. 8, Ordinance n° 2011-839 – *JORF* (official gazette) n° 0163 of 16 July 2011, p. 12290. Chapter VI (Art. L. 176-1 to L. 176-5) 'Civil liability insurance relating to a space operation' added to the legislative section, Book I: The contract, Title VII: Insurance contracts in the marine, air, aeronautical, river and lake sectors for goods transported by all means and for civil liability in space.
59 On the issue of potential overlaps or treatment discrepancies under RT, according to the type of the Space system, or as regard the REI-CSG's provisions or other applicable international standards, *see* the 'concordance table' in Annex IV.

6 THE DEVELOPMENT STAGES OF LEGISLATION ON SPACE OPERATIONS, FROM THE FIRST STUDIES IN 1999 TO ITS ENTRY INTO FORCE IN DECEMBER 2010

The framework for application of the regulations in the 2008 act is based on[60] three Council of State decrees[61]; in other words, decrees by the Prime Minister cosigned by the ministers concerned, following an opinion from the Council of State. These three decrees were issued on 9 June 2009, one of them on the authorization regime (no. 2009-643), a second one on CNES (no. 2009-644), and the third on Space-based data (no. 2009-640).

The three public main entities concerned by these decrees, the ministry in charge of space affairs, CNES and its President, and the SGDSN (French Secretariat-General for Defence and National Security), were also granted 'administrative authority' prerogatives that will allow them to sovereignly adopt general or individual regulatory decisions in the form of 'orders' in their respective areas of competence.

Moreover, the relevant ministers and governmental authorities retain all capacity to make decisions at an intermediate level in the form of a 'simple decree', without seeking the opinion of the Council of State, in application of the first decrees or, more generally, in the context of their general powers relating to matters which, under the constitution, do not require such consultation.[62]. This is the case of the simple decree of 19 July 2013 on monitoring the activity of primary operators of SBD (n° 2013-654 issued in application of implementing decree n° 640).

6.6.1 The Authorisation Decree of 2009 (D-A)

This decree is the main implementing text for this legislation on the authorization and monitoring of space operations. It enables the law to be implemented by providing clarifications that come under regulatory or administrative authority within the meaning of the French Constitution.[63]

This implementing decree firstly appointed the ministry in charge of space as the famous 'administrative authority' issuing, monitoring, and sanctioning the implementation of *authorizations* and *licenses*, in collaboration with CNES, its technical arm. According to the French Constitution, it is indeed by a decree taken by the French President, adopted in the Council of Ministers after opinion of the Council of State[64], that are defined the

---

60 For more details on the hierarchy of laws and the preparation of texts under French law, cf.*Guide de légistique* published since 2005 by the Secretary General of the Government and the Vice-President of the Council of State and available on the official Legifrance website: https://www.legifrance.gouv.fr/Droit-francais/Guide-de-legistique

61 These decrees can be identified by the following text in their preamble: 'The Council of State heard' or '*le Conseil d'Etat entendu.*'

62 Decree n° 2009-643 of 9 June 2009 on authorizations issued in application of the space operations act n° 2008-518 of 3 June 2008. *JORF* (official gazette) n° 0132 of 10 June 2009, p. 9406.

63 *Cf.* Arts. 34 and 37 of the Constitution of the French Republic, dated 4 October 1958; www.conseil-constitutionnel.fr

64 That is to say, a decision taken at government or executive level and not at legislative level.

ministers' organization allocation of competence and supervision over public bodies like CNES. As mentioned in Part 1[65] it is at the regulatory level that supervision of the space sector can be redistributed, if need be, upon each government's formation or reshuffling, at the level of the French President, in the form of a decree 'issued by the Council of Ministers' or in French 'décret pris en Conseil des Ministres.' However, paradoxically, as underlined in §1.1 above, the bylaws and missions of CNES, as a public state body (EPIC), were set out in 1961 at the level of the act and not by a decree.

Beyond these preliminary considerations on hierarchy of laws regarding FSOA and CNES, we may retain among the specifications introduced by this FSOA's decree the following items on the authorization process.

6.6.1.1 Administrative and Financial Authorization Criteria

This authorization decree specifies the conditions for issuing and monitoring the authorization, by distinguishing the **administrative part**, under the leadership of the minister in charge of space and concerning operator aptitude (moral, financial, and professional guarantees) and the **technical part** for which compliance monitoring was entrusted to CNES. It also specifies processing times according to authorization and license types (D-A. Art. 1-11).

6.6.1.2 The Concept of Technical Event

It introduced the notion of 'technical event' (D-A. Art. 7) namely: 'the implementation or knowledge by the operator of an event not provided for by the authorization or a technical incident affecting the conditions of the space operation as was authorized, subsequent to the issuing of the authorization.' Knowledge of any technical event obliges the operator to inform CNES promptly. This concept of technical event is of great legal importance in the authorization and monitoring process under the SOA. To some extent, it reverses the burden of proof after issuance of the authorization: it is the responsibility of the operator to indicate to the administrative authority, in all circumstances, during preparation of the operation until its total completion, that it remains within the framework set out by the authorization.

By analogy with the 'good faith' theory applicable to contracts under French law,[66] it could be considered that any failure in this respect by the operator could render it liable

---

65   *Cf.* above on Part. 1, §2.1.1.2 'Supervision on space policy and CNES... Evolution of the ministerial supervision on space policy and CNES from 1961 to 2018.'

66   'Good faith' can be defined as the belief or knowledge that a person has that they are in a lawful situation, and an awareness of carrying out actions without infringing on the rights of others. In its former Art. 1134, the Civil Code mentions the obligation of good faith only in the area of contract *enforcement* by providing in para. 3 that agreements lawfully entered into 'must be performed in good faith.' Building on case law, the new Art. 1104 of the Civil Code (post-2016 version, following the Order of 10 February 2016 on the reform of contract law, the general regime and proof of obligations) broadened the scope of action by pro-

for simple negligence, or even intentional fault. This is the approach that the finance act adopted under the SOA[67] seems to take, in the case of a serious breach or intentional fault, to deny the benefit of the financial guarantee granted to an authorized operator. Indeed, this act stipulates that the state guarantee "applies, except in the case of intentional fault or serious failure to comply with the specifications of the authorization." On its side, Article 15 of the *application decree* expressly provides for the possibility for the administrative authority to revoke an authorization or a license in the case (§1) of a *false declaration or false information*, (§3) in the case of failure to comply with the related specifications (in particular, technical specifications), and (§4) if conditions, in particular, technical conditions, to which it is subject are no longer met.

6.6.1.3 A New Procedure for Pre-Certification of Procedures and Systems

The 'authorisation decree' also introduced a *pre-authorisation procedure* (D-A Art. 11) allowing 'certification in stages' by CNES of compliance of new space systems with technical regulations, from the start of the design and development of these systems, provided that they are intended to be operated under SOA status. This possibility is open to any individual or legal entity concerned, laboratories, space agencies, manufacturers, or future operators. It is therefore not confined to operators, who are not always known or involved at this design stage. This procedure is *optional*, at the discretion of the development manager, but the certifications granted by CNES at each critical milestone will be validly *enforceable* in the technical field examined at the time of application for the authorization proper to put said systems into operation.

This procedure, which is not legally obligatory, is therefore strongly recommended as an opportunity for researchers, manufacturers, or future operators to avoid any bad surprises at the time of application for the final authorization with respect to noncompliance of the design, which could have been identified and corrected at lower cost and in less time earlier in the development phase. This procedure was notably used in the development of Ariane 6 by ESA and Airbus Safran Launchers,[68] or by the industry to develop new Earth-observation systems.

This is also an opportunity for the administrative authority and CNES to adapt or develop technical regulations or legislation to address issues related to innovative or

---

viding that 'contracts must be negotiated, entered into and performed in good faith. This is a *public policy* provision (*i.e.*, mandatory, without the possibility of exemption in the terms of the contract).'

67 Art. 119 of the Amending Finance Act n° 2008-1443 of 30 December 2008, that fixed, in accordance with the provisions of Arts. 16 and 17 of the SOA, the amount below which and above which, relating to space operations, the State is authorised to guarantee compensation for damage caused to third parties in the context of an authorised space operation....

68 'Airbus Safran Launchers' was renamed 'Ariane Group' in May 2017 and, in the context of the Ariane 6 program, became 'the design authority' for the launch system in its development phase; this authority had previously been exercised since 1973 (Ariane I to V) by CNES under a delegated authority from ESA.

breakthrough systems in the event that their promoters had opted for this prior certification procedure. These might include, currently, space launch systems and orbital systems that can be reused, refueled, repaired, or manned, *Space tugs* or suborbital flights, which are not dealt with by current legislation to the full extent of their technical or legal complexity.

6.6.1.4 Various Clarifications Brought on some FSOA's Items

The *authorisation decree* then refines some points of the law:
- The response time of the ministry to the applicant in the case of operations conducted from abroad or on their behalf (D-A. Article 12 supplementing the provisions of Article 4-4° of the SOA).
- The status of orbital operations (DA Article 13 supplementing the provisions of Articles 1.5°, 2.3°, and 20 of the SOA).
- The *in-orbit* transfer of control regime (DA Article 14 supplementing the provisions of Article 3 of the SOA).
- The conditions for revoking authorizations, including the case of a *false declaration or false information* that can be related with the occurrence of a *technical event* with reference to D-A Article 7 (D-A Article 15, supplementing the provisions of Article 9 of the SOA).
- The financial guarantees or insurance that may be taken out by the operator (D-A Articles 16 to 18, supplementing the provisions of Article 6 of the SOA): see details in §6.6.1.5 below.
- The process for inspecting the preparation and implementation of the authorized space operations, included the empowerment of commissioned and sworn officers (D-A Articles 19 to 23, supplementing Articles 7 to 11 of the SOA).

6.6.1.5 Adjustments to the Obligation for the Operator to Take Out a Financial Guarantee or Insurance under Article 6 of the SOA

The decree specifies the *nature of the financial guarantees* to be provided for under FSOA's Article 6. These *financial guarantees*: shall be furnished by means of a written commitment from a credit institution or an insurance company, a joint and several *guarantee* (in French a '*caution*'), a *first-demand guarantee* or *liquid assets* (in French '*actifs liquidables*').The operator shall send the minister responsible for space (the administrative authority) a document furnishing proof of the financial guarantees before the commencement of the space operation. In addition, with the purpose of limiting the cost of insurance throughout the duration of routine orbital control operations, Article 18 of the decree provides for the possibility of a special exemption from insurance or guarantees for *station-keeping satellites in geostationary orbit*. Insurance, therefore, only continues to be required for changes in orbital position, in particular end-of-life maneuvers. In Article 17, the decree also provided for the possibility of an insurance exemption of limited duration in the event of it being impossible to take out insurance because of *poor market status of the insurance market*.

6.6.1.6 Determination of the Date of Entry into Force of the Act

Finally, in its Article 24, this implementing decree determined the date of entry into force of the SOA by subjecting it to the publication of the order enacting the *technical regulations* (cf. §6.6.4.2 below) and, at the latest, eighteen months after its own publication so that the discussions undertaken with the operators and manufacturers regarding these regulations would not stall the effective implementation of the law.

6.6.2 The CNES' Decree of 2009 (CNES-D)

This decree no. 644 of 9 June 2009 supplements CNES decree no. 84-510 of 28 June 1984 as amended which organized its supervision and governance (cf. §2.1).

It added a title III on the *Space Objects Register* (relating to the provisions of Art. 12 of the SOA) and a title IV that details the *powers of its President at the Guiana Space Centre*.[69] Finally, it added a title V including a single article (D-CNES Art. 14-17) on the powers delegated to the President of CNES by law (SOA Arts. 8 and 21) more broadly for *emergency measures* required for the safety of individuals and property and the protection of public health and the environment, to authorize him to delegate his signature by means of an order. These emergency measures apply to all space operations in the SOA jurisdiction and not only to activities conducted at CSG.

6.6.2.1 Powers of the President of CNES at CSG

These powers of the President of CNES at the Guiana Space Centre (hereinafter CSG) concern:
- on the one hand, his special policing authority in respect of the *safeguarding mission* (D-CNES Art. 14-8 to 14-10);
- on the other hand, a mission of *coordination of safety measures*, under the authority of the Prefect of French Guiana (D-CNES Art. 14-11 to 14-14).

The terms according to which the President can delegate his authority for these two missions are also specified (D-CNES Art. 14-15 and 14-16).

The *safeguarding mission* and related policing and regulatory powers *of the President of CNES* at CSG mainly concern measures for monitoring activities at the base relating to

---

[69] *Cf.* D-CNES Art. 14-7 to 14-16 in application of Art. 21 of the SOA supplementing the missions of CNES in its constitutive act, in Art. L. 331-6 of the Research Code.

the design, preparation, production, storage, and transport of space objects and their constitutive parts, as well as testing and operations conducted within or from the Guiana Space Centre. In this respect, the President adopts, in a form of *administrative order*, measures on the establishment, safety, and protection of installations and serious decisions on the suspension or banning of activities, or even neutralization of launchers (destruction in flight). The decree also provides for the possibility of delegation of powers by the President. In practice, such delegation is granted in its entirety to the Director of CSG, except on the signature of the *Operating Regulations for Installations* (the REI-CSG developed hereunder in 6.6.4.1).

Safety coordination powers at CSG (D-CNES chapter II) are essential, in addition to the obligations binding the various private companies,[70] in relation to themselves and their employees, concerning their civil and criminal liability as 'company director' 'chief of the site' (or '*chef d'établissement*') or under other *public order legislation* in force such as: work or occupational safety (or '*sécurité du travail*'), legislation on classified installations for the protection of the environment (or '*Installation Classées pour la protection de l'environnement*', ICPE), legislation applicable to 'operators of vital importance' (or '*Opérateurs d'Importance Vitale*', OIV) and other legislation regarding national security, etc.

The President of CNES' coordination measures therefore cover this companies' so-called 'overflow' risks with regard to overall capacity limits at the base in terms of installations, networks, and other mutual resources within the entire perimeter of the base. Indeed, a company can generate 'overflow risks' (or '*risques débordants*') by its activities even while observing safety or environmental rules that apply intrinsically, if such an activity, carried out in addition to that of other companies without consultation or coordination, is likely to undermine mutual capacity, affecting base safety, for example, by preventing proper functioning of information technology systems or electricity production, or by giving rise to insufficient availability of fire prevention measures or mutual medical emergency services.

Another example is that such coordination can take place between *development activities*, such as building launch pads, under the responsibility of ESA,[71] dangerous *industrial manufacturing* or integration activities for solid propellant boosters by the companies Regulus or Europropulsion,[72] and the proper functioning of sensitive operations relating

---

70 Currently, the best known companies being Arianespace, Airbus Safran Launchers (renamed ArianeGroup in 2017), ELV or AVIO, Regulus, Europropulsion, Air Liquide, technical assistance companies, etc.
71 Work for which project ownership is generally delegated by ESA to the Ground Systems Sub-Directorate of the CNES Launcher Directorate.
72 Regulus is a joint subsidiary of Avio (Italy) and Safran (France). It operates the French Guiana propellant production facility (UPG) and currently produces loaded segments S2 and S3 for the solid propellant stages of Ariane 5 and the loaded P80 for the VEGA launcher.
    Europropulsion, a joint subsidiary of Safran (France) and Avio (Italy), is also a French-Italian company governed by French law that operates the Booster Integration Building (BIP), for the integration of the solid propellant stages of Ariane 5 and is in charge of integration of the P80 engine into VEGA and integration of the engine for these stages.

to actual *launch campaigns* between Ariane, Soyuz, or Vega launchers. It was therefore necessary to formalize the *primacy of the President of CNES' coordination role at this base*, which comes above safety issues in his list. The coordination mission formalized by the SOA thus substitutes the empirical role, recognized within the CISG and UEBS[73] in the mid-2000s, which made CNES the 'leader of all the establishments at the base.' This power, now recognized by the law as being held by the President of CNES, is formally exercised under the authority of the Prefect. Indeed, the latter primarily represents the State in his authority concerning safety and security in Guiana[74] and can on his own impose sensitive arbitrations, as a last resort, between various industrial and business activities, including those of CNES, outside special policing mission of the latter mentioned above, as manager of the base and of certain industrial installations, such as for example the payload or satellite preparation complexes (EPCU, etc.).

This decree also highlights[75] the notion of 'technical event' for activities conducted at CSG. Therein, this concept is drafted as follows (D-CNES, Art. 14-7 para. 2):

> The President of CNES shall be promptly informed by all persons referred to in the previous paragraph (*i.e., all persons located at or conducting operations at CSG*) of any event, incident or accident, relating to his missions under Article L. 331-6 of the above-mentioned Code (*these powers at CSG*). He shall keep the State representative in the department (the Prefect) informed.

These technical events are processed by means of a well-established procedure at CSG since the beginning of its operations, called 'safeguard submission procedure.' This procedure is detailed below in §6.6.4.1 in the Operating Regulations for Installations at Guiana Space Centre (cf. REI-CSG Art. 26 *et seq.*).

To conclude on the subject of the powers of the President of CNES or his representative at CSG, it should be noted that these must be respected not only directly by the Space Operator (the only entity referred to by the SOA) but also by all individuals or legal entities,

---

73 The CISG (Guiana Space Industry Community) is a joint consultative body of the industrial and operational establishments present at CSG. It brings together CSG's main decision makers: CNES, Arianespace, Airbus Safran Launchers, Air Liquide Spatial Guyane, Regulus, Europropulsion, Safran, and ESA (as an observer member).
The UEBS (Union of Space Base Employers) brings together members of the CISG and the 37 subcontractors with employer responsibilities at CSG. Its aim is to harmonize social policy and coordinate the employment and training of staff at CSG.
74 Decree n° 89-314 of 16 May 1989 as amended on the coordination of safety procedures for space launch operations in French Guiana. Art. 1: "The Prefect of Guiana, as a Government Delegate, is responsible for ensuring the **external security** of the installations and resources located in the department of French Guiana **involved in Guiana Space Centre activities, in particular, launch operations**. In this respect, his competence extends to coordinating civil defence and military measures."
75 Like the authorisation decree (D-A. Art. 7) mentioned above in §6.6.1.

public or private, and all operators of installations working within the CSG enclosure solely by virtue of the fact that they are located within the geographical perimeter of the Guiana Space Centre (D-CNES, Art. 14-7 paragraph 1).

It should be noted that the entire SOA mechanism applicable to CSG (SOA Art 21, Decree CNES Title IV, REI below) refers to a well-defined territorial enclosure, on the basis of *Ratione loci,* whereas the other provisions of the SOA refer either to space operations (*Ratione materiae*) or the operator (*Ratione personae*). It should be emphasized here that one of the main aims of the SOA was to define the legal framework of CNES' missions and those of its President at CSG, since the status and functioning of the center were not explicitly recognized by any specific national law or regulation[76] before 2008, except in the 1960s for needs relating to its installation.[77] Consequently, the authority for safeguarding and the coordination mission of the President of CNES at this launch base were through SOA provided for under specific internal legislation, with all related prerogatives in terms of policing regulations and sanctions, while complying with existing contractual and partnership frameworks, both at the intergovernmental level of ESA[78] (CSG agreements with France and Launchers declarations on production or exploitation phases) and with private players at the base in CISG and UEBS. Nevertheless, overall responsibility for *operational management and functioning of the launch range complex*[79] remains strongly attached to the contractual and partnership framework cited above and was not mentioned

---

76 The few references to CSG in regulations prior to the SOA come from indirect sources such as the Decree of 16 May 1989 mentioned above on the coordination of safety procedures for space launch operations in French Guiana. This text only mentions CSG activities incidentally, without specifying their dependence on CNES or its President, or referring to the internal safety regime at this base.

77 Decree 65-388 of 21 May 1965 on the *declaration of public utility and the urgent need* for CNES to carry out certain site work. *JORF* (Official gazette) 25 May 1965, p. 4267; this decree provides that the plots to be used as the implantation site of the future satellite launch base (as defined in a map attached to the decree), may be purchased amicably or by way of expropriation. Assignment deed between the State (Ministry of the Economy and Finance) and CNES for buildings in the private State domain located in the territories of the municipalities of Cayenne, Kourou, Macouria, and Sinnamary dated 20 October 1971. Private agreement filed in the archives of the Prefecture of Cayenne, recorded on 2 December 1971, and published in the Cayenne mortgage registry on 2 December 1971, filing 60/816 vol. 372 n° 64.

78 In particular, the abovementioned agreements between the French government and the European Space Agency relating to CSG since 1975, the successive Declarations since 1980 between European States on the production or operational phases of Ariane, Vega, and Soyuz launchers (see §1.2.2.3, §1.2.3).

79 Operational responsibility which, when compared for instance to the domestic organization of a civil airport, corresponds to that assigned to the *Aéroports de Paris* (ADP) group in France (at Roissy-CdG and Orly), which provides overall management of the airport, facilities, networks, services, logistical coordination between various airlines, maintenance, supplies, catering, and businesses. On the other hand, and still in comparison to the air sector, the sovereign powers conferred by FSOA to the President of CNES in relation to safeguarding within the CSG perimeter are closer to those of the DGAC (Directorate-General for Civil Aviation). In France, this Directorate guarantees the safety and security of air transport, in particular, its Directorate of Air Navigation Services (DSNA), which controls air traffic, notably, takeoffs, and landings at airports.

as such in this CNES' decree which only affects the *sovereign missions* of the President of CNES and his representatives.

In view of the difficulty of separating these responsibilities from each other in the optimal operation of this base, France, ESA, and the manufacturing community are always committed to promoting coherence between various applicable legal instruments by organizing ongoing consultations between themselves. As already pointed out, this spirit of cooperation was notably obvious during consultations initiated by the Minister in charge of Space to define the application of the SOA at CSG.

6.6.2.2 Emergency Measures

This decree provides for the possibility of the President of CNES delegating, by way of an order, his signature to carry out his functions under Article 8 of the SOA[80] in the event of danger due to an uncontrolled situation, or one that is uncontrollable by the operator. These special powers in the case of an emergency are separate from the safeguarding prerogatives at CSG referred to by this Article 21 in the first paragraph. In concrete terms, this means that, in the case of an emergency, the President of CNES may, under his responsibility, delegate to the competent Director, his capacity to give instructions and impose all measures he deems necessary upon operators or, as the case may be, their suppliers, in the interests of the safety of individuals and property and the protection of public health and the environment. In this case, it is a *delegation of signature* and not a *delegation of power*, as was granted to the Director of CSG (CR L.331-6), and the President remains responsible for the actions committed by his delegated representative in relation to third parties or the administrative authority.

This delegation is notably granted to directors of launchers, directors of the Toulouse Space Centre (CST) and the Guiana Space Centre as *heads of centers* with monitoring and tracking facilities under their authority. This delegation can be activated in the case of uncontrolled reentry of a space vehicle, or in the case of sensitive satellite maneuvers following a failed launch or end-of-life maneuvers. It is important, for the person exercising it, to verify that the decisions it makes do fall within the prerogatives of the President of CNES, with regard to the delegation of power that the latter disposes of himself from the administrative authority, and to ensure that operators are consulted for any critical decisions concerning their space vehicles, except in the case of immediate danger as specified in the last paragraph of Article 8 of the SOA.

---

80 Powers that themselves are delegated to him by the administrative authority (Minister in charge of space affairs) pursuant to Art. 21 of the SOA in its second amendment of the constitutive act of CNES, codified in the Research Code (addition of a new Art. L. 331-7).

6.6.2.3 Maintenance of the Space Objects Register by CNES: CNES Decree and the August 2011 Registration Order

The other component of the CNES decree was to set out this body's prerogatives for maintaining the national register of space objects. This decree specified procedures for the transmission, recording, modification, and publication by CNES to the Minister of Foreign Affairs of information concerning objects to be registered by France under the United Nations Convention of 14 January 1975 on the registration of space objects launched into outer space (SOA, Art. 12).

It stipulated that an order to be issued by the minister in charge of space (D-CNES, Art. 14-1) would set out the information required to identify a space object. This order was issued two years later, on 12 August 2011 (hereinafter A-I).[81] The requirements for this national register went beyond those of the international register resulting from the abovementioned United Nations Convention. The additional requirements introduced by this national system include:

- a deadline requiring the operator to forward its information to CNES at the latest 60 days following the launch (D-A. Art 14-2);
- additional technical and legal information to be provided concerning the space object and its history,[82] namely the name of its manufacturer (A-I. Art. 1-3°), the history of its ownership, and any real or personal security interests in the latter (A-I. Art. 1-4°), its control mode in outer space (A-I. Art. 1-7°), and any anomalies encountered during its orbit insertion or during its functioning as a space vehicle (A-I. Art. 1-8°).

It should be underlined that declarations relating to the national registration procedure for these space objects or objects in orbit play an essential role in facilitating the monitoring of operations and in determining legal liability (see §7.1.2.1.). They also allow connections to be made with the application of other related legislation and authorization regimes of the French state concerning the same space systems and their uses such as licenses on frequencies and on information services and networks, defense and security concerns, etc. (see §7.5).

Finally, to conclude this paragraph on the 'CNES decree' (n° 2009-644), it should be noted that this text did not provide details of any of the main competences of this body in the authorization and monitoring process for space operations or in the development of technical regulations (cf. Art. 28 of the SOA) since these CNES prerogatives were included

---

81 Order of 12 August 2011 (A-I.) setting out the list of information required to identify a space object in application of title III of Decree n° 84-510 of 28 June 1984 on CNES. *JORF* (official gazette) n° 0208 of 8 September 2011, p. 15127.
82 Cf. Art. 1 of the 'registration' order (A-I.) above compared to Art. IV of the United Nations Convention of 14 January 1975 referred to above.

6   THE DEVELOPMENT STAGES OF LEGISLATION ON SPACE OPERATIONS, FROM THE FIRST
    STUDIES IN 1999 TO ITS ENTRY INTO FORCE IN DECEMBER 2010

in the 'implementing decree' (D-A. 2009-643) above. This legislative choice aimed to make the latter text the main autonomous implementing decree for the act.

6.6.3   *The Space-Based Data Decree of 2009[83] (SBD-D) and Following Texts*

Adoption of the SOA was an opportunity to establish a new specific legal framework, in parallel, to govern control of access to and dissemination of certain 'primary space-based data'. This regime, defined in title VII of the SOA, concerns, in substance, certain civil data for Earth observation collected by satellites orbiting the Earth to be disseminated or sold to users on the ground[84] if their resolution and clarity characteristics mean they are sensitive in terms of defense and security for France, in particular, in the context of its international commitments.

This regime is separable, in its content, from the other provisions of the SOA proper. It was not subject to any particular debate or amendments during its examination by Parliament and its enforcement regime was discussed in a restricted interministerial context under the auspices of the General Secretariat for Defence and National Security. In view of the unique nature of this regime, all of its implementing regulations, simple decrees and orders, are presented in a consolidated manner in §7.4.

6.6.4   *Development of Technical Regulations for Systems and Procedures (RT) and Operating Regulations for Installations at CSG (REI) – between 2008 and 2011*

This preparation of regulations continued in line with the consultations undertaken with industry professionals and operators for the act and implementing decrees. It was enriched by the lessons learnt by a delegation of CNES experts in Washington D.C. in the United States organized by NASA[85] from 2 to 6 March 2009. This mission was an opportunity to meet the entities in charge of studying or proposing the various components of space regulations in this country, namely the FAA, FCC, NOAA, DoS, and NASA.[86] These experts

---

83 Decree n° 2009-640 of 9 June 2009 implementing the provisions of title VII of law n° 2008-518 of 3 June 2008 on space operations, amended by Decree n° 2013-653 of 19 July 2013.
84 This activity is also known as *remote sensing* or *space-based imaging*.
85 Thanks to the good offices of Michael Wholley, NASA's General Counsel, and his deputy Jay Steptoe.
86 The Federal Aviation Administration (FAA) is in charge of launch licences and permits for suborbital flights. The Federal Communications Commission (FCC) is in charge of licenses for telecommunications or broadcasting systems (spatial or otherwise) as regards frequencies, installations, and content. The National Oceanic and Atmospheric Administration (NOAA) is the research and operational agency in charge of meteorology and monitoring the environment, the atmosphere, and the ocean. It operates its own satellites and is the authority in charge of granting licences to the private sector in this area. Its French closer correspondents are: Météo-France (France's national meteorological service), a part of the IGN (French National

shared their extensive experience of putting in place new space legislation with their French counterparts, in particular, for the transitional phase concerning systems that are already operational in competition with new systems designed and developed by the private sector.

6.6.4.1 The Order of 9 December 2010 Regulating the Operation of Installations at the Guiana Space Centre (REI-CSG)

It should be recalled here that the initial and primary objective of FSOA was to give greater legal security to the *safeguarding* (*or safety or sauvegarde*) mission of CNES at CSG in view of opening up the latter to launchers other than Ariane, namely launchers like Soyuz and Vega, which were not or would no longer be developed under the 'design authority' of CNES.

More generally, the *safeguarding role of CNES* aims to ensure proper control of the technical hazards arising from all its hazardous activities conducted on or from its sites or by its representatives. It thus covers *safeguarding on the ground* (risks in the field in close proximity to the launch or mission site) and safeguarding *in flight* (risks in orbit and falling parts) for all operations with space vehicles, such as prevention of space debris, use of nuclear energy sources by space systems, planetary protection (to avoid contamination of the moon and other celestial bodies), but also balloon flights (stratospheric balloons) or mini-rockets operations for educational purposes.

Concerning the texts sources, this mission came under the 'CNES Safeguarding Doctrine,' a single document that describes, in exhaustive detail, the policy and strategy of this public body under key international treaties adopted by France (UN, ESA, ICAO, sea convention, etc.) down to practices in force relating to its know-how and its own experience, including all regulations applicable in France like the rules of the air, regulations on Installations Classified for Environmental Protection (ICPE), those on toxic substances, hazardous materials and pyrotechnics, the Labour Code, the Public Health Code, the Civil Aviation Code, etc. This doctrine is set out in detail for each activity in 'safeguarding regulations' issued and applied by the *facility managers* or the *directors responsible*. These regulations resemble *manuals* or *operating instructions* intended for *experienced industry professionals*. Despite their name, from a legal perspective, these instructions had no 'regulatory value' within the meaning of Art. 37 of the French Republic Constitution of

---

Geographic Institute) and IFREMER (French Research Institute for Exploitation of the Sea), operational departments of the Ministry of the Environment and CNES for certain scientific programs concerning oceanography (Jason, Argos, etc.). The Department of State (DoS) is in charge of international relations, the equivalent of the French *ministère des affaires étrangères* (Ministry of Foreign Affairs). DoS is the correspondent of CNES for national satellite's registrations. The National Aeronautics and Space Administration (NASA) is the United States' civilian governmental space agency. Its French counterpart, in this respect, is CNES as Space agency, given however that NASA is not involved in the national licensing process for Space systems operations, contrary to the CNES. NASA also has competence for aeronautic research and, in this respect, its French equivalent is ONERA (French Aerospace Lab.).

6 THE DEVELOPMENT STAGES OF LEGISLATION ON SPACE OPERATIONS, FROM THE FIRST STUDIES IN 1999 TO ITS ENTRY INTO FORCE IN DECEMBER 2010

4 October 1958. Aside from the specific case of CNES employees where a 'subordinate relationship' to the employer applies, the enforceability of these safeguarding regulations as such, and the resulting authority of CNES, are only based on the *tacit or express agreement (contract)* of the parties concerned, under the auspices of UEBS, CISG, and the high-level agreements between ESA and the French government.[87]

The safeguarding role that interests us here is the one that concerns all the activities conducted at the CSG base, considered as a single establishment under the authority of CNES, without prejudice to the legal and contractual obligations that may also apply to other companies (to their directors) permanently established on this site.[88] Prior to the SOA, this authority was only legally recognized at the level of intergovernmental agreements on CSG between ESA and the French government, with no accompanying measures to implement them in national legislation or regulations. The challenge was to transpose this operational document, based on professional practices, which was put in place by CNES along with industry players and Arianespace under the Ariane program to manage risks, to the new SOA architecture and to the new *administrative and policing authority of CNES*.

It was thus necessary to produce a regulatory document based on clear *generic objectives* and not resources or means, know-how or methods. In other words, the text would have to be as neutral as possible in terms of the choice of technical and managerial solutions for the attention of new entrants or systems (Soyuz, Vega, and future systems), independent of CNES. This redrafting once again took place in close collaboration with the main players concerned, namely Arianespace and EADS Space Transportation, replaced today by ArianeGroup.

The finalized text was signed on 9 December 2010, the day before entry into force of the SOA, under the number 2010-1 and the title 'Operating Regulations for Installations at Guiana Space Centre' (REI-CSG) by Yannick d'Escatha, President of CNES, holder of regulatory authority at CSG.[89] This signature is, in fact, the only prerogative that the President of CNES retains as such; the latter grants delegation of the rest of his powers, on a permanent basis, to the Director of CSG to implement these regulations and issue enforcement measures.

It should be noted that it was not considered appropriate from a media perspective to use the term 'police' in the title of the REI, a term that is not legally necessary, to avoid perturbing the spirit of responsibility and cooperation that existed between all players at this base. This text was published in the *register of administrative acts of the Prefecture of*

---

87 *See above*: §5.2-§6.6.2.
88 Namely, Arianespace as the launch operator, Airbus Group and Avio as project managers for the manufacture and final assembly of Ariane and Vega launchers, Regulus and Europulsion as manufacturer of the Ariane 5 Boosters, Air Liquide for the propellants and all the technical assistance companies, all of them linked by a site agreement under the UEBS and the CISG.
89 *Cf.* the last lines of Art. L331-6 of the Research Code created by Art. 21 of the SOA: "[...] For this purpose, it adopts the special regulations applicable within the perimeter mentioned above."

French Guiana. The CNES has since set up its own register of administrative acts, which should be accessible on its website.

The REI was accompanied by implementing measures known as 'Regulatory Instructions' (IR, for *'Instructions Réglementaires'*)[90] issued by the Director of CSG under his permanent delegated powers mentioned above, in respect of the safeguarding mission and related administrative sanctions.[91] These instructions are called 'Coordination Instructions' (IC, for *'Instructions de Coordination'*) when they come under the mission to coordinate safety measures carried out under the delegated authority of the Prefect of French Guiana.[92] These instructions may deal, in detail, with practical issues as varied as issuing access passes, traffic and parking of vehicles at the base, in particular, bicycles, evacuation of tourists and the residents of the Salvation Islands (in French *Iles du Salut*), recruitment and supervision of trainees, etc. These instructions (IR or IC) are published or notified to their addressees by CSG. Depending on the subject, some of them may be for restricted, confidential, or individual distribution.

6.6.4.2 The Order on Technical Regulations of 31 March 2011 (TR or RT)

The authorization and monitoring regime for space operations laid down by the SOA is based on *stringent technical criteria* set out in technical regulations (Arts. 4 and 28 of the SOA). It should be noted that such stringency is not systematic in national space legislation. Other legislations in force in Europe, like that of the United Kingdom from 1986 (18 July) or more recently the Luxembourg law of 20 July 2017 on the exploration and use of space resources, are not accompanied by any technical regulations and puts more emphasis on administrative, legal, contractual, and even financial requirements in terms of insurance or financial guarantees to the benefit of the government to cover the latter's potential liability as *launch State* on an international level.[93] The option chosen by the SOA to implement the French government's duty of 'authorization and ongoing surveillance' under Article VI of the Outer Space Treaty of 1967 was to maintain stringent safety requirements for all systems and procedures operated in its jurisdiction, or under its flag or its *liability*, for damage to third parties.

This issue was the subject of debate because strict technical standards and stringent requirements can also discourage innovation or contribute to making French space systems more expensive and ultimately affect their competitiveness in the market compared to others who are less constrained by their legislation. In fact, beyond France's international

---

90 Research Code L. 336-2 I, D-CNES Art. 14-8 to 14-10, REI: definitions.
91 Decree 2009-644 CNES, Art. 14.9: fifth class fine, *i.e.*, currently €1,500, or €3,000 maximum in the case of a repeat offence, without prejudice to criminal sanctions provided for by other regulations.
92 Research Code L. 336-2 II, D-CNES Art. 14-11 to 14-14, REI: definitions.
93 Within the meaning of Art. VII of the 1967 Treaty and the United Nations Convention of 1972 mentioned above.

commitments concerning legal liability and moral responsibility, it was found that the competitiveness of such space systems that are complex, costly and uncertain in their functioning, remains inseparable from their reliability and their technical performance and, consequently, from the safety and quality assurance rules applied to them from the fore *design stage*. These technical regulations, therefore, apply to the design, preparation, and production of all space operations conducted from France, or by French operators or in French jurisdiction (Arts. 2 and 3 of the SOA).

The only exemption possible, provided for by Article 4-4° of the act,[94] concerns operations conducted in a foreign jurisdiction,[95] provided that, in the eyes of the administrative authority, sufficient guarantees have been given from the State concerned (legislation, specific commitments, prevailing practices, etc.). The act provides (Art. 28 f) that these technical regulations are developed by CNES but adopted by the administrative authority. By this same Article (in its 'g'), the CNES is also vested with delegated authority to inspect compliance with these technical regulations during processing of authorization requests and for the monitoring of the preparation and implementation of the space operation.

Development of the RT was also discussed in close consultation with industry professionals and operators in the field of launch systems and orbital systems (notably satellites).

In the first part, these regulations include provisions that are common to these two systems, namely the various definitions necessary including the scope of this text (RT Art. 2). Then there is a subdivision between each operational phase, the *launch* on the one hand and the *control* and *return* to Earth of a space object on the other, which broadly corresponds to the current division of competence within CNES between the experts of the DLA (Directorate of Launch Vehicles) and CST (orbital systems) and the divisions existing in the industry that manufactures or operates these systems. Here again, the text was broadly inspired by *safeguarding doctrine and regulations* and *quality assurance rules* applicable to the development and implementation of these systems.[96] As a precaution and for pedagogic purposes toward FSOA authorization applicants, these regulations were drafted in a 'free-standing' manner to be as exhaustive as possible in each of its component sections, with the risk of repetitions and reproducing articles from a higher level verbatim, and sometimes at the risk of causing difficulties in interpretation, if the latter are themselves amended at a later date.[97]

The launcher section was developed from the safeguarding doctrine and regulations at CSG, by extracting provisions relating to the *design* and *on-board* sections, some of

---

94 Supplemented by Art. 12 of authorisation decree n° 2009-643.
95 *E.g.*, the launching of a French satellite from a launcher abroad.
96 *See* Annex IV for comparison between these TR provisions and the ones of international instruments on the same area as to Space debris mitigation measures (UN COPUOS Guidelines, IADS Guidelines, ISO Requirements, European Code of Conduct principles, etc.).
97 On this issue of potential duplications, discrepancies, or gaps, *see* the working document appended in Annex IV herein.

which were reproduced nevertheless in REI-CSG, which was based on the same source. To avoid confusion over who is responsible with regard to CNES inspections toward the operator, its suppliers or other CSG establishments, a single point of contact, the 'RAC,'[98] was set up at CSG level with the appointment of a sole Technical Compliance Manager at a given moment in time, who passes the reins between the DLA and CSG in the final phase of the campaign. A joint formal confirmation of technical compliance is issued in the name of CNES before each flight at CSG. Aside from setting out result specifications in a determined manner, these regulations have the peculiarity, *in legal or even ethics or moral terms*, of being able to set *quantitative and statistical objectives for the safety of individuals according to operation type*.[99] In fact, these quantitative and statistical objectives correspond to international standards for space activity (see this Annex IV), in particular, those set originally since the 1960s by NASA for its own missions.

These thresholds are, of course, without prejudice, where applicable, to the full and total liability of the operator in relation to the victim, in the case of an accident, and to application of the State guarantee (SOA Art. 13 et seq., RT Art. 1). Other innovative, even pioneering, provisions of these regulations include the integration of international measures which, until then, fell under best practice and best efforts within civilian governmental agencies, into a legally binding text for private players. In particular, the prevention measures concerning debris set out in Articles 21, 24, and 39 to 41 of the RT which transposes recommendations from the IADC in particular,[100] a space agency forum with the mission of reducing production of space debris, on a voluntary basis, or limiting its effects. Rules were thus re-transcribed on the protection of certain useful and potentially crowded

---

98   RAC for '*Responsable d'Avis de Conformité*' or Responsible for the Conformity Notice.
99   For example, RT Art. 20 on launches specifies permissible thresholds, with the maximum probability of at least one victim, for a risk of catastrophic damage, which varies for launch risks, from 2×10^{-5} (2/100,000) for the whole phase or 10^{-7} (1/10,000,000) per fall back of non-orbited parts (boosters), or for re-entry risks, from 10^{-7} (1/10,000,000) in nominal that could be reduced to 10^{-4} (1/10,000) on a 'best efforts' basis, in the event of 'proven impossibility'. Article 44 on the return of space objects sets this threshold at 2×10^{-5} (2/100,000) for a controlled return of this integrated or destroyed object and at 10^{-4} (1/10,000) on a 'best efforts' basis, in the case of 'proven impossibility'.
100 The Inter-Agency Space Debris Coordination Committee (IADC) is an international forum of governmental bodies, namely of space agencies, for the coordination of activities related to the issues of man-made and natural debris in space. The primary purpose of the IADC is to exchange information on space debris research activities between member space agencies, to facilitate opportunities for cooperation in space debris research, to review the progress of ongoing cooperative activities, and to identify debris mitigation options. One of its achievements is to recommend debris mitigation guidelines that can be considered during planning and design of spacecraft and launch vehicles in order to minimize or eliminate generation of debris during operations.
     Members of the IADC are the Italian Space Agency (ASI), British National Space Centre (BNSC), Centre National d'Etudes Spatiales (CNES), China National Space Administration (CNSA), Deutsches Zentrum fuer Luft-und Raumfahrt e.V. (DLR), European Space Agency (ESA), Indian Space Research Organisation (ISRO), Japan Aerospace Exploration Agency (JAXA), National Aeronautics and Space Administration (NASA), the National Space Agency of Ukraine (NSAU), and Russian Space Agency (Roskosmos).

orbits (region A in low orbit less than or equal to 2000 km and region B for geostationary orbits at an altitude of 35786 km + or -200 km) recommending *controlled atmospheric reentries*, or *de-orbiting* of the space objects concerned to *graveyard orbits*, at the *end of the mission* or within 25 years after the launch, depending on the case.

The RT (Arts. 26 and 43, in particular) also introduced *planetary protection measures*, namely, non-contamination of the moon and other celestial bodies by space objects or their component parts, in accordance with the non-legally binding recommendations of COSPAR (Committee on Space Research). This provision may be applicable to the project of *exploitation of space resources (space mining)*. To avoid affecting systems already in orbit or in the design phase, Article 55 of the RT provided for *deferred implementation measures* in its provisions.

This RT was firstly submitted for publication and notice to the European Commission[101] in accordance with the provisions of the notification procedure of Directive 98/34/EC of 22 June 1998 in the field of technical standards and regulations and rules relating to information society services.

6.6.4.3 Best Practice Guide (GBP)

The need for a best practice guide to accompany the technical regulations arose from consultations with industry professionals during development of the latter text. It results from RT Art. 54. The principle was for the existing players, well-versed in proven safety practices and systems in relation to CNES, when they did not originate from the latter itself (!), not to be obliged, once again, to prove compliance with the new regulations being developed.

This approach was strengthened by the CNES 'benchmarking' mission in the United States in March 2009.[102] The authorities of this country also opted to maintain certain proven practices, known as 'grandfather practices,'[103] which correspond to 'acquired rights' (in French '*droits acquis*'), during development of their initial legislation on launches (CSLA). Then, the GBP was based on practices validated through experience acquired in the development, operation, and monitoring of space systems. It refers, in particular, to standards and normative technical specifications, as well as standards recognized by the profession on the safety of property, individuals, public health, and the environment, in the context of conducting space operations. Proper observation, therefore, of the practices, methods, and resources referenced in this guide, on the part of the latter, shows compliance with the RT, in particular, in terms of meeting its statistical goals.

---

101 Notice n° 2010/0687/F.
102 Mentioned below in the introduction to this §6.6.4.
103 A 'grandfather clause' is an exception that allows an old rule to continue to apply to some existing situations when a new rule will apply to all future situations.

This is an *optional measure*. It cannot be imposed on the operator, who remains free to demonstrate this by any other means. This guide is however *binding on CNES* and the administrative authority, if it is duly complied with by the operator.

In terms of content, this guide was mainly inspired, with regard to launches, by the *Ariane management specifications (SMA, Spécifications de Management Ariane)*,[104] for which CNES is the 'custodian' under the authority of ESA. These specifications were developed since the beginning of the 1970s in consultation with all industry players. The best practice guide also has the vocation of recognizing certain *software tools* designed by CNES and granted free of charge to the operators concerned to assist them in their authorization application. These software tools can concern, for example, calculation methods for fragmentation of space objects or debris generation in the case of a collision or explosion, and their impact on the ground or in space according to their trajectory and their composition and external factors, with regard to the restrictive and preventive requirements set out in the RT. Limitations of usage or dissemination of the *best practice guide* may be set up by CNES in order to protect technologies in the broad sense, *i.e.*, *defense secrets, export control* rules on sensitive products and technologies, *protection of national scientific and technical property, trade secret, industrial and business confidentiality,intellectual property rights* relating to software, and *know-how* relating to systems and processes used. According to the provisions of Article 54 of the RT, the best practice guide is prepared by CNES in consultation with industry professionals in the context of a working group representative of the operators and manufacturers concerned

6.6.4.4 Common Features Between RT and REI-CSG

Among the legal specificities common to such regulatory orders of a technical nature (REI-CSG, RT and GBP) is that they can contain 'obligations of means' or 'best effort' (for '*obligation de moyens*') and that they explicitly open up possibilities for 'exemption' (in RT's French language '*dérogation*') when something is 'demonstrated' or 'proven' to be impossible. This possibility is a departure from classic regulatory texts accompanied by administrative policing measures[105] that are based on the obligation to produce specific, objective, and readily measurable results. Of course, such exemptions are only admissible if the *technical events* concerned have previously been declared, in complete transparency. As a matter of fact, the *ex-ante* 'safeguarding submission procedure' in case of 'technical event' is particularly developed in the CSG regulations.

These specificities are no less admissible legally, provided that they target *experienced professionals* and that they are adopted and implemented in a *nondiscriminatory manner*,

---

104 This is a reference document, at the operational level, setting out the organization and the roles of each participant from design to operation of the Ariane launcher between the different players.
105 *Cf.* the powers of authorized officers (SOA Art. 7) and the powers of the President of CNES (SOA Art. 21).

in complete *neutrality as regards technical resources used*, and in the *public interest* to *reduce risks of damage to property, individuals and the environment* and, incidentally, to limit the potential liability of the operators concerned or of the French State. They also oblige CNES to adopt stringent requirements in terms of expertise and independence when it approves these exemptions in the context of its delegated authority. This justifies the measures taken to avoid all sources of *conflict of interest*, even technical ones, with its other space agency activities (*see* Part I, §4.3).

6.7 Extension of Application of the SOA to ESA Activities, on a Negotiated Basis between 2009 and March 2013

Following the publication of the implementing decrees on 9 June 2009, the President of CNES, Yannick d'Escatha, sent a letter on 2 November 2009 to the ESA Director General, Jean-Jacques Dordain, outlining this new legislation and inviting this agency to participate in the consultation conducted by CNES to develop technical regulations (RT), the best practice guide, and operating regulations for installations at CSG (REI-CSG) by proposing to set up a joint working group bringing together technical experts in the areas of 'launchers and manned flights' and legal experts from the two bodies. The Director General of ESA responded favorably by a letter dated 23 December 2009. Although the latter pointed out that this legislation would not directly apply to space operations conducted under the agency's programs,[106] he recognized the need to lay down procedures so that the agency's programs and activities would be conducted in line with French technical and safeguarding regulations.

This need is based on the fact that such a European research and development agency could not propose and produce space systems that are not exploitable in an operational phase, or on a recurring basis, with regard to legislation adopted by its own Member States to ensure the safety and protection of individuals and property. A CNES-ESA working group was thus set up to propose a specific agreement on the application by ESA of this legislation. On this basis, ESA, the ministry, and CNES reached an agreement, in 2011, to extend the application of SOA technical regulations, on a voluntary basis, *to future launch*

---

106 Pursuant to Annex I 'Privileges and Immunities' of the 'Convention for the establishment of a European Space Agency' signed in Paris on 30 May 1975 and entered into force on 30 October 1980.
Nevertheless, as an incentive for ESA to cooperate on enforcement of this legislation, Art. XXII (§1) of this Annex provides that 'the Agency shall cooperate, at all times, with the competent authorities of Member States in order to facilitate the proper administration of justice, to ensure the observance of police regulations and regulations concerning the handling of explosives and inflammable material, public health, labour inspection or other similar national legislation, and to prevent any abuse of the privileges, immunities and facilities provided for in this Annex."
Furthermore, Art. XXIII of this same Annex reaffirms that "Each Member State shall retain the right to take all precautionary measures in the interests of its security."

systems of this European organization (namely, Vega and Ariane 6), as from the development phase. This voluntary application of the technical part of the SOA by ESA for launch systems operated at CSG was formalized on two levels.

- The first was based on an exchange of letters between *ESA and the minister* in charge of space to benefit from the prior authorization regime provided for by Article 11 of the Authorisation Decree (2009-643). This regime was to apply to ESA *development programs for launchers intended to be launched from CSG*, in particular, Vega, which was then at the end of the development phase.[107] Its benefits were accorded to this intergovernmental organization (that is not subject to the SOA) and its beneficiaries, as future operators in the operational phase, namely Arianespace to date.
- The second level, finalized on 15 December 2011, concerns an arrangement entered into by *ESA and CNES*[108] to coordinate *exchanges of information* between *CNES' compliance monitoring missions* under RT-SOA and REI-SOA concerning safety of individuals and property with regard to ESA launch systems in the development and/or operational phase and those under the responsibility of ESA, regarding the same systems and phases, as the 'qualifying authority' for compliance with its program and performance specifications.

An identical arrangement was entered into on 13 March 2013 between ESA and CNES on safety coordination of ESA *orbital systems operated from French soil*,[109] in particular, from CNES' CST installations.

These agreements allowed for organization of consistency in the respective technical reviews during design, development, and operation, it being understood that these phases could be inverted, for example, in the case of re-qualification of all or part of a system in operation, due to corrective developments following contingencies or in-flight failure, for example. Such consistency helps avoid any duplication or deficiencies between ESA and CNES, while saving human and financial resources and at the same time strengthening safety, reliability, and performance of the space systems concerned.

It should be recalled, however, that the accepted application of the SOA to ESA only concerns the technical part, *i.e.*, quite often the part delegated to CNES. The administrative part, *i.e.*, decisions regarding the appropriateness of launching and conducting a program, remains under the full sovereignty of the Council of ESA or its Director General, and not

---

107 This process was documented in an exchange of letters, after a referral to the Director General of ESA, Jean-Jacques Dordain, on 27 May 2011 and a reply from the Minister, Laurent Wauquiez, on 5 December 2011.
108 Arrangement of 15 December 2011 between the *Centre National d'Etudes Spatiales* (CNES) and the European Space Agency on safety coordination for ESA launch systems operated at the Guiana Space Centre and verification of their qualification status.
109 For example: operations to dock ATV to the International Space Station (ISS), positioning of navigation satellites of the European Galileo's constellation, or maneuvers of the Rosetta probe's Philae module around the Churyumov-Gerasimenko comet.

obviously of the French minister in charge of space. With respect to governance, a parallel can be drawn with CNES, itself exonerated from the scope of the act, under Article 27 of the SOA, as a space agency for its activities that come under public interest missions. To launch its programs and related space operations, therefore, this body only needs a decision at the level of its Board of Directors, which acts in place of the administrative authority pursuant to its constitutive act.[110]

---

110 Art. L332-2 (b) of the Research Code and Art. 4.1 of Decree 84-510 of the Decree of 28 June, as amended, on the *Centre national d'études spatiales* (CNES) (*cf.* above Part I, §2.2).

7 The French Space Operations Act's Regimes

Chapter 7 analyzes FSOA's regime under a global and consolidated approach. It discusses step by step different issues that appear in the functioning frame of this space operation's regimes for authorization, control, and liability. In other words, it provides basic answers to the questions what, who, where, when, and how upon the 2008 Space Operation Act.

Chapter 7 includes the authorization and control regime (§7.1), the operator's liability, insurance and State guarantee conditions for damage caused to third parties (§7.2), the legal relationships between private stakeholders participating in a space operation (§7.3), and the specific rules for space-based data (§7.4). Other legal operators' obligations required in France related to frequency, telecommunication services, or export control are addressed in §7.5.

7.1 Authorization and Control Regime for Space Operations

7.1.1 Architecture

Figure 1   Legal Arborescence of FSOA, Philippe Clerc 2016

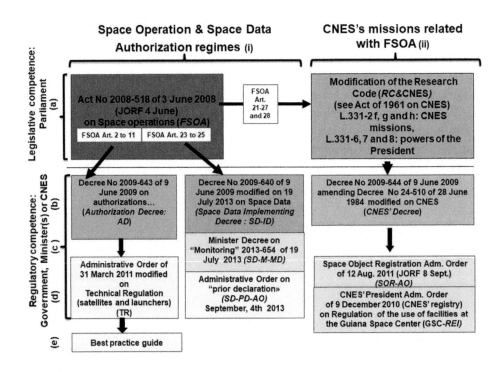

Figure 1: Legal Arborescence of FSOA, Philippe Clerc 2016

For a comprehensive view, diagram 1 above named 'Legal Arborescence of FSOA' gathers all texts created or modified under FSOA law-making process, as detailed in Chapter 6, so as to highlight the hierarchy of these different legal norms. This hierarchy appears from the legislative level, on the top, to the different regulatory levels down (diagram's vertical scale from 'a' to 'e'). This diagram also distinguishes, at the horizontal level, the FSOA's core legal framework (column 'i') from the related amendments introduced to the CNES legal status and missions (column 'ii').

Its first row (a) brings together legislative texts being passed through the form of an 'Act' or Statute law (*loi* in French) following a parliamentary adoption.[1] It includes, from the first left box, the FSOA of 3 June 2008 that lays down principles for space operations' authorization and control (as heading of column 'i') and, following on the right, the CNES' 1961 codified Act (as heading column 'ii') as being specifically amended by FSOA to complete the competences of this space agency related to the new legal framework.

At the regulatory competence level now[2], each act is supplemented by its 'Implementation Decree' or 'Application Decree' (*décret d'application*) as set in the second row (b). These application decrees were all adopted the same day on 9 June 2009[3] by the prime minister, on behalf of the government, after approval of the Council of State (*Conseil d'Etat*):

- The first application decree (n° 643), commonly called the 'Authorisation Decree'[4] (AD), details the authorization procedure to operate a Space Object and designates the Ministry of Research in charge of Space activities as the 'Administrative Authority.'
- The second application decree (n° 640) on 'Space-based data'[5] specifies the technical characteristics of such data according to which, following FSOA's Title VII, the relevant 'Primary Space-based data operator'[6] shall submit a formal declaration to the competent Administrative Authority, *i.e.*, the General Secretariat for Defence and National Security (SGDSN). This application decree is completed by a 'simple decree' (*décret simple*) n° 654 of 19 July 2013 on monitoring Primary Space-Based Operator (see third row 'c'). This 'Monitoring Decree'[7] organizes administrative procedures relating to the collection, record, and dissemination of such SBD.

---

1   Matters of legislative competence (*i.e.* Statutes, Statute Law, or Act) are listed in Art. 34 of the French Republic Constitution of 4 October 1958. As relates to matters regarding this act, we may underline in this Art. 34 that: "Statutes the shall determine the rules concerning: civic rights and the fundamental guarantees granted to citizens for the exercise of their civil liberties; freedom, nationality, the status and capacity of persons, the determination of serious crimes and other major offences and the penalties they carry [...] Statutes shall also lay down the basic principles of the general organisation of national defence, the preservation of the environment, systems of ownership, property rights and civil and commercial obligations [...]" As regard to CNES' bylaws and competence, it is mentioned later in the text that "statutes shall also determine the rules governing... the setting up of categories of public legal entities."
2   Matters of regulation (*i.e.* Application Decrees under consultation with the Council of State, Simple Decrees, Orders, etc.) are characterized pursuant Art. 37 of the French Republic Constitution of 4 October 1958. The relevant decisions are taken by the competent executive power (presidency, government, ministry, administration's department, public legal entity, or local and regional authorities). The regulatory competence is defined by default in Art. 37 as follows: "Matters other than those coming under the scope of statute law shall be matters for regulation."
3   And also published at the same date on 10 June 2009 at the French official gazette (*Journal Officiel de la République Française – JORF*).
4   Acronym AD, or D-A in French.
5   Acronym SBD-ID or SBD-AD, or D-DOS in French.
6   Acronym PSBDO or EPDOS in French for 'Exploitant Primaire de Données d'Origine Spatiales.'
7   Acronym SBD-MD or DS-EPDOS in French for 'Décret Surveillance - Exploitants Primaire de Données d'Origine Spatiale'.

- The third application decree (n° 644), relating to CNES Act, completes its actual *functioning decree* of 28 June 1984[8] (see above Part I, §2.2), without redrafting the latter, to specify this agency's competences on the maintenance of the national registry of Space Objects (following FSOA Art. 12) and the specific powers of its president under Article L 331-6 of the Research code (created by FSO Art. 21-1°) for the exploitation of the facilities of the Guiana Space Centre, including the conditions in which he may delegate such powers under Article L 331-8 of the same code (created by FSO Art. 21-2).

Each application decree has been completed at least by one 'administrative order' (*arrêté*) taken by ministers, their directors of departments, or by the CNES' President according to their respective competence on the relevant matter (see fourth row 'd'). Insofar, the Ministry of Research in charge of Space activities as the 'Administrative Authority'[9] adopted on 31 March 2011 the FSOA's *Technical Regulation* (TR or TR)[10] under proposal of CNES[11]. Under the same form, this ministry set up the list of necessary information to furnish to CNES to identify Space Objects on the national registry. On its side, the President of the CNES adopted the *police regulation* related with the activities at the Guiana Space Centre (REI-CSG).

Last but not least, as provided for in TR Art. 54, CNES, French Space operators and industry adopted consensual documents between adopted in a form of a 'guide of good practice' in order to recognize optional but enforceable practical solutions, including software algorithms, to comply with such technical regulation (see fifth row 'e'). This guide is divided into two documents: one on Space Launch Systems and the second on Orbital Systems. Since these documents may contain know-how or proprietary information, they are only accessible through CNES to the allowed operators and their contractors subject to an appropriate agreement.

---

8   Acronym CNES-D, or D-CNES in French.
9   AD Art. 1 pursuant FSOA Art. 4 second para.
10 TR in French for 'Réglementation technique.'
11 Pursuant FSOA Art. 28 completing Art. L.331-2 of the Research Code on CNES' missions by a f) stating 'to assist the government in the definition of the technical regulations relating to Space operations.'

7.1.2 Definition of Activities and Operators

7.1.2.1 Scope of the French Space Operation Act

The FSOA provides in its first article the definitions of Space activities and Operators subjected to the French government's acceptance and supervision.[12]

Space operations

Starting with the jurisdictional *rationa materae* criterion, in other words through an approach of activity domain, sector or even, a 'Space Operation' is defined by the first Act's Article (1-3) as 'any activity consisting in **launching or attempting to launch an Object in Outer Space**, or in **ensuring the command of a Space Object** during its journey in Outer Space [...], as well as during its return on Earth.'

In addition, for the legal purpose of establishing a clear handover of responsibility and attribution of potential liability toward third parties between successive operations, this legislation introduced definitions of 'Launching Phase,' 'Command phase' (in-orbit), and 'Return to Earth phase.' Thus, as to the 'Launching phase' the responsibility of the *Launch Operator* starts at the instant the *launch operations become irreversible* and ends with the *separation* between the launcher and the satellite, subject to more specific provisions contained, if necessary, in the authorization issued to the operator (FSOA Art. 1 §4).

The 'Command Phase' starts at the moment when the object to be put in outer Space is separated from its launch vehicle and ends when the first of the following events occurs:
- when the final maneuvers for de-orbiting and the passivation activities have been completed;
- when the operator has lost control over the Space Object;
- the return to Earth or the full disintegration of the Space Object into the atmosphere.

Accordingly, except in case of *willful misconduct*, the Space Operator's special liability under FSOA Art. 13 ends when all the obligations set out in the authorization or the license as to its own phase of responsibilities are fulfilled, or at the latest one year after the date on which these obligations should have been fulfilled. The Government shall be liable in the operator's place for damages occurring after this period.

As a result, we may assume that the final landing of the Space Object on the ground or in the sea marks the end of application of this FSOA as a special legal system, and consequently the end of any further legal obligation as to the associated operator(s). However,

---

12 For a better understanding, a definition list of legal and technical terms used in this FSOA, its technical regulations, and those of IADC, UN-COPUOS, ISO Space Debris Mitigation measures is specially drafted in ANNEX III.

the ordinary law may remain opposable yet again according to the French Civil Code as relates to the vehicle or its wreck, with respect to its 'real owner' or the 'Guardian of the thing'.[13] For instance, the *ordinary law* may be opposed to the incumbent owner or the relevant former Space operator, to repair damage or cover recycling or repatriation's expenses caused by a wreck, such as a former launcher's fairing, drifting on the sea or stranding in a beach.

Space operators
Taking now into consideration the related person or legal body governed by the law, in other words the *ratione personae* criterion, this act provides that the authorization process only applies to the Space Operator, namely **any individual or corporate entity carrying out a Space Operation under its own responsibility and in an independent manner** (FSOA Art. 1-2°).

Thus, notwithstanding the condition of *nationality* which is addressed further in §7.1.3, the characterization of the quality of a Space Operator under this act goes back to the assessment of its actual responsibilities in the achievement of a Space Operations, as the name indicates. In fact, this definition of the 'Operator,' resulted from extensive discussions during the preparatory work within the Council of State, the French government and Parliament following their consultations with operators and manufacturers. This led to the adoption of a short definition, with an interpretation which appears today widely shared by all these stakeholders. Accordingly, the qualification of Operator is to be kept for those who, at a given time, have the *effective control or command* and the (delegated) *power to dispose of the spacecraft* (the 'abusus'), in other words, the one who behaves as the real decision maker, even if not being the owner, in particular when it comes to engaging the spacecraft's *end-of-life maneuvers*.

As a result, **there can be only one Operator at the time**, who shall be the only one responsible as the Authorization holder and, eventually, liable for damages caused to third parties by the Space Object in its control. Based on the same logic, the act has retained the **possibility of multiple operators acting 'in series'** on the command of same Space Object. For instance, the transfer of command of a satellite to another operator can be formally authorized, in a final or a reversible manner, once nominally positioned in-orbit. The successor operator will be then solely and fully responsible in controlling all operations under the act. For instance, the Administrative Authority may grant, subject to a prior compliant application by the prime Operator, an authorization or a global license allowing a transfer of responsibilities between a 'routine operator' to a 'specialized operator' for the achievement of given critical or hazardous maneuver(s), *i.e.,* change of orbit positioning, docking, reparation, end-of-life. Such authorization or license may be reversible in allowing

---

13   Currently Art. 1242 (old numbering, before 2016: Art. 1384).

a reallocation of responsibilities, and associated third party's liability, to the nominal or routine operator once such critical maneuvers have been properly achieved, according to the Administrative Authority's decision based on CNES' review.

This act (Art. 3) also expressively provides for a ***transferring command*** **between French and foreign operators** relating to systems already placed in orbit. This transfer shall be authorized or licensed in both ways under FSOA:
- Paragraph 1 of Article 3 refers to the transfer of commanding between a French operator, holding an authorization under FSOA, and a foreign Operator (as subjected to a foreign law).
- The second paragraph applies to a French operator intending to take the control of a Space Object whose launching or control has not been authorized under the present act, in other words to the takeover under FSOA's scope of a Space system being previously subject to a foreign jurisdiction.

Such application procedure for bilateral transfer of command provide in any circumstances the French government with the opportunity: (i) to obtain from the operator the necessary guarantees regarding the national and international commitments made by that foreign State as well as its legislation and practices regarding the safety of persons and property, the protection of public health and the environment, and liability indemnification,[14] and/or (ii) to enter into negotiation directly with the appropriate state in order agree. The criterion 'independent manner' means that the characterization of Space Operator is reserved to the sole 'effective and final decision maker' and thus that FSOA does not affect subcontractors who have no autonomy of action or decision-making powers at critical moments, or owners such as financial or capital structure who are not involved in the operations.

However, the owner of the satellite may be *presumed* to being the operator in case of a confusing situation in the contractual or operational scheme/chain, whether or not arising from a deliberate situation among the different stakeholders. Basically, the difficulty of identifying the genuine Space Operator may arise with regard to the satellite end-of-life period, at the time of making a decision of the starting or not of disposal maneuvers. In this situation a conflict of interest may arise between the economic user or owner of the satellite, wishing to extend the working life of its asset, and the technical operator that remains accountable to the FSOA's regulations and its associated penalties. The question then is one of determining who will independently make the final decision.

Accordingly, following the same pragmatic approach, a subcontractor who unequivocally acts independently as an operator may be qualified as such. For example, may be qualified as the actual 'space operator', the *satellite manufacturer* that achieves the satellite in-orbit

---

14 FSOA Art. 4.4°, DA Art. 12.

positioning maneuvers in application of an 'In-Orbit delivery contract' on behalf of its *customer*. The latter may later be the future satellite owner or the final nominal space operator.

Finally, this criterion of 'independent manner' proves to be the stumbling block of the FSOA's allocation regime of responsibility and liability. Such condition is a prerequisite for the attribution of the governmental authorization or licenses and for identifying the future person potentially liable for any damage caused by the Space Object. This criterion also dramatically affects the organization of the contractual and financial framework between all stakeholders involved in the Space venture.

Governmental space activities (including CNES' operations)
FSOA's procedures do not apply to the **Ministry of Defence** with respect to ballistic missiles[15] and/or to **CNES** for its own operations as a Space agency.[16]

With regard to the *Ministry of Defence*, we may assume furthermore that this administration, as directly acting on behalf of the State, may be exempted in full or in part of the FSOA's formal authorization process, at least from the *administrative review* performed by the Ministry of Research and from the *obligation of insurance* (FSOA Art. 6) and the specific State guaranty benefit. Indeed, under the French Republic Constitution or 1958, the internal organization and procedures within the Administration and ministries belong to the scope of the regulatory power, namely pursuant Government's decree. Thus the Ministry of Defence which legally, administratively and financially merges with the State has its proper administrative *modus operandi*, especially as regards to its core defense activity and remains accordingly its self-insurer under the general umbrella of the State as an affiliate department, without being obliged to subscribe the private insurance required under FSOA (Art. 6) nor resorting to the specific government guarantee for Space liability damages (Art. 15).

Indeed, it should be pointed out that the main FSOA's administrative requirement (Art. 4) to "not jeopardize national defence interests or the respect by France of its international commitments" is already the critical essence of this ministry's competence, under the authority of the Prime minister (and SGDSN) and the President of Republic, and shall not be assessed as such by the Ministry of Research and Space on an administrative standpoint. As a result, the administrative decision process on Space defense systems does not differ from the one applicable to this ministry's other programs while being at the same time consistent with FSOA's regime. Consistently, the decision process does not preclude the application of the FSOA's Technical Regulation as to such Space systems.

---

15   FSOA Art. 26.
16   FSOA Art. 27.

The associated compliance monitoring also remains basically delegated to dedicated CNES staff (see §4.3.3 and 7.1.7) who are fully empowered to deal with any sensible data. Furthermore, all Space Objects operated by or on behalf the Ministry of Defence are recorded in the national registry with an information made to the Secretary-General of the United Nations according to Article II of the Convention dated 14 September 1975 relating to Registration of Objects launched into Outer Space.

For Space system building and operations directly awarded by this ministry to the private sector, CNES acts in its technical control mission under the ordinary procedure of FSOA, at the service of the Administrative Authority. The Ministry of Defence may also delegate to CNES, in its quality of as a national Space agency, full or part or its management responsibilities during the development, industrialization, and operational phases of a new system. Thus, the FSOA's technical monitoring may be implemented by CNES as the case may be under a direct public delegation, as contracting authority from the Ministry of Defence[17] or as technical assistant[18] of the same.

The status of *CNES* for its own operations is also remarkable. This Space agency was set up in 1961 under a specific act as national public agency entitled with autonomous legal and financial capacity, but embodied as an 'EPIC' being authorized to undertake industrial or commercial activities.[19] FSOA made it more necessary than ever to avoid any source of business competition from CNES to those private operators whose operations would be likely subjected to its technical control on behalf of the French government under the same Act. This concern was also raised as relates to CNES' historical safeguard responsibilities on the Guiana launch base, initially resulting from an empirical definition according to the agreements between the French government and ESA, and now being formalized through a formal authority of administrative police granted to its President.

It has hence become necessary to outline CNES' responsibilities under this new act to avoid any source of *conflicts of interests*[20] or misunderstanding on its statutory mission. The solution was[21] to exempt CNES from FSOA's provisions applicable to Space Operators (Titles II and IV) provided that such operations already fell under the scope of its assigned public mission, after approval by the Administrative Authority[22], namely its board of directors[23]. This exclusion has been consistently extended to its activities on Earth obser-

---

17 Basically, through the DGA (for *Direction générale de l'armement*), its armament technical and procurement directorate.
18 In French: *Délégation de maîtrise d'ouvrage publique* or *Assistance à Maîtrise d'ouvrage (AMO)*.
19 Acronym for *Etablissement public à caractère industriel et commercial* or a national public body of industrial and commercial nature, according to the CNES' constituent Act as codified in Art. L 331-1 of the French Code of Research. *Seeabove* in Part I.
20 On this issue, *see above* in Part 1, §4.3.
21 *Ibid.* FSOA Art. 27.
22 Under the fourth paragraph (or paragraph 'b') of Art. L. 331-2 (CNES' constituent Act) of the Research Code.
23 Art. 4-1° of decree n° 84-510 of 28th June 1984 (modified) relating to the Centre National d'Etudes Spatiales.

vation satellite and the reception of Earth observation data as relates to the provisions of Title VII of FSOA.

As a result, CNES does not perform any longer operations on a commercial basis in the free open market in potential competition with applicants on FSOA' authorization or licenses. Its scope of operations services is limited to its public Space agency's activities of general interest, namely: scientific vehicles, technological satellites, Space application demonstrators, satellites for civil public services (observation, meteorology, navigation, localization, etc.), or any other similar activity delegated by public entities, at the national, European, or international level, including from defense authorities as mentioned above. CNES also pursue its policy of progressively withdrawing from commercial companies' shareholding. This withdrawal from commercial activities or shareholding has been specially provided for in Annex II of the Senate Report on behalf of the Economics Affairs Commission by Mr. Henri Revol, titled 'Direct and indirect interest of CNES in competitive activities.'[24] Indeed its Annex II lists CNES' situation (1) on main commercial activities and (2) on affiliates and shareholdings with the associated inventory of measures already taken or planned.

To summarize, for the sake of clarity as relates to the wording of Art. VI the UN Outer Space Treaty of 1967, we may assume that CNES henceforth shall act only as a governmental agency, and not as 'nongovernmental entities.'[25]

Space industry activities
Prime contractors or industrial suppliers are not directly covered by the authorization process as far as they act as manufacturers only, without performing operations involving delivery in orbit. The genuine industrial activities involved in the production of a Space Object indeed remain outside the framework of the FSOA, pursuant to Article 2.

This exclusion marks a difference with *Aviation and Air Law* to which the *aircraft industry* is directly submitted, in particular with regard to the governmental procedures to obtain the airworthiness certificate for their craft. This difference should be taken into account when designing a future legislation dedicated on suborbital flights.

However, Spacecraft manufacturers are indirectly concerned through their contractual obligations, when running the delivery of their equipment to the FSOA's Operator in compliance with the latest specifications that obviously incorporate the ones of the Technical Regulation. Spacecraft manufacturers may also directly benefit from the procedure

---

24 *Ibid.* footnote n° 24, Senate – Report on Economics Affairs Commission, January 15th 2008, n° 161 and n° 328 (2007-2008), Annex II, p. 93 and 94.
25 'Non-governmental entities' (in other words private or commercial bodies) according to the wording of the Art. VI of the 1967 Outer Space Treaty (ibid) which is the original legal source of any national Space legislation, and as such of this FSOA.

of 'prior certification' stated by Article 11 of the authorization decree for the purpose of any critical Space system under development, since their early design phase. In addition, notwithstanding its status out of the FSOA's scope, a non-operator manufacturer can also benefit from the specific governmental guarantee in case of damage caused during the launch phase if it has been condemned by a foreign court to compensate a third party for this damage in place of the incumbent French Space Operator[26].

European space activities (ESA and EU)
The European Space Agency (ESA) and the European Union (EU) for operations that they may carry out from French territory are also outside the scope of this law as intergovernmental organisms endowed by their constitutive treaty with *privileges and immunities* from any national jurisdiction. Bridges have been built on a voluntary basis with ESA[27], which nevertheless has its own rules governing international liability in case of damage, having made a *declaration of acceptance* to that effect under the UN Convention of 29 March 1972.[28]

The interest for this international organization of being submitted to the FSOA's monitoring technical compliance process is to be able to justify, toward its sponsoring Members States, that Space systems developed[29] under its responsibility are to be designed in compliance with the legal requirements that will be applicable along its *exploitation phase*, which is to be outside its jurisdiction, in particular concerning commercial or recurrent systems to be further operated by third parties. Thus, the reference made to the requirements of the French Space Operation Act makes sense as long as that the latest will be finally applicable, or potentially representative or equivalent with other national rules that may be applicable during the Space system's industrial and commercial exploitation phase.

7.1.2.2 Registration of Space Objects

According to article II of the 1975 UN Convention on Registration of Objects Launched Into Outer Space and the article VIII of the 1967 UN Outer Space Treaty, the registration by the *launching state* of a *space object*[30] allows to the latter to retain jurisdiction and control

---

26 FSOA Art. 15, last para. (*cf.* below Chapter 2) and Art 18.
27 See §6.7 above.
28 Resolution of the Council of the European Space Agency on the Agency's Legal Liability (ESA/C/XXII/Res.3) adopted by the ESA Council on 13 December 1977. ESA's Declaration of Acceptance of the Astronauts Agreement, the Liability Convention and the Registration Convention: adopted by the ESA Council on 12 December 1978, deposited on 2 January 1979, applied retroactively as of 20 September 1976 and completed by an additional declaration in 2000.
29 For more details on the application of the FSOA procedure as to the development phase of a new Space systems, *see under* Section 6 the pre-certification procedure established by Art. 11 of the AD.
30 I.e., basically any spacecraft, its components parts (launcher stages…) or other object being launched into the Earth orbit or beyond.

over such object, and over any personnel thereof, while in outer space or on a celestial body. This jurisdiction basically affects any human driven or automatized activity carried out within or from this space object, in particular through telemetry. In addition, the *Registering State* is thus deemed liable for any damaged caused to a third party by the registered object whether in the ground, in the airspace or in outer space.

However, any other *Launching State* may be successfully sued and sanctioned by a victim on the basis of the *absolute liability* set up by Art. IV.1 (a) of the 1972 UN Liability Convention for damage suffered I the Earth ground or airspace. Another *non-registering Launching State* can be held liable for a third party damage in orbit while ensuring the *effective monitoring* of a space object on the basis the fault liability regime set up by article Art. IV.1 (b) of the aforesaid 1972 UN Liability Convention.

In these conditions, the detailed list of information that France have to furnish to the Secretary-General of the United Nations (Art. IV of Registration Convention) concerning each space object carried on its registry is of great importance.

Requirements of the French national register under FSOA, according to the August 2011 Registration Order, are more detailed than those of the article IV of the UN Registration Convention. According to the specifications on space object registry provided for in the CNES' decree (Title III, Art. 14-2), the Space Object Operator shall transmit its information to CNES at the latest sixty days following its launch, namely after the separation of the satellite from the launcher in accordance with FSOA Art. 1.4°. The Order information list is detailed below:

Description of the space object and the general function of the object (A-I. Art. 1-1° and 2°)
The description of the general function of the space object, resulting from Article IV-(e) of the United Nations Convention refers to the actual mission of the orbital system in its various *potential applications*, namely as the case may be: telecommunications, broadcasting, observation, meteorology, navigation, science, defense, transport of individuals and freight *in-orbit, on-orbit* maintenance, repairing, fueling, or repositioning, manned stations, manned stations on the Moon or another celestial body, etc. As mentioned previously, aside from the special regime of Earth observation (SOA title VII on SBD), the SOA does not govern the legal framework of such services provided on Earth from space. Indeed, the latter are subject to the legislation that is applicable to them 'on Earth,' according to the activity sector concerned. In this respect, damage caused by signal failure of these user services is explicitly excluded from the SOA liability regime (SOA Art 1-1°). Despite this exclusion of services by the SOA, the ministry in charge of space, acting as the administrative authority retains full competence, based on the information given at the time of registration, to verify that these other governmental authorizations relating to satellite missions and services have indeed been requested or obtained following examination by the relevant

national authority, in particular, concerning radio spectrum allocation[31] or the exploitation of said services.[32] Furthermore, depending on the adequacy of the information provided by the registrant, the administrative authority retains all its capacity under SOA monitoring to ban or suspend services in orbit "of a nature that could compromise national defence interests or the fulfilment by France of its international commitments" (SOA Art. 4, para. 2; Art. 9, para. 1).

Name of the manufacturer (A-I. Art. 1-3°)
This information, which was not required under SOA,[33] was a first step toward *Air Law*, since such legislation is also applicable to *aircraft manufacturers*, in particular, for their certification requirements, beyond the rights and obligations of the *carrier (Airline)*, which is the equivalent of our Space Operator. This was a first source of rapprochement between the two laws which could prove useful for legislative developments aiming to include *suborbital flights*. In the case of an anomaly during launch or during orbital control, the vehicle manufacturer can thus be also subjected to inspections by authorized or sworn officers appointed by the administrative authority (SOA Art. 7-II.). These verifications may also help determine, if necessary, whether the latter exercised an operator's responsibility within the meaning of the SOA (SOA Art 1-2[34]), for example, independent control of the space object after its separation from the launcher, as can happen in the case of a delivery-in-orbit contract, to the benefit of a customer who may or may not (foreign party) be subjected to the SOA.

History of its ownership and any real or personal security interests in the space object (A-I. Art. 1-4°)
This information allows a legal connection to be made, if necessary, with the international guarantee registration system provided for in the *UNIDROIT Protocol*. This history also enables the administrative authority to know who was the real Space Operator responsible for the satellite in orbit within the meaning of Article 1-2 of the SOA (*cf.* §7.1.2.1) for certain successive or sensitive maneuvers in orbit, in particular when failing any relevant stipulation in the contract(s) between those taking part in the operation. Indeed, it often occurs that the satellite owner, or his creditor, has the real last word, over the one of the service provider in charge of the technical conduct of the space object, concerning critical decisions for the

---

31 Under the framework of the ANFR, the French frequency agency.
32 Depending on the case, from the ARCEP, the French electronic communications and postal regulation authority, or the CSA, the French broadcasting authority.
33 The authorization, monitoring, and liability regimes for operations under the SOA only apply to *Space Operators* within the meaning defined in its Art. 1-2, but FSOA's Art. 15 last paragraph allows industry to benefit from the State Guarantee for damage.
34 Which defines 'space operator' or 'operator' as: any individual or legal entity that leads a space operation, **under its responsibility and in an independent manner.**

satellite's service life, in particular, when deciding whether or not to instigate end-of-life maneuvers with regard to requirements provided for in this respect under the authorization or the technical regulations. As a result, consideration of the ownership of spacecraft may help to determine who is the effective 'independent and responsible' *Space Operator* according to FSOA's Article 1.2.

Description of control mode in outer space (A-I. Art. 1-7°)
Descriptions of the control mode of the space object in its different phases, its maneuverability, its control network, participants and its legal and technical conditions can make it easier to determine the operator responsible during each given phase and, if relevant, to enable assessment of the existence and degree of fault committed by the latter in controlling the vehicle, during an investigation following an anomaly or an accident.

Revelation of any anomalies encountered during orbit insertion or in the functioning of the object as a space vehicle (A-I. Art. 1.8° and 2)
The obligation to reveal such anomalies is in line with the reference to *technical events* provided for in the implementing decrees (D-A. Art.7; D-CNES Art. 14-7 par. 2); it can inverse the burden of proof toward the 'registrant operator' if the latter made omissions. Furthermore, it can be applied retroactively against previous operators. This *declaration of anomalies* dates all incidents encountered before registration after separation of its space object (satellite) from the launcher at each phase of satellite positioning until its orbital stabilization (A-I. Art. 1.8). Then the operator shall notify immediately any modification with regard to its registered information, in particular any significant event susceptible to affect life in orbit of the space object, in particular its de-orbitation, its end of the exploitation or loss of control (A-I. Art. 2).

The question therefore arises, in the case of damage, to what extent can the operator or owner of a vehicle in orbit rely on this declaration to rule out their own liability, reserve their rights against (the) previous operator(s), or finally share liability with the latter for all anomalies prior to their taking control. This question affects both non-contractual[35] and contractual liability between the parties concerned, up to the limits of the well-known saying that "no-one can constitute proof themselves"[36] when legal facts are involved like

---

35   Otherwise known under French law as tortious liability or liability for damage caused to third parties.
36   Or the principle of a ban on 'self-constituted proof.' According to a judgment by the civil chamber of the *Cour de Cassation* on 6 February 2014, the highest jurisdiction in France stated that under French law, the principle according to which 'no-one can constitute proof themselves' is in no case applicable to **proof of a legal fact**. A 'legal fact' is defined as a situation producing consequences beyond the control of the parties, which is notably the case of an anomaly. In non-contractual civil liability, proof of a 'legal fact' can be provided by any means (freedom of proof) following the logic of a body of accurate and consistent evidence, at the sovereign discretion of the judge. In this context, such a prior declaration of anomaly may constitute the beginning of written proof and it may have probative value if it is supplemented by other forms of proof

in this case. Indeed, an objection should be made to this declaration of anomaly to avoid liability.

More generally to conclude on the French *registration regime*, it should be underlined, that the requirements of this register, which were laid down by a simple order, produce considerable legal consequences regarding responsibility and liability under FSOA and beyond in connection with other applicable legislation on services (SBD applications, telecommunication or broadcasting services, etc.). In the event of damage, they have an impact on the determination of non-contractual liability (in relation to third parties) or contractual liability (between parties) and, possibly, the State guarantee or insurance, or exclusion clauses.

7.1.2.3 FSOA's Exclusions or Exemptions

Activities excluded
Some Space-related activities remain out of this legislation' scope, explicitly or implicitly, either fully or in part.

Space Applications and frequency spectrum allocations

The term of 'damage' as defined by FSOA's Art. 1-1° refers to the one 'directly *caused by a Space Object as part of a Space Operation,* to the exclusion of the consequences arising from the use of the signal transmitted by this Object.' As a result, any exploitation of the signal of a satellite's payload does not fall within the scope this specific legislation's liability regime (FSOA Title IV) and associated insurance obligation (FSOA Art. 6) and shall not be subject to its procedures of authorization and control. This exclusion affects any information services from the satellite's payload such as telecommunication, broadcasting, localization, and navigation. This exclusion may be explained firstly by the fact that Space applications' legal background have remained out of the scope of the binding United Nation Space Treaties (1967, 1972, 1975, etc.). Indeed, Remote Sensing of the Earth and Direct Television Broadcasting are the only applications being addressed by its General Assembly Principles but in a form of *non-constraining instruments*.[37]

The second reason for excluding Space application from national Space law was to avoid interference or duplication with other legislations on study in France, Europe or in other jurisdiction dealing with the same services toward users (see §5.1.1 on the 'LSI,'

(witness accounts, other written documents from the opponent describing the same facts, etc.) to determine liability for resulting damage.

37 Principles Relating to Remote Sensing of the Earth from Outer Space, adopted by the U.N. General Assembly 95th plenary meeting on 3 December 1986 (resolution 41/65). Principles Governing the Use by States of Artificial Earth Satellites for International Direct Television Broadcasting, adopted by the U.N. General Assembly on 10 December 1982 (resolution 37/92).

§5.1.2 on 'data policy'). Thus, *Space applications legal frameworks* are integrated into other relevant governmental licensing procedures and legislations, as developed in this book in §7.5. The Space application solely subjected to the FSOA's provisions relates to Earth Observation pursuant to its Title VII on Space-Based Data (SBD). This SBD regime is developed in this book under §6.6.3 and §7.4.

We may assume however more broadly, based on the core provisions of FSOA, that the Administrative Authority could deny or suspend any authorization to launch or to operate any *application spacecraft*, the use of which would be likely to *jeopardize national defense interests* or the respect by France of its *international commitments* pursuant to its Article 4, 2° paragraph.

Notwithstanding the above, we have also to retain that consistent with international treaties or standards, in particular regarding the IADC, UNGA-COPUOS, ISO and EU ICOC Space Debris Mitigation measures,[38] the FSOA's associated technical regulation has introduced indirectly a 'legal link' between the Spacecraft *mission, i.e.,* satellite's capacity to deliver 'services' or 'applications' toward users, and the Space operator's responsibilities in commanding the same satellite as a 'vehicle' or 'Spacecraft'.[39] This regulation indeed imposes to the space operator to initiate the end-of-life maneuvers on its Space Object 'once the Object has completed its *operational phase*' or 'mission'[40] This means that a satellite shall be de-orbited when its *servicing capacity* (its *instrument payload*) toward users is definitely over, even if this satellite as such remains fully maneuverable, as a spacecraft. The purpose of this rule is of general interest on *Space sustainability* to preserve a rational use of available Space orbits and frequencies as limited resources and to reduce the risk of collision and the associated liability as regards only to fully operational satellites.

---

38   IIADC-SDMG (2007) or IADC: Inter-Agency Space Debris Coordination Committee (IADC) Space Debris Mitigation Guidelines (SDMG), IADC-02-01-Revision 1, September 2007, action item 22.4, issued by Steering Group and Working Group 4.
     – UNGA-COPUOS-SDMG 62/217 (2007) or UNGA 62/217: United Nations General Assembly (UNGA), Resolution 62/217 adopted on 22 December 2007, based on the Report of the Scientific and Technical Subcommittee (STC) of the Committee of the Peaceful Uses of Outer Space (COPUOS) on Space Debris Mitigation Guidelines (SDMG), annexed in 62th session, official records, supplement n° 20 (A/62/20) of 1 February 2008.
     – ISO-SDMR 24113 (2011) or ISO: International Standard Organisation (ISO) 24113 of May 2011, 2nd edition 2011-05-15, 'Space Systems – Space Debris Mitigation Requirements.'
     – EU ICOC draft (2014): 'European Union's Draft of International Code of Conduct for Outer Space Activities,' version of 31 March 2014.
     For a comparison between these organizations' guidelines and FSOA's related provisions, *see* the Concordance Table in this Annex IV.
39   For details, *see* Annex III, the comparison list of definition and acronyms between TR-FSOA and IADC, UNGA and ISO instruments: End of Mission, Mission Phase, Operational Phase, and Space System. *See also* Annex IV as to the concordance and content of the relevant technical provisions.
40   TR Art. 40.4 and 40.5 in particular.

Finally, it has to be specified in addition that national allocation of frequency bands relating to a Space vehicle both for its command telemetry that for its payload services to Earth (data transmitting, broadcasting, etc.), as being formerly managed under the International Telecommunication Union (ITU), comes in France under the jurisdiction of the French Electronic Communications and Postal Code (Art. L. 97-2...) as specified bellow in §7.5. The relevant license has to be given, on behalf of the French government, by the Minister in charge of electronic communications, after obtaining the opinion of the 'assigning authorities' for the frequencies concerned.

Human space flights

The term 'Operation,' within the meaning of this legislation,[41] only concerns any activity relating to a 'Space Object,' during a 'Space operation'; meanwhile, the term of 'damage'[42] remains limited to the one 'directly caused by a Space Object as part of a Space Operation.' As a result, FSOA does not covers as such the *regime of Human Beings* in Space, in particular the commercial passenger, except to guarantee specifically the victims' rights, for damage suffered on ground or airspace, under the third-party liability regime (Art. 13) and its related insurance regime (Art. 6) and the associated State Guarantee (Art. 14...). In the same line, as to Outer Space activities, the FSOA's Technical Regulation (Art. 22) lays down provisions to prevent the risks of accidental collision with manned Space Objects, such as potentially the ISS, for which the orbital parameters are accurately known and available.

The more obvious reason why manned Spaceflights are not considered directly by FSOA is that such activities, as a matter of fact, currently already fall under the legal framework of the International Space Station (ISS) with its intergovernmental agreement (IGA) between the fifteen governments involved in this project and the associated Memorandum of Understanding (MoU) between the National Aeronautics and Space Administration (NASA) and the European Space Agency (ESA), both signed on 29 January 1998. So, there is no need for any specific regulation since there is no other prospected Space-manned program or cooperation supported by France at the national or bilateral level.

However, on a strict legal standpoint, we may consider that any extension of this SOA to manned mission would seriously challenge its current liability regime relating to 'persons taking part in the Space operation,'[43] which results from a delicate balance between with the ordinary law and international practices deeply rooted among the Space community. This issue may be developed as follows:

---

41 Pursuant Art 1.3 and 1.4,
42 Pursuant Art 1.1.
43 As laid down in FSOA' Title IV, Chapter II Art. 19 and 20.

On the one hand, as noted by the Council of State in its appraisal report of 6 April 2006,[44] in line with higher legal principles of the French Constitution of 1958,[45] the Civil Code,[46] and the associated jurisprudence of the Court of Cassation, the specific system of cross-waivers of recourse and hold harmless clause to be set forth in this FSOA's provisions may not be extended as such toward a victim being a 'natural person,' being 'nonprofessional,' or 'consumer' or in a case of 'serious injury or death' or even more as a result of 'inexcusable fault' or of a willful misconduct. These obstacles do not seem limited to the French legal regime since the corresponding high value legal principle on responsibility and liability have been derived from those of prevalent international commitments such as the Universal Declaration of Human Rights (UDHR) of 1948[47] recognized by many countries.

On the other hand, we have to consider the current legal and contractual instruments in effect among the international *market of Space Launch Services*. Basically, this current responsibility and liability regime was shaped and standardized empirically from the 1980s under the lead of its major providers, Arianespace and its competitors, their stakeholders and customers with the appropriate support of governments regarding regulation and guarantees. Such a business sector remained focused on commercial Space launch services provided by *unmanned* and *non-reusable spacecrafts*[48] with the objective of placing unmanned spacecraft in orbit (satellites). Then, the related risk consists in material loss only that could be covered by appropriate legal, financial and governmental remedies (securities, insurance, stock, guarantees, etc.). To this end, this *Space community* has built among its stakeholders a *global risk management scheme* based on *cross-waiver of claim*, or even *best effort obligations* for Space operators, that allows to each supplier along the industrial chain to be released from any liability and responsibility, as relates to the *delivery of its goods or service* toward its respective customer, since the conclusion of the final *acceptance review*, the latest being always executed on or from the ground. At the end of

---

44 This report is discussed in Chapter 6, §6.3. Regarding the content of this report on third party liability *See* its Part 2 , para. 2.2.2, *responsabilité à l'égard des partenaires contractuels*, p. 109-113.

45 According to its Preamble that recognize in particular as higher legal value the French Declaration of Human and Civil Rights of 26 October 1789, Art. 4 of which states that "liberty consists in the freedom to do everything that does not arm others [...]."

46 As to the Civil Code: on Civil liability rights, *see* Art. 1240 (Art. 1382 in old numbering before 2016) stating that 'Any act committed by a person who causes damage to another person shall render the person through whose fault the damage was caused liable to make reparation for it (*tout fait quelconque de l'homme, qui cause à autrui un dommage, oblige celui par la faute duquel il est arrivé à le réparer*). On Liability of the "*guardian of the thing*" (*gardien de la chose*) see Art. 1242 (Art 1384 in old numbering before 2016). On product liability or on clause limiting or exonerating the producer or professionals, *see* Art. 1244-14 currently (Art. 1986-15 in old numbering before 2016) and Art. 1643 (hidden defect).

47 Adopted by the United Nations General Assembly at its 3rd session on 10 December 1948

48 The U.S. Space Manned Shuttle, which was designed to provide services for commercial missions, ceased this activity as a consequence of the tragic accident of 'Challenger' 28 January 1986, few seconds after its liftoff.

the chain, the launch service provider operator is required to extend the 'cross-waiver of claim' or 'hold harmless' clauses[49] to its customer, *i.e.,* the satellite owner or operator and its/their respective stakeholders.

Finally, the *satellite customer* is bearing the economic loss of its asset since the launch, and may underwrite appropriate insurances, while the *launch operator* will be liable for any third-party damage up to the separation of the satellite and shall underwrite corresponding insurance up to the ceiling amount guaranteed by its government. As a result, the 'stumbling block' of this risk management system balance is inseparable from the existence of an appropriate *guarantee from State*(s) covering the liability burden toward third parties for damages that could not be supported by the sole insurance market. To this particular point, it is recalled that rationales for such State guarantee arise from the latest's obligations as *Launch State* under the UN Space Treaties,[50] but also from strategic and general considerations related to the maintenance of an independent and sustainable access to Space for public interest needs: exploration, science, technology, telecommunication, observation navigation, defense, including domestic economic development and industry competitiveness.

In conclusion, we may assume that extending current national Space law to *manned Space* operation is a common difficult issue of most *Space powers* which focus on the definition of an appropriate regime of liability among participants to the Space operation, especially toward 'passengers' or 'consumers.' To this extent, current State guarantee systems should be readdressed to deal with human space transportation activities to be managed by the private sector. Beyond non-negotiable human rights and ethical guidelines, this review process should then consider, on the legal and political perspectives, the specific benefits generated by this emerging activity as to society and public interests as regards the general limits affecting such public aids to the competitive sector.

Suborbital flights

Beyond the reasons developed above regarding *Manned Spaceflights*, *Suborbital Flights* may be excluded from the scope of this national Space law, as far as they don't meet its fundamental criterion of its Article 1.3 for which a 'Space activity,' means 'any activity consisting in launching or attempting to launch an **Object into outer Space**, or of ensuring the commanding of a **Space Object** during its journey in outer Space... and, if necessary, during its return to Earth.' This approach is consistent with the famous 'functionalism theory' that is reiterated in a constant manner by the French delegation at the COPUOS

---

49 On FSOA's regime of cross-waiver of claim see §7.3. Legal Relationships between private stakeholders participating to in a space operation.
50 *Ibid.,* 1967 OST (art VII) and 1972 Liability Convention.

Legal Subcommittee as a criterion for the application of UN Space Treaties. The same criterion also applies by default to operations on sounding rockets (without orbiting function of any object into outer space) and stratospheric balloons that definitely fall under the scope of Air law in France.

The issue of the status of *hybrid systems* is a difficult one. These systems may be defined as vehicles designed both to flight in and *beyond Airspace* with *human on board*, with the trajectory passing through Outer Space, and to be used for Space Operations, in particular for orbiting small satellites. The difficulty results from the fundamental legal differences between Space law and Air law, at the international and European level. Should the Outer Space Treaty of 1967 be applicable to these activities, namely with regard to vehicles designed to place an object in orbit under the 'functionalist' criterion,[51] the FSOA regime will be applicable. The French government then shall be responsible to authorize and control the operations under its jurisdiction or liability (Art. VI, VII VIII of 1967 OST treaty and Art. 2 of FSOA). The French State thus as launching State shall bear, jointly or severally, an absolute liability for damage caused to foreign third parties on the ground or in the Airspace, and thereof shall grant to the relevant private Suborbital and Space Operator the appropriate guarantee or ceiling.

On this matter of jurisdiction as mentioned above in §6.5.4.1, except on the issue of State guarantee or ceiling, French Space law like any other national Space legislation in Europe does not fall into the harmonization competence of the EU.[52] For its part, Air Law is applicable for civil vehicles using *air lift force*. Unlike Space law statutes, Air law provides that States retain their *territorial jurisdiction (ratione loci)* on the Airspace above their frontiers. The civil and nongovernmental aviation law is built at the international level of the International Civil Aviation Organization (ICAO-*OACI*, Chicago Convention signed on 7 December 1944). The goal of this law is to organize civil international 'transport' in a 'safe and orderly manner,' air transport services being to be 'established on the basis of equality of opportunity and operated soundly and economically.'

---

51 Notwithstanding other criteria, in particular of physical or technical sources, that may be used at associated technical regulation levels such as: airlift (or not), altitude (<30 km for Airspace, >100 km for Outer space, in between for Suborbital space), energy or thrust magnitude, ballistic or flying mode, reusable or expendable systems (or subsystems), controlled or uncontrolled re-entry.
52 TFEU or Lisbon Treaty Art. 189:
    1. To promote scientific and technical progress, industrial competitiveness and the implementation of its policies, the Union shall draw up a European space policy. To this end, it may promote joint initiatives, support research and technological development, and coordinate the efforts needed for the exploration and exploitation of space.
    2. To contribute to attaining the objectives referred to in paragraph 1, the European Parliament and the Council, acting in accordance with the ordinary legislative procedure, shall establish the necessary measures, which may take the form of a European space program, **excluding any harmonization of the laws and regulations of the Member States.**
    3. The Union shall establish any appropriate relations with the European Space Agency.
    4. This Article shall be without prejudice to the other provisions of this Title.

At the European level, Air transport fall within the entire harmonization competence of the EU in transports (TFEU Art. 4.g and Title VI Art. 90 to 100) and its safety regime is organized under the auspices of the European Aviation Safety Agency (EASA-EASE).

Among other important discrepancies as to Space law, we may underline that:
- *Aircraft registration* rules apply to vehicles or mobiles designed to travel and return on Earth (E to E) and not to be left permanently on Earth orbit or beyond to fulfill their main mission, like Space Objects or Space stations (E to S).
- Air law provides licensing on both sides of *Aircraft certification* and *Airlines companies'* operations, whereas FSOA focuses on the appropriate *Space Operator* and *Space Operation* and does not affect directly spacecraft and manufactures.
- As to *Liability regimes*, Space law considers only Third Party indemnification and remains uncertain with regard to the status of victims 'participating to the space operation'[53] as Air transport law is especially relevant on this matter toward passengers or crew as contracting parties (transport or employment contract).
- *Air Transport Contracts* and its liability and guaranty regimes are for a long time internationally standardized under the Warsaw Convention[54] that has been modernized by the Montreal Convention.[55] These conventions provide appropriate indemnification ceiling applicable by default, on damages to human death or injury and freight or baggage losses.
- As to *Development Governance*, the design and development phases of new civil Aircrafts are for many decades under the full responsibility of the private sector, with government support capacity being limited to *reimbursable aids* under the potential control of WTO and/or EU or USA's domestic laws and appropriate mechanisms and courts. Innovative Space systems or critical technology, even nowadays in the context of *New Space*, largely remain under the management or support of Space Agencies, at the national level.[56] This support may be achieved directly through traditional civil or defense agencies' Research & Technology Development programs or through procurement or partnership contracts for developing innovative systems or technology or for purchasing future associated services.[57]

---

53 UN Liability Convention of 1972, Art. VII.
54 12 October 1929 and 'The Hague Protocol' of 28 September 1955.
55 Convention of Montreal done on 28 May 1999, entered into force in Europe on 28 June 2004, ratified in France by Act n° 2003-380 of 24 April 2003 and published by Decree n° 2004-578 of 17 June 2004 at the official gazette (*JORF*) n° 143 of 22 June 2004 page 11205.
56 Even at the European level, within the framework of the European space agency (ESA) under the principle of geographical return (*i.e.* on principle, an allocation of contract to the domestic industry guaranteed in proportion of the relevant government contribution to ESA budget program).
57 For instance the NASA COTS program (Commercial Orbital Transportation Services), established by President G.W Bush in 2004, supporting Space X on Falcon 9 Launch services to the ISS, or even lately the

- The *Air traffic management* affects *civil transport of commercial aircrafts* using proven standardized template systems, operations control centers and procedures in all over the world under the auspices of the ICAO. Space traffic management, now still at the state of questioning, involves several kinds of space vehicles (controlled or not, manned or not), launching bases (on ground, sea, aircraft, launcher stage, etc.), orbits, radiofrequencies and missions (telecommunication, observation, navigation, Earth monitoring, defense applications, etc.) without any legal relation with transport services. This issue involves decision on priority rights on which even UN COPUOS may have limited competence at the international level.[58]

Obviously, all these differences of solution between Air transport law and Space law may be resolved by negotiation at the international level between by governments and stakeholders in order to develop suborbital flight activities. To that extent, it is worth noting the effort of the Office of Commercial Space Transportation (AST) of the U.S. Federal Aviation Administration (FAA) to promote an open dialogue at the international level.[59] AST-FAA has established the International Affairs Program to foster a common understanding of, and approach to, developing internationally consistent operational safety principles and procedures for commercial launch and reentry operations. Specifically, AST is sharing its regulatory philosophy with countries[60] interested in developing new spaceports and/or hosting U.S. commercial launch vehicles. Discussions on regulatory issues have been engaged with French representatives of CNES and DGAC since 2009.

To go back to concrete propositions of convergence on behalf of suborbital flights, we may consider a *sequential or cumulative application* of TRs and safety of Air law and Space law following the nature of operational phases. In any case, irrespective of the activity or the vehicle nature, common status will have to be retained at least with regard to:
- Human civil rules and victim's status respectively as third party, passengers or crew in particular, with regard to indemnification for death and injury;
- State's third-party liability and guarantees for a uniform protection of human interests (safety regulations, indemnification regime, etc.) and to avoid distortion of competition in the international market between private operators.

U.S. government pre-purchase of Earth Observation high resolution data on the 90s to its domestic private sector.
58 On the issue frequency spectrum: competence of IUT - on Space application services: competence of WTO, EU, etc. - on defence matters: UN security council or regional treaties (NATO), etc.
59 https://www.faa.gov/about/office_org/headquarters_offices/ast/programs/international_affairs.
60 Such as Sweden, United Kingdom, Spain, France, Japan, Singapore, Curacao, Italy, New Zealand, the European Union, and the European Aviation Safety Agency.

A closed dedicated working group created in France in 2015 under the auspices of the COSPACE (see below Chapter 8) has been assigned with the task to clarify the issue of licensing such flying systems and their associated ground facilities and operation services under French jurisdiction, regarding FSOA and/or aviation law. This study group, co-driven by CNES and the General directorate for Civil Aviation (DGAC), achieved its first report named 'Suborbital crafts – French Position' on 29 February 2016. It continued to be effective in 2018 in carrying out its consultations with industry in order to propose to the relevant authorities an enhanced appraisal report with associate buildings blocks of an appropriate legal framework. In any case, as of now, any person designing such suborbital systems may initiate an authorization application at any step through the procedure laid down in Article 11 of FSOA's Application decree of 9 June 2009.

Reusable space system, on-orbit services…
Launching or commanding a Space system in orbit or for its reentry to Earth are qualified as 'Space Operation' according to FSOA's scope, but some associated maneuvers regarding reusable Space system or in-orbit services (refueling, repairing in orbit, removal of Spacecraft, ground refurbishment process, technical event management, etc.) are not specifically addressed by its current French technical regulations which remain based on existing systems or systems known as being in a planned development. Furthermore, we may assume that the introduction of such systems will challenge the existing cross-waiver of claim as a well-established international custom between private stakeholders being associated in a given Space venture within their contractual chain.

Indeed, since any Spacecraft defects in functioning could be henceforth definitely proved in orbit or after a return on ground, customers, insurance companies or 'non-Space stakeholders' in particular may become more reluctant to accept exemptions or limitations of expected performances from their suppliers. As a result, current legislation, like the French one (FSOA's Art. 20), as making such clauses compulsory 'between persons taking part in the Space operation' regarding Space Object damage during the launch phase, or at least applicable by default during a Space Object command phase in orbit, may be reconsidered by lawmakers in order to render these waivers less systematic.

This also challenges the third-party liability regime based on the 'fault' for damage caused in-orbit (break up, system malfunction, etc.) pursuant to Article III of the 1972 Liability Convention which has been translated into the FSOA in its Article 13. As a matter of fact, this 'fault' regime has never been duly specified by any international authorized texts or any prominent case law. Whatsoever, studies are currently underway at the CNES level as relates to the relevant European Space projects in order to complete at first the necessary provisions in the technical regulations.

Exploitation of land or mining resources of celestial bodies (Moon, Mars, other planets, asteroids, etc.)

France has signed the 1979's UN 'Moon Agreement' which provides that the Moon and other Celestial Bodies and their natural resources are the common heritage of mankind (Art. 11.1 to 11.3) and that an international regime should be established to govern the exploitation of such resources when such exploitation is about to become feasible (Art. 11.5). However, France has not ratified so far this treaty so that the latest is not legally opposable up to now to the French State and not transposed into its domestic legislation. As a result, FSOA does not contain specific provisions for exploiting ground resources on celestial bodies but does not prevent any operations on a Space Object that could help such exploitation provided that, under FSOA's Art. 4:

- Such activities are compliant with the Technical Regulation[61] set forth for the safety of persons and property, the protection of public health and the environment.
- The systems intended to be implemented are not likely to jeopardize national defense interests or the respect by France of its international commitments, in particular the principle of non-appropriation under Article II of the 1967 UN Outer Space Treaty.[62]

FSOA regime also recognizes:

- The conservation of property rights on Space Objects launched or operated and registered under its framework (FSOA's Art. 12, Application decree Art. 14.1 to 14.6, Registration Order of 12 August 2011).
- Existing or created Intellectual Property Rights from Space Objects registered in France according to FSOA (Art. 22).

In addition, we may also underline the famous principle of 'freedom of trade and industry,' resulting from the 'Le Chapelier Act of 1792,' that was elevated by the jurisprudence of the Council of States to the level of 'general principle of law.'[63] This domestic principle may be enhanced by the European one of 'freedom of establishment' set out by of the Treaty on the Functioning of the European Union[64] and the case law of the Court of Justice of the European Union.

Indeed, these legal principles promoting the 'entrepreneurial freedom' may reverse the burden of the proof at the expense of administrations and on behalf of such private entrepreneurs, as far as security and safety regulations are satisfied. In this context, France

---

61 In particular, its provisions on the planetary protection in its Arts. 26 and 43.
62 Art. II: Outer Space, including the Moon and other celestial bodies, is not subject to national appropriation by claim of sovereignty, by means of use or occupation, or by any other means.
63 See 'Daudignac,' 22 June 1951, n° 00590 02551, published in Recueil Lebon.
64 TFUE Art. 49 and 54.

is advocating a prior international consensus on this matter before completing its national Space legislation on exploitation of land or mining resources of celestial bodies.

Other launch base than the Guiana Space Centre (CSG)

Current French technical regulations do not lay down any requirements on launch site design and operations except the one related to the CSG. The reason for this legal loophole on generic technical requirements as relates new launch bases is essentially practical and political. Firstly, practical because there is basically no special need for such regulation since the CSG's regulation (CSG)-REI is rendered fully enforceable as a consequence of FSOA enactment. Secondly political to address any concerns, even purely theoretical, that may be felt by the French budget authorities, ESA Member States and the associated industry stakeholders, as to the possibility of encouraging thereby a development of a competition with the CSG, the actual European Spaceport which monopolizes huge European investments and resources.

Indeed, Article 27 of the technical regulation (TR) only refers to the REI-CSG regulation for operations to be run from this site and for operations run from another launch site considers only the foreign sites in order to consider derogation that may be allowed in such circumstances under FSOA's Art. 4. However, nothing in this act shall prevent a private company to apply for an authorization, according to FSOA Article 2.1, to develop such ground facilities as an appropriate system "to proceed with the launching of a Space Object from the French territory." For that purpose, the applicant may use for a Space system, since the earliest development stage, the 'pre-application' procedures provided by Article 11 of the FSOA Authorization Decree, as detailed below in §7.1.6. This procedure indeed allows any person responsible for designing or developing a system or a subsystem that is critical having regard for the safety of people and property and the protection of public health and the environment, and which is intended to be used as part of a Space operation, to submit a file to the CNES describing the general technical characteristics and the development plan, so as to enable this center to certify its compliance, in whole or in part, with the FSOA's technical regulation.

In this regard, we may assume by analogy that the actual requirements provided for foreign sites will be the minimum set of specifications for new sites in France. Accordingly, an applicant for a new Space launching site should at least:
– furnish proof of the existence of the systems and procedures specific to said site, in particular concerning positioning, neutralization, and telemetry, designed to protect individuals, property, public health, and the environment during the course of the operation;
– furnish proof of the compatibility of the abovementioned systems and procedures with the requirements of this Technical Regulation;

– demonstrate that the launcher is designed and produced to ensure compatibility with the abovementioned systems and procedures.

In any case, here also, the current lack of specific legal or regulation framework shall not be construed as an obstacle for the development of new Space systems but a real opportunity to design, through appropriate consultation between the government department and the relevant private stakeholders, a 'tailor-made' regulation that would set out the best from the FSOA, REI, and TR background as well as proposing innovative and adapted solutions to the benefit of these enterprises. For this purpose, the procedure for preliminary certification set up through Article 11 of the Authorization Decree (see §7.1.6 below) not only helps the industry to secure the compliance of its new systems since the early design phases, but also enables CNES and the Administrative Authority to provide necessary adjustments on the existing legal and regulatory framework as to be ready to examine application under the formal authorization purpose of FSOA, of the new designed system once fully developed.

FSOA's exemptions
Derogations expressly provided for in the FSOA
In accordance with FSOA's principles on responsibility and safety, *exemption or derogation* may be granted by the Administrative Authority for a given Space Operation along its design phase or exploitation phase, either on a temporary basis or upon appropriate demonstration in light of the actual technical, financial, or legal circumstances. Thus, the term 'derogation' shall not be assimilated hereby to the one of 'exclusion' above which refers to matters actually *outside the scope of this SOA*. Basically, on a legal and global standpoint, an exemption may be granted in any legal decision or measure according to the prominent principle of 'parallelism of competence' under the French administrative law. This means that any regulatory decision taken by a competent authority, or in other words acted in compliance with higher legal norms (Constitution, Statute Law, Application Decree, etc.), can be cancelled or amended by the same authority, under the same formalism, subject to the non-retroactive effect of laws and if so, the respect for individual vested rights.

Possibilities of exemption or derogation have also been expressively provided for in by the Act subject to specification to be set forth in a decree passed at the Council of State,[65] namely in the FSOA's Application decree. Among the main derogations specially allowed by the act itself:

---

65 Consistent with Art. 37, second sentence, of the French Constitution, which states that: 'Provisions of statutory origin (*i.e. from an act*) enacted in regulation may be amended by decree issued after consultation with the Council of State.'

- The famous Article 4. 4° regards the possibility for the Administrative Authority to exempt the applicability, in all or in part, of the **Technical Regulation** compliance checking control for an operation which is to be carried out from the territory of a **foreign State** or from means or facilities falling under the jurisdiction of a foreign State. This exemption is however subjected to specific conditions in particular, that the national and international commitments made by that State as well as its legislation and practices include sufficient guarantees regarding the safety of persons and property and the protection of public health and the environment, and liability matters. Reference of this exemption is accordingly made in Article 12 of the Authorization Decree.
- Article 6. 1°, second paragraph, regards the **compulsory insurance or financial guarantee** required for Space operators to cover third-party damage. It provides for a decree to be passed at the Council of State to set forth the terms of such insurance or the nature of the financial guarantees that may be accepted by the competent authority but also to specific conditions in which the Administrative Authority may exempt the operator from such insurance and guaranty requirements.

As a consequence, Article 17 of the Authorization Decree allows the Ministers responsible for Space and for Budget to jointly decide to exempt the operator, for a limited period of time, from its *obligation of insurance*, if it is impossible, given the situation of the insurance market, to cover the operation by an insurance policy or to furnish one of the financial guarantees. Another exemption is provided for by Article 18 of the same decree on behalf of geostationary satellites in exploitation during its nominal station-keeping period, when there are no orbit position changes or other maneuver terminating satellite station-keeping.

The Technical Regulations also bear a lot of exemptions but, as a common rule, *any derogation* to a given requirement shall be firstly provided for in the relevant regulation and secondly be *duly justified*, on the operator's burden, by an impossibility of meeting this initial requirement. Furthermore, in no way such impossibility should relieve the operator from its obligations of safety being understood that any derogation allowed bears its alternative or mitigation solutions that shall be then respected. The rationale behind these exemptions may result from the same *risk management norms* from which the technical regulations have been extracted, in particular norms for the management, *engineering and product assurance* in Space projects extracted or derived from respective standards of ECSS,[66] IADC, or ISO, as being established within Space agencies as mission requirements for planned Spacecraft and orbital stages.

---

66 European Cooperation for Space Standardization (ECSS), cooperation under the auspices of the European Space Agency.

As relates to the ECSS ones, the Space Project Risk Management standard[67] provides for the possibility of 'acceptance of risks'[68] as a 'decision to cope with consequences, should a risk scenario materialize' in association with two notes stating:
- "A risk can be accepted when its magnitude is less than a given threshold defined in the risk management policy."
- "In the context of risk management, acceptance can mean that even though a risk is not eliminated, its existence and magnitude are acknowledged and tolerated."

Regarding the IADC's Space Debris Mitigation Guidelines as being translated into a resolution of the United Nation's General Assembly on 22 December 2007,[69] we may also retain the same logic of requirements of doing or nor doing something in *normal or nominal situations* with associated exemption or alternative mitigations measures should such requirements cannot be met. As a matter of fact, these international organizations propose guidelines that should be considered for the mission planning, design, manufacture, and operational (launch, mission, and disposal) phases of any Spacecraft and launch vehicle orbital stages. Thus, one of the unique features of FSOA's Technical Regulation was to translate such not legally binding guidelines or principles into *enforceable provisions* but associated with the same *enforceable exemptions*.

---

67 'Space Project Management – Risk Management,' ECTS-M-ST-80C, Published by ESA Publication Division, ESTEC, P.O. Box 299, 2200 AG Noordwijk, The Netherlands. Copyright: 2008 © by the European Space Agency for the members of ECSS.
68 See ECTS-M-ST-80C above, under Article Art. 3-2 terms specific to the present standard, §3-2-1 'Acceptance of (risk)'.
69 The Inter-Agency Space Debris Coordination Committee (IADC) is an inter-Space agency technical forum founded in 1993, whose aim is to coordinate efforts to deal with debris in orbit around the Earth. Its membership comprises major Space agencies: Agenzia Spaziale Italiana (ASI), Centre National d'Etudes Spatiales (CNES), China National Space Administration (CNSA), Canadian Space Agency (CSA), German AeroSpace Center (DLR), European Space Agency (ESA), Indian Space Research Organisation (ISRO), Japan AeroSpace Exploration Agency (JAXA), Korea AeroSpace Research Institute (KARI), National Aeronautics and Space Administration (NASA), Russian Federal Space Agency (ROSCOSMOS), State Space Agency of Ukraine (SSAU), United Kingdom Space Agency (UKSA). Its working group n° 4 adopted in September 2007 the IADC Mitigation Guidelines (IADC-02-01 September 2007 – action item 22-4).
The Space Debris Mitigation Guidelines were then adopted by the Scientific and Technical Subcommittee of the United Nation Committee on the Peaceful Uses of the Outer Space (UN-COPUOS) at its 673rd meeting (STSC 44th session, A/AC.105/890, para. 99, Annexe IV) and endorsed by the full Committee at its 572nd meeting (COPUOS 50th session. In report of the COPUOS – Official Records of the General Assembly, 62nd Session, supplement n° 20 (A/62/20), paras. 117 and 118, and the Annex, p. 47-50) and then by the U.N. General Assembly on 22 December 2007 (Agenda item 31, Resolution n° 62/217, para. 26).
CNES proper standard on debris management were initially compiled in 'Standards Collection, Method and Procedure Space Debris – Safety Requirements' (RNC-CNES-Q40-512) (1999).

Other legal exemptions on space operations: turnover taxes, fees ...
Independently from the FSOA's scope, it is worth to underline in this section on legal exemptions the derogatory tax regime established on behalf of Space operations, and more particularly on 'turnover' generated thereof. The tax scheme for Space services has been developed between the 1970s and 1980s in France through several individual decisions taken by the French Tax Authorities[70] that were directly notified to the interested parties. These decisions regarding new outer Space activities were taken consistently with existing General Principle of French Tax Law, in accordance with the EU's common system of value-added tax (VAT),[71] under the supervision of the famous Tax Legislation Department.

This led to the tax exemption on launch services from the French Guiana based on the principle that *'Outer Space is an export territory'*[72] as regards French tax law, being understood that a delivery in-orbit is a transaction beyond the territorial jurisdiction of such law. This exemption on export delivery however, as a general VAT rule for any export, does not call into question the right to deduct the amount of VAT paid on acquired goods or services in any EU country for the purpose of carrying out this Space service. Such right to deduct 'input VAT' may also be shifted into a right to be fully reimbursed the associated VAT paid or even to obtain a general exemption for any transaction upstream associated with such Space operation (*e.g.,* launcher manufacturing) for the benefit of all stakeholders involved in the manufacturing of the launcher, its satellite, or other payload launched in outer Space.

It should be emphasized that notwithstanding these upstream *export exemptions* on behalf of space operations, states retain the full capacity to tax *downlink services* (telecommunications, data, broadcasting, etc.) rendered or consumed in their territory, according to the general rules of VAT on *imports*. Basically exemptions in Europe on export delivery operates two times: firstly, for *deliveries* of spacecraft (launcher satellite and associate components) from Europe, included from French's European territory, to French Guiana; and secondly, for the supply of launch services from Guiana, since such overseas department has its own tax system based on business turnover called 'Octroi de Mer.' As a result, any delivery from the European territory associated with a good to be launched outer Space from the CSG launch base in French Guiana will be at least exported

---

70 The DGFIP (*Direction Générale des finances publiques*) of the Ministry of Budget, its Tax Legislation Department (*Direction de la Legislation Fiscale*) or its executive Tax General Directorate, the DGI (*Direction Générale des Impôts*).
71 The EU's common system of value added tax (VAT) is now currently codified by Council Directive 2006/112/EC of 28 November 2006 on the common system of value added tax. Successive amendments and corrections have been incorporated into the basic text by the following texts, in particular Council Directive 2009/132/EC of 19 October 2009 determining the scope of Art. 143(b) and (c) of Directive 2006/112/EC as regards exemption from value added tax on the final importation of certain goods (OJ L 292, 10.11.2009, p. 5-30).
72 This principle is recalled in many coherent decisions taken by the DGI and notified directly to the space industry and CNES for the needs of given projects since the 1970's.

and exempted twice with regard to VAT and 'Octroi de Mer', the one between Europe's mainland[73] and Guiana and the second from Guiana territory to 'outer-Space export'.

The time at which the *service delivery* takes effect regarding *VAT generator event* is the moment when the launching operations become irreversible, namely the ignition of powder booster engines for Ariane 5 or the opening of the gantry's hook for Soyuz or Ariane 4. This time refers to the starting of the launch phase regarding Article 1.4 of FSOA and not to the end of such Space operation performance which shall occur when the 'Space Object' (satellite or other payload) is separated from its launch vehicle. At this point it is worth reminding a cause and effect relationship between FSOA's regime, tax law, and current international agreement practices since the event of irreversible launch is also generally retained in contracts of sale between the satellite manufacturer and its customer as the effective time of transfer of ownership and risks. The same event is also retained in most Launch Services Agreements (LSA) as the effective time of transferring the 'risk of loss' between the launch service provider and its satellite operator's customer regarding the latest's launched payload.

Thus, let's recall that it may appear surprising to any ordinary observer that the transfer of risks (*i.e.*, the burden of the loss on the asset) could be achieved notwithstanding the fact that the service provider has not yet achieved its contract performance as to delivering the satellite in the agreed orbit! The rationale for such singular contractual provision still results from the traditional 'best effort clauses' set up in LSA to the benefit of the launch service provider's performance, as well as the associated 'waivers of claim.' The whole clause system thus excludes any contractual responsibility from the service provider once its launcher basically switches into an automatic phase, *i.e.*, just after its irreversible liftoff.

To conclude this development on Space operation tax regimes exemption, we may retain upstream that any delivery made to ESA with regard to its programs and facilities is exempted from any kind of taxes, duties, and fees consistent with this international organization's status. Such exemption was subsequently extended to the production or exploitation phase of these ESA-developed launcher systems. It can be deduced therefore that the French government shall refrain from any domestic taxation on launcher services transaction as being generated from the entire European stakeholder community.

Last but not least, the FSOA regime has not provided for any application fees or tax to be paid by the private sector on the Space operation authorizing or licensing process.

7.1.3 Authorization or License Application – Actors Concerned

As stated before, the Administrative Authority responsible for the authorization and control of operations is the ministry in charge of Space, namely the Ministry of Higher Education

---

73 Or 'Europe métropolitaine' under the French expression.

and Research under section 1 of the authorization decree (AD). The CNES therefore has no decision-making power in this regard. Nonetheless, according to this act (Art. 28), CNES remains solely responsible, on behalf of the Administrative Authority, for proposing TRs, ensuring monitoring compliance with them and keeping the register of Space Objects.[74] Moreover, the President of the CNES is vested with proper regulatory and administrative police powers as regard to activities performed in the launch range facilities of the Guiana Space Centre. Such powers are actually delegated to the Director of the CSG.[75]

7.1.3.1 Authorizations for a French Launch Operator or for any Person Providing a Launch Service in the French Territory

Regarding launches or returns to Earth, any operator intending to launch or return a Space Object to *French territory*, or to means or *facilities under French jurisdiction* must request authorization to do so. This is a classic application of the territorial criterion of the law (jurisdictional *ratione loci*). Also covered are operators of French nationality who intend to carry out the same operations outside any jurisdiction (on the high seas or from Space, for example) or abroad, even if the French government has no sovereignty in the country within the meaning of Article VI[76] of the 1967 Space Treaty. This is the application of the personal criterion of the law (jurisdictional *ratione personae*). The purpose of this was for the legislator, despite its lack of territorial jurisdiction, to leave to the French State a means of controlling, at least on the legal or contractual level, any such operation that might entail its liability as a 'launch State' if there is damage, within the meaning of the UN 1972 Convention.

Accordingly, Article 4 §4 of the FSOA[77] may provide for an exemption from monitoring compliance with its Technical Regulations given that France has no jurisdiction to effectively

---

74 FSOA Art. 28 – AD Art. 3 et seq. D – CNES Art. 14.
75 FSOA Art. 21, D-CNES Arts. 14-7 to 14-16.
76 Art. VI of the 1967 Outer Space Treaty: States Parties to the Treaty shall bear international responsibility for national activities in outer Space, including the Moon and other celestial bodies, whether such activities are carried on by governmental agencies or by *nongovernmental entities*, and for assuring that national activities are carried out in conformity with the provisions set forth in the present Treaty. The activities of nongovernmental entities in outer Space, including the Moon and other celestial bodies, shall require *authorization and continuing supervision* by the *appropriate State Party* to the Treaty. When activities are carried on in outer Space, including the Moon and other celestial bodies, by an international organization, responsibility for compliance with this Treaty shall be borne both by the international organization and by the States Parties to the Treaty which are part of that organization.
77 FSOA Art. 4 §4: 'A decree passed at the Council of State shall set forth the terms of application of the present article. It shall specify in particular: … 4° When an authorization is solicited for an operation which is to be carried out from the territory of a foreign State or from means or facilities falling under the jurisdiction of a foreign State, the conditions in which the administrative authority may exempt the applicant from all or any part of the compliance checking mentioned in the first paragraph, when the national and international commitments made by that State as well as its legislation and practices include sufficient guarantees regarding the safety of persons and property and the protection of public health and the environment, and liability matters.'

enforce such monitoring abroad. This exemption on Technical Regulation's application may therefore be conditional on the presentation by the applicant operator of equivalent guarantees in technical, financial, and contractual terms to be granted by the foreign State or the local operator. The conditions for such *equivalent guarantees* to are described in fairly general terms in Article 12 of the AD.[78]

7.1.3.2   Authorizations for a French Satellite Operator

The satellite in-orbit command phase begins after separation from the launcher with the stationing of the satellite on its mission orbit and continues with its station-keeping during its stay in outer Space until the engagement of end-of-life operations. It includes several operations from the necessary readjustment maneuvers in the routine mode, to the case by case avoidance of other Space Objects or debris, and any changes in orbits, and lastly to the end-of-life maneuvers such as passivation, placing in a graveyard orbit, controlled or accelerated return to Earth, etc. This means the command phase may itself cover several successive phases of interventions sometimes conducted by several operators acting in series on the same Space vehicle, as mentioned in §7.1.2.1 above for FSOA operators and §7.1.2.2 on registration of space objects. Thus, each operator shall be required to get a dedicated authorization to cover its obligations in the corresponding phase of operation, namely its potential liability and guarantee for damage caused to third parties.

Accordingly, any French person who intends to command a satellite must obtain firstly an authorization to proceed with its launch and secondly to ensure its command during its stay in outer Space. This therefore means the number of authorization permit to be requested by the operator is two. However, adjustments have been provided as relates to the procured launch, whether from domestic or foreign origin:
- When the launch is to be carried out in France, according to Article 6 of the 'authorization decree',[79] the launch may be relieved of the technical compliance control if it provides the authorization already issued under FSOA to the launch provider concerned. This exemption makes it possible to avoid a duplicate review of the technical compliance

---

78   AD Art. 12: "When the authorization application relates to an operation to be conducted from the territory of a foreign State or from means or facilities placed under the jurisdiction of a foreign government, the applicant shall, as applicable, furnish all the information needed to assess the existence of the guarantees referred to in section 4° of Art. 4 of the abovementioned Act of 3 June 2008 which exempts it from all or part of the compliance control provided for in the first paragraph of the same article. In the manner set forth in Art. 5, the Minister shall inform the applicant of his decision, either to grant the exemption sought, or the reasons for his decision to deny it."
79   AD Art. 6: "If, in support of an application to have a Space Object launched, a French operator furnishes the launch authorization obtained by the operator responsible for launching said Space Object, it shall not be required to furnish the technical part described in II of Art. 1 of this decree. In the case provided for in the previous paragraph, the authorization to have the Object launched shall be deemed granted if the Minister responsible for Space has not replied within a month of the date of registration of the application."

for the same launch. It applies in particular to those made by Arianespace from French Guiana in which the client is French and subject to the FSOA, which is the case for example of Eutelsat.
- When the launch is to be carried out outside French jurisdiction, Article 4 §4 of the FSOA may provide for an exemption from monitoring compliance with the *technical regulations* (TR) as discussed in §7.1.3.1.

Conversely, a foreign satellite operator procuring a launch service from a French Space Operator under FSOA is not personally subject to this act as to such launch procurement and *a fortiori* for any operation beyond this launching phase, *i.e.*, the satellite phase of command, whose responsibility and associated liability is handed back to such foreign operator in association with the appropriate Registration or Launching State according to the UN Space Treaties.

7.1.3.3 Disposals and Transfer of the Command of a Satellite in Orbit by or for a French Operator

Over and above these situations already considered by the three main United Nations treaties on Space, the national authorization system has extended its application to commercial transactions (sales, corporate mergers and acquisitions, satellite assignments, etc.), provided they result in transfers of command's responsibility between national and foreign operators on satellites already in orbit. The purpose of this is for the French state to obtain on such occasions all the necessary guarantees, both from private entities and the other launch States concerned:

- *In case of sale, with transfer of command and jurisdiction, of a French registered satellite to a foreign operator*, the French government will seek to ensure that the assignee or its own State assumes liability, or vouches for it in case of third-party claims, for any future damage caused by the transferee, but which may be incumbent upon France at the first level, as the originally declared Launching State under the UN 1972 Liability Convention.
- *Conversely, if a national operator acquires the ownership and command of a foreign satellite already in orbit*, the French government will have to ensure when considering the authorization request that the risks of a satellite that may soon be a wreck are not transferred to it. Thus the satellite's operations must comply with the TRs or, failing that, the State of the assignor or the assignor itself must provide France with all the necessary guarantees.

7.1.4   Administrative and Technical Criteria

With regard to government granting and controlling authorizations to operate Space vehicles, this legislation has sought to define *objective criteria* recognized by best practices. The authorization request is subject to a double review of compliance with the *technical and administrative criteria*, which are intended to meet the same objective, *i.e.*, the interest of 'the safety of persons and property, the protection of public health and the environment' (FSOA Art. 4, 5, 8, etc.).

7.1.4.1   The Administrative Review

'Administrative compliance' is assessed at the governmental level in coordination between the Minister for Space and those Ministers for Foreign Affairs and Finance. This review mainly focuses on the *operator's moral, financial, and technical aptitude*, and its *compliance with France national defense interests or international commitments* (FSOA Art. 4 first and second paragraph – AD Art. 1 part 1). As a matter of fact, most of these conditions about the current operators (Arianespace, Eutelsat, etc.) are accepted once and for all by their *administrative license* granted for 10 years as detailed in §7.1.5 below. The administrative review is then limited to status changes, to specific terms and conditions or derogations on the financial guaranty or insurance covers.[80]

For the purpose of exempting from monitoring compliance with the TR for operations to be conducted abroad or outside French jurisdiction, this administrative review may have to evaluate whether requirements are met with regard to national and international commitments made by the relevant State. Such review considers whether this foreign legislation and practices, on the technical, conventional, or financial terms, from the *State or the local operator*, offer sufficient guarantees regarding the safety of persons and property and the protection of public health and the environment. The burden of proof on 'sufficient guarantees' rests with the applicant (FSOA Article 4 §4. – AD Art. 12). As a result, on this sole hypothesis of an operation implemented outside French jurisdiction, *i.e.*, for the procurement of a foreign service to launch a French satellite or to transfer the latest of command, we may assume that the administrative review can be the substitute for the technical review, as being detailed in §7.1.4.2 below.

The administrative review also provides the opportunity, for the Ministry for Space, to consult where appropriate the relevant ministries' departments in charge of granting other authorizations or licenses affecting the same Space systems, as relates to its frequency band allocations, payload services exploitation (broadcast, telecommunication, Earth

---

80   Derogations under the Arts. 17 and 18 of the Authorization Decree: *see below* Chapter 2, first bullet: 'The scope of liability for damage to third parties and associated insurance.'

observation, etc.) or export control concerns[81]. This role of single administrative point of contact played by the Minister for Space is essential to check the consistency of the respective decisions to be taken on a same Space system in the name of the French government taking into account its national and international responsibilities.

7.1.4.2 The Technical Review on Systems and Procedures Implemented in Space Operation

The high standard set by FSOA in terms of technical compliance review is one of the main characteristics of this national authorization regime in comparison to other similar regimes, in particular within Europe.[82]

Basically, the FSOA's higher requirements is due to the importance of launching activities in the CSG that this legislation is the only one to address in Europe. This high standard is also presented by the French government as the fair counterpart to its guarantee offered to private operators for the indemnification of damage caused to third parties. The investigation of the operator's systems and procedures compliance with the Technical Regulation is entrusted to the CNES under the terms of the act itself (FSOA Art. 28). The President of the CNES or his/her delegate is also responsible for ensuring compliance with the Guiana Space Centre Safety Regulations (REI) if the system is operated from the CSG (FSOA Art 21). This technical compliance assessment is compulsory for any operation under the scope of FSOA, with the exception for operations to be conducted abroad or outside French jurisdiction based on the guarantees obtained as mentioned above (FSOA Article 4 §4. – AD Art. 12).

According to the Authorization decree, the *operator's technical file* must describe the Space operation to be conducted and the systems and procedures to be implemented. This file includes (AD Art. 1 II) the common requirements for all operations and systems:

a) The General **Notice of compliance** with the technical regulations. Through this solemn declaration the operator certifies the completeness of its systems and procedure compliance with the provisions of the Technical regulation.

b) The internal standards and **quality management** provisions applicable as part of the Space operation to be carried out. These provisions regarding the given operation complete general information required on the administrative part of the file (AD Art. 1, I, 2°) about the applicant's company quality management systems and internal staff qualification and training policies.

---

81 As detailed below in §7.5 'Other procedures and legislations to be respected in France order to operate a satellite or satellite payload services.'

82 For instance, the United Kingdom Space Act of 1986 presently in force remains more demanding on the operator's legal and financial guarantees toward the State in terms of liability. The Luxembourg licensing process, which affects the major worldwide telecommunication satellite's operators (such as SES and Intelsat) has not formalized up to now technical requirements.

c) All the **measures**, including the **hazard studies** and **risk management plans** to ensure the safety of people and property and the protection of public health and the environment.d) **Impact studies on the environment** and the measures designed to avoid, reduce, or offset the adverse effects on the environment:
- The risk prevention plan relating to hazards caused by the fall-back to Earth of the Space Object or fragments thereof,
  - The environmental damage prevention plan as defined in Article L.161-1 of the environment code,
  - The Space debris limitation plan,
  - The collision risk prevention plan,
  - As applicable, the nuclear safety plan,
  - As applicable, the planetary protection plan.

e) The **risk management measures during the conduct of the operation** (*i.e.*, flight safety, ground safety)

f) The planned **emergency measures**

Then, the technical regulation issued by order of 31 March 2011 develops the rational basis of the compliance control, in particular concepts of hazard studies, impact studies, risk management plan and associated measures set out above (in c to f).

This regulation stipulates the technical *objectives of safety, quantitatively and qualitatively*, that any system and its associated procedures shall meet to be authorized for operations under the FSOA. As mentioned above (§6.6.4), this technical regulation represents an autonomous legal instrument, derived from existing practices both on engineering quality assurance and safety control. These practices were defined and enforced by CNES since its inception in its capacity of national Space agency and contracting authority for the needs of its Space projects. Basically, this technical authority results from its responsibilities in the launching base of CSG as recognized at least since 1975 in the same name agreement between the French government and ESA.

More specifically, the background of this technical regulations stems from provisions of the actual CNES' *Safeguard (or Safety) Doctrine*, as formulated into several sectorial internal Safeguard Regulation,[83] as well as other existing quality control standards or rules such as the *Ariane Management Specification (SMA)* regarding launcher exploitation. When the FSOA was issued, these technical standards and rules were already widely adopted by industry and private operators being in contractual relationship with CNES and have been copied for the needs of their own follow-up private systems. The rationale of all these technical rules results from the importance of risks for person and goods associated with

---

83   Sectorial Safeguard Regulations were actually safety, work, or operating instruction issued by the head of centers or directors concerned.

Space operations, in particular due to the huge quantity of energy and hazardous materials stored in launchers and satellites.

These 'risk mastery' regulations are thus closely linked with the quality standard of CNES[84] on system design based on the famous motto 'reliability is the first barrier of safety.' On the other hand, as an exception to the principle 'dura lex, sed lex'[85] these regulations may have a pragmatic and protective approach in allowing as much as possible in non-nominal[86] situations, *i.e.*, an unexpected situation, to save the success of the mission lives of the Space vessels and their payload.

In any case, it must be reminded (TR Art. 2 §4) that compliance with such requirements may in no way relieve the operator of its liability for any damage caused to third parties, as specified in FSOA's Art. 13, nor the French government's one as Launching State under OST Art. VII and the 1972 Liability Convention. However, any willful infringement of TR's provisions or severe inobservance shall deprive the relevant operator of its rights regarding the State guarantee coverage set in FSOA Articles 14 to 17, and probably, as a result, of its private insurance compensation, as subscribed under FSOA Article 6.

The TR's methodology is generated pursuant to its Article 7 for a launch of a Space Object and Article 32 for control and return to Earth of a Space Object.[87]

It consists firstly to identify, in the **hazard (or risk) study** (or assessment),[88] the *'feared event'* (FE)[89] as material or human failures capable of generating catastrophic or severe consequences, in terms of damage to persons, property, public health, and the environment. Basically, it is implied that the 'feared events' were formerly identified originally during the qualification process of the system during its design and development phase. This hazard or risk study includes a description of all the hazards related to the operation in nominal and accidental operating situations, whether their cause is internal or external.

On launch services, such 'feared events' (TR Art. 7) are listed as follows:
- Damage linked to fallback of elements designed to separate from the launcher;
- Damage linked to controlled or uncontrolled reentry of launcher elements placed in earth orbit;

---

84 To that effect see TR's Arts. 11 to 19 for the launch of a Space Object and Arts. 35and 38 for the control and return to Earth of a Space Object.
85 'The law is harsh but it is the law'.
86 Situation that is contrary to a 'Nominal' situation, the latest corresponding, according to TR Art. 1, to the specifications or performance levels announced by the operator or designer of the Space Object.
87 For articles of reference on this methodology on launch systems conformity to the technical regulation, see C. Aussilhou & D. Miot, 'Launch Systems Conformity Training Process and Academic Methodology'; CNES, Launcher s' Directorate, caroline.assilhou@cnes.fr..François Cahuzac, Stephane Louvel (CNES) 'Implementation of the French act Space Operation Act for launchers and contribution to the control of risks' IAC-12, E7,5,13,x16006.
88 The 'hazard study' is mentioned in AD Art. 1 II (c) ,its French name is Etude de danger or EdR.
89 In French: *Evenement Redouté* or ER.

- Damage linked to failure of the launch vehicle;
- Collision with manned Space Objects, for which the orbital parameters are precisely known and available;
- Damage linked to explosion of a stage in orbit;
- Collision with a celestial body

Regarding orbit control or return to Earth operations on Space Object, the *fear events* are listed as follow:[90]
- Human injury caused by a reentry to Earth,
- Production of Space debris following an explosion,
- Collision with a manned Space Object,
- Injection in a degraded orbit leading to premature reentry,
- Collision with a satellite in geostationary orbit, whose orbital parameters are precisely known and available, during station acquisition, repositioning, or disposal maneuvers,
- Dispersion of radioactive material,
- Planetary contamination.

The *hazard study* must include an exhaustive analysis of the causes and consequences as well as the probabilities of the abovementioned FE. Its purpose is to appreciate the *criticality of risks* which is expressed by multiplying the 'severity' of the event by its 'probability.' The launch operator must therefore demonstrate **compliance with the 'quantity' requirement**[91] **regarding 'catastrophic damage'**[92] **to individuals**. This *quantity requirement* requires from the operator to respect at any time a maximum allowable probability of causing at least one casualty or one victim. This *probability* 'Allocation'[93] varies according to the considered *period of risk event*.[94] Its calculation has to take into account many factors listed respectively in Articles 20-2 and 44-2 but no specific enforceable formula has been released. This demonstration of compliance however can be made by using some tools made available

---

90 TR. Art. 32.
91 As set in Art. 20 for the launch of a Space Object and Arts. 44 and 45 for the control and return to Earth of a Space Object.
92 'Catastrophic damage' is defined in TR Art. 1 as an immediate or deferred loss of human life, or serious human injury (bodily injuries, other irreversible health impairments, occupational invalidity or illness, either permanent or temporary).
93 'Allocation' is defined in TR Art. 1 as a "level of probability given to the occurrence of a critical or specified event, when determining the safety Objective."
94 2×10^{-5} for the entire launch phase; 10^{-7} by nominal fall back of those launchers elements not designed be placed in orbit (*e.g.*, the boosters EAP for Ariane V); 2×10^{-5} for a controlled atmospheric re-entry of those launcher elements placed in orbit, with a reduction tolerated up to 10^{-4} if the impossibility of a controlled atmospheric re-entry can be duly proven by the operator.

by CNES[95] for that purpose to operators, as provided for in the Best Practice Guide mentioned below.

The launch operator must also evaluate more globally the **effects of any accidents on public health and the environment**. In line with the 'authorization decree' Art. 1 II (d),[96] the operator must carry out an **environmental** *impact assessment* that covers *nominal operation* of the launch system. This study covers the impact of the *planned operation* on the (Earth) environment and on public health, in particular with regard to the provisions of Article L 161-1 of the French Environment Code, as well as the impact in terms of production of Space debris, in accordance with the provisions of TR (Art. 21 or 40).

On the basis of the conclusions of the **hazard and impact assessments** above, the launch operator draws up and implements **hazard management plans** according to TR Art. 9[97]. This risks management policy, as promoted by this regulation regarding 'Feared Events,' rests on two main pillars:

- **Risk (or hazard) prevention.** These measures consist in getting rid of **causes,** or limiting their occurrence, by strengthening the launcher reliability, by changing the wrong equipment if possible, by choosing another launcher trajectory path. However it should be pointed out that risk prevention measures may be jeopardized, on a proven qualified and industrialized Space system, by technical difficulties, delays, or high cost of changing its designed architecture or components, being understood that any change requires an additional qualification process and may introduce new other risks on the reliability or safety of such system.
- **Risk treatment.** These measures which do not affect the initial design of the system or its existing implementation process consist only in mitigating the **effects** of the FE. This means to find solutions to make risk tolerable, such as to limit the number of persons locally exposed to the risk on ground, to limit the launcher hazardousness (*e.g.,* its 'neutralization'[98]).

---

95 STELA to verify that the satellite will remain outside the protected region A and B (Art. 40 §4 and 5). DEBRISK to identify the satellite elements which would reach the ground during atmospheric re-entry. ELECTRA to evaluate the risk for Earth re-entry (downloadable http://logiciels.cnes.fr/STELA).
96 As set in TR: Art. 8 for the launch of a Space Object and Art. 33 for the control and return to Earth of a Space Object.
97 Art. 9 for the launch of a Space Object and Art. 34 for the control and return to Earth of a Space Object.
98 The concept of *Neutralisation* is defined both in the TR and REI-CSG (Articles Art. 1) as an "action taken on the launcher in order to minimise damage to individuals and property. It can in particular be characterised by an action to destroy or stop the thrust of a launch vehicle, in order to terminate the flight of the considered vehicle or a stage which is no longer functioning correctly."

This hazard management policy also highlight the difference between **nominal**[99] and **non-nominal** situations, **controlled and not controlled reentries**[100]. It is understood however that an **uncontrolled** reentry of an end-of-life Space Object may be a **nominal situation** (*e.g.,* the situations to managed under TR Art. 45). To this end, in accordance with the requirements of Articles 18 to 26 for the launch of a Space Object, and Articles 39 to 49 for the control (command or mastery) and return to Earth of a Space Object, the operator shall draw up and implement the following risk management plans: an environmental damage prevention plan, a Space debris limitation plan, a fallback prevention plan of Space Objects or fragments, a collision risks prevention plan, an emergency measures plan, and, as applicable, a nuclear safety plan or a planetary protection plan.

Among these requirements, we may focus on *debris mitigation*, in particular as it relates to noncontrolled Space Objects (Cubesat, nanosat, very small satellites, etc.), planetary protection, technical requirements concerning the launch site, and launching phase for GEO satellites.

In Article 39 of the TR, the 'Ability to control (or command) the Space Object' implies that the latter must be designed, produced, and implemented in such a way that the operator, for the duration of the operation, can receive information about its status and send it commands, in particular those necessary to:

- Reduce the risk on the ground in case of **non-nominal reentries** (premature or accidental) according to Art 47;
- Perform the **disposal (end-of-life) maneuvers** as specified in paragraphs 3, 4, and 5 of Article 40, namely:[list]
- **Passivation of storage tanks** (3): all the onboard energy reserves are permanently depleted or placed in such a condition that they entail no risk of generating debris, all the means for producing energy onboard are permanently deactivated.
- **Protected Region A**[101] – Low Earth Orbit (4): withdrawal (or de-orbitation) of the Space Object with controlled atmospheric reentry to the Earth, or if impossibility duly proven, it must be operated so that it is no longer present in protected region A **twenty-five years after the end of the operational phase.**

---

99 As defined in TR Art.1: Nominal: corresponding to the specifications or performance levels announced by the operator or designer of the Space Object (*e.g.,* flight corridor around nominal trajectory in Art. 17.6). On the contrary, a premature or accidental re-entry is defined as non-nominal according to Art. 47.

100 As defined in TR Art.1: Controlled *(non-controlled)* re-entry: atmospheric re-entry of a Space Object **with a predefined contact or ground impact zone** (*for which it is not possible to predefine the ground impact zone)* **for** *(by)* the Object or fragments thereof.

101 **Protected region A**, low Earth orbit (LEO) – spherical region extending from the surface of the Earth up to an altitude (Z) of 2,000 km.

- **Protected Region B**[102] – Geostationary orbit (5): The Space Object must be operated in such a way that, once it has completed its operational phase, it shall be placed in an orbit which does not interfere with region B. This orbit must be such as, under the effect of natural disturbances, the Object does not return to protected region B within one hundred years following the end of the operation.[/list]

Equivalent rules are set to protect the same regions from launcher's components or debris generated after the end of the launching phase (TR Art. 21 paragraph 5).[103]

In this regards it should be recalled that RFOA's technical regulations, in particular the prevention measures concerning debris set out in Articles 21, 24, and 39 to 41, have transposed into a legally binding text for private players, international mitigation guidelines from IADC, ISO, etc. which, until then, fell under recommendations or best practice appliqued on a voluntary basis within the most demanding governmental space agencies. However, most of the existing launching systems[104] as well as very small satellites (Cubesats) have not been designed to be controlled after being launched. In other words, these Space Objects nominally were not supposed to be commanded once orbited. Thus, FSOA's technical regulations have provided several solutions to authorize such subsystems not designed to be controlled nominally.

The first set of solution is based on exemptions or tolerances allowed regarding *quantitative safety objectives*[105] 'if the impossibility to respect specifications applicable on controlled atmospheric reentry can be duly proven by the operator.' In this case the operator makes its best efforts to meet the reduced[106] *quantitative objective* assigned, regarding the system and mission design or mitigation measures during operations. It can be noted, regarding the end-of-life maneuvers and the 'Region A Protection' by noncontrolled satellites (nanosatellites), that the starting point of the 25-year period is the beginning of

---

102 **Protected region B**, geosynchronous region (GEO) – segment of the spherical envelope defined as follows:
  – lower limit = geostationary altitude minus 200 km
  – upper limit = geostationary altitude plus 200 km
  – $-15° \leq$ latitude $\leq +15°$
  – geostationary altitude (GEO) = 35,786 km (altitude of geostationary terrestrial orbit).
103 Art. 21 TR provisions on Space debris limitation for *launchers and their components* are to be compared to those of Art. 39 and 40 on *space objects* (i.e. satellites). For clarification, the Annex IV 'Table of Concordance as to technical provisions' make bridges firstly within Technical Regulation (RT) itself between launcher and space object requirements and secondly between those of the latter and International Instruments on Space Debris Mitigation Measures (IADC, UNGA res.62/217, ISO, etc.).
104 Of which the Ariane launcher family for its third (orbited) stage, before Ariane VI currently under development.
105 See Art 20.1, (b) first *v.* second para. and Art. 44.1. See §7.1.2.3 more broadly on the *exemption logic* of FSOA's technical regulations.
106 10^{-4} instead of 2×10^{-5} with regard to Art 20.1, (b) first vs second paragraph and Art. 44.1.

the 'command phase' (after separation with the launcher) and not the *end of* 'exploitation' of such satellite.

The second solution results from the non-retroactive character of these regulations as provided by Article 55 (*Interim provisions*).

Beyond the issue of orbital space debris pollution, existing international principles and standards of planetary protection have been expressly translated by FSOA's regulatory system[107] into domestic legally binding provisions. This standard refers 'Planetary protection policy' as published by the Committee on Space Research (COSPAR) for implementation of Article IX of the 1967 Outer Space Treaty. The relevant operator must design and implement therefore an appropriate planetary protection plan. These provisions on planetary protection are to be applied, for instance, to any authorized exploitation activity on the Moon, on Mars, or other celestial bodies including asteroids (if any mining activities).

Lastly, with regard to the technical requirements concerning the launch site, FSOA's legislative and regulatory system does not foresee generic rules for the design and the management of a launch base.[108] Such a generic regime did not appear useful in the early 2000's when designing FSOA's regime since the Guiana Space Center was the unique existing Space launch base in France and Europe (in French Guiana) to be regulated. In this context, TR Article 27 distinguishes between operations run from the Guiana Space Centre, and operations from another launch site. In the first case, the regulations simply refer to the Order of 9 December 2010 regulating the operation on CSG facilities (REI-CSG). In the second case, subject to the waivers that may be granted by the Administrative Authority under FSOA Article 4.4 for foreign operations, the relevant French operator (of launch or satellite, under FSOA Art. 2) must furnish proofs either of the existence comparable technical regulations in such site and of compliance of its systems and procedure with these local regulations.

7.1.4.3 The Best Practice Guide

In order to avoid unnecessarily constraints to the incumbent operators, namely Arianespace and Eutelsat, regarding their already proven systems and procedures, the **Best Practice Guide**[109] has been set up by the technical regulations (TR Art. 54[110]) as a practical solution

---

107 Art. 1 of the abovementioned decree of 9 June 2009 and TR Art. 26 and 43.
108 *See above* §7.1.2.2 *other launch base than the CSG*.
109 *See above* §6.6.4.3.
110 Decree of 31 March 2011 relating to the technical regulations (TR) – *JORF* n° 0126 31 May 2011
TR Art. 54:
1. A guide of good practices is drawn up by the Centre national d'études spatiales, jointly with the profession, within the framework a working group representative of the operators and industry stakeholders, in order to characterize certain practices in force that help to demonstrate compliance with this technical regulation. This guide is based on practices validated by the experience that have been validated through experience acquired in the development, operation, and control of Space systems. It is in particular based on standards, technical specifications constituting standards, and standards recognized by the profession relating to the

allowing the operator to demonstrate compliance with such regulations. This guide, which has been drafted and validated by CNES in conjunction with the operators and manufacturers concerned, can be used to recognize certain existing practices as complying with a given article of the regulations. This guide can validate or confirm the use of tools or software whose use are already widely recognized by the profession by industrial and Space operators as well as government agencies. This means that CNES may make available to operators its own software related, for example, to the necessary hazard studies.[111]

Obviously, the practices of assessment or mitigation of risks validated by the guide are not the only solutions to comply with the technical regulations, but the advantage for the operator in using them is that it does not have to demonstrate their own compliance.

From a legal point of view, we may say that this guide offers subjective, empirical realization methods of respecting the Technical Regulation as the latter just provides generic objectives to be achieved, remaining *neutral* as to the *originality and creativity* of the proposed technical solutions. As a result, this guide is not compulsory, but consistent compliance is binding on the Administrative Authority under the regulations, especially regarding CNES technical compliance control.

7.1.5 Licenses to Simplify the Authorization Processes

The law provides, for different types of licenses, the simplification of recurrent authorization application requests, for the benefit of experienced operators or systems that have already been qualified and proven. The maximum validity period of a license is ten years. The minister may, on the basis of a substantiated decision, grant a license for a period less than what has been requested (AD Art. 8).

7.1.5.1 The 'Administrative' License Noting the Applicant's Moral, Financial, and Professional Guarantees

This license covers the portion other than technical or related to the operated system in the authorization file. It concerns information about the *applicant* as natural or juridical person: its name or company name, legal form, the address of its headquarters, and the

---

safety of life, property, public health, and the environment within the context of Space operations. The contents of this guide comply with the applicable provisions regarding protection of intellectual property as well as industrial and scientific assets.

2. Compliance with all or part of the requirements of this technical regulation is deemed to be acquired if the operator can demonstrate compliance with the relevant recommendations of this guide.

The use of the guide of good practices shall neither be mandatory nor exclusive.

111 *See, e.g.,* Modelling software of the fragmentation of a Space system in case of explosion in order to calculate the impact on the ground in terms of damage to persons, at each instant on a given trajectory, in response to the requirements defined by Art. X of the technical regulations. For a list of software opposable under GBP, see § 7.1.4.2, footnote n° 95.

signatory of the application. It allows to recognize in a long-term view the operator's specific capability to carry out its missions and assess the existence of its moral, financial, and professional guarantees. As such, the applicant must prove (AD Art. 1):
- the conditions of good repute and, in particular, the lack of personal bankruptcy of the individuals that are to conduct the Space operation;
- the company's financial standing and corporate governance;
- the quality management systems implemented within the company;
- the qualification and personnel training policies.

The benefit of such a license is the exempt for its holder from having to provide these supporting documents a second time, except in cases of changes affecting them.

7.1.5.2 Operator License Noting the Technical Compliance of its Systems and Procedures

In this case, the recurring approval concerns a system or its implementing procedures in the so-called basic configuration.[112] Its interest lies in reducing the volume of technical files of recurrent authorization applications only to information which is new or differs from the generic system already 'licensed.' The other advantage on behalf of the operator is that it reduces the investigation lead time to 1 month for the total process, of which 2 weeks for the CNES, compared with 4 months and 2 months for the CNES, respectively, in the normal authorization mode (AD Art. 3 and 5).

7.1.5.3 License Constituting Authorization

The beneficiary of such a license no longer needs to obtain an authorization in each case. He/she only needs to inform the Administrative Authority of the proposed operation at least one month before its implementation. In case of changes to the content of the license, the Administrative Authority may, after the CNES has been notified, formulate requirements or oppose the authorization.

7.1.6 *Procedure for Preliminary Certification to Accompany the Development of New Systems*

The Application Decree of 2009 provided for *an original pre-certification system*[113] to support the development of new systems and prepare new entrants well ahead of the feasibility of the FSOA authorization application itself in order to facilitate the success at the end of the formal authorization procedure. This decree (Article 11) defines a procedure

---

112 E.g., platforms of the Eurostar or Spacebus type, Ariane 5 ECA launcher, etc.
113 *See above* §6.6.1.3.

which allows any interested party, not necessarily an operator, such as a Start Up, a laboratory, an engineering school, a supplier, an industrial prime contractor, or a Space agency having an interest such as ESA to submit the first technical sections of an authorization file to the CNES several years in advance.

The new system examination is submitted by the interested party directly to CNES as of the first project feasibility studies in order to obtain throughout the project development phase one or more certificates of compliance certifying the achievement of critical technical milestones, which will not need to be validated again subsequently while examining the final authorization application. The process of this preliminary conformity control is detailed in the TR in its Articles 50 to 53 (Part 4). Conversely, this upstream procedure also allows the government and CNES to prepare in parallel, through appropriate consultations, necessary adjustments to make upon the legislation and regulations to meet the needs of such newly designed Space systems.

7.1.7 Controlling the Preparation and the Implementation of a Space Operation after Its Authorization

7.1.7.1 Obligations of the Authorization Holder

From the *preparation* to the *performance* of its operations to those of the Space Object's *end of life* (*return to Earth* or into the atmosphere or placed in a *graveyard orbit*), the holder of the authorization is required to comply with its obligations under the law, decrees, technical regulations and, where applicable, in the case of launches from French Guiana, the Guiana Space Centre Safety Regulations (REI-CSG). It must also respect the '**requirements**' (*prescription* in French) of a technical or legal nature expressly mentioned in the authorization issued (FSOA Art. 5).

The operator must also promptly notify to CNES events not covered by the authorization and any technical incident affecting the conditions of the Space operation as authorized (AD Art. 7). These events are known as '**Technical events**' (cf. above §6.6.1.2). The REI-CSG applies this obligation through the preliminary procedure referred to as '**safeguard submission**.' This duty to provide information is important because in the event of a serious breach, the defaulting operator may lose the benefit of the governmental guarantee if this shortcoming is the source of injury to a third party (cf. below end of §7.2. – LFR n° 2008-1443, Art. 119).

7.1.7.2 Persons Empowered to Control Granted Authorizations[114]

The *technical inspectors* or *basic controllers* are CNES' employees who are daily involved in monitoring that the systems and procedures implemented by the Space operators comply with the technical regulation (FSOA Art. 28 g), either during the examination of authorization requests, the preparation of operations, or their implementation. These persons are not necessarily 'Authorized Agents' as defined below but being subject to the regulatory status of CNES personnel, they are subject to the same rules governing civil servants in terms of confidentiality, integrity, and ethics.

The *Commissioned officers* or *Authorized Agents*, empowered under the provisions of FSOA Art. 7, are appointed by the Administrative Authority, within government departments, CNES, or other public agencies to conduct the necessary controls to check the compliance of the obligations of the authorization holder. If necessary, they carry out intrusive checks on the operator's premises or, if applicable, at its contractors' premises. They thus have access to the plants, premises, and facilities from which Space operations are carried out as well as access to the Space Object. They can obtain all the relevant documents or evidence. They can also be mandated in case of emergency or danger to give appropriate instructions and impose appropriate measures (see below §7.1.8). They are entrusted with a power of '**administrative police**,' which basically means a '**preventive police**.'

The Sworn Officers or Sworn Agents (FSOA Art. 10) are authorized agents who are qualified, under the prosecutor's department authority, to investigate criminal offences prescribed by law (FSOA Art. 11, see below at §7.1.9 'penalties'). They are subject to **judicial or criminal police,** which means a repressive police as provided for in the Criminal Procedure Code.

7.1.8 Emergency Measures

At any time during a launch, from the command in orbit or the return to Earth of a Space Object, in case of emergency, incident or loss of control, the minister, or the agents acting under its authority, may at any moment give instructions and require any measures they consider necessary for the safety of persons and property, the protection of public health and the environment (FSOA Art. 8). These exceptional measures may lead to the forced recovery of the control of the Space Object, its de-orbiting or passivation.

The President of the CNES has a specific delegation in this regard (FSOA Art 21).[115] At the CSG, the President of the CNES or his/her delegate under the mission of safeguard

---

114 See §4.3.3 and §6.4
115 *See* §4.3.2, §6.4.4, §6.5.1.3 and §6.6.2.1.

may take similar steps up to the *destruction of the launcher in flight*.[116] Procedural implementation of this emergency measures is specified by the Technical Regulation in several article (see concordance table in Annex IV).

7.1.9 Penalties

The law provides for administrative sanctions or criminal penalties depending on the seriousness of the offence.

7.1.9.1 Withdrawal and Suspension of the Authorization (Administrative Sanctions)

The Administrative Authority can withdraw or suspend an authorization in cases of infringement by the operator of its obligations under the FSOA, the authorisation decree, the technical regulations or the requirements specified in the authorization, or when the operations for which they were sought are likely to jeopardize the national defense interests or the respect by France of its international commitments (FSOA Art. 9, §1). Such measures may also be enforced in case of *unforeseen incidents* or *technical events* which require the *reassessment of the authorization* (AD Article 7). In case of suspension or withdrawal of the license, the Administrative Authority may require the operator to take, at its own expenses, appropriate measures to limit the risks (FSOA Art. 9 §2).

7.1.9.2 Fines (Criminal Sanction)

FSOA Art. 11 provides for criminal penalties that include fines of up to € 200,000 for the most egregious offences such as proceeding to launch, command, or transfer a Space Object without authorization or infringing an administrative measure or court decision ordering its stoppage or suspension. These fines may appear rather low with regard to the seriousness of the offense but it appeared during the parliamentary debate that basically the major penalty for a private space operator, toward its shareholders, stakeholders (contractors, bank, insurances) and customers, remains to be publicly condemned, regarding its brand image, and being deprived entirely or partially of its business capacity with regard to its license or authorization rights and even more to be denied from the benefit of the State guarantee in case of damage caused to third party.

---

116 As a consequence of FSOA Art. 21 (Research Code's Art. L331-6) and REI-CSG's Art. 63, Chapter VI-2.

7.2 Operators Liability, Insurance, and State Guarantee for Damage Caused to Third Parties

7.2.1 The Scope of Liability for Damage to Third Parties and Associated Insurance

The purpose of the FSOA rules governing liability for damage caused to third parties is to channel the responsibility to a single operator for a given damage. According to the UN Convention on International Liability for Damage caused by Space Objects of 29 March 1972, the FSOA retains in its Article 13 an **Objective liability or absolute liability** (of the type in Art. 1242 of the French Civil Code[117]) for damage caused to a victim on the ground or in the airspace and **liability for misconduct** (of the type in Art. 1240 or 1241 of the French Civil Code[118]) for damage caused in outer Space.

Following the proposals made by industrialists, operators and insurers consulted by M.P. Pierre Lasbordes, examination by the French National Assembly (§6.5.2.5 above) led to a *limitation of that liability* ***in time***. As a result, other than in cases of willful misconduct, the operator's responsibility (and the related liability of its insurer) ceases when all of the obligations set forth by the authorization or the license are met or, at the latest, one year after the date on which such requirements should have been met. The State replaces the operator for damage occurring after this deadline. Article 6 of the FSOA therefore requires the operator to take out an insurance or to have an equivalent financial guarantee approved by the competent authority in order to cover its liability incurred in the above conditions of Article 13 and up to the extent of their liability indicated in the following paragraph.

The authorization decree n° 2009-643 of 9 June 2009 (D-A. Art 16) specifies terms and conditions of such financial guarantee or insurance covers. Some exceptions can be allowed by the Administrative Authority:
- if it appears impossible, given the situation of the insurance market, for the operator to be covered by an insurance policy or to furnish one of the financial guarantees (D-A Art. 17), or;
- on behalf of geostationary satellites operations during the time of conservative station-keeping. However, these financial guarantees or insurance covers again become mandatory for any change of orbit, orbital position, or upon any other maneuver terminating the satellite station-keeping (D-A Art. 18).

---

117 *Alias* Art. 1384 of the former numbering (before Year 2016).
118 *Alias* Art.1382 and 1383 of the former numbering (before Year 2016).

7.2.2 Governmental Guarantees (FSOA Art. 16 and 17)

A governmental guarantee or recourse action for indemnity capped by the latter is used to place a ceiling on the liability of the operator, for certain damages to third parties, except in case of willful misconduct of the operator, depending on the nature of the action brought by the victim.

The **Guarantee** of the French government is called into play (FSOA Art. 15) to cover damages exceeding the amount that the operator would have to indemnify when it is directly prosecuted and convicted by a court in France or abroad:
- for damage *caused during the launch phase*, on the ground, in airspace, and also in Space for other satellites by the launcher, and;
- to damage *caused on the ground or in airspace <u>after</u> the launch phase*, especially in case of a return to Earth of a 'poorly orbited' satellite or the return to Earth of a stage of the launcher.

Conversely, the damage caused by the operator's fault to other satellites in outer Space is not covered by the governmental guarantee. This guarantee can also benefit to contractors, subcontractors, customers, and/or the latter insurers for damage caused during the launch phase, in the exceptional case in which they are sued directly, instead of the operator, by a victim in particular abroad (FSOA Art.18).

Following this logic, **the recourse action** for indemnity by the French State (FSOA Art. 14) may be implemented against the FSOA's operator having caused the damage, when it was required to compensate the victim as part of its *liability* as the *launching State* under the UN Convention of 29 March 1972 on the international liability for damage caused by Space Objects. This recourse action for indemnity by the State against the operator is limited in the same range than the above State guarantee's ceiling. However, contrary to the guarantee above, this recourse ceiling plays in favor of the operator, for any damage caused *after* the launch phase, *regardless of the location of the damage*. This is because damage in Outer Space was not excluded by Article 14 §2, which covers every situation *after the launch phase* contrary to Article 15 §2 on State guarantee benefit that retains only after the launch phase, the 'damage caused on the ground or in the airspace.'

The final amount below for which **recourse action** for indemnity by the State applies, or beyond which the ***governmental guarantee applies***, is determined by the authorization, given the risks involved (Art. 16 and 17), according to a range established in the ***2008 Finance Act***[119] between € 50 and 70 million. This amount is basically set at € 60 million for damage caused during the launch phase, corresponding to the strict amount defined

---
119 Ibid. LFR No. 2008-1443 of 30 December 2008 Article 119.

since 1980 by the European states in the Launchers Exploitation Declaration for Ariane launchers' family and then for Soyuz and Vega as being launched from the CSG.

The same *2008 Finance Act*, rather discreetly, introduced a new restriction under the governmental guarantee stating that it is implemented 'except in cases of... *serious failure* to comply with the requirements of the authorization.' This reserve is more severe for the operator than the only exception foreseen in the Space Operations Act, which only applies in cases of **willful misconduct**.

The table below gives synthetic information on FSOA's different liability regimes and associated state guarantee or recourse solutions depending on damage localization, operator's behavior assumptions, and victims' claim judicial procedure:

	Damage on Ground or in the Air SpaceAbsolute liability regime (under UN 1972 Liab Convention and FSOA)	**Damage in the Outer SpaceLiability/ fault regime (under UN 1972 Liab Convention and FSOA)**
During the launch phase Except willful misconduct	Foreign victim's state liability action under UN 1972 convention against French government as launching state: ⇨ **Government's recourse action** for indemnity' against the operator limited to the ceiling amount set by the Authorization (between 50 and 70M€) *(Art 14.1°)*	
	Victim's liability action in a civil court against an Authorized Space Operator or any other entity taking part to the authorized operation undertaken from France or other European country: ⇨ **State guarantee** on behalf of the relevant entity beyond the compensation amount set by the Authorization (>50 to 70M€), except severe nonobservance of authorization requirements /Art. 119 of LFR 2008. *(Art 15.1° or 15 last paragraph[120])*	
After the launch phase (phase of command), including when the Space Object returns to Earth	Foreign victim's State liability action under UN 1972 Convention against French government as Launching State: ⇨ **Government's recourse action** for indemnity' against the Authorized Operator limited to the ceiling amount set by the Authorization (between 50 and 70M€) *(Art 14.2°)*	
	Ground or Air victim's liability action in a civil court against the Authorized Space Operator or any other entity taking part to the authorized operation undertaken from France or other European country: ⇨ **State guarantee** on behalf of the relevant entity beyond the compensation amount set by the authorization (>50 to 70M€), except severe inobservance of	On-Space victim's liability action in a civil court against the Authorized Space Operator: ⇨ **No guarantee from State** ⇨ **Unlimited liability of the Authorized Operator** *(Art 15.2°)*

---

120 Art. 15 last paragraph takes into account a civil foreign claim directed against a *participant to the production* of the relevant space object (in place of the FSOA authorized space operator): "In the case of damage caused during the launching phase, the governmental guarantee shall benefit, *if necessary* and in the conditions set out in the paragraphs above, *to the persons who are not third parties* to a Space operation pursuant to the present Act."

	Damage on Ground or in the Air Space Absolute liability regime (under UN 1972 Liab Convention and FSOA)	Damage in the Outer Space Liability/ fault regime (under UN 1972 Liab Convention and FSOA)
	authorization requirements /Art. 119 of LFR 2008. (Art 15.2 or 15 last paragraph)	
After completion of all Authorization Requirements, or one year after…Except willful misconduct or severe nonobservance of the authorization requirements…	⇨ End of the period of responsibility and liability of the Authorized Space Operator ⇨ Full indemnification or compensation from the French State, as the case may be, to the victim or the Authorized Operator (Art. 13, last paragraph)	
After complete landing on Earth (land or sea) of any- disused authorized space object or its components parts (fairing, wreck, etc;)	Verification of the relevant authorization: ⇨ A priori, damage on land and sea, after the complete achievement of the space operation, is out of scope of FSOA as specific liability system (FSOA Art. 1. 4° and 5°):[121] return to the ordinary law regime of the Civil Code Art 1242 (liability for guardian of the thing).	Not applicable

FSOA's Liability Board, 2017. Working document of Philippe Clerc

7.3 Legal Relationships between Private Stakeholders Participating in a Space Operation

To ensure greater safety of transactions among participants involved in a Space operation, the law focuses on validating a widespread practice in the Space sector, that of exclusion clauses or the cross-waiver of liability or guarantee clauses. Such clauses are typically concluded between all the participants in a Space operation and the production of a Space Object, *e.g.*, between the operator and its customer or between the customers and their respective contractors, including the insurers. This recognition was necessary to resolve uncertainties of common law jurisprudence limiting the validity of such limitations for professionals in the same sector of activity.

This measure was therefore included in Article 20 of the act. Despite its reciprocity between the parties concerned, the purpose of such clauses is mainly to protect the *industrial Space manufacturers*, and in particular *suppliers of the Space Operator*, in the event of damage caused by a *latent defect* (or *hidden defect*, or in French 'vices cachés') in their product, against any appeals of the Space Operator or the latter customers (*e.g.*, satellite

---

121 See §7.1.2.1.

owner or satellite service provider), in connection with third-party victims' compensations that would be incommensurate with the price of their own service. This provision results in protecting, if necessary, any industrial provider having caused damage on ground to a third party in connection with a Space Operation. This solution makes sense since in this case, the operator's liability is already covered by the law by the compulsory insurance (FSOA Art. 6) for up to 60 million euros actually and capped beyond that amount by the government. There is no reason therefore for the act to allow other possibilities of chain actions to recover damages leading to the manufacturer when the victim already qualifies for compensation under the same law.

The widespread use of this *hold harmless pact (or exclusion pact)* leads each *stakeholder* to insure its own risks and losses, without having to file claims against each other. These provisions are extended to the *insurers* thus waiving their *right for subrogation*. These waivers apply by default between all participants involved in the Space operation or the production of the Space Object and those who are bound by contracts, in other words, between those who are not 'third parties' within the meaning of FSOA Art. 1 §6. It is therefore a matter of *public policy, namely* a mandatory legal provision that cannot be dismissed by agreement between parties.

The only possibility provided by law to contractually waive this clause concerns compensation for damage caused during the production of an object designed to be commanded in Space (*i.e.*, a satellite) or during its command in orbit. This openness is explained by the fact that damage between satellites in outer Space (collision), which happens rarely as a matter of fact, is treated on the basis of *proven fault* (FSOA's article 13. 2°, consistent with the 1972 UN Convention) and is no longer covered by the governmental guarantee in this case, except during the launch phase. This exemption is also consistent with a practice developed by industry, between space operators and the satellite industry, following the repetition of failures in orbit that resulted in several lawsuits from the 1990s onward in the United States. Quite logically, these exclusion clauses cannot be invoked by a perpetrator of willful misconduct. This measure leads to global savings throughout the sector in terms of litigation costs and collateral inconvenience. It has also helped to create or maintain solidarity between industrialists in the same sector, in particular among the Ariane's stakeholders.

This unusual system with regard to normal business practice has become acceptable for customers of Space systems (or their insurers) by the existence of the constraints of the technical regulations associated with the FSOA, under the independent compliance monitoring by the CNES opposable to the operator and the suppliers of the latter.

These technical requirements to ensure the safety of Space operations with respect to third parties have also helped enhance the reliability of the systems for the benefit of the various economic parties involved in the operation.

***

To summarize the above regarding the liability for damage to third parties in the FSOA[122]:
- The liability for damage is **channeled** to the sole authorized operator;
- The authorized operator is therefore presumed to bear alone any and all litigation related to the damage;
- Except willful misconduct or severe nonobservance of authorization requirements, the operator can benefit from the **governmental guarantee** (Article 15) for any damage caused during the launch phase and after only damage on the ground or in airspace beyond a certain amount (between € 50 and 70 million, in actual fact € 60 million). Thus, this guarantee does not cover the operator for damage it has caused during the in-orbit command phase (Art. 15.2);
- When the State was ordered to repair damage under the international responsibility of the UN Convention of 1972, it had a **recourse action** for indemnity against the authorized operator concerned within the limit of the above amount. This recourse action is capped, for the benefit of the operator, even for damage caused during the in-orbit command phase (Art. 14 §2) while the same damage is not eligible for governmental guarantee above (Art. 15.2);
- The operator must be insured for liabilities over the amounts (Article 6.1) covered by the government (actually under 60 M€);
- If, despite all of the above, an industrial subcontractor is sued directly by a third party instead of the authorized operator (or the French government), for damage caused during the launch phase and is sentenced by a court (*a priori* foreign, etc.), the FSOA provides, by way of exception, the possibility for the industrial to benefit directly from the governmental guarantee (Art. 15, last paragraph).

7.4 Specific Rules for High-Resolution Space-based Data (FSOA Art. 23-25)

It should be recalled that this specific declaratory regime does not concern space operations as such but the use of a satellite's payload for observation services from space, which are programmed, processed, and delivered on Earth. The legal framework applicable to this high-resolution observation service falls more under laws on privacy protection, the monitoring of sensitive technology and data, disclosure of government data, or intellectual property and competition regulation, than law on space activities, which is the core subject of FSOA.

So, the two administrative regimes remained completely independent in terms of French State control. For space operations (prior authorization regime) there is a prior

---

122 *I.e.* aside from the case below in Article 20 of the FSOA, which applies only to the contractual relations between participants in the operation or in the production of the Space Object.

inspection at the time of the authorization application, based on objective criteria of technical compliance and safety of individuals and property. For observation (declaratory regime), it is only a retrospective inspection following the declaration, which takes place on a case-by-case basis during operation of the service, based on more sensitive and subjective criteria relating to security threats and national defense, but mitigated by observance of fundamental rights, in particular freedom of information and trade.

7.4.1 Data concerned: High-Resolution Space-Based Data (SBD)

The technical characteristics of the data concerned by this regime are defined in a decree. They include resolution, location accuracy, observation frequency band, and the quality of Earth-observation data received or subject to satellite system programming (SOA, Art. 23).

The first version of the implementing decree of 9 June 2009,[123] adopted following the Council of State's opinion, stated that these characteristics of the data would be determined by a future 'simple' decree. The aim was to be able to revise these thresholds more easily according to developments in technology and threats. In the end, it was on the contrary this first 2009 high-level decree that was amended[124] on 19 July 2013 to specify under its proper provisions these technical thresholds in order to give stronger regulatory foundations to them.

Activities exercised by primary operators of SBD are therefore subject to prior declaration when they concern the following:
- Data from panchromatic optical sensors with onboard resolution less than or equal to two meters;
- Data from multispectral optical sensors with onboard resolution less than or equal to eight meters or with a number of spectral bands greater than or equal to ten;
- Data from stereoscopic optical sensors with resolution less than or equal to ten meters or with altimeter accuracy less than or equal to ten meters in relative value (fifteen meters in absolute value);
- Data from infrared sensors with resolution less than or equal to five meters;
- Data from radar sensors with resolution less than three meters;
- Data with intrinsic location accuracy less than ten meters (circle of error at 90%).

---

123 *Cf.* Art. 1 of Decree 2009-640 of 9 June 2009 in its initial version in the *JORF* (official gazette) of 10 June 2009. The original version of this decree n° 2009-640 is translated in Annex II.
124 Decree n° 2013-653 of 19 July 2013 amending Decree n° 2009-640 of 9 June 2009 implementing the provisions of title VII of law n° 2008-518 of 3 June 2008 on space operations. *JORF* (official gazette) n° 0168 of 21 July 2013, p. 12190.

7.4.2 The Entity Concerned: 'Primary Operator of Space-Based Data' (EPDOS)

Unlike the regime for space operations, exploitation of SBD does not require prior authorization but is based on a *declarative system*. The entity subject to this specific regime is not the space operator of the satellite as such but the 'primary operator of the space-based data'. The French government chose the strictest definition of a *primary operator of space-based data* following the proposals by the Ministry of the Economy, Finance and Industry in charge of the digital economy, conscious not to impede *freedom of information* and exploitation of the data, and to promote the development of this strategic industry, while simplifying State control.

The *Primary Operator of the Space-based data* is defined as any individual or legal entity that *programs* a satellite system for Earth observation or that *receives* Earth-observation data from space (SOA Art. 1-7). In fact, it is the single entity that controls programming of the satellite payload[125] or the entity that directly receives the data from the satellite from its installations on the ground. This operator is thus the first and only independent point of contact on French soil that controls the *acquisition or dissemination* of such data, hence the term 'primary' operator.

The details above are important because State monitoring introduced by this law is limited solely to the activities of this operator and cannot intervene upstream or downstream. This solution appeared to strike a balance between the need for effective monitoring for defense and safety requirements and the need to protect key constitutional principles such as freedom of expression, communication, information, trade and industry. The civilian vocation of this observation activity, in particular, within the meaning of the United Nations' 1986 principles on remote sensing,[126] to which France is committed, did not seem to allow the introduction of systematic inspection in France prior to any selling or dissemination of data, like, for example 'Shutter control' in the United States.[127]

Consequently, any future operator whose data and products fall under the thresholds set out above must make a declaration, two months before any activity, on a form for which

---

125 That is, control of sensor activation, parameter adjustment for image acquisition, in particular, aiming at the Earth, metric or radiometric resolution, stereoscopic or simple mode, etc.
126 *Cf.* Principles on remote sensing adopted by the General Assembly in its resolution 41/65 of 3 December 1986. "Principle I: For the purposes of these principles with respect to remote sensing activities: a) The term '*remote sensing*' means the sensing of the Earth's surface from space by making use of the properties of electromagnetic waves emitted, reflected or diffracted by the sensed objects, *for the purpose of improving natural resources management, land use and the protection of the environment*; [...]"
127 'Shutter control' in the United States bans the purchase or dissemination, as the case may be, of images acquired by satellite. To date, it is codified in: Public Law 111-314, Title 51, National and Commercial Space Programs (2010), Subchapter III, 60121 and 60122 -15 CFR 960. Licensing of Private RS Systems under the NOAA - 18 CFR 793-797 and EO 10104 Chapter 37. Espionage and Censorship ...

the template was defined by an order dated 4 September 2013.[128] The absence of a response from the administration two months after a declaration does not mean that the activity is prohibited; on the contrary, this authority is obliged to provide individual notification of any reservations during this period.

7.4.3 The Supervisory Authority: the SGDSN and the Interministerial Committee on Space-Based Data

The competent *administrative authority* for this regime is the SGDSN (*Secretary-General for Defence and National Security* or *Secrétaire Général de la Défense et de la Sécurité Nationale*). This authority, that reports directly to the Prime Minister, may impose restrictive measures on the activities declared to it. In its mission, it relies on the opinions of an *interministerial committee*, whose tasks, composition, and organization are set out by the 'simple decree' *(the SBD's Monitoring Decree)* adopted on 19 July 2013.[129]

According to Article 4 of the latter decree, the interministerial committee on SBD is composed of: the Secretary-General for Defence and National Security or his representative, and a representative each of the Minister of Foreign Affairs, the Minister of the Interior, and the Minister of Space. The President of CNES or his representative can also be invited to participate in the meetings of the committee when so justified by a particular item on the agenda.

7.4.4 Restrictions on the Purchase and Dissemination of Data

The restrictions provided for in the implementing decree 2009-640 can result in immediate, total, or partial suspension of satellite programming or of data reception or of the production of images for a temporary, renewable period. These activities may be simply deferred or forbidden on a permanent basis. Restrictions can also concern the technical quality of the data or the geographical location of the image-acquisition areas. The simple decree of 19 July 2013 specifies in its Article 3 that the restrictions extend to the production of new data or images and to the dissemination of primary data already archived. The content of these decisions regarding restrictions can be protected according to legislation on the confidentiality of national defense matters and related criminal sanctions.

---

128 Order of 4 September 2013 on prior declaration of an activity carried out by primary operators of space-based data, *JORF* (official gazette) n° 0213 of 13 September 2013.
129 Decree n° 2013-654 of 19 July 2013 on monitoring the activity of primary operators of space-based data *JORF* (official gazette) n° 0168 of 21 July 2013.

7.4.5   Regime for CNES' Earth-observation Activities

It should also be noted concerning CNES (SOA, Art. 27) and its own space operations that its 'satellite activities for Earth observation and reception of Earth-observation data are not subject to this regime applicable to SBD (SOA, title VII). This exclusion is also justified by the fact that these observation activities must necessarily concern a mission of general or public interest for which the funding and approval of the State or the relevant administrative authority (the minister in charge of space or the SGNSN) is already solicited within the CNES' own governance through its Board of Directors.[130]

It should also be noted that concerning these SBD issues, CNES has no formal role alongside the administrative authority, the SGDSN, with respect to procedures for examining and verifying declarations by primary operators of SBD. CNES' only prerogative here is to be able to be invited to participate in the works of the interministerial advisory committee on SBD.

It is not any less bound by the same rules preventing conflict of interest as the case may be with regard to its own Earth-observation programs due to its potential participation in the committee or to the technical authorization process for space operations regarding observation satellite (launch, orbital control, end-of-life maneuvers) falling within the scope of the general regime of the SOA (titles II to VI) or lastly to its public responsibilities regarding the associate radiofrequency spectrum (cf. §7.5.1).

In any case, in mid-2008, before the entry into force of the general regime of the SOA in 2010 and the current Title VII on SBD in 2013, CNES transferred to a company of the EADS group (today known as Airbus Defence and Space) its total interest in the capital of the company Spot Image, its subsidiary in charge of global commercial distribution of data and products from the SPOT family of civil satellites and from the civil channel of the dual system Pleiades (cf. §5.1.2).

7.4.6   Other Restrictions on SBD Dissemination

In addition to State monitoring of high-resolution SBD flow for reasons of security and national defense as resulting from the SOA, the legislation on surveillance of *sensitive exports* applies to *foreign sales of receiving stations* for such data. More generally, the law

---

130 Under Art. 1 of Decree n° 84-510 of 28 June 1984 on CNES (version consolidated in April 2017), CNES is placed under the supervision of the Minister of Defence, the minister in charge of space and the minister in charge of research. The highest decision-making body of CNES, its Board of Directors (*see* Part 1. §2.1.1), is composed of eighteen members, twelve of which are appointed by decree. Among these people appointed by the State, five are chosen based on their competence following a proposal by the three supervisory ministers above (the 'qualified prominent figures' and seven representatives of their respective ministers), namely: The **Prime Minister (SGDSN)** and ministers of industry, the budget, **defence, foreign affairs**, research, and space.

provides for other restrictions on the dissemination of SBD in the interests of the protection of privacy,[131] business confidentiality,[132] or simply in application of common liability law[133] in the case of damage caused to others (tortious liability, unfair competition, etc.).

7.5 OTHER PROCEDURES AND LEGISLATIONS TO BE RESPECTED IN FRANCE IN ORDER TO OPERATE A SPACE OBJECT OR ITS PAYLOAD SERVICES

Basically, the scope of the French Space Operations Act (FSOA) affects independent operation or command on a Space Object or a vessel, or more specifically operations on its bus or its platform with its technical easements by the way of the associated telemetry network. Except the particular regime of Space-Based Data discussed above in §7.4, FSOA does not apply to the payload services, in other words Space applications, such as telecommunication, localization, navigation, meteorology, or broadcasting.

The risk to be contained by FSOA, according to its Article 1 §1, is focused on potential damage to persons or property, and in particular to public health or to the environment, *directly caused by a Space Object* as part of a Space operation "to the exclusion of the consequences arising from the use of the signal transmitted by this Object for users." As a consequence, any other responsibility or liability of the Space operator, in particular on the integrity, availability, or reliability of the signal or services provided by its Space Object, remains governed by the statutory law or the relevant applicable sectorial legislation. The study of such other regimes is beyond the framework of the present book dedicated to Space operation law. However, it could be useful to highlight the main ones to the attention of new players in Space business in France.

It must be kept in mind that despite the fact that several licenses or authorization could be necessary to be granted on a given satellite on behalf of the French State, there is no formal governmental 'one-stop shop,' but, as a general principle of administrative law, the FSOA's Administrative Authority has the responsibility to forward matters beyond its competence to the right ministry or Administrative Authority.

---

131 In particular, in application of the EU General Data Protection Regulation (or GDPR): Regulation (EU) 2016/679 of 27 April 2016 on the protection of natural persons with regard to the processing of personal data and on the free movement of such data.

132 In particular, in application of the directive (EU) 2016/943 of 8 June 2016 on the protection of undisclosed know-how and business information (trade secrets) against their unlawful acquisition, use and disclosure. This directive was not transposed in French law at the date of March 2018 due to a difficult domestic debate regarding possible threat to the *press freedom*.

133 Art 1240 and 1241 of the French Civil Code (former numbering 1382 and 1383) and their associated case-law. Official Journal of the European Union, 15.6.2016, L 157/1.

7.5.1 Authorization to Use the Frequency Spectrum

The operator must apply for an authorization to use frequencies to the ANFr (the French National Frequencies Board). According to article L. 97-2 of the French Electronic Communications and Postal Code (CPCE),[134] the procedure is twofold:
- Request for allocation to the *ANFr* who checks conformity with the national Table of Frequency Band Allocations, declare the allocation to the IUT, and takes fees.
- Authorization of the Minister in charge of electronic communications, after obtaining the opinion of the 'assigning authorities' for the frequencies concerned.

It should be noted here that *CNES remains one of the assigning authorities* for certain frequency bands related to Spacecraft command services or, by default, on unique Space services such as exploration, observation, navigation, and meteorology from Space according to the Order of 9 July 1987.[135] The operator must respect these procedures of frequency allocation in each country aimed for deployment and ask for the required authorization from the national agencies and assigning authorities.

7.5.2 Authorization for Satellite Telecommunication Network or Services Open to the Public

Beyond the allocation of frequencies above, whose purpose is to allow coordination between different systems at the international, regional and national levels, and more specifically to prevent the risk of jamming, a specific application is required for any operator undertaking to provide or operate satellite telecommunication networks or to provide satellite telecommunications open to the public in France. Such prior declaration set out in Article L. 33 of the *French Electronic Communications and Postal Code (CPCE)*,[136] focuses in particular on the content of the service delivered to public user or consumer. The operator must make this prior declaration to the *ARCEP*, the French 'Electronic Communications and Postal Regulatory Authority.' Inversely, an 'independent network' as reserved to the

---

134 As settled by Act n° 2004-575 dated 21 June 2004 and decree n° 2006-1015 dated 11 August 2006.
135 *JORF* 1 August 1987, p. 865 1. The CNES is the 'assigning authority' for the frequency band attributed to the T.E.C. user (telecommunications for various users) in the national Table of Frequency Band Allocations, for the following frequency bands: **Space exploitation** (E.X.S., E.X.E., E.X.T.), **Earth exploration** by satellite (E.T.S., E.T.E., E.T.T.), **Earth exploration** by satellite by **passive sensors** (E.P.S., E.P.E., E.P.T.), Space research (R.E.S., R.E.E., R.E.T.), **Space research** by passive sensors (R.P.S.), **radio navigation** by satellite (R.N.S., R.N.E., R.N.T.), and **meteorology** by satellite (A.E.S., A.E.E., A.E.T.). *Arrêté* (ministry order) of 9 July 1987 (*JORF* 1 August 1987, page 8651) *relatif à l'utilisation de certaines bandes de fréquences par le CNES* (regarding the use of certain frequency bands by CNES). *See above* §4.1.1.3 'Frequency Spectrum.'
136 In application of Act n° 2004-669 dated 9 July 2009.

use of one or more persons in a close group of users for the exchange of private internal communications does not require such declaration.

7.5.3 Open Data Legislation

While France introduced its SBD monitoring regime via the SOA (*see* for detail §7.4), the European Union advocated legislation aiming to force the Member States to *open up their data for public interest needs*. This European *open data legislation* is however focused on 'common' data, i.e. *data other* than the high-resolution ones governed by dedicated law on security and national defense such as FSOA Title VII in France or 'SatDSiG' in Germany.[137]

These European measures on opening data are based on two directives[138]:
- the *PSI Directive* which applies to the *reuse* by the private sector of 'Public Sector Information.'[139]
- The *INSPIRE Directive* which aimed to cover information requirements in the area of *environmental protection*.

The PSI Directive was transposed by the law on access to administrative documents known as CADA no. 78-753 of 17 July 1978 amended several times, then codified since 19 March 2016 in the 'Code of relations between the public and the administration' (Art. L300-1 et seq.). The last specific transposition text is the law of 28 December 2015 on the terms of *reusing public sector information free-of-charge*.[140] Article 2 of this text concerns data (already) made available in electronic format and states that this information must, if possible be "in an open-standard readily-reusable format, in other words machine-readable." This legislation promoting the opening of data was strengthened within the administration and extended to all public and private bodies by the law of 7 October 2016 on the *Digital*

---

137 Since November 2007, the distribution of 'high-grade' satellite-based Earth observation data is regulated in Germany by the 'Satellitendatensicherheitsgesetz' (SatDSiG), which can be translated to 'Act to Safeguard the Security Interests of the Federal Republic of Germany from Endangerment by the Distribution of High-Grade Earth Remote Sensing Data,' or the Satellite Data Security Act. G. v. 23.11.2007 BGBl. I S. 2590 (Nr. 58); zuletzt geändert durch Artikel 92 G. v. 29.03.2017 BGBl. I S. 626 - Geltung ab 01.12.2007, abweichend siehe § 35; FNA: 700-6 Wirtschaftsverwaltung.
138 See Ibid §4.2 and §5.1.2 on PSI and INSPIRE. See also the French debates on this issue of 'open data' developed on Chapter 5 §5.1.2.
139 'PSI' Directive n° 2003/98/EC of 17 November 2003 on the reuse of public sector information, JOUE (official gazette) 31 December 2003 (L 345/90), amended by Directive 2013/37/EU 26 June 2013 (2013/37). JOUE L175 of 27 June 2013.
140 Law n° 2015-1779 of 28 December 2015 on the terms of reusing public sector information, free-of-charge, JORF (official gazette) n° 0301 of 29 December 2015.

7   THE FRENCH SPACE OPERATIONS ACT'S REGIMES

Republic (the so-called 'Lemaire Act')[141] while adding some restrictions to it, in particular, restrictions regarding privacy and copyright. Such restrictions are also developed elsewhere in application of the expanded General Regulation on Personal Data of 2016 enforceable from 25 May 2018[142].

As for the INSPIRE directive (2007/2/EC of 14 March 2007), it aimed to facilitate the production and exchange of data to develop an infrastructure for European geographic information to promote environmental protection. This aim was extended to the operational plan by the *Copernicus program* developed on the basis of Article 189 of TFEU in cooperation between the European Union and the ESA. *Copernicus* is therefore the first European satellite infrastructure, with dedicated satellites and ground segment, to cover the public interest needs of users and ensure continuity of programs initiated by the agencies, like the first *SPOT family* of satellites from CNES, in France. This INSPIRE directive was also transposed in France by the *CADA law* and in the legislative and regulatory sections of the Environmental Code.

In this respect, an implementing decree of 2 January 2008 should be highlighted as it introduced free access to data relevant to the safety of individuals and property to the benefit of local authorities, for needs relating to the implementation of preventive measures for major *natural disasters* falling under their competences.[143]

---

141 Law n° 2016-1321 of 7 October 2016 for a digital Republic, *JORF* (official gazette) n° 0235 of 8 October 2016.
142 Regulation (EU) 2016/679 of 27 April 2016 on the protection of natural persons with regard to the processing of personal data and on the free movement of such data (General Data Protection Regulation or GDPR).
143 Decree n° 2008-5 of 2 January 2008 implementing Art. L. 563-5 of the Environmental Code and on the communication of data relevant to the safety of individuals and property in the context of major natural disaster prevention, *JORF* (official gazette) n° 0003 of 4 January 2008, p. 268.
This decree, in chapter III of title VI of book V of the regulatory section of the Environmental Code, section 5 entitled: 'Communication of data relevant to the safety of individuals and property' was drafted as follows:
"Art. R. 563-16. – Without prejudice to the provisions of Arts. L. 564-1 to L. 564-3, local authorities, or associations thereof, **have free access to data available to the State and its public bodies, at their request, motivated by the safety of individuals and property pursuant to Art. L. 563-5, to implement preventive measures for major natural disasters falling under their competences.**
For this sole purpose, and **subject to third-party rights**, raw physical data from sensors may be freely communicated to these local authorities or associations thereof, **with the exception of satellite data**, after correction of manifest errors collected by the State and its public bodies, which is not already freely accessible to them and which they need to use to:
1. Prepare informative and regulatory maps of major natural disasters that they are responsible for producing under the Environmental Code and the Town Planning Code;
2. Prepare and exercise the policing measures incumbent upon them under the General Local Authorities Code, the Environmental Code and law n° 2004-811 of 13 August 2004 on modernization of civil security;
3. Carry out protective works and construct protective structures against risks, for which they are the contracting authority;
4. Include risk prevention in their infrastructure and facilities projects."

However, after consultation with the bodies concerned, including CNES, this decree expressly excluded satellite data from its scope. This exception is in line with data policies applicable in France[144] and to a certain extent those of other space powers in Europe relating to SBD.

To sum up, Space data for which an *exception* may be claimed in respect of the obligation for open and free dissemination, includes:

- Data collected and distributed outside of a strictly designated formal public service context. In this respect, it should be noted that CNES, as a space agency and research center, has neither the statutory mission nor the allocated budget to distribute data in an ongoing operational manner. Its activity is structured program by program with allocated budgets. Its statutory mission is therefore limited upstream to developing innovative satellites and onboard instruments, demonstrating their technological and operational feasibility and then transferring them to public or private operators for long-term recurrent exploitation. This restriction was, however, mitigated by the so-called 'Lemaire Act' of 7 October 2016, mentioned above.
- Data that are unusable as they are, in particular, data that require extraction from archives, algorithms, or specific processing software or the provision of ancillary data. Indeed, these sensitive and costly operations exceed the normal framework of simple reproduction or uploading of data already produced and used by the public sector.
- Data from systems developed in the context of international cooperation with third parties (*e.g.*, Jason, Argos, [...] with NASA, ISRO, and Eumetsat) or under the ESA because these data are subject to a specific intergovernmental data policy involving third-party rights.
- Data or derived products[145] protected by or protectable by copyright (Spot or Pleiades data).
- Data subject to restrictions concerning the confidentiality of national defense matters (cf. SBD/SOA), business confidentiality or privacy.
- Data from the fields of research and education or from the promotion of research institutions. This restriction was however mitigated by the so-called Lemaire(Axelle) Act' of 7 October 2016, mentioned above.

Of course, these legally justified exceptions do not prevent the bodies concerned, including CNES, from disseminating such data, on a voluntary and organized basis, free of charge, to institutional users for *public interest missions* recognized under national, European, and

---

144 *Cf.* above, §5.1.2.
145 For example, when it is technically possible to extract the initial data, which itself were protected, by reverse engineering on the corresponding product (*e.g.*, digital map).

international legislation or programmes, the actions of which are undertaken under the 'Charter on Space and Major Disasters,' ISIS programme, etc.

7.5.4 Export Control Procedures

Any launch outside France of a Space Object (satellite or launcher) manufactured in France or from a foreign country on behalf of a French Space operator is considered as an export (of good, technology, or service) subject to export control regulations applicable in France or, as the case may be, according to the legislation of the relevant foreign country from which such Space Object or its components have been imported. To this extent, all exchanges of technology or information affecting a launch service from French Guiana may also be subject to foreign export control legislation such as the ITAR or EAR[146] one from the United States of America. The applicable export control regime is determined by the first exporting country and depends on the security sensibility of on-board technology as marked per list of 'dual use' or 'military' goods or technologies.

7.5.4.1 For Dual-use Goods

As formalized by decision n° 2015-2420 of the European Commission dated 12 October 2015, the European Regulation EC 428/2009 and its Annex I being updated every year contains the list of goods controlled under this regulation. This control only applies to exports finally aimed for non-European countries, being understood that exchange limited to EU Member states are not considered as an export under European regulation. In France, transfer and export of dual-use goods are examined by the French service for dual-use goods (SBDU), after having obtained the opinion of the French Interministerial Commission for dual-use goods (CIBDU). Actually, most of the space systems and technology fall within the scope of 'military regime' below rather than dual-use ones.

7.5.4.2 For Specifically Military Goods and Technologies

Article L. 2335-18 of the French Defence Code[147] assimilates as export of *military goods and technologies* (and not only dual) any of the following *Space devices*:

---

146 The International Traffic in Arms Regulations (ITAR) and the Export Administration Regulations (EAR) are the two important U.S. export control laws that affect the manufacturing, sales, and distribution of technology.
   The legislation seeks to control access to specific types of technology and the associated data. Its goal is to prevent the disclosure or transfer of sensitive information to a non-U.S. national.
   ITR contains a United States Munitions List (USML) of restricted articles and services. EAR contains a Commerce Control List (CCL) of regulated commercial items, including those items that have both commercial and military applications (dual-use items). *See below* footnotes.

147 As set up by Act n° 2011-702 dated 22 June 2011(Art. 1) and implemented by decree n° 2012-901 dated 20 July 2012 relating to import and export outside the European Union of war material, arms and munitions

1° The satellites of detection or *observation*, their equipment of observation and shots as well as their ground exploitation stations, designed or modified for a military use or *on which their characteristics confer military capacities*;
2° Spacecraft, other satellites, their ground stations of exploitation, their equipment specially designed or modified for a military use;
3° Engines and thrust systems specially designed or modified for the materials mentioned in 1 and 2;
4° *Rockets and Space launchers with military ballistic capacity, their equipment and components as well as the specialized facilities of production, test, and launch*;
5° The parts, the components, the accessories, and the specific materials of environment, including the maintenance equipment of materials mentioned in 1 in 3;
6° Specialized *tools for manufacturing* the materials mentioned in 1 in 4.

The transfer of such equipment outside of France is subject to a prior authorization of the French Prime Minister even to other Member States of the European Union. This decision is made upon advice of the French Interministerial Commission on the study of war material exports (CIEEMG or *Commission interministérielle pour l'étude des exportations de matériel de guerre*). The authorization is refused when the transfer is likely to compromise the essential interests of the safety.

7.5.4.3   Re-export of Imported Sensitive Goods

Any export out of France of a Space equipment, formerly imported under upstream foreign export license shall require a specific authorization for its reexport outside of France under such foreign regulation's 'end-destination control' regime. For example, a launch from France of an U.S.-manufactured satellite or of a French satellite containing a significant part of U.S. components, beyond the necessary authorization under French national legislation on export or import of dual use or military goods and technologies, may be subject to the U.S. export regulation of ITAR (International Traffic in Arms Regulations[148]) or EAR[149] as far as U.S. equipment are concerned.

---

and related items, and to intra-community transfers of defence-related goods, as a transposition in France of the Directive 2009/43/CE dated 6 May 2009 on intra-community transfers of defence-related goods (directive 'TIC').

148   ITAR [regulated by 22 CFR 120-130] is a strict regulatory regime whose purpose is to ensure U.S. security in a global meaning. There is no balancing of commercial or research objectives. Its covers military items or defence articles. It normally regulates goods and technology designed to kill or defend against death in a military setting but it includes Space-related technology because of application to missile technology. It also includes technical data related to defence articles and services.

149   EAR [regulated by 15 CFR 730-774] regulates dual-use items, *i.e.*, items or technology designed for commercial purpose but which could have military applications (computers, civilian aircraft, pathogens). The licensing regime encourages balancing competing interests, availability, commercial, and research objectives with national security.

7.5.5   Other Optional Procedures

Subjected to EU-dedicated exemption framework on its own public aids regulation,[150] it may be possible for a French Space operator or manufacturer to apply for insurance or financial guarantee like COFACE (itself secured by government guarantee) that covers export risks toward foreign customers.

---

150 *See* Communication from the Commission to the Member States on the application of Arts. 107 and 108 of the Treaty on the Functioning of the European Union to short-term export-credit insurance (2012/C 392/01 – *EU Official Journal* 19 December 2012.

8 Conclusion: Assessment and Perspectives for the French Space Operation Act

8.1 Feedback from the Triennial Inventories of 2013 and 2017

Since the entry into force of the FSOA in December 2010, two triennial inventories were organized by the Ministry in charge of Space activities with the help of CNES to review the implementation of the FSOA, the first on 4 December 2013, the second recently on 14 March 2017. These assessments were achieved in relation to industrialists, operators, and insurers, more specifically regarding the daily implementation of technical rules and administrative procedures of the TR and REI-CSG. Their conclusion can be summarized positively: no authorizations have been denied nor failures or victims associated with authorized operations, nor has there been any litigation in connection with the law. We can also consider that the overall safety of the relevant space systems was enhanced by the technical compliance controls which have a direct effect on the reliability of launchers and satellite all together with their operational performances, to the whole satisfaction of their economic sponsors and customers. Procedure and criteria brought by FSOA's technical regulations indeed also serve actually as a set of common standard of quality assurance plans for private operators in their contractual relations. Thus, this reference can even be applied to enhance operations ultimately not subject to the FSOA, representing a 'quality label' for the commercialization of the same Space systems or services especially for Export purposes.

It should be noted that this label remains free of fees as any application procedure for authorization or license under FSOA nowadays. The existence of the independent expertise of CNES in monitoring the technical compliance of the systems to be operated appears to be a prerequisite of trust of the customer who does not belong to the Space community. This includes private media broadcasting or satellite telecommunications operators with regard to their launch service provider, but also with regard to the latter, bankers or insurers or foreign governments which invest significant amounts in a space programme while refraining from any claim according to the practice of waivers and hold harmless clauses (§7.3 above).

CNES on its side, as a public institution of an industrial and commercial nature, has logically abandoned its activities remunerated in competition or business relations with Space operators that are potentially subject to the FSOA authorization system (§4.3). The establishment has therefore refocused its interventions in line with its public interest missions to serve scientific and technical research in the development of innovative Space systems, or to satisfy the operational needs of other public bodies such as Defense, the ESA, or the EU that cannot currently be borne by the competitive market. This refocusing of CNES on noncompetitive activities also helps to prevent potential conflicts of interest and possible sources of litigation. This gave the opportunity to CNES to reboot its activities and resources on behalf of its core mission as a Space agency serving innovation and the common good.

Furthermore, beyond the mandatory effect of FSOA, the continuous involvement of the Space community (manufacturers, operators, scientist, research centers, universities, CNES, and ESA) in the consultation process on technical regulation process and in its implementation has contributed to promote best practices and a common sense of responsibility shared by this community. This consensus around a common set of shared values led to a large adoption in June 2015 of the 'Collective for Space Care Charter' that aims to contribute to the mitigation of the risk associated with Space operation as to allow the development of such activity in a sustainable way.

8.2 The 'Collective for Space Care' as an Ethical Spin-off of the FSOA

The Collective for Space Care[1] initiative can be presented as an ethical spin-off of the FSOA process. It unites on a voluntary basis within a nonprofit society chaired by the CNES President, Space operators, and partners who jointly acknowledge responsibility for complying with international treaties and principles pertaining to Space matters, compliant with applicable Space legislations[2] and applying the best practices derived from them.

These charter commitments include:
- Technical quality of projects, high level of performance, risk mitigation
- Protection of Space environment (limiting debris, preventing collision)
- Contribution to the Sustainability of Space community activities during all phases, including design, manufacturing, and operations
- Sharing practices, tools, and information which facilitate compliance with existing safety rules and principles for the benefit of security and Space activity development
- Promotion of research and good practices for risk assessments and mitigation
- Exemplarity based on high moral principles, for the benefit of humanity, in the interests of scientific endeavor.

---

1   The charter was signed on 17 June 2015 at the 51st International Paris Air Show by heads of Airbus Defence and Space, Airbus Safran Launchers, Arianespace, the European Space Agency (ESA), Eutelsat, Thales Alenia Space, and the University of Montpellier.
2   Included but not limited to FSOA.

The charter also recalls expressively that its ethical principles are consistent with the maintaining of its partners' competitiveness at the international level. On the contrary, it could reasonably be expected that this charter may promote business development of its private partners, beyond the attractiveness of its ethical values, toward their potential investors or customers, to the extent that risk mitigation in Space operations always goes hand in hand with technical quality and performance.

8.3 Challenges with the New Space Economy at the Beginning of the Twenty-First Century

Basically, FSOA has paved the way for a national legislation framework to meet the needs of existing launchers and satellite systems operations in accordance with the UN, ESA, and UE legal framework and taking into account privatization of these activities as it has been evolving over since the 1980s in the manufacturing industry. This exercise has been made within the limits of the current technologies and designed systems as well as the contemporary capacity of the private sector to develop new systems, Space operations services, and value-added applications.

That said, the Law would not stand as a concrete block toward the future and this Space law irresistibly will evolve to meet its new challenges such as those arising in entering soon in the 2020s. Among these challenges, since the early 2000s a second wave of privatization and reconfiguration of the space industry ensued, with the rising power of a new class of entrepreneurs,[3] like the well-known GAFA companies,[4] wishing to apply to the Space sector their own new-economy business model, namely that of Silicon Valley.

This phenomenon, known as 'New Space,'[5] bears some common features that tackle the current Space stakeholders, both private and public. Posed in a broad manner, we summarize the key ones as follows:

---

3   Jeff Bezos (Amazon and Blue Origin – Launcher New Shepard), Paul Allen (cofounder of Microsoft, sponsor of Space Ship One and of Strato Launch System), Sergei Brin and Larry page (founders of Google, constellation Terra Bella), Elon Musk (Founder of PayPal, Tesla, and Space X commercializing the Falcon launchers' family and capsule Dragon), Richard Branson (Virgin Galactic And Space Ship Two suborbital crafts), Greg Wyler (president of OneWeb satellite constellation and founder of O3b Networks).
4   GAFA for Google Apple Facebook Amazon.
5   For publications on the New Space phenomenon, *see* A. Dupas, *Demain nous vivrons tous dans l'espace* (F) (Tomorrow we will all live in Outer Space), Rober Laffont éditions, Paris, March 2011, ISBN: 2-221-12512-6. Alain Dupas is an expert in politics, technology, and spatial strategy. Having previously worked for CNES, the French Space agency, he is currently an expert for the EBRD (European Bank for Reconstruction and Development) and a research fellow at George Washington University (extract from a biography of Robert Laffont, 2010).

- These New Space's entrepreneurs have been previously successful players in the digital economy, where they have fast developed worldwide monopolistic companies from successful start-up, thanks to an original concept of new Internet and network services applications for mobile end users.
- Their ambitions are global. This matches with the worldwide capacity of *Space application services*. Beyond innovative Space application's services to be delivered onto the Earth, they also aim to develop Space Exploration and the Human Conquest of the solar system planets such as Mars.
- To achieve their end, New Space industry has an incremental approach starting by developing reliable, cheap, well-proven technology systems. The second step consists in allowing them to be reused, resupplied, repaired, or refurbished on-orbit in order to reduce their operating costs and finally adapting their capacity to long-run missions.
- New Space's visions are inseparable from the personal identity of their Founding entrepreneurs. This personalization approach of business, that may turn to a 'personality cult,' sharply contrasts with the anonymous stock feature and governance of the major traditional incumbent actors of the worldwide aerospace industry and their measured media policy. In this respect, let us recall that the traditional space industry[6] has been shaped step by step since the 1960s under public procurement and industrial policy of governmental Space and Defense agencies;
- These investors have also particular financial leverage because before entering in Space affairs they made a considerable fortune allowing them to inject seed money and raise more easily capital from institutional investors or crowdfunding sites to support their Space ambitions.
- New Space actors originating from a fully liberalized, innovative and risky market do not feel comfortable with traditional Space agency procedures or with governmental procurement or design authorities.
- Last but not least, 'law suit' is not tabooed for these new players as a potential leverage to gain new market against a competitor benefiting from an anchor or monopolistic tenancy from traditional public procurement. One can interpret in that sense the April 2014 Elon Musk's SpaceX law suit against the U.S. Air Force over a huge government contract for rocket components reserved for the United Launch Alliance (ULA), the joint operation of Boeing and Lockheed Martin. It is worth remembering that such a legal dispute is still not of frequent use in the traditional space sector, including among competitors, where the 'waivers of claim clauses' has remained the standard condition, as mentioned in Chapter 7[7]).

---

6 Of which Boeing, Lockheed, Airbus D&S, Thales Alenia Space, Ariane Group, Arianespace.
7 Specifically, in §7.1.2.3 on exclusions regarding space or suborbital human flights and in §7.3 about the liability regime within entities taking part in a space operations authorized under FSOA.

8 Conclusion: Assessment and Perspectives for the French Space Operation Act

Notwithstanding this challenging private initiative, Space activities development indeed remains essentially supported and shaped by national government policies and their program resources. Beyond the prestige attached to the Space conquest in the 1960s as reflected by the Moon Race between the United States and the former USSR, Space capacities become a critical asset to offer a worldwide facility of global information dissemination, access, or control without foreign interference.[8]

As a matter of fact, and also from a legal point of view, it is possible from Space, at least for civil purposes, to freely discuss, exchange any information and data, including for entertainment, localize, navigate, operate ground network systems, observe people, economic activities, and resources.

Basically, the independent capacity to launch Space vessels and to operate them has become one of the major components of full sovereignty of any State or nation. As a result, any major State is willing to attain or to maintain its autonomy or its leadership in Space activities in the international scene. This necessity or willingness may be furthered by the concept of 'Space Dominance,' as theorized in the United States by the end of the 1990s and claimed under the presidency of Bill Clinton.[9] This approach is based on a common view, basically challenging all nations –whether they are a Space power or not – that the

---

[8] As a consequence of the Principle on Freedom of Outer Space Exploration under Art. 1 of the UN OST 1967.
On the U.S. declination of this principle to the 'non-interference on Space system passage,' see National Space Policy (The White House, National Science and Technology Council, 19 September 1996, Fact Sheet, Appendix F-2, page 1, §3). 'The United States considers the Space systems of any nation to be national property with the right of passage through and operations in Space without interference. Purposeful interference with Space systems shall be viewed as an infringement on sovereign rights.'

[9] Quoted in ibid U.S. NSP 1996, measures page 1, §1 "For over three decades, the United States has led the world in the exploration and use of outer Space. Our achievements in Space have inspired a generation of Americans and people throughout the world. We will maintain this leadership role by supporting a strong, stable, and balanced national Space program that serves our goals in national security, foreign policy, economic growth, environmental stewardship, and scientific and technical excellence. Access to and use of Space are central for preserving peace and protecting U.S. national security as well as civil and commercial interests."
A national Security for a New Century; The White House December 1999:
- Page 12: 'We are committed to maintaining U.S. leadership in Space. Unimpeded access to and use of Space is a vital national interest – essential for protecting U.S. national security, promoting our prosperity and ensuring our well-being. Consistent with our international obligations, we will deter threats to our interests in Space, counter hostile efforts against U.S. access to and use of Space, and maintain the ability to counter Space systems and services that could be used for hostile purposes against our military forces, command and control systems, or other critical capabilities. We will maintain our technological superiority in Space systems, and sustain a robust U.S. Space industry and a strong, forward-looking research base.'
- Page 25: 'Space has emerged in this decade as a new global information utility with extensive political, diplomatic, military and economic implications for the United States. We are experiencing an ever-increasing migration of capabilities to Space as the world seeks to exploit the explosion in information technology. Telecommunications, telemedicine, international financial transactions and global entertainment, news, education, weather and navigation all contribute directly to the strength of our economy – and all are dependent upon Space capabilities.'

control of Space is to be in the 21st century the key prerequisite of State independence and national economy development, and beyond that of dominance. This consideration is notably based on a comparison with the mastery of the Sea (*i.e.*, Sea Dominance) which was in the 19th century the essence of the United Kingdom's Empire domination of the worldwide economy.

On its military extension, 'Space dominance' leads to the 'full-spectrum superiority' of the national defense's doctrine, which is defined[10] as 'the cumulative effect of dominance in the air, land, maritime, and Space domains and information environment (which includes cyberSpace) that permits the conduct of joint operations without effective opposition or prohibitive interference.' Under these circumstances, Space systems have a major role to play in all these dimensions of the global mastery of information.

Such considerations also explain, at the European level, the willingness of old nations to aggregate their efforts to develop a common and coherent Space policy and programs as a cement of the European integration. This joint effort is concretized, either under the civil flags of the European Space agency and the European Union than through original bilateral or multilateral cooperation models for undertaking dual and defense projects among their Member States on a case by case basis (Pleiade, Helios in Earth observation, Syracuse, Athena-Fidus in Telecommunication, etc.).

In addition to this consideration of global information dominance, States also need with regard to their national interests to drive or at least to monitor the new forms of Space conquest in the field of 'on-orbit services,' ground space resource exploitation, and associated human occupation in Space, as initiated today by the private industry in the context of New Space. This implies investments to master new cost-efficient technology for disrupting Space systems being reusable, refurbish-able, repairable, more controllable, environmentally friendly for Space and safe on a wide public scale. The same goes for any scientific, technological, operational, commercial needs as much for civil than strategic and defense purposes.

Thus the issue for the next steps in law making is not to discuss the respective weaknesses of private and public investments on Space activities, or to focus on one model to the detriment of the other, but to face the challenge of strengthening both the private initiative and public support to combine their resources to the better satisfaction of the general interest of developing application from Space and exploitation of the latter resources on orbit or in the celestial bodies.

---

10   Department of Defence Dictionary of Military and Associated Terms (DOD Dictionary) – May 2017.

8.4 Next Legal Challenges and Consequences on the FSOA

Then we are reaching the limit of this exercise. A legal study indeed must remain within fixed data and substantive law. With reference to lessons learned from my fellow space lawyer Ram Jakhu,[11] I like to repeat that "Law is nothing but a crystallized policy", but the reverse is not true!

It is indeed of policy and legislative responsibilities of directing, making, altering and repealing law or regulations and not on experts or technicians' ones. From this pragmatic perspective, prospective legal studies should firstly focus in dealing with issues raised by developing space businesses already engaged and not yet fully addressed in the current positive legislation. Among these issues, one can resume those already mentioned here above with regard to space activities currently out of any FSOA specific provisions (see §7.1.2.3 above), namely:

- **Space applications and their related frequency spectrum allocation and other** administrative requirements. One basic issue is to harmonize licensing regimes of both payload activities and bus or platform vehicle operations as affecting a same space system. Standard rules and procedures should also be set up with respect to data collection, protection, processing, archiving, management, distribution, and access of data.
- **Human space flight and human space occupation.** Legal issues affect firstly the needs of a standard law on orbital transport contract with extended solutions on issues of third-party liability and liability, waivers, labor, police, criminal law, manufacturing, commerce, intellectual or real property acquisition.
- **Suborbital flights and hybrid extra-atmospheric operations.** Harmonization issues affect in this matter: crafts' registration and certification, liability regime included toward passengers and crew, damage indemnification ceiling and guaranties, contractual responsibility borne by professionals and associated waivers authorized or not, State guaranty scope, R&D public aids regimes, coordinated Air and Space management traffic regime, frequency spectrum coordination, appropriate space(air)port regulations, competent authorities (UN-OOSA &-UN-COPUOS/OACI, UE-AESA/national governments, DGAC/CNES).
- **Reusable space system, on-orbit service.** The main future issues are related to potential adaptations to the related definitions of space object, operation, and operator with regards to FSOA's licensing regime, the necessary complement to provide for in the technical regulations, and the space operator contractual and extra contractual

---

11 Ram Jakhu is professor at the Faculty of Law of McGill University in Montreal and Director of the Research Center and the Institute of Air and Space Law (IASL). He was Philippe Clerc's teacher when he attended the Master of Space Studies course of the International Space University in Strasbourg (first session 1995-1996).

responsibility regime (including insurance regime and validity of waivers in contracts). On-orbit services also raise additional issues on traffic management with regard to operations arising between space objects previously authorized or registered under different licensing regime or jurisdictions.
- **Exploitation of land or mining resources of celestial bodies,** Moon, Mars, other planets, asteroids... The problem with this activities is mainly political and diplomatic as reflected by the State's reluctance or hesitation to join the 1979 UN Moon international regime[12] as proposed by its Article 11 §5. To this extent, it is worth underlining that France remains in a position of 'mediation,' being a signatory to the agreement without having ratified it. In any case, a prior consensual solution has to be found at the international level to regulate licensing on uses of land and resources from space accommodating freedom of entrepreneurship, protection of investments, planetary protection, and the peacekeeping for humanity.
- **Other cross-sectorial issues** should be addressed such as tax law (VAT on space services, taxation on space assets), competition law and public procurement with respect to public aids control, data policy (free dissemination versus protection, liability on signal...), intellectual property for inventions made in space, judicial, and police cooperation, common medical assistance and repatriation, global standards (ISO) for interconnection between different systems and networks, standardized space operations agreements (included for in-orbit services), space brokers status, etc. And last but not least, new public-private trans-national models, integrating company law and public international law, as referred to the limited partnerships dual model of Indies companies in Europe in the 17th century.

These issues need to be addressed after appropriate consultations, in particular under the aegis of the UN's specialized organizations (COPUOS, OACI, UIT, OMC) in order to complete or adapt existing international hard and soft law and subsequent national legislations. The same applies to the design of new forms of cooperation between or within public and private sectors to support innovative space enterprises.

In this perspective, France is also subjected to its European commitments and interests of both the ESA and the EU. ESA is committed for its competence in the development of new European space systems and EU has to play its shared competence in space policy

---

12 Agreement Governing the Activities of States on the Moon and Other Celestial Bodies. The Moon Agreement was considered and elaborated by the COPUOS Legal Subcommittee from 1972 to 1979. The Agreement was adopted by the General Assembly in 1979 in resolution 34/68. Its Art. 11 §5 states that "States Parties to this Agreement hereby undertake to establish an international regime, including appropriate procedures, to govern the exploitation of the natural resources of the moon as such exploitation is about to become feasible."

and its own space programs since 2007 without prejudice of its traditional legislative competence in any economic matter.

To cope with these challenges, France, at the national level, has already set up several mechanisms to facilitate consultation between stakeholders on space policy and law and to facilitate public support on behalf of these new private ventures.

CNES' support tools and procurement instruments toward the private sector already benefit from appropriate procedures authorized by its status and by the new 2015 Ordinance on public market (as to 'Innovation Partnership,' R&D and Defense regimes, etc.).

Moreover, CNES as EPIC (Public Body of *an Industrial and Commercial Nature*) holds the legal capacity to support the setting up of innovative startups or to contribute to their capital stock, at least during the seed period.

On the French government side, it is worth mentioning the new bottom up supporting instrument set up in 2010 to foster more broadly the innovative private initiative: the so-called Future Investment Program *(Plan d'Investissement d'Avenir-PIA)* renamed 'Investment plan' in 2017. This program serves to finance innovative and exemplary projects proposed by industry included on Space systems and related services. CNES as a Space agency may be selected as facilitator and/or contract officer on behalf of the government to support such projects.

Lastly, with regard to consultations on new space policy, governance, and law in France, we may recall the mission of the high level Committee CoSpace (for State Industry Consultative Committee on Space) established in September 2013 to enable an open and permanent consultation toward the Space industry, operators, and application users for the design of future Space policy and programs.

Incidentally, the CNES initiative 'Collective for Space Care' launched in June 2014, among public and private space operators, may also serve as a consultation forum to prepare next evolution of the Space Law. It can therefore be concluded at this stage that all necessary preparations are in place to accompany the evolution of Space law in France.

As a final conclusion, the absence of prior regulation associated with the FSOA as such shall never imply from a legal point of view a prior refusal nor a delayed assessment's decision from the French government with regard to any innovative private undertaking based on new space systems or operations.

Indeed, Article 11 of the 2009 FSOA's Application decree provides that "any person responsible for designing or developing a system or a sub-system that is critical having regard for the safety of people and property and the protection of public health and the environment […], may submit a file to the *Centre National d'Etudes Spatiales*." Should the related technical regulation not exist or not be fully appropriated for assessing such new space systems, CNES shall first propose appropriate modifications to this regulation[13] and then, while waiting for that, move forward with its current technical compliance assessment background based on general space standard of safety and quality assurance.[14]

Last but not least we must recall the famous French principle of 'freedom of trade and industry,' resulting from the Le Chapelier Act of 1792, as elevated to the level of 'general principle of law,' that reverses the burden of the proof at the expense of administrations and on behalf of such private entrepreneurs!

It is on this positive note ahead to the future that we should conclude this study on legislation for Space activities in France. Thus, we may retain that this law has remained definitely attached to serve at the same time the Space policy ambitions of France and Europe, safety of people and property, protection of public health and the Earth and Space environment, and private entrepreneurship; and all that without jeopardizing a peaceful and fruitful future for the human space conquest!

---

13   According to FSOA's Art. 28 completing by an 'f' the Art. L-331-2 of the Research Code stating that "among CNES' responsibilities is: ... f) To assist the Government in the definition of the technical regulations relating to space operations."
14   Such solution was practiced during the transitory period of FSOA's entry into force, between 10 December 2010 (DA 2009, Art. 24) and 31 May 2011 this date corresponding with the publication of the 31st March Technical Regulation Order.

ANNEXES I - Original législation – French version

List of annexes

Annexe 1.1	Loi relative au CNES codifiée au code de la recherche (Loi CNES)
Annexe 1.2	Loi n°2008-518 du 3 juin 2008 relative aux opérations spatiales (LOS)
Annexe 1.3	Décret n° 2009-643 du 9 juin 2009 relatif aux autorisations délivrées en application de la loi n° 2008-518 du 3 juin 2008 relative aux opérations spatiales (DA)
Annexe 1.4	Décret n° 2009-644 du 9 juin 2009 modifiant le décret n° 84-510 du 28 juin 1984 relatif au Centre national d'études spatiales (D-CNES)
Annexe 1.4 bis	Arrêté du 12 août 2011 fixant la liste des informations nécessaires à l'identification d'un objet spatial en application du titre III du décret n° 84-510 du 28 juin 1984 relatif au Centre national d'études spatiales (AI)
Annexe 1.5	Décret n° 2009-640 du 9 juin 2009 portant application des dispositions prévues au titre VII de la loi n° 2008-518 du 3 juin 2008 relative aux opérations spatiales (D-DOS)
Annexe 1.5 bis	Décret n° 2013-653 du 19 juillet 2013 modifiant le décret n° 2009-640 du 9 juin 2009 portant application des dispositions prévues au titre VII de la loi n° 2008-518 du 3 juin 2008 relative aux opérations spatiales (D-DOS)
Annexe 1.5 ter	Décret n° 2013-654 du 19 juillet 2013 relatif à la surveillance de l'activité des exploitants primaires de données d'origine spatiale (D-DOS-S)
Annexe 1.5 quater	Arrêté du 4 septembre 2013 relatif à la déclaration préalable d'activité effectuée par les exploitants primaires de données d'origine spatiale (A-DOS-D)
Annexe 1.6	Arrêté du 31 mars 2011 relatif à la réglementation technique en application du décret n° 2009-643 du 9 juin 2009 relatif aux autorisations délivrées en application de la loi n° 2008-518 du 3 juin 2008 relative aux opérations spatiales (RT)
Annexe 1.6 bis	Arrêté du 11 juillet 2017 modifiant l'arrêté du 31 mars 2011 relatif à la réglementation technique (RT)
Annexe 1.7	Arrêté du 9 décembre 2010 portant sur réglementation de l'exploitation des installations du centre spatial guyanais (REI-CSG)

Annexe 1.1

Loi relative au CNES codifiée au code de la recherche (Loi CNES)

Loi relative au CNES[1] codifiée au code de la recherche
Version consolidée Mai 2017[2]
Chapitre Ier: Centre national d'études spatiales (CNES).

Article L331-1
(Statut)[3]
Le Centre national d'études spatiales est un établissement public national, scientifique et technique, à caractère industriel et commercial, doté de l'autonomie financière.

Article L331-2[4]
(Mission)
Le Centre national d'études spatiales a pour mission de développer et d'orienter les recherches scientifiques et techniques poursuivies en matière spatiale.
Il est notamment chargé:
a) De recueillir toutes informations sur les activités nationales et internationales relatives aux problèmes de l'espace, son exploration et son utilisation;
b) De préparer et de proposer à l'approbation de l'autorité administrative les programmes de recherche d'intérêt national dans ce domaine;
c) D'assurer l'exécution desdits programmes, soit dans les laboratoires et établissements techniques créés par lui, soit par le moyen de conventions de recherche passées avec d'autres organismes publics ou privés, soit par des participations financières;
d) De suivre, en liaison avec le ministère des affaires étrangères, les problèmes de coopération internationale dans le domaine de l'espace et de veiller à l'exécution de la part des programmes internationaux confiée à la France;

---

[1] Texte issu de la loi n°61-1382 du 19 décembre 1961 instituant un Centre national d'études spatiales (JORF 20 décembre 1961) codifié aux articles L331-1 à L331-6 du Code de la recherche par l'ordonnance n°2004-545 du 11 juin 2004 relative à la partie législative de ce code (JORF n°138 du 16 juin 2004 page 10719) et modifié et complété par la loi n°2008-518 du 3 juin 2008 (articles 21 et 28) relative aux opérations spatiales dite LOS.

[2] Chemin d'accès: Code de la recherche, Partie législative, Livre III les établissements publics à caractère industriels et commercial.

[3] Les titres suivant les numéros d'articles (texte en italique et entre parenthèse) ont été ajoutés par l'auteur pour une meilleure lisibilité. Ils n'ont aucune valeur légale particulière.

[4] Modifié par Loi n°2008-518 du 3 juin 2008 (LOS) - art. 28.

e) D'assurer soit directement, soit par des souscriptions ou l'octroi de subventions la publication de travaux scientifiques concernant les problèmes de l'espace;
f) D'assister l'Etat dans la définition de la réglementation technique relative aux opérations spatiales;
g) D'exercer, par délégation du ministre chargé de l'espace, le contrôle de la conformité des systèmes et des procédures mis en œuvre par les opérateurs spatiaux avec la réglementation technique mentionnée au f);
h) De tenir, pour le compte de l'Etat, le registre d'immatriculation des objets spatiaux.

Article L331-3
(Administration)
Le Centre national d'études spatiales est administré par un conseil d'administration comprenant des représentants de l'Etat, des personnalités choisies en raison de leur compétence dans le domaine d'activité du centre et des représentants du personnel élus dans les conditions prévues par le chapitre II du titre II de la loi n° 83-675 du 26 juillet 1983 relative à la démocratisation du secteur public.

Article L331-4
(Financement)
Pour le financement de ses missions, le Centre national d'études spatiales dispose notamment de crédits budgétaires ouverts pour les recherches spatiales par la loi de finances, de subventions publiques ou privées, de redevances pour services rendus, de dons et legs, de produits financiers et autres produits accessoires.

Article L331-5[5]
(Gestion budgétaire et comptabilité publique)
Le Centre national d'études spatiales assure sa gestion financière et présente sa comptabilité suivant les règles relatives aux établissements publics à caractère industriel et commercial dotés d'un agent comptable.

Article L331-6[6]
(Pouvoirs confiés au président du CNES au CSG au titre de la LOS)
I. - Le président du Centre national d'études spatiales exerce, au nom de l'Etat, la police spéciale de l'exploitation des installations du Centre spatial guyanais dans un périmètre délimité par l'autorité administrative compétente. A ce titre, il est chargé d'une mission

---

5   Modifié par le Décret n°2012-1247 du 7 novembre 2012 (art. 107) pour le soumettre aux dispositions des titres Ier et III du décret n° 2012-1246 du 7 novembre 2012 (art. 49) relatif à la gestion budgétaire et comptable publique. Voir note 8.
6   Modifié par Loi n°2008-518 du 3 juin 2008 (LOS) - art. 21.

générale de sauvegarde consistant à maîtriser les risques techniques liés à la préparation et à la réalisation des lancements à partir du Centre spatial guyanais afin d'assurer la protection des personnes, des biens, de la santé publique et de l'environnement, au sol et en vol, et il arrête à cette fin les règlements particuliers applicables dans les limites du périmètre mentionné ci-dessus.

II. - Le président du Centre national d'études spatiales coordonne, sous l'autorité du représentant de l'Etat dans le département, la mise en œuvre, par les entreprises et autres organismes installés dans le périmètre défini au I, des mesures visant à assurer la sûreté des installations et des activités qui y sont menées, et s'assure du respect, par ces entreprises et organismes, des obligations qui leur incombent à ce titre.

III. - Dans la mesure strictement nécessaire à l'accomplissement des missions prévues aux I et II, les agents que le président du Centre national d'études spatiales habilite ont accès aux terrains et locaux à usage exclusivement professionnel et occupés par les entreprises et organismes installés au Centre spatial guyanais dans le périmètre défini au I.

Article L331-7[7]

(Délégation au président du CNES pour les mesures d'urgences prévues par la LOS)

Le président du Centre national d'études spatiales peut, par délégation de l'autorité administrative mentionnée à l'article 8 de la loi n° 2008-518 du 3 juin 2008 relative aux opérations spatiales et pour toute opération spatiale, prendre les mesures nécessaires prévues au même article pour garantir la sécurité des personnes et des biens ainsi que la protection de la santé publique et de l'environnement.

Article L331-8[8]

(Renvoi à un décret d'application[9] en Conseil d'Etat)

Un décret en Conseil d'Etat fixe les conditions d'application du présent chapitre, notamment les conditions dans lesquelles le président du Centre national d'études spatiales peut déléguer sa compétence mentionnée à l'article L. 331-6.

---

7   Créé par Loi n°2008-518 du 3 juin 2008 (LOS) - art. 21.
8   Créé par Loi n°2008-518 du 3 juin 2008 (LOS) - art. 21.
9   Le décret d'application en vigueur est le décret n°84-510 du 28 juin 1984 modifié relatif au Centre national d'études spatiales (accessible en version consolidée sous le site de LEGIFRANCE https://www.legifrance.gouv.fr/). Ce texte a été modifié notamment en 2009 (dans ses articles actuels 14-1 à 14-17 créés en lieu et place de l'article 14) pour tenir compte du décret d'application de la LOS du 3 juin 2008 (cf. Décret n°2009-644 du 9 juin 2009) puis en 2012 (dans ses articles actuels 3, 4, 5, 13) par le Décret n°2012-1247 du 7 novembre 2012 (art. 107) pour le soumettre aux dispositions des titres Ier et III du décret n° 2012-1246 du 7 novembre 2012 (art. 49) relatif à la gestion budgétaire et comptable publique.

ANNEXE 1.2

Loi n°2008-518 du 3 juin 2008 relative aux opérations spatiales (LOS)

LOI n° 2008-518 du 3 juin 2008 relative aux opérations spatiales[1]
L'Assemblée nationale et le Sénat ont adopté,
Le Président de la République promulgue la loi dont la teneur suit:

TITRE IER: DEFINITIONS

Article 1
(Définitions)[2]
Pour l'application de la présente loi, on entend par:
1° « Dommage »: toute atteinte aux personnes, aux biens, et notamment à la santé publique ou à l'environnement directement causée par un objet spatial dans le cadre d'une opération spatiale, à l'exclusion des conséquences de l'utilisation du signal émis par cet objet pour les utilisateurs;
2° « Opérateur spatial », ci-après dénommé « opérateur »: toute personne physique ou morale qui conduit, sous sa responsabilité et de façon indépendante, une opération spatiale;
3° « Opération spatiale »: toute activité consistant à lancer ou tenter de lancer un objet dans l'espace extra-atmosphérique ou à assurer la maîtrise d'un objet spatial pendant son séjour dans l'espace extra-atmosphérique, y compris la Lune et les autres corps célestes, ainsi que, le cas échéant, lors de son retour sur Terre;
4° « Phase de lancement »: la période de temps qui, dans le cadre d'une opération spatiale, débute à l'instant où les opérations de lancement deviennent irréversibles et qui, sous réserve des dispositions contenues, le cas échéant, dans l'autorisation délivrée en application de la présente loi, s'achève à la séparation du lanceur et de l'objet destiné à être placé dans l'espace extra-atmosphérique;
5° « Phase de maîtrise »: la période de temps qui, dans le cadre d'une opération spatiale, débute à la séparation du lanceur et de l'objet destiné à être placé dans l'espace extra-atmosphérique et qui s'achève à la survenance du premier des événements suivants:

---

1   Consolidated French version of the FSOA on May 2017.
2   The final version of this Act retains wording only at the 'Title' and 'Chapter' levels. Wording on the level of 'Article' have been added (in italics and into brackets) for information on this text, based on the one used for drafts during legislative proceedings.

- lorsque les dernières manœuvres de désorbitation et les activités de passivation ont été effectuées;
- lorsque l'opérateur a perdu le contrôle de l'objet spatial;
- le retour sur Terre ou la désintégration complète dans l'atmosphère de l'objet spatial;

6° « Tiers à une opération spatiale »: toute personne physique ou morale autre que celles participant à l'opération spatiale ou à la production du ou des objets spatiaux dont cette opération consiste à assurer le lancement ou la maîtrise. Notamment, ne sont pas regardés comme des tiers l'opérateur spatial, ses cocontractants, ses sous-traitants et ses clients, ainsi que les cocontractants et sous-traitants de ses clients;

7° « Exploitant primaire de données d'origine spatiale »: toute personne physique ou morale qui assure la programmation d'un système satellitaire d'observation de la Terre ou la réception, depuis l'espace, de données d'observation de la Terre.

TITRE II: AUTORISATION DES OPERATIONS SPATIALES

CHAPITRE IER: OPERATIONS SOUMISES A AUTORISATION

Article 2
(Champ d'application des autorisations)
Doit préalablement obtenir une autorisation délivrée par l'autorité administrative:
1° Tout opérateur, quelle que soit sa nationalité, qui entend procéder au lancement d'un objet spatial à partir du territoire national, de moyens ou d'installations placés sous juridiction française ou qui entend procéder au retour d'un tel objet sur le territoire national, sur des moyens ou des installations placés sous juridiction française;
2° Tout opérateur français qui entend procéder au lancement d'un objet spatial à partir du territoire d'un Etat étranger, de moyens ou d'installations placés sous la juridiction d'un Etat étranger ou d'un espace non soumis à la souveraineté d'un Etat ou qui entend procéder au retour d'un tel objet sur le territoire d'un Etat étranger, sur des moyens ou des installations placés sous la juridiction d'un Etat étranger ou sur un espace non soumis à la souveraineté d'un Etat;
3° Toute personne physique possédant la nationalité française ou personne morale ayant son siège en France, qu'elle soit ou non opérateur, qui entend faire procéder au lancement d'un objet spatial ou tout opérateur français qui entend assurer la maîtrise d'un tel objet pendant son séjour dans l'espace extra-atmosphérique.

Article 3
(Autorisation des transferts d'objets spatiaux)

Le transfert à un tiers de la maîtrise d'un objet spatial ayant fait l'objet d'une autorisation au titre de la présente loi est soumis à l'autorisation préalable de l'autorité administrative. Conformément aux dispositions du 3° de l'article 2, tout opérateur français qui entend prendre la maîtrise d'un objet spatial dont le lancement ou la maîtrise n'a pas été autorisé au titre de la présente loi doit obtenir à cette fin une autorisation préalable délivrée par l'autorité administrative.

Les modalités d'application du présent article sont fixées par décret en Conseil d'Etat.

CHAPITRE II: CONDITIONS DE DELIVRANCE DES AUTORISATIONS

Article 4
(Délivrance des autorisations)

Les autorisations de lancement, de maîtrise et de transfert de la maîtrise d'un objet spatial lancé et de retour sur Terre sont délivrées après vérification, par l'autorité administrative, des garanties morales, financières et professionnelles du demandeur et, le cas échéant, de ses actionnaires, et de la conformité des systèmes et procédures qu'il entend mettre en œuvre avec la réglementation technique édictée, notamment dans l'intérêt de la sécurité des personnes et des biens et de la protection de la santé publique et de l'environnement.

Les autorisations ne peuvent être accordées lorsque les opérations en vue desquelles elles sont sollicitées sont, eu égard notamment aux systèmes dont la mise en œuvre est envisagée, de nature à compromettre les intérêts de la défense nationale ou le respect par la France de ses engagements internationaux.

Des licences attestant, pour une durée déterminée, qu'un opérateur spatial justifie des garanties morales, financières et professionnelles peuvent être délivrées par l'autorité administrative compétente en matière d'autorisations. Ces licences peuvent également attester la conformité des systèmes et procédures mentionnés au premier alinéa avec la réglementation technique édictée. Elles peuvent enfin valoir autorisation pour certaines opérations.

Un décret en Conseil d'Etat fixe les conditions d'application du présent article. Il précise notamment:

1° Les renseignements et documents à fournir à l'appui des demandes d'autorisation et la procédure de délivrance de ces autorisations;
2° L'autorité administrative compétente pour délivrer les autorisations et pour édicter la réglementation technique mentionnée au premier alinéa;
3° Les conditions dans lesquelles peuvent être délivrées les licences mentionnées au troisième alinéa ainsi que les modalités selon lesquelles le bénéficiaire d'une licence informe l'autorité administrative des opérations spatiales auxquelles il procède;
4° Les conditions dans lesquelles l'autorité administrative peut dispenser le demandeur de tout ou partie du contrôle de conformité prévu au premier alinéa, lorsqu'une

autorisation est sollicitée en vue d'une opération devant être conduite à partir du territoire d'un Etat étranger ou de moyens et d'installations placés sous la juridiction d'un Etat étranger et que les engagements nationaux ou internationaux, la législation et la pratique de cet Etat comportent des garanties suffisantes en matière de sécurité des personnes et des biens, de protection de la santé publique et de l'environnement, et de responsabilité.

CHAPITRE III: OBLIGATIONS DES TITULAIRES D'AUTORISATION

Article 5
(Prescriptions conditionnant les autorisations)
Les autorisations délivrées en application de la présente loi peuvent être assorties de prescriptions édictées dans l'intérêt de la sécurité des personnes et des biens et de la protection de la santé publique et de l'environnement, notamment en vue de limiter les risques liés aux débris spatiaux.
Ces prescriptions peuvent également avoir pour objet de protéger les intérêts de la défense nationale ou d'assurer le respect par la France de ses engagements internationaux.

Article 6
(Obligation d'assurance ou de garantie financière)
I. – Tout opérateur soumis à autorisation en application de la présente loi est tenu, tant que sa responsabilité est susceptible d'être engagée dans les conditions prévues à l'article 13 et à concurrence du montant mentionné aux articles 16 et 17, d'être couvert par une assurance ou de disposer d'une autre garantie financière agréée par l'autorité compétente. Un décret en Conseil d'Etat précise les modalités d'assurance, la nature des garanties financières pouvant être agréées par l'autorité compétente et les conditions dans lesquelles il est justifié du respect des obligations mentionnées au premier alinéa auprès de l'autorité qui a délivré l'autorisation. Il précise en outre les conditions dans lesquelles l'opérateur peut être dispensé par l'autorité administrative de l'obligation prévue à l'alinéa précédent.
II. – L'assurance ou la garantie financière doit couvrir le risque d'avoir à indemniser, dans la limite du montant mentionné au I, les dommages susceptibles d'être causés aux tiers à l'opération spatiale.
III. – L'assurance ou la garantie financière doit bénéficier, dans la mesure de la responsabilité pouvant leur incomber à raison d'un dommage causé par un objet spatial, aux personnes suivantes:
1°   L'Etat et ses établissements publics;
2°   L'Agence spatiale européenne et ses Etats membres;
3°   L'opérateur et les personnes qui ont participé à la production de l'objet spatial ou à l'opération spatiale.

Article 7
(Personnes habilitées au contrôle)
– Modifié par LOI n°2013-431 du 28 mai 2013 - art. 31

I. – Sont habilités à procéder aux contrôles nécessaires en vue de vérifier le respect des obligations du présent chapitre:

1° Les agents commissionnés par l'autorité administrative mentionnée à l'article 2, dans des conditions déterminées par décret en Conseil d'Etat, appartenant aux services de l'Etat chargés de l'espace, de la défense, de la recherche, de l'environnement ou à ses établissements publics qui exercent leurs missions dans les mêmes domaines;

2° Les agents habilités à effectuer des contrôles techniques à bord des aéronefs;

3° Les membres du corps de contrôle des assurances mentionné à l'article L. 612-18 du code monétaire et financier;

4° Les agents mentionnés à l'article L. 1421-1 du code de la santé publique;

5° Les administrateurs des affaires maritimes, les officiers du corps technique et administratif des affaires maritimes, les fonctionnaires de catégories A et B affectés dans les services exerçant des missions de contrôle dans le domaine des affaires maritimes sous l'autorité ou à la disposition du ministre chargé de la mer, les commandants des bâtiments de l'Etat et les commandants de bord des aéronefs de l'Etat chargés de la surveillance en mer.

Les agents mentionnés aux 1° à 5° sont astreints au secret professionnel dans les conditions et sous les sanctions prévues aux articles 226-13 et 226-14 du code pénal.

II. – Les agents mentionnés au I ont accès à tout moment aux établissements, aux locaux et aux installations où sont réalisées les opérations spatiales ainsi qu'à l'objet spatial. Au plus tard au début des opérations de contrôle, l'opérateur spatial est avisé qu'il peut assister à la visite et se faire assister de toute personne de son choix, ou s'y faire représenter. Lorsque les locaux ou une partie de ceux-ci constituent un domicile, les visites sont autorisées dans les conditions définies à l'article 7-1.

III. – Dans le cadre de leur mission de contrôle, hormis les saisies réalisées selon la procédure prévue à l'article 7-1, les agents mentionnés au I peuvent demander communication de tous les documents ou pièces utiles, quel qu'en soit le support. Ils peuvent en prendre copie et recueillir sur convocation ou sur place les renseignements et justifications nécessaires.

Les agents ne peuvent emporter des documents qu'après établissement d'une liste contresignée par l'opérateur. La liste précise la nature des documents et leur nombre.

L'opérateur est informé par l'autorité administrative mentionnée à l'article 2 des suites du contrôle. Il peut lui faire part de ses observations.

IV. – Si l'opérateur ou la personne ayant qualité pour autoriser l'accès à l'installation ne peut être atteint ou s'il s'oppose à l'accès, les agents mentionnés au I peuvent y être autorisés dans les conditions prévues à l'article 7-1.

Article 7-1
- Modifié par LOI n°2011-94 du 25 janvier 2011 - art. 31

I. - La visite prévue à l'article 7 est autorisée par ordonnance du juge des libertés et de la détention du tribunal de grande instance dans le ressort duquel sont situés les lieux à visiter. L'ordonnance comporte l'adresse des lieux à visiter, le nom et la qualité du ou des fonctionnaires habilités à procéder aux opérations de visite et de saisie ainsi que les heures auxquelles ils sont autorisés à se présenter.

L'ordonnance est exécutoire au seul vu de la minute.

II. - L'ordonnance est notifiée sur place, au moment de la visite, à l'occupant des lieux ou à son représentant qui en reçoit copie intégrale contre récépissé ou émargement au procès-verbal de visite. En l'absence de l'occupant des lieux ou de son représentant, l'ordonnance est notifiée, après la visite, par lettre recommandée avec demande d'avis de réception. La notification est réputée faite à la date de réception figurant sur l'avis. A défaut de réception, il est procédé à la signification de l'ordonnance par acte d'huissier de justice.

L'acte de notification comporte mention des voies et délais de recours contre l'ordonnance ayant autorisé la visite et contre les contestations sur le déroulement des opérations de visite. Il mentionne également que le juge ayant autorisé la visite peut être saisi d'une demande de suspension ou d'arrêt de cette visite.

III. - La visite et la saisie de documents s'effectuent sous l'autorité et le contrôle du juge des libertés et de la détention qui les a autorisées. Le juge des libertés et de la détention peut, s'il l'estime utile, se rendre dans les locaux pendant l'intervention. A tout moment, il peut décider la suspension ou l'arrêt de la visite. La saisine du juge des libertés et de la détention aux fins de suspension ou d'arrêt des opérations de visite et de saisie n'entraîne pas la suspension de celles-ci.

IV. - La visite ne peut commencer avant 6 heures et après 21 heures. Elle est effectuée en présence de l'occupant des lieux ou de son représentant, qui peut se faire assister de l'avocat de son choix. En l'absence de l'occupant des lieux, les agents chargés de la visite ne peuvent procéder à celle-ci qu'en présence de deux témoins qui ne sont pas placés sous leur autorité.

Les agents habilités, l'occupant des lieux ou son représentant peuvent seuls prendre connaissance des pièces et documents avant leur saisie.

Un procès-verbal relatant les modalités et le déroulement de l'opération et consignant les constatations effectuées est dressé sur-le-champ par les agents habilités à procéder à la visite. Un inventaire des pièces et documents saisis lui est annexé s'il y a lieu. Le procès-verbal et l'inventaire sont signés par les agents habilités et par l'occupant des lieux ou, le cas échéant, son représentant et les témoins. En cas de refus de signer, mention en est faite au procès-verbal.

Les originaux du procès-verbal et de l'inventaire sont, dès qu'ils ont été établis, adressés au juge qui a autorisé la visite. Une copie de ces mêmes documents est remise ou adressée par lettre recommandée avec demande d'avis de réception à l'occupant des lieux ou à son représentant.

Le procès-verbal et l'inventaire mentionnent le délai et les voies de recours.

Les pièces saisies sont conservées pour les besoins de la procédure, à moins qu'une décision insusceptible de pourvoi en cassation par les parties n'en ordonne la restitution.

V. - L'ordonnance autorisant la visite peut faire l'objet d'un appel devant le premier président de la cour d'appel suivant les règles prévues par le code de procédure civile. Les parties ne sont pas tenues de constituer avocat.

Cet appel est formé par déclaration remise ou adressée par pli recommandé au greffe de la cour dans un délai de quinze jours. Ce délai court à compter de la notification de l'ordonnance. Cet appel n'est pas suspensif.

Le greffe du tribunal de grande instance transmet sans délai le dossier de l'affaire au greffe de la cour d'appel où les parties peuvent le consulter.

L'ordonnance du premier président de la cour d'appel est susceptible d'un pourvoi en cassation, selon les règles prévues par le code de procédure civile. Le délai du pourvoi en cassation est de quinze jours.

VI. - Le premier président de la cour d'appel connaît des recours contre le déroulement des opérations de visite ou de saisie autorisées par le juge des libertés et de la détention suivant les règles prévues par le code de procédure civile. Les parties ne sont pas tenues de constituer avocat.

Le recours est formé par déclaration remise ou adressée par pli recommandé au greffe de la cour dans un délai de quinze jours. Ce délai court à compter de la remise ou de la réception soit du procès-verbal, soit de l'inventaire, mentionnés au premier alinéa. Ce recours n'est pas suspensif.

L'ordonnance du premier président de la cour d'appel est susceptible d'un pourvoi en cassation selon les règles prévues par le code de procédure civile. Le délai du pourvoi en cassation est de quinze jours.

VII. - Le présent article est reproduit dans l'acte de notification de l'ordonnance du juge des libertés et de la détention autorisant la visite.

Article 8
(Missions de l'autorité administrative en cas d'urgence)
S'agissant du lancement ou de la maîtrise d'un objet spatial, l'autorité administrative ou, sur délégation de celle-ci, les agents habilités par elle à cet effet peuvent à tout moment donner les instructions et imposer toutes mesures qu'ils considèrent comme nécessaires dans l'intérêt de la sécurité des personnes et des biens et de la protection de la santé publique et de l'environnement.

L'autorité administrative ou les agents habilités agissant sur sa délégation consultent l'opérateur au préalable, sauf dans le cas où existe un danger immédiat.

Un décret en Conseil d'Etat précise les modalités de délégation et d'habilitation des agents chargés de l'application du présent article.

CHAPITRE IV: SANCTIONS ADMINISTRATIVES ET PENALES

Article 9
(Retrait et suspension des autorisations)
Les autorisations délivrées en application de la présente loi peuvent être retirées ou suspendues en cas de manquement du titulaire aux obligations qui lui incombent, ou lorsque les opérations en vue desquelles elles ont été sollicitées apparaissent de nature à compromettre les intérêts de la défense nationale ou le respect par la France de ses engagements internationaux.

En cas de suspension ou de retrait de l'autorisation de maîtrise d'un objet spatial lancé, l'autorité administrative peut enjoindre à l'opérateur de prendre, à ses frais, les mesures propres, au regard des règles de bonne conduite communément admises, à limiter les risques de dommage liés à cet objet.

Article 10
(Constatation des infractions – agents assermentés)
Outre les officiers et agents de police judiciaire agissant conformément aux dispositions du code de procédure pénale, les agents mentionnés au I de l'article 7 et assermentés ont qualité pour rechercher et constater les infractions aux dispositions du présent chapitre et aux textes pris pour son application. Ils disposent, à cet effet, des pouvoirs prévus aux II à IV du même article.

Ils constatent ces infractions par des procès-verbaux qui font foi jusqu'à preuve contraire. Ils sont adressés au procureur de la République dans les cinq jours qui suivent leur clôture. Un décret en Conseil d'Etat précise les modalités d'application du présent article.

Article 11
(Sanctions pénales ou amendes)
I. – Est puni d'une amende de 200 000 euros le fait:
1° Pour tout opérateur, quelle que soit sa nationalité, de procéder sans autorisation au lancement d'un objet spatial à partir du territoire national ou de moyens ou installations placés sous juridiction française ou au retour d'un tel objet sur le territoire national ou sur des moyens ou installations placés sous juridiction française;
2° Pour tout opérateur français, de procéder sans autorisation au lancement d'un objet spatial à partir du territoire d'un Etat étranger, de moyens ou d'installations placés sous la juridiction d'un Etat étranger ou d'un espace non soumis à la souveraineté d'un Etat ou au retour d'un tel objet sur le territoire d'un Etat étranger, sur des moyens

ou des installations placés sous la juridiction d'un Etat étranger ou sur un espace non soumis à la souveraineté d'un Etat;
3° Pour toute personne physique possédant la nationalité française ou personne morale ayant son siège en France, de faire procéder sans autorisation au lancement d'un objet spatial ou d'en assurer la maîtrise sans autorisation pendant son séjour dans l'espace extra-atmosphérique.

II. – Est puni d'une amende de 200 000 euros le fait:
1° De transférer à un tiers sans autorisation la maîtrise d'un objet spatial dont le lancement ou la maîtrise a été autorisé au titre de la présente loi;
2° Pour tout opérateur français, de prendre sans autorisation la maîtrise d'un objet spatial dont le lancement n'a pas été autorisé au titre de la présente loi.

III. – Est puni d'une amende de 200 000 euros le fait pour un opérateur:
1° De poursuivre l'opération spatiale en infraction à une mesure administrative ou à une décision juridictionnelle d'arrêt ou de suspension;
2° De poursuivre l'opération spatiale sans se conformer à une mise en demeure de l'autorité administrative de respecter une prescription.

IV. – Est puni d'une amende de 200 000 euros le fait pour un opérateur ou une personne physique de faire obstacle aux contrôles effectués en application de l'article 7.

TITRE III: IMMATRICULATION DES OBJETS SPATIAUX LANCES

Article 12
(Tenue du registre national d'immatriculation)
Dans les cas où l'obligation d'immatriculer incombe à la France en vertu de l'article II de la convention du 14 janvier 1975 sur l'immatriculation des objets lancés dans l'espace extra-atmosphérique et, le cas échéant, d'autres accords internationaux, les objets spatiaux lancés sont inscrits sur un registre d'immatriculation tenu, pour le compte de l'Etat, par le Centre national d'études spatiales selon des modalités fixées par décret en Conseil d'Etat.

TITRE IV: RESPONSABILITES

CHAPITRE IER: RESPONSABILITE A L'EGARD DES TIERS

Article 13
(Canalisation de la responsabilité)
L'opérateur est seul responsable des dommages causés aux tiers du fait des opérations spatiales qu'il conduit dans les conditions suivantes:
1° Il est responsable de plein droit pour les dommages causés au sol et dans l'espace aérien;

2°   En cas de dommages causés ailleurs qu'au sol ou dans l'espace aérien, sa responsabilité ne peut être recherchée que pour faute.

Cette responsabilité ne peut être atténuée ou écartée que par la preuve de la faute de la victime.

Sauf cas de faute intentionnelle, la responsabilité prévue aux 1° et 2° cesse quand toutes les obligations fixées par l'autorisation ou la licence sont remplies ou, au plus tard, un an après la date où ces obligations auraient dû être remplies. L'Etat se substitue à l'opérateur pour les dommages intervenus passé ce délai.

Article 14
(Action récursoire de l'Etat)
Lorsqu'en vertu des stipulations du traité du 27 janvier 1967 sur les principes régissant les activités des Etats en matière d'exploration et d'utilisation de l'espace extra-atmosphérique, y compris la Lune et les autres corps célestes, ou de la convention du 29 mars 1972 sur la responsabilité internationale pour les dommages causés par des objets spatiaux, l'Etat a réparé un dommage, il peut exercer une action récursoire contre l'opérateur à l'origine de ce dommage ayant engagé la responsabilité internationale de la France, dans la mesure où il n'a pas déjà bénéficié des garanties financières ou d'assurance de l'opérateur à hauteur de l'indemnisation.

Si le dommage a été causé par un objet spatial utilisé dans le cadre d'une opération autorisée en application de la présente loi, l'action récursoire s'exerce:
1°   Dans la limite du montant fixé dans les conditions mentionnées à l'article 16 en cas de dommage causé pendant la phase de lancement;
2°   Dans la limite du montant fixé dans les conditions mentionnées à l'article 17 en cas de dommage causé après la phase de lancement, y compris à l'occasion du retour sur Terre de l'objet spatial.

En cas de faute intentionnelle de l'opérateur, les limites prévues aux 1° et 2° ne s'appliquent pas.

L'Etat n'exerce pas d'action récursoire en cas de dommage causé par un objet spatial utilisé dans le cadre d'une opération autorisée en application de la présente loi et résultant d'actes visant les intérêts étatiques.

Article 15
(Garantie financière de l'Etat)
Lorsqu'un opérateur a été condamné à indemniser un tiers à raison d'un dommage causé par un objet spatial utilisé dans le cadre d'une opération autorisée en application de la présente loi, et à la condition que l'opération en cause ait été conduite depuis le territoire de la France ou d'un autre Etat membre de l'Union européenne ou partie à l'accord sur l'Espace économique européen, ou à partir de moyens ou installations placés sous la juri-

diction de la France ou d'un autre Etat membre de l'Union européenne ou partie à l'accord sur l'Espace économique européen, cet opérateur bénéficie, sauf cas de faute intentionnelle, de la garantie de l'Etat selon les modalités prévues par la loi de finances:
1° Pour la part de l'indemnisation excédant le montant fixé dans les conditions mentionnées à l'article 16 en cas de dommage causé pendant la phase de lancement;
2° Pour la part de l'indemnisation excédant le montant fixé dans les conditions mentionnées à l'article 17 en cas de dommage causé au sol ou dans l'espace aérien après la phase de lancement, y compris à l'occasion du retour sur terre de l'objet spatial.

En cas de dommage causé pendant la phase de lancement, la garantie de l'Etat bénéficie, le cas échéant et dans les conditions prévues aux alinéas précédents, aux personnes qui n'ont pas la qualité de tiers à une opération spatiale, au sens de la présente loi.

Article 16
(Plafond de la garantie de l'état applicable pendant la phase de lancement)
Dans le cadre fixé par la loi de finances[3], l'autorisation délivrée en application de la présente loi fixe, compte tenu des risques encourus, eu égard notamment aux caractéristiques du site de lancement, le montant en deçà duquel et au-delà duquel sont, respectivement, en cas de dommages causés pendant la phase de lancement, exercée l'action récursoire et octroyée la garantie de l'Etat.

Article 17
(Plafond de la garantie de l'Etat applicable après la phase de lancement)
Dans le cadre fixé par la loi de finances, l'autorisation délivrée en application de la présente loi fixe, compte tenu des risques encourus, le montant en deçà duquel et au-delà duquel sont, respectivement, en cas de dommages causés après la phase de lancement, exercée l'action récursoire et octroyée la garantie de l'Etat.
NOTA:
Conformément à l'article 29 de la loi n° 2008-518 du 3 juin 2008, les articles 16 et 17 de la loi entrent en vigueur à compter de la publication de la loi de finances qui fixe le minimum et le maximum entre lesquels est compris le montant au-delà duquel est octroyée la garantie de l'Etat.

Article 18
(Direction du procès)
Toute personne mise en cause devant une juridiction à raison d'un dommage au titre duquel elle serait susceptible de bénéficier de la garantie de l'Etat en informe l'autorité administrative compétente qui peut, au nom de l'Etat, exercer tous les droits de la défense

---

3 See footnote under article 29 below.

dans le procès. A défaut d'une telle information, la personne mise en cause est réputée avoir renoncé au bénéfice de la garantie de l'Etat.

CHAPITRE II: RESPONSABILITE A L'EGARD DES PERSONNES PARTICIPANT A L'OPERATION SPATIALE

Article 19
(Renonciation mutuelle à recours en cas de dommage causé à un tiers)
Lorsque, pour indemniser un tiers, l'assurance ou la garantie financière mentionnées à l'article 6 ainsi que, le cas échéant, la garantie de l'Etat ont été mises en jeu, la responsabilité de l'une des personnes ayant participé à l'opération spatiale ou à la production de l'objet spatial à l'origine du dommage ne peut être recherchée par une autre de ces personnes, sauf en cas de faute intentionnelle.

Article 20
(Clauses limitatives de responsabilité en cas de dommage causé à un partenaire contractuel)
En cas de dommage causé par une opération spatiale ou la production d'un objet spatial à une personne participant à cette opération ou à cette production, la responsabilité de toute autre personne participant à l'opération spatiale ou à la production de l'objet spatial à l'origine du dommage et liée à la précédente par un contrat ne peut être recherchée à raison de ce dommage, sauf stipulation expresse contraire portant sur les dommages causés pendant la phase de production d'un objet spatial destiné à être maîtrisé dans l'espace extra-atmosphérique ou pendant sa maîtrise en orbite, ou cas de faute intentionnelle.

TITRE V: DISPOSITIONS RELATIVES AU CODE DE LA RECHERCHE

Article 21[4]
(Rôle du Président du CNES)
Le code de la recherche est ainsi modifié:
1°   L'article L. 331-6 est ainsi rédigé:
   « Art. L. 331-6.-I. – Le président du Centre national d'études spatiales exerce, au nom de l'Etat, la police spéciale de l'exploitation des installations du Centre spatial guyanais dans un périmètre délimité par l'autorité administrative compétente. A ce titre, il est chargé d'une mission générale de sauvegarde consistant à maîtriser les risques techniques liés à la préparation et à la réalisation des lancements à partir du Centre spatial guyanais afin d'assurer la protection des personnes, des biens, de la santé publique

---

[4]   Modifies articles L331-6 and L331-7 (V) of the Research Code. Creates article L331-8 (V) of the Research Code.

et de l'environnement, au sol et en vol, et il arrête à cette fin les règlements particuliers applicables dans les limites du périmètre mentionné ci-dessus.

« II. – Le président du Centre national d'études spatiales coordonne, sous l'autorité du représentant de l'Etat dans le département, la mise en œuvre, par les entreprises et autres organismes installés dans le périmètre défini au I, des mesures visant à assurer la sûreté des installations et des activités qui y sont menées, et s'assure du respect, par ces entreprises et organismes, des obligations qui leur incombent à ce titre.

« III. – Dans la mesure strictement nécessaire à l'accomplissement des missions prévues aux I et II, les agents que le président du Centre national d'études spatiales habilite ont accès aux terrains et locaux à usage exclusivement professionnel et occupés par les entreprises et organismes installés au Centre spatial guyanais dans le périmètre défini au I. »;

2°   Après l'article L. 331-6, sont insérés deux articles L. 331-7 et L. 331-8 ainsi rédigés:
« Art. L. 331-7.-Le président du Centre national d'études spatiales peut, par délégation de l'autorité administrative mentionnée à l'article 8 de la loi n° 2008-518 du 3 juin 2008 relative aux opérations spatiales et pour toute opération spatiale, prendre les mesures nécessaires prévues au même article pour garantir la sécurité des personnes et des biens ainsi que la protection de la santé publique et de l'environnement.
« Art. L. 331-8.-Un décret en Conseil d'Etat fixe les conditions d'application du présent chapitre, notamment les conditions dans lesquelles le président du Centre national d'études spatiales peut déléguer sa compétence mentionnée à l'article L. 331-6. »

TITRE VI: PROPRIETE INTELLECTUELLE

Article 22[5]
(Extension des règles de brevets d'invention)
I. – L'article L. 611-1 du code de la propriété intellectuelle est complété par un alinéa ainsi rédigé:
« Sauf stipulation contraire d'un engagement international auquel la France est partie, les dispositions du présent article s'appliquent aux inventions réalisées ou utilisées dans l'espace extra-atmosphérique y compris sur les corps célestes ou dans ou sur des objets spatiaux placés sous juridiction nationale en application de l'article VIII du traité du 27 janvier 1967 sur les principes régissant les activités des Etats en matière d'exploration et d'utilisation de l'espace extra-atmosphérique, y compris la Lune et les autres corps célestes. »

II. – L'article L. 613-5 du même code est complété par un e) ainsi rédigé:

---

5   Modifies art. L611-1 (V) and art. L613-5 (M)art. L331-2 (V) of the Intellectual Property Code.

« e) Aux objets destinés à être lancés dans l'espace extra-atmosphérique introduits sur le territoire français. »

TITRE VII : DONNEES D'ORIGINE SPATIALE

Article 23
(Déclaration préalable)
Tout exploitant primaire de données d'origine spatiale exerçant en France une activité présentant certaines caractéristiques techniques définies par décret en Conseil d'Etat doit préalablement en faire la déclaration à l'autorité administrative compétente.
Ces caractéristiques techniques sont notamment fonction de la résolution, de la précision de localisation, de la bande de fréquence d'observation et de la qualité des données d'observation de la Terre faisant l'objet de la programmation d'un système satellitaire ou reçues.

Article 24
(Contrôle de l'autorité administrative)
L'autorité administrative compétente s'assure que l'activité des exploitants primaires de données d'origine spatiale ne porte pas atteinte aux intérêts fondamentaux de la Nation, notamment à la défense nationale, à la politique extérieure et aux engagements internationaux de la France.
A ce titre, elle peut, à tout moment, prescrire les mesures de restriction à l'activité des exploitants primaires de données d'origine spatiale nécessaires à la sauvegarde de ces intérêts.

Article 25
(Amendes - ou sanctions pénales)
Est puni d'une amende de 200 000 euros le fait, par tout exploitant primaire de données d'origine spatiale, de se livrer à une activité présentant les caractéristiques techniques mentionnées à l'article 23 :
1° Sans avoir effectué la déclaration mentionnée à l'article 23 ;
2° Sans respecter les mesures de restriction prises sur le fondement de l'article 24.

ANNEXE 1.2

TITRE VIII: DISPOSITIONS TRANSITOIRES ET FINALES

Article 26
(Exclusion des activités de défense)
La présente loi ne s'applique pas au lancement et au guidage, pour les besoins de la défense nationale, d'engins dont la trajectoire traverse l'espace extra-atmosphérique, notamment les missiles balistiques.
Ne sont pas soumises aux dispositions du titre VII les activités d'exploitant primaire de données d'origine spatiale exercées par le ministère de la défense.

Article 27
(Exclusion de certaines activités du CNES du champ d'application de la loi)
En tant qu'elles relèvent d'une mission publique confiée au Centre national d'études spatiales après approbation de l'autorité administrative en application du quatrième alinéa de l'article L. 331-2 du code de la recherche, ne sont pas soumises aux dispositions des titres II et IV les opérations de lancement, de retour sur terre, de maîtrise ou de transfert de maîtrise d'un objet spatial et aux dispositions du titre VII les activités satellitaires d'observation de la Terre et de réception des données d'observation de la Terre.

Article 28[6]
(Attributions nouvelles du CNES)
L'article L. 331-2 du code de la recherche est complété par un f, un g et un h ainsi rédigés:
« f) D'assister l'Etat dans la définition de la réglementation technique relative aux opérations spatiales;
« g) D'exercer, par délégation du ministre chargé de l'espace, le contrôle de la conformité des systèmes et des procédures mis en œuvre par les opérateurs spatiaux avec la réglementation technique mentionnée au f;
« h) De tenir, pour le compte de l'Etat, le registre d'immatriculation des objets spatiaux. »

Article 29
(Entrée en vigueur des articles 16 et 17)
Les articles 16 et 17 de la présente loi entrent en vigueur à compter de la publication de la loi de finances[7] qui fixe le minimum et le maximum entre lesquels est compris le montant au-delà duquel est octroyée la garantie de l'Etat.

---

6 Modifies article L331-2 (V) of the Research Code.
7 See Amending Finance Act (Loi de finance rectificative) n°2008-1443 of 30 December 2008 - Annex 6 Article 119, JORF 31 December 2008:
'I- In conformity with the provisions of the provisions of the Space Operation Act N° 2008-518 of June 3rd, 2008 , the Government is authorized to guarantee the compensation of the damage caused to third parties in

Article 30
(Applicabilité outre-mer)
La présente loi est applicable en Nouvelle-Calédonie, en Polynésie française, dans les îles Wallis et Futuna et dans les Terres australes et antarctiques françaises.

La présente loi sera exécutée comme loi de l'Etat.

Fait à Paris, le 3 juin 2008.

Nicolas Sarkozy

Par le Président de la République:
Le Premier ministre,
François Fillon
La ministre de l'intérieur,
de l'outre-mer et des collectivités territoriales,
Michèle Alliot-Marie
Le ministre des affaires étrangères
et européennes,
Bernard Kouchner
La ministre de l'enseignement supérieur
et de la recherche,
Valérie Pécresse
Le ministre de la défense,
Hervé Morin

(1) Travaux préparatoires: loi n° 2008-518.
Sénat:
Projet de loi n° 297 (2006-2007);
Rapport de M. Henri Revol, au nom de la commission des affaires économiques, n° 161 (2007-2008);
Discussion et adoption le 16 janvier 2008 (TA n° 50).
Assemblée nationale:

---

connection with a space operation authorized under the aforementioned act and carried out from a territory of the European Economic Area. This coverage applies, <u>except wilful misconduct or serious departure from the requirement of the authorization</u>, beyond a ceiling fixed in the same authorization. This ceiling shall be between 50 million euros and 70 million euros.
II. paragraph I above is applicable in New Caledonia, in French Polynesia, on islands Wallis and Futuna and in the French Southern and Antarctic Lands.'

Projet de loi, adopté par le Sénat, n° 614;

Rapport de M. Pierre Lasbordes, au nom de la commission des affaires économiques, n° 775;

Discussion et adoption le 9 avril 2008 (TA n° 120).

Sénat:

Projet de loi n° 272 (2007-2008);

Rapport de M. Henri Revol, au nom de la commission des affaires économiques, n° 328 (2007-2008);

Discussion et adoption le 22 mai 2008 (TA n° 97).

Annexe 1.3

Décret n° 2009-643 du 9 juin 2009 relatif aux autorisations délivrées en application de la loi n° 2008-518 du 3 juin 2008 relative aux opérations spatiales (DA)

Décret n° 2009-643 du 9 juin 2009 relatif aux autorisations délivrées en application de la loi n° 2008-518 du 3 juin 2008 relative aux opérations spatiales[1]

NOR: ESRR0825834D

ELI: https://www.legifrance.gouv.fr/eli/decret/2009/6/9/ESRR0825834D/jo/texte
Alias: https://www.legifrance.gouv.fr/eli/decret/2009/6/9/2009-643/jo/texte

Le Premier ministre,
Sur le rapport de la ministre de l'enseignement supérieur et de la recherche,
Vu le code de l'environnement, notamment son article L. 161-1;
Vu le code monétaire et financier, notamment ses articles L. 431-7 à L. 431-7-5;
Vu le code de procédure pénale, notamment son article 28;
Vu le code de la recherche, notamment le chapitre Ier du titre III du livre III;
Vu la loi n° 2008-518 du 3 juin 2008 relative aux opérations spatiales;
Vu le décret n° 84-510 du 28 juin 1984 relatif au Centre national des études spatiales;
Vu le décret n° 97-1189 du 19 décembre 1997 pris pour l'application au ministre de l'éducation nationale, de la recherche et de la technologie du 1° de l'article 2 du décret n° 97-34 du 1er janvier 1997 relatif à la déconcentration des décisions administratives individuelles;
Vu l'avis du comité consultatif de la législation et de la réglementation financières en date du 1er avril 2009;
Le Conseil d'Etat (section des travaux publics) entendu,
Décrète:

TITRE IER: AUTORISATION ET LICENCE

CHAPITRE IER: PROCEDURE D'AUTORISATION

---

[1] JORF n° 0132 du 10 juin 2009

Article 1

Les autorisations prévues aux articles 2 et 3 de la loi du 3 juin 2008 susvisée sont délivrées par le ministre chargé de l'espace. Ce dernier arrête la réglementation technique prévue au premier alinéa de l'article 4 de la même loi.

La demande d'autorisation est adressée au ministre en trois exemplaires par courrier ainsi que par voie électronique. Elle comporte deux parties:

I. - Une partie administrative qui comprend:
1° S'il s'agit d'une personne physique: ses nom, prénoms et domicile; s'il s'agit d'une personne morale: sa dénomination ou sa raison sociale, sa forme juridique, l'adresse de son siège social ainsi que la qualité du signataire de la demande;
2° Les éléments permettant d'apprécier l'existence des garanties morales, financières et professionnelles du demandeur. A ce titre, le demandeur doit justifier:
   – des conditions d'honorabilité et, notamment, d'absence de faillite personnelle des personnes physiques qui conduisent l'opération spatiale;
   – de la situation financière et des conditions de gouvernance de l'entreprise;
   – des systèmes de gestion de la qualité mis en œuvre au sein de l'entreprise;
   – de la qualification et des politiques de formation du personnel;
3° S'il en dispose, la licence attestant que l'opérateur spatial justifie des garanties morales, financières et professionnelles mentionnées au troisième alinéa de l'article 4 de la loi du 3 juin 2008 susvisée. Dans ce cas, le demandeur ne fournit que les pièces mentionnées aux 1° et 2° ci-dessus qui n'ont pas été transmises au titre de la demande de licence;
4° Les modalités de garanties financières envisagées pour l'opération, notamment leur nature, leur montant et leur délai de constitution.

II. - Une partie technique qui comprend:
1° La description de l'opération spatiale devant être conduite et des systèmes et procédures que le demandeur entend mettre en œuvre;
2° Un dossier dont la composition est précisée par arrêté pris par le ministre chargé de l'espace en fonction du type d'opération envisagée et qui comprend tout ou partie des éléments suivants:
   a) La notice générale de conformité à la réglementation technique;
   b) Les normes internes et dispositions de gestion de la qualité applicables dans le cadre de l'opération spatiale devant être conduite;
   c) L'ensemble des mesures, y compris les études de dangers et les plans de maîtrise des risques, mises en œuvre par le demandeur pour assurer la sécurité des biens et des personnes et la protection de la santé publique et de l'environnement;
   d) Les études d'impact sur l'environnement et les mesures destinées à éviter, réduire ou compenser les effets néfastes sur l'environnement qui comprennent:

- le plan de prévention des risques induits par la retombée de l'objet spatial ou de ses fragments;
- le plan de prévention des dommages environnementaux tels que définis à l'article L. 161-1 du code de l'environnement;
- le plan de limitation des débris spatiaux;
- le plan de prévention des risques de collision;
- le cas échéant, le plan de sûreté nucléaire;
- le cas échéant, le plan de protection planétaire;

e) Les mesures de maîtrise des risques prévues lors de la conduite de l'opération spatiale;

f) Les mesures de secours prévues;

3° S'il en dispose, la licence attestant la conformité des systèmes et procédures mentionnés au troisième alinéa de l'article 4 de la loi du 3 juin 2008 susvisée. Dans ce cas, le demandeur ne fournit que les éléments mentionnés aux 1° et 2° qui n'ont pas été transmis au titre de la demande de licence.

Article 2

Le ministre chargé de l'espace, le cas échéant après avoir invité le demandeur à compléter son dossier, en accuse réception, en indiquant au demandeur la date d'enregistrement du dossier, un mois au plus tard après la réception du dossier complet.

Article 3

Le dossier est transmis au Centre national d'études spatiales, qui contrôle la conformité des systèmes et procédures que le demandeur entend mettre en œuvre avec la réglementation technique, en vue d'assurer la sécurité des personnes et des biens et la protection de la santé publique et de l'environnement. Il peut, à tout moment, inviter le demandeur à lui communiquer des informations complémentaires.

Le président du Centre national d'études spatiales transmet son avis au ministre chargé de l'espace dans un délai de deux mois à compter de la date d'enregistrement du dossier. Si le demandeur est titulaire d'une licence mentionnée au troisième alinéa de l'article 4 de la loi du 3 juin 2008 susvisée attestant de la conformité des systèmes et procédures, le Centre national d'études spatiales vérifie que l'opération dont l'autorisation est demandée est conforme à cette licence. Son avis doit alors être rendu dans un délai de quinze jours à compter de la date d'enregistrement du dossier.

Article 4

Préalablement à sa décision, le ministre porte à la connaissance du demandeur le projet d'arrêté statuant sur sa demande. Le demandeur dispose d'un délai de quinze jours pour présenter ses éventuelles observations. Ces dispositions ne sont pas applicables lorsque le demandeur est titulaire d'une licence mentionnée au troisième alinéa de l'article 4 de la loi du 3 juin 2008 susvisée et que la demande est instruite dans les délais d'instruction réduits mentionnés aux articles 3 et 5.

Article 5
Le ministre chargé de l'espace prend sa décision dans les quatre mois suivant la date d'enregistrement du dossier mentionnée à l'article 2. Il peut, par décision motivée et notifiée au demandeur, proroger ce délai pour une durée qui ne peut excéder deux mois. Lorsque le demandeur est titulaire d'une licence mentionnée au troisième alinéa de l'article 4 de la loi du 3 juin 2008 susvisée, le délai mentionné à la première phrase de l'alinéa précédent est de un mois.
L'autorisation peut être assortie de prescriptions édictées dans l'intérêt de la sécurité des biens et des personnes, de la protection de la santé publique, de l'environnement et des intérêts de la défense nationale ainsi que pour assurer le respect par la France de ses engagements internationaux. Ces prescriptions prévoient notamment les modalités selon lesquelles les agents habilités dans les conditions prévues à l'article 7 de la loi du 3 juin 2008 précitée suivent la préparation de l'opération, en particulier la phase technique de la préparation.
L'autorisation est délivrée pour toute la durée de l'opération spatiale concernée. Toutefois, si l'opération n'a pas commencé dans les dix ans qui suivent la date d'octroi de l'autorisation, l'autorisation est caduque et l'opérateur doit présenter une nouvelle demande.

Article 6
Si un opérateur français fournit, à l'appui d'une demande d'autorisation de faire procéder au lancement d'un objet spatial, l'autorisation de lancement obtenue par l'opérateur chargé de procéder au lancement dudit objet spatial, il est dispensé de fournir la partie technique décrite au II de l'article 1er du présent décret.
Dans ce cas, l'autorisation de faire procéder au lancement est réputée accordée si le ministre chargé de l'espace n'a pas fait connaître sa réponse dans un délai d'un mois à compter de la date d'enregistrement de la demande.

Article 7
Si, postérieurement à la délivrance de l'autorisation, l'opérateur met en œuvre ou a connaissance d'événements non prévus par l'autorisation ou d'incidents techniques affectant les conditions de l'opération spatiale telle qu'elle a été autorisée, il en informe sans délai le Centre national d'études spatiales.
Celui-ci peut, après consultation ou sur proposition de l'opérateur, proposer au ministre des mesures correctives à apporter à l'autorisation accordée. Celui-ci, après avoir mis en

mesure l'opérateur de présenter ses observations, peut modifier en conséquence l'autorisation. Sa décision est notifiée à l'opérateur.

Si, malgré ces éventuelles mesures correctives, les événements ou incidents techniques mentionnés au premier alinéa aggravent substantiellement les risques au regard de la sécurité des personnes et des biens et de la santé publique et de l'environnement, le ministre, sur proposition du Centre national d'études spatiales, invite l'opérateur à présenter une nouvelle demande. L'autorisation initiale reste en vigueur jusqu'à la notification de la nouvelle décision du ministre chargé de l'espace.

Si le Centre national d'études spatiales estime qu'il n'y a pas lieu de modifier l'autorisation accordée, il l'indique au ministre qui informe le demandeur de sa décision.

CHAPITRE II: LICENCES

Article 8
Les licences mentionnées au troisième alinéa de l'article 4 de la loi du 3 juin 2008 susvisée sont attribuées selon les modalités prévues pour les autorisations au chapitre Ier du présent décret.

La durée maximale de validité d'une licence est de dix ans. Le ministre peut, par décision motivée, accorder une licence pour une durée inférieure à celle qui a été demandée.

Article 9
Les licences mentionnées à la deuxième phrase du troisième alinéa de l'article 4 de la loi du 3 juin 2008 susvisée peuvent attester tout ou partie de la conformité des systèmes et procédures prévus par l'opérateur spatial avec la réglementation technique.

Article 10
Les demandes de licence valant autorisation pour certaines opérations sont accompagnées d'une description précise de chaque type d'opération concernée. Toute opération qui ne répond pas à la description contenue dans cette licence doit faire l'objet d'une demande d'autorisation selon les modalités prévues au chapitre Ier ci-dessus.

Le titulaire d'une licence valant autorisation pour certaines opérations informe le ministre chargé de l'espace un mois avant la mise en œuvre de toute opération mentionnée dans ladite licence. Lorsque, en raison de l'urgence, ces dispositions ne peuvent être respectées, l'opérateur justifie auprès du ministre, dans les meilleurs délais, de la nécessité de l'opération et des motifs de sa décision.

Article 11
Toute personne responsable de la conception ou du développement d'un système ou d'un sous-système critique au regard de la sécurité des personnes et des biens et de la protection

de la santé publique et de l'environnement au sens de la réglementation technique prévue au premier alinéa de l'article 4 de la loi du 3 juin 2008 susvisée, destiné à être utilisé dans le cadre d'une opération spatiale, peut soumettre au Centre national d'études spatiales un dossier en décrivant les caractéristiques techniques générales ainsi que son plan de développement, en vue de permettre au centre d'en attester la conformité, en tout ou partie, à la réglementation technique précitée.

Le Centre national d'études spatiales prescrit les contrôles, essais et analyses requis par la réglementation technique. Au terme de cet examen, le président du centre remet au soumissionnaire, pour chaque étape du développement réalisée, un document attestant la conformité du système ou du sous-système critique à la réglementation technique, qui peut être produit à l'appui d'une demande d'autorisation présentée dans les conditions prévues au chapitre Ier ci-dessus.

Les documents attestant de cette conformité ne sauraient valoir autorisation au sens de l'article 2 de la loi du 3 juin 2008 susvisée. Ils ne préjugent pas de la conformité dudit système ou sous-système à la réglementation technique pour une utilisation dans un cadre autre que celui prévu dans le dossier technique soumis pour l'opération spatiale considérée.

CHAPITRE III: OPERATIONS CONDUITES A PARTIR DU TERRITOIRE D'UN ETAT ETRANGER OU DE MOYENS OU D'INSTALLATIONS PLACES SOUS LA JURIDICTION D'UN ETAT ETRANGER

Article 12

Lorsque la demande d'autorisation concerne une opération devant être conduite à partir du territoire d'un Etat étranger ou de moyens ou d'installations placés sous la juridiction d'un Etat étranger, le demandeur fournit, le cas échéant, tous éléments permettant d'apprécier l'existence des garanties mentionnées au 4° de l'article 4 de la loi du 3 juin 2008 susvisée qui le dispensent de tout ou partie du contrôle de conformité prévu au premier alinéa du même article.

Dans les conditions de l'article 5, le ministre informe le demandeur de sa décision soit d'accorder la dispense demandée, soit des raisons qui motivent son refus.

CHAPITRE IV: MAITRISE D'UN OBJET SPATIAL

Article 13

Toute autorisation de maîtrise d'un objet spatial est donnée pour l'ensemble des opérations techniques nécessaires à cette maîtrise, qu'elles soient réalisées par l'opérateur lui-même ou par une ou des personnes agissant sous son autorité, notamment les manœuvres de mise et de maintien à poste, les manœuvres orbitales ainsi que la désorbitation.

Article 14

I. – L'autorisation de transfert de la maîtrise d'un objet spatial prévue au premier alinéa de l'article 3 de la loi du 3 juin 2008 susvisée est délivrée par le ministre chargé de l'espace sur présentation d'une demande conjointe de l'opérateur ayant la maîtrise de l'objet spatial et de l'opérateur récipiendaire, sous réserve des dispositions du II ci-dessous.

La demande mentionne la nature de l'objet spatial à transférer et comprend, en ce qui concerne l'opérateur récipiendaire, les pièces mentionnées aux I et II de l'article 1er ou, si l'opérateur en dispose, la licence prévue à l'article 4 de la loi du 3 juin 2008 susvisée.

Le ministre chargé de l'espace statue dans le mois suivant la date de réception de la demande mentionnée à l'article 2.

II. – Pour les transferts pour lesquels l'opérateur récipiendaire n'est pas soumis aux dispositions de la loi du 3 juin 2008 précitée, la demande d'autorisation de transfert est présentée par l'opérateur ayant la maîtrise de l'objet spatial; elle mentionne la nature de l'objet spatial à transférer et comprend les pièces justifiant que l'opérateur récipiendaire n'est pas soumis aux dispositions de la loi susmentionnée et donnant toutes garanties que l'objet spatial à transférer sera immatriculé après le transfert et que le transfert sera notifié au secrétaire général de l'Organisation des Nations unies.

CHAPITRE V: RETRAIT DE L'AUTORISATION OU DE LA LICENCE

Article 15

L'autorisation ou la licence délivrée en application du présent décret peut être retirée par le ministre chargé de l'espace:

1° En cas de fausse déclaration ou de faux renseignement;
2° Lorsque son maintien risque de porter atteinte à la défense nationale ou au respect par la France de ses engagements internationaux;
3° En cas de non-respect des prescriptions dont est, le cas échéant, assortie l'autorisation ou la licence;
4° Lorsque les conditions auxquelles est subordonnée l'autorisation ou la licence ne sont plus réunies.

Le retrait ne peut intervenir qu'après que le titulaire de l'autorisation ou de la licence a été à même de faire valoir ses observations dans un délai de trente jours.

TITRE II: GARANTIES FINANCIERES

Article 16

Les garanties financières prévues à l'article 6 de la loi du 3 juin 2008 susvisée résultent de l'engagement écrit d'un établissement de crédit ou d'une entreprise d'assurance, d'une caution personnelle et solidaire, d'une garantie à première demande ou d'actifs liquidables.

L'opérateur transmet au ministre chargé de l'espace un document prouvant la constitution des garanties financières avant le début de l'opération spatiale.

Article 17
Le ministre chargé de l'espace et le ministre chargé du budget peuvent, par une décision conjointe, dispenser l'opérateur, pour une durée limitée, de l'obligation prévue au I de l'article 6 de la loi du 3 juin 2008 susvisée, en cas d'impossibilité, compte tenu de l'état du marché de l'assurance, d'être couvert par une assurance ou de disposer d'une des garanties financières mentionnées à l'article 16 du présent décret.
L'opérateur présente dans sa demande de dispense un document attestant de sa solvabilité.

Article 18
Le ministre chargé de l'espace peut dispenser l'opérateur de l'obligation prévue au I de l'article 6 de la loi du 3 juin 2008 susvisée lorsque l'opération envisagée prévoit le maintien à poste d'un satellite sur l'orbite géostationnaire pendant une durée déterminée. Pendant cette durée, l'opérateur n'est pas tenu de disposer d'une des garanties financières ou d'assurance prévues à l'article 16. Lors de chaque changement d'orbite, de position orbitale ou de toute autre manœuvre qui met fin au maintien à poste du satellite, l'opérateur doit pouvoir attester de l'obligation prévue à l'article 6 de la loi du 3 juin 2008 précitée selon les modalités prévues à l'article 16.
L'opérateur présente, dans ce cas, au ministre chargé de l'espace, dès la mise en œuvre de l'opération spatiale, un document attestant de sa solvabilité.

TITRE III: CONTROLES

Article 19
Le ministre chargé de l'espace habilite, par arrêté, parmi les fonctionnaires et agents placés sous son autorité et les agents du Centre national d'études spatiales, les personnes à procéder aux contrôles prévus à l'article 7 de la loi du 3 juin 2008 susvisée. L'arrêté précise l'objet et la durée de l'habilitation.

Article 20
Les agents mentionnés à l'article 19 peuvent, après avis du procureur de la République auprès du tribunal de grande instance de leur résidence administrative, être habilités par arrêté du ministre chargé de l'espace à rechercher et à constater, par procès-verbal, les infractions prévues au chapitre IV de la loi du 3 juin 2008 susvisée.

L'arrêté précise l'objet et la durée de l'habilitation.

Les agents mentionnés au premier alinéa prêtent serment devant le tribunal de grande instance de leur résidence administrative.

La formule du serment est la suivante: « Je jure et promets de bien et loyalement remplir mes fonctions et d'observer en tout les devoirs qu'elles m'imposent. Je jure également de ne rien révéler ou utiliser de ce qui sera porté à ma connaissance à l'occasion de l'exercice de mes fonctions. »

Article 21

Les habilitations prévues au présent décret peuvent être retirées par arrêté du ministre chargé de l'espace et, le cas échéant, pour les personnes placées sous son autorité, à la demande du président du Centre national d'études spatiales, lorsque cette mesure est justifiée par les nécessités du service ou compte tenu du comportement du fonctionnaire ou de l'agent dans l'exercice de ses fonctions. Dans ce dernier cas, l'intéressé doit avoir été mis à même de présenter ses observations.

Article 22

Une carte professionnelle portant mention de l'habilitation, de son objet et de sa durée est délivrée par le ministre chargé de l'espace ou par le président du Centre national d'études spatiales, chacun pour ce qui le concerne, aux fonctionnaires et agents habilités placés sous leur autorité.

Le modèle de la carte professionnelle est établi par les autorités susmentionnées, chacune pour ce qui la concerne.

La mention de la prestation de serment est portée sur la carte.

Article 23

Dans les cas mentionnés à la dernière phrase du II et au IV de l'article 7 de la loi du 3 juin 2008 susvisée, le magistrat est saisi à la requête du ministre chargé de l'espace ou du président du Centre national d'études spatiales. Il statue conformément aux dispositions prévues aux articles 7 et 7-1 de la même loi. La représentation n'est pas obligatoire.

TITRE IV: DISPOSITIONS TRANSITOIRES

Article 24

Les dispositions du présent décret entrent en vigueur un an après la publication de l'arrêté édictant la réglementation technique mentionnée au premier alinéa de l'article 4 de la loi du 3 juin 2008 susvisée et, au plus tard, dix-huit mois après la publication du présent décret.

Article 25
Le paragraphe 2 « Recherche » du titre II de l'annexe au décret du 19 décembre 1997 susvisé est complété par la rubrique suivante:

Autorisation d'opération spatiale.Suspension ou retrait d'autorisation d'opération spatiale.	Décret n° 2009-643 du 9 juin 2009 relatif aux autorisations délivrées en application de la loi n° 2008-518 du 3 juin 2008 relative aux opérations spatiales.

Article 26
La ministre de l'enseignement supérieur et de la recherche et le ministre du budget, des comptes publics et de la fonction publique sont chargés, chacun en ce qui le concerne, de l'exécution du présent décret, qui sera publié au Journal officiel de la République française.

Fait à Paris, le 9 juin 2009.
François Fillon

Par le Premier ministre:
La ministre de l'enseignement supérieur
et de la recherche, Valérie Pécresse

Le ministre du budget, des comptes publics
et de la fonction publique, Eric Woerth

Annexe 1.4

Décret n° 2009-644 du 9 juin 2009 modifiant le décret n° 84-510 du 28 juin 1984 relatif au Centre national d'études spatiales (D-CNES)

Décret n° 2009-644 du 9 juin 2009 modifiant le décret n° 84-510 du 28 juin 1984 relatif au Centre national d'études spatiales[1]

Le Premier ministre,
Sur le rapport de la ministre de l'enseignement supérieur et de la recherche,
Vu la Convention du 14 janvier 1975 sur l'immatriculation des objets spatiaux lancés dans l'espace extra-atmosphérique;
Vu le code de la recherche, notamment ses articles L. 331-6 et L. 331-8;
Vu le code de la défense, notamment ses articles R. * 1311-1 à R. * 1311-10, R. * 1311-34 et R. * 1311-37;
Vu la loi n° 2008-518 du 3 juin 2008 relative aux opérations spatiales, notamment ses articles 12 et 21;
Vu le décret n° 84-510 du 28 juin 1984 relatif au Centre national d'études spatiales;
Vu le décret n° 89-314 du 16 mai 1989 relatif à la coordination des actions de sécurité lors des opérations de lancements spatiaux en Guyane;
Vu le décret n° 2004-374 du 29 avril 2004 relatif aux pouvoirs des préfets, à l'organisation et à l'action des services de l'Etat dans les régions et les départements;
Le Conseil d'Etat (section des travaux publics) entendu,
Décrète:

Article 1
Après l'article 14 du décret du 28 juin 1984 susvisé, il est inséré un titre III, un titre IV et un titre V ainsi rédigés:

« **TITRE III**

« **DISPOSITIONS RELATIVES AU REGISTRE D'IMMATRICULATION DES OBJETS SPATIAUX**
« Art. 14-1.-Pour l'exercice de la mission confiée au Centre national d'études spatiales par l'article 12 de la loi n° 2008-518 du 3 juin 2008 relative aux opérations spatiales, tout

---
[1] JORF n° 0132 du 10 juin 2009.

opérateur spatial au sens de l'article 1er de cette loi fournit au centre les informations qui sont nécessaires à l'identification de l'objet spatial et dont la liste est fixée par arrêté du ministre chargé de l'espace.

« Art. 14-2.-L'opérateur transmet ces informations au Centre national d'études spatiales au plus tard soixante jours après le lancement.

« Art. 14-3.-Le Centre national d'études spatiales attribue pour chaque objet spatial lancé sur une orbite terrestre ou au-delà un numéro d'immatriculation et l'inscrit sur le registre national d'immatriculation.

« Art. 14-4.-Toute modification des informations prévues à l'article 15 du présent décret est transmise immédiatement par l'opérateur concerné au Centre national d'études spatiales, qui apporte la modification au registre national d'immatriculation.

« Art. 14-5.-Le registre d'immatriculation est public et peut être consulté librement sur demande adressée au Centre national d'études spatiales. Toutefois, les informations relatives à l'identification du propriétaire ou du constructeur de l'objet spatial et aux éventuelles sûretés, réelles ou personnelles, constituées sur celui-ci, ne sont communiquées qu'après accord préalable des intéressés.

« Art. 14-6.-Le Centre national d'études spatiales transmet au ministre des affaires étrangères les informations issues du registre d'immatriculation requises par la convention du 14 janvier 1975 sur l'immatriculation des objets spatiaux lancés dans l'espace extra-atmosphérique. Il l'informe de tout événement affectant la vie en orbite de l'objet spatial inscrit sur le registre d'immatriculation, en particulier la désorbitation, la fin de l'exploitation ou la perte de l'objet spatial.

« Le ministre des affaires étrangères communique ces informations au secrétaire général de l'Organisation des Nations unies.

« TITRE IV

« POUVOIRS DU PRÉSIDENT DU CENTRE NATIONAL D'ÉTUDES SPATIALES AU CENTRE SPATIAL GUYANAIS

« Art. 14-7.-Le président du Centre national d'études spatiales exerce les pouvoirs qu'il tient de l'article L. 331-6 du code de la recherche sur l'ensemble des installations exploitées ou détenues par toute personne physique ou morale, publique ou privée, situées dans les limites du périmètre du centre spatial guyanais, fixé par arrêté du ministre chargé de l'espace.

« Le président du Centre national d'études spatiales est informé sans délai par toute personne visée à l'alinéa précédent de tout fait, incident ou accident, relatif aux missions qu'il tient de l'article L. 331-6 du code précité. Il en tient informé le représentant de l'Etat dans le département.

Chapitre Ier: Mission de sauvegarde

« Art. 14-8.-Sans préjudice des pouvoirs de police du préfet, en particulier en matière d'installations classées, le président du Centre national d'études spatiales exerce la police spéciale du centre spatial guyanais au titre des dispositions du I de l'article L. 331-6 du code de la recherche.

« A cet effet, il arrête les mesures de sauvegarde applicables aux installations situées à l'intérieur du périmètre du centre spatial guyanais, notamment en ce qui concerne les activités relatives à la conception, à la préparation, à la production, au stockage et au transport des objets spatiaux et de leurs éléments constitutifs, ainsi qu'aux essais et aux opérations réalisés dans le périmètre ou à partir du centre spatial guyanais.

« A ce titre, il arrête notamment:

« – le schéma relatif à l'implantation des installations, voies et réseaux situés sur le site du centre spatial guyanais;

« – les règles relatives à l'accès des personnes et des véhicules au centre spatial guyanais et aux installations situées dans son périmètre, ainsi que les règles de circulation des personnes et des véhicules au sein du site du centre spatial guyanais;

« – les règles particulières applicables au sol et en vol en matière de sécurité des personnes, des biens et de l'environnement pour les activités réalisées à l'occasion de chaque lancement, ainsi que les procédures de sauvegarde permettant de s'assurer de la conformité des activités visées au deuxième alinéa du présent article avec ces règles;

« – les zones à protéger pendant les opérations de lancement et les limites du couloir de vol acceptables;

« – les conditions météorologiques permettant de procéder aux opérations de lancement et les mesures correspondantes;

« – les règles applicables concernant la neutralisation des lanceurs et les mesures correspondantes.

« Lorsque l'exercice d'une des activités visées au deuxième alinéa du présent article présente un danger sérieux pour les personnes ou les biens ou pour la protection de l'environnement ou de la santé publique, le président du Centre national d'études spatiales peut prendre toutes mesures consistant à interdire, suspendre ou arrêter ladite activité; il peut procéder à l'évacuation de l'installation ou de la zone où se déroule l'activité en cause.

« Art. 14-9.-Le président du Centre national d'études spatiales peut prononcer une amende administrative d'un montant prévu pour les contraventions de la 5e classe à l'encontre de toute personne physique ou morale visée à l'article 14-7 exerçant une activité en violation de la réglementation prévue à l'article 14-8 sans préjudice des sanctions pénales prévues par d'autres réglementations.

« Lorsque les manquements constatés revêtent un caractère particulièrement grave, le président peut suspendre l'activité en cause après avoir, au préalable, mis en demeure l'intéressé. En cas d'urgence, il peut suspendre cette activité sans préavis.

« Art. 14-10.-Les manquements font l'objet de constats écrits dressés par les agents mentionnés à l'article 14-15.

« Les constats sont notifiés à la personne concernée par tout moyen faisant preuve certaine. Ils portent la mention des sanctions encourues.

« La personne concernée a accès à l'ensemble des éléments de son dossier. Elle doit pouvoir être entendue par le président du Centre national d'études spatiales ou par la personne désignée par celui-ci à cet effet. Elle peut se faire représenter ou assister par la personne de son choix.

« Aucune amende ne peut être prononcée plus de deux ans après la constatation d'un manquement.

« Les amendes et mesures de suspension font l'objet d'une décision motivée notifiée à la personne concernée par tout moyen faisant preuve certaine. Les amendes sont recouvrées selon les modalités prévues pour le recouvrement des créances de l'Etat étrangères à l'impôt et au domaine.

Chapitre II - Mission de coordination des mesures de sûreté

« Art. 14-11.-Pour l'exercice des pouvoirs de coordination qui lui sont conférés au II de l'article L. 331-6, le président du Centre national d'études spatiales agit sous l'autorité du représentant de l'Etat dans le département pour l'exercice de ses attributions en matière de sûreté des installations et des activités menées au centre spatial guyanais.

« Art. 14-12.-Le président du Centre national d'études spatiales coordonne:

« – la constitution et la transmission aux autorités compétentes des dossiers dans le cadre des procédures propres à chaque réglementation;

« – la préparation avec les personnes visées à l'article 14-7 des inspections des autorités compétentes au déroulement desquelles il est convié. Les personnes visées à l'article 14-7 le tiennent informé des résultats de ces inspections et, le cas échéant, de la façon dont elles s'acquittent des obligations en découlant;

« – l'information des autorités compétentes de tout manquement aux obligations relatives à la sûreté et à la sécurité dont il a connaissance.

« Il participe à la préparation et à l'exécution des mesures d'interdiction, de suspension ou d'arrêt d'une activité et d'évacuation d'une zone ou d'une installation prises par le représentant de l'Etat dans le département auquel il fait rapport.

« Il coordonne l'élaboration des plans de secours propres à chaque installation et élabore les plans de secours pour l'ensemble du centre spatial guyanais et met en œuvre les moyens correspondants. Il en rend compte au représentant de l'Etat dans le département.

« Art. 14-13.-Le président du Centre national d'études spatiales met en œuvre, sous l'autorité du représentant de l'Etat dans le département, les mesures visant à la protection du patrimoine scientifique et technique à l'intérieur des installations et à celle des installations contre les malveillances.

« Art. 14-14.-Le président du Centre national d'études spatiales centralise et coordonne l'information fournie par les exploitants relative aux risques présentés par les installations et leur exploitation, notamment dans le cadre d'instance de concertations prévues par d'autres réglementations.

Chapitre III - Modalités du contrôle
« Art. 14-15.-Le président du Centre national d'études spatiales peut habiliter les agents placés sous son autorité à procéder aux contrôles nécessaires à l'accomplissement des missions prévues par l'article L. 331-6 du code de la recherche.
« Ils informent, le cas échéant, le président du Centre national d'études spatiales de tout trouble susceptible d'affecter l'accomplissement de ces missions.
« Art. 14-16.-Conformément aux dispositions de l'article L. 331-8 du code de la recherche, le président du Centre national d'études spatiales peut déléguer une partie des pouvoirs prévus à l'article L. 331-6 au directeur de l'établissement du centre spatial guyanais, ainsi qu'aux responsables des activités de sauvegarde, de sûreté et de sécurité du centre spatial guyanais.

« TITRE V
« MESURES D'URGENCE NÉCESSAIRES À LA SÉCURITÉ DES PERSONNES ET DES BIENS ET À LA PROTECTION DE LA SANTÉ PUBLIQUE ET DE L'ENVIRONNEMENT
« Art. 14-17.-Lorsqu'il exerce les compétences prévues à l'article L. 331-7 du code de la recherche, le président du Centre national d'études spatiales peut déléguer sa signature par arrêté. »

Article 2
La ministre de l'intérieur, de l'outre-mer et des collectivités territoriales, le ministre des affaires étrangères et européennes et la ministre de l'enseignement supérieur et de la recherche sont chargés, chacun en ce qui le concerne, de l'exécution du présent décret, qui sera publié au Journal officiel de la République française.

Fait à Paris, le 9 juin 2009.
François Fillon

Par le Premier ministre:
La ministre de l'enseignement supérieur
et de la recherche,
Valérie Pécresse
La ministre de l'intérieur,

de l'outre-mer et des collectivités territoriales,
Michèle Alliot-Marie
Le ministre des affaires étrangères
et européennes,
Bernard Kouchner

Annexe 1.4 (bis)

Arrêté du 12 août 2011 fixant la liste des informations nécessaires à l'identification d'un objet spatial en application du titre III du décret n° 84-510 du 28 juin 1984 relatif au Centre national d'études spatiales (AI)

Arrêté du 12 août 2011 fixant la liste des informations nécessaires à l'identification d'un objet spatial en application du titre III du décret n° 84-510 du 28 juin 1984 relatif au Centre national d'études spatiales[1]

Le ministre de l'enseignement supérieur et de la recherche,
Vu le code de la recherche, notamment l'article L. 331-2;
Vu la loi n° 2008-518 du 3 juin 2008 modifiée relative aux opérations spatiales;
Vu le décret n° 84-510 du 28 juin 1984 relatif au Centre national d'études spatiales, modifié notamment par le décret n° 2009-644 du 9 juin 2009,
Arrête:

Article 1
Les informations devant être fournies par tout opérateur spatial au sens de l'article 1er de la loi n° 2008-518 du 3 juin 2008, permettant l'identification de l'objet spatial lancé sur une orbite terrestre ou au-delà en vue de son inscription dans le registre national d'immatriculation par le Centre national d'études spatiales, sont les suivantes:
1° La désignation de l'objet spatial;
2° La fonction générale de l'objet;
3° Le nom du constructeur;
4° L'historique de la propriété et des éventuelles sûretés, réelles ou personnelles, constituées sur celui-ci;
5° La date et le lieu du lancement;
6° Les paramètres de l'orbite finale, y compris la période nodale, l'inclinaison, l'apogée et le périgée;
7° Le mode de maîtrise dans l'espace extra-atmosphérique;
8° Les éventuelles anomalies rencontrées lors de la mise en orbite ou dans le fonctionnement en tant que véhicule spatial.

---

[1] JORF n° 0208 du 8 septembre 2011

Article 2
L'opérateur transmet immédiatement toute modification des informations prévues à l'article précédent, en particulier tout événement significatif susceptible d'affecter la vie en orbite de l'objet spatial, notamment la désorbitation, la fin de l'exploitation ou la perte de l'objet spatial.

Article 3
Le directeur général pour la recherche et l'innovation est chargé de l'exécution du présent arrêté, qui sera publié au Journal officiel de la République française.

Fait le 12 août 2011.

Pour le ministre et par délégation:
Par empêchement du directeur général
Pour la recherche et l'innovation:
L'adjointe au directeur général
Pour la recherche et l'innovation,
C. Gaudy

Annexe 1.5

Décret n° 2009-640 du 9 juin 2009 portant application des dispositions prévues au titre VII de la loi n° 2008-518 du 3 juin 2008 relative aux opérations spatiales (D-DOS)

Décret n° 2009-640 du 9 juin 2009 portant application des dispositions prévues au titre VII de la loi n° 2008-518 du 3 juin 2008 relative aux opérations spatiales (D-DOS)

Le Premier ministre,

Sur le rapport de la ministre de l'enseignement supérieur et de la recherche et du ministre de la défense,
Vu le code pénal, notamment ses articles 413-9 et suivants;
Vu la loi n° 78-753 du 17 juillet 1978 modifiée portant diverses mesures d'amélioration des relations entre l'administration et le public et diverses dispositions d'ordre administratif, social et fiscal, notamment son article 6;
Vu la loi n° 2000-321 du 12 avril 2000 modifiée relative aux droits des citoyens dans leurs relations avec l'administration;
Vu la loi n° 2008-518 du 3 juin 2008 relative aux opérations spatiales, notamment ses articles 1er et 23 à 27;
Vu le décret n° 97-34 du 15 janvier 1997 relatif à la déconcentration des décisions administratives individuelles, modifié en dernier lieu par le décret n° 2007-139 du 1er février 2007;
Vu le décret n° 97-1184 du 19 décembre 1997 pris pour l'application au Premier ministre du 1° de l'article 2 du décret n° 97-34 du 15 janvier 1997 relatif à la déconcentration des décisions administratives individuelles;
Vu le décret n° 98-608 du 17 juillet 1998 relatif à la protection des secrets de la défense nationale;

Le Conseil d'Etat (section des travaux publics) entendu,
Décrète:

Article 1
Sont considérées comme « données d'origine spatiale » dont l'exploitation primaire est soumise à une déclaration préalable à l'autorité administrative, pour l'application du titre VII de la loi du 3 juin 2008 susvisée, les données issues de capteurs optiques panchroma-

tiques, de capteurs optiques multi-spectraux, de capteurs optiques stéréoscopiques, de capteurs infrarouges et de capteurs radar, dont les caractéristiques de résolution et de précision sont fixées par décret.

Article 2
L'autorité administrative mentionnée à l'article 23 de la loi du 3 juin 2008 susvisée est le secrétaire général de la défense nationale.

Article 3
La déclaration mentionnée à l'article 1er doit être adressée à l'autorité administrative au moins deux mois avant le début de l'exploitation. Le formulaire de déclaration et la liste des pièces à fournir par le déclarant sont définis par arrêté du Premier ministre.
Lorsqu'elle estime que la déclaration est en la forme irrégulière ou incomplète, l'autorité administrative invite le déclarant à régulariser ou à compléter sa déclaration.
Préalablement au dépôt de la déclaration, l'exploitant primaire de données d'origine spatiale doit avoir obtenu une habilitation pour traiter les informations classifiées qui pourraient lui être transmises conformément au décret du 17 juillet 1998 susvisé.

Article 4
L'autorité administrative donne récépissé de la déclaration et communique, le cas échéant, au déclarant une copie des mesures de restriction qui auraient été prises en application de l'article 5 ci-après.
Tout changement envisagé du mode d'exploitation doit faire l'objet d'une déclaration complémentaire de l'exploitant primaire au moins deux mois avant ce changement.

Article 5
Pour assurer la sauvegarde des intérêts mentionnés à l'article 24 de la loi du 3 juin 2008 susvisée, le secrétaire général de la défense nationale peut prononcer, après avis d'une commission interministérielle dont les missions, la composition et l'organisation sont fixées par décret, des mesures de restriction aux activités qui lui ont été déclarées. En cas d'urgence, l'avis des membres de la commission peut, le cas échéant, être recueilli par courrier ou par courrier électronique. Ces mesures peuvent, notamment, consister en:
- la suspension immédiate, totale ou partielle, de la programmation ou de la réception pour une durée temporaire reconductible;
- l'obligation de différer la programmation, la réception ou la production des images pour une durée temporaire reconductible;
- l'interdiction permanente de programmation ou de réception;
- la limitation de la qualité technique des données;
- la limitation géographique des zones de prises de vue.

Les décisions de restriction peuvent être protégées conformément aux dispositions relatives à la protection du secret de la défense nationale.

L'autorité administrative informe les membres de la commission interministérielle des décisions prises.

Article 6

L'annexe prévue au décret du 19 décembre 1997 susvisé est ainsi complétée:
« Décisions relatives à l'activité des exploitants primaires de données d'origine spatiale prévues aux articles 23 à 25 de la loi n° 2008-518 du 3 juin 2008 relative aux opérations spatiales. »

Article 7

La ministre de l'enseignement supérieur et de la recherche et le ministre de la défense sont chargés, chacun en ce qui le concerne, de l'exécution du présent décret, qui sera publié au Journal officiel de la République française.

Fait à Paris, le 9 juin 2009.

François Fillon

Par le Premier ministre:
La ministre de l'enseignement supérieur
et de la recherche,
Valérie Pécresse
Le ministre de la défense,
Hervé Morin

Annexe 1.5 (bis)

Décret n° 2013-653 du 19 juillet 2013 modifiant le décret n° 2009-640 du 9 juin 2009 portant application des dispositions prévues au titre VII de la loi n° 2008-518 du 3 juin 2008 relative aux opérations spatiales (D-DOS)

Décret n° 2013-653 du 19 juillet 2013 modifiant le décret n° 2009-640 du 9 juin 2009 portant application des dispositions prévues au titre VII de la loi n° 2008-518 du 3 juin 2008 relative aux opérations spatiales (D-DOS)

Publics concernés: tout exploitant primaire de données d'origine spatiale exerçant son activité en France.

Objet: déterminer les caractéristiques techniques de l'activité des exploitants primaires de données d'origine spatiale soumise à une déclaration préalable à l'autorité administrative.

Entrée en vigueur: le texte entre en vigueur le lendemain de sa publication.

Notice: le décret définit les caractéristiques techniques de l'activité des exploitants primaires de données d'origine spatiale soumise à une déclaration préalable à l'autorité administrative. Ces caractéristiques sont notamment fonction de la résolution, de la précision de localisation, de la bande de fréquence d'observation et de la qualité des données d'observation de la Terre.

Le décret prévoit également le délai imparti aux exploitants primaires exerçant déjà une telle activité à la date de publication du texte pour soumettre la déclaration préalable.

Références: le décret est pris pour l'application de l'article 23 de la loi n° 2008-518 du 3 juin 2008 relative aux opérations spatiales. Il peut être consulté sur le site Légifrance (http://www.legifrance.gouv.fr).

Le Premier ministre,

Sur le rapport du ministre de la défense et de la ministre de l'enseignement supérieur et de la recherche,

Vu la loi n° 2008-518 du 3 juin 2008 modifiée relative aux opérations spatiales, notamment ses articles 1er, 23, 26 et 27;

Vu le décret n° 2009-640 du 9 juin 2009 portant application des dispositions prévues au titre VII de la loi n° 2008-518 du 3 juin 2008 relative aux opérations spatiales;

Le Conseil d'Etat (section des travaux publics) entendu,

Décrète:

Article 1
L'article 1er du décret du 9 juin 2009 susvisé est remplacé par les dispositions suivantes:

« Art. 1er. -Est soumise à la déclaration préalable prévue à l'article 23 de la loi du 3 juin 2008 susvisée l'activité exercée par les exploitants primaires des données d'origine spatiale suivantes:
a) Les données issues de capteurs optiques panchromatiques dont la résolution à bord est inférieure ou égale à deux mètres;
b) Les données issues de capteurs optiques multi-spectraux dont la résolution à bord est inférieure ou égale à huit mètres ou dont le nombre de bandes spectrales est supérieur ou égal à dix;
c) Les données issues de capteurs optiques stéréoscopiques dont la résolution est inférieure ou égale à dix mètres ou la précision altimétrique inférieure ou égale à dix mètres en valeur relative (quinze mètres en valeur absolue);
d) Les données issues de capteurs infrarouges dont la résolution est inférieure ou égale à cinq mètres;
e) Les données issues de capteurs radar dont la résolution est inférieure à trois mètres;
f) Les données dont la précision de localisation intrinsèque est inférieure à dix mètres (cercle d'erreur à 90 %). »

Article 2
Les exploitants primaires de données d'origine spatiale exerçant à la date de publication du présent décret une des activités mentionnées à l'article 1er soumettent la déclaration préalable dans les deux mois qui suivent la publication de l'arrêté prévu à l'article 3 du décret du 9 juin 2009 susvisé.

Article 3
Le ministre de la défense et la ministre de l'enseignement supérieur et de la recherche sont chargés, chacun en ce qui le concerne, de l'exécution du présent décret, qui sera publié au Journal officiel de la République française.

Fait le 19 juillet 2013.

Jean-Marc Ayrault

Par le Premier ministre:

Le ministre de la défense,
Jean-Yves Le Drian

Annexe 1.5 (bis)

La ministre de l'enseignement supérieur
et de la recherche,
Geneviève Fioraso

Annexe 1.5 (ter)

Décret n° 2013-654 du 19 juillet 2013 relatif à la surveillance de l'activité des exploitants primaires de données d'origine spatiale (DDOS- S)

Décret n° 2013-654 du 19 juillet 2013 relatif à la surveillance de l'activité des exploitants primaires de données d'origine spatiale

Publics concernés: administration de l'Etat et exploitants primaires de données d'origine spatiale.

Objet: commission interministérielle des données d'origine spatiale; définition des mesures de restriction à l'activité des exploitants primaires de données d'origine spatiale.

Entrée en vigueur: le texte entre en vigueur le lendemain de sa publication.

Notice: le décret définit les missions, la composition et l'organisation de la commission interministérielle des données d'origine spatiale, chargée de conseiller l'autorité administrative pour la détermination et la coordination du suivi de la politique nationale en matière de surveillance de l'activité des exploitants primaires de données d'origine spatiale. Le décret précise également la nature de certaines mesures de restriction à l'activité des exploitants primaires de données d'origine spatiale que l'autorité administrative peut édicter pour assurer la sauvegarde des intérêts fondamentaux de la nation.

Références: le décret est pris pour l'application de l'article 24 de la loi n° 2008-518 du 3 juin 2008 relative aux opérations spatiales; il est également pris pour l'application de l'article 5 du décret n° 2009-640 du 9 juin 2009 portant application des dispositions prévues au titre VII de la loi n° 2008-518 du 3 juin 2008 relative aux opérations spatiales. Il peut être consulté sur le site Légifrance (http://www.legifrance.gouv.fr).

Le Premier ministre,

Sur le rapport du ministre des affaires étrangères, du ministre de l'intérieur, du ministre de la défense et de la ministre de l'enseignement supérieur et de la recherche,

Vu le code pénal, notamment ses articles 413-9 et suivants;

Vu le code de la défense, notamment ses articles R. 2311-1 à R. 2311-9;

Vu la loi n° 2008-518 du 3 juin 2008 modifiée relative aux opérations spatiales, notamment ses articles 1er et 23 à 27;

Vu le décret n° 97-1184 du 19 décembre 1997 modifié pris pour l'application au Premier ministre du 1° de l'article 2 du décret n° 97-34 du 15 janvier 1997 relatif à la déconcentration des décisions administratives individuelles;

Vu le décret n° 2006-672 du 8 juin 2006 relatif à la création, à la composition et au fonctionnement de commissions administratives à caractère consultatif;

Vu le décret n° 2009-640 du 9 juin 2009 portant application des dispositions prévues au titre VII de la loi n° 2008-518 du 3 juin 2008 relative aux opérations spatiales, notamment son article 5,
Décrète:

Article 1
La commission interministérielle instituée à l'article 5 du décret du 9 juin 2009 susvisé, dénommée ci-après « commission interministérielle des données d'origine spatiale », conseille l'autorité administrative mentionnée à l'article 2 du même décret pour la détermination et la coordination du suivi de la politique nationale en matière de surveillance de l'activité des exploitants primaires de données d'origine spatiale.

Les départements ministériels représentés au sein de la commission interministérielle peuvent saisir l'autorité administrative de tout fait susceptible de nécessiter son intervention.

Article 2
La commission interministérielle des données d'origine spatiale:
1° Emet un avis sur les mesures de restriction que l'autorité administrative envisage de prendre en application de l'article 24 de la loi du 3 juin 2008 susvisée;
2° Propose des orientations et conseille l'autorité administrative sur l'opportunité de projets de directives en matière de surveillance de l'activité des exploitants primaires de données d'origine spatiale;
3° Appelle l'attention de l'autorité administrative sur les atteintes aux intérêts fondamentaux de la Nation que peut faire naître tout projet d'accord ou de contrat de programmation, de réception directe ou de production de données d'origine spatiale issues de satellites opérés par les exploitants primaires.

Article 3
Les mesures de restriction mentionnées à l'article 24 de la loi du 3 juin 2008 susvisée portent notamment sur la programmation, sur la réception directe en vue de la production de nouvelles données ou sur la diffusion des données primaires archivées sous la responsabilité des exploitants primaires de données d'origine spatiale concernant une zone ou un territoire donné suivant les modalités prévues à l'article 5 du décret du 9 juin 2009 susvisé.

Les mesures de restriction à la diffusion des données peuvent notamment consister en:
a) La suspension immédiate, totale ou partielle, de la délivrance des données concernant des zones géographiques déterminées, pour une durée temporaire reconductible;
b) L'obligation, totale ou partielle, de différer la délivrance des données concernant des zones géographiques déterminées, pour une durée temporaire reconductible;

c) La limitation, totale ou partielle, de la qualité technique des données concernant des zones géographiques déterminées pouvant être délivrées, pour une durée temporaire reconductible;
d) La limitation permanente de la qualité technique des données concernant certaines zones du territoire national pouvant être délivrées.

Article 4

La commission interministérielle des données d'origine spatiale comprend:
a) Le secrétaire général de la défense et de la sécurité nationale ou son représentant, président;
b) Un représentant du ministre de la défense;
c) Un représentant du ministre des affaires étrangères;
d) Un représentant du ministre de l'intérieur;
e) Un représentant du ministre chargé de l'espace.

Le président de la commission interministérielle peut inviter le président du Centre national d'études spatiales ou son représentant à participer aux réunions de la commission lorsqu'une question particulière de l'ordre du jour le justifie.

Le président de la commission interministérielle peut inviter toute personne dont il juge la participation utile aux travaux de la commission interministérielle.

Le secrétariat de la commission interministérielle est assuré par le secrétariat général de la défense et de la sécurité nationale.

Article 5

La commission interministérielle des données d'origine spatiale se réunit au moins une fois par an, sur convocation de son président ou à la demande de l'un de ses membres.
Elle peut également être consultée par courrier ou par courrier électronique à la demande de son président ou sur proposition de l'un de ses membres.

Article 6

Le ministre des affaires étrangères, le ministre de l'intérieur, le ministre de la défense et la ministre de l'enseignement supérieur et de la recherche sont chargés, chacun en ce qui le concerne, de l'exécution du présent décret, qui sera publié au Journal officiel de la République française.

Fait le 19 juillet 2013.

Jean-Marc Ayrault

Par le Premier ministre:

Le ministre des affaires étrangères,
Laurent Fabius
Le ministre de l'intérieur,
Manuel Valls
Le ministre de la défense,
Jean-Yves Le Drian
La ministre de l'enseignement supérieur
et de la recherche,
Geneviève Fioraso

Annexe 1.5 (quater)

Arrêté du 4 septembre 2013 relatif à la déclaration préalable d'activité effectuée par les exploitants primaires de données d'origine spatiale (A-DOS-D)

Arrêté du 4 septembre 2013 relatif à la déclaration préalable d'activité effectuée par les exploitants primaires de données d'origine spatiale

Le Premier ministre,
Vu la loi n° 2008-518 du 3 juin 2008 relative aux opérations spatiales;
Vu le décret n° 2009-640 du 9 juin 2009 modifié portant application des dispositions prévues au titre VII de la loi n° 2008-518 du 3 juin 2008 relative aux opérations spatiales,
Arrête:

Article 1
La déclaration préalable prévue par l'article 23 de la loi du 3 juin 2008 susvisée est effectuée au moyen du formulaire annexé au présent arrêté. Ce formulaire contient la liste des pièces et des informations qui doivent être fournies par le déclarant à l'autorité administrative.

Article 2
Lorsque la déclaration est complète, l'autorité administrative l'enregistre et délivre à l'exploitant un récépissé attestant le respect de l'obligation de déclaration. Le récépissé indique la date de l'enregistrement.

Article 3
Le délai de deux mois prévu par l'article 3 du décret du 9 juin 2009 susvisé court à compter de la date d'enregistrement de la déclaration.

Article 4
Le secrétaire général de la défense et de la sécurité nationale est chargé de l'exécution du présent arrêté, qui sera publié au Journal officiel de la République française.

Annexe

DÉCLARATION D'ACTIVITÉ DES EXPLOITANTS PRIMAIRES DE DONNÉES D'ORIGINE SPATIALE

Formulaire à adresser en trois exemplaires sur papier ainsi que par voie dématérialisée au secrétariat général de la défense et de la sécurité nationale, direction des affaires internationales, stratégiques et technologiques, 51, boulevard de La Tour-Maubourg, 75700 Paris 07 SP (téléphone: + 33 [0]1-71-75-80-79, télécopie: + 33 [0]1-71-75-80-60).
Numéro de dossier (réservé à l'administration):
Date d'enregistrement de la déclaration:
A. – Déclarant
A1. – Société (ou personne physique le cas échéant)
Joindre un document général présentant la société et un extrait K bis du registre du commerce et des sociétés datant de moins de trois mois:
Dénomination sociale (ou nom):
Numéro SIRET:
Adresse:
Numéro de téléphone: Numéro de télécopie:
Adresse électronique:
Adresse du site internet:
A2. – Habilitation de l'exploitant
Ministère ou organisme ayant délivré l'habilitation:
Niveau d'habilitation:
Date et durée de l'habilitation:
Numéro de l'habilitation:
B. – Personne chargée du dossier administratif
Nom et prénom(s):
Nationalité:
Niveau d'habilitation:
Numéro d'habilitation:
Ministère d'habilitation:
Date et durée d'habilitation:
Adresse:
Numéro de téléphone:
Numéro de télécopie:
Adresse électronique:
C. – Activité faisant l'objet d'une déclaration (1)
C1. – Systèmes exploités (2)

Annexe 1.5 (quater)

Nom du système:

Type de données produites:

Caractéristiques des données (résolution, facteur de mérite, précision de géolocalisation, précision altimétrique, nombre de bandes spectrales, définition de chaque bande spectrale):

Performances du système:

Architecture du segment sol et système de stockage et d'archivage:

Mode de programmation et de réception des données:

Nature de la protection des transmissions (programmation et télémesure image):

La cessation d'une activité ayant fait l'objet d'une déclaration doit, dès qu'elle prend effet, être communiquée à l'autorité administrative dont les coordonnées figurent en tête de ce formulaire.

C2. – Modes d'exploitation des systèmes

Organisation de l'exploitant (descriptif sommaire à joindre):

Produits issus de l'exploitation des données:

Coopération (le cas échéant pour chaque système):

Répartition géographique et localisation des stations de réception des données: descriptif à joindre (mise à jour en fonction des implantations):

Type de contrat lié à l'exploitation de chaque station de réception (durée de validité, systèmes concernés, données concernées, priorités de programmation accordées...):

C3. – Projets d'accord ou de contrats

Le déclarant transmet pour avis à l'autorité administrative les projets d'accord et de contrats de programmation, de réception directe ou de production de données qu'il souhaite négocier ou conclure avec ses clients potentiels.

C4. – Identité de l'exploitant primaire

s'il est différent du déclarant

Nom:

Adresse:

Numéro de téléphone:

Numéro de télécopie:

Adresse électronique:

Adresse du site internet:

Nota. – Tout changement conduisant à modifier les informations concernant une activité déclarée doit faire l'objet d'une nouvelle déclaration à l'autorité administrative selon les modalités prévues par les dispositions de l'article 3 du décret n° 2009-640 du 9 juin 2009.

D. - Autres renseignements relatifs au système exploité

Immatriculation des satellites:

Attribution des fréquences:

Autres:
(1) L'ensemble des données techniques demandées dans cette partie pourront faire l'objet d'une annexe technique séparée. (2) Les rubriques doivent être renseignées pour chaque système exploité.
Fait le 4 septembre 2013.
Pour le Premier ministre et par délégation:
Le secrétaire général de la défense
et de la sécurité nationale,
F. Delon

Annexe 1.6

Arrêté du 31 mars 2011 relatif à la réglementation technique en application du décret n° 2009-643 du 9 juin 2009 relatif aux autorisations délivrées en application de la loi n° 2008-518 du 3 juin 2008 relative aux opérations spatiales (RT)

Arrêté du 31 mars 2011 relatif à la réglementation technique en application du décret n° 2009-643 du 9 juin 2009 relatif aux autorisations délivrées en application de la loi n° 2008-518 du 3 juin 2008 relative aux opérations spatiales[1]

La ministre de l'enseignement supérieur et de la recherche,
Vu la directive 98/34/CE du Parlement européen et du Conseil du 22 juin 1998 prévoyant une procédure d'information dans le domaine des normes et réglementations techniques et des règles relatives aux services de la société de l'information, et notamment la notification n° 2010/0687/F;
Vu le code de la recherche, notamment le chapitre Ier du titre III du livre III;
Vu la loi n° 2008-518 du 3 juin 2008 modifiée relative aux opérations spatiales;
Vu le décret n° 2009-643 du 9 juin 2009 relatif aux autorisations délivrées en application de la loi du 3 juin 2008 relative aux opérations spatiales, et notamment son article 1er,
Arrête:

PREMIERE PARTIE: DEFINITIONS ET DISPOSITIONS PRELIMINAIRES

Article 1 - Définitions.
Au sens du présent arrêté, on désigne par:
« Allocation »: niveau de probabilité affecté à l'occurrence d'un événement redouté ou spécifié, lors de l'élaboration des objectifs de sécurité;
« Coefficient de sécurité »: rapport entre la limite admissible d'un paramètre caractérisant un système ou un élément et sa valeur maximale attendue en fonctionnement nominal. Sa valeur intègre la notion de dispersion propre à chaque domaine concerné;
« Couloir de vol »: volume dans lequel le véhicule de lancement est susceptible d'évoluer et au-delà duquel il est neutralisé;
« Débris spatial »: tout objet spatial non fonctionnel d'origine humaine, y compris des fragments et des éléments de celui-ci, en orbite terrestre ou rentrant dans l'atmosphère terrestre;

---

[1] JORF n° 0126 du 31 mai 2011

« Dispositif bord de neutralisation »: ensemble des moyens embarqués concourant à la neutralisation du véhicule de lancement en vol;

« Dommage catastrophique »: perte de vie humaine, immédiate ou différée, ou blessures graves aux personnes (lésions corporelles, autres atteintes irréversibles à la santé, invalidité ou maladie professionnelle, permanente ou temporaire);

« Fin de vie »: fin de la phase de retrait de service de l'objet spatial ou perte de contrôle de celui-ci;

« Instant irréversible »: pour une opération de lancement, instant de passage de l'ordre qui conduit irrémédiablement au décollage du véhicule de lancement;

« Marge de sécurité »: rapport entre la limite admissible d'un paramètre caractérisant un système ou un élément et sa valeur maximale attendue en fonctionnement normal multipliée par le coefficient de sécurité;

« Neutralisation »: intervention sur le lanceur tendant à minimiser les dommages aux personnes et aux biens. Elle peut notamment se caractériser par une action permettant de provoquer la destruction ou l'arrêt de la poussée d'un véhicule de lancement, pour mettre fin au vol dudit véhicule ou d'un étage ne fonctionnant plus correctement;

« Niveau de risque »: estimation probabiliste caractérisant l'insécurité d'un système vis-à-vis d'un événement redouté, exprimée par la probabilité d'occurrence de cet événement;

« Nominal » correspondant aux spécifications ou aux performances annoncées par l'opérateur ou le concepteur de l'objet spatial;

« Objet spatial »: tout objet d'origine humaine, fonctionnel ou non durant son lancement, son séjour dans l'espace extra-atmosphérique ou son retour, y compris les éléments d'un lanceur mis en orbite;

« Phase de retrait de service »: phase finale de l'opération spatiale pendant laquelle sont menées les actions de mise en sécurité de l'objet spatial visant à limiter les risques liés aux débris spatiaux;

« Phase opérationnelle »: période de temps qui, dans le cadre d'une opération de maîtrise dans l'espace extra-atmosphérique, débute à l'instant où l'opérateur prend la maîtrise de l'objet spatial et s'achève au début de la phase de retrait de service;

« Procédure »: manière spécifiée d'effectuer une activité ou un processus;

« Processus »: ensemble d'activités corrélées ou interactives qui transforment des éléments d'entrée en éléments de sortie;

« Régions protégées »:

1. Région protégée A, orbite terrestre basse (LEO) – région sphérique qui s'étend depuis la surface de la Terre jusqu'à une altitude (Z) de 2 000 km;
2. Région protégée B, région géosynchrone – segment de l'enveloppe sphérique défini comme suit:
   - limite inférieure = altitude géostationnaire moins 200 km;
   - limite supérieure = altitude géostationnaire plus 200 km;

- latitude comprise entre – 15 et + 15 degrés;
- altitude géostationnaire » (Z GEO) = 35 786 km (altitude de l'orbite terrestre géostationnaire);

« Rentrée non contrôlée »: rentrée atmosphérique d'un objet spatial pour laquelle il n'est pas possible de prédéfinir la zone d'impact au sol de l'objet ou de ses fragments;

« Rentrée contrôlée »: rentrée atmosphérique d'un objet spatial avec une zone prédéfinie de contact ou d'impact au sol de l'objet ou de ses fragments;

« Retour »: période qui commence à la rentrée de l'objet spatial dans l'atmosphère terrestre et prend fin lorsqu'il est immobilisé sur la Terre, dans le cadre d'une rentrée contrôlée ou non contrôlée;

« Risque technique »: risque d'origine technologique, industrielle, opérationnelle, humaine ou naturelle. Expression utilisée pour différencier le risque de nature technique de tout autre type de risque, notamment à caractère financier ou lié à la sûreté des installations;

« Sécurité »: ensemble des dispositions destinées à maîtriser les risques dans le but d'assurer la protection des personnes, des biens et la protection de la santé publique et de l'environnement;

« Système spatial »: ensemble constitué par un ou plusieurs objets spatiaux et par les équipements et installations qui leur sont associés pour remplir une mission déterminée. S'agissant d'une opération de lancement, le système spatial est un ensemble constitué du lanceur, de la base de lancement en interface, y compris les stations de poursuite, et de l'objet spatial destiné à être lancé;

S'agissant d'une opération de maîtrise, le système spatial est un ensemble constitué de l'objet spatial et du segment sol en interface;

« Véhicule de lancement »: ensemble constitué du lanceur et des objets spatiaux destinés à être mis en orbite.

Article 2 - Dispositions préliminaires.

1. Le présent arrêté a pour objet de préciser la réglementation technique sur la base de laquelle le ministre chargé de l'espace délivre, après exercice d'un contrôle de conformité par le Centre national d'études spatiales, une autorisation de conduite d'une opération spatiale, conformément à la loi du 3 juin 2008 susvisée.
2. Les dispositions du présent arrêté s'appliquent aux opérations spatiales mentionnées aux articles 2 et 3 de la loi du 3 juin 2008 susvisée, à l'exception de celles pour lesquelles une dispense du contrôle de conformité est accordée dans les conditions du quatrième alinéa de l'article 4 de la loi précitée.
3. Les dispositions du présent arrêté s'appliquent uniquement:
    a) A une opération de lancement qui remplit les trois critères cumulatifs suivants:
        - décollage depuis le sol;
        - propulsion par réaction;

- vol non habité;
b) A une opération de maîtrise dans l'espace extra-atmosphérique d'un objet spatial non habité;
c) A une opération de retour sur Terre d'un objet spatial non habité.

La réglementation technique applicable aux opérations spatiales non mentionnées ci-dessus fera l'objet d'un arrêté spécifique.
4. Le respect des exigences du présent arrêté ne saurait exonérer l'opérateur de sa responsabilité en matière de dommages causés aux tiers, telle que prévue à l'article 13 de la loi du 3 juin 2008 susvisée.
5. Les agents qui, en application de l'article 7 de la loi du 3 juin 2008 susvisée, sont habilités à effectuer le contrôle du respect des prescriptions techniques édictées par référence à la présente réglementation technique et annexées à l'arrêté d'autorisation sont placés sous l'autorité du président du Centre national d'études spatiales dans les conditions fixées par l'arrêté les habilitant.

DEUXIEME PARTIE: LANCEMENT D'UN OBJET SPATIAL

TITRE IER: CHAMP D'APPLICATION

Article 3
Les dispositions de la présente partie s'appliquent à l'opération de lancement, jusqu'à la fin de vie des étages et éléments du lanceur.

TITRE II: DOSSIER TECHNIQUE

CHAPITRE IER: DOCUMENTATION A FOURNIR

Article 4 - Description de l'opération spatiale et des systèmes et procédures.
La description de l'opération spatiale et des systèmes et procédures mentionnée au II (1°) de l'article 1er du décret du 9 juin 2009 susvisé présente les composantes du système de lancement, les caractéristiques de l'objet spatial destiné à être lancé et de la mission envisagée.

Article 5 - Notice générale de conformité.
1. L'opérateur de lancement établit, conformément au II (2°, a) de l'article 1er du décret du 9 juin 2009 susvisé, une notice générale de conformité à la présente réglementation technique.
2. Cette notice générale de conformité identifie les documents fournis au titre des articles 6 à 10 du présent arrêté et établit l'état de conformité en résultant.

Article 6 - Normes internes et dispositions de gestion de la qualité.
L'opérateur de lancement établit, conformément au II (2°, b) de l'article 1er du décret du 9 juin 2009 susvisé, les documents justifiant du respect des dispositions du chapitre 2 du présent titre.

Article 7 - Etude des dangers.
L'opérateur de lancement réalise, conformément au II (2°, c) de l'article 1er du décret du 9 juin 2009 susvisé, une étude exposant les dangers que peut présenter l'opération spatiale envisagée.
Cette étude comprend une description de l'ensemble des dangers liés à l'opération dans les cas de fonctionnement nominal et accidentels, que leur cause soit d'origine interne ou externe. L'étude précise la nature et l'étendue des conséquences que peuvent avoir tous ces cas de fonctionnement. S'agissant des éléments du véhicule de lancement faisant l'objet d'un retour ou d'une retombée et susceptibles d'atteindre le sol, l'étude présente les constituants de ces éléments en indiquant les dimensions, les masses et les matériaux utilisés.
L'opérateur de lancement doit à ce titre:
- démontrer le respect des dispositions de l'article 20 du présent arrêté s'agissant des risques de dommages aux personnes;
- évaluer les effets sur la santé publique et l'environnement dans les cas accidentels.

Cette étude doit traiter des événements suivants, dans les conditions prévues au chapitre III du présent titre:
- dommages liés à la retombée d'éléments prévus de se détacher du lanceur;
- dommages liés à la rentrée contrôlée ou non contrôlée des éléments du lanceur placés sur une orbite terrestre;
- dommages liés à la défaillance du véhicule de lancement;
- collision avec les objets spatiaux habités dont les paramètres orbitaux sont connus avec précision et disponibles;
- dommages liés à l'explosion d'un étage en orbite;
- collision avec un corps céleste.

L'étude doit présenter l'analyse exhaustive des causes et des conséquences ainsi que les probabilités des événements redoutés mentionnés ci-dessus. Les mesures de réduction des risques permettant de respecter les dispositions des articles 18 à 26 du présent arrêté sont listées dans les plans de maîtrise des risques prévus à l'article 9 du présent arrêté.

Article 8 - Etude d'impact.
L'opérateur de lancement réalise, conformément au II (2°, d) de l'article 1er du décret du 9 juin 2009 susvisé, l'étude d'impact sur l'environnement de l'opération envisagée.
L'étude d'impact doit traiter, lors du fonctionnement nominal du système de lancement, de l'impact de l'opération envisagée sur la santé publique et l'environnement au regard

des dispositions de l'article L. 161-1 du code de l'environnement ainsi que de l'impact en matière de génération de débris spatiaux conformément aux dispositions de l'article 21 du présent arrêté.

Cette étude d'impact prend en compte:
- le fonctionnement des moteurs, notamment la caractérisation de la nature et la quantification des débits des produits de combustion atmosphérique et extra-atmosphérique, en phase propulsée;
- la retombée des éléments du lanceur, notamment la caractérisation de la nature et la quantification des produits retombant sur terre, en mer ou sur un corps céleste.

Cette étude traite également de l'impact de:
- la production de débris spatiaux;
- le cas échéant, l'emport de matières radioactives à bord du véhicule de lancement.

Article 9 - Mesures de maîtrise des risques.

L'opérateur de lancement établit et met en œuvre, conformément au II (2°, e) de l'article 1er du décret du 9 juin 2009 susvisé, à partir des conclusions des études de danger et d'impact mentionnées aux articles 7 et 8 ci-dessus, les plans de maîtrise des risques suivants:
- le plan de prévention des dommages environnementaux qui liste les mesures prises pour modérer les impacts négatifs sur l'environnement identifiés dans l'étude d'impact mentionnées à l'article 8 du présent arrêté, à l'exception de celles relatives à la limitation des débris spatiaux et à la sûreté nucléaire;
- le plan de limitation des débris spatiaux, qui démontre le respect des dispositions de l'article 21 du présent arrêté;
- le plan de prévention des risques induits par la retombée de l'objet spatial ou de ses fragments, qui démontre le respect des dispositions des articles 20, 23 et 24 du présent arrêté;
- le plan de prévention des risques de collision, qui démontre le respect des dispositions de l'article 22 du présent arrêté;
- le cas échéant, le plan de sûreté nucléaire, qui démontre le respect des dispositions de l'article 25 du présent arrêté;
- le cas échéant, le plan de protection planétaire, qui démontre le respect des dispositions de l'article 26 du présent arrêté.

Article 10 - Mesures de secours.

L'opérateur de lancement liste, conformément au II (2°, f) de l'article 1er du décret du 9 juin 2009 susvisé, les mesures de secours prévues et l'organisation mise en place aux fins de protection des personnes.

En particulier, cette liste doit inclure les moyens nécessaires à la mise en œuvre du troisième alinéa de l'article 23 du présent arrêté.

ANNEXE 1.6

CHAPITRE II: EXIGENCES SYSTEME QUALITE

Article 11 - Assurance qualité.
1. L'opérateur de lancement doit mettre en œuvre et gérer, pour la conduite de l'opération spatiale, un système de management de la qualité ainsi que des normes internes et des dispositions de gestion de la qualité conformément à l'article 1er du décret du 9 juin 2009 susvisé. Ce système de management doit traiter de l'assurance qualité, de la sûreté de fonctionnement, de la gestion de configuration et de la conduite des travaux.
2. Le système spatial doit être conçu, produit, intégré et mis en œuvre de manière à maîtriser les risques induits par les activités critiques. Une activité est critique si une erreur humaine ou une défaillance de moyens utilisés augmente les risques de dommage aux personnes durant l'opération de lancement.
3. Un système de surveillance et de maîtrise des dérives de fabrication et de mise en œuvre doit être mis en place. Ce système doit permettre la traçabilité des faits techniques et organisationnels affectant les activités d'ingénierie et de production.
4. Le système de management de la qualité doit traiter, en particulier, des faits techniques ou d'organisation suivants:
   - les écarts (anomalies, évolutions) par rapport à la configuration (définition, processus de production et mise en œuvre du système de lancement) ayant fait l'objet de l'autorisation ou, le cas échéant, de la licence;
   - les écarts (anomalies, évolutions) issus de l'exploitation des paramètres enregistrés en vol susceptibles de remettre en cause les conditions dans lesquelles l'autorisation ou le cas échéant la licence ont été acquises.
5. La description et la justification du comportement du lanceur ainsi que la définition des matériaux utilisés doivent être conservés jusqu'à la fin de l'opération spatiale concernée. A l'issue de celle-ci, ces éléments sont transmis au Centre national d'études spatiales avec la description de l'état atteint.

Article 12 - Compétence, moyens, organisation et installations.
L'opérateur de lancement doit disposer des compétences, des moyens et de l'organisation nécessaires pour préparer et mettre en œuvre l'opération de lancement envisagée:
- installations et organisation appropriées;
- équipements, outils et matériels adaptés à l'opération envisagée;
- documentation relative aux tâches et aux procédures;
- accès aux données utiles à la préparation de l'opération envisagée;
- enregistrement, exploitation et archivage des données techniques;
- postes clés et processus de formation associé.

Article 13 - Visibilité technique.
L'opérateur de lancement doit mettre en place une organisation lui permettant d'informer sans délai, au titre de l'article 7 du décret du 9 juin 2009 susvisé, le Centre national d'études spatiales de tous les faits techniques ou d'organisation mentionnés au quatrième alinéa de l'article 11 du présent arrêté.

Article 14 - Revues techniques.
1. Des revues techniques visant à la vérification de la mise en œuvre des dispositions du présent arrêté doivent être planifiées par l'opérateur de lancement. Ces revues peuvent être également pratiquées dans le cadre de revues conduites par ailleurs.
2. L'opérateur de lancement doit informer le Centre national d'études spatiales des revues préalables au lancement. Les agents habilités au titre de l'article 7 de la loi du 3 juin 2008 susvisée peuvent y assister dans les conditions fixées au même article.

Article 15 - Cocontractants, sous-traitants et clients.
1. L'opérateur de lancement doit faire appliquer par ses cocontractants, sous-traitants et clients des dispositions nécessaires à l'établissement et au maintien de la conformité à la présente réglementation technique.
2. L'opérateur de lancement doit faire appliquer, sous sa responsabilité, par les personnes visées ci-dessus des dispositions liées à l'organisation, l'assurance qualité et l'ingénierie conformes à des normes et pratiques reconnues par la profession.
3. L'opérateur de lancement doit faire appliquer, sous sa responsabilité, par ses clients les dispositions permettant de garantir la compatibilité (géométrique, mécanique, dynamique, thermique, électromagnétique et radioélectrique) entre les objets spatiaux destinés à être mis en orbite et le système de lancement, et en vérifie la prise en compte.

CHAPITRE III: EXIGENCES TECHNIQUES SPECIFIQUES POUR LES OPERATIONS DE LANCEMENT

SECTION 1: EXIGENCES TECHNIQUES GENERALES LIEES A L'OPERATION DE LANCEMENT

Article 16 - Justifications requises.
1. Pour assurer la maîtrise technique du système et des procédures vis-à-vis des événements redoutés mentionnés à l'article 7 du présent arrêté, l'opérateur de lancement doit justifier:
   a) Le référentiel normatif technique retenu;
   b) La prise en compte de l'environnement climatique dans lequel le système est opéré;
   c) L'aptitude du système de lancement et de ses sous-systèmes à remplir la mission.

Ceci inclut:
- la description, le dimensionnement;
- les essais et/ou les modélisations, le recalage et la précision des modèles associés qui doivent mettre en exergue les interfaces et interactions entre les différents sous-systèmes et entre les différentes disciplines;
- les coefficients de sécurité et marges de sécurité;
- les réglages des moyens sol de lancement en interface avec le lanceur (seuils de surveillance);

d) La maîtrise et la reproductibilité, le cas échéant, des processus industriels de fabrication, de contrôle et de mise en œuvre;

e) La prise en compte, dans la conception, des analyses de sûreté de fonctionnement, comprenant les évaluations de fiabilité et les identifications de criticité;

f) La prise en compte des mesures issues des analyses de risque du système de lancement et des analyses de risque en opérations;

g) La prise en compte du retour d'expérience lié au traitement des faits techniques de développement, de production, des essais et des vols;

h) Les scénarios de fragmentation et de génération de débris spatiaux à la rentrée ou à la neutralisation du véhicule de lancement.

2. Les justifications mentionnées au premier alinéa ci-dessus doivent être apportées dans chacun des cas suivants:
   - domaine de vol (cas nominal, cas avec incertitudes associées aux dispersions et aux méconnaissances);
   - domaine extrême;
   - cas non nominaux (pannes).

   Lesdites justifications doivent couvrir:
   - l'ensemble des phases de vie du système;
   - l'ensemble des phases stabilisées et transitoires rencontrées.

3. Les justifications doivent porter sur:
   a) La caractérisation de l'enveloppe des évolutions nominales et extrêmes du véhicule de lancement (libre évolution à six degrés de liberté du véhicule de lancement);
   b) La démonstration de la fiabilité du lanceur dans cette enveloppe, en particulier:
      - la justification de sa tenue mécanique (systèmes propulsifs, structures principales et sous-système);
      - la justification de la performance des systèmes propulsifs et pyrotechniques;
      - la justification de la performance des chaînes de conduite du vol (notamment systèmes électriques, hydrauliques, logiciels);
      - s'il est requis, la fiabilité du dispositif bord de neutralisation et son effet sur les zones de retombée.

c) La caractérisation mécanique spécifique aux études de rupture du lanceur:
   - la détermination de la valeur minimale en termes d'incidence et de pression dynamique garantissant la rupture structurale;
   - la détermination de la fragmentation (nombre de débris, géométrie, masse, caractéristiques matériaux) de tout ou partie du véhicule de lancement en fonction de l'origine des scénarios de destruction, mécanique ou thermique.
d) Les analyses suivantes en ce qui concerne la mise en œuvre au sol:
   - l'analyse de la chronologie de l'opération de lancement, démontrant l'atteinte de l'état attendu à l'instant irréversible;
   - l'analyse de l'innocuité des opérations de préparation sur la fiabilité du véhicule de lancement pendant l'opération de lancement, à partir de l'analyse de tous les processus d'opérations de fabrication, d'intégration et de contrôle réalisés directement par intervention humaine, ou à distance via un système de contrôle-commande.

Article 17 - Analyse spécifique de mission.

En complément des justifications prévues à l'article 16 du présent arrêté, liées à la justification générique du système de lancement pour une famille de mission donnée, l'opérateur de lancement doit apporter les éléments suivants inhérents à l'opération envisagée:

1° La démonstration du respect du domaine d'utilisation du véhicule de lancement;
2° La démonstration de la compatibilité des objets destinés à être mis en orbite avec les ambiances véhicule de lancement (géométrique, mécanique, dynamique, thermique, électromagnétique et radioélectrique);
3° La détermination des niveaux de charges du véhicule de lancement, incluant les objets spatiaux destinés à être lancés (charges dynamiques et thermiques);
4° La démonstration que les caractéristiques réelles du spécimen de lanceur utilisé pour la mission sont conformes à la définition théorique présentée conformément à l'article 16 du présent arrêté;
5° Le cas échéant, la justification que les écarts (anomalie, évolutions) par rapport à la configuration ayant fait l'objet d'une licence, conformément aux dispositions de l'article 16 du présent arrêté (définition, processus de production, mise en œuvre) et ceux issus de l'exploitation des paramètres enregistrés en vol sont analysés et rendus techniquement acceptables;
6° La justification de la trajectoire spécifique à la mission optimisée au regard des risques encourus;
7° La définition du couloir de vol autour de la trajectoire nominale, jusqu'à l'injection en orbite;
8° Le dimensionnement et position des taches de retombée pour les éléments non mis en orbite, y compris pour l'information relative à la circulation aérienne et maritime;

9° La définition des choix de fin de vie pour les éléments mis en orbite conformément aux dispositions de l'article 20 et des quatrième, cinquième, sixième et septième alinéas de l'article 21 du présent arrêté et, le cas échéant, la détermination des zones de retombée;

10° La validation des paramètres d'habillage du contrôle de vol et du logiciel de vol adaptés à la mission permettant de justifier le bon fonctionnement du logiciel de vol;

11° Concernant les moyens automatiques embarqués de neutralisation du véhicule de lancement, le cas échéant:
  – la définition des réglages à partir de l'analyse des trajectoires simulées des cas non nominaux;
  – le dimensionnement et la position des taches de retombée faisant suite à la neutralisation;
  – la validation des seuils des algorithmes spécifiques du logiciel de vol permettant de neutraliser le véhicule de lancement, afin d'en démontrer le bon fonctionnement.

Article 18 - Moyens embarqués de neutralisation.

Pour la phase de lancement:

Une étude exhaustive des cas de pannes à l'origine des situations anormales conduisant le véhicule de lancement à devenir dangereux doit être menée par l'opérateur de lancement, notamment dans les cas suivants:
– sortie du couloir de vol prédéfini;
– retombée dangereuse des éléments prévus de se détacher;
– comportement non nominal du contrôle de vol;
– non-placement en orbite du composite supérieur.

Cette étude doit justifier de manière qualitative et quantitative de la nécessité ou non de moyens automatiques embarqués permettant de neutraliser le véhicule de lancement avant l'instant où la tache d'impact est tangente aux eaux territoriales du premier Etat rencontré le long de la trajectoire nominale. Dans le cas où de tels moyens sont nécessaires, cette étude doit présenter leur définition ainsi que les éléments demandés au titre de l'article 17 du présent arrêté.

Pour la rentrée contrôlée:

Une étude exhaustive des cas de pannes à l'origine des situations anormales conduisant l'élément propulsif du lanceur mis en orbite à devenir dangereux doit être menée par l'opérateur de lancement, notamment dans le cas de non-maîtrise du niveau ou de la direction de la poussée.

Cette étude doit présenter les moyens automatiques embarqués permettant d'effectuer la rentrée contrôlée de l'élément propulsif mis en orbite.

Article 19 - Suivi du volet retour d'expérience associé.
Les paramètres de fonctionnement du véhicule de lancement, incluant les positions et vitesses de ce dernier, ayant un impact sur la maîtrise des risques résultant des études mentionnées aux articles 7 et 8 du présent arrêté doivent être acquis, retransmis au sol, enregistrés et exploités par l'opérateur de lancement. Toute déviation de ces paramètres par rapport à l'état de référence attendu constitue un fait technique dont une analyse doit être menée a posteriori pour tout système de lancement récurrent.

SECTION 2: OBJECTIFS QUANTITATIFS POUR LA SECURITE DES PERSONNES

Article 20 - Objectifs quantitatifs pour la sécurité des personnes.
1. Pour la somme des risques de dommages catastrophiques, l'opérateur de lancement doit respecter les objectifs quantitatifs suivants, exprimés en probabilité maximale admissible de faire au moins une victime (risque collectif):
   a) Risque au lancement:
      - $2*10^{-5}$ pour l'ensemble de la phase de lancement, comprenant la prise en compte des cas dégradés du système de lancement et incluant la retombée des éléments prévus de se détacher du lanceur sans être mis en orbite;
      - 10^{-7} par retombée nominale d'élément pour les éléments prévus de se détacher du lanceur sans être mis en orbite, conformément au premier alinéa de l'article 23 du présent arrêté.
   b) Risque à la rentrée:
      - $2*10^{-5}$ pour la phase de retour de chaque élément du lanceur mis en orbite dans le cadre d'une rentrée atmosphérique contrôlée, incluant, conformément au premier alinéa de l'article 23 du présent arrêté, une allocation spécifique de 10^{-7} pour le retour nominal de l'élément. L'opérateur de lancement met en œuvre cette rentrée contrôlée conformément aux 1 et 5 de l'article 21 du présent arrêté.
      - En cas d'impossibilité dûment justifiée de procéder à une rentrée atmosphérique contrôlée telle que prévue ci-dessus, l'opérateur de lancement doit faire ses meilleurs efforts pour respecter un objectif quantitatif de 10^{-4} pour la phase de retour de chaque élément du lanceur mis en orbite. Dans ce cas, les choix d'architecture et des matériaux des éléments mis en orbite faisant l'objet d'une rentrée non contrôlée doivent être justifiés vis-à-vis de l'objectif de limiter le nombre et l'énergie (cinétique et explosible) des fragments susceptibles d'atteindre le sol.
2. Les exigences mentionnées au premier alinéa ci-dessus doivent être évaluées avec une méthode de calcul prenant en compte:

- l'ensemble des phénomènes conduisant à générer un risque de dommage catastrophique (phase de montée, retombée d'étage après séparation, rentrée atmosphérique d'un étage mis en orbite);
- les trajectoires avant fragmentation (atmosphérique ou extra-atmosphérique), en fonction des instants de vol et des pannes considérées;
- les scénarios de fragmentation et de génération des débris correspondants, à la rentrée ou à la neutralisation du véhicule de lancement;
- la dispersion au sol des débris et l'évaluation de leurs effets;
- la fiabilité du lanceur pour la phase de lancement;
- la fiabilité de la manœuvre de désorbitation de l'élément propulsif du lanceur mis en orbite, dans le cas de la rentrée contrôlée.
3. Des allocations quantitatives spécifiques pour un risque de dommage catastrophique particulier peuvent être prescrites, dans le respect des objectifs mentionnés au 1 du présent article, conformément à l'article 5 du décret du 9 juin 2009 susvisé.

SECTION 3: LIMITATION DES DEBRIS SPATIAUX ET PREVENTION DES RISQUES DE COLLISION

Article 21 - Limitation des débris spatiaux.

Le système de lancement mis en œuvre par l'opérateur de lancement doit être conçu, produit et mis en œuvre de façon à respecter les dispositions suivantes pour les éléments évoluant dans l'espace extra-atmosphérique:

1. Le lanceur doit être conçu, produit et mis en œuvre de manière à limiter au maximum la production de débris au cours des opérations nominales, y compris au-delà de la fin de vie du lanceur ainsi que de ses éléments constitutifs. L'opérateur de lancement met notamment en œuvre, à ce titre, les dispositions suivantes:
   - dans le cadre du lancement d'un objet spatial unique, un seul élément (par exemple, un étage) du lanceur peut être placé en orbite;
   - dans le cadre du lancement de plusieurs objets spatiaux, au maximum deux éléments (par exemple, un étage ou la structure d'adaptation) du lanceur peuvent être placés en orbite.

Les dispositions ci-dessus ne sont pas applicables:
- aux systèmes pyrotechniques. Ceux-ci ne doivent toutefois pas générer de produits de taille supérieure ou égale à 1 mm dans leur plus grande dimension;
- aux propulseurs à poudre. Ceux-ci ne doivent toutefois pas générer de débris de combustion de taille supérieure ou égale à 1 mm dans la région protégée B. S'agissant de la conception et de l'utilisation des propulseurs à poudre, l'opérateur de lancement met en œuvre des méthodes permettant d'éviter de mettre durablement en

orbite des produits de combustion solide qui pourraient contaminer la région protégée A.
2. Le lanceur doit être conçu, produit et mis en œuvre de façon à ce que les débris produits dans le respect des dispositions du 1 ci-dessus qui parviennent à atteindre la surface de la Terre ne présentent pas de risque excessif pour les personnes, les biens, la santé publique ou l'environnement, notamment du fait d'une pollution de l'environnement par des substances dangereuses.
3. La probabilité d'occurrence d'une désintégration accidentelle doit être inférieure à 10^3 jusqu'à la fin de vie de l'objet spatial; son calcul doit inclure les modes de pannes des systèmes de propulsion et de puissance, les mécanismes et les structures, mais ne prend pas en compte les impacts extérieurs.
Les fragmentations volontaires d'éléments du lanceur sont interdites.
4. Le lanceur doit être conçu, produit et mis en œuvre de façon à ce que, à l'issue de la phase de retrait de service:
   – toutes les réserves d'énergie à bord soient épuisées de façon permanente, ou placées dans un état tel que l'épuisement des réserves d'énergie à bord soit inéluctable, ou dans un état tel qu'elles ne présentent pas de risque de générer des débris;
   – tous les moyens de production d'énergie à bord soient désactivés de façon permanente.
5. Le lanceur doit être conçu, produit et mis en œuvre de façon à ce que, après la fin de la phase de lancement, ses éléments constitutifs mis sur des orbites traversant la région protégée A soient désorbités dans le cadre d'une rentrée atmosphérique contrôlée.
En cas d'impossibilité, dûment justifiée, à respecter cette disposition, il doit être conçu, produit et mis en œuvre de façon à ce que ses éléments constitutifs ne soient plus présents dans la région protégée A, vingt-cinq ans après la fin de la phase de lancement. Ce résultat est obtenu de préférence par une rentrée atmosphérique non contrôlée ou, à défaut, par la mise sur une orbite dont le périgée reste, dans les cent ans qui suivent la fin de l'opération, au-dessus de la région protégée A.
6. Le lanceur doit être conçu, produit et mis en œuvre de façon à ce que, après la fin de la phase de lancement, ses éléments constitutifs mis sur une orbite incluse dans ou traversant la région protégée B soient mis sur une orbite n'interférant pas avec cette région au-delà d'une année. Cette orbite doit être telle que, sous l'effet des perturbations naturelles, le lanceur ou ses éléments constitutifs ne reviennent pas dans la région protégée B dans les cent ans qui suivent la fin de l'opération.
7. La probabilité de pouvoir réaliser avec succès les manœuvres de retrait de service mentionnées aux quatrième, cinquième et sixième alinéas ci-dessus doit être au moins de 0,9. Cette probabilité est évaluée sur la durée totale de l'opération; son calcul, effectué avant le début de l'opération spatiale, doit prendre en compte tous les systèmes, sous-systèmes et équipements utilisables pour ces manœuvres, leurs niveaux de redondance

éventuels et leur fiabilité, en tenant compte des effets du vieillissement atteint au moment où il est prévu que ces manœuvres seront exécutées, ainsi que la disponibilité des moyens et ressources en énergie nécessaires pour ces manœuvres.

Article 22 - Prévention des risques de collision.
Les systèmes doivent être conçus, produits et mis en œuvre et leur mission définie de façon à limiter, pendant l'opération spatiale et les trois jours qui suivent la fin de la phase de retrait de service, les risques de collision accidentelle avec des objets habités dont les paramètres orbitaux sont connus avec précision et disponibles.

SECTION 4: EXIGENCES LIEES A LA RETOMBEE SUR TERRE

Article 23 - Prévention des risques induits par la retombée du lanceur ou de ses fragments.
1. Dans le cas où le lanceur comporte des éléments prévus pour s'en détacher en phase de lancement ou s'agissant de l'élément propulsif mis en orbite dans le cadre d'une rentrée atmosphérique contrôlée, la zone de retombée sur Terre doit être maîtrisée par l'opérateur de lancement. La zone de retombée, associée à une probabilité de 99,999 %, ne doit pas interférer avec le territoire, y compris les eaux territoriales, de tout Etat, sauf accord de ce dernier.
   A cet effet, l'opérateur de lancement met en œuvre les dispositions suivantes:
   - prise en compte des trajectoires avant fragmentation (atmosphérique ou extra-atmosphérique), en fonction des instants de séparation des étages et prenant en compte les dispersions de fonctionnement des sous-systèmes du véhicule de lancement;
   - modélisation des scénarios de fragmentation et de génération des débris correspondants;
   - analyse de la dispersion des débris arrivant en mer.
2. Dans l'hypothèse où une zone de retombée se situe dans une région caractérisée par un fort trafic maritime (rail maritime essentiellement) ou par la présence de plates-formes pétrolières fixes et occupées, une analyse particulière doit être menée dans le cadre de l'étude des dangers prévue à l'article 7 du présent arrêté.
3. L'organisation et les moyens mis en place par l'opérateur de lancement doivent permettre au président du Centre national d'études spatiales:
   - d'informer les autorités compétentes en charge du contrôle aérien et maritime des zones de retombées en cas nominal, en précisant les taches à 99 % de ces retombées;
   - en situation non nominale, de transmettre, sans délai, aux autorités compétentes les informations relatives à la zone de retombée d'éléments permettant d'avertir au plus tôt les autorités des Etats concernés;

- de fournir toutes informations utiles en vue de l'établissement et de la mise en œuvre des plans d'intervention nécessaires par les autorités compétentes.

Article 24 - Epaves et récupération d'éléments du lanceur.

1. Tout lanceur doit être conçu, produit et mis en œuvre de telle sorte que ses étages propulsifs prévus pour retomber sur Terre ne présentent pas de risque technique consécutif à la création d'une épave maritime. Les épaves ne doivent pas constituer, ni menacer de constituer, un obstacle ou un danger pour la navigation, la pêche ou l'environnement, ni un écueil ou un obstacle dans un port, une passe d'accès ou une rade.
2. Lorsque des étages doivent être récupérés, leur dispositif de neutralisation doit être inhibé en cas de séparation nominale, mais doit fonctionner en cas de séparation intempestive ou de rupture d'étage. Ce dispositif doit pouvoir être remis en sécurité avant toute manutention de récupération.

SECTION 5: RISQUES PARTICULIERS

Article 25 - Sûreté nucléaire.

Tout opérateur de lancement ayant l'intention de transporter des matières radioactives à bord du véhicule de lancement se conforme à la réglementation applicable en vigueur et justifie de son application dans le plan de sûreté nucléaire prévu au II (2°, d) de l'article 1er du décret du 9 juin 2009 susvisé.

Article 26 - Protection planétaire.

Tout opérateur de lancement procédant à un lancement vers un autre corps céleste, incluant ou non un retour de matière extraterrestre, se conforme à la norme internationale « Politique de protection planétaire » publiée par le Committee on Space Research (COSPAR) pour l'application de l'article IX du Traité sur les principes régissant les activités des Etats en matière d'exploration et d'utilisation de l'espace extra-atmosphérique, y compris la Lune et les autres corps célestes et justifie de son application dans le plan de protection planétaire prévu au II (2°, d) de l'article 1er du décret du 9 juin 2009 susvisé.

CHAPITRE IV: EXIGENCES TECHNIQUES LIEES AU SITE DE LANCEMENT

Article 27

1. S'agissant d'une opération conduite depuis le Centre spatial guyanais, le lanceur doit être conçu et produit de façon à être compatible avec les systèmes et procédures issus de l'arrêté portant réglementation de l'exploitation des installations du Centre spatial guyanais édicté par le président du Centre national d'études spatiales.

2. S'agissant d'une opération conduite depuis un autre site de lancement et sous réserve des dispenses accordées au titre de l'article 4.4 de la loi du 3 juin 2008 susvisé, l'opérateur:
   - justifie de l'existence de systèmes et procédures propres audit site, notamment en matière de localisation, de neutralisation et de télémesure, visant lors du déroulement de l'opération à la protection des personnes, des biens, de la santé publique et de l'environnement;
   - justifie de la compatibilité des systèmes et procédures susmentionnés avec les dispositions du présent arrêté;
   - démontre que le lanceur est conçu et produit de façon à être compatible avec les systèmes et procédures susmentionnés.

TROISIEME PARTIE: MAITRISE ET RETOUR SUR TERRE D'UN OBJET SPATIAL

TITRE IER: CHAMP D'APPLICATION

Article 28

Les dispositions de la présente partie ne s'appliquent pas à la maîtrise et au retour des étages et des éléments de lanceur auxquels s'appliquent les dispositions de la deuxième partie du présent arrêté.

TITRE II: DOSSIER TECHNIQUE

CHAPITRE IER: DOCUMENTATION A FOURNIR

Article 29 - Description de l'opération spatiale et des systèmes et procédures.

La description de l'opération spatiale et des systèmes et procédures mis en œuvre, mentionnée au II (1°) de l'article 1er du décret du 9 juin 2009 susvisé, présente le système spatial utilisé pour l'opération envisagée, constitué du segment sol et de l'objet spatial. Cette description présente également les divers sous-systèmes dudit objet.

S'agissant d'un objet spatial devant effectuer une rentrée en fin de vie, la description présente les constituants de la plate-forme et de la charge utile, ainsi que leurs équipements, susceptibles d'atteindre le sol, en indiquant les dimensions, les masses et les matériaux utilisés.

Cette description comprend une analyse de mission présentant l'orbite de référence, les moyens pour y accéder (injection, mise à poste) et pour s'y maintenir (maintien à poste) avec les repères espace et temps associés, les mesures pour restituer l'orbite avec la précision prévue, la capacité de contrôler l'objet (existence et visibilité des stations sol ou des satellites relais, du centre de contrôle ou d'une autonomie bord) ainsi que la stratégie de retrait de

service. Elle indique les modèles relatifs aux systèmes spatiaux utilisés pour mener cette analyse de mission.
Cette description comprend la capacité de maîtrise prévue à l'article 39 du présent arrêté.

Article 30 - Notice générale de conformité
1. L'opérateur établit, conformément au II (2°, a) de l'article 1er du décret du 9 juin 2009 susvisé, une notice générale de conformité à la présente réglementation technique.
2. Cette notice générale de conformité:
   - identifie les documents fournis au titre des articles 31 à 34 ainsi que 47 et 48 du présent arrêté;
   - établit l'état de conformité en résultant.

Article 31 - Normes internes et dispositions de gestion de la qualité
L'opérateur établit conformément au II (2°, b) de l'article 1er du décret du 9 juin 2009 susvisé, les documents justifiant du respect des dispositions du chapitre II du présent titre.

Article 32 - Etude des dangers
L'opérateur réalise, conformément au II (2°, c) de l'article 1er du décret du 9 juin 2009 susvisé, une étude exposant les dangers que peut présenter l'opération spatiale envisagée pour les personnes, les biens, la santé publique et l'environnement, notamment les dangers liés à la génération de débris spatiaux.
Cette étude comprend une description de l'ensemble des dangers liés à l'opération dans les cas de fonctionnement nominal et accidentels, que leur cause soit d'origine interne ou externe, et en précise la nature et l'étendue des conséquences.
Cette étude doit traiter notamment des événements suivants, dans les conditions prévues aux chapitres III et IV du présent titre:
- dommages aux personnes à l'occasion d'une rentrée sur Terre;
- production de débris spatiaux à la suite d'une explosion;
- collision avec un objet spatial habité;
- mise en orbite dégradée conduisant à une rentrée prématurée;
- collision avec un satellite en orbite géostationnaire, dont les paramètres orbitaux sont connus avec précision et disponibles, lors des manœuvres de mise à poste, de changement de localisation ou de retrait de service;
- dispersion de matière radioactive;
- contamination planétaire.

Le contenu de l'étude des dangers doit être en relation avec la gravité et la probabilité d'occurrence des événements redoutés susceptibles d'être engendrés par l'opération envisagée.

Article 33 - Etude d'impact

L'opérateur réalise, conformément au II (2°, d) de l'article 1er du décret du 9 juin 2009 susvisé, l'étude d'impact de l'opération envisagée sur l'environnement terrestre ainsi que l'impact en matière de génération de débris spatiaux conformément aux dispositions de l'article 40 du présent arrêté.

Cette étude d'impact identifie et évalue, lors du fonctionnement nominal, les impacts sur l'environnement de l'opération et les mesures prises modérant les impacts négatifs. Cette étude d'impact identifie, en particulier, les débris créés ou susceptibles d'être créés par la mise en œuvre de l'objet spatial. Le contenu de cette étude d'impact doit être en relation avec les incidences prévisibles et les effets directs ou indirects temporaires et permanents de l'opération envisagée sur l'environnement.

Article 34 - Mesures de maîtrise des risques.

L'opérateur établit et met en œuvre, conformément au II (2°, e) de l'article 1er du décret du 9 juin 2009 susvisé, à partir des conclusions des études de danger et d'impact mentionnées aux articles 32 et 33 ci-dessus, les plans de maîtrise des risques suivants:

- le plan de limitation des débris spatiaux, qui démontre le respect des dispositions de l'article 40 du présent arrêté;
- le plan de prévention des dommages environnementaux, qui démontre que les matériaux et les sources d'énergie choisis pour l'objet spatial ne sont pas de nature à créer des dommages environnementaux, ainsi que le respect du deuxième alinéa de l'article 45 du présent arrêté;
- le plan de prévention des risques induits par la retombée de l'objet spatial ou de ses fragments, qui démontre le respect des dispositions des articles 44 à 46 du présent arrêté;
- le plan de prévention des risques de collision, qui démontre le respect des dispositions de l'article 41 du présent arrêté;
- le cas échéant, le plan de sûreté nucléaire, qui démontre le respect des dispositions de l'article 42 du présent arrêté;
- le cas échéant, le plan de protection planétaire, qui démontre le respect des dispositions de l'article 43 du présent arrêté.

CHAPITRE II: EXIGENCES SYSTEME QUALITE

Article 35 - Compétence, moyens, organisation et installations.

1. L'opérateur doit mettre en œuvre et gérer, pour la conduite de l'opération spatiale, un système de management de la qualité ainsi que des normes internes et dispositions de gestion de la qualité, conformément à l'article 1er du décret du 9 juin 2009 susvisé. Ce

système de management doit traiter de l'assurance qualité, de la sûreté de fonctionnement, de la gestion de configuration et de la conduite des travaux.
2. Il doit disposer des compétences, des moyens et de l'organisation nécessaires pour préparer et mettre en œuvre l'opération envisagée:
   – installations et organisation appropriées;
   – équipements, outils et matériels adaptés à l'opération envisagée;
   – documentation relative aux tâches et aux procédures;
   – accès aux données utiles à la préparation de l'opération envisagée;
   – enregistrement, exploitation et archivage des données techniques;
   – postes clés et processus de formation associé.
3. La description et la justification des constituants de l'objet spatial critiques vis-à-vis de la protection des personnes, des biens, de la santé publique et de l'environnement, notamment en ce qui concerne la production de débris spatiaux, ainsi que la définition des matériaux utilisés doivent être conservés jusqu'à la fin de l'opération spatiale concernée. Après les manœuvres de retrait de service, ces éléments sont transmis au Centre national d'études spatiales avec la description de l'état atteint.

Article 36 - Faits techniques et d'organisation.
L'opérateur doit mettre en place une organisation lui permettant:
– de connaître et de traiter, pendant la préparation et la conduite de l'opération spatiale, tous les faits techniques et d'organisation susceptibles d'affecter les conditions de l'opération spatiale telle qu'elle a été autorisée, notamment la stratégie de retrait de service;
– d'informer, sans délai, au titre de l'article 7 du décret du 9 juin 2009 susvisé, le Centre national d'études spatiales de tous ces faits techniques et d'organisation.

Article 37 - Revues techniques.
Des points clés visant à la vérification de la mise en œuvre des dispositions du présent arrêté doivent être planifiés par l'opérateur. L'opérateur doit informer le Centre national d'études spatiales des points clés préalables au lancement et à l'engagement des manœuvres de retrait de service de l'objet spatial.

Article 38 - Cocontractants et sous-traitants.
1. L'opérateur doit faire appliquer, par ses cocontractants et sous-traitants, toutes dispositions nécessaires à l'établissement et au maintien de la conformité à la présente réglementation technique.
2. L'opérateur doit faire appliquer, par les personnes visées ci-dessus, des dispositions liées à l'organisation, l'assurance qualité et l'ingénierie conformes à des normes et pratiques reconnues par la profession.

ANNEXE 1.6

CHAPITRE III: EXIGENCES TECHNIQUES SPECIFIQUES COMMUNES A LA MAITRISE EN ORBITE ET AU RETOUR SUR TERRE D'UN OBJET SPATIAL

Article 39 - Capacité de maîtrise de l'objet spatial.

L'objet doit être conçu, produit et mis en œuvre de façon à permettre à l'opérateur, pendant toute la durée de l'opération, de recevoir des informations sur son état et de lui envoyer des commandes nécessaires notamment à l'application des articles 47 et 48 du présent arrêté.

Article 40 - Limitation des débris spatiaux.

Les systèmes mis en œuvre par l'opérateur doivent être conçus, produits et mis en œuvre de façon à respecter les dispositions suivantes:
1. Les systèmes doivent être conçus, produits et mis en œuvre de façon à ne pas générer de débris au cours des opérations nominales de l'objet spatial.
   La disposition ci-dessus n'est pas applicable:
   – aux systèmes pyrotechniques. Ceux-ci ne doivent toutefois pas générer des produits de taille supérieure ou égale à 1 mm dans leur plus grande dimension;
   – aux propulseurs à poudre. Ceux-ci ne doivent toutefois pas générer de débris de combustion de taille supérieure ou égale à 1 mm dans la région protégée B. S'agissant de la conception et de l'utilisation des propulseurs à poudre, l'opérateur met en œuvre des méthodes permettant d'éviter de mettre durablement en orbite des produits de combustion solide qui pourraient contaminer la région protégée A.
2. La probabilité d'occurrence d'une désintégration accidentelle doit être inférieure à 10^{-3} jusqu'à la fin de vie de l'objet spatial; son calcul doit inclure les modes de pannes des systèmes de propulsion et de puissance, les mécanismes et les structures, mais ne prend pas en compte les impacts extérieurs.
   En cas de détection d'une situation entraînant une telle défaillance, l'opérateur doit pouvoir planifier et mettre en œuvre des mesures correctives afin d'éviter toute désintégration.
3. Les systèmes doivent être conçus, produits et mis en œuvre de façon à ce que, à l'issue de la phase de retrait de service:
   – toutes les réserves d'énergie à bord soient épuisées de façon permanente ou placées dans un état tel qu'elles ne présentent pas de risque de générer des débris;
   – tous les moyens de production d'énergie à bord soient désactivés de façon permanente.
4. Les systèmes doivent être conçus, produits et mis en œuvre de façon à ce que l'objet spatial ayant achevé sa phase opérationnelle sur une orbite traversant la région protégée A soit désorbité avec rentrée atmosphérique, de manière contrôlée.

En cas d'impossibilité, dûment justifiée, à respecter cette disposition, il doit être conçu, produit et mis en œuvre de façon à ce qu'il ne soit plus présent dans la région protégée A, vingt-cinq ans après la fin de la phase opérationnelle. Ce résultat est obtenu, de préférence, par une rentrée atmosphérique non contrôlée ou, à défaut, par la mise sur une orbite stable dont le périgée reste, dans les cent ans qui suivent la fin de l'opération, au-dessus de la région protégée A.

5. L'objet spatial doit être conçu, produit et mis en œuvre de façon à ce que, lorsqu'il a achevé sa phase opérationnelle sur une orbite incluse dans ou traversant la région protégée B, il soit mis sur une orbite n'interférant pas avec cette région. Cette orbite doit être telle que, sous l'effet des perturbations naturelles, dans les cent ans qui suivent la fin de l'opération, l'objet ne revienne pas dans la région protégée B.
6. La probabilité de pouvoir disposer des ressources en énergie nécessaires pour réaliser avec succès les manœuvres de retrait de service mentionnées aux 3, 4 et 5 ci-dessus doit être au moins de 0,9.
7. L'opérateur doit évaluer la probabilité de pouvoir réaliser avec succès les manœuvres de retrait de service mentionnées aux 3, 4 et 5 ci-dessus. Cette évaluation, qui n'inclut pas la disponibilité des ressources en énergie, doit être effectuée par l'opérateur sur la durée totale de l'opération et prend en compte tous les systèmes, sous-systèmes et équipements utilisables pour ces manœuvres, leurs niveaux de redondance éventuels et leur fiabilité, en tenant compte des effets du vieillissement atteint au moment où il est prévu que ces manœuvres seront exécutées.

Article 41 - Prévention des risques de collision.
Les systèmes doivent être conçus, produits et mis en œuvre et leur mission définie de façon à limiter, pendant l'opération spatiale et les trois jours qui suivent la fin de l'opération, les risques de collision accidentelle avec les objets habités et les satellites en orbite géostationnaire dont les paramètres orbitaux sont connus avec précision et disponibles.

Article 42 - Sûreté nucléaire.
Tout opérateur ayant l'intention de mettre en œuvre des matières radioactives à bord de l'objet spatial se conforme à la réglementation applicable en vigueur et justifie de son application dans le plan de sûreté nucléaire prévu à l'article 1er du décret du 9 juin 2009 susvisé.

Article 43 - Protection planétaire.
Tout opérateur ayant l'intention de conduire une mission vers un autre corps céleste, incluant ou non un retour de matière extraterrestre, se conforme à la norme internationale « Politique de protection planétaire » publiée par le Committee on Space Research (COSPAR) pour l'application de l'article IX du Traité sur les principes régissant les activités

des Etats en matière d'exploration et d'utilisation de l'espace extra-atmosphérique, y compris la Lune et les autres corps célestes. L'opérateur justifie de son application dans le plan de protection planétaire prévu à l'article 1er du décret du 9 juin 2009 susvisé.

CHAPITRE IV: EXIGENCES TECHNIQUES SPECIFIQUES POUR LE RETOUR D'UN OBJET SPATIAL

Article 44 - Objectifs quantitatifs pour la sécurité des personnes pour le retour sur Terre d'un objet spatial.

1. S'agissant du retour d'un objet spatial, les objectifs quantitatifs de sauvegarde, exprimés en probabilité maximale admissible de faire au moins une victime (risque collectif), sont définis comme suit:

    $2*10^{-5}$ pour un retour intègre;

    $2*10^{-5}$ pour une rentrée atmosphérique contrôlée avec destruction de l'objet spatial.

    En cas d'impossibilité dûment justifiée de procéder à une rentrée atmosphérique contrôlée avec destruction de l'objet spatial telle que mentionnée ci-dessus, l'opérateur doit faire ses meilleurs efforts pour respecter un objectif quantitatif de 10^{-4} pour une rentrée non contrôlée avec destruction de l'objet spatial.

2. Les dispositions mentionnées au premier alinéa ci-dessus doivent être évaluées avec une méthode de calcul reposant sur:
    – la prise en compte de l'ensemble des phénomènes conduisant à générer un risque de dommage catastrophique;
    – la prise en compte des trajectoires avant fragmentation;
    – la modélisation des scénarios de fragmentation et de génération des débris correspondants à la rentrée;
    – la dispersion au sol des débris et l'évaluation de leurs effets;
    – la prise en compte de la fiabilité de l'objet spatial.

3. Ces objectifs comprennent le risque associé au retour nominal de l'objet ou de ses fragments ainsi que celui associé aux cas non nominaux. Ces objectifs sont sans préjudice des dispositions des articles 42 et 45 du présent arrêté.

Article 45 - Exigences liées à la rentrée non contrôlée de l'objet spatial prévue en fin de vie.

1. Les choix d'architecture et des matériaux des objets spatiaux faisant l'objet d'une rentrée non contrôlée doivent être justifiés vis-à-vis de l'objectif de limiter le nombre et l'énergie (cinétique et explosible) des fragments susceptibles d'atteindre le sol.

2. Les systèmes doivent être conçus, produits et mis en œuvre de façon à ce que les éléments qui parviennent à atteindre la surface de la Terre ne présentent pas de risque

inacceptable pour les personnes, les biens, la santé publique ou l'environnement, notamment du fait d'une pollution de l'environnement par des substances dangereuses.

Article 46 - Prévention des risques induits par la retombée de l'objet spatial ou de ses fragments lors d'une rentrée contrôlée.
1. L'opérateur détermine les zones de retombée de l'objet spatial et de ses fragments pour toute rentrée atmosphérique contrôlée sur Terre, associées respectivement à une probabilité de 99 % et de 99,999 %. Ces zones de retombée doivent prendre en compte les incertitudes associées aux paramètres de rentrée.
2. La zone de retombée associée à une probabilité de 99,999 % ne doit pas interférer avec le territoire, y compris les eaux territoriales, de tout Etat, sauf accord de ce dernier.
   Dans l'hypothèse où une zone de retombée se situe dans une région caractérisée par un fort trafic maritime (rail maritime essentiellement) ou par la présence de plates-formes pétrolières fixes et occupées, une analyse particulière doit être menée, dans le cadre de l'étude des dangers mentionnée à l'article 32 du présent arrêté.
3. L'organisation et les moyens mis en place par l'opérateur doit permettre au président du Centre national d'études spatiales:
   - d'informer les autorités compétentes en charge du contrôle aérien et maritime des zones de retombées en cas nominal, en précisant les taches à 99 % de ces retombées;
   - de transmettre aux autorités compétentes les informations relatives à la zone de retombée d'éléments permettant d'avertir au plus tôt les autorités des Etats concernés, en situation dégradée;
   - de fournir toutes informations utiles en vue de l'établissement et de la mise en œuvre des plans d'intervention nécessaires par les autorités compétentes.

TITRE III: OBLIGATIONS LIEES A LA CONDUITE DE L'OPERATION SPATIALE

Article 47 - Rentrées non nominales.
Dans le cas d'une rentrée prématurée ou accidentelle, l'opérateur met prioritairement en œuvre toutes mesures permettant de réduire le risque au sol.

Article 48 - Etat de l'objet spatial.
1. L'opérateur tient à jour un état justifiant de la capacité de l'objet spatial à accomplir les manœuvres de retrait de service visées aux 3, 4 et 5 de l'article 40 du présent arrêté et notamment de la disponibilité des ressources en énergie nécessaires à cette manœuvre. Cet état est transmis au Centre national d'études spatiales chaque fois que survient un événement affectant cette capacité.
2. L'état de l'objet spatial obtenu à l'issue des opérations de retrait de service sera transmis au Centre national d'études spatiales.

Article 49 - Destruction intentionnelle.
1. L'opérateur doit éviter la destruction intentionnelle de tout objet spatial en orbite.
2. Lorsque l'opérateur entend procéder à une destruction intentionnelle, il fait état de sa nécessité auprès du président du Centre national d'études spatiales. Ces destructions ne peuvent avoir lieu qu'à des altitudes suffisamment basses pour limiter la durée de vie en orbite des fragments produits.

QUATRIEME PARTIE: CONFORMITE PRELIMINAIRE A LA REGLEMENTATION TECHNIQUE

TITRE IER: CHAMP D'APPLICATION

Article 50
Au titre de l'article 11 du décret du 9 juin 2009 susvisé, les systèmes et sous-systèmes critiques suivants peuvent être soumis au Centre national d'études spatiales:
- le système spatial;
- l'objet spatial;
- la plate-forme d'un objet spatial, le cas échéant associée à un système de commande et de contrôle;
- le sous-système propulsif d'un objet spatial;
- les installations de lancement d'un objet spatial.

Article 51
Le dossier prévu au premier alinéa de l'article 11 du décret du 9 juin 2009 susvisé est constitué conformément aux dispositions de l'article 50 du présent arrêté. Il est soumis au Centre national d'études spatiales pendant le développement du système ou du sous-système concerné, au plus tôt à l'issue de la phase de conception préliminaire.
Le document attestant la conformité préliminaire à la présente règlementation technique peut être délivré par le Centre national d'études spatiales à l'issue des étapes de la conception et du développement du système ou du sous-système suivantes:
- conception préliminaire;
- conception détaillée;
- production et essais au sol destinés à vérifier le respect des dispositions du présent arrêté pour le système ou sous-système concerné;
- qualification.

TITRE II: PROCEDURE DE DELIVRANCE DU DOCUMENT ATTESTANT CONFORMITE

Article 52 - Pièces à fournir.
1. Pour un système de lancement, le soumissionnaire fournit tout ou partie, selon le système concerné, des documents prévus aux articles 4 à 10 du présent arrêté.
   Pour un sous-système propulsif d'un système de lancement, le Centre national d'études spatiales établit la liste des documents à fournir et le calendrier associé après fourniture du plan de développement prévu au premier alinéa de l'article 11 du décret du 9 juin 2009 susvisé.
2. Pour un système spatial autre qu'un système de lancement, le soumissionnaire fournit tout ou partie, selon le système concerné, des documents prévus aux articles 29 à 34 du présent arrêté.

Article 53 - Contrôles, essais et analyses.
Sur la base des pièces fournies au titre de l'article 52 du présent arrêté, le Centre national d'études spatiales prescrit tous contrôles, essais et analyses tels que prévus au deuxième alinéa de l'article 11 du décret du 9 juin 2009 susvisé.
S'agissant d'un système de lancement, ces demandes peuvent également être relatives à la compatibilité avec les systèmes et procédures du site depuis lequel l'opération spatiale est conduite.

CINQUIEME PARTIE: GUIDE DES BONNES PRATIQUES

TITRE UNIQUE

Article 54
1. Un guide des bonnes pratiques est établi par le Centre national d'études spatiales, en concertation avec la profession dans le cadre d'un groupe de travail représentatif des opérateurs et des industriels concernés afin de caractériser certaines pratiques en vigueur qui permettent de contribuer à démontrer le respect de la présente réglementation technique.
   Ce guide repose sur des pratiques validées par l'expérience acquise dans le développement, l'exploitation et le contrôle des systèmes spatiaux. Il s'appuie notamment sur des normes, des spécifications techniques à vocation normative ainsi que des standards reconnus par la profession, se rapportant à la sécurité des biens, des personnes, de la santé publique et de l'environnement dans le cadre de la conduite d'opérations spatiales. Le contenu de ce guide respecte les dispositions applicables en matière de la protection de la propriété intellectuelle ainsi que du patrimoine industriel et scientifique.

2. La conformité à tout ou partie des dispositions de la présente réglementation technique est présumée acquise dans le cas où l'opérateur démontre le respect des recommandations afférentes de ce guide.

L'utilisation du guide des bonnes pratiques ne saurait présenter un caractère obligatoire ou exclusif.

SIXIEME PARTIE: DISPOSITIONS TRANSITOIRES ET FINALES

Article 55 - Dispositions transitoires

1. S'agissant des opérations de lancement d'un objet spatial, il est fait application des dispositions transitoires suivantes:
   a) Les dossiers de demande d'autorisation pour les opérations de lancement qui utilisent un système de lancement dont la première opération a eu lieu depuis le territoire français avant le 4 juin 2008 peuvent faire référence aux dossiers techniques déjà instruits par le Centre national d'études spatiales notamment dans le cadre des accords internationaux existants, en particulier ceux conclus avec ou dans le cadre de l'Agence spatiale européenne.

   Dans ce cas, les dispositions du sixième alinéa de l'article 21 du présent arrêté ne sont pas applicables. En cas d'impossibilité dûment justifiée d'appliquer les dispositions du cinquième alinéa de l'article 21 du présent arrêté, l'opérateur de lancement fait ses meilleurs efforts pour se rapprocher des seuils mentionnés.

   b) Pour les systèmes dont le premier lancement depuis le territoire français a lieu entre le 4 juin 2008 et le 31 décembre 2011, les dispositions du sixième alinéa de l'article 21 du présent arrêté ne sont pas applicables;

   c) Pour les systèmes dont le premier lancement depuis le territoire français a lieu postérieurement au 31 décembre 2011, les dispositions du présent arrêté sont pleinement applicables.

2. S'agissant des opérations de maîtrise et de retour d'un objet spatial, il est fait application des dispositions transitoires suivantes:
   a) Pour les objets spatiaux lancés avant le 10 décembre 2010:
      - s'agissant des dispositions des articles 32 et 33, les études ne traiteront que des dangers et impacts associés aux procédures mises en œuvre postérieurement au 10 décembre 2010;
      - les dispositions de l'article 38, celles des 1, 2, 6 et 7 de l'article 40 ainsi que celles de l'article 45 ne sont pas applicables;
      - s'agissant des dispositions des 3, 4 et 5 de l'article 40 ainsi que celles de l'article 41, l'opérateur doit mettre en œuvre la meilleure stratégie possible compte tenu de la définition de l'objet spatial;

- s'agissant des dispositions de l'article 44, l'opérateur doit mettre en œuvre la meilleure stratégie possible compte tenu de la définition de l'objet spatial et procéder à une estimation du risque.
b) Pour les objets spatiaux dont le lancement intervient entre le 10 décembre 2010 et le 31 décembre 2020:
    - les dispositions des 1 à 2 de l'article 40 ainsi que celles de l'article 45 ne sont pas applicables;
    - s'agissant des dispositions des 3 à 6 de l'article 40 ainsi que celles de l'article 41, l'opérateur doit mettre en œuvre la meilleure stratégie possible compte tenu de la définition de l'objet spatial;
    - s'agissant des dispositions de l'article 44, l'opérateur doit mettre en œuvre la meilleure stratégie possible compte tenu de la définition de l'objet spatial et procéder à une estimation du risque.

Article 56
Le président du Centre national d'études spatiales est chargé de l'exécution du présent arrêté, qui sera publié au Journal officiel de la République française.

Fait le 31 mars 2011.
Pour la ministre et par délégation:
Le directeur général
pour la recherche et l'innovation,
R. Stephan

Annexe 1.6 (bis)

Arrêté du 11 juillet 2017 modifiant l'arrêté du 31 mars 2011 relatif à la réglementation technique (RT)

Arrêté du 11 juillet 2017 modifiant l'arrêté du 31 mars 2011 relatif à la réglementation technique en application du décret n° 2009-643 du 9 juin 2009 relatif aux autorisations délivrées en application de la loi n° 2008-518 du 3 juin 2008 relative aux opérations spatiales

La ministre de l'enseignement supérieur, de la recherche et de l'innovation,
Vu la directive 2015/1535/CE du Parlement européen et du Conseil du 9 septembre 2015 prévoyant une procédure d'information dans le domaine des réglementations techniques et des règles relatives aux services de la société de l'information, notamment la notification n° 2017/114/F;
Vu le décret n° 2009-643 du 9 juin 2009 modifié relatif aux autorisations délivrées en application de la loi du 3 juin 2008 relative aux opérations spatiales, notamment son article 1er;
Vu l'arrêté du 31 mars 2011 relatif à la réglementation technique en application du décret n° 2009-643 du 9 juin 2009 relatif aux autorisations délivrées en application de la loi n° 2008-518 du 3 juin 2008 relative aux opérations spatiales,
Arrête:

Article 1
L'arrêté du 31 mars 2011 susvisé est modifié conformément aux articles 2 à 13 du présent arrêté.

Article 2
Le cinquième alinéa de l'article 1er est remplacé par les dispositions suivantes:
« " Couloir de vol " »: volume dans lequel le véhicule de lancement est susceptible d'évoluer compte tenu des dispersions normales; »

Article 3
Au dernier alinéa de l'article 10, les mots: « du troisième alinéa de l'article 23 du présent arrêté » sont remplacés par les mots: « du 3 de l'article 23 du présent arrêté ».

Article 4
Au second alinéa de l'article 13, les mots: « au quatrième alinéa de l'article 11 du présent arrêté » sont remplacés par les mots: « au 4 de l'article 11 du présent arrêté ».

Article 5
Dans la première phrase du 2 de l'article 16, les mots: « au premier alinéa ci-dessus » sont remplacés par les mots: « au 1 du présent article ».

Article 6
Au 9° de l'article 17, les mots: « des quatrième, cinquième, sixième et septième alinéas de l'article 21 du présent arrêté » sont remplacés par les mots: « des 4,5,6 et 7 de l'article 21 du présent arrêté ».

Article 7
L'article 20 est remplacé par les dispositions suivantes:
« Art. 20.-Objectifs quantitatifs pour la sécurité des personnes.
« 1. Pour la somme des risques de dommages catastrophiques, l'opérateur de lancement doit respecter les objectifs quantitatifs suivants, exprimés en probabilité maximale admissible de faire au moins une victime (risque collectif):
« a) Risque au lancement:
« $2* 10-5$ pour l'ensemble de la phase de lancement, comprenant la prise en compte des cas dégradés du système de lancement et incluant la retombée des éléments prévus de se détacher du lanceur sans être mis en orbite;
« $10-7$ par retombée nominale d'élément pour les éléments prévus de se détacher du lanceur sans être mis en orbite, conformément au 1 de l'article 23 du présent arrêté.
« b) Risque à la rentrée:
« $2* 10-5$ pour la phase de retour de chaque élément du lanceur mis en orbite dans le cadre d'une rentrée atmosphérique contrôlée, incluant, conformément au 1 de l'article 23 du présent arrêté, une allocation spécifique de $10-7$ pour le retour nominal de l'élément. L'opérateur de lancement met en œuvre cette rentrée contrôlée conformément aux 1 et 5 de l'article 21 du présent arrêté.
« En cas d'impossibilité dûment justifiée de procéder à une rentrée atmosphérique contrôlée telle que prévue ci-dessus, l'opérateur de lancement doit faire ses meilleurs efforts pour respecter un objectif quantitatif de $10-4$ pour la phase de retour de chaque élément du lanceur mis en orbite. Dans ce cas, les choix d'architecture et des matériaux des éléments mis en orbite faisant l'objet d'une rentrée non contrôlée doivent être justifiés vis-à-vis de l'objectif de limiter le nombre et l'énergie (cinétique et explosible) des fragments susceptibles d'atteindre le sol.

« 2. Les exigences mentionnées au 1 du présent article doivent être évaluées avec une méthode de calcul prenant en compte:

«-l'ensemble des phénomènes conduisant à générer un risque de dommage catastrophique (phase de montée, retombée d'étage après séparation, rentrée atmosphérique d'un étage mis en orbite);

«-les trajectoires avant fragmentation (atmosphérique ou extra-atmosphérique), en fonction des instants de vol et des pannes considérées;

«-les scénarios de fragmentation et de génération des débris correspondants, à la rentrée ou à la neutralisation du véhicule de lancement;

«-la dispersion au sol des débris et l'évaluation de leurs effets;

«-la fiabilité du lanceur pour la phase de lancement;

«-la fiabilité de la manœuvre de désorbitation de l'élément propulsif du lanceur mis en orbite, dans le cas de la rentrée contrôlée.

« 3. Des allocations quantitatives spécifiques pour un risque de dommage catastrophique particulier peuvent être prescrites, dans le respect des objectifs mentionnés au 1 du présent article, conformément à l'article 5 du décret du 9 juin 2009 susvisé. »

Article 8

L'article 21 est ainsi modifié:

1° A la première phrase du 3, les mots: « inférieure à 103 » sont remplacés par les mots: « inférieure à 10-3 »;

2° Le 5 est remplacé par les dispositions suivantes:

« 5. Respect zone A

« a) Le lanceur doit être conçu, produit et mis en œuvre de façon à ce que, après la fin de la phase de lancement, ses éléments constitutifs mis sur des orbites traversant la région protégée A soient désorbités dans le cadre d'une rentrée atmosphérique contrôlée.

« b) En cas d'impossibilité, dûment justifiée, à respecter cette disposition, il doit être conçu, produit et mis en œuvre de façon à ce que ses éléments constitutifs ne soient plus présents dans la région protégée A, vingt-cinq ans après la fin de la phase de lancement. Ce résultat est obtenu de préférence par une rentrée atmosphérique non contrôlée ou, à défaut, par la mise sur une orbite dont le périgée reste, dans les cent ans qui suivent la fin de l'opération, au-dessus de la région protégée A.

« c) Si l'orbite visée par les éléments constitutifs du lanceur après les manœuvres de retrait de service est dans ou traverse la zone A et a une excentricité inférieure à 0,25, elle doit permettre le respect des exigences édictées aux a) et b) du 5 du présent article avec une probabilité d'au moins 0,5 en prenant en compte l'effet des perturbations orbitales naturelles.

« d) Si l'orbite visée par les éléments constitutifs du lanceur après les manœuvres de retrait de service a une excentricité supérieure à 0,25, elle doit permettre le respect des exigences édictées aux a) et b) du 5 du présent article avec une probabilité d'au moins 0,9 en prenant en compte l'effet des perturbations orbitales naturelles et les incertitudes associées. »

3° Le 6 est remplacé par les dispositions suivantes:
« 6. Respect zone B
« a) Le lanceur doit être conçu, produit et mis en œuvre de façon à ce que, après la fin de la phase de lancement, ses éléments constitutifs mis sur une orbite incluse dans ou traversant la région protégée B soient mis sur une orbite n'interférant pas avec cette région au-delà d'une année. Cette orbite doit être telle que, sous l'effet des perturbations naturelles, le lanceur ou ses éléments constitutifs ne reviennent pas dans la région protégée B dans les cent ans qui suivent la fin de l'opération.
« b) Si l'orbite visée par les éléments constitutifs du lanceur après les manœuvres de retrait de service a une excentricité supérieure à 0,25, elle doit permettre le respect des exigences édictées au a) du 6 du présent article avec une probabilité d'au moins 0,9 en prenant en compte l'effet des perturbations orbitales naturelles et les incertitudes associées. ».

4° Au 7, la première phrase est remplacée par la phrase suivante:
« La probabilité de pouvoir réaliser avec succès les manœuvres de retrait de service mentionnées aux 4,5 et 6 du présent article doit être au moins de 0,9. »

Article 9
A la fin de la première phrase du deuxième alinéa de l'article 29, après le mot: « spatial », sont insérés les mots: «, ainsi que la durée maximale de l'opération spatiale prévue initialement. »

Article 10
Au quatrième alinéa de l'article 34, les mots: « le respect du deuxième alinéa de l'article 45 du présent arrêté » sont remplacés par les mots: « le respect du 2 de l'article 45 du présent arrêté ».

Article 11
L'article 40 est remplacé par les dispositions suivantes:
« Art. 40.-Protection de l'environnement spatial.
« Les systèmes mis en œuvre par l'opérateur doivent être conçus, produits et mis en œuvre de façon à respecter les dispositions suivantes:
« 1. Les systèmes doivent être conçus, produits et mis en œuvre de façon à ne pas générer de débris au cours des opérations nominales de l'objet spatial.

« La disposition ci-dessus n'est pas applicable:
«-aux systèmes pyrotechniques. Ceux-ci ne doivent toutefois pas générer des produits de taille supérieure ou égale à 1 mm dans leur plus grande dimension;

«-aux propulseurs à poudre. Ceux-ci ne doivent toutefois pas générer de débris de combustion de taille supérieure ou égale à 1 mm dans la région protégée B. S'agissant de la conception et de l'utilisation des propulseurs à poudre, l'opérateur met en œuvre des méthodes permettant d'éviter de mettre durablement en orbite des produits de combustion solide qui pourraient contaminer la région protégée A.
Toutefois la libération en orbite d'un unique module de propulsion additionnel est admise. Ce module, en tant qu'objet spatial, doit respecter l'ensemble des dispositions de la troisième partie du présent arrêté.
« 2. La probabilité d'occurrence d'une désintégration accidentelle doit être inférieure à 10^{-3} jusqu'à la fin de vie de l'objet spatial.
« Son calcul doit inclure les modes de pannes des systèmes de propulsion et de puissance, les mécanismes et les structures, mais ne prend pas en compte les impacts extérieurs.
« En cas de détection d'une situation entraînant une telle défaillance, l'opérateur doit pouvoir planifier et mettre en œuvre des mesures correctives afin d'éviter toute désintégration.
« 3. Les systèmes doivent être conçus, produits et mis en œuvre de façon à ce que, à l'issue de la phase de retrait de service:
«-toutes les réserves d'énergie à bord soient épuisées de façon permanente ou placées dans un état tel qu'elles ne présentent pas de risque de générer des débris;
«-tous les moyens de production d'énergie à bord soient désactivés de façon permanente;
«-toutes les capacités d'émission radioélectrique de la plateforme et de la charge utile doivent être interrompues de façon permanente.
« Les dispositions du 3 du présent article ne sont pas applicables aux rentrées contrôlées.
« 4. Respect zone A
« a) Les systèmes équipés d'éléments propulsifs permettant de modifier l'orbite doivent être conçus, produits et mis en œuvre de façon à ce que l'objet spatial ne soit plus présent dans la région protégée A vingt-cinq ans après avoir achevé sa phase opérationnelle sur une orbite traversant la région protégée A.
« b) Ce résultat est obtenu, de préférence, par une rentrée atmosphérique ou, à défaut, par la mise sur une orbite stable dont le périgée reste, dans les cent ans qui suivent la fin de l'opération, au-dessus de la région protégée A.
« c) Les systèmes non équipés d'élément propulsif permettant de modifier l'orbite doivent être conçus, produits et mis en œuvre de façon à ce que l'objet spatial ne soit plus présent dans la région protégée A vingt-cinq ans après l'injection en orbite.

« d) Si l'orbite visée par l'objet spatial après les manœuvres de retrait de service est dans ou traverse la zone A et a une excentricité inférieure à 0,25, elle doit permettre le respect des exigences édictées aux a), b) et c) du 4 du présent article avec une probabilité d'au moins 0,5 en prenant en compte l'effet des perturbations orbitales naturelles.

« e) Si l'orbite visée par l'objet spatial après les manœuvres de retrait de service a une excentricité supérieure à 0,25, elle doit permettre le respect des exigences édictées aux a), b) et c) du 4 du présent article avec une probabilité d'au moins 0,9 en prenant en compte l'effet des perturbations orbitales naturelles et les incertitudes associées.

« 5. Respect zone B

« a) L'objet spatial doit être conçu, produit et mis en œuvre de façon à ce que, lorsqu'il a achevé sa phase opérationnelle sur une orbite incluse dans ou traversant la région protégée B, il soit mis sur une orbite n'interférant pas avec cette région. Cette orbite doit être telle que, sous l'effet des perturbations naturelles, dans les cent ans qui suivent la fin de l'opération, l'objet ne revienne pas dans la région protégée B.

« b) Si l'orbite visée par l'objet spatial après les manœuvres de retrait de service a une excentricité supérieure à 0,25, elle doit permettre le respect des exigences édictées au 5 du présent article avec une probabilité d'au moins 0,9 en prenant en compte l'effet des perturbations orbitales naturelles et les incertitudes associées.

« c) Si l'orbite visée par l'objet spatial après les manœuvres de retrait de service a une excentricité inférieure à 0,1, elle doit permettre le respect des exigences édictées au 5 du présent article et être située au-dessus de la zone B.

« 6. La probabilité de pouvoir réaliser avec succès les manœuvres de retrait de service mentionnées aux 3,4 et 5 du présent article doit être au moins de 0,85. Cette probabilité, qui n'inclut pas la disponibilité des ressources en énergie consommable, doit être calculée avant le lancement par l'opérateur sur la durée de la phase de maitrise pour laquelle le système a été qualifié et prend en compte tous les systèmes, sous-systèmes et équipements utilisables pour ces manœuvres, leurs niveaux de redondance éventuels et leur fiabilité.

« 7. La probabilité, calculée avant le lancement et, à chaque instant pendant la mission, de disposer lors de l'engagement des manœuvres de retrait de service mentionnées aux 3,4 et 5 du présent article, des ressources en énergie consommables nécessaires aux manœuvres de fin de vie pour les réaliser avec succès, doit être au moins de 0,99. »

Article 12

L'article 44 est ainsi modifié:

1° Le 1 est remplacé par les dispositions suivantes:

« 1. S'agissant du retour d'un objet spatial, l'objectif quantitatif de sauvegarde, exprimé en probabilité maximale admissible de faire au moins une victime (risque collectif), est de 10^{-4}. »

2° Le 2 est remplacé par les dispositions suivantes:

« 2. Les dispositions mentionnées au 1 du présent article doivent être évaluées en prenant en compte:
la stratégie de rentrée atmosphérique (contrôlée ou non contrôlée);
«-la population à la date de rentrée prévue;
«-l'ensemble des phénomènes conduisant à générer un risque de dommage catastrophique;
«-les trajectoires avant fragmentation;
«-la modélisation des scénarios de fragmentation et de génération des débris correspondants à la rentrée;
«-la dispersion au sol des débris et l'évaluation de leurs effets;
«-la fiabilité de l'objet spatial. »

Article 13
L'article 55 est ainsi modifié:
1°   Le 4e alinéa est remplacé par les dispositions suivantes:
« Dans ce cas, les dispositions du 6 de l'article 21 du présent arrêté ne sont pas applicables. En cas d'impossibilité dûment justifiée d'appliquer les dispositions du 5 de l'article 21 du présent arrêté, l'opérateur de lancement fait ses meilleurs efforts pour se rapprocher des seuils mentionnés. »
2°   Au 5e alinéa, les mots: « les dispositions du sixième alinéa de l'article 21 du présent arrêté » sont remplacés par les mots: « les dispositions du 6 de l'article 21 du présent arrêté »
3°   Le 11e alinéa est remplacé par les dispositions suivantes:
«-s'agissant des dispositions des 3 à 7 de l'article 40 ainsi que celles de l'article 41, l'opérateur doit mettre en œuvre la meilleure stratégie possible compte tenu de la définition de l'objet spatial ».

Article 14
Le présent arrêté sera publié au Journal officiel de la République française.
Fait le 11 juillet 2017.
Pour la ministre et par délégation:
Le directeur général de la recherche et de l'innovation,
A. Beretz

ANNEXE 1.7

Arrêté du 9 décembre 2010 portant sur réglementation de l'exploitation des installations du centre spatial guyanais (REI-CSG)

Arrêté portant reglementation de l'exploitation des installations du centre Spatial Guyanais (CSG) (REI - CSG)

Preambule

Le Président du Centre national d'études spatiales,
Vu:
L'accord entre le Gouvernement de la République française et l'Agence spatiale européenne du 16 décembre 2008 relatif au centre spatial guyanais et aux prestations associées;
la loi n° 2008-518 du 3 juin 2008 relative aux opérations spatiales (ci-après la « loi relative aux opérations spatiales »);
le décret n° 65-388 du 21 mai 1965 et sa modification par décret du 25 juillet 1967 portant déclaration d'utilité publique et d'urgence la réalisation par le Centre national d'études spatiales des travaux d'implantation d'une base de lancement de satellites dans le département de la Guyane française ainsi que les acquisitions corrélatives des terrains d'assises de ladite base;
le décret n° 89-314 du 16 mai 1989 modifié relatif à la coordination des actions de sécurité lors des opérations de lancements spatiaux en Guyane;
le décret du 22 janvier 2001 fixant l'étendue des zones et les servitudes applicables au voisinage du centre radioélectrique de Kourou (Guyane) n° 9730510314 pour la protection des réceptions radioélectriques contre les perturbations électromagnétiques;
le décret n° 2009-643 du 9 juin 2009 relatif aux autorisations délivrées en application de la loi n° 2008- 518 du 3 juin 2008 relative aux opérations spatiales;
le décret n° 84-510 du 28 juin 1984 relatif au Centre national d'études spatiales, tel que modifié notamment par le décret n° 2009-644 du 9 juin 2009 (ci-après le « décret relatif au CNES »);
l'arrêté du 2 juin 1988 relatif à la création d'une zone réglementée (circulation aérienne) (centre spatial guyanais de Kourou);
l'arrêté du 2 juin 2006 fixant la liste des secteurs d'activités d'importance vitale et désignant les ministres coordonnateurs desdits secteurs;

l'arrêté relatif à la réglementation technique en application du décret n° 2009-643 du 9 juin 2009 relatif aux autorisations délivrées en application de la loi n° 2008-518 du 3 juin 2008 relative aux opérations spatiales (ci-après la « réglementation technique »);
l'acte administratif du 10 octobre 1971 relatif aux Îles du Salut.

Arrête:

PARTIE 1 - DISPOSITIONS GENERALES

CHAPITRE 1.1 DISPOSITIONS PRELIMINAIRES

Article 1 - Définitions
Activité à risque: activité mettant en œuvre un ou des produit(s) dangereux ou un ou des systéme(s) à risque, ou se déroulant dans une zone de danger.

Les activités à risque sont classées en deux catégories en fonction de l'évolution de l'état du système au cours de leur déroulement:
- activité à risque en phase dynamique: activité à risque au cours de laquelle au moins un élément à risque du système supporte un changement d'état (notamment mécanique, électrique, pneumatique ou chimique) volontaire ou subi;
- activité à risque en phase statique: activité à risque au cours de laquelle aucun élément à risque du système ne supporte de changement d'état.

Agents habilités: ensemble des personnes habilitées, dans les conditions prévues à l'article 14-15 du décret relatif au CNES susvisé, chargées de procéder aux contrôles nécessaires à l'accomplissement des missions prévues à l'article L. 331-6 du code de la recherche.
Allocation: conformément à l'article 1er de la réglementation technique, niveau de probabilité affecté à l'occurrence d'un événement redouté ou spécifié, lors de l'élaboration des objectifs de sécurité.
Atmosphère confinée: atmosphère dans laquelle le renouvellement de l'air peut être insuffisant pour permettre à une personne d'y séjourner en sécurité.
Atmosphère explosible: atmosphère susceptible de devenir explosive du fait de conditions locales particulières.
Atmosphère à risque toxique: atmosphère susceptible de contenir des substances toxiques pour l'homme.
Barrière de sécurité: fonction, produit, matériel, logiciel ou intervention humaine qui s'oppose à l'apparition ou au cheminement d'un événement préjudiciable à la sécurité.

Ce peut être notamment:
- une propriété physique;

– une caractéristique intrinsèque du produit, matériel ou logiciel;
– un dispositif technologique.

A titre exceptionnel, et de façon dûment justifiée, cette barrière peut consister en une procédure. L'efficacité d'une barrière de sécurité est évaluée par sa fiabilité.

Barrière passive de sécurité: barrière de sécurité dont la fonction est assurée sans intervention humaine et sans énergie stockée afin de se prémunir d'une éventuelle panne avance.

Centre spatial guyanais (CSG): complexe technique, industriel et opérationnel, dont le périmètre est délimité par arrêté du ministre chargé de l'espace, regroupant des établissements, des entreprises, des organismes de statuts divers et l'ensemble des moyens nécessaires aux activités de préparation et de réalisation des lancements. Ces activités sont notamment relatives à la conception, à la préparation, à la production, au stockage et au transport des objets spatiaux et de leurs éléments constitutifs, ainsi qu'aux essais et aux opérations réalisés dans ou à partir de ce périmètre.

Chaîne de neutralisation: ensemble des équipements embarqués concourant à la neutralisation du lanceur en vol.

Charge utile: objet (satellite, sonde...) destiné à être embarqué sur un lanceur en vue de son lancement dans l'espace extra atmosphérique.

CNES/Centre spatial guyanais (CNES/CSG): établissement ou ensemble d'établissements du Centre national d'études spatiales implanté(s) dans le périmètre du CSG. Il regroupe l'ensemble des installations et du personnel placé sous la responsabilité ou l'autorité directe du directeur de l'établissement du CSG.

Critères d'intervention prédictifs: critères de neutralisation du véhicule de lancement avant la fin de la mission de sauvegarde et d'intervention telle que précisée à l'- Article 63 - du présent arrêté, basé sur l'impossibilité du véhicule spatial d'atteindre une orbite stable en termes de sécurité des personnes et des biens en tenant compte de différents cas de panne modélisés ou en tenant compte de la possibilité de retombée d'étage sur des terres.

Coefficient de sécurité: conformément à l'article 1er de la réglementation technique, rapport entre la limite admissible d'un paramètre caractérisant un système ou un élément et sa valeur maximale attendue en fonctionnement nominal sa valeur intègre la notion de dispersion propre à chaque domaine concerné.

Coefficient de sécurité à rupture (Jr): rapport entre la limite admissible à rupture d'un paramètre caractérisant un système ou un élément et sa valeur maximale attendue en fonctionnement normal. Pour tout élément d'un système à fluide sous pression, il s'agit du rapport entre la pression admissible à rupture (la pression admissible à rupture est la pression relative de rupture calculée, validée lors des essais de qualification) et la pression maximale attendue en service (ci-après « pms »).

Coefficient de sécurité instantané (Js): rapport entre la pression admissible à rupture et la pression relative atteinte à l'instant considéré par le système en cause.

Coefficient de timbrage (Jt): rapport entre la pression de timbrage et la pression maximale atteinte en présence de personnel pour un système à fluide donné.

Couloir de vol: conformément à l'article 1 de la réglementation technique, volume dans lequel le véhicule de lancement est susceptible d'évoluer et au-delà duquel il est neutralisé.

Déclarant: tout organisme, établissement, exploitant, maître d'ouvrage, maître d'œuvre ou mandataire des précédents qui entend procéder à la construction d'une installation nouvelle ou à la modification d'une installation existante dans le périmètre du CSG.

Élément à risque: partie constitutive d'un système à risque ou partie d'un système, pouvant en cas de défaillance(s) matérielle(s) ou humaine(s) engendrer un événement redouté à conséquence catastrophique ou grave.

Ensemble de lancement (EL): ensemble des installations nécessaires à la mise en œuvre et au contrôle d'un type de lanceur en vue de son lancement. Exemples: Ensemble de lancement ARIANE (ELA), Ensemble de lancement SOYOUZ (ELS), Ensemble de lancement VEGA (ELV.9).

Entité de sauvegarde: entité, au sein de chaque établissement situé dans le périmètre du CSG, qui fait respecter les mesures de sauvegarde dans son établissement et qui est l'interlocuteur privilégié des agents habilités. Cette entité est indépendante de celles chargées de la production ou de l'exploitation, au sein de ce même établissement.

Epreuve de timbrage: épreuve de mise en pression d'un système à une pression spécifiée dite pression de timbrage.

Etablissement: ensemble des installations destinées à des activités de production et d'exploitation, relevant de la responsabilité d'un même exploitant et situées généralement sur un même site, y compris leurs équipements et activités connexes quand l'une au moins des installations est soumise aux législations relatives aux installations classées pour la protection de l'environnement et à la sécurité pyrotechnique. Cette définition s'entend sans préjudice de la qualification donnée par d'autres législations (notamment par le code du travail, le code des impôts, le code de la défense, le code de l'environnement et le code du commerce).

Etude de sûreté de fonctionnement: étude qui identifie tous les risques techniques et fonctionnels, démontre l'atteinte des objectifs de sûreté recherchés, permet la prise en compte dès la conception de la hiérarchisation des risques ainsi que la vérification de la bonne application des mesures de maîtrise des risques.

Fail Operational (FO): apte à la mission après une panne.

Fail Safe (FS): en sécurité après une panne. Le maintien en sécurité après deux pannes indépendantes est dénommé FS/FS.

Fait technique: tout événement volontaire ou non survenant sur un matériel ou logiciel susceptible d'engendrer un écart prévu avec la définition d'origine, y compris en matière de performance (modification), ou un écart non prévu (anomalie).

Flegmatisation: réduction de la sensibilité d'une matière ou d'un dispositif pyrotechnique à un type donné d'agression.

Indépendant(e): deux dispositifs, éléments, fonctions, informations, systèmes, etc., sont dits indépendants s'ils n'ont pas de mode commun de défaillance et s'ils ne génèrent aucune action réciproque entre eux.

Industriel charge utile: entreprise, liée par contrat directement ou indirectement à l'opérateur de lancement, responsable des activités de préparation et de mise en œuvre d'une charge utile à l'intérieur du périmètre du CSG, en vue de son lancement.

Instruction de coordination: mesure prise par le président du Centre national d'études spatiales dans le cadre du pouvoir de coordination des mesures de sûreté prévu aux articles 14-11 à 14-14 du décret relatif au CNES susvisé.

Instruction réglementaire: acte réglementaire pris par le président du Centre national d'études spatiales ou son délégataire en application d'une disposition spécifique du présent arrêté.

Interception: interruption de la continuité du cheminement potentiel d'un événement redouté ou d'une fonction spécifiée dans un système à risque. La levée d'une interception est soumise à l'accord de l'entité de sauvegarde et est appelée "autorisation sauvegarde".

Jr: voir coefficient de sécurité à rupture.

Js: voir coefficient de sécurité instantané.

Jt: voir coefficient de timbrage.

L.B.B. (Leak Before Burst): mode de défaillance d'une capacité sous pression dont la conception permet pour tout type de défaut structurel de limiter les risques en évitant la projection d'éclat. Seuls la fuite de fluide et ses dangers potentiels sont à considérer dans ce cas.

Limite de dangers: limite géographique au-delà de laquelle aucune zone de dangers susceptible d'être engendrée par un système ou une activité à risque au sol ou en vol ne doit exister. Elle constitue la frontière entre la zone protégée et la zone non protégée.

Neutralisation: conformément à l'article 1er de la réglementation technique, intervention sur le lanceur tendant à la sécurité des personnes et des biens et à la protection de la santé publique et de l'environnement. Elle peut notamment se caractériser par une action permettant de provoquer la destruction ou l'arrêt de poussée d'un véhicule de lancement, pour mettre fin au vol dudit véhicule ou d'un étage ne fonctionnant plus correctement.

Niveau de risque: conformément à l'article 1er de la réglementation technique, estimation probabiliste caractérisant l'insécurité d'un système vis-à-vis d'un événement redouté, exprimée par la probabilité d'occurrence de cet événement.

Nominal: correspondant aux spécifications ou aux performances annoncées par l'opérateur ou le concepteur de l'objet spatial, conformément à l'article 1er de la réglementation technique.

Objet spatial: conformément à l'article 1er de la réglementation technique, tout objet d'origine humaine, fonctionnel ou non durant son lancement, son séjour dans l'espace extra atmosphérique ou son retour, y compris les éléments d'un lanceur mis en orbite.
Panne avance: réalisation d'une fonction sans qu'elle soit désirée.
Panne retard: non réalisation d'une fonction lorsqu'elle est désirée.
Phase de retrait de service: conformément à l'article 1•r de la réglementation technique, phase finale de l'opération spatiale pendant laquelle sont menées les actions de mise en sécurité de l'objet spatial visant à limiter les risques liés aux débris spatiaux.

Phase de vol d'un objet spatial: les différentes phases de vol d'un objet spatial sont les suivantes:
- <u>Phase de lancement</u>: a le sens prévu à l'article 1er de la loi relative aux opérations spatiales susvisée;
- <u>Phase de retour ou retour</u>: conformément à l'article 1er de la réglementation technique, période qui démarre à la rentrée de l'objet spatial dans l'atmosphère terrestre et prend fin lorsqu'il est immobilisé à la surface de la Terre, dans le cadre d'une rentrée contrôlée ou non contrôlée.

Poursuite: détermination à distance des variables caractéristiques des mouvements relatifs d'un objet spatial.
Pression maximale attendue en service (pms): pression relative maximale qu'une capacité, un organe ou un composant à fluide sous pression est susceptible de subir durant sa vie opérationnelle, dans le cadre de son environnement opérationnel.
Produit ou fluide dangereux: produit ou fluide susceptible de causer un dommage par ses propriétés intrinsèques (mécaniques, physiques, chimiques, biologiques, nucléaires, thermiques, etc.), ou par réaction avec le milieu environnant. Cette notion inclut notamment toutes les substances et préparations dangereuses telles que définies dans la réglementation en vigueur, les gaz neutres liquéfiés réfrigérés (azote, hélium, etc.) en tant que fluides cryotechniques, ainsi que les fluides chauds.
Réglementation technique: arrêté pris par le ministre en charge de l'espace en application de l'article 4 de la loi relative aux opérations spatiales précitée.
Rentrée non contrôlée: conformément è l'article 1°' de la réglementation technique, rentrée atmosphérique d'un objet spatial pour laquelle il n'est pas possible de prédéfinir la zone d'impact au sol de l'objet ou de ses fragments.
Rentrée contrôlée: conformément à l'article 1er de la réglementation technique, rentrée atmosphérique d'un objet spatial avec une zone prédéfinie de contact ou d'impact au sol de l'objet ou de ses fragments.
Risque: grandeur à deux dimensions, associée à une circonstance précise de la vie du système et caractérisant un événement redouté par la gravité de ses conséquences et par la probabilité de son occurrence.

Risque technique: conformément à l'article 1er de la réglementation technique, risque d'origine technologique, industrielle, opérationnelle, humaine ou naturelle. Expression utilisée pour différencier le risque de nature technique de tout autre type de risque, notamment è caractère financier ou lié è la sûreté des installations.

Safe-life: durée et nombre de cycles requis durant lesquels il est démontré par essai ou analyse qu'une structure, même si elle renferme la plus grande fêlure non décelable par les moyens de contrôle, ne présente pas de défaillance sous la charge et l'environnement de service attendus.

Sauvegarde (mission générale de): conformément à l'article 21 de la loi relative aux opérations spatiales susvisée et au chapitre Ier du titre IV du décret relatif au CNES précité, ensemble des dispositions destinées à maîtriser les risques techniques liés à la préparation et à la réalisation des lancements afin d'assurer la sécurité des personnes et des biens et la protection de la santé publique et de l'environnement, au sol et en vol.

Sauvegarde au sol

Ensemble des dispositions:
- destinées à maîtriser les risques techniques issus d'activités se déroulant au sol et concourant au vol d'un véhicule de lancement;
- relatives aux compléments de la réglementation applicable en matière de sécurité rendus nécessaires par les particularités des activités du site.

Sauvegarde en vol

Ensemble des dispositions destinées à maîtriser les risques techniques durant le vol d'un véhicule de lancement contrôlé depuis le CSG.

Ces dispositions ont pour objectif d'assurer la sécurité des personnes et des biens et la protection de la santé publique et de l'environnement à la surface de la Terre, pour les aéronefs en vol ou dans l'espace atmosphérique, vis-à-vis de tout dommage pouvant résulter des évolutions en vol dudit véhicule.

Schéma d'implantation (ou schéma directeur): document prévu è l'article 14-8 du décret relatif au CNES précité lié à l'occupation des sols au CSG:
- synthétisant les contraintes règlementaires en matière de sécurité des personnes et des biens, de protection de la santé publique et de l'environnement et de mise en œuvre d'équipements liées à l'utilisation actuelle des terrains du CSG et de sa zone périphérique;
- caractérisant chaque zone (zone de lancement, zone industrielle, zone naturelle);
- déterminant les potentialités des zones libres et leur devenir envisageable.

Seuil des effets irréversibles (SEI): seuil délimitant la zone des dangers significatifs pour les personnes. Les valeurs seuil SEI sont définies par la législation relative aux installations classées pour la protection de l'environnement.

Sûreté (mesures de): mesures relatives à la protection des personnes et des installations prévues par la législation et la réglementation applicables et dont la mise en œuvre est placée sous la coordination du président du Centre national d'études spatiales, au titre de l'article 14-11 du décret relatif au CNES précité.

Système à risque: système qui répond à l'un au moins des deux critères suivants:
- il contient un ou plusieurs produits ou fluide dangereux;
- il est constitué d'un ou plusieurs éléments à risque.

Système de neutralisation: ensemble des moyens sol de télécommande et des chaînes de neutralisation bord concourant à la neutralisation du véhicule de lancement en vol.

Système spatial: conformément à l'article 1" de la réglementation technique, ensemble constitué par un ou plusieurs objets spatiaux et par les équipements et installations qui leur sont associés pour remplir une mission déterminée. S'agissant d'une opération de lancement, le système spatial est un ensemble constitué du lanceur, de la base de lancement en interface, y compris les stations de poursuite, et de l'objet spatial destiné à être lancé. S'agissant d'une opération de maîtrise, le système spatial est un ensemble constitué de l'objet spatial et du segment sol en interface.

Trajectographie: détermination, reconstitution et représentation de la trajectoire d'un véhicule de lancement à partir notamment de moyens de poursuite lanceur.

TCN: station de télécommande de neutralisation.

Valeur limite de court terme (VLCT): valeur de la concentration d'une substance toxique dans l'atmosphère d'un lieu de travail, admise pour une durée maximale d'exposition du personnel de quinze minutes, sans risque d'altération pour la santé. Cette valeur est définie par le code du travail.

Valeur limite de moyenne d'exposition (VME): valeur de la concentration d'une substance toxique dans l'atmosphère d'un lieu de travail, admise pour une durée maximale d'exposition du personnel sur la durée d'un poste de travail (8 heures), sans risque d'altération pour la santé. Cette valeur est définie par le code du travail.

Véhicule de lancement: conformément à l'article 1°' de la réglementation technique, ensemble constitué du lanceur et des objets spatiaux destinés à être mis en orbite.

Zone de danger (ou zone dangereuse, ou zone à risque, ou zone d'effet): zone pouvant être le siège d'effet(s) susceptible(s) d'occasionner un dommage, du fait de la proximité d'un ou plusieurs systèmes à risque.

Zone proche: domaine autorisé pour l'évolution du véhicule de lancement durant les premiers instants de vol. La zone proche prend fin au plus tard à l'horizon radio électrique ou à la limite de portée de la TCN du CNES/CSG.

Article 2 - Champ d'application

Le présent arrêté porte réglementation de police spéciale de l'exploitation des installations du centre spatial guyanais (CSG). Il définit les mesures de police administrative applicables aux activités conduites dans ou à partir du périmètre du CSG, en application du 1. de l'article L.331-6 du code de la recherche et des articles 14-7 à 14-10 ainsi que 14-15 et 14-16 du décret relatif au CNES précité, sans préjudice des législations et réglementations par ailleurs applicables.

Article 3 - Modalités de contrôle

Toute personne visée à l'article 14-7 du décret relatif au CNES précité désigne un interlocuteur privilégié des agents habilités à procéder aux contrôles nécessaires à l'accomplissement de la mission de police spéciale de l'exploitation des installations du CSG, au titre de l'article 14-15 du même décret.

Les agents habilités ont accès aux terrains et locaux dans les conditions fixées au Ill. de l'article L.331-6 du code de la recherche.

Leur présence est obligatoire dans les centres de lancement lors de la chronologie finale de lancement, afin de contrôler en temps réel le traitement des éventuels particularités et aléas mettant en cause la sauvegarde, en liaison étroite avec les représentants désignés par l'opérateur de lancement. Dans ce cadre, l'opérateur de lancement met à disposition des agents habilités les moyens techniques et logistiques et informations nécessaires.

CHAPITRE 1.2 - EXIGENCES ORGANISATIONNELLES ET PROFESSIONNELLES

Article 4 - Obligations générales des exploitants ou détenteurs d'installations

Toute personne visée à l'article 14-7 du décret relatif au CNES précité est soumise aux obligations suivantes:
- maîtriser la configuration de ses installations et de leurs évolutions;
- exploiter et maintenir ces installations dans les conditions de sécurité requises;
- mettre en place une entité de sauvegarde propre à son établissement telle que définie à l'article 1 - du présent arrêté;
- tenir informé sans délai le président du Centre national d'études spatiales de toute modification de matériel, système, configuration, plan d'opération, procédure, ainsi que de tout fait technique, incident ou accident, qui sont susceptibles, au sens de l'article 21 - et de l'Article 23 - du présent arrêté, de porter atteinte à la sécurité des personnes et des biens et à la protection de la santé publique et de l'environnement ou de générer de nouveaux risques.

Article 5 - Organisation, installations et moyens
Toute personne visée à l'article 14-7 du décret relatif au CNES précité doit disposer des compétences et moyens nécessaires pour préparer et mettre en œuvre les activités qu'elle conduit, notamment:
- organisations et installations appropriées en matière de fabrication, d'intégration, d'essai, de préparation du véhicule de lancement et de réalisation de l'opération de lancement;
- processus et procédés industriels qualifiés;
- personnels qualifiés en nombre adapté;
- équipements, outils, logiciels et matériels adaptés à l'activité envisagée;
- documentation relative aux tâches, aux responsabilités et aux procédures;
- accès aux données utiles à la préparation de l'activité envisagée;
- enregistrement, exploitation et archivage des données techniques;
- traitement des faits techniques.

Article 6 - Sous-traitants, fournisseurs et clients
Toute personne visée à l'article 14-7 du décret relatif au CNES précité doit:
- informer ses sous-traitants et fournisseurs de l'application du présent arrêté dans le périmètre du CSG;
- faire appliquer, sous sa responsabilité, par ses sous-traitants et fournisseurs intervenant à l'intérieur du périmètre de son établissement les dispositions du présent arrêté.
- L'opérateur de lancement doit en outre faire appliquer, sous sa responsabilité, par ses clients et le cas échéant par l'industriel charge utile les dispositions du présent arrêté.

PARTIE II -. REGLES D'ACCES ET DE CIRCULATION

Article 7 - Articulation avec la réglementation relative à la sécurité des installations
Le régime d'accès et de circulation prévu au présent arrêté est sans préjudice de l'application de la réglementation relative aux activités d'importance vitale, notamment de l'arrêté du 2 juin 2006 désignant l'espace comme secteur d'activités d'importance vitale, et des mesures de sécurité liées au classement du centre spatial guyanais en Etablissement à Régime Restrictif d'accès par le Secrétariat Général de la Défense et de la Sécurité Nationale, aux termes desquelles la majorité des installations réparties à l'intérieur du périmètre du CSG est également classée en Installations d'importance Vitale. Ces installations sont sectorisées en zones protégées soumises aux dispositions des articles 413-7 et 413-8 du code pénal. Le président du Centre national d'études spatiales coordonne et s'assure de la mise en œuvre de cette réglementation dans les installations à l'intérieur du périmètre du CSG et prend à cet égard toute instruction de coordination nécessaire, conformément aux dispositions de l'article 14-13 du décret précité relatif au CNES.

Annexe 1.7

Article 8 - Règles d'accès des personnes et des véhicules
1. Toute personne pénétrant à l'intérieur d'une installation située dans le périmètre du CSG est formellement identifiée et autorisée.

    Cette identification et cette autorisation se matérialisent par l'octroi d'un badge individuel d'accès adapté aux différentes situations d'accès. Le badge indique l'organisme d'appartenance des personnes et sa durée de validité.

    Ce badge, propriété du Centre national d'études spatiales, est délivré au nom du président du Centre national d'études spatiales et est restitué selon les modalités précisées lors de sa délivrance ou à la demande du Centre national d'études spatiales.

    Le suivi de la formation sauvegarde prévue à - l'article 9 - du présent arrêté conditionne l'obtention ou le renouvellement de ce badge d'accès.

    Les conditions spécifiques d'accès des personnes et des véhicules aux installations sont précisées par instruction réglementaire du président du Centre national d'études spatiales.

    Pour des raisons de sécurité, les agents en charge de la sécurité peuvent effectuer, à n'importe quel moment, des fouilles sur des véhicules, en présence du conducteur, aux sorties et aux entrées des zones clôturées et filtrées du CSG. Ces fouilles peuvent également être réalisées au sein des établissements, en accord avec les chefs d'établissements concernés.

    Pour les mêmes raisons, ces agents peuvent faire procéder à l'enlèvement ou au déplacement d'un véhicule en cas de stationnement gênant.

2. Dans les installations, le contrôle des accès des personnes à certains locaux ou zones s'effectue par programmation de carte électronique, selon des critères liés:
    - à des mesures de sécurité et de sauvegarde mises en œuvre dans le local ou la zone concernés;
    - au besoin d'en connaître pour le déroulement de l'activité du personnel concerné;
    - à l'habilitation de défense requise pour l'accès à certains locaux ou zones ou pour participer à certaines activités.

    Le besoin d'accès à ces locaux ou zones fait l'objet d'une demande de programmation par le chef d'établissement concerné auprès du président du Centre national d'études spatiales.

3. Dans une zone à risque, un moyen de liaison permanent entre l'entité de sauvegarde concernée et les personnes procédant à l'activité dans la zone est exigé. En cas d'activité sur un système à risque, une équipe de deux personnes au minimum est exigée. Néanmoins, le nombre de personnes admises à se trouver simultanément dans les zones de danger d'une opération à risque est aussi réduit que possible.

    En cas d'activité dans une zone à risque sans intervention sur un système à risque, une personne seule peut intervenir. La liaison permanente exigée avec l'entité de sauvegarde concernée peut être remplacée dans ce cas par une liaison permanente avec les centres de secours des sapeurs-pompiers du CSG.

Les accès à certaines zones peuvent être subordonnés à la nature des risques engendrés par les activités et à l'utilisation d'équipements de protection collective ou individuelle adaptés.

Article 9 - Formation « sauvegarde

Toute personne susceptible de se déplacer sans accompagnateur dans le périmètre du CSG doit recevoir une formation « sauvegarde » dont le contenu et les conditions sont précisés par instruction réglementaire du président du Centre national d'études spatiales.

La formation sauvegarde constitue un préalable minimal à toute habilitation pyrotechnique délivrée au titre de la législation applicable relative aux établissements pyrotechniques.

Article 10 - Mesures de contrôle d'accès

Certaines zones et locaux font l'objet de mesures de contrôle d'accès par des moyens de surveillance électronique et vidéo. A cet effet, le président du Centre national d'études spatiales spécifie par instruction réglementaire les différents systèmes de sécurité ainsi que leurs modalités d'installation et de mise en œuvre permettant d'assurer la cohérence globale et la compatibilité technique avec les systèmes et réseaux existants.

Article 11 - Règles de circulation à l'intérieur du périmètre du CSG

Le code de la route s'applique sur l'ensemble des routes et voies situées à l'intérieur du périmètre du CSG. Les pouvoirs de police du président du Centre national d'études spatiales en matière de circulation sont exercés sans préjudice des pouvoirs de police générale en matière de circulation publique du préfet de Guyane.

Le président du Centre national d'études spatiales peut être amené à fermer ou à restreindre la circulation publique sur tout ou partie des routes ou voies situées à l'intérieur du périmètre du CSG, pour des contraintes de sécurité ou de sûreté liées à la conduite d'activités au sein du CSG.

L'arrêt et le stationnement sont interdits aux véhicules de toutes catégories sur les accotements de la portion de la route de l'Espace comprise entre le tronçon de Carapa et le poste de garde Orchidée. Des panneaux réglementaires signalent cette interdiction.

Article 12 - Evacuation d'une installation ou d'une zone

Conformément à l'article 14-8 du décret relatif au CNES précité, le président du Centre national d'études spatiales peut, s'agissant de l'exercice d'une activité présentant un danger sérieux pour les personnes ou les biens ou pour la protection de l'environnement ou de la santé publique, procéder à l'évacuation de toute installation ou de toute zone construite ou naturelle, située à l'intérieur du périmètre du CSG.

Les activités visées comprennent notamment les opérations liées au transfert des charges utiles et du lanceur et à la chronologie de lancement.

Article 13 - Accès, circulation, séjour et évacuation des Îles du Salut
Les conditions d'accès, de circulation et de séjour des Îles du Salut, qui comportent des installations techniques opérationnelles liées aux activités spatiales et des installations à caractère hôtelier et touristique et qui sont notamment soumises à une servitude de protection conclue avec le conservatoire de l'espace littoral et des rivages lacustres, sont précisées par instruction réglementaire du président du Centre national d'études spatiales.

Le président du Centre national d'études spatiales peut être amené à interdire l'accès à ces îles ainsi qu'à en prononcer l'évacuation dans les conditions prévues à l'article 12 - du présent arrêté.

En tout état de cause, les personnes extérieures à l'activité de lancement sont évacuées des Îles en chronologie de lancement.

Article 14 - Accès et évacuation de la zone de loisirs
Le président du Centre national d'études spatiales peut être amené à interdire l'accès à la zone de loisirs, qui comprend notamment l'aérodrome du CSG et des infrastructures sportives et associatives, ainsi qu'à en prononcer l'évacuation dans les conditions prévues à l'article 12 - du présent arrêté.

En tout état de cause, la zone de loisirs est évacuée en chronologie de lancement.

Article 15 - Transport de marchandises dangereuses
Le transport de marchandises dangereuses à l'intérieur du périmètre du CSG est régi par la réglementation relative au transport de marchandises dangereuses sur route (ADR).

En cas d'impossibilité de mise en œuvre des dispositions réglementaires de l'ADR, liée à la spécificité des objets spatiaux ou de leurs éléments constitutifs, le transport de ces objets ou éléments fait l'objet de mesures de sauvegarde et de sécurité spécifiques, qui sont précisées par instruction réglementaire et instruction de coordination du président du Centre national d'études spatiales.

Tout projet de livraison à l'intérieur du périmètre du CSG d'objets de la classe 1, à l'exclusion des objets classés 1.4S en emballage de transport, et de la classe 7, au sens de l'ADR, fait l'objet d'une demande spécifique d'accès au président du Centre national d'études spatiales au plus tard dans les 30 jours précédant la date prévue de leur arrivée.

PARTIE III - REGLES D'IMPLANTATION DES INSTALLATIONS

Article 16 - Implantation des installations
Il est rappelé que la propriété des terrains sur lesquels a été implanté le CSG ainsi que celle des Îles du Salut ont été transférées au Centre national d'études spatiales par l'Etat par acte administratif de cession du 20 octobre 1971. Une partie de ces terrains est mise à disposition de l'Agence spatiale européenne par le Centre national d'études spatiales à la demande de l'Etat, dans le cadre de l'Accord entre le Gouvernement français et l'Agence spatiale européenne relatif au CSG et aux prestations associées susvisé.

Toute création ou modification d'installation ou de construction à l'intérieur du périmètre du CSG soumise à permis de construire ainsi que toute modification d'installation à risque ou située dans une zone de danger ou pouvant affecter les voies et grands réseaux du CSG doit être conforme au schéma relatif à l'implantation des installations, voies et réseaux, arrêté par instruction réglementaire du président du Centre national d'études spatiales, aux dispositions de la présente PARTIE Ill, ainsi qu'à celles du CHAPITRE V.1 et du CHAPITRE V.2 du présent arrêté.

Article 17 - Mise à disposition des terrains
Le président du Centre national d'études spatiales délimite le périmètre des terrains affectés à l'implantation envisagée, en cohérence avec les études constituées dans le cadre des législations relatives aux installations classées pour la protection de l'environnement et à la sécurité pyrotechnique.

Le maître d'ouvrage de l'installation matérialise l'emprise du terrain dès la construction par une clôture d'enceinte ou une signalisation appropriée.

Le président du Centre national d'études spatiales tient à jour le plan de référence des terrains mis à disposition.

Article 18 - Exploitation des installations
Tout détenteur ou exploitant d'une installation située dans l'emprise des terrains qui lui sont affectés est tenu de garantir l'entretien global de l'emprise et de maintenir la signalisation ou la clôture la matérialisant.

Article 19 - Changement d'exploitant
Tout projet de changement d'exploitant sur une installation du CSG est soumis au président du Centre national d'études spatiales qui vérifie notamment que le nouvel exploitant répond aux dispositions prévues à l'- Article 5 - du présent arrêté.

Article 20 - Cessation d'activité

Tout détenteur ou exploitant d'une installation dont l'exploitation cesse doit, à ses frais, avant la cessation d'activité, la remettre dans un état tel qu'elle ne puisse porter atteinte à la sécurité des personnes et des biens et à la protection de la santé publique et de l'environnement et qu'elle soit compatible avec le schéma directeur du CSG. Avant la cessation d'activité, le président du Centre national d'études spatiales peut, à cet égard, sans préjudice de l'application de la législation relative aux installations classées pour la protection de l'environnement, imposer au frais du détenteur ou de l'exploitant la réhabilitation, le démantèlement, la destruction des installations et la remise à l'état initial des terrains affectés.

PARTIE IV. - REGLES GENERALES DE SAUVEGARDE

CHAPITRE IV.1 - OBJECTIFS GENERAUX DE SAUVEGARDE

Article 21 - Classes de risques relatives aux activités menées au sol

Deux catégories de classe de risques sont définies dans le cadre du présent arrêté, selon la gravité des dommages:

Classes de risque	*définition des dommages*
Risque à conséquence catastrophique	– **Perte de vie humaine, immédiate ou différée** – **Invalidité permanente** – **Atteinte à la santé publique irréversible**
Risque à conséquence grave	– **Blessures graves aux personnes n'entraînant ni perte de vie humaine, ni d'invalidité permanente** – **Atteinte à la santé publique réversible** – **Dommages importants aux biens:** – destruction totale ou partielle de biens publics ou privés – destruction totale ou partielle d'une installation critique pour l'opération de lancement – **Dommages importants à l'environnement**

Il est précisé que les risques environnementaux catastrophiques sont contenus dans la classe de risque à conséquence catastrophique pour la vie humaine et la santé publique, car ils entraînent l'un des dommages définis pour cette classe.

Article 22 - Exigences relatives aux activités menées au sol
Principes:
Tout système à risque identifié dans les conditions prévues à l'- Article 29 -, à l'- Article 30 -et à l'- Article 31 - du présent arrêté et mis en œuvre dans le cadre d'activités au sol doit satisfaire à un objectif de fiabilité clairement identifié et compatible avec les exigences

qualitatives et quantitatives ci-dessous. Cet objectif de fiabilité doit explicitement contribuer à la sécurité des personnes et des biens et à la protection de la santé publique et de l'environnement.

La démonstration de la tenue de l'objectif de fiabilité doit prendre en compte les aspects liés aux matériels et à leur mise en œuvre, et peut s'appuyer sur des règles et des méthodes de sûreté de fonctionnement reconnues dans le guide des bonnes pratiques prévu à l'article 54 de la réglementation technique.

Exigences qualitatives:
1. Pour toute activité à risque conduite à l'intérieur du périmètre du CSG ou à partir du CSG, les systèmes spatiaux, les systèmes de sécurité, les étages intégrés et les systèmes sol associés à ces derniers doivent répondre aux exigences suivantes:
   - **activité présentant des risques à conséquence grave: critère de la panne unique**
   Aucune défaillance (panne simple ou erreur humaine) ne doit présenter de risque à conséquence grave ou a *fortiori* catastrophique (caractère dit "Fail Sale" (FS)).
   Cependant, le respect du critère de la panne unique n'est pas exigé:
   - pour un système de lancement à partir de l'instant où l'opération de lancement devient irréversible, et jusqu'à sa remise en sécurité dans le cas d'une tentative de lancement avortée;
   - pour les éléments structuraux d'un lanceur ou d'une charge utile dans le cas où l'application dudit critère n'est pas réalisable dans des conditions économiquement acceptables, compte tenu de l'état des connaissances et des pratiques et de la vulnérabilité du milieu dans lequel ledit lanceur est susceptible d'évoluer.
   - **activité présentant des risques à conséquence catastrophique: critère de la double panne**
   Aucune combinaison de deux défaillances (panne ou erreur humaine) ne doit présenter de risque à conséquence catastrophique (FS/FS ou FO/FS).
   Le critère de la double panne ne s'applique pas à la combinaison de deux erreurs humaines.
2. Les exigences qualitatives prévues au 1°' alinéa ci-dessus ne s'appliquent pas aux éléments structuraux, qui sont dimensionnés conformément à des normes et selon des méthodes d'ingénierie adaptées, afin d'assurer un niveau de sécurité équivalent. Une instruction réglementaire du président du Centre national d'études spatiales précise ces normes et méthodes.

Exigences quantitatives:
Pour toute activité à risque à conséquence catastrophique conduite à l'intérieur du périmètre du CSG, la probabilité maximale admissible de faire au moins une victime (risque collectif), prise en compte pour le dimensionnement des systèmes de lancement, des bancs d'essais et des moyens techniques associés, est de 10-• par campagne de préparation d'un lancement ou d'essais.

Article 23 - Classes de risques relatives aux activités en vol

Une seule classe de risques est définie dans le cadre du présent arrêté pour les évènements en vol pouvant conduire à des dommages à la surface de la Terre.

Classes de risque	définition des dommages
Risque à conséquence catastrophique	– **Perte de vie humaine, immédiate ou différée** – **Blessures graves** – **Atteintes irréversibles à la santé des personnes**

Il est précisé que les risques environnementaux catastrophiques sont contenus dans la classe de risque à conséquence catastrophique pour la vie humaine et la santé publique, car ils entraînent l'un des dommages définis pour cette classe.

Article 24 - Exigences relatives aux activités menées en vol
Principes
Tout système à risque identifié dans les conditions prévues à l'- Article 32 - du présent arrêté et mis en œuvre dans le cadre du vol doit satisfaire à un objectif de fiabilité clairement identifié et compatible avec les exigences qualitatives et quantitatives ci-dessous. Cet objectif de fiabilité doit explicitement contribuer à la sécurité des personnes et des biens et à la protection de la santé publique et de l'environnement.
La démonstration de la tenue de l'objectif de fiabilité doit prendre en compte les aspects liés aux matériels et à leur mise en œuvre, et s'appuyer sur des règles et des méthodes de sûreté de fonctionnement reconnues dans le guide des bonnes pratiques prévu à l'article 54 de la réglementation technique.
Exigences quantitatives
Les exigences liées au vol relèvent du cadre général fixé par la réglementation technique.
Exigences qualitatives
Les activités présentant des risques à conséquence catastrophique doivent satisfaire au critère de la double panne, défini comme suit: aucune combinaison de deux défaillances (panne ou erreur humaine) ne doit présenter de risque à conséquence catastrophique (FS/FS ou FO/FS).
Le critère de la double panne ne s'applique pas à la combinaison de deux erreurs humaines.

Article 25 - Logiciels
Les logiciels contribuant de manière directe ou indirecte à la sécurité des personnes et des biens et à la protection de la santé publique et de l'environnement, et en particulier ceux constituant des barrières de sécurité, font l'objet d'analyses de criticité pour en déduire les exigences de conception, de développement et de validation ainsi que les mesures en diminution de risque appropriées à leur criticité.

Ces éléments sont soumis au président du Centre national d'études spatiales conformément aux dispositions prévues au CHAPITRE IV.2 du présent arrêté.

CHAPITRE IV.2 PROCEDURE DE SAUVEGARDE

Article 26 - Processus de soumission sauvegarde
Un processus dit de soumission de dossier relatif à la sauvegarde (« soumission sauvegarde »), itératif et continu, permet au président du Centre national d'études spatiales de vérifier le respect des dispositions du présent arrêté par toute personne visée à l'article 14-7 du décret relatif au CNES précité.

Cette personne, pour chaque activité à risque qu'elle entend conduire:
- identifie et évalue les risques définis aux - Article 21 - et - Article 23 - du présent arrêté;
- met en place, le cas échéant, un programme de réduction de risques.

Elle fournit dès que possible et par écrit au président du Centre national d'études spatiales un dossier comprenant la démonstration du respect des dispositions spécifiques à chaque type de soumission sauvegarde, telles que prévues respectivement par les dispositions des - Article 29 - à - Article 32 - du présent arrêté.

Article 27 - Traitement des modifications
Toute modification d'un lanceur, d'une charge utile, d'une installation sol et de matériels associés dont l'utilisation ou la mise en œuvre présentent des risques à conséquence grave ou catastrophique tels que définis à l'- Article 21 - et à l' - Article 23 - du présent arrêté fait l'objet d'une nouvelle soumission sauvegarde, selon la procédure prévue à l'- Article 26 - du présent arrêté.

Article 28 - Traitement des non-conformités
En cas d'impossibilité de se conformer à une ou plusieurs dispositions du présent arrêté, toute personne visée à l'article 14-7 du décret relatif au CNES précité, adresse par écrit une demande de dérogation au président du Centre national d'études spatiales, assortie d'un dossier justificatif qui doit préciser et motiver:
- l'impossibilité, dans le cas considéré, de prendre toutes les mesures permettant l'établissement, le maintien ou le rétablissement de la conformité aux dispositions du présent arrêté;
- les mesures prises pour se rapprocher autant que faire se peut d'une conformité aux dispositions du présent arrêté;
- le niveau de risque résiduel découlant de la non-conformité.

Le président du Centre national d'études spatiales peut accorder par décision expresse une dérogation à caractère exceptionnel, liée notamment aux conditions d'environnement opérationnel du moment.

Article 29 - Cas des installations sol
Le déclarant est clairement identifié. A défaut d'identification, le déclarant est le maître d'ouvrage dans le cadre d'une installation nouvelle ou l'exploitant concerné en cas de modification d'une installation existante.

Le déclarant soumet au président du Centre national d'études spatiales le dossier prévu au titre de l'- Article 26
- du présent arrêté, qui justifie du respect d'une part des dispositions du présent article et d'autre part des régies applicables aux installations sol prévues au CHAPITRE V.1 et au CHAPITRE V.2 du présent arrêté.

Phase 0 - Faisabilité
Le dossier de faisabilité doit comprendre une étude préliminaire de risques établie à partir des éléments suivants:
- les caractéristiques concernant:
- la nature et les dangers des produits envisagés;
- les quantités maximales de chacun de ces produits dans l'installation.
- la liste des systèmes à risque ainsi que leur description préliminaire;
- le descriptif des modes opératoires et des options techniques envisagées, notamment:
- le type d'activités effectuées dans l'installation;
- les moyens matériels associés éventuellement utilisés;
- les contraintes opérationnelles liées aux activités, notamment l'évacuation de zones, l'incompatibilité d'activités ou la limitation du nombre de personnes présentes;
- les interfaces de l'installation avec les voies et grands réseaux existants.
- les trajectoires de référence dans le cas de l'implantation d'une zone de lancement. Cette étude doit démontrer:
- que l'implantation envisagée de l'installation est conforme à ['- Article 16 - du présent arrêté;
- le respect des dispositions législatives et réglementaires applicables en matière d'installations classées pour la protection de l'environnement et de sécurité pyrotechnique.

Phase 1 - Conception
Le déclarant fournit les dossiers de définition de l'installation et de ses équipements intégrant les spécifications et les remarques formulées par le président du Centre national d'études spatiales à l'issue de la phase O.
Les modes opératoires définis au cours de cette phase sont suffisamment détaillés pour que la prise en compte des contraintes opérationnelles définies en phase de faisabilité puisse être contrôlée.
Le déclarant réalise ou fait réaliser les études réglementaires nécessaires à l'obtention des autorisations d'exploiter au titre des législations relatives aux installations classées pour la protection de l'environnement et à la sécurité pyrotechnique, dans les conditions prévues par ces législations.
Ces études sont fournies au président du Centre national d'études spatiales, dans les conditions prévues par l'instruction édictée par celui-ci dans le cadre de sa mission de coordination des mesures de sûreté, telle que définie au II. de l'article L. 331-6 du code de la recherche.
La phase 1 est close à la réception du permis de construire.

Phase 2 - Réalisation
Les agents habilités doivent pouvoir à tout moment pendant la phase de réalisation de l'installation, dans les conditions prévues à l'- Article 3 - du présent arrêté:
– effectuer des visites de chantier;
– vérifier et confirmer l'opérabilité de l'installation conformément au plan de déploiement opérationnel et aux modes opératoires prévus; à ce titre ils assistent aux réceptions et aux qualifications techniques et opérationnelles des systèmes dont le dysfonctionnement peut être préjudiciable à la sécurité des personnes et des biens et à la protection de la santé publique et de l'environnement;
– vérifier l'innocuité des installations sur la fiabilité et la sécurité des voies et grands réseaux.
La phase 2 est close à l'issue de la réception technique de l'installation.

Phase 3 - Mise en œuvre
Le déclarant soumet au président du Centre national d'études spatiales un dossier attestant de la maîtrise de la configuration de toute installation à risque et du maintien dans le temps de la conformité aux dispositions du présent arrêté.
L'ouverture de la soumission de dossier de phase 3 est indépendante de la clôture des phases O à 2 mentionnées ci-dessus. Elle doit débuter le plus tôt possible, dès que la définition de l'installation et ses modes opératoires de validation et d'exploitation sont suffisamment connus.

Le dossier doit comprendre les documents suivants:
- les spécifications de mise en œuvre;
- les procédures de mise en œuvre;
- les consignes de sécurité liées au site et aux activités qui s'y déroulent.

Article 30 - Cas des charges utiles

L'industriel charge utile, sous la responsabilité de l'opérateur de lancement, soumet au président du Centre national d'études spatiales le dossier prévu au titre de I'- Article 26 - du présent arrêté, qui comprend la justification du respect des dispositions du présent article ainsi que des règles applicables aux charges utiles prévues au CHAPITRE V.1 et au CHAPITRE V.3 du présent arrêté.

Lorsque le système a été conçu à partir d'un système ayant déjà fait l'objet d'un dossier de soumission, la nouvelle soumission peut se faire « par différence ». Ce type de soumission « par différence » ne peut être mis en œuvre que deux fois sur une période de trois ans. Au-delà, une nouvelle soumission d'un dossier complet doit alors être réalisée.

Les phases 1, 2, et 3 peuvent être menées en parallèle, l'ouverture d'une phase n'étant pas conditionnée par la fermeture de la précédente.

Phase 0 - Faisabilité

La phase de faisabilité est facultative, sauf pour les nouvelles plateformes utilisant des technologies innovantes. Le dossier de faisabilité comprend au minimum:
- la liste des systèmes à risque ainsi que leur description;
- une présentation des choix techniques envisagés;
- une liste des risques liés au système bord et matériels sol spécifiques associés;
- le cas échéant, la liste des législations, réglementations et normes applicables au projet.

Phase 1 - Conception

Le dossier de conception comprend au minimum:
- le descriptif détaillé des systèmes à risque, de leurs circuits de contrôle et de commande ainsi que de leurs équipements sol associés. Ce descriptif comprend également les éléments constitutifs des systèmes ainsi que les données de fiabilité permettant d'évaluer le niveau de risque;
- le plan de fréquences envisagé des émetteurs et des récepteurs accompagné des caractéristiques des émissions (spectre, puissance, modulation, codage, etc.);
- l'analyse préliminaire des risques, même partielle;
- les plans de qualification des éléments importants des systèmes à risque.

Phase 2 - Qualification
Le dossier de qualification comprend au minimum:
- les résultats des essais de qualification, partiels ou globaux, des systèmes à risque;
- le plan des essais de réception, partiels ou globaux, des systèmes à risque;
- toute étude particulière ou note de calcul permettant de juger des caractéristiques des systèmes à risque (notamment l'analyse de la fracture);
- le document définissant les interfaces entre la charge utile et les matériels associés et les diverses installations du CSG;
- l'analyse préliminaire de risques enrichie des données issues de la phase en cours;
- le cas échéant les modifications du plan de fréquences et des caractéristiques des émissions.

Phase 3 - Mise en œuvre
La phase de mise en œuvre débute au plus tard six mois avant le lancement et est close avant le démarrage de chacune des activités à risque. Le dossier correspondant comprend:
- les procédures de conduite d'activités, y compris les procédures relatives aux activités de remise en sécurité et les procédures d'urgence en cas d'incident. Ces procédures doivent mettre en œuvre les mesures suivantes:
- identifier les activités à risque;
- prendre en compte les spécificités du CSG (sites, moyens, appellations, etc.);
- préciser, pour chaque étape, le nombre et la fonction des personnes indispensables dans les zones de danger;
- préciser la liste des moyens et produits utilisés;
- préciser étape par étape la procédure de remise en sécurité;
- indiquer les durées des activités, y compris celles de remise en sécurité, ainsi que les interruptions éventuelles.
- l'analyse de conformité aux exigences de sauvegarde du lanceur au sol pour les activités de mise en configuration et remise en sécurité des charges utiles en zone de lancement;
- les résultats des essais de réception de certains composants des systèmes à risque, en particulier les certificats d'épreuve des appareils à pression de gaz; ces documents peuvent être fournis à l'arrivée du matériel à l'intérieur du périmètre du CSG;
- les autorisations de détention et d'utilisation des matériels soumis à autorisation administrative (exemple: objet émettant des rayonnements ionisants);
- les certificats d'aptitude médicale pour les personnels travaillant sur certains systèmes à risque, notamment ceux émettant des rayonnements ionisants ou renfermant des produits toxiques. Ces documents peuvent être fournis à l'arrivée desdits systèmes à l'intérieur du périmètre du CSG;
- les certificats d'habilitation des personnels pour la manipulation des produits pyrotechniques;

- le plan d'opérations satellite en version définitive comportant en particulier la liste finale des procédures, les fiches d'opérations et le planning des opérations.

Article 31 - Cas des lanceurs au sol

L'opérateur de lancement, ou toute personne responsable de la conception ou du développement du lanceur, notamment le maitre d'ouvrage, soumet au président du Centre national d'études spatiales le dossier prévu au titre de l' - Article 26 -du présent arrêté, qui comprend la justification du respect des dispositions du présent article ainsi que des règles applicables aux lanceurs prévues au CHAPITRE V.1 et au CHAPITRE V.3 du présent arrêté.

Phase 0 - Faisabilité

Le dossier de faisabilité comprend:
- le cahier des charges du projet;
- la description des choix et solutions techniques envisagés pour le projet;
- la liste des systèmes à risque ainsi que leur description préliminaire;
- les allocations d'objectifs de sécurité;
- une première évaluation quantitative des niveaux de risque des différentes options techniques de conception envisagées;
- l'analyse préliminaire des risques liés à la conception et à la mise en œuvre du projet en identifiant les risques au niveau du système, les circonstances et les événements potentiellement à risque;
- l'identification des aspects critiques vis-à-vis de la sécurité des personnes et des biens et de la protection de la santé publique et de l'environnement;
- les principes de prévention des risques à appliquer;
- la liste des législations, réglementations, normes et spécifications applicables.

Phase 1 - Conception

Le dossier de conception comprend:
- l'évaluation des choix de conception retenus;
- l'identification des risques et les études préliminaires démontrant leur minimisation;
- les règles de qualification applicables aux systèmes à risque et en particulier aux chaînes de sauvegarde;

Phase 2 - Réalisation / qualification

Le dossier de réalisation / qualification comprend:
- un complément d'analyse des risques et d'évaluation du niveau de risque du système et des matériels associés pour démontrer la tenue des objectifs de sauvegarde;
- les modalités de gestion des paramètres critiques;

- les plans de qualification des systèmes classés à risque;
- l'évaluation des résultats de qualification des équipements classés à risque;
- le plan des opérations de mise en œuvre du système et les activités à risque qui en découlent.

Phase 3 - Mise en œuvre
Le dossier de mise en œuvre comprend:
- la liste des activités de contrôle et de mise en œuvre du système, qui doit couvrir toutes les étapes de la préparation et du lancement, ou de l'essai pour les spécimens d'essais, depuis la sortie des composants à risque hors des stockages jusqu'au lancement ou à la fin de l'essai ainsi que la remise en état de l'ensemble de lancement ou du banc d'essais;
- les plans d'opérations;
- les procédures de mise en œuvre couvrant les situations nominales et dégradées.

Le président du Centre national d'études spatiales peut demander communication des documents suivants:
- les spécifications de mise en œuvre du lanceur et de ses étages ou du spécimen d'essais;
- les procès-verbaux de réception de tous les matériels et les certificats d'épreuve des capacités sous pression;
- les autorisations de détention et d'utilisation des matériels soumis à autorisation administrative dans le cadre de l'application des réglementations pertinentes (exemple: objet émettant des rayonnements ionisants).

L'opérateur de lancement soumet au résident du Centre national d'études spatiales le document définitif fixant les procédures d'activités standard et les plans standard d'opérations.

Toute modification d'une procédure standard en procédure spécifique doit recevoir l'approbation de l'entité de sauvegarde avant soumission au président du Centre national d'études spatiales.

Article 32 - Cas de la sauvegarde vol
L'opérateur de lancement, ou toute personne responsable de la conception ou du développement du lanceur, notamment le maître d'ouvrage:
- soumet au président du Centre national d'études spatiales le dossier prévu au titre de l'- Article 26 - du présent arrêté, qui comprend la justification du respect des dispositions du présent article ainsi que des règles applicables aux lanceurs prévues dans la PARTIE VI du présent arrêté, notamment s'agissant des équipements contribuant à la sauvegarde, de la trajectoire prévue du véhicule de lancement, des données de réglage des équipements et des algorithmes contribuant à la sauvegarde;

– fournit tous les informations, données et faits techniques nécessaires à l'exercice de ses missions au titre du présent arrêté, telles que définies à l'- Article 63 -et à l'- Article 64 - du présent arrêté.

a) Phases de faisabilité, de conception et de réalisation

L'opérateur de lancement ou toute personne responsable de la conception ou du développement du lanceur, notamment le maître d'ouvrage, soumet au président du Centre national d'études spatiales un dossier comprenant:
– la liste des systèmes à risque intervenant dans le cadre de la mission de sauvegarde et d'intervention définie à l'- Article 63 - du présent arrêté;
– ses méthodes de sauvegarde contribuant à la sécurité des personnes et des biens et à la protection de la santé publique et de l'environnement;
– la conception et la réalisation du dispositif sol/bord, conformément aux dispositions de la PARTIE VI du présent arrêté.

b) Phase de préparation au vol

L'opérateur de lancement ou toute personne responsable de la conception ou du développement du lanceur, notamment le maître d'ouvrage, soumet au président du Centre national d'études spatiales un dossier comprenant:
– la configuration de mission (version du lanceur, type de mission, trajectoire et moyens sol associés) sous l'aspect sauvegarde;
– les informations et données permettant la mise en œuvre des règles et des calculs de sauvegarde applicables;
– les informations et données attestant du bon fonctionnement du dispositif d'intervention (bord/sol);
– les informations et données permettant la vérification de la déclaration de réservation des zones de retombées nominales d'étages en prévision du lancement, au profit des usagers aériens et maritimes.

c) Phase de lancement et phase de retrait de service

L'opérateur de lancement soumet au président du Centre national d'études spatiales un dossier comprenant:
– les informations et données permettant la mise en œuvre des règles et des calculs de sauvegarde applicables;
– les informations et données permettant la maîtrise des risques engendrés au sol et dans l'atmosphère par le véhicule de lancement;

- les informations et données permettant l'élaboration et la transmission des informations relatives à la zone de retombée d'éléments ou de produits dangereux, dans le cadre des plans de secours.

PARTIE V. - REGLES DE SAUVEGARDE APPLICABLES AU SOL

CHAPITRE V.1 REGLES COMMUNES

Article 33 - Règles générales de sauvegarde au sol
Les règles de la présente PARTIE V s'appliquent à la maîtrise des risques pour les activités menées au sol, sur les installations sol, le lanceur et les charges utiles à l'exception des activités menées au sol lors du vol du véhicule spatial, qui relèvent de la PARTIE VI du présent arrêté.

En vue d'assurer la sécurité des personnes et des biens et la protection de la santé publique et de l'environnement, la conception, la réalisation et la mise en œuvre des systèmes sol et bord classés à risque conformément à l'- Article 21 -du présent arrêté reposent sur:
- la fiabilité desdits systèmes et le respect des coefficients de sécurité satisfaisant aux spécifications de sûreté de fonctionnement et aux exigences de sauvegarde;
- la mise en place de barrières de sécurité, d'interceptions à la disposition de l'entité de sauvegarde sur l'installation concernée, la visualisation ou les comptes rendus d'état des interceptions, permettant de contrôler la configuration des systèmes à risques;
- la mise en place de procédures, de commandes à distance et d'automatismes permettant de limiter le nombre de personnes exposées;
- la mise en sécurité des personnes exposées par des protections individuelles adaptées aux risques encourus.

Article 34 - Organisation des activités
Sur chacune des installations situées à l'intérieur du périmètre du CSG, l'organisation des activités au sol en phase de production, de campagne de lancement ou d'essais doit comprendre une entité de sauvegarde.
La fonction sauvegarde est assurée en permanence grâce à la mise en place d'un système d'astreinte et par une surveillance constante des alarmes de sécurité.
Toute personne visée à l'article 14-7 du décret relatif au CNES précité transmet au président du Centre national d'études spatiales l'organisation opérationnelle et de sécurité qu'il met en place.
Sur un site (bâtiment, plateforme, poste de travail, etc.) où se déroule une activité à risque, celle-ci est indiquée aux personnes extérieures à l'activité par une signalisation claire.

La nature, le lieu et les heures de début et de fin de toute activité dont les risques débordent du périmètre de l'établissement sont signalés au président du Centre national d'études spatiales.

Article 35 - Procédures de conduites d'activités
Tous les processus d'action ou d'intervention relatifs à la sécurité des personnes et des biens et à la protection de la santé publique et de l'environnement mis en œuvre par les personnes visées à l'article 14-7 du décret relatif au CNES précité sont formalisés par écrit sous forme de:
- procédures de cas nominaux et de situations dégradées;
- consignes de sécurité;
- documents fixant la conduite à tenir en cas d'incident ou d'accident.

Les procédures sont conçues de manière à être réversibles, c'est à dire de manière qu'à l'occasion d'un certain nombre de points clés au cours de l'activité, il soit possible de revenir dans une situation où le système concerné est en sécurité.
Les procédures de conduite d'activités à risque sont approuvées par l'entité de sauvegarde de l'établissement et soumises au président du Centre national d'études spatiales pour les activités dont les risques débordent du périmètre de l'établissement.
Avant qu'un système ne soit en configuration à risque, l'entité de sauvegarde est informée de la vérification de la configuration et du bon fonctionnement des circuits du système.

Article 36 - Missions et moyens de l'entité de sauvegarde
Une activité à risque ne peut débuter qu'après avoir obtenu l'accord de l'entité de sauvegarde de l'établissement concerné. Cette entité vérifie à cette fin que les moyens et conditions nécessaires au déroulement en sécurité de l'opération, tels que les moyens de protection incendie, le gardiennage, la surveillance météorologique, la mise en alerte de moyens médicaux, la présence sur les lieux d'un représentant de l'entité de sauvegarde, l'évacuation d'une zone particulière ou la compatibilité avec les activités menées en parallèle, sont réunis.

Toute entité de sauvegarde doit disposer des moyens techniques nécessaires à la supervision des activités à risque et en particulier:
- des moyens vidéo nécessaires pour surveiller les activités sur le site;
- des moyens de communication pour conserver la liaison avec les personnels concernés et pour assurer le recueil et la diffusion d'informations ou d'alertes, en liaison avec le président du Centre national d'études spatiales.

Tout représentant de l'entité de sauvegarde peut assister aux activités sur le terrain à son initiative, dans le respect des études de sécurité établies dans le cadre des réglementations applicables.

Article 37 - Anomalies, incidents ou accidents
Pour toutes anomalies, incidents ou accidents intervenant sur un système ou élément à risque et tous événements à conséquence grave ou catastrophique survenus au cours des activités à risque, notamment en campagne ou en chronologie de lancement, toute personne visée à l'article 14-7 du décret relatif au CNES précité:
- prend les mesures d'urgence nécessaires telles que l'alerte des moyens de secours et la remise en sécurité des installations;
- s'assure que ces anomalies, incidents ou accidents sont portés immédiatement à la connaissance de son entité de sauvegarde;
- porte immédiatement ces anomalies, incidents ou accidents à la connaissance du président du Centre national d'études spatiales;
- s'assure que ces anomalies font l'objet d'une instruction technique permettant d'en identifier les causes et de définir les actions correctrices.

Postérieurement à l'instruction technique mentionnée ci-dessus, les enseignements tirés en matière de sauvegarde et les mesures adoptées sont portés à la connaissance de l'entité de sauvegarde et du président du Centre national d'études spatiales.

Article 38 - Barrières de sécurité
Des barrières de sécurité sont exigées pour les circuits ou systèmes à risques pouvant être activés intempestivement, soit par défaillance matérielle, soit par erreur humaine.

Leur nombre minimal dépend de la gravité de l'événement redouté:
- trois barrières pour un événement à conséquence catastrophique;
- deux pour un événement à conséquence grave.

Pour les circuits ou systèmes à risques, l'organe situé sur ledit circuit ou système, qui commande le passage du fluide ou du courant, est considéré comme une barrière.
Les barrières s'opposant à un même événement redouté sont indépendantes et, si possible, de natures différentes. Elles peuvent être de nature mécanique, électrique, logicielle ou être des procédures lorsque que des barrières physiques sont technologiquement impossibles.
Les procédures de mise en œuvre des barrières sont conçues de manière que plusieurs barrières d'un même circuit ou système ne soient pas levées simultanément.

Article 39 - Interceptions

Pour les circuits ou systèmes dont les risques sont à conséquence catastrophique au sens de l'- Article 21 - du présent arrêté, l'entité de sauvegarde de l'établissement concerné doit disposer:
- d'une part, de la commande de l'une des barrières ou de l'interdiction de la levée de celle-ci;
- d'autre part, du compte rendu d'état de la barrière concernée.

Cette barrière est dénommée "interception". Elle ne doit pas pouvoir être techniquement surpassée.

Une absence d'énergie dans les circuits d'une interception ne doit pas faire changer l'état du système ou du circuit.

Après levée de l'interception et exécution de la commande, la remise en place de cette interception ne doit avoir aucune action sur le circuit ou système considéré.

Article 40 - Systèmes pyrotechniques

Les composants des systèmes pyrotechniques, ainsi que les matières pyrotechniques, si elles sont à nu lors d'une activité nominale ou si la structure de l'objet qui les contient n'apporte pas de protection, sont choisis en fonction de leur faible sensibilité aux agressions externes d'origine thermique (point chaud, incendie), mécanique (chute, choc, impact, frottement, vibration), électrique (électricité statique, foudre, émission électromagnétique) et chimique (compatibilité chimique).

Pour l'exécution d'une fonction, l'opérateur de lancement ou l'industriel charge utile s'assure qu'il a choisi l'objet ou la matière pyrotechnique présentant le moindre danger quand il est soumis à une agression externe.

Tout moteur à propergol solide constitutif du système de propulsion d'un étage du lanceur est conçu et mis en œuvre de manière à empêcher tout risque d'envol incontrôlé pour toutes les phases de vie du moteur: production, stockage, transport, essai, intégration sur le lanceur, jusqu'au plus tard de la chronologie de lancement.

Les dispositifs bord ou sol, assurant l'anti-envol, sont préférentiellement de type barrière passive de sécurité.

Les initiateurs électro-pyrotechniques (inflammateurs, amorces-détonateurs) doivent procurer un niveau de sécurité au moins équivalent à ceux du type 1 A, 1 W, 5 mn non feu.

En sus des règles particulières de conception des systèmes électriques définies à l'· Article 41 - du présent arrêté, les circuits électriques des systèmes pyrotechniques sont conçus de manière à limiter le courant induit sur le circuit de mise à feu à au moins 20 dB au-dessous du courant maximal de non feu, lorsqu'ils sont exposés à un champ électromagnétique défini par l'environnement électromagnétique généré par les moyens sol, le lanceur et les charges utiles.

Dans le cas où un filtre est adjoint au circuit, il est monté au plus près de l'initiateur à protéger, et la portion des circuits située entre le filtre et l'initiateur est blindée.

Les composants sont capables de supporter sans allumage ni dégradation une décharge de:
- 25 000 V fournis par un condensateur de 470 à 500 pF à travers une résistance pure de 5 000 n, la tension étant appliquée aux bornes du composant;
- 25 000 V fournis par un condensateur de 470 à 500 pF, sans résistance, la tension étant appliquée entre les bornes court-circuitées du composant et son boîtier.

La source d'alimentation électrique des circuits des systèmes pyrotechniques est préférentiellement une source de courant continu.

Dans le cas contraire, la source d'alimentation électrique doit respecter les exigences de compatibilité électromagnétique telles que définies à l'- Article 43 - du présent arrêté.

L'intensité délivrée par les équipements de contrôle des dispositifs électro-pyrotechniques est telle qu'il ne puisse se produire d'amorçage intempestif ou de flegmatisation de l'initiateur. L'intensité de contrôle est limitée à au moins 20 dB au-dessous du courant maximal de non feu.

L'entité de sauvegarde de l'établissement s'assure que le matériel de contrôle électrique est homologué. Un circuit de mise à feu ne doit pas pouvoir accumuler de charge électrostatique éventuelle.

Les éléments électro-pyrotechniques sont dans une configuration de sécurité pendant le stockage, les manipulations et après montage prenant en compte notamment la possibilité d'agressions extérieures. Leur raccordement est précédé d'une vérification d'absence de tension.

Les périodes de silence radio sont indiquées dans les procédures.

La mise en place des électro détonateurs et/ou le raccordement des chaînes électro pyrotechniques classées à risque doit se faire le plus tard possible dans la séquence de préparation du lanceur ou de la charge utile. Dès leur raccordement, l'entité de sauvegarde de l'établissement doit pouvoir avoir accès au contrôle de l'état des chaînes pyrotechniques.

En complément des dispositions contenues dans les fiches de données de sécurité des objets et matières pyrotechniques, il est précisé:
- la classification en division de risque pyrotechnique au travail;
- les résultats d'essais de sécurité aux agressions mécaniques (choc, chute, friction, vibration), thermiques (point chaud, incendie), électriques (électricité statique, émission électromagnétique, foudre), chimiques (compatibilité chimique) auxquelles les composants des systèmes pyrotechniques et les matières pyrotechniques considérés peuvent être soumis durant toutes leurs phases de vie au CSG;

— les effets pyrotechniques attendus en mode nominal de fonctionnement et en mode dégradé lorsqu'ils sont soumis à une agression externe.

Les objets pyrotechniques inutilisés ou ayant atteint leur date limite d'emploi sont récupérés par leur propriétaire puis détruits. La procédure de destruction est soumise au président du Centre national d'études spatiales.

Article 41 - Systèmes électriques
Les systèmes électriques, même conformes à la réglementation française, sont considérés comme système à risque, sans limitation de tension, de courant ou de fréquence, lorsque l'une des conditions suivantes est remplie:
- le système électrique active des systèmes ou organes contenant un ou plusieurs produits dangereux;
- le système électrique peut, en cas de défaillance(s), délivrer une énergie (électrique, thermique, etc.) ou des effluents susceptibles d'occasionner un dommage direct (effet d'origine électrique) ou indirect (effet sur un système à risque relié au système électrique).

Les systèmes électriques à risque sont protégés contre les surintensités et les surtensions transitoires.

Les équipements sont conçus pour que les parties métalliques externes et les blindages puissent être mis à la masse.

Les règles suivantes sont applicables aux câbles:
- les câbles doivent résister et être protégés contre l'abrasion et la torsion;
- les câbles sont choisis en fonction de critères de résistance au feu, de génération de fumées et de leur compatibilité avec les fluides environnants;
- les blindages de câbles ne doivent pas être utilisés comme conducteur de mise à la terre ni comme ligne signal (sauf câbles coaxiaux pour ce dernier cas);
- les conducteurs des circuits électriques à risque ne doivent pas cheminer dans les mêmes câbles ou dans les mêmes passages que ceux utilisés pour d'autres circuits;
- les liaisons redondantes doivent cheminer dans des câbles et des passages différents;
- les structures ne doivent pas présenter d'arêtes vives dans les zones d'implantation des câbles de façon à éviter les risques de blessure des câbles.

Les règles suivantes sont applicables aux connecteurs des systèmes à risque:
- les connecteurs sont conçus de manière que leur branchement ne présente pas d'ambiguïté (détrompage mécanique des connecteurs). Le code couleur peut être utilisé mais ne se substitue pas au détrompage mécanique;

- les connecteurs sont guidés de manière appropriée lors de l'enfichage pour que les contacts femelles et mâles ne subissent aucune contrainte durant l'accouplement ou le désaccouplement;
- les connecteurs sont guidés et retenus de manière à ne transmettre aux contacts aucune contrainte affectant leur bon fonctionnement;
- les connecteurs sont à contacts femelles du côté de la source d'énergie et à contacts mâles du côté de l'utilisation;
- la détérioration d'une connexion (écrasement du connecteur ou mise en contact de deux broches voisines) ne doit pas entraîner d'événement catastrophique ou grave;
- les connecteurs utilisés pour les circuits à risque doivent pouvoir être verrouillés;
- la position des broches doit permettre d'éviter tout risque de court-circuit entre deux broches et entre une broche et la fiche;
- les conducteurs des circuits à risque doivent disposer de connecteurs et d'embases spécifiques qui ne peuvent en aucun cas être communs avec d'autres circuits.

+Les règles suivantes sont applicables aux batteries:
- les batteries doivent pouvoir être facilement déconnectées;
- si la batterie n'est pas connectée, les plots de connexion sont munis d'une protection permettant d'éviter les risques de court-circuit;
- en cas de court-circuit, les projections d'électrolytes sont maîtrisées.

Article 42 - Electricité statique
Les systèmes électriques à risque ainsi que les systèmes électriques concourant à la sécurité ou au maintien en condition de sécurité des installations sont conçus de manière à être insensibles à une décharge électrostatique.

Un matériau est jugé conducteur au sens électrostatique lorsque sa résistivité électrique volumique est inférieure à 10^8 Om.

Les systèmes au sein desquels l'électricité statique peut présenter un risque à conséquence grave ou catastrophique au sens de l'- Article 21 -du présent arrêté sont conçus et réalisés de manière à limiter la création et l'accumulation de charges électrostatiques par l'emploi de matériaux conducteurs.

Les éléments conducteurs (métalliques ou non métalliques) fixes ou mobiles constitutifs de ces systèmes sont interconnectés par des liaisons équipotentielles et reliés à la terre. Ces liaisons font l'objet de contrôles électriques.

Lors de leur mise en œuvre, les différents éléments de la charge utile, du lanceur et leurs matériels respectifs associés ainsi que des installations sol ne doivent pas accumuler de charges électrostatiques au cours des activités d'intégration ainsi qu'au cours des transferts. La mise en place de dispositifs de protection individuelle empêchant l'accumulation des charges électrostatiques est obligatoire lors de la manipulation d'objets ou de matières

explosibles sensibles aux décharges électrostatiques. Ces protections peuvent consister en des chaussures ou bandelettes conductrices associées à un sol conducteur, des bracelets conducteurs, des vêtements de travail conducteurs.
Elles sont réalisées, utilisées, entretenues et contrôlées selon les règles de l'art.

Article 43 - Compatibilité électro magnétique (CEM)
Les lanceurs, charges utiles, installations sol et matériels associés sont conçus de manière à assurer la compatibilité électromagnétique entre les différentes installations et équipements électriques.

Les règles de l'art sont respectées, notamment celles relatives:
- à la constitution de réseaux maillés ou de plans de masse interconnectés, reliés à la terre;
- aux liaisons équipotentielles, vis à vis des courants haute fréquence, des masses électriques, des masses métalliques des équipements, des blindages et des écrans;
- au câblage et au cheminement des câbles courants forts et courants faibles;
- à la continuité électrique des chemins de câble et goulottes métalliques, entre les différents châssis, aux passages de parois et avec les équipements desservis;
- à la séparation des organes courants forts perturbateurs des organes courants faibles sensibles;
- à la continuité électrique et la reprise de blindage câbles/connecteurs, connecteurs/embases et embases/équipements connectés.

Les dispositions ci-dessus sont mises en œuvre en prenant en compte les contraintes d'environnement (corrosion notamment) et sont vérifiées lors de leur mise en service, ou le cas échéant après avoir subi une modification de structure, puis périodiquement.

Article 44 - Systèmes à fluides
Un circuit contenant un ou plusieurs fluides dangereux est considéré comme système à risque.
Un circuit contenant un ou plusieurs fluides sous pression et conforme à la réglementation française des équipements sous pression est considéré comme système à risque si au moins un des fluides est un fluide dangereux.

Les circuits à risque sont conçus de manière que:
- les mélanges de fluides incompatibles soient impossibles;
- les connexions soient détrompées mécaniquement (raccord, longueur) chaque fois qu'il y a un risque d'erreur de montage ou lorsque le composant est propre à un fluide déterminé;

- les lubrifiants et matériaux utilisés soient compatibles avec les fluides concernés (agression chimique, thermique, mécanique, etc.);
- toute rétention soit impossible, à l'exception des éléments dont la fonction implique une rétention (filtres, pièges à vapeurs, etc.).

Les systèmes recevant des fluides dangereux doivent systématiquement subir avant remplissage un test d'étanchéité à au moins la pression maximale attendue en présence de personnel.

Les éléments ou équipements des systèmes à fluides à contrôler avant chaque campagne doivent figurer dans un plan de revalidation.

Toutes les parties conductrices, métalliques ou non métalliques, fixes ou mobiles, des réservoirs, circuits de transfert et organes associés (vanne, filtre, etc.), sont interconnectées par des liaisons équipotentielles et reliées à la terre avant et pendant tout transvasement de fluide.

Article 45 - Systèmes mécaniques et électromécaniques

Les systèmes mécaniques et électromécaniques utilisés à l'occasion d'activités à risque font l'objet d'une étude de sûreté de fonctionnement.

Article 46 - Atmosphère confinée

Les locaux à atmosphère confinée font l'objet d'une signalisation conforme à la législation du travail.

Le personnel devant pénétrer dans une zone à atmosphère confinée doit prendre connaissance et appliquer les consignes particulières de sécurité fixant la conduite à tenir pour prévenir les risques d'anoxie avant de pouvoir accéder au lieu concerné, dans les conditions définies à l'- Article 8 - du présent arrêté.

Tout le personnel doit avoir à sa disposition un masque d'air respirable ou une tenue étanche alimentée en air respirable quand il pénètre dans un local difficile d'évacuation. Ce local est ventilé en permanence et un surveillant extérieur est présent pendant toute la durée de l'activité.

Avant que du personnel pénètre dans une zone à atmosphère confinée, le taux d'oxygène est vérifié.

Tout travail en atmosphère confinée avec risque de sous-oxygénation nécessite la présence d'au moins deux détecteurs indépendants dont un fixe, munis chacun d'une alarme basse, effectuant en permanence le contrôle de l'atmosphère. Le niveau d'alarme basse à prendre en compte pour la détection est de 19% d'oxygène (pourcentage en volume).

Dans le cas particulier des installations sol, tout local à risque de sous oxygénation est équipé d'un système fixe de détection de la teneur en oxygène équipé d'une alarme déportée ainsi que d'une alarme locale sonore et lumineuse.

Lorsque des personnes doivent pénétrer dans des installations à atmosphère confinée non accessibles habituellement, l'entité de sauvegarde conduit une analyse de sécurité pour prendre en compte les règles ci dessus.

Article 47 - Circuits d'air respirable
Les circuits d'air respirable sont conçus de manière à ne pas être pollués. A cet effet, les connexions mobiles et les raccords sont détrompés mécaniquement (raccords, longueurs).

Article 48 - Atmosphère à risque toxique
Les locaux ou installations à atmosphère à risque toxique font l'objet d'une signalisation. Le personnel devant pénétrer dans une zone à atmosphère à risque toxique doit prendre connaissance et appliquer les consignes particulières de sécurité fixant la conduite à tenir pour prévenir les risques d'inhalation de produits toxiques avant de pouvoir accéder au lieu concerné, dans les conditions définies à l'- Article 8 - du présent arrêté.

Tout travail dans une zone à atmosphère à risque toxique nécessite la présence d'un détecteur effectuant en permanence le contrôle de l'atmosphère, équipé d'une alarme.

Dans le cas particulier des installations sol, tout local à atmosphère à risque toxique est équipé d'un système fixe de détection de la teneur en vapeur/gaz toxique avec une alarme conçue conformément aux dispositions de !'- Article 52 - du présent arrêté, ainsi que d'une alarme locale sonore et lumineuse.

Pour toute activité impliquant un fluide toxique, des mesures de toxicité sont effectuées avant, pendant et après l'activité.

Tout détecteur est réglé pour que l'alarme se déclenche lorsque la concentration en substance toxique dans l'atmosphère du lieu de travail est supérieure à 90 % de la valeur limite de court terme (VLCT). Si la VLCT d'une substance toxique n'est pas définie, le déclenchement de l'alarme est réglé à 90% de sa valeur limite moyenne d'exposition (VME).

Tout le personnel doit avoir à sa disposition un masque à cartouche filtrante adaptée aux différents risques considérés ou une tenue étanche alimentée en air respirable en fonction des risques générés par l'activité, conformément au tableau ci-dessous:

Type d'activité	*Equipement de protection individuelle*
Présence dans un local à atmosphère à risque toxique ou activité sur zone de stockage de fluides toxiques	Tenue anti acide et masque à cartouche filtrante en bandoulière.
Activités sur réseaux pollués par un fluide toxique	Tenue antiacide et masque à air respirable, éventuellement complétés par une protection vis-à-vis des projections d'égouttures.
Activités de transfert d'ergols et remplissage, activités sur des systèmes contenant des fluides toxiques pressurisés	Tenue étanche résistant aux projections des fluides toxiques, alimentée en air respirable

Les travaux ou activités nécessitant la mise à l'air libre d'organes ayant contenu des fluides toxiques sont précédés par leur vidange, et les intervenants sont protégés si les organes n'ont pas été décontaminés.

Chaque rejet volontaire d'effluents toxiques, liquides ou gazeux doit obtenir l'accord de l'entité de sauvegarde de l'établissement, qui vérifie que ce rejet est effectué conformément à la législation relative aux installations classées pour la protection de l'environnement.

Les limitations d'accès des personnels en zone dangereuse et l'utilisation de commandes à distance sont définies en fonction de l'agressivité des fluides dangereux et des risques qu'ils génèrent.

Article 49 - Atmosphère explosible
Dans le cas des systèmes renfermant des fluides inflammables et toxiques, les installations et équipements ne doivent pas générer d'atmosphère explosible en fonctionnement normal, à l'extérieur de ces derniers.

Article 50 - Radionucléides
Outre les dispositions en matière de transport de marchandises dangereuses prévues à l'- Article 15 - du présent arrêté, tout détenteur ou utilisateur de radionucléides au sens des dispositions pertinentes du code de la santé publique, sous forme de source radioactive, de produits ou dispositifs en contenant, transmet au président du Centre national d'études spatiales une copie des dossiers d'autorisation de détention et d'utilisation, ainsi que les noms et coordonnées des personnes compétentes en radioprotection (PCR).

Article 51 - Appareils à rayonnement laser
Tout détenteur ou utilisateur d'appareil à rayonnement laser à risque à conséquence grave ou catastrophique au sens de l'- Article 21 - du présent arrêté transmet au président du Centre national d'études spatiales le dossier descriptif dudit appareil incluant sa classification et les risques associés, ainsi que son lieu et sa configuration d'utilisation et de stockage.

CHAPITRE V.2 REGLES SPECIFIQUES RELATIVES AUX INSTALLATIONS SOL ET AUX MATERIELS ASSOCIES

Article 52 - Systèmes d'alarme et de sécurité
Les systèmes d'alarme et de sécurité font l'objet d'études de sûreté de fonctionnement justifiant la conformité aux exigences de l'- Article 22 - du présent arrêté.

Leurs défaillances sont signalées par une alarme.

Les alarmes des détecteurs fixes d'incendie et de vapeurs toxiques sont reportées vers les centres de secours des sapeurs-pompiers du CSG.

Article 53 - Systèmes électriques
Tous les systèmes électriques des matériels sol associés aux lanceurs et charges utiles doivent disposer d'une coupure d'urgence des alimentations électriques permettant en une seule manœuvre de couper en charge tous les conducteurs actifs. Les coupures d'urgence sont facilement accessibles et aisément reconnaissables.

Les systèmes de sécurité font l'objet d'une analyse détaillée afin d'identifier les systèmes devant être maintenus actifs en cas de coupure d'urgence.

A l'intérieur d'un local où se déroule une activité à risque, un éclairage de secours est mis en place pour permettre d'assurer la mise en sécurité de l'activité en cours.

Les locaux de stockage et de charge des batteries sont suffisamment ventilés pour garantir que la concentration des vapeurs émises soit inférieure à 25% de la limite inférieure d'explosivité (LIE).

Article 54 - Compatibilité électro magnétique (CEM)
Les systèmes électriques à risque, et les systèmes électriques concourant à la sécurité ou au maintien en condition de sécurité des installations, sont insensibles à une émission électromagnétique rayonnée (radar, foudre, radiocommunication, téléphone) et à une émission conduite par les différents réseaux courant fort, courant faible, et autres réseaux conducteurs (fluides par exemple).

Article 55 - Circuits contenant des fluides dangereux
En complément des dispositions générales édictées à l'- Article 44 - les règles suivantes sont applicables.

Les circuits commandés à distance contenant des fluides dangereux doivent comporter des vannes se mettant automatiquement en position de sécurité (soit ouvertes, soit fermées) en cas de perte d'énergie (électrique, hydraulique, pneumatique, etc.).

Les circuits à fluide (cryotechnique, corrosif, inflammable) pouvant endommager le matériel électrique sont conçus de manière qu'une fuite ne risque pas de détériorer les lignes électriques de contrôle-commande au point de générer un risque à conséquence grave ou catastrophique au sens de l'- Article 21 -du présent arrêté.

Les réservoirs de stockage de fluides dangereux sont munis de vannes d'isolement du circuit de distribution pouvant être manœuvrées dans les conditions maximales de pression et de débit possibles par construction.

Pour les dispositifs mobiles (notamment les karts), les évents des soupapes et organes de pressurisation des fluides toxiques ou inflammables sont prévus pour être collectés et raccordés aux évents des installations fixes.

Article 56 - Protection contre la foudre
Les dispositions relatives à la protection contre la foudre prévues dans Je cadre de la législation relative aux installations classées pour la protection de l'environnement est applicable au véhicule de lancement au sol dans toutes ses phases de mise en œuvre.
Cette protection contre la foudre est faite préférentiellement par des moyens de protection passive et à défaut par des moyens de protection active. Dans ce dernier cas, cette protection est compatible avec les capacités de prévision météorologique et de protection contre la foudre du CNES/CSG.

CHAPITRE V.3 REGLES AU SOL SPECIFIQUES AUX LANCEURS ET AUX CHARGES UTILES

Article 57 - Systèmes électriques embarqués
Un système électrique embarqué est considéré à risque dès lors qu'il peut délivrer un courant de contact pouvant provoquer un choc électrique et des brûlures, d'une intensité supérieure ou égale à:
- 3,5 mA pour les courants continus et alternatifs jusqu'à une fréquence de 10 kHz;
- 350*f mA (f étant la fréquence exprimée en MHz) pour les courants alternatifs d'une fréquence variant de 10 kHz à 100 kHz;
- 35 mA pour les courants alternatifs d'une fréquence supérieure à 100 kHz.

Avant tout transfert du lanceur ou de la charge utile, les circuits électriques classés à risque sont contrôlés et maintenus en sécurité pendant toute la durée du transfert.
Les liaisons ombilicales des circuits électriques è risque sont contrôlées avant connexion à la charge utile.

Article 58 - Critères de classement à risque pour les systèmes embarqués à fluides

Les systèmes à fluides embarqués sous pression sont considérés comme systèmes è risque dès lors que les dimensions et pressions d'utilisation de chacun des organes distincts (récipient ou tuyauterie) sont les suivantes:

Nature du fluide	Recipient (capacite)	Tuyauterie
GAZ. ou liquides dont la pression de vapeur à la température maximale admissible est supérieure de 0,5 bar à la pression atmosphérique normale.	P > 0.5 bar And V > 1 litre And PxV > 50 bar x 1 Or P > 1000 bar	P > 0.5 bar And DN > 32 And PxDN > 1000 bar
LIQUIDES dont la pression de vapeur à la température maximale admissible est inférieure ou égale de 0,5 bar à la pression atmosphérique normale.	P > 10 bar And PxV > 10000 bar x 1 Or P > 1000 bar	P > 10 bar And DN > 200 And PxDN > 5000 bar

V: volume interne du récipient en litre
P: pression manométrique en bar
DN: dimension nominale en mm. - Désignation numérique de la dimension commune à tous les éléments d'un système de tuyauterie autres que les éléments indiqués par leur diamètre extérieur ou par la taille du filet.
Il s'agit d'un nombre arrondi è des fins de référence et qui n'a pas de relation stricte avec les cotes de fabrication.
La taille nominale est indiquée par DN suivi d'un nombre.
Il est précisé que les organes sont considérés comme distincts lorsque la déchirure de l'un ne peut se propager à l'autre.

Article 59 - Systèmes embarqués à fluides sous pression classés à risque

Les systèmes fluides embarqués sous pression et classés à risque au sens de l'- Article 58 - du présent arrêté sont conformes à une norme reconnue ou à minimâ aux exigences définies à l'- Article 44 - du présent arrêté et des règles ci-après.

1. Les capacités sous pression des systèmes à fluide embarqués sont dimensionnées pour les charges de pression avec un coefficient de sécurité à rupture Jr au moins égal à 2. Dans certains cas particuliers, ce coefficient peut être abaissé jusqu'à 1,5 en fonction des modes de défaillance possibles démontrés par des études et des essais.

   Une capacité sous pression de type LBB, utilisée dans le domaine de pression requis pour obtenir le caractère LBB, ne génère une zone dangereuse qu'en raison de la fuite possible du fluide contenu. Dans ce cas, seul le danger lié à ce fluide est pris en compte pour déterminer la zone de danger.

   Les capacités doivent subir un programme d'essais et de tests dans le but de confirmer leur bon dimensionnement et la qualité de leur réalisation.

2. Les systèmes à fluides embarqués et leurs composants doivent avoir subi leurs épreuves de timbrage telles que décrites ci-après avant leur arrivée dans le périmètre du CSG:
   On définit un coefficient de timbrage Jt tel que la pression de timbrage est réalisée à Jt fois la pression maximale atteinte en présence de personnel.
   Si le coefficient de sécurité à rupture Jr est supérieur ou égal à 2, $Jt = 1,5$.
   Si le coefficient de sécurité à rupture Jr est inférieur à 2,

$$Jt = \frac{1 + Jr}{2}$$

En cas d'impossibilité démontrée, due à la conception, d'effectuer cette épreuve de timbrage sur l'ensemble du système, des épreuves peuvent être réalisées par parties. Le montage final de l'ensemble du système fait l'objet de dispositions qualité adaptées afin de garantir la tenue mécanique de l'ensemble lors de la mise sous pression. Tout écart accepté par rapport aux procédures qualités applicables est justifié et porté à la connaissance du président du Centre national d'études spatiales.

3. La configuration d'épreuve de timbrage ne doit pas subir d'évolution ou d'incident technique susceptible de remettre en cause sa validité.

Après épreuve du système, la pression maximale attendue en service ne doit jamais être dépassée.

Les capacités sous pression en service ne doivent avoir subi aucune agression (mécanique, thermique, électrique, etc.) susceptible d'affecter ses caractéristiques.

En cas de réparation ou d'entretien, un essai d'étanchéité représentatif est requis avant toute remise en service. En outre, si l'activité n'est pas limitée à un démontage/remontage mais comprend des interventions plus importantes (soudage, formage, etc.}, le système sous pression est inspecté et éprouvé.

4. Les vitesses de pressurisation et de dépressurisation ne doivent pas créer de situations dangereuses incontrôlables (gradient de température, coup de bélier, etc.).

La pression relative en millibar s'exerçant sur un organe où l'on intervient manuellement (démontage, réparation, serrage ou desserrage de raccords, etc.) est telle que le produit de cette pression par la section de passage qui est pratiquée (exprimée en cm2 soit inférieur à 1000.

Tout assemblage des éléments contenant un fluide sous pression est du type "Safe-Life" tel que défini à l' - Article - 1 du présent arrêté.

Dans le cas particulier d'un système assemblé par soudage, les soudures entre ces différentes parties sont contrôlées après assemblage par un procédé non destructif reconnu dans le domaine aérospatial. Tout écart constaté lors de ces contrôles est porté à la connaissance du président du Centre national d'études spatiales.

5. Pendant les phases dynamiques de pressurisation ou de dépressurisation et en phase statique, les contraintes opérationnelles sont fixées par référence au coefficient de sécurité instantané J_s défini comme le rapport entre la pression admissible à rupture et la pression relative atteinte à l'instant considéré par le système en cause:

J_s = Pression admissible à rupture / Pression relative instantanée considérée

Ce coefficient variable J_s est en outre tel que J_s supérieur ou égal à J_r.

L'accès aux zones de dangers générées par un système à fluides embarqué sous pression est subordonné aux règles particulières suivantes:

Coefficient de sécurité Js	Accès phase statique	Accès phase dynamique (2)
$Js \geq 4$	Aucune contrainte	Aucune contrainte
$3 s Js < 4$	Aucune contrainte	Accès contrôlé (1)
$2 s Js < 3$	Accès contrôlé (1)	Accès limité (3)
$Js < 2$	Accès interdit (4)	Accès interdit (4)

(1) Seules les personnes directement concernées par les activités pour lesquelles leur présence en zone dangereuse est indispensable sont admises. Ces activités peuvent concerner tout autre élément du lanceur que la capacité en cause.
(2) La phase dynamique inclut les mouvements de fluides et les manutentions de capacités sous pression, mais exclut les paliers à respecter pour l'équilibrage des températures après les mises en pression.
(3) Seules les personnes concernées par l'activité de pressurisation/dépressurisation sont admises, dans le cas où la réalisation de l'activité ne peut se faire à distance.
(4) Dans le cas particulier des capacités sous pression de type LBB, l'accès peut être contrôlé dans les conditions définies au nota (1) jusqu'à $Js \geq 1,5$.

Article 60 - Systèmes pyrotechniques

Les parties conductrices externes (métalliques ou non métalliques) et les blindages des composants d'une chaîne pyrotechnique, d'un initiateur, d'un boîtier de sécurité et d'armement, des composants de transmission et de distribution et des dispositifs fonctionnels (réglettes de destruction, cordeaux de découpe, fusées, vannes, vérins, etc.) sont équipotentiels et mis à la masse.

Pour les systèmes pyrotechniques présentant un risque à conséquence catastrophique au sens de l'- Article 21 -du présent arrêté, la barrière à proximité de la source de risque est obligatoirement constituée d'une barrière mécanique (le boîtier de sécurité et d'armement) qui doit empêcher la mise à feu intempestive du système.

Les boîtiers de sécurité et d'armement sont réalisés de telle sorte que:
– la barrière une fois positionnée dans un des états « armé » ou « désarmé » ne puisse pas quitter cette position en l'absence de commande ou sous l'effet d'une sollicitation extérieure (chocs, vibrations, phénomène électrostatique, etc.) dans un environnement normal ou accidentel;
– la barrière soit interceptée conformément aux dispositions de l'- Article 39 -du présent arrêté;
– le compte rendu d'état de positionnement soit représentatif de l'état réel « armé » ou « désarmé » et puisse être déporté;
– l'état « armé » ou « désarmé » soit visualisé par un indicateur physiquement lié au dispositif d'interception;
– ils soient commandés à distance mais qu'un désarmement manuel soit toujours possible;
– le montage du détonateur soit impossible physiquement si le boîtier n'est pas en position « désarmé ».

L'implantation des boitiers de sécurité et d'armement doit permettre un accès facile pour le montage et le raccordement des détonateurs et le désarmement manuel.

Les boîtiers de sécurité et d'armement sont en position de sécurité en présence de personnel. Cette position de sécurité doit pouvoir être contrôlée pour s'assurer de l'état du système.

PARTIE VI. - REGLES DE SAUVEGARDE EN VOL

CHAPITRE Vl.1 REGLES GENERALES EN VOL

Article 61 - Définition et délimitation des zones et niveau de protection associé
1. Trois zones géographiques sont définies pour l'exercice de la mission de sauvegarde et d'intervention (MSI) définie à l' - Article 63 - du présent arrêté en cas de situation accidentelle en vol.
   a) *Zone à risques au lancement (ZRL)*
   La zone à risques au lancement est définie comme le domaine terrestre et maritime pour lequel le vol d'un véhicule de lancement peut engendrer en situation nominale ou accidentelle des risques au sens de l' - Article 23 - du présent arrêté qu'ils soient de nature mécanique, thermique ou toxique.
   En conséquence, la partie terrestre de cette zone est évacuée par le président du Centre national d'études spatiales au moment de la chronologie de lancement sans préjudice des mesures que peut prendre le Préfet, notamment au titre du décret n° 89-314 du 16 mai 1989 susvisé. Toutefois, certains bâtiments dimensionnés pour supporter tous les effets redoutés peuvent abriter les personnels strictement nécessaires au déroulement de la chronologie.
   b) *Zone protégée (ZPJ*
   La zone protégée est le complément terrestre et maritime de la zone à risques au lancement (ZRL)
   En cas de défaillance du lanceur, ce dernier est neutralisé de sorte qu'il ne puisse engendrer de risques dans cette zone, au sens de l'- Article 23 - du présent arrêté, qu'ils soient de nature mécanique, thermique ou toxique.
   c) *Zones à risque toxique au lancement (ZRTL!*
   Une zone à risque toxique au lancement est une zone terrestre exposée aux risques toxiques mais protégée des risques de nature thermique et mécanique (fragments lourds) au sens de l'- Article 23 - du présent arrêté, engendrés par un accident du lanceur. Une ZRTL est spécifique à un type de mission pour un lanceur donné. L'ensemble des ZRTL est précisé par instruction réglementaire du président du Centre national d'études spatiales.
   Dans cette zone, la présence de personnes est subordonnée à l'existence de mesures particulières assurant notamment la protection contre les effets toxiques encourus ou contre la retombée de fragments légers déportés par le vent.

En cas de danger sérieux, le président du Centre national d'études spatiales peut toutefois faire évacuer cette zone conformément aux dispositions de l'- Article 12 - du présent arrêté.

2. Les limites entre les zones définies ci-dessus sont décrites ci-après:

   a) ***Limite de dangers (LD)***

   La limite de dangers est la frontière entre la ZP et la ZRL. Au-delà de cette limite, le public en ZP n'est pas exposé aux risques tels que définis à l'- Article 23 - du présent arrêté.

   Les coordonnées géographiques des points définissant la limite de danger sont spécifiées en annexe du présent arrêté.

   b) ***Limite des impacts (LI)***

   La limite des impacts est la frontière entre la ZRL et la ZRTL.

   Le schéma de principe ci-après illustre ces définitions.

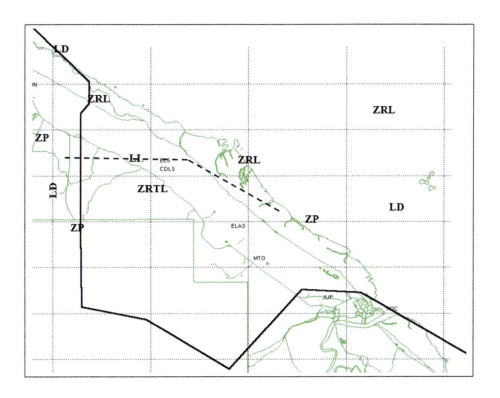

Article 62 - Couloir de vol
Le couloir de *vol* est un domaine dans lequel le véhicule de lancement suit une trajectoire compatible avec sa mission. En dehors de ce domaine, la mission lanceur est considérée comme perdue et le président du Centre national d'études spatiales peut décider d'une neutralisation commandée du véhicule de lancement.
Le couloir de *vol*, défini conformément à l'article 17 de la réglementation technique, ainsi que la méthode retenue pour l'obtenir, sont fournis au président du Centre national d'études spatiales par l'opérateur de lancement.

Article 63 - Mission de sauvegarde et d'intervention (MSI)
Dans le cadre de sa mission de sauvegarde liée à la réalisation des lancements, le président du Centre national d'études spatiales exerce une mission dite de sauvegarde et d'intervention (MSI) consistant à:
- apprécier à tout instant le caractère dangereux représenté par le véhicule de lancement en vol;
- intervenir à tout instant pour neutraliser le véhicule de lancement;
- vérifier les zones de retombée d'éléments dans les cas nominaux et dégradés;
- connaître l'état des moyens concourant à cette mission.

La mission de sauvegarde et d'intervention débute à l'instant où le lanceur quitte le sol et prend fin au terme de la capacité d'intervention depuis le CSG.
Le vol de tout véhicule de lancement doit pouvoir être interrompu de façon volontariste depuis le sol par le président du Centre national d'études spatiales pendant l'exercice de la mission de sauvegarde et d'intervention avant que les conditions de vol ne permettent plus d'assurer la sécurité des personnes et des biens et la protection de la santé publique et de l'environnement.
A cette fin, le véhicule de lancement doit disposer d'un moyen de neutralisation télécommandé en zone proche par le sol. La décision et la mise en œuvre de la neutralisation sont du ressort du président du Centre national d'études spatiales.
Dans le cas de risques à conséquence catastrophique au sens de l'Article 23 - du présent arrêté, le critère FS/FS s'applique comme suit: la première panne étant la défaillance du véhicule de lancement, une panne sur le système de neutralisation ne doit donc pas conduire à un risque à conséquence catastrophique. Aussi, tous les moyens sol et bord concourant à l'application des mesures de neutralisation doivent respecter le critère "Fail Operational" (FO). Toutefois, dans le cas de la neutralisation à partir de critères d'intervention prédictifs tels que définis à l'- Article 66 - du présent arrêté, l'opérateur de lancement doit se conformer autant que faire se peut au respect du critère FO.

Article 64 - Mission de surveillance et d'alerte (MSA)

Outre sa mission de sauvegarde liée à la réalisation des lancements, le président du Centre national d'études spatiales exerce également une mission dite de surveillance et d'alerte (MSA) consistant à:
- assurer après la fin de la MSI, un suivi de vol du véhicule de lancement lancé depuis le CSG afin d'en vérifier le bon déroulement;
- transmettre en cas de défaillance du véhicule de lancement aux autorités compétentes, en particulier au ministre chargé de l'espace, les informations relatives à la zone de retombée d'éléments, permettant d'avertir au plus tôt les autorités des Etats concernés. Ces informations sont également transmises à l'opérateur de lancement.

La mission de surveillance et d'alerte débute au terme de la mission de sauvegarde et d'intervention telle que définie à l'- Article 63 - du présent arrêté et prend fin à la fin de la phase de retrait de service du dernier étage du lanceur. Lorsque la phase de retrait de service conduit à une rentrée contrôlée immédiate, la mission de surveillance et d'alerte se poursuit jusqu'à l'évaluation de la zone de retombée.

Article 65 - Exigences communes à la mission de sauvegarde et d'intervention (MSI) et à la mission de surveillance et d'alerte (MSA)

L'opérateur de lancement met à disposition du président du Centre national d'études spatiales les moyens et données issus du bord nécessaire à l'exercice de la MSI et de la MSA, pour lui permettre d'analyser:
- la localisation du véhicule de lancement;
- le comportement du véhicule de lancement dès le décollage;
- le caractère dangereux ou non du vol;
- l'état du dispositif d'intervention à bord;
- la réaction du dispositif d'intervention à bord lorsqu'il est activé;
- la zone impactée suite à un accident en vol ou à l'activation du dispositif d'intervention à bord.

Article 66 - Exigences spécifiques à la MSI

En zone proche, l'analyse des trajectoires déviées physiquement réalistes permet d'assurer de façon volontariste la neutralisation du lanceur dans l'intérêt de la sécurité des personnes et des biens et de la protection de la santé publique et de l'environnement. A chaque instant du vol, le président du Centre national d'études spatiales doit pouvoir, dans le cadre de sa MSI, neutraliser le véhicule de lancement de sorte qu'il ne puisse engendrer de risques, au sens de l'- Article 23 - du présent arrêté dans la zone protégée (ZP), qu'ils soient de nature mécanique, thermique ou toxique.

L'opérateur de lancement transmet à cette fin au président du Centre national d'études spatiales toutes données nécessaires, notamment celles prévues aux articles 16 à 19 de la réglementation technique.

Des critères d'intervention dits prédictifs pourront être mis en œuvre par le président du Centre national d'études spatiales à partir du sol, notamment en fonction des études menées dans le cadre de l'article 18 de la réglementation technique, afin de neutraliser le lanceur avant le survol des terres. L'opérateur de lancement fournit à cette fin tous les éléments nécessaires au président du Centre national d'études spatiales.

CHAPITRE VI.2 SYSTEME DE NEUTRALISATION

Article 67 - Objectifs du système de neutralisation
Le système de neutralisation est constitué d'un dispositif bord d'intervention télécommandé depuis le sol.

Des automatismes à bord peuvent compléter ce dispositif sans pouvoir s'y substituer. Leur utilisation exclusive n'est possible qu'à partir de l'instant où le système de télécommande sol est dans l'incapacité de garantir un bilan de liaison suffisant.

L'opérateur de lancement doit s'assurer que le dispositif bord d'intervention est compatible avec les moyens du CNES/CSG.

L'opérateur de lancement s'assure que les éléments bord du système de neutralisation sous sa responsabilité permettent de neutraliser le véhicule de lancement. Cette neutralisation doit permettre à partir d'un ordre unique depuis le sol, pour tous les étages:
- d'assurer que la zone de danger induite par la neutralisation est compatible avec les contraintes liées aux différentes zones à protéger;
- de minimiser l'impact sur l'environnement;
- de provoquer l'arrêt de la poussée;
- d'inhiber l'allumage de tout étage susceptible de propulsion;
- d'empêcher toute autopropulsion de chaque étage;
- d'assurer la dispersion directe ou indirecte des ergols toxiques, avec ou sans combustion;
- d'éviter la détonation des ergols solides ou liquides aussi bien en altitude qu'à l'impact éventuel au sol;
- d'empêcher la retombée de fragments d'une masse incompatible avec le dimensionnement des installations au sol à protéger.

Article 68 - Fonctions du système de neutralisation
L'opérateur de lancement s'assure que le dispositif d'intervention à bord peut exécuter les différentes fonctions ci-après:
- **neutralisation commandée:** une télécommande du sol provoque l'exécution de la fonction de neutralisation simultanément sur tous les étages. Lors de sa mise en œuvre, aucun processus fonctionnel bord ne doit pouvoir inhiber ou retarder l'exécution de cette fonction.
- **neutralisation automatique instantanée:** un dispositif automatique embarqué commande instantanément l'exécution de la fonction de neutralisation de tous les étages, lorsqu'une séparation non nominale ou une rupture d'étage survient ou en cas de dérive par rapport à des conditions spécifiées;
- **neutralisation automatique retardée:** un dispositif automatique embarqué commande l'exécution de la fonction avec un retard spécifié, pour neutraliser un étage après séparation nominale, sans induire de risque sur les étages supérieurs, avant l'impact au sol, et en assurant la dispersion des ergols résiduels;
- **inhibition du dispositif bord de réception de la télécommande:** ce dispositif bord de réception télécommande est inhibé au terme de la MSI.

Article 69 - Conception du système de neutralisation
L'opérateur de lancement s'assure que les éléments bord constitutifs du système de neutralisation sous sa responsabilité respectent les critères suivants:
- cohérence globale en matière d'allocation de fiabilité, notamment entre le bord et le sol;
- redondance et ségrégation géographique dans les limites physiques du véhicule de lancement des chaînes de sauvegarde embarquées (critère FO);
- niveaux de fiabilité relatifs à la panne avance et à la panne retard cohérents entre eux. Ces niveaux doivent également être cohérents individuellement avec l'objectif de sécurité et l'objectif de réussite de la mission du lanceur. Les niveaux requis de fiabilité sont précisés par instruction réglementaire du président du Centre national d'études spatiales;
- les fonctions sauvegarde de neutralisation sont de préférence indépendantes du fonctionnel bord. A défaut, tout lien (bus de dialogue, masse électrique, ordre séquentiel, etc.) entre les équipements réalisant des fonctions sauvegarde de neutralisation et les équipements du fonctionnel bord ne doit pas retarder ou inhiber (quelle que soit la panne) les capacités des fonctions de neutralisation.

Article 70 - Eléments bord constitutifs de la chaîne de neutralisation
Les éléments bord constitutifs de la chaîne de neutralisation mentionnés ci-dessous font l'objet du processus de soumission tel que défini à l'- Article 32 - du présent arrêté:
- organes d'exécution permettant d'agir sur le véhicule de lancement (chaîne pyrotechnique de sauvegarde, vannes, etc.);
- organes de commande pouvant être soit un récepteur bord d'un signal émis par le sol, soit un dispositif spécifique embarqué;
- alimentations en énergie de ces organes;
- circuits de puissance et de communication.

Les chaînes de sauvegarde bord sont redondées et ségréguées (critère FO), conformément aux dispositions de l'- Article 63 - du présent arrêté. Elles sont conçues pour résister aux agressions pouvant être rencontrées pendant la chronologie de lancement et la phase de lancement.

En cas d'impossibilité de respecter la règle de ségrégation ci-dessus pour certains systèmes existants ainsi que pour les nouveaux systèmes, une étude de sûreté fonctionnement doit démontrer la tenue des objectifs de sécurité tels que prévus à l' - Article 24 - du présent arrêté.

Lorsque la neutralisation est déclenchée, le fonctionnement des organes de chaque étage du véhicule de lancement est assuré au niveau de performance requis et le système doit fonctionner dans les conditions d'environnement les plus sévères pouvant résulter de la défaillance du véhicule de lancement.

Article 71 - Mise en œuvre des chaînes de neutralisation
L'opérateur de lancement fournit au président du Centre national d'études spatiales les informations nécessaires à la prise en compte et à la vérification de tous les effets de l'explosion en vol du véhicule de lancement ainsi que ceux issus de l'utilisation du système de neutralisation.

A ce titre, l'opérateur de lancement fournit:
- les scénarios de neutralisation (explosion, retombée intègre, rupture, etc.);
- les données de fragmentation et d'explosion;
- les énergies à l'impact;
- les données aérodynamiques de tout ou partie du lanceur retombant.

Article 72 - Ordres envoyés depuis le sol

Les éléments sol du système de neutralisation doivent permettre d'envoyer les trois ordres suivants:
- maintien;
- neutralisation commandée;
- inhibition (ou OFF).

L'opérateur de lancement justifie que les chaînes de neutralisation bord sont capables d'exécuter les fonctions associées à chacun de ces ordres, selon les modalités fixées à l'- Article 32 - du présent arrêté.

Article 73 - Récepteurs télécommande bord (RTC)

A bord, les ordres sont reçus simultanément par deux récepteurs embarqués qui commandent deux chaînes de sauvegarde bord.

Le délai théorique de traitement, de réception et d'exécution par le bord est soumis au président du Centre national d'études spatiales au cours de la phase de conception telle que prévue à l'- Article 32 - du présent arrêté.

Pour chaque vol, l'opérateur de lancement mesure le délai réel de traitement, de réception et d'exécution par le bord pendant les activités de campagne et vérifie sa conformité avec le délai théorique. L'opérateur de lancement transmet ces informations au président du Centre national d'études spatiales dès que possible et, au plus tard, avant le transfert en zone de lancement.

Article 74 - Limite de visibilité de la TCN

Le bilan de liaison de la TCN est défini par:
- la limite de visibilité géométrique, fixée à 2,5 degrés de site géométrique afin de se prémunir de la chute rapide des contrôles automatiques de gain observée en fin de visibilité radioélectrique au moment du passage sous l'horizon et des éventuelles perturbations d'origine radioélectrique;
- la limite de portée prenant en compte les pertes de propagation radioélectrique et les marges définies par instruction réglementaire du président du Centre national d'études spatiales. Elle dépend de la distance entre la station sol de télécommande et le lanceur ainsi que de l'antenne utilisée;
- la réception réelle au niveau de chaque RTC du véhicule de lancement, comprise dans une plage de -30 dBm à -90 dBm, le long de la trajectoire nominale pendant la MSI.

L'opérateur de lancement doit concevoir la trajectoire du véhicule de lancement en optimisant le bilan de liaison.

Article 75 - Qualification et contrôles
Les éléments du lanceur contribuant à la neutralisation, chaque sous-ensemble ainsi que le dispositif complet avec ses constituants (câblages, prises, raccords, etc.) sont qualifiés en prenant en compte les conditions d'ambiance représentatives de la défaillance du véhicule de lancement.
L'opérateur de lancement doit démontrer cette qualification par des essais dimensionnants dédiés.
L'opérateur de lancement doit également démontrer par essais le bon fonctionnement du matériel après intégration du lanceur.
Les spécifications relatives à l'ensemble de ces essais sont soumises au président du Centre national d'études spatiales dans les conditions prévues à l'- Article 32 - du présent arrêté.

CHAPITRE VI.3 SYSTEME DE LOCALISATION

Article 76 - Eléments du système de localisation
Les éléments sol et bord du système permettant la localisation du véhicule de lancement et la détermination de la zone de retombée potentielle sont soumis au président du Centre national d'études spatiales dans les conditions prévues à l'- Article 32 - du présent arrêté pendant leur phase de conception et de réalisation. Cette soumission porte notamment sur:
- la fréquence de mise à disposition des données;
- la précision de la restitution;
- les délais et les temporisations diverses.

Les équipements bord contribuant à la fonction de localisation sont compatibles avec les systèmes et procédures du CNES/CSG. L'opérateur de lancement fournit les éléments nécessaires au président du Centre national d'études spatiales lui permettant de s'assurer de cette compatibilité.
Pour l'exercice de la MSI, le président du Centre national d'études spatiales doit disposer à tout instant du vol propulsé des informations de localisation. Ces informations sont issues au minimum de deux chaînes de localisation indépendantes. Au moins une de ces chaînes doit utiliser des moyens externes au véhicule de lancement.
Pour l'exercice de la MSA, le président du Centre national d'études spatiales doit disposer des informations de localisation dans les conditions prévues à l'- Article 85 - et à l'- Article 86 - du présent arrêté.

Article 77 - Conception du système de localisation
L'opérateur de lancement s'assure que les éléments bord du système de localisation sous sa responsabilité respectent les critères suivants:
- cohérence globale en matière d'allocation de fiabilité, notamment entre le bord et le sol;
- redondance et ségrégation géographique des chaînes de localisation (critère FO);
- niveaux de fiabilité relatifs à la panne avance et à la panne retard cohérents entre eux. Ces niveaux sont cohérents individuellement avec l'objectif de sécurité et l'objectif de réussite de la mission du véhicule de lancement;
- la fonction de localisation utilisée dans le cadre de la MSI est indépendante de la fonction de navigation active pour la mission du véhicule de lancement. Tout lien (bus de dialogue, masse électrique, ordre séquentiel, etc.) entre les équipements réalisant des fonctions de localisation et les équipements du fonctionnel bord ne doit pas retarder ou inhiber (quelle que soit la panne) les capacités des fonctions de localisation.

Article 78 - Visualisation du véhicule de lancement
L'opérateur de lancement doit mettre à disposition du président du Centre national d'études spatiales les images permettant d'observer en temps réel le comportement du véhicule de lancement. Ces images sont compatibles avec les systèmes et procédures du CNES/CSG et permettent au minimum une visualisation dans deux plans orthogonaux en champ large couvrant la plage d'espace verticale entre O et 250 mètres sur une largeur de champ d'environ 600 mètres.

Article 79 - Localisation par les radars
Le véhicule de lancement est équipé de répondeurs radar indépendants et compatibles avec les systèmes et procédures du CNES/CSG. Toute chaine de localisation externe est conçue de telle manière qu'il soit possible de déterminer les conditions cinématiques du véhicule de lancement à tout instant de la trajectoire et en situations nominale ou dégradées.

Article 80 - Localisation avec les moyens bord
L'opérateur de lancement doit s'assurer de la précision et de la robustesse de la localisation par des moyens internes au lanceur dans tous les cas de pannes possibles. Conformément aux dispositions de l'- Article 77 - du présent arrêté, les données de localisation interne ne peuvent être prises en compte que lorsqu'elles ne participent pas aux fonctions de navigation, de guidage et de pilotage du véhicule de lancement.
Le traitement sol et bord par l'opérateur de lancement de ces données de localisation ne doit pas conduire à leur altération (garantie d'intégrité).

Article 81 - Précision des moyens de localisation
L'opérateur de lancement fournit au président du Centre national d'études spatiales les éléments nécessaires à la détermination des erreurs de localisation en position et en vitesse. Ces fournitures sont définies au cours du processus de soumission sauvegarde tel que prévu à l'- Article 32 - du présent arrêté.

Article 82 - Qualification et contrôles
Les éléments du lanceur contribuant à la localisation, chaque sous-ensemble ainsi que le dispositif complet avec ses constituants (câblages, prises, raccords, etc.) sont qualifiés en prenant en compte les conditions d'ambiance représentatives de la défaillance du véhicule de lancement.
L'opérateur de lancement doit démontrer cette qualification par des essais dimensionnant dédiés.
L'opérateur de lancement doit également démontrer par essais le bon fonctionnement du matériel après intégration du lanceur.
Les spécifications relatives à l'ensemble de ces essais sont soumises au président du Centre national d'études spatiales dans les conditions prévues à l'- Article 32 - du présent arrêté.

CHAPITRE VI.4 - SYSTEME DE TELEMESURE
Article 83 - Objectifs du système de télémesure

L'opérateur de lancement transmet au président du Centre national d'études spatiales les données de télémesure permettant:
- de caractériser l'état de la liaison bord-sol télécommande, avant le décollage et en vol;
- d'apprécier l'état des chaînes de sauvegarde à bord, avant le décollage et en vol;
- de recevoir le compte rendu d'acquisition bord des ordres télécommandés;
- de suivre l'état des automatismes bord liés à la fonction sauvegarde incluant les fonctions de désorbitation et de passivation;
- d'acquérir les paramètres permettant la mise en œuvre des critères d'intervention prédictifs par le sol;
- d'acquérir la localisation du lanceur;
- de recevoir l'état de bon fonctionnement du lanceur (propulsion, contrôle de vol, équipements électriques).

Article 84 - Utilisation de la télémesure pour la MSI
A tout instant du vol propulsé, le président du Centre national d'études spatiales doit disposer en temps réel, aux fins d'exercice de sa mission de sauvegarde et d'intervention telle que prévue à l'- Article 63 - du présent arrêté:
- des données de localisation détaillées;
- de l'état du dispositif d'intervention à bord;
- des données sur le déroulement du séquentiel de vol;
- des données bord relatives au fonctionnement du véhicule de lancement.

Le contenu détaillé des données nécessaires à la MSI fait l'objet d'une instruction réglementaire du président du Centre national d'études spatiales pour chaque système de lancement considéré.

Article 85 - Utilisation de la télémesure pour la MSA
Lors des phases propulsées, de la séparation des étages, de la désorbitation et de la phase de mise en conditions initiales pour une rentrée contrôlée des éléments du véhicule de lancement, l'opérateur de lancement doit mettre à la disposition du président du Centre national d'études spatiales les paramètres temps réel suivants, aux fins d'exercice de sa mission de surveillance et d'alerte telle que prévue à l'- Article 64 - du présent arrêté:
- données de localisation détaillées;
- données sur le déroulement du séquentiel de vol;
- données bord relatives au fonctionnement du véhicule de lancement. En cas de difficulté d'application due aux besoins de la mission, des trous de télémesure en phase de régime stabilisé (hors allumage, extinction ou changement de régime commandé) peuvent être admis dans les conditions suivantes:
- justification par l'opérateur de lancement de ces difficultés et propositions associées;
- mise en place d'un enregistrement à bord;
- orbite osculatrice de périgée supérieur à 120 km pendant tout la durée du trou télémesure;
- durée du trou de télémesure compatible avec la garantie d'acquisition par la station suivante dans tous les cas non nominaux (hors explosion pendant la phase de trou de télémesure).

La mise en œuvre de ces mesures est soumise par l'opérateur de lancement au président du Centre national d'études spatiales.

Le contenu détaillé des données nécessaires à la MSA fait l'objet d'une instruction réglementaire du président du Centre national d'études spatiales pour chaque système de lancement considéré.

Article 86 - Utilisation de la télémesure pour le retrait de service des étages
Lors des phases de retrait de service des étages du véhicule de lancement, le président du Centre national d'études spatiales doit disposer en temps réel:
- de données sur le déroulement du séquentiel de vol;
- de données relatives au bon fonctionnement du véhicule de lancement.

En cas de difficulté d'application due aux besoins de la mission, un trou de réception de télémesure peut être admis. Il est soumis par l'opérateur de lancement au président du Centre national d'études spatiales.

Le contenu détaillé des données nécessaires fait l'objet d'une instruction réglementaire du président du Centre national d'études spatiales pour chaque système de lancement considéré.

Article 87 - Système de télémesure du CSG
Le CSG dispose de moyens adaptés de réception de télémesure pour assurer la poursuite du véhicule de lancement lors des missions de lancement GTO standard vers l'est.

Pour les autres missions, l'opérateur de lancement doit fournir les moyens et données d'entrée nécessaires à la constitution du réseau de stations spécifiques. Dans ce cas, ces moyens font l'objet de la soumission sauvegarde prévue à l'- Article 32 - du présent arrêté. Les moyens mis en œuvre à bord pendant le lancement sont compatibles avec les systèmes et procédures du CNES/CSG.

Article 88 - Qualifications et contrôles
Les éléments du lanceur contribuant à la télémesure, chaque sous-ensemble ainsi que le dispositif complet avec ses constituants (câblages, prises, raccords, etc.) sont qualifiés.

L'opérateur de lancement doit démontrer cette qualification par des essais dédiés.

L'opérateur de lancement doit également démontrer par essais le bon fonctionnement du matériel après intégration du lanceur.

Les spécifications relatives à l'ensemble de ces essais sont soumises au président du Centre national d'études spatiales dans les conditions prévues à l'- Article 32 - du présent arrêté.

Article 89 - Exploitation des données de vol
L'opérateur de lancement doit effectuer une analyse systématique, postérieurement au vol, des données transmises par le lanceur concernant les systèmes contribuant à la sauvegarde. Une synthèse de ces exploitations est transmise par écrit au président du Centre national d'études spatiales. Cette synthèse comprend à minimâ les éventuelles anomalies rencontrées pouvant avoir des incidences sur la sauvegarde et le traitement prévu de ces anomalies.

PARTIE VII. CONDITIONS PERMETTANT DE PROCEDER AU LANCEMENT EN CHRONOLOGIE FINALE

Article 90 - Conditions nécessaires au lancement
En application de l'article 14-8 du décret relatif au CNES précité, le président du Centre national d'études spatiales arrête la chronologie de lancement si l'un des critères définis à l'- Article 91 - et à l'- Article 92 - du présent arrêté n'est pas respecté.

Article 91 - Critères météorologiques
- **Vent au sol**

L'opérateur de lancement fournit les quantités et types d'ergols permettant de définir le critère de vent au sol en zone proche afin d'assurer la sécurité des personnes et des biens et la protection de la santé publique et de l'environnement.

Le critère de vent au sol est établi comme le vent maximum admissible pour rester dans le seuil des effets toxiques définis dans la limite de danger.

- **Vent en altitude**

Le vent est pris en compte le jour de lancement au travers de radio sondages.

Pour chaque lancement, des simulations en tenant compte des vents issus du dernier radio sondage au plus près du HO sont réalisées par le président du Centre national d'études spatiales pour s'assurer du respect de la limite de dangers conformément à l'- Article 61 - du présent arrêté.

- **Foudre**

Les critères applicables liés au risque de foudroiement du lanceur sont les suivants:
- C1: Pas de risque foudre dans un rayon de 10 km autour du lanceur.
- C2: Pas de nuages convectifs de plus de 6500 m d'épaisseur dans un rayon de 10 km autour du pas de tir au HO.
- C3: Pas d'enclume de Cumulonimbus à la verticale du pas de tir, si la cellule orageuse est à moins de 20 km

Article 92 - Critères techniques
- **Fonction sauvegarde vol**

Le lancement est subordonné à l'état des chaînes de sauvegarde à bord, au bon fonctionnement des dispositifs de commande sol, ainsi qu'à l'état des éventuels dispositifs de désorbitation afin de garantir que le lanceur est « localisable, télémesurable et neutralisable » dans les conditions prévues dans la PARTIE VI du présent arrêté.

Le dernier contrôle du bon fonctionnement du dispositif bord de neutralisation, de localisation et de télémesure est effectué dans une configuration la plus proche possible de celle du vol et le plus tard possible dans la chronologie de lancement.

Le dernier contrôle du dispositif d'intervention à bord doit être effectué dans la configuration la plus proche possible de celle de vol.

- **Autorisation et mesures du ministre chargé de l'espace**

Le lancement est subordonné à l'existence et au maintien de l'autorisation de procéder au lancement délivrée par le ministre chargé de l'espace au titre de la loi relative aux opérations spatiales précitée.

L'application des dispositions du présent arrêté est sans préjudice de la mise en œuvre par le ministre, ou, par délégation, par le président du Centre national d'études spatiales, des instructions et mesures nécessaires dans l'intérêt de la sécurité des personnes et des biens et de la protection de la santé publique et de l'environnement, telles que prévues à l'article 8 de la loi relative aux opérations spatiales précitée et à l'article L. 331-7 du code de la recherche.

- **Collision en orbite**

Dans le cadre de sa mission de sauvegarde liée à la réalisation des lancements, le président du Centre national d'études spatiales s'assure de la protection des objets spatiaux habités.

A cette fin, le vol du véhicule de lancement dans la fenêtre de lancement envisagée est compatible avec la position des objets spatiaux habités dont les paramètres orbitaux sont connus avec précision et disponibles.

- **Vacuité des zones à risques au lancement**

Conformément aux dispositions de l'- Article 61 - du présent arrêté, la ZRL est évacuée en chronologie de lancement. Seules sont autorisées à demeurer dans certains bâtiments renforcés de la ZRL, les personnes nécessaires au lancement et en ZRTL, celles placées sous le contrôle du président du Centre national d'études spatiales.

Article 93 - Protection externe du CSG

Le président du Centre national d'étude spatial peut également arrêter la chronologie de lancement sur demande du représentant de l'Etat chargé de la protection externe, dans les conditions prévues au décret du 16 mai 1989 précité.

PARTIE VIII. - Sanctions

Article 94 - Amende administrative
Conformément à l'article 14-9 du décret relatif au CNES précité, le président du Centre national d'études spatiales peut prononcer une amende administrative d'un montant prévu pour les contraventions de la 5• classe à l'encontre de toute personne physique ou morale visée à l'article 14-7 du même décret exerçant une activité en violation des dispositions du présent arrêté.

PARTIE IX. - Dispositions administratives

Article 95 - Communication des informations, données et dossiers
L'ensemble des informations, données et dossiers devant être transmis ou soumis au président du Centre national d'études spatiales dans le cadre de l'application des dispositions du présent arrêté sont adressés au directeur du centre spatial guyanais.

Article 96 - Recours
Le présent arrêté est susceptible de recours devant le tribunal administratif territorialement compétent par le demandeur dans un délai de deux mois suivant sa notification.

Dans le même délai de deux mois, le demandeur peut présenter un recours gracieux. Le silence gardé par le président du CNES pendant plus de deux mois sur la demande de recours gracieux emporte décision implicite de rejet de cette demande conformément à l'article R. 421-2 du code de justice administrative.

Article 97 - Entrée en vigueur et publication
Les dispositions du présent arrêté prennent effet à compter sa publication au recueil des actes administratifs de la Préfecture de Guyane.
Le présent arrêté est librement consultable au local de remise des badges du Centre spatial guyanais.

Fait à Paris, le 9 décembre 2010.

Appendix

Annexe 1: Coordonnées géographiques des points définissant laLimite de Danger

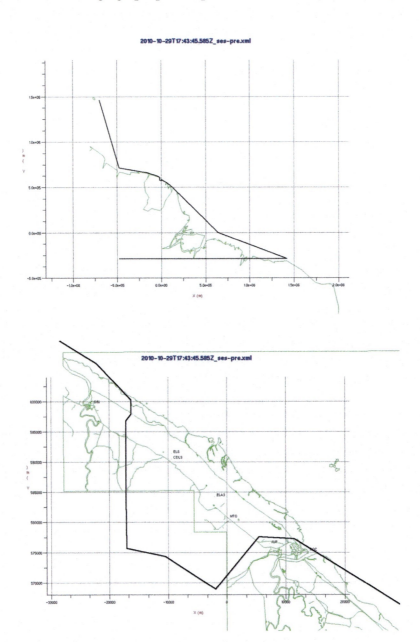

ANNEXE 1.7

Coordonnées WGS84 des points définissants la Limite de Danger (Longitude Latitude en degrés décimaux)	
59.000000°W	13.0000000°N
57.000000°W	06.4000000°N
54.200000°W	05.9000000°N
53.120000°W	05.5400000°N
52.950000°W	05.4390000°N
52.896667°W	05.3850000°N
52.896667°W	05.3633333°N
52.904100°W	05.3539000°N
52.904167°W	05.2416667°N
52.903500°W	05.1650000°N
52.840400°W	05.1507000°N
52.768100°W	05.1043000°N
52.701400°W	05.1820000°N
52.647944°W	05.1788889°N
52.179300°W	04.8959000°N
51.847000°W	04.6691000°N
51.508900°W	04.4032000°N
47.000000°W	00.0000000°N
40.000000°W	02.6000000°S
57.000000°W	02.6000000°S

ANNEXES II "ORIGINAL LEGISLATION" ENGLISH VERSION (NON-OFFICIAL TRANSLATION)

List of Annexes

Annex 2.1	CNES' constituent Act of 1961 as consolidated in the French Code of Research (CNES' Act)
Annex 2.2	Space Operation Act of 3rd June, 2008 (FSOA 2008)
Annex 2.3	Decree 2009-643 of 9th June, 2009 on authorization issued in accordance with SOA 2008 (Authorization Decree)
Annex 2.4	Decree 2009-644 of 9th June, amending the 1984 CNES' Decree (CNES Decree)
Annex 2.5	Decree 2009-640 of 9th June, 2009 on Space-Based Data (SBD Decree)
Annex 2.6	Order of 31st March, 2011 on Technical Regulation (RT)
Annex 2.7	Order of 9th December, 2010 regulating the operations on CSG facilities (REI)

ANNEX 2.1

CNES' constituent Act of 1961 as consolidated in the French Code of Research (CNES' Act)

The CNES' constituent Act[1] as codified in the French Code of Research[2]

Chapter 1. Centre National d'Etudes Spatiales (CNES) – National Center for Space Studies

Article L331-1
(Statute)[3]
The Centre National d'Etudes Spatiales is a national public body of industrial and commercial nature, with scientific and technical missions, and financial autonomy.

Article L331-2[4]
(Missions)
The mission of the CNES is to develop and to guide scientific and technical researches in the field of space.
Among the Centre National d'Etudes Spatiales responsibilities is:
a) to collect all information on national and international activities concerning space questions and space uses and exploitation;
b) to prepare and put forward proposals to the administrative authority for programmes of national interest in the field of space;
c) to ensure implementation of these programmes, either by laboratories and technical bodies set up by Centre National d'Etudes Spatiales, or through research agreements made with other public or private bodies, or through shareholding funds;

---

1 Issued from law n°61-1382 dated December 19th 1961 creating the National Center for Space Studies, Official Journal of the French Republic (OJFR), codified at articles L331-1 à L331-6 of the French Code of Research by par order n°2004-545 dated June 11th 2004 relating to the legal section of this Code, OJFR n°138 date June 16th 2004 page 10719, modified by law n°2008-518 dated June 3rd 2008 (articles 21 and 28) relating to space operations, the French Space Operation Act (FSOA).
2 Code of Research, Legislative Section, Book III. Public commercial and industrial bodies
3 Titles following an article's number (text in italics and in brackets) have been added by the author for a better understanding of the text. They have no particular legal value.
4 Modified by law n°2008-518 date June 3rd 2008 (FSOA) – art. 28.

d) to develop international cooperation in the field of space in conjunction with the Ministry of Foreign Affairs and to ensure execution of France's contributions to international programmes;
e) to guarantee, either directly or indirectly through grants or funding, publication of scientific papers concerning space issues;
f) to assist the State in the elaboration of technical regulations relating to space operations;
g) by delegation of the Ministry in charge of space, to control that systems and procedures implemented by space operators comply with the technical regulations mentioned above (f);
h) to hold the registry of space objects on behalf of the State.

Article L331-3
(Administration)
The Centre National d'Etudes Spatiales shall be administered by a Governing Board, composed of State's representatives, persons chosen for their competence in the field of CNES's activity and staff representatives elected according to the conditions stated in Chapter II Title II of the Act n°83-675 dated July 26th 1983 relating to public-sector democratisation.

Article L331-4
(Funding)
To fund its missions, the Centre National d'Etudes Spatiales shall dispose of budgetary appropriations open for space researches by the Finance Law, of public or private grants, of payments for services rendered, of donations and legacies, of financial revenues and other accessory products.

Article L331-5[5]
(Budget management and Public accountancy)
The Centre National d'Etudes Spatiales shall assume its financial management and present its accountancy according to the rules on public bodies of industrial and commercial nature, provided with an accounting officer.

---

5   Modified by decree n°2012-1247 dated November 7th 2012 (art. 107), to fit the dispositions under Title I and III of decree n°2012-1246 dated November 7th 2012 (art. 49) relating to budget management and public accountancy. See footnote 8.

Article L331-6[6]
(Powers entrusted to the CNES's President at GSC under the FSOA)
I. – The President of the Centre National d'Etudes Spatiales shall exercise on behalf of the State the special Police for the exploitation of the facilities of the Guiana Space Centre, within a perimeter defined by the competent administrative authority. As such, it shall be in charge of a general mission of safeguard consisting in controlling the technical risks related to the preparation and carrying out of the launches from the Guiana Space Centre in order to ensure the protection of persons, property, public health and the environment, on the ground and during the flight, and it shall set out to this end the specific regulations applicable within the limits of the perimeter defined above.

II. – Under the authority of the Government representative in the *Département* of Guiana, the President of the Centre National d'Etudes Spatiales shall coordinate the implementation by companies and other entities settled in the perimeter defined in part I. above of measures taken in order to ensure the security of the facilities and of the activities undertaken therein, and shall verify that those companies and agencies fulfil their obligations in this respect.

IIII. – To the extent strictly necessary for the accomplishment of the missions set out in parts I. and II., the agents empowered by the President of the Centre National d'Etudes Spatiales have access to the land and premises used exclusively for professional purposes and occupied by the companies and agencies settled at the Guiana Space Centre in the perimeter defined in part I. above.

Article L 331-7[7]
(Emergency measures delegated to the CNES' President under the FSOA)
The President of the Centre National d'Etudes Spatiales may take for any space operation, by delegation of the administrative authority mentioned in Article 8 of the Act n° 2008-518 dated June 3rd relating to space operations, the necessary measures provided for in the same article to ensure the safety of persons and property, as well as the protection of public health and the environment.

---

[6] Modified by law n°2008-518 date June 3rd 2008 (FSOA) – art. 21.
[7] Created by law n°2008-518 date June 3rd 2008 (FSOA) – art. 21.

Article L331-8[8]
(Application decree[9]*)*
A decree passed at the Council of State shall set forth the terms of implementation of the present chapter, particularly the conditions in which the President of the Centre National d'Etudes Spatiales may delegate its competence mentioned in Article L. 331-6.

Legislative references on CNES' Act (ORIGINAL ACT OF 1961)

Text:
- CNES Constitutive Act, 19 December 1961 n° 1961-1382, codified by Legal Ordinance of 11 June 1 2004 n° 2004-545, into the French Code of Research (here after CR), Articles L. 331-1 to L331-6, being amended by article 21 and 28 of French Space Operations Act June 3rd 2008 adding article L 331-7 and 8.

Preliminary works:

National Assembly *(Assemblée nationale)* – Minutes in « Documents de l'Assemblée Nationale1961 »
- Act Draft N° 1429 and report N° 1460 by Michel Sy. First session 12 September 1961. Session of 13 October 1961, p 569.
- Final discussion and adoption on 18 October 1961 session.

Senate *(Sénat)* - Minutes in the 1961-1962 Session Senate Journal
- Act Draft N° 29 and Report N°97by Jacques Baumel. First session 24 October. Session of 30 November 1961.
- Final discussion and adoption on 7 décembre 1961, session FSOA Preliminary works

---

8   Created by law n°2008-518 date June 3rd 2008 (FSOA) – art. 21.
9   The implementing decree in force is the modified decree n°84-510 dated June 28th 1984 relating to the National Center for Space Studies (available in its consolidated version at the following website LEGIFRANCE https://www.legifrance.gouv.fr/). In particular, this text has been modified in 2009 (in its actual articles 14-1 to 14-7 replacing article 14) to take consideration of the implementing decree of the FSOA dated June 3rd 2008 (decree n°2009-644 dated June 9th 2009), then modified in 2012 (in its actual articles 3, 4, 5, 13) by decree n°2012-1247 dated November 7th 2012 (art. 107), to fit the dispositions under Title I and III of decree n° 2012-1246 dated November 7th 2012 (art. 49) relating to budget management and public accountancy.

ANNEX 2.2

Space Operation Act of 3rd June, 2008 (FSOA 2008)

French Space Operations Act n°2008-518 of 3rd June, 2008 (FSOA 2008)[1]

The National Assembly and the Senate adopted,
The President of the French Republic promulgate the following Law:

TITLE I: Definitions

Article 1
(Definitions)
For the purposes of this Act:
- The term "damage" means damage to persons or property, and in particular to public health or to the environment, directly caused by a space object as part of a space operation, to the exclusion of the consequences arising from the use of the signal transmitted by this object for users;
- The term "space operator", thereafter referred to as "the operator": means any natural or juridical person carrying out a space operation under its responsibility and independently;
- The term "space operation" means any activity consisting in launching or attempting to launch an object into outer space, or of ensuring the commanding of a space object during its journey in outer space, including the Moon and other celestial bodies, and, if necessary, during its return to Earth;
- The term "launching phase" means the period of time which, as part of a space operation, starts at the moment when the launching operations become irreversible and which, without prejudice to provisions contained, if necessary, in the authorization granted pursuant to the present act, ends when the object to be put in outer space is separated from its launch vehicle.

---

[1] Non-official English Translation of the text « Loi n° 2008 -518 du 3 juin 2008 relatives aux opérations Spatiales' as published on the French official gazette (JORF) on the 4th of June 2008 based on CNES Legal Department's internal document of May 2017.
The final version of this Act retains wording only at the 'Title' and 'Chapter' levels. Wording of Articles have been added for information on this text, based on the one used for drafts during legislative proceedings. All data in italics, included foot notes, have been added by the Author.

- The term "phase of command" means the period of time starting as part of a space operation at the moment when the object to be put in outer space is separated from its launch vehicle and ending when the first of the following events occurs:
  - when the final manoeuvres for de-orbiting and the passivation activities have been completed;
  - when the operator has lost control over the space object;
  - the return to Earth or the full disintegration of the space object into the atmosphere;
- The term "third party to a space operation" means any natural or juridical person other than those taking part in the space operation or in the production of the space object(s) the launch or command of which is part of the operation. In particular, the space operator, its contractors, its subcontractors and its customers, as the contractors and subcontractors of its customers, are not regarded as third parties.
- The term "space-based data primary operator" means any natural or juridical person ensuring the programming of an Earth observation satellite system or the reception of Earth observation data from outer space.

Title II: Authorization of space operations
(Autorisation des opérations spatiales)

Chapter 1: Operations subject to authorization
(Opérations soumises à autorisation)

Article 2
Scope of Authorizations
(Champ d'application des autorisations)
The following shall obtain an authorization from the administrative authority:
1° Any operator, whatever its nationality, intending to proceed with the launching of a space object from the national territory or from means or facilities falling under French jurisdiction, or intending to proceed with the return of such an object onto the national territory or onto facilities falling under French jurisdiction;
2° Any French operator intending to proceed with the launching of a space object from the territory of a foreign State or from means or facilities falling under the jurisdiction of a foreign State or from an area that is not subject to the sovereignty of a State, or intending to proceed with the return of such an object onto the territory of a foreign State or onto means and facilities falling under the jurisdiction of a foreign State or onto an area that is not subject to the sovereignty of a State;
3° Any natural person having French nationality or juridical person whose headquarters are located in France, whether it is an operator or not, intending to procure the

launching of a space object or any French operator intending to command such an object during its journey in outer space.

Article 3
Authorization for transferring command of space objects
(Autorisation des transferts d'objets spatiaux)
The transfer to a third party of the commanding of a space object which has been authorized pursuant to the terms of the present act is subject to prior authorization from the administrative authority.
Pursuant to the provisions of paragraph 3 of Article 2, any French operator intending to take the control of a space object whose launching or control has not been authorized under the present act shall obtain to this end a prior authorization from the administrative authority.
The terms of application of the present article are set forth by decree passed at the Council of State.

Chapter 2: Conditions for granting authorizations
(Conditions de délivrance des autorisations)

Article 4
Granting authorization
(Délivrance des autorisations)
Authorizations to launch, to command or to transfer the commanding of a space object launched and to proceed with its return to Earth are granted once the administrative authority has checked the moral, financial and professional guarantees of the applicant, and if necessary of its shareholders, and has ascertained that the systems and procedures that it intends to implement are compliant with the technical regulations set forth, in particular for the safety of persons and property, the protection of public health and the environment.
Authorizations cannot be granted when the operations for which they were requested, regarding in particular the systems intended to be implemented, are likely to jeopardise national defence interests or the respect by France of its international commitments.
Licenses certifying for a determined time period that a space operator satisfies moral, financial and professional guarantees may be granted by the administrative authority competent for issuing authorizations. These licenses may also attest the compliance of the systems and procedures referred to in the first paragraph with the technical regulations set forth. Lastly, these licenses may be equivalent to authorizations for certain operations.
A decree passed at the Council of State shall set forth the terms of application of the present article. It shall specify in particular:

1° The information and documents to be provided to support applications for authorizations, as well as the granting procedure for these authorizations;
2° The administrative authority competent for granting authorizations and for setting forth the technical regulations referred to in the first paragraph;
3° The conditions in which the licenses mentioned in the third paragraph can be granted, and the modes in which the beneficiary of such a license informs the administrative authority of the space operations he undertakes;
4° When an authorization is solicited for an operation which is to be carried out from the territory of a foreign State or from means or facilities falling under the jurisdiction of a foreign State, the conditions in which the administrative authority may exempt the applicant from all or any part of the compliance checking mentioned in the first paragraph, when the national and international commitments made by that State as well as its legislation and practices include sufficient guarantees regarding the safety of persons and property and the protection of public health and the environment, and liability matters.

Chapter III: Obligations of authorizations holders
(Obligations des titulaires d'autorisation)

Article 5
Conditional requirements for granting authorization
(Prescriptions conditionnant les autorisations)
The authorizations granted pursuant to the present act may include requirements set forth for the safety of persons and property, protection of public health and the environment, in particular in order to limit risks related to space debris.
These requirements may also be set forth in order to protect the national defence interests or to ensure the respect by France of its international commitments.

Article 6
Compulsory insurance or financial guarantee
(Obligation d'assurance ou de garantie financière)
I. – Any operator subject to authorization pursuant to the present act shall have and maintain, as long as it can be held liable pursuant to Article 13 and for the amount set out in Articles 16 and 17, insurance or another financial guarantee approved by the competent authority.

A decree passed at the Council of State shall set forth the terms of insurance, the nature of the financial guarantees that may be accepted by the competent authority and the conditions in which the fulfilment of the requirements referred to in the previous paragraph is proved to the authority having granted the authorization. It also specifies conditions in which the administrative authority may exempt the operator from the requirements set out in the previous paragraph.

II. – The insurance or financial guarantee must cover the risk of having to compensate for the damages that could be caused to third parties to the space operation up to the amount mentioned in the first paragraph.

III> – The insurance or financial guarantee must cover the following persons to the extent of their liability for the damage caused by a space object:
- The Government and its public bodies;
- The European Space Agency and its Member States;
- The operator and the persons having taken part in the production of the space object or in the space operation.

Article 7
Persons empowered to control
(Personnes habilitées au contrôle)

I. – The following are empowered to proceed with the necessary controls in order to ascertain that the obligations set out in the present chapter are fulfilled:

1° The agents commissioned by the administrative authority mentioned in Article 2 in the conditions set forth in a decree passed at the Council of State, and belonging to the Government departments in charge of Space, Defence, Research, Environment or to its public bodies carrying out their missions in the same fields;
2° The agents empowered to perform technical checkings aboard aircrafts;
3° The members of the Insurance Control Body mentioned in Article L. 310-13 of the Insurance Code;
4° The agents mentioned in Article L. 1421-1 of the Public Health Code;
5° The administrators and inspectors of maritime affairs, the officers from the technical and administrative body of maritime affairs, the maritime affairs controller, the commandants of the State ships and aircrafts in charge of maritime surveillance.

The agents mentioned above are bound by professional confidentiality under the conditions and penalties set out by Article 226-13 and 226-14 of the Penal Code.

II. – Agents mentioned in part I. above shall have access at any time to the buildings, premises and facilities where space operations are conducted and to the space object itself. These provisions are not applicable to the part of the premises being used as a residence, except between 6 a.m. and 9 p.m. upon authorization from the President of the *tribunal de grande instance* (court of first instance of general jurisdiction) or by the judge it empowered to do so.

The operator is informed at the latest when the controlling operations begin that he may attend the operations and be assisted by any person of his choice, or that he can be represented for that purpose.

III. – As part of their controlling assignment, the agents mentioned in part I. above can ask for any document or useful item, irrespective of their *medium*. They can make copies and gather any necessary information and justification, *in situ* or upon notification.

The agents can take documents away only after having established a list countersigned by the operator. This list specifies the nature and quantity of the documents.

The operator shall be informed by the administrative authority mentioned in Article 2 of the control follow up and may transmit its observations.

If the operator or the person empowered to grant access to the building, premise or facility cannot be contacted or if he denies access, the agents mentioned in part I. above may seek permission from the President of the *Tribunal de grande instance*, or from the judge empowered to do so.

Article 8
Emergency tasks of the administrative authority in case of risk of damage
(Missions de l'autorité administrative en cas d'urgence)

Concerning the launching or the control of the space object, the administrative authority, or the agents acting on its authority and empowered by it to this end, may at any moment give instructions and require any measures they consider necessary for the safety of persons and property, the protection of public health and the environment.

The administrative authority and the agents acting on its authority shall consult the operator beforehand, unless there is an immediate danger.

A decree passed at the Council of State shall specify the terms of delegation and capacitation of the agents in charge of the enforcement of the present article.

Chapter IV: Administrative and penal sanctions
(Sanctions administratives et pénales)

Article 9
Revocation or suspension of authorizations
(Retrait et suspension des autorisations)

The authorizations granted according to the terms of the present Act can be revoked or suspended in case the holder contravenes to its obligations, or when the operations for which they were sought are likely to jeopardise the national defence interests or the respect by France of its international commitments.

In case of suspension or withdrawal of the authorization to command a launched space object, the administrative authority may enjoin the operator to take, at its own expenses, the appropriate measures regarding the commonly admitted good rules of conduct to limit the risks of damage due to that object.

Article 10
Ascertainment of infringements – Sworn officers
(Constatation des infractions – agents assermentés)
In addition to the judicial police officers and agents acting following the prescriptions of the Code of Criminal Procedure, the sworn agents mentioned in the first paragraph of Article 7 are authorized to investigate and record breaches to the prescriptions of the present Chapter and of the texts issued for its enforcement. To this end, they exercise the powers set out in paragraphs II. and IV. of the same article.

They record these breaches in reports which are considered authentic unless the contrary is proved. They are sent to the *Procureur de la République* (Head of the Prosecution Department at courts of first instance of general jurisdiction) within five days after their issuing.

A decree adopted passed at the Council of State shall set forth the terms of application of the present article.

Article 11
Penalties (or fines)
(Sanctions pénales ou amendes)
I. – The following shall give rise to a fine of € 200 000:
1° Any operator, whatever its nationality, proceeding without authorization to the launching of a space object from the national territory or from means or facilities falling under French jurisdiction, or to the return of such an object onto the national territory or onto means or facilities falling under French jurisdiction;
2° Any French operator proceeding without authorization to the launching of a space object from the territory of a foreign State, from means or facilities falling under the jurisdiction of a foreign State, or from an area not subject to a State's sovereignty or to the return of such an object onto the territory of a foreign State, onto means or facilities falling under the jurisdiction of a foreign State or onto an area not subject to a State's sovereignty.
3° Any natural person having French nationality or juridical person having its headquarters in France procuring the launching of a space object without authorization, or commanding it without authorization during its journey into outer space.
II. – The following shall give rise to a fine of € 200 000:
1° Transferring to a third party without authorization the commanding of a space object which launching or commanding has been authorized according to the terms of the present act;
2° Any French operator undertaking without authorization the commanding of a space object which launching has not been authorized according to the present law.
III. – An operator shall be fined € 200 000 in the case of:

1°   pursuing the space operation in breach of an administrative measure or court decision ordering its ceasing or suspension;
2°   pursuing the space operation without complying with an administrative summon to comply with a prescription.

IV. – Is fined € 200 000 the fact for operators or individuals to prevent controls undertaken pursuant to Article 7.

Title III: Registration of launched space objects
(Immatriculation des objets spatiaux lancés)

Article 12
Keeping of national space object register
(Tenue du registre national d'immatriculation)
In the event France has a registration obligation according to Article II of the Convention dated 14 September 1975 relating to Registration of objects launched into outer space, and, if necessary, of other international agreements, the launched space objects are registered in a registry hold by the Centre National d'Etudes Spatiales on behalf of the State, following the prescriptions set out in a decree passed at the Council of State.

Title IV: Liability
(Responsabilités)

Chapter 1: Liability towards third parties
(Responsabilité à l'égard des tiers)

Article 13
Channelling of liability
(Canalisation de la responsabilité)
The operator shall be solely liable for damages caused to third parties by the space operations which it conducts in the following conditions:
1°   He shall be absolutely liable for damages caused on the ground or in airspace;
2°   He shall be liable only due to his fault for damages caused elsewhere than on the ground or in airspace.

This liability may only be reduced or set aside in case the fault of the victim is proven.
Except in case of willful misconduct, the liability set forth in 1° and 2° ends when all the obligations set out in the authorization or the license are fulfilled, or at the latest one year after the date on which these obligations should have been fulfilled. The Government shall be liable in the operator's place for damages occurring after this period.

Article 14
Government's recourse action for indemnity
(Action récursoire de l'Etat)
When the Government has paid compensation for damage according to the stipulations of the Treaty dated 27 January 1967 relating to Principles Governing the Activities of States in the Exploration and Use of outer Space, including the Moon and other Celestial Bodies, or of the Convention dated 19 march 1972 relating to International Liability for Damage caused by Space Objects, it may present a claim for indemnification against the operator having caused the damage for which France was held internationally liable, to the extent that the Government has not already benefited from the insurance or financial guarantees of the operator up to the amount of the compensation.
If the damage was caused by a space object used as a part of an operation authorized according to the terms of the present Act, the claim for indemnification may be brought:
1° within the limit of the amount set out pursuant to the conditions mentioned in article 16 in the case of damage caused during the launching phase;
2° within the limit of the amount set out pursuant to the conditions mentioned in Article 17 in the case of damage caused after the launching phase, including when the space object returns to Earth.
In case of a wilful misconduct of the operator, the limitations set out in 1° and 2° shall not apply.
The Government shall not present a claim for indemnification if the damage was caused by a space object used as a part of an operation authorized according to the terms of the present Act and resulting from acts targeting governmental interests.

Article 15
Government's financial guarantee
(Garantie financière de l'Etat)
When an operator has been condemned to compensate a third party for a damage caused by a space object used as a part of an operation authorized according to the terms of the present Act, and if that operation has been undertaken from the French territory or from the territory of another Member State of the European Union or from the territory of a State party to the European Economic Area Agreement, or from means or facilities falling under the jurisdiction of France or another Member State of the European Union or of a State party to the European Economic Area Agreement, that operator shall benefit, except in case of a wilful misconduct, from the governmental guarantee, according to the terms of the Finance Act:
1° For the part of the compensation exceeding the amount set out in the conditions mentioned in Article 16, in the case of a damage caused during the launching phase;

2° For the part of the compensation exceeding the amount set out in the conditions mentioned in Article 17, in the case of a damage caused on the ground or in airspace after the launching phase, including when the space object returns to Earth.

In the case of damage caused during the launching phase, the governmental guarantee shall benefit, if necessary and in the conditions set out in the paragraphs above, to the persons who are not third parties to a space operation pursuant to the present Act.

Article 16
Government's guarantee ceiling applicable during the launching phase
(Plafond de la garantie de l'état applicable pendant la phase de lancement)
Within the framework set forth in the Finance Act,[2] the authorization granted pursuant to the present Act shall set out, given the risks incurred and regarding in particular the characteristics of the launching site, the amount respectively below and beyond which the claim for indemnification is exercised and the governmental guarantee is granted, in the case of a damage caused during the launching phase.

Article 17
Government's guarantee ceiling applicable after the launching phase
(Plafond de la garantie de l'Etat applicable après la phase de lancement)
Within the framework set forth in the Finance Act, the authorization granted pursuant to the present Act shall set out, given the risks incurred, the amount respectively below and beyond which the claim for indemnification is exercised and the governmental guarantee is granted, in the case of a damage caused after the launching phase.

Article 18
Supervision of the proceedings
(Direction du procès)
Any person questioned before a court because of a damage for which he could benefit from the governmental guarantee shall inform the competent administrative authority, which may exercise all the defence rights in the proceedings on behalf of the Government. If he fails to do so, the questioned person shall be deemed to having waived to the governmental guarantee.

Chapter II: Liability towards persons taking part in the space operation
(Responsabilité à l'égard des personnes participant à l'opération spatiale)

---

2 See footnote under article 29 below.

Article 19
Cross waiver of claims for damage caused to a third party
(Renonciation mutuelle à recours en cas de dommage causé à un tiers)
When the insurance or financial guarantee mentioned in Article 6 as well as, if necessary, the governmental guarantee have been laid out to indemnify a third party, one of the persons having taken part in the space operation or in the production of the space object which caused the damage cannot be held liable by another of these persons, except in case of a wilful misconduct.

Article 20
Limitation of liability clause for damage caused to a contracting partner
(Clauses limitatives de responsabilité en cas de dommage causé à un partenaire contractuel)
In the case of a damage caused by a space operation or the production of a space object to a person taking part in this operation or in that production, any other person taking part in the space operation or in the production of the space object having caused the damage and bound to the previous one by a contract cannot be held liable because of that damage, unless otherwise expressly stipulated regarding the damage caused during the production phase of a space object which is to be commanded in outer space or during its commanding in orbit, or in case of a wilful misconduct.

Titre V: Provisions relating to the Research Code
(Dispositions relatives au code de la recherche)

Article 21
The role of CNES' President
(Rôle du Président du CNES)
The Research Code is amended as follows:
– Article L. 331-6 is drafted as follows:
   "*Art. L. 331-6.* – I. – The President of the Centre National d'Etudes Spatiales shall exercise on behalf of the State the special Police for the exploitation of the facilities of the Guiana Space Centre, within a perimeter defined by the competent administrative authority. As such, it shall be in charge of a general mission of safeguard consisting in controlling the technical risks related to the preparation and carrying out of the launches from the Guiana Space Centre in order to ensure the protection of persons, property, public health and the environment, on the ground and during the flight, and it shall set out to this end the specific regulations applicable within the limits of the perimeter defined above.
   "II. Under the authority of the Government representative in the *Département* of Guiana, the President of the Centre National d'Etudes Spatiales shall coordinate the

implementation by companies and other entities settled in the perimeter defined in part I. above of measures taken in order to ensure the security of the facilities and of the activities undertaken therein, and shall verify that those companies and agencies fulfil their obligations in this respect.

"III. To the extent strictly necessary for the accomplishment of the missions set out in parts I. and II., the agents empowered by the President of the Centre National d'Etudes Spatiales have access to the land and premises used exclusively for professional purposes and occupied by the companies and agencies settled at the Guiana Space Centre in the perimeter defined in part I. above."

– Articles L. 331-7 and L. 331-8 are inserted after Article L. 331-6 and are drafted as follows:

"*Art. L. 331-7.* – The President of the Centre National d'Etudes Spatiales may take for any space operation, by delegation of the administrative authority mentioned in Article 8 of the Act n° 2008-518 dated June 3rd relating to space operations, the necessary measures provided for in the same article to ensure the safety of persons and property, as well as the protection of public health and the environment."

"*Art. L. 331-8.* – A decree passed at the Council of State shall set forth the terms of application of the present chapter, particularly the conditions in which the President of the Centre National d'Etudes Spatiales may delegate its competence mentioned in Article L. 331-6."

Title VI: Intellectual Property
(Propriété intellectuelle)

Article 22
Extension of rules on patent for invention
(Extension des règles de brevets d'invention)

I. – Article L. 611-1 of the Intellectual Property Code is completed by a paragraph drafted as follows:

"Unless otherwise provided in an international agreement to which France is a party, the provisions of the present article apply to the inventions made or used in outer space, including onto celestial bodies and into or onto space objects placed under national jurisdiction according to article VIII of the Treaty dated 27 January 1967 relating to Principles Governing the Activities of States in the Exploration and Use of Outer Space, including the Moon and other celestial bodies."

II. – Article L. 613-5 of the same Code is completed by an *e)* drafted as follows:

"*e)* To the objects intended to be launched in outer space brought onto the French territory."

Title VII: Space-Based Data
(Données d'origine spatiale)

Article 23
Preliminary declaration
(Déclaration préalable)
Any primary space-based data operator undertaking in France an activity having certain technical characteristics defined in a decree passed at the Council of State must preliminarily declare it to the competent administrative authority.

These technical characteristics are related in particular to the resolution, location accuracy, observation frequency band and quality of the Earth observation data which are received or for which a satellite system is programmed.

Article 24
Administrative Authority's control
(Contrôle de l'autorité administrative)
The competent administrative authority ascertains that the activity undertaken by the primary operators of space-based data does not harm fundamental interests of the Nation, particularly defence matters, foreign policy and international commitments of France.

To this end, it may at any time prescribe measures restraining the activity of the primary space-based data operators, which are necessary to safeguard these interests.

Article 25
Fines (or Penalties)
(Amendes – ou sanctions pénales)
Any primary space-based data operator undertaking an activity showing the technical characteristics mentioned in Article 23 shall be fined € 200 000 in the case:
- it fails to proceed with the declaration mentioned in Article 23;
- it fails to comply with the restriction measures taken pursuant to Article 24.

Title VIII: Transitory and Final Provisions
Dispositions transitoires et finales

Article 26
Exclusion of Defence activities
(Exclusion des activités de défense)
The present Act does not apply to the launching and guiding, for the needs of national defence, of vehicles which trajectory passes through outer space, in particular ballistic missiles.

The activities of the Ministry of Defence acting as primary space-based data operator are not subject to the provisions of Title VII.

Article 27
Exclusion of CNES' activities from the scope of this act
(Exclusion de certaines activités du CNES du champ d'application de la loi)
As they fall under the scope of a public mission assigned to the Centre National d'Etudes Spatiales after approval by the administrative authority pursuant to paragraph 4 of Article L. 331-2 of the Research Code, the operations of launching, returning to Earth, commanding or transfer of commanding of a space object are not subject to the provisions of Titles II and IV, and the Earth observation satellite activities and the reception of Earth observation data are not subject to the provisions of Title VII

Article 28
New attributions assigned to the CNES
(Attributions nouvelles du CNES)
Article L. 331-2 of the Research Code is completed by an *f)*, a *g)* and an *h)* drafted as follows:
"*f)* To assist the Government in the definition of the technical regulations relating to space operations;
"*g)* To verify, by delegation of the minister in charge of space, that the systems and procedures implemented by the space operators comply with the technical regulation mentioned in paragraph *f)*;
"*h)* To hold the register of the space objects on behalf of the Government."

Article 29
Entry into force of articles 16 and 17 (Governement's guarantee ceiling)
(Entrée en vigueur des articles 16 et 17)
Articles 16 and 17 of the present Act shall enter into force at the date of publication of the Finance Act[3] setting out the minimum and the maximum amounts between which is included the amount beyond which the governmental guarantee is granted.

---

3   See Amending Finance Act (Loi de finance rectificative) n°2008-1443 of 30 December 2008 – Annex 6 Article 119, JORF 31 December 2008:
    '*I- In conformity with the provisions of the provisions of the Space Operation Act N° 2008-518 of June 3rd, 2008, the Government is authorized to guarantee the compensation of the damage caused to third parties in connection with a space operation authorized under the aforementioned act and carried out from a territory of the European Economic Area. This coverage applies, <u>except wilful misconduct or serious departure from the requirement of the authorization,</u> beyond a ceiling fixed in the same authorization. This ceiling shall be between 50 million euros and 70 million euros.*
    II. paragraph I above is applicable in New Caledonia, in French Polynesia, on islands Wallis and Futuna and in the French Southern and Antarctic Lands.'

Article 30
Applicability of the Act to the French overseas communities
(Applicabilité outre-mer)
The provisions of the present Act are applicable in New-Caledonia, in French Polynesia, in the Islands of Wallis and Futuna and in the French southern and Antarctic lands.

This Act shall be implemented as a State Act.

Paris, 3rd of June 2008

Preliminary works:

Ministry for Research and new technology in charge of Space affairs:
- Study report "Evolution of Space law in France", February 2003, MRNT, Technology Directorate Space and Aeronautics Department (synthesis available in English), www.recherche.gouv.fr.

Council of State (Conseil d'Etat):
- Appraisal Studies, April 6th 2006, "A Legal Policy for Space Activities" (*Pour une politique juridique des activités spatiales*), edited by La Documentation Française, Paris 2006.

Senate (Sénat):
- Mr. Henri Revol's report, on behalf of the Economics Affairs Commission, January 15th 2008, n° 161 et n° 328 (2007-2008).

National Assembly (*Assemblée Nationale*):
- Mr. Pierre Lasbordes's report, on behalf of the Economics Affairs Commission, April 2nd 2008, n° 775.

ANNEX 2.3

Decree 2009-643 of 9th June, 2009 on authorization issued in accordance with SOA 2008 (Authorization Decree)

Decree 2009-643 of 9th June, 2009 on authorization issued in accordance with SOA 2008 (Authorization Decree)

Minister of Higher Education and Research

Decree n°2009-643 of 9th June 2009 On the authorizations issued in accordance with French Act no. 2008-518 of 3rd June 2008 relative to space operations

The Prime Minister,
On the basis of the report drafted by the Minister of Higher Education and Research,
Having regard for the environment code, in particular article L.161-1;
Having regard for the money and finance code, in particular articles L. 431-7 to L. 431-7-5;
Having regard for the code of criminal procedure, in particular article 28;
Having regard for the code of research, in particular Book III, Title III, Chapter 1;
Having regard for Act no. 2008-518 of 3rd June 2008 on space operations;
Having regard for decree no. 84-510 of 28th June 1984 relative to the Centre National d'Etudes Spatiales (French space agency);
Having regard for decree no. 97-1189 of 19 December 1997 applying to the Minister of Education, Research and Technology section 1° of article 2 of decree no. 97-34 of 1st January 1997 on the devolution of individual administrative decisions;
Having regard for the opinion of the advisory committee on financial legislation and regulations of 1st April 2009.
Having heard the Council of State (public works department),
Decrees:

TITLE I: AUTHORIZATION and LICENSE

Chapter I: Authorization procedure

Article 1
The authorizations provided for in articles 2 and 3 of the above-mentioned Act of 3rd June 2008 are issued by the Minister responsible for space who formulates the technical regulation provided for in section one of article 4 of the same Act.
Authorization applications are sent to the Minister in three copies, by post or electronically. Such application consists of two parts;

I. – An administrative part comprising;
1° For a private individual: surname, first name (s) and address; for a legal entity: company name, legal form, head office address and the capacity of the person signing the application;
2° Information demonstrating the existence of moral, financial and professional guarantees of the applicant. In this respect, the applicant must furnish proof of:
    - its worthiness and particularly the lack of any personal bankruptcy of the private individuals conducting the space operation,
    - the company's financial situation and terms of governance,
    - quality management systems applied in the company,
    - staff qualification and training policies;
3° If any, the license certifying that the space operator has the moral, financial and professional guarantees referred to in section three of article 4 of the above-mentioned Act of 3rd June 2008. In this case, the applicant shall only furnish the documents listed in 1° and 2° above which were not sent for the license application;
4° The details of all financial guarantees contemplated for the operation, namely the type and amount thereof and the time required to create them.

II. – A technical part comprising:
1° A description of the space operation to be conducted and of the systems and procedures that the applicant intends to implement;
2° A file to be prepared in accordance with an order made by the Minister responsible for space according to the type of operation contemplated, and which includes all or part of the following:
    a) The general notification of compliance with the technical regulations;
    b) The internal standards and quality management provisions applicable to the space operation to be conducted;
    c) All the measures, including surveys of hazards and risk control plans, taken by the applicant to guarantee the safety of people and property and to protect public health and the environment;
    d) The environmental impact studies and measures designed to avoid, reduce or offset the harmful effects on the environment, including;
        - the risk prevention plan relating to risks caused by the fall-back of the space object or fragments thereof,

- the prevention plan relating to environmental damage, as defined in article L.161-1 of the environment code,
- the space debris limitation plan,
- the collision prevention plan,
- as applicable, the nuclear safety plan,
- as applicable, the planetary protection plan;

e) The risk control measures planned during the performance of the space operation;

f) The emergency measures planned.

3° If any, the license certifying the conformity of the systems and procedures stipulated in section three of article 4 of the above-mentioned Act of 3rd June 2008. In this case, the applicant shall only furnish the documents listed in 1° and 2° above which were not sent for the license application.

Article 2

No later than one month after receiving the full application and, as required, after asking the applicant to complete its application, the Minister responsible for space shall acknowledge receipt informing the applicant of the date of registration thereof.

Article 3

The application shall be transmitted by the Minister in charge of space to the Centre National d'Etudes Spatiales which shall check that the systems and procedures that the applicant intends to implement are compliant with the technical regulation, with a view to the safety of people and property and for public health and environmental protection. It may ask the applicant for further information at any time.

The President of the Centre National d'Etudes Spatiales shall send his opinion to the Minister responsible for space within two months of the date of registration of the application.

If the applicant holds a license listed in section three of article 4 of the above-mentioned Act of 3rd June 2008 certifying the conformity of the systems and procedures, the Centre National d'Etudes Spatiales shall check that the operation for which the authorization application is filed complies with such license. Its opinion must then be given within fifteen days of the date of registration of the application.

Article 4

Prior to making his decision, the Minister shall advise the applicant of the draft order governing its application. The applicant shall then have fifteen days in which to make any observations. These provisions shall not apply when the applicant holds an authorization stipulated in section three of article 4 of the above-mentioned Act of 3rd June 2008 and where the application is examined within the shorter times referred to in articles 3 and 5.

Article 5
The Minister responsible for space shall make his decision within four months of the date of registration of the application stipulated in article 2. He may extend this time limit by two months at the most, by notifying a reasoned decision to the applicant.

When the applicant holds a license stipulated in section three of article 4 of the above-mentioned Act of 3rd June 2008, the time limit referred to in the first sentence of the previous paragraph is one month.

The authorization may be issued together with instructions enacted for the purpose of the safety of people and property, protection of public health, of the environment and of the interests of national defense as well as to ensure that France fulfils its international undertakings. Such instructions shall namely set out the manner in which the agents authorized as provided for in article 7 of the above-mentioned Act of 3rd June 2008 monitor the preparation of the operation, particularly the technical stage of the preparation.

The authorization shall be issued for the entire length of the space operation in question. However, if the operation has not commenced within ten years of the date of award of the authorization, the latter shall lapse and the operator must file another application.

Article 6
If, in support of an application to have a space object launched, a French operator furnishes the launch authorization obtained by the operator responsible for launching said space object, it shall not be required to furnish the technical part described in II of article 1 of this decree.

In the case provided for in the previous paragraph, the authorization to have the object launched shall be deemed granted if the Minister responsible for space has not replied within a month of the date of registration of the application.

Article 7
If, subsequent to the authorization being issued, the operator makes use of or has knowledge of events not foreseen for by the authorization or of technical mishaps affecting the conditions of the space operation as authorized, it shall promptly inform the Centre National d'Etudes Spatiales thereof.

The latter may, after consulting or following a proposal by the operator, suggest to the minister corrective measures to be made to the authorization granted. After allowing the operator to put forward any observations, the minister may alter the authorization accordingly and notify the operator of his decision.

If, despite these possible corrective measures, the events or technical incidents referred to in the first paragraph substantially increase the risks relating to the safety of people and property and to public health and the environment, the minister, on the proposal of the Centre National d'Etudes Spatiales, shall ask the operator to file a new application. The initial authorization shall remain in force until the new decision made by the Minister responsible for space has been notified.

If the Centre National d'Etudes Spatiales believes that there is no need to alter the authorization granted, it shall advise the minister accordingly who shall inform the applicant of his decision.

Chapter II: Licenses

Article 8

The licenses referred to in section three of article 4 of the above-mentioned Act of 3rd June 2008 are awarded in the manner stipulated for the authorizations in Chapter I of this decree.

A license shall be valid for ten years at the most. The minister may, by means of a reasoned decision, grant a license for a shorter amount of time than the requested duration.

Article 9

The licenses stipulated in the second sentence of section three of Article 4 of the above-mentioned Act of 3rd June 2008 may certify all or part of the compliance of the systems and procedures planned by the space operator with the technical regulation.

Article 10

Applications for license carrying authorization for certain operations shall include a precise description of each type of operation in question. Any operation which does not fit the description contained in that license must give rise to an authorization in the manner set forth in Chapter 1 above.

The holder of a license carrying valid authorization for certain operations shall inform the Minister responsible for space one month before the performance of any operation referred to in said license. When, owing to the urgency, these provisions cannot be observed, the operator shall prove to the minister, as soon as possible, the need for the operation and the reasons for his decision.

Article 11

Any person responsible for designing or developing a system or a sub-system that is critical having regard for the safety of people and property and the protection of public health and the environment within the meaning of the technical regulation provided for in paragraph one of article 4 of the above-mentioned Act of 3rd June 2008, intended to be used as part of a space operation, may submit a file to the Centre National d'Etudes Spatiales describing the general technical characteristics and the development plan, so as to enable the centre to certify its compliance, in whole or in part, with the above-mentioned technical regulation.

The Centre National d'Etudes Spatiales shall recommend the inspections, tests and analyses required by the technical regulation. At the end of this examination, the President of the Centre shall give the tenderer, for each step in the development carried out, a document certifying the compliance of the critical system or sub-system with the technical regulation and such documents may be produced in support of an authorization application filed in the manner set forth in Chapter 1 above.

The documents certifying such compliance shall not carry authorization for the purposes of article 2 of the above-mentioned Act of 3rd June 2008. They do not prejudge the compliance of said system or sub-system with the technical regulation for any use outside the framework contemplated in the technical file submitted for the space operation in question.

Chapter III: Operations conducted out of the territory of a foreign State or from means or facilities placed under the jurisdiction of a foreign government

Article 12

When the authorization application relates to an operation to be conducted from the territory of a foreign State or from means or facilities placed under the jurisdiction of a foreign government, the applicant shall, as applicable, furnish all the information needed to assess the existence of the guarantees referred to in section 4° of article 4 of the above-mentioned Act of 3rd June 2008 which exempt it from all or part of the compliance control provided for in the first paragraph of the same article.

In the manner set forth in article 5, the Minister shall inform the applicant of his decision, either to grant the exemption sought, or the reasons for his decision to deny it.

Chapter IV: Space object control

Article 13

Any authorization to control a space object is granted for all the technical operations necessary for such control, whether they are performed by the operator itself or by one or more of the individuals acting under its authority, in particular stationing and station-keeping maneuvers, as well as orbital and de-orbiting maneuvers.

Article 14

I. – The authorization to transfer the control of a space object set forth in paragraph 1 of Article 3 of the above-mentioned Act of 3rd June 2008 is granted by the Minister responsible for space upon submission of a joint application by the operator controlling the space object and the receiving operator, subject to the provisions of point II hereinafter.

The application shall stipulate the nature of the space object to be transferred and shall include, as regards the receiving operator, the documents listed in points I and II of Article 1, or, in the event that the operator has one, the license set forth in Article 4 of the above-mentioned Act of 3rd June 2008.

The Minister responsible for space shall make a decision within a month of the date of receipt of the application stipulated in Article 2.

II. – Concerning transfers for which the receiving operator is not subject to the provisions of the above-mentioned Act of 3rd June 2008, the transfer authorization application shall be submitted by the operator controlling the space object; it shall specify the nature of the space object to be transferred and shall include the documents proving that the receiving operator is not subject to the provisions of the above-mentioned Act and furnishing all guarantees that the space object to be transferred shall be registered after the transfer and that the transfer shall be notified to the Secretary General of the United Nations Organization.

Chapter V: Authorization or license withdrawal

Article 15

The authorization or license granted pursuant to this decree may be withdrawn by the Minister responsible for space;

1°   In the event of misrepresentation or false information;
2°   Where maintaining it is likely to jeopardize national defense or the fulfillment by France of its international undertakings;
3°   In the event of failure to comply with any requirements of the license or authorization;
4°   Where the conditions to which the authorization or license is subject are no longer met.

The authorization or license may only be withdrawn when the holder thereof has been able to make its observations within a period of thirty days.

TITLE II: Financial GUARANTEES

Article 16

The financial guarantees provided for in Article 6 of the above-mentioned Act of 3rd June 2008 shall be furnished by means of a written commitment from a credit institution or an insurance company, a joint and several guarantor, a first-demand guarantee or liquid assets.

The operator shall send the Minister responsible for space a document furnishing proof of the financial guarantees before the commencement of the space operation.

Article 17
The Minister responsible for space and the budget minister may jointly decide to exempt the operator, for a limited period of time, from the obligation set forth in point I of Article 6 of the above-mentioned Act of 3rd June 2008, if it is impossible, given the situation of the insurance market, to be covered by an insurance policy or to furnish one of the financial guarantees stipulated in Article 16 hereof.
The operator shall furnish a document proving its solvency in its exemption application.

Article 18
The Minister responsible for space may exempt the operator from the obligation set forth in point I of Article 6 of the above-mentioned Act of 3rd June 2008 where the planned operation includes the station-keeping of a satellite on the geostationary orbit for a determined length of time. During that time, the operator is not required to have one of the financial guarantees or insurance covers provided for in Article 16 hereof. Whenever the orbit or orbit position changes or upon any other maneuver terminating the satellite station-keeping, the operator must be able to furnish proof of the obligation set forth in Article 6 of the above-mentioned Act of 3rd June 2008 in the manner provided for in Article 16 hereof.
In this case, and as soon as the space operation is performed, the operator shall submit a document proving its solvency to the Minister responsible for space.

TITLE III: INSPECTIONS

Article 19
By way of an order, the Minister responsible for space shall, from the civil servants and agents under his authority and the agents of the Centre National d'Etudes Spatiales, appoint the individuals authorized to proceed with the inspections provided for in Article 7 of the above-mentioned Act of 3rd June 2008. The order shall specify the purpose and duration of the appointment.

Article 20
The agents referred to in Article 1 hereof may, after notification has been given by the State Prosecutor to the Regional Court of Justice having competent jurisdiction in their administrative place of residence, be authorized by way of an order by the Minister responsible for space to investigate and report the breaches provided for in chapter IV of the above-mentioned Act of 3rd June 2008.
The order shall specify the purpose and duration of the authorization.
The agents referred to in section 1 shall take an oath before the Regional Court of Justice of competent jurisdiction in their administrative place of residence.

The oath shall be as follows: "I swear and promise to properly and faithfully assume my role and to fulfill all the relevant duties inherent therein. I further swear not to disclose or use the information brought to my knowledge in the performance of my duties."

Article 21

The authorizations provided for in this decree may be revoked by an order of the Minister responsible for space and, as applicable, for individuals acting under his authority, on request from the President of the Centre National d'Etudes Spatiales, where such a measure is justified by service requirements or given the behavior of the civil servant or agent in the performance of his duties. In the latter case, the individual in question must have been given the opportunity to make his observations.

Article 22

A business card mentioning such an authorization, as well as the purpose and duration thereof, shall be issued either by the Minister responsible for space or by the President of the Centre National d'Etudes Spatiales to the civil servants and agents respectively under their authority.

The template of the business card shall be drawn up by the above-mentioned authorities respectively for the individual(s) of their concern.

The oath-taking shall be indicated on the card.

Article 23

The matter considered in the last sentence of Points II and IV of Article 7 of the above-mentioned Act of 3rd June 2008, is referred to the magistrate by the Minister responsible for space or the President of the Centre National d'Etudes Spatiales. He shall give a decision by reasoned order, in accordance with the provisions of Articles 7 and 7-1 of the same law. Representation is not compulsory as part of such proceedings.

TITLE IV: TRANSITIONAL PROVISIONS

Article 24

The provisions hereof come into effect one year after the publication of the order specifying the technical regulation referred to in section 1 of Article 4 of the above-mentioned Act of 3rd June 2008 and no later than eighteen months after the publication hereof.

Article 25

Paragraph 2 "Research" of Title II of the Appendix to the above-mentioned decree of 19th December 1997 is completed with the following section:

Space operation authorization Suspension or withdrawal of space operation authorization	Decree No. 2009- 643 of 9th June 2009 relating to the permits granted in accordance with Act No. 2008-518 of 3rd June 2008 on space operations.

Article 26

The Keeper of the Seals, Minister of Justice, the Minister of Higher Education and Research and the Minister responsible for the Budget, Public Accounts and the Civil Service are each responsible, as far as they are concerned, for enforcing this decree that shall be published in the French Republic Official Journal.

ANNEX 2.4

Decree 2009-644 of 9th June, amending the 1984 CNES' Decree (CNES Decree)

Decree 2009-644 of 9th June 2009 amending the 1984 CNES' Decree (CNES Decree)

Minister of Higher Education and Research

Decree n°2009-644 of 9th June 2009 amending decree no. 84-510 of 28th June 1984 relating to the Centre National d'Etudes Spatiales (CNES)

The Prime Minister,
On the basis of the report drafted by the Minister of Higher Education and Research,
Having regard for the Convention of 14th January 1975 on the registration of space objects launched into outer space,
Having regard for the Research Code, in particular articles L. 331-6 and L. 331-8;
Having regard for the Defense Code, in particular articles R.* 1311-1 to R.* 1311-10, R.* 1311-34 and R.* 1311-37;
Having regard for Act No. 2008-518 of 3rd June 2008 relating to space operations, in particular articles 12 and 21;
Having regard for decree no. 84-510 of 28th June 1984 relating to the Centre National d'Etudes Spatiales;
Having regard for decree no. 89-314 of 16th May 1989 relating to the coordination of safety measures during space launches in French Guiana;
Having regard for decree no. 2004-374 of 29th April 2004 relating to the prefects' powers, to the organization and to the action of Government services in the regions and *départements*;
Having heard the Council of State (public works department),
Decrees:

Article 1
After Article 14 of the above-mentioned decree of 28th June 1984, a title III, a title IV and a title V are inserted as follows:

"TITLE III

"**Provisions relating to the keeping of the space object register by the Centre National d'Etudes Spatiales**

"*Art.14-1.* – To fulfill the assignment entrusted to the Centre National d'Etudes Spatiales by Article 12 of Act No. 2008-518 of 3rd June 2008 relating to space operations, any space operator within the meaning of Article 1 of the above-mentioned Act shall furnish the Centre National d'Etudes Spatiales with the information necessary to identify the space object, the list of which is determined by an order[1] made by the Minister responsible for space.

"*Art.14-2.* – The operator shall send this information to the Centre National d'Etudes Spatiales no later than sixty days after the launch.

"*Art.14-3.* – The Centre National d'Etudes Spatiales shall allocate a register number for each earth-orbiting space object or space object launched beyond the Earth, and enter it on the national register.

"*Art.14-4.* – Any change to the information provided for in Article 15 of this decree shall be sent immediately by the relevant operator to the Centre National d'Etudes Spatiales, which shall enter the change on the national register.

"*Art. 14-15.* – The register is public and may be freely consulted upon request sent to the Centre National d'Etudes Spatiales. However, the information concerning the identification of the owner or manufacturer of the space object and any real or personal warrants on the same is only disclosed with the prior consent of the interested parties.

"*Art. 14-6.* – The Centre National d'Etudes Spatiales shall send the Minister of Foreign affairs the information taken from the register required by the convention of 14th January 1975 on the registration of space objects launched into outer space. It shall inform him of any event affecting the life in orbit of the space object entered on the register, in particular the de-orbiting, the end of the operation or the loss of the space object.

"The Minister of Foreign Affairs shall send this information to the Secretary General of the United Nations Organization.

"TITLE IV:

"**Powers of the president of the Centre National d'Etudes Spatiales at the Guiana Space Centre**

"*Art. 14-7.* – The powers specified in Article L. 331-6 of the Research Code are conferred upon the president of the Centre National d'Etudes Spatiales and are exercised on all the facilities operated or owned by any individual or legal entity, be it public or private, within

---

1 Order August 12th, 2011, JORF n°0208 September 8th 2011

the perimeter of the Guiana Space Centre, established by an order of the Minister responsible for space.

"The president of the Centre National d'Etudes Spatiales shall be immediately informed by any person referred to in the previous section of any fact, incident or accident relating to the assignments he has under Article L. 331-6 of the above-mentioned code. He shall immediately inform the Government representative in the French *département* thereof.

"Chapter I: "Safety mission

"*Art.14-8.* – Without prejudice to the prefect's police powers, in particular concerning listed facilities in the frame of public and environmental protection law, the president of the Centre National d'Etudes Spatiales shall be responsible for the special safety of the Guiana Space Centre under the provisions of paragraph I of Article L. 331-6 of the Research Code.

"To that end, he shall enact the safety actions applicable to the facilities located within the perimeter of the Guiana Space Centre, in particular as regards the activities of designing, preparing, producing, storing and transporting space objects and their constitutive parts, as well as the tests and operations performed within the perimeter or out of the Guiana Space Centre.

"Therefore, he shall formulate in particular:
- the plan relating to the layout of the facilities, roads and networks located on the site of the Guiana Space Centre;
- the rules governing the access of individuals and vehicles to the Guiana Space Centre and to the facilities within its perimeter, as well as the rules governing the movement of individuals and vehicles within the site of the Guiana Space Centre;
- the specific rules applicable on the ground and in flight relating to the safety of people, property and the environment for the activities carried out for each launch, as well as the safety procedures applied to ensure that the activities referred to in section 2 of this article comply with those rules;
- the areas to be protected during launching operations and the acceptable limits of the air corridor;
- the meteorological conditions in which launching operations can be carried out and the corresponding actions;
- the applicable rules concerning the neutralization of launchers and the corresponding actions.

Where exercising one of the activities referred to in section 2 of this article involves a serious risk for life or property or for the protection of the environment or public health, the president of the Centre National d'Etudes Spatiales may take any measures consisting in prohibiting, suspending or stopping the said activity; he may ask for the facility or area in which the activity in question is carried out to be evacuated.

"*Art. 14-9.* – The president of the Centre National d'Etudes Spatiales may issue an administrative fine of an amount equal to that set for Class 5 offences against any individual or legal entity referred to in Article 15-6 carrying out an activity in breach of the regulation set forth in Article 15-8 without prejudice to the legal sanctions provided for by other regulations.

"Where the breaches are particularly serious, the president may suspend the activity in question after giving the interested party prior notice. In the event of an emergency, he may suspend the activity in question without notice.

"*Art. 14-10.* – Breaches shall give rise to written reports drawn up by the agents stipulated in Article 14-15.

"The reports shall be notified to the individual in question by any means being convincing proof and they shall mention the penalties incurred.

"The individual in question may access all of the information in his/her file. He/she must be allowed to be heard by the president of the Centre National d'Etudes Spatiales or by the person appointed thereby for that purpose. He/she may be represented or assisted by the person of their choice.

"No fine may be decided more than two years after establishing a breach.

"Fines and suspension measures must be the result of a reasoned decision sent to the individual in question by any means being convincing proof. Fines shall be collected in the manner set forth for the collection of Government debts unrelated to tax and property.

"**Chapter 2 – "Safety and security measure coordination**

"*Art. 14-11.* – To exercise the coordination powers specified in II of Article L. 3316 and conferred upon him, the president of the Centre National d'Etudes Spatiales shall act under the authority of the Government representative in French Guiana to perform his tasks relating to safety and security of the facilities and the activities carried out at the Guiana Space Centre.

"*Art. 14-12.* – The president of the Centre National d'Etudes Spatiales shall coordinate:
- "the preparation and transmission to the competent authorities of files within the framework of the procedures specific to each regulation;
- "the preparation with the individuals referred to in Article 14-7 of the inspections by the competent authorities which he shall be asked to attend. The individuals referred to in Article 14-7 shall keep him informed of the results of these inspections and, as applicable, of the manner in which they fulfill the resulting obligations;
- "the notification to the competent authorities of any breach of the obligations relating to safety and security of which he has knowledge.

"He shall take part in the preparation and application of measures taken by the Government representative in French Guiana to whom he reports to prohibit, suspend or stop an activity and to evacuate an area or facility.

"He shall coordinate the drafting of the emergency plans specific to each facility, he shall draft the emergency plans for the entire Guiana Space Centre, and he shall implement the relevant means. He shall report thereon to the Government representative in French Guiana.

"*Art. 14-13.* – The president of the Centre National d'Etudes Spatiales shall, under the authority of the Government representative in French Guiana, take measures to protect the facilities and the scientific and technical assets inside the facilities against malicious intent.

"*Art. 14-14.* – "He shall centralize and coordinate the information provided by the operators relating to the risks of the facilities and their operation, in particular as part of the consultation boards provided for by other regulations.

"**Chapter 3 – "Terms and conditions of inspection**

"*Art. 14-15.* – The president of the Centre National d'Etudes Spatiales may empower the agents under his authority to conduct the inspections necessary to fulfill the assignments as provided in Article L. 331-6 of the Research Code.

They shall, as applicable, inform the president of the Centre National d'Etudes Spatiales of any problem likely to affect the accomplishment of these assignments.

"*Art. 14-16.* – In accordance with the provisions of Article L. 331-8 of the Research Code, the president of the Centre National d'Etudes Spatiales may delegate a part of the powers provided for in Article L. 331-6 to the director of the Guiana Space Centre, and to the individuals responsible for safety and security of the Guiana Space Centre.

"TITLE V

"**Emergency measures necessary for the safety of people and property and for the protection of public health and the environment**

"*Art.14-17.* – When he exercises the powers provided for in Article L. 331-7 of the Research Code, the president of the Centre National d'Etudes Spatiales may delegate his signing authority by way of an order.

Article 2

The Minister of Foreign and European affairs, the Minister of the Interior, Overseas territories and Local governments, and the Minister for Higher education and Research are each responsible, as far as they are concerned, for enforcing this decree that shall be published in the French Republic Official Journal.

ANNEX 2.5

Decree 2009-640 of 9th June, 2009 on Space-Based Data (SBD Decree)

Decree no. 2009-640 of 9 June 2009 applying the provisions of Title VII of act no. 2008-518 of 3 June 2008 on space operations
NOR: PRMX0830 126D

The Prime Minister,

On receipt of the report of the Minister of Higher Education and Research and the Minister of Defence,
Having regard to the penal code and particularly articles 413-9 et seqq;
Having regard to act no. 78-753 of 17 July 1978 as amended, on various measures to improve relations between the Civil Service and the public and on various arrangements of an administrative, social or fiscal nature, especially article 6;
Having regard to act no. 2000-321 of 12 April 2000 as amended, on citizens' rights in relations with the Civil Service;
Having regard to act no. 2008-518 of 3 June 2008 on space operations, especially articles 1 and 23 to 27;
Having regard to decree no. 97-34 of 15 January 1997 on the devolution of individual administrative decisions, last amended by decree no. 2007-139 of 1 February 2007;
Having regard to decree no. 97-1184 of 19 December 1997 for application to the Prime Minister of point 1 of article 2 of decree no. 97-34 of 15 January 1997 on the devolution of individual administrative decisions;
Having regard to decree no. 98-608 of 17 July 1998 on the protection of national defence secrets;
Having heard the Council of State (public works section),
Decrees:

Article 1
Data from panchromatic optical sensors, multispectral optical sensors, stereoscopic optical sensors, infrared sensors and radar sensors whose resolution and precision are set by decree are considered to be "space data" subject to a prior declaration by the primary operator to an administrative authority with a view to application of Title VII of the abovementioned act of 3 June 2008

Article 2
The administrative authority mentioned in article 23 of the abovementioned act of 3 June 2008 is the Secretary General for National Defence.

Article 3.
The declaration mentioned in article 1 shall be addressed to the administrative authority at least two months prior to processing. The declaration form and list of documents to be provided by the declarant are defined by order of the Prime Minister.
Should the administrative authority consider the declaration non-compliant or incomplete, it shall ask the declarant to rectify or complete its declaration.
Prior to declaration, the primary space data operator shall have been cleared to process the classified information it may receive in compliance with the abovementioned decree of 17 July 1998.

Article 4.
The administrative authority shall acknowledge receipt of the declaration and, if necessary, give the declarant a copy of the restrictive measures taken in compliance with article 5 below.
Any planned change in the operating mode shall be subject to an additional declaration by the primary operator at least two months prior to this change.

Article 5.
To safeguard the interests mentioned in article 24 of the abovementioned act of 3 June 2008, the Secretary General for National Defence can decide, following consultation of an interministerial committee whose tasks, composition and organization are set by decree, to apply restrictive measures to the declared activities. If urgent, the opinion of committee members may, if necessary, be received by mail or e-mail. These measures may, in particular, consist of the:
- immediate total or partial suspension of imagery programming or reception for a renewable temporary period;
- requirement to postpone the programming, reception or production of imagery for a renewable temporary period;
- permanent ban on programming or reception;
- limitation of the data's technical quality;
- geographical limitation of coverage areas.

Decisions on restrictive measures may be protected as per the provisions relating to the protection of national defence secrets.

The administrative authority shall inform the interministerial committee members of decisions taken.

Article 6.

The annex provided for in the abovementioned decree of 19 December 1997 is completed thus:

"Decisions relating to the activity of primary space data operators provided for by articles 23 to 25 of act no. 2008-518 of 3 June 2008 on space operations."

Article 7.

The Minister of Higher Education and Research and the Minister of Defence are tasked, each for his/her part, with the implementation of the present decree, to be published in the Official Gazette of the French Republic.

Signed in Paris on 9 June 2009.
François Fillon

Prime Minister:
Minister of Higher Education and Research,
Valérie Pécresse
Minister of Defence,
Hervé Morin

Annex 2.6

Order of 31st March, 2011 on Technical Regulation (RT)

Order of 31st March 2001 on Technical Regulation (RT)

Order of 31st of March, 2011 on Technical Regulation implementing decree No. 2009-643 of 9th June, 2009 on the authorizations issued in accordance with act No. 2008-518 of 3rd June, 2008 Relative to Space Operations
NOR: *ESRR1103737A*

The Ministry for Higher Education and Research,

Having regard to the Research Code, in particular chapter 1 of part III of book III;
Having regard Act no. 2008-518 of 3rd June 2008 concerning space operations, as amended;
Having regard to decree no. 2009-643 of 9th June 2009 concerning licenses issued pursuant to the Act of 3rd June 2008 concerning space operations, in particular its article 1;

Orders:

PART ONE: DEFINITIONS AND PRELIMINARY PROVISIONS

Article 1– Definitions
The following definitions are used in this decree:

"**Allocation**": level of probability given to the occurrence of a critical or specified event, when determining the safety objectives;
"**Catastrophic damage**": immediate or deferred loss of human life, or serious human injury (bodily injuries, other irreversible health impairments, occupational invalidity or illness, either permanent or temporary);
"**Controlled re-entry**": atmospheric re-entry of a space object with a predefined contact or ground impact zone for the object or fragments thereof;
"**Disposal phase**": final phase of the space operation during which the space object is made safe in order to limit the risks related to space debris.;
"**End of life**": end of the disposal phase of the space object or loss of control of it;
"**Flight corridor**": volume within which the launch vehicle is liable to fly and outside of which it is neutralised;

"**Hazard level**": probabilistic estimate characterising the "lack of safety" of a system with regard to a critical event, expressed by the probability of occurrence of this event;
"**Irreversible moment**": for a launch operation, time at which the last order leading to launch vehicle lift-off is sent;
"**Launch vehicle**": assembly comprising the launcher and the space objects intended to be placed into orbit.
"**Neutralisation**": action taken on the launcher in order to minimise damage to individuals and property. It can in particular be characterised by an action to destroy or stop the thrust of a launch vehicle, in order to terminate the flight of the considered vehicle or a stage which is no longer functioning correctly;
"**Nominal**": corresponding to the specifications or performance levels announced by the operator or designer of the space object;
"**On-board neutralisation device**": on-board means involved in neutralising the launch vehicle in flight;
"**Operational phase**": period of time which, during an operation involving control in extra-atmospheric space, begins at the moment the operator takes control of the space object and ends with the beginning of the disposal phase;
"**Procedure**": specified way of carrying out an activity or process;
"**Process**": Set of correlated or interactive activities which transform input elements into output elements;
"**Protected regions**":
1) protected region A, low Earth orbit (LEO) – spherical region extending from the surface of the Earth up to an altitude (Z) of 2,000 km;
2) protected region B, geosynchronous region – segment of the spherical envelope defined as follows:
    - lower limit = geostationary altitude minus 200 km
    - upper limit = geostationary altitude plus 200 km
    - -15 degrees ≤ latitude ≤ +15 degrees
    - geostationary altitude " (Z GEO) = 35,786 km (altitude of geostationary terrestrial orbit);

"**Return**": period which starts at re-entry of the space object into the Earth's atmosphere and ends when it is immobilised on the ground, as part of a controlled or uncontrolled re-entry;
"**Safety**": set of arrangements intended to control risks in order to ensure protection of people, property and public health and the environment.
"**Safety coefficient**": the ratio between the allowable limit of a parameter characterising a system or an element and its maximum expected value in nominal operation. Its value includes the scattering specific to each field concerned;

"**Safety margin**": margin between the allowable limit of a parameter characterising a system or an element and its maximum value reached in normal operation, multiplied by the safety coefficient;

"**Space debris**": any non-functional human made object, including fragments and elements thereof, in Earth orbit or re-entering the Earth's atmosphere;

"**Space object**": any human made object, functional or not, during its launch time, its time spent in extra-atmospheric space or its return, including the elements of a launcher placed into orbit;

"**Space system**": arrangement consisting of one or more space objects and the associated equipment and installations needed to perform a specified mission. With regard to a launch operation, the space system contains the launcher, the interfaced launch base, including the tracking stations, and the space object to be launched. With regard to a control operation, the space system consists of the space object and the interfaced ground segment.

"**Technical hazard**": hazard of technological, industrial, operational, man-made or natural origin. Expression used to differentiate between a technical hazard and all other types of hazards, in particular financial or related to installations safety;

"**Uncontrolled re-entry**": atmospheric re-entry of a space object for which it is not possible to predefine the ground impact zone by the object or fragments thereof.;

Article 2 – Preliminary provisions
1. The purpose of this order is to specify the technical regulation on the basis of which the Minister in charge of space, following a conformity verification by the Centre national d'études spatiales (CNES), grants an authorization to carry out a space operation, pursuant to the above-mentioned Act of 3rd June 2008.
2. The provisions of this order apply to the space operations mentioned in articles 2 and 3 of the above-mentioned Act of 3rd June 2008, except those for which the conformity verification is waived in the conditions of paragraph 4 of article 4 of the above-mentioned Act.
3. The provisions of this order apply only:
   a) to a launch operation which meets all of the following criteria:
      – lift-off from the ground;
      – rocket propulsion;
      – unmanned flight.
   b) to an operation to control an unmanned space object in extra-atmospheric space;
   c) to an operation to return an unmanned space object to Earth.

   The technical regulation applicable to the space operations not mentioned above, will be the subject of a specific order.

Compliance with the requirements of this order may in no way relieve the operator of its liability for any damage caused to third parties, as specified in article 13 of the above-mentioned Act of 3rd June 2008.

4. Personnel who, pursuant to article 7 of the above-mentioned Act of 3rd June 2008, are authorised to verify compliance with the provisions stipulated with reference to these technical regulation and appended to the licensing order, are placed under the authority of the President of the Centre national d'études spatiales in the conditions stipulated in the order to authorise them.

PART TWO: LAUNCH OF A SPACE OBJECT

SECTION I: SCOPE

Article 3
The provisions of this part apply to the launch operation, up until the end-of-life of the stages and launcher elements.

SECTION II: TECHNICAL FILE

Chapter 1 – Required documentation

Article 4 – Description of the space operation and systems and procedures
The description of the space operation and systems and procedures mentioned in II.1° of article 1 of the above-mentioned decree of 9th June 2009 presents the components of the launch system, the characteristics of the space object to be launched and the intended mission.

Article 5 – General notice of conformity
1. In accordance with II.2°a) of article 1 of the above-mentioned decree of 9th June 2009, the launch operator establishes a general notice of conformity with this technical regulation.
2. This general notice of conformity:
   - identifies the documents supplied in accordance with articles 6 to 10 of this order;
   - establishes the resulting conformity.

Article 6 – Internal standards and quality management provisions
In accordance with II.2°b) of article 1 of the above-mentioned decree of 9th June 2009, the launch operator produces documents justifying compliance with the requirements of chapter 2 of this section.

Article 7 – Hazard study

In accordance with II.2°c) of article 1 of the above-mentioned decree of 9th June 2009, the launch operator carries out a study of the potential hazards involved in the planned space operation.

This study includes a description of all the hazards related to the operation in nominal and accidental operating situations, whether their cause is internal or external. The study specifies the nature and scope of the possible consequences of all these operating situations. When dealing with elements of the launch vehicle which are returned or which fall-back and are liable to reach the ground, the study presents the components of these elements, stating their dimensions, masses and materials used.

The launch operator must therefore:
- demonstrate compliance with the requirements of article 20 of this order, with regard to the risk of injury to individuals;
- evaluate the effects of any accidents on public health and the environment.

This study must cover the following events, in the conditions stipulated in chapter 3 of this section:
- damage linked to fallback of elements designed to separate from the launcher;
- damage linked to controlled or uncontrolled re-entry of launcher elements placed in earth orbit;
- damage linked to failure of the launch vehicle;
- collision with manned space objects, for which the orbital parameters are precisely known and available;
- damage linked to explosion of a stage in orbit;
- collision with a celestial body.

The study must present an exhaustive analysis of the causes and consequences, as well as the probabilities of the above-mentioned critical events. The risk reduction measures such as to comply with the requirements of articles 18 to 26 of this order are listed in the risk management plans laid out in article 9 of this order.

Article 8 – Impact assessment

In accordance with II.2°d) of article 1 of the above-mentioned decree of 9th June 2009, the launch operator carries out an environmental impact assessment for the planned operation. During nominal operation of the launch system, the impact assessment must cover the impact of the planned operation on the environment and on public health, having regard to the provisions of article L 161-1 of the Environment Code, as well as the impact in terms of generation of space debris, in accordance with the provisions of article 21 of this order. This impact assessment takes account of:

- working motor phases, in particular characterisation of the nature and quantification of the rates of atmospheric and extra-atmospheric combustion products during the powered flight;
- fall-back of launcher elements, in particular the characterisation of the nature and quantification of the products falling back on land, sea or onto a celestial body.

This assessment also covers the impact of:
- the production of space debris;
- as applicable, the carriage of radioactive materials on-board the launch vehicle.

Article 9 – Hazard management measures

In accordance with II.2°e) of article 1 of the above-mentioned decree of 9th June 2009, and on the basis of the conclusions of the hazard and impact assessments mentioned in articles 7 and 8 above, the launch operator draws up and implements the following hazard management plans:
- the environmental damage prevention plan, which lists the steps taken to mitigate the negative environmental impacts identified in the impact assessment mentioned in article 8 of this order, except for those concerning the space debris limitation and nuclear safety;
- the space debris limitation plan, demonstrating compliance with the requirements of article 21 of this order;
- the prevention plan concerning hazards resulting from the fall-back of space objects or fragments thereof, demonstrating compliance with the requirements of articles 20, 23 and 24 of this order;
- the prevention plan concerning the risks of collision, demonstrating compliance with the requirements of article 22 of this order;
- as applicable, the nuclear safety plan, demonstrating compliance with the requirements of article 25 of this order;
- as applicable, the planetary protection plan, demonstrating compliance with the requirements of article 26 of this order.

Article 10 – Emergency measures

In accordance with II.2°f) of article 1 of the above-mentioned decree of 9th June 2009, the launch operator lists the emergency measures planned and the organisation implemented for the protection of human safety.

This list must in particular include the means necessary for implementing paragraph 3 of article 23 of this order.

ANNEX 2.6

Chapter 2 – Quality system requirements

Article 11 – Quality assurance

1. When carrying out the space operation, the launch operator must implement and manage a quality management system as well as internal standards and quality management requirements in conformity with article 1 of the above-mentioned decree of 9th June 2009. This management system must cover quality assurance, dependability and safety (RAMS : reliability, availability, maintainability, safety), configuration management and supervision of work.
2. The space system must be designed, produced, integrated and implemented in such a way as to control the hazards induced by the critical activities. An activity is said to be critical if a human error or failure of the resources employed increases the risk of human injury during the launch operation.
3. A system for monitoring and controlling any drift in manufacturing and implementation must be installed. This system should allow traceability of technical and organisational events affecting engineering and production activities.
4. The quality management system in particular deals with the following technical or organisational events:
    – deviations (anomalies, evolutions) in relation to the configuration (definition, launch system production and implementation process) which has been subject of the authorization or, as applicable, the license,
    – deviations (anomalies, evolutions) resulting from exploitation of parameters recorded in-flight, likely challenging the conditions in which the authorization or, as applicable, the license, was granted.
5. The description and justification of launcher behavior, and the definition of the materials used, must be retained until the end of the space operation concerned. Following it, these elements are transmitted to the Centre national d'études spatiales with the description of the state reached.

Article 12 – Competence, resources, organisation and installations

The launch operator must have the competence, resources and organisation necessary for preparing and implementing the planned launch operation:
– appropriate installations and organisation,
– equipment and tools appropriate to the planned operation,
– documentation concerning tasks and procedures,
– access to data of use for preparation of the planned operation,
– recording, analysis and archival of technical data,
– key jobs and associated training process.

Article 13 – Technical visibility
The launch operator must set up an organisation enabling it, in compliance with article 7 of the above-mentioned decree of 9th June 2009 and without delay, to inform the Centre national d'études spatiales of any technical or organisational events as mentioned in the 4th paragraph of article 11 of this order.

Article 14 – Technical reviews
1. Technical reviews to check implementation of the provisions of this order must be scheduled by the launch operator. These reviews can also be carried out as a part of reviews conducted elsewhere.
2. The launch operator must inform the Centre national d'études spatiales of the reviews prior to launch. The personnel qualified in compliance with article 7 of the above-mentioned Act of 3rd June 2008 may attend them in the conditions laid down in the same article.

Article 15 – Co-contractors, subcontractors and customers
The launch operator must ensure that its co-contractors, subcontractors and customers apply the provisions required for establishing and maintaining conformity with these technical regulation.
1. The launch operator must, under its own responsibility, ensure that the above-mentioned persons apply the provisions relating to organisation, quality assurance and engineering as stipulated by the standards and practices acknowledged by the profession.
2. The launch operator must, under its own responsibility, ensure that its customers apply the provisions such as to guarantee compatibility (geometrical, mechanical, dynamic, thermal, electromagnetic and radioelectric) between the space objects to be placed in orbit and the launch system, and must check that this has been taken into account.

Chapter 3 – Specific technical requirements for the launch operations

Sub-section 1 – General technical requirements linked to the launch operation

Article 16 – Required proof
1. To ensure technical control of the system and procedures with respect to the critical events mentioned in article 7 of this order, the launch operator must furnish proof of:
   a) the technical standards framework utilised;
   b) consideration of the climatic environment in which the system is operated;
   c) the ability of the launch system and its subsystems to perform the mission. This includes:
      – description, dimensions;

- tests and/or modelling, readjustment and precision of the associated models, which must highlight the interfaces and interactions between the different subsystems and between the different disciplines;
- the safety coefficients and safety margins;
- the parameters of the ground launch resources interfacing with the launcher (surveillance thresholds);

d) the management and reproducibility, as necessary, of the industrial manufacturing, inspection and deployment processes;

e) incorporation into the design of RAMS analyses, including reliability assessments and identification of critical points;

f) incorporation of measures resulting from the launch system hazard analyses and operational hazard analyses;

g) incorporation of experience feedback from processing of technical events during development, production, testing and flight;

h) scenarios for fragmentation and generation of space debris at re-entry or neutralisation of the launch vehicle.

2. The proof mentioned in the first paragraph above must be provided in each of the following cases:
   - flight envelope (nominal case, case with uncertainties associated with dispersion and lack of data);
   - extreme envelope;
   - non-nominal cases (failures).

   Said proof must cover:
   - all system life of the system;
   - all stabilised and transitional phases encountered.

3. The proof must concern:
   a) characterisation of the launch vehicle nominal and extreme movements envelope (free movement with six degrees of freedom of the launcher);
   b) demonstration of launcher reliability within this envelope, in particular:
      - proof of its mechanical strength (propulsion systems, main structures and subsystem);
      - proof of the performance of the propulsion and pyrotechnical systems;
      - proof of the performance of the flight control systems (in particular electrical and hydraulic systems and software);
      - as required, the reliability of the on-board neutralisation system and its effect on the fall-back areas.

c) mechanical characterisation specific to the launcher break-up studies:
   - determination of the minimum value in terms of incidence and dynamic pressure guaranteeing structural break-up;
   - determination of fragmentation (number of debris pieces, geometry, mass, characteristics of materials) of all or part of the launch vehicle, depending on the mechanical or thermal origin of the destruction scenarios.
d) the following analyses concerning ground operations:
   - analysis of the chronology of the launch operation, demonstrating that the expected status is reached at the irreversible moment;
   - analysis of the harmlessness of the preparation operations for the reliability of the launch vehicle during the launch operations, based on an analysis of all the manufacturing, integration and inspection processes carried out directly by man or remotely via an instrumentation and control system.

Article 17 – Specific mission analysis
In addition to the proof specified in article 16 of this order, relating to generic justification of the launch system for a given mission family, the launch operator must furnish the following, elements inherent in the planned operation:
1. demonstration of compliance with the operating envelope of the launch vehicle;
2. demonstration of the compatibility of the objects intended to be placed in orbit with the launch vehicle environments (geometrical, mechanical, dynamic, thermal, electromagnetic and radioelectric);
3. determination of the load levels on the launch vehicle, including the space objects intended to be launched (dynamic and thermal loads);
4. demonstration that the actual characteristics of the specific launcher used for the mission are in conformity with the theoretical definition presented in compliance with article 16 of this order;
5. as applicable, proof that the deviations (anomalies, evolutions) in relation to the configuration which was licensed, in accordance with the requirements of article 16 of this order (definition, production process, implementation) and those resulting from utilisation of the parameters recorded in-flight, are analysed and made technically acceptable;
6. proof of the specific mission trajectory, optimised with respect to the potential hazards;
7. definition of the flight corridor around the nominal trajectory, up to orbital injection;
8. the sizing and position of the fall-back zones for the elements not placed in orbit, including with regard to notification of air and maritime traffic;
9. definition of the end-of-life choices for the elements placed in orbit in compliance with the requirements of article 20 and paragraphs 4, 5, 6 and 7 of article 21 of this order and, as applicable, determination of the fall-back zones;

10. validation of the customized parameters for flight control and the flight software, tailored to the mission, such as to be able to furnish proof of correct working of the flight software;
11. with regard to the launch vehicle on-board automatic neutralisation systems, as applicable:
    - definition of the settings based on analysis of simulated non-nominal trajectories;
    - sizing and positioning of the fall-back zones following neutralisation;
    - validation of the flight software specific algorithm thresholds allowing neutralisation of the launch vehicle, in order to demonstrate correct operation.

Article 18 – On-board neutralisation systems

For the launch phase:

An exhaustive study of the failure scenarios at the origin of abnormal situations leading the launch vehicle to become a hazard must be carried out by the launch operator, in particular in the following cases:
- deviation from the predetermined flight corridor,
- dangerous fallback of elements designed to separate,
- non-nominal behaviour of flight control,
- failure to place the upper composite into orbit.

This study must give qualitative and quantitative proof of the need or otherwise for on-board automatic systems in order to neutralise the launch vehicle before the moment at which the impact zone is tangent to the territorial waters of the first State encountered along the nominal trajectory. If such resources prove to be necessary, this study must define them as well as the elements required by article 17 of this order.

For controlled re-entry:

An exhaustive study of the failure scenarios at the origin of abnormal situations leading for the propulsion element of the launcher placed in orbit to become a hazard must be carried out by the launch operator, in particular in the case of failure to control the level or direction of thrust.

This study must present the on-board automatic systems for ensuring controlled re-entry of the propulsion element placed in orbit.

Article 19 – Flight tracking and associated experience feedback

The launch vehicle operating parameters, including its positions and speeds, which have an impact on risk management as resulting from the studies mentioned in articles 7 and 8 of this order must be acquired, transmitted to the ground, recorded and analysed by the launch operator. Any deviation of these parameters from the expected reference state constitutes a technical event which must be subsequently analysed for any recurring launch system.

Sub-section 2 – Quantitative objectives for human safety

Article 20 – Quantitative objectives for human safety
1. For the cumulative catastrophic damage risks, the launch operator must respect the following quantitative objectives, expressed as a maximum allowable probability of causing at least one casualty (collective risk):
   a) Lift-off risk
      – $2*10^{-5}$ for the entire launch phase, including consideration of degraded launch system situations and fall-back of elements designed to separate from the launcher without being placed in orbit,
      – 10^{-7} by nominal fall-back of those elements designed to separate from the launcher without being placed in orbit, in accordance with paragraph 1 of article 23 of this order.
   b) Re-entry risk
      – $2*10^{-5}$ for the return phase of each launcher element placed in orbit, in a controlled atmospheric re-entry, including – in accordance with 1 of article 23 of this order – a specific allocation of 10^{-7} for nominal return of the element. The launch operator implements this controlled re-entry in accordance with paragraphs 1 and 5 of article 21 of this order.
      – If the impossibility of a controlled atmospheric re-entry as specified above can be duly proven, the launch operator must do it its best efforts to meet a quantitative objective of 10^{-4} for the return phase of each launch element placed in orbit. In this case, the choice of the architecture and materials of the elements placed in orbit and subject to uncontrolled re-entry must be justified with respect to the objective of limiting the number and energy (kinetic and explosive) of the fragments liable to reach the ground.
2. the requirements mentioned in the first paragraph above must be evaluated using a calculation method taking account of:
   – all the phenomena leading to a risk of catastrophic damage (ascent phase, stage fall-back after separation, atmospheric re-entry of a stage placed in orbit);
   – the trajectories before fragmentation (atmospheric or extra-atmospheric), depending on the flight times and failures considered;
   – the scenarios for fragmentation and generation of the corresponding debris, at re-entry or at neutralization of the launch vehicle;
   – dispersion of debris on the ground and evaluation of their effects;
   – launcher reliability for the launch phase;

- the reliability of the de-orbiting maneuver for the launcher propulsion element placed in orbit, in the case of controlled re-entry.
3. Specific quantitative allocations for a risk of particular catastrophic damage may be specified, in compliance with the objectives mentioned in the first paragraph of this article, in accordance with article 5 of the above-mentioned decree of 9th June 2009.

Sub-section 3 – Space debris limitation and prevention of collision risks

Article 21 – Space debris limitation
The launch system implemented by the launch operator must be designed, produced and implemented such as to comply with the following requirements for the elements operating in extra-atmospheric space:
1. The launcher must be designed, produced and implemented in such a way as to minimise the production of debris during nominal operations, including after the end-of-life of the launcher and its component parts. The launch operator in particular takes the following measures in this respect:
   - for launch of a single space object, a single launcher element (for example a stage) may be placed in orbit;
   - for launch of several space objects, a maximum of two launcher elements (for example a stage or the adapter structure) may be placed in orbit.
   - The above requirements do not apply:
   - to pyrotechnic systems. The largest dimension of any products generated must be less than 1 mm;
   - to solid propellant boosters. The size of any combustion debris generated in protected region B must be less than 1 mm. With regard to the design and operation of solid propellant boosters, the launch operator takes steps to avoid placing solid combustion products in long-term orbit which could contaminate protected region A.
2. The launcher must be designed, produced and implemented so that the debris produced in compliance with the requirements of the first paragraph above and which do manage to reach the surface of the Earth, constitute no excessive risk for individuals, property, public health or the environment, in particular as a result of environmental pollution by hazardous substances.
3. The probability of occurrence of accidental break-up must be less than 10^{-3} until the end-of-life of the space object. This calculation must include failure modes of propulsion and power systems, mechanisms and structures but does not take account of any external impacts.
Intentional fragmentations of launcher elements are prohibited.

4. The launcher must be designed, produced and implemented so that, following the disposal phase:
   - all the on-board energy reserves are permanently depleted or placed in a state such that depletion of the on-board energy reserves is inevitable, or in such a condition that they entail no risk of generating debris;
   - all the means for producing energy production means are permanently deactivated.
5. The launcher must be designed, produced and implemented so that, after the end of the launch phase, its components placed in orbits passing through protected region A are de-orbited by controlled atmospheric re-entry.
   If the impossibility of meeting this requirement can be duly proven, the launcher must be designed, produced and implemented so that its components are no longer present in protected region A twenty-five years after the end of the launch phase. This result is preferably achieved by uncontrolled atmospheric re-entry or, failing that by placing them to an orbit for which the perigee remains above protected region A for one hundred years following the end of the operation.
6. The launcher must be designed, produced and implemented so that, after the end of the launch phase, its components stationed in an orbit in or passing through protected region B, are placed in an orbit which does not interfere with this region for more than one year. This orbit must be such that, under the effect of natural disturbances, the launcher or its components do not return to protected region B within one hundred years following the end of the operation.
7. The probability of successfully completing the disposal maneuvers mentioned in paragraphs 4, 5 and 6 above must be at least 0.9. This probability is evaluated for the total duration of the operation. Its calculation, carried out before the beginning of the space operation, must take account of all the systems, subsystems and equipment usable for these maneuvers, their redundancy levels as applicable and their reliability, taking account of the effects of the ageing reached at the time for which their use is scheduled, along with the availability of the means and energy resources necessary for these maneuvers.

Article 22 – Prevention of risks of collision

The systems must be designed, produced and implemented and their mission defined so that, during the space operation and the three days following the end of the disposal phase, the risks of accidental collision with manned objects for which the orbital parameters are accurately known and available are limited.

Sub-section 4 – Requirements related to fall-back to Earth

Article 23 – Prevention of risks arising from fall-back by the launcher or fragments thereof

1. If the launcher comprises elements designed to separate during the launch phase, or in the case of the propulsion element placed in orbit for controlled atmospheric re-entry, the fall-back zone on Earth must be controlled by the launch operator. The fall-back zone, associated with a probability of 99.999%, must not impinge on the territory, including the territorial waters, of any State, without its agreement. The launch operator thus implements the following measures:
   - takes account of the trajectories before fragmentation (atmospheric or extra-atmospheric), depending on the moments of stage separation and taking account of operating dispersions of the launch vehicle subsystems;
   - modelling of the scenarios covering fragmentation and the corresponding generation of debris;
   - analysis of dispersion of the debris falling on the sea.
2. In the event of a fall-back zone being situated in a region with heavy maritime traffic (mainly shipping lanes) or in which fixed and manned oil platforms are located, a special analysis must be carried out to deal with the hazards described in article 7 of this order.
3. The organisation and resources put into place by the launch operator must enable the President of the Centre national d'études spatiales or the Minister with responsibility for space:
   - to inform the competent authorities in charge of air and maritime traffic control of the fall-back zones in a nominal situation, specifying the zones receiving 99% of these fall-backs;
   - without delay to transmit to the competent authorities the information concerning the fall-back zone of elements, so that the authorities of the states concerned can be warned as early as possible of any non-nominal situation;
   - to provide all useful information at its disposal so that the necessary response plans can be determined and implemented by the competent authorities.

Article 24– Wrecks and recovery of launcher elements

1. All launchers must be designed, produced and implemented so that the propulsion stages designed to fall back to Earth do not constitute a technical hazard following the creation of a maritime wreck. Wrecks must not constitute or threaten to constitute an obstacle or hazard for navigation, fishing, or the environment, or a shipping hazard or obstacle in a port, approach channel or road.

2. When the stages are to be recovered, their neutralisation system must be inhibited in the event of nominal separation, but must function in the event of uncommanded separation or stage break-up. It must be possible to make this system safe before any recovery operation.

Sub-section 5 – Particular hazards

Article 25 – Nuclear safety
Any launch operator intending to transport radioactive materials on-board the launch vehicle conforms to the applicable regulation in force and demonstrates application thereof in the nuclear safety plan required in II.2°d) of article 1 of the above-mentioned decree of 9th June 2009.

Article 26 – Planetary protection
Any launch operator conducting a launch to another celestial body, whether or not including the return of extraterrestrial materials, must comply with the international "Planetary protection policy" standard published by the *Committee on Space Research* (COSPAR) for implementation of article IX of the Treaty on Principles Governing the Activities of States in the Exploration and Use of Outer Space, Including the Moon and Other Celestial Bodies and demonstrate application thereof in the planetary protection plan required in II.2°d) of article 1 of the above-mentioned decree of 9th June 2009.

Chapter 4 – Technical requirements concerning the launch site

Article 27
1. For operations run from the Guiana Space Centre, the launcher must be designed and produced to ensure compatibility with the systems and procedures contained in the order constituting the special policing regulation issued by the President of the Centre national d'études spatiales.
2. For operations run from another launch site and subject to the waivers granted under article 4.4 of the above-mentioned Act of 3rd June 2008, the operator:
    – furnishes proof of the existence of the systems and procedures specific to said site, in particular concerning positioning, neutralisation and telemetry, designed to protect individuals, property, public health and the environment during the course of the operation;
    – furnishes proof of the compatibility of the above-mentioned systems and procedures with the requirements of this order;
    – demonstrates that the launcher is designed and produced to ensure compatibility with the above-mentioned systems and procedures.

ANNEX 2.6

PART THREE: Command *(or Control)* and RETURN to earth of a space object

SECTION I: SCOPE

Article 28
The provisions of this part do not apply to the control and return of stages and launcher elements covered by the provisions of the second part of this order.

SECTION II: TECHNICAL FILE

Chapter 1 – Documentation to be provided

Article 29 – Description of the space operation and associated systems and procedures
The description of the space operation and the implemented systems and procedures as mentioned in II.1° of article 1 of the above-mentioned decree of 9th June 2009 presents the space system used for the planned operation, consisting of the ground segment and the space object. This description also presents the various subsystems of said object.

When dealing with space object performing re-entry at end of life, the description presents the platform and payload components, as well as their equipment, able to reach the ground, stating the dimensions, masses and materials used.

This description comprises a mission analysis presenting the reference orbit, the means of attaining it (injection, station acquisition) and maintaining it (station-keeping) with the associated space and time coordinates, the measures for reconstructing the orbit with the intended degree of precision, the ability to control the object (existence and visibility of ground stations or relay satellites, of the control centre or on-board autonomous capability), as well as the disposal strategy. It states the space system models used to perform this mission analysis.

This description comprises the control capability covered by article 39 of this order.

Article 30 – General notice of conformity
1. In accordance with II.2°a) of article 1 of the above-mentioned decree of 9th June 2009, the operator establishes a general notice of conformity with this technical regulation.
2. This general notice of conformity:
   – identifies the documents supplied under articles 31 to 34 and 47 and 48 of this order;
   – establishes the resulting status of conformity.

Article 31 – Internal standards and quality management provisions
In accordance with II.2°b) of article 1 of the above-mentioned decree of 9th June 2009, the operator produces documents proving compliance with the requirements of chapter 2 of this section.

Article 32 – Hazard Study
In accordance with II.2°c) of article 1 of the above-mentioned decree of 9th June 2009, the operator carries out a study of the potential hazards of the planned space operation for individuals, property, the environment and public health, in particular hazards related to the generation of space debris.
This study includes a description of all the hazards relating to the operation in the case of both nominal and accidental operating situations, whether the cause is internal or external in nature, and specifies the nature and scope of the consequences.

This study must in particular cover the following events, in the conditions laid out in chapters 3 and 4 of this section:
- human injury caused by a re-entry to Earth,
- production of space debris following an explosion,
- collision with a manned space object,
- injection in a degraded orbit leading to premature re-entry,
- collision with a satellite in geostationary orbit, whose orbital parameters are precisely known and available, during station acquisition, repositioning or disposal maneuvers,
- dispersion of radioactive material,
- planetary contamination.

The contents of the hazards study must be commensurate with the severity and probability of occurrence of the critical events liable to be caused by the planned operation.

Article 33 – Impact assessment
In accordance with II.2°d) of article 1 of the above-mentioned decree of 9th June 2009, the operator carries out an assessment of the impact of the planned operation on the Earth's environment, as well as the impact in terms of generation of space debris, in compliance with the provisions of article 40 of this order.
This impact assessment, for nominal operation, identifies and evaluates the environmental impacts of the operation and the measures taken to mitigate any negative impacts. This impact assessment in particular identifies debris created or liable to be created by deployment of the space object. The content of this impact assessment must be commensurate with the foreseeable incidence and the direct or indirect, temporary or permanent effects of the planned operation on the environment.

Article 34 – Risk management measures

In accordance with II.2°e) of article 1 of the above-mentioned decree of 9th June 2009, and on the basis of the conclusions of the hazard study and impact assessment mentioned in articles 32 and 33 above, the operator draws up and implements the following risk management plans:
- the space debris limitation plan, demonstrating compliance with the requirements of article 40 of this order;
- the environmental damage prevention plan, demonstrating that the materials and energy sources chosen for the space object are not such as to create environmental damage, as well as compliance with paragraph 2 of article 45;
- the prevention plan concerning hazards resulting from the fallback of a space object or fragments thereof, demonstrating compliance with the provisions of articles 44 to 46 of this order;
- the prevention plan concerning the risks of collision, demonstrating compliance with the requirements of article 41 of this order;
- as applicable, the nuclear safety plan, demonstrating compliance with the requirements of article 42 of this order;
- as applicable, the planetary protection plan, demonstrating compliance with the requirements of article 43 of this order.

Chapter 2 – Quality system requirements

Article 35 – Competence, resources, organisation and installations

1. For performance of the space operation, the operator must implement and manage a quality management system as well as internal standards and quality management provisions in conformity with article 1 of the above-mentioned decree of 9th June 2009. This management system must cover quality assurance, dependability and safety, configuration management and supervision of work.
2. It must have the competence, resources and organisation necessary for preparing and implementing the planned operation:
   - appropriate installations and organisation,
   - equipment and tools and material appropriate to the planned operation,
   - documentation concerning tasks and procedures,
   - access to data of use for preparation of the planned operation,
   - recording, processing and archival of technical data,
   - key posts and associated training process.
3. The description and justification of the critical components of the space object with regard to protection of individuals, property, the environment and public health, in particular with regard to the production of space debris, and the definition of the

materials used, must be kept until the end of the space operation concerned. After the disposal manoeuvres, these elements are sent to the Centre national d'études spatiales with a description of the state attained.

Article 36 – Technical and organisational events
The operator must set up an organisation enabling it:
- during the preparation and performance of the space operation, to identify and deal with all technical and organisational events liable to affect the conditions of the space operation as authorised, in particular the disposal strategy;
- as specified in article 7 of the above-mentioned decree of 9th June 2009, to inform the Centre national d'études spatiales without delay of all these technical and organisational events.

Article 37 – Technical reviews
Key points defined to check implementation of the provisions of this order must be scheduled by the operator. The operator must inform the Centre national d'études spatiales of the key points prior to launch and to initiation of the space object disposal manoeuvres.

Article 38 – Co-contractors and subcontractors
1. The operator must ensure that its co-contractors and subcontractors apply all the measures necessary for establishing and maintaining conformity with this technical regulation.
2. The operator must ensure that the persons mentioned above apply the provisions relating to organisation, quality assurance and engineering in compliance with the standards and practices acknowledged by the profession.

Chapter 3 – Specific technical requirements common to control in orbit and return to Earth of a space object

Article 39 – Ability to "command" (control) the space object
The object must be designed, produced and implemented in such a way that the operator, for the duration of the operation, can receive information about its status and send it commands, in particular those necessary for implementation of articles 47 and 48 of this order.

Article 40 –Space debris limitation
The systems implemented by the operator must be designed, produced and implemented such as to comply with the following requirements:
1. The systems must be designed, produced and implemented so as to avoid generating debris during nominal operations of the space object.
   The above requirement does not apply:
   - to pyrotechnic systems. The largest dimension of any products they generate must however be less than 1 mm;
   - to solid propellant boosters. The size of any combustion debris they generate in protected region B must however be less than 1 mm. With regard to the design and operation of solid propellant boosters, the operator implements measures allowing to avoid placing durably in orbit solid combustion products which could contaminate protected region A.
2. The probability of occurrence of accidental break-up must be less than 10^{-3} until the end of life of the space object. This calculation must include failure modes of propulsion and power systems, mechanisms and structures, but does not take into account external impacts.
   If a situation leading to such a failure is detected, the operator must be able to schedule and implement corrective measures to prevent any break-up.
3. The systems must be designed, produced and implemented so that, following the disposal phase:
   - all the on-board energy reserves are permanently depleted or placed in such a condition that they entail no risk of generating debris,
   - all the means for producing energy on-board are permanently deactivated.
4. The systems must be designed, produced and implemented so that, once the space object has completed its operational phase in an orbit passing through protected region A, the space object is de-orbited with controlled atmospheric re-entry.
   If the impossibility of meeting this requirement can be duly proven, it must be designed, produced and implemented so that it is no longer present in protected region A twenty-five years after the end of the operational phase. This result is preferably achieved by uncontrolled atmospheric re-entry or, failing that, by placing in a stable orbit for which the perigee remains above protected region A for one hundred years following the end of the operation.
5. The space object must be designed, produced and implemented so that, once it has completed its operational phase in an orbit in or passing through protected region B, it is placed in an orbit which does not interfere with this region. This orbit must be such that, under the effect of natural disturbances, the object does not return to protected region B within one hundred years following the end of the operation.

6. The probability of having sufficient energy resources to successfully carry out the disposal maneuvers mentioned in paragraphs 3, 4 and 5 above must be at least 0.9.
7. The operator must evaluate the probability of being able to successfully carry out the disposal maneuvers mentioned in paragraphs 3, 4 and 5 above. This evaluation, which does not include the availability of energy resources, must be made by the operator for the total duration of the operation and take account of all systems, subsystems and equipments usable for these maneuvers, their level of redundancy, if any, and their reliability, taking account of the effects of the ageing reached at the time they are scheduled to be carried out.

Article 41 – Prevention of risks of collision
The systems must be designed, produced and implemented and their mission defined so that during the space operation and the three days following the end of the operation, the risks of accidental collision with manned objects and satellites in geostationary orbit for which the orbital parameters are precisely known and available is limited.

Article 42 – Nnuclear safety
Any operator intending to utilise radioactive materials on-board the space object conforms to the applicable regulation in force and demonstrates application thereof in the nuclear safety plan required in article 1 of the above-mentioned decree of 9th June 2009.

Article 43 – Planetary protection
Any operator intending to conduct a mission to another celestial body, whether or not including the return of extraterrestrial materials, must comply with the international "Planetary protection policy" standard published by the *Committee on Space Research* (COSPAR) for implementation of article IX of the Treaty on Principles Governing the Activities of States in the Exploration and Use of Outer Space, Including the Moon and Other Celestial Bodies. The operator demonstrates implementation thereof in the planetary protection plan required by article 1 of the above-mentioned decree of 9th June 2009.

Chapter 4 – Specific technical requirements for the return of a space object

Article 44 – Quantitative human safety objectives for return of a space object to Earth
1. With regard to the return of a space object, the quantitative safety objectives, expressed as the maximum probability of causing at least one casualty (collective risk) are defined as follows:
    - $2*10^{-5}$ for return of an integral object;
    - $2*10^{-5}$ for controlled atmospheric re-entry with destruction of the space object;

- If it can be duly proven that controlled atmospheric re-entry with destruction of the space object as mentioned above is impossible, the operator must do its best efforts to meet a quantitative objective of 10^{-4} for uncontrolled re-entry with destruction of the space object.
2. The provisions mentioned in the first paragraph above must be evaluated using a calculation method based on:
    - consideration of all phenomena leading to a risk of catastrophic damage;
    - consideration of the trajectories before fragmentation;
    - modelling of the fragmentation and debris generation scenarios corresponding to re-entry;
    - dispersion of the debris on the ground and evaluation of their effects;
    - consideration of the reliability of the space object.
3. These objectives comprise the risk associated with nominal return of the object or fragments thereof as well as that associated with non-nominal cases. These objectives in no way prejudice the provisions of articles 42 and 45 of this order.

Article 45 – Requirements concerning uncontrolled re-entry of an end-of-life space object

1. The choice of architecture and materials of the space objects undergoing uncontrolled re-entry must be justified with the aim of limiting the number and energy (kinetic and explosive) of the fragments liable to reach the ground.
2. The systems must be designed, produced and implemented so that the elements which manage to reach the surface of the Earth entail no unacceptable risk for individuals, property, public health or the environment, in particular through pollution of the environment by hazardous substances.

Article 46 – Prevention of risks arising from fall-back of the space object or fragments thereof during controlled re-entry

1. The operator determines the fall-back zones of the space object and fragments thereof for any controlled atmospheric re-entry to Earth, associated with a probability of 99% and 99.999% respectively. These fall-back zones must take account of the uncertainties linked to the re-entry parameters.
2. The fall-back zone associated with a probability of 99.999% should not impinge on the territory, including the territorial waters, of any State, without its agreement.
   In the event of a fall-back zone being situated in a region with heavy maritime traffic (mainly shipping lanes) or in which fixed and manned oil platforms are located, a special analysis must be carried out within the hazards study described in article 32 of this order.

3. The organisation and resources put into place by the operator must enable the President of the Centre national d'études spatiales:
   - to inform the competent authorities in charge of air and maritime traffic control of the fall-back zones in a nominal situation, specifying the zones receiving 99% of these fall-backs;
   - to transmit to the competent authorities the information concerning the fall-back zone of elements in any non-nominal situation, so that the authorities of the states concerned can be warned as early as possible;
   - to provide all useful information at its disposal so that the necessary response plans can be determined and implemented by the competent authorities.

SECTION III: OBLIGATIONS RELATED TO PERFORMANCE OF THE SPACE OPERATION

Article 47 – Non-nominal re-entries
In the case of premature or accidental re-entry, the operator as a priority implements all measures such as to reduce the risk on the ground.

Article 48 – Status of the space object
1. The operator keeps an up-to-date status demonstrating the ability of the space object to perform the disposal maneuvers specified in paragraphs 3, 4 and 5 of article 40 of this order and in particular the availability of the energy resources needed for this maneuvers. This status is transmitted to the Centre national d'études spatiales whenever an event affecting this capacity occurs.
2. The space object status attained following the disposal operations will be transmitted to the Centre national d'études spatiales.

Article 49 – Intentional destruction
1. The operator must avoid the intentional destruction of any space object in orbit.
2. When the operator intends to proceed with intentional destruction, it notifies the President of the Centre national d'études spatiales of the need to do so. This destruction may only take place at altitudes that are low enough to limit the lifetime in orbit of the fragments produced.

ANNEX 2.6

PART FOUR: PRELIMINARY CONFORMITY WITH THE TECHNICAL REGULATION

SECTION I: SCOPE

Article 50
Under article 11 of the above-mentioned decree of 9th June 2009, the following critical systems and subsystems may be submitted to the Centre national d'études spatiales:
- the space system;
- the space object;
- the space object platform, associated with a monitoring and controlling system as applicable;
- the propulsion subsystem of a space object;
- the launch installations of a space object.

Article 51
The file stipulated in the first paragraph of article 11 of the above-mentioned decree of 9th June 2009 is created in accordance with the requirements of article 50 of this order. It is submitted to the Centre national d'études spatiales during development of the system or subsystem concerned, and no earlier than the end of the preliminary design phase.

The document certifying preliminary conformity with this technical regulation may be issued by the Centre national d'études spatiales following the following design and development steps of the system or subsystems:
- preliminary design;
- detailed design;
- production and ground testing designed to check compliance with the requirements of this order for the system or subsystem concerned;
- qualification.

SECTION II: PROCEDURE FOR ISSUE OF THE DOCUMENT CERTIFYING CONFORMITY

Article 52 – Documents to be provided
1. For a launch system, and depending on the system concerned, the bidder supplies all or some of the documents specified in articles 4 to 10 of this order.
   For a launch system propulsion subsystem, the Centre national d'études spatiales draws up the list of documents to be supplied and the associated schedule, after supplying

the development plan stipulated in the first paragraph of article 11 of the above-mentioned decree of 9th June 2009.
2. For a space system other than a launch system, and depending on the system concerned, the bidder supplies all or part of the documents stipulated in articles 29 to 34 of this order.

Article 53 – Checks, tests and analyses
On the basis of the items supplied pursuant to article 52 of this order, the Centre national d'études spatiales specifies all the checks, tests and analyses as provided for in the second paragraph of article 11 of the above-mentioned decree of 9th June 2009.
With regard to a launch system, these requests can also concern compatibility with the systems and procedures of the site from which the space operation is carried out.

PART FIVE: GUIDE OF GOOD PRACTICES
SINGLE SECTION

Article 54
1. A guide of good practices is drawn up by the Centre national d'études spatiales, jointly with the profession, through a working group representative of the operators and industrial firms concerned, in order to characterise certain practices in force, that help to demonstrate compliance with these technical regulation.
   This guide is based on practices validated by the experience acquired in the development, operation and inspection of space systems. It is in particular based on standards, technical specifications constituting standards, and standards recognised by the profession relating to the safety of life, property, public health and the environment within the context of space operations. The contents of this guide comply with the applicable requirements for protection of intellectual property as well as industrial and scientific assets.
2. Conformity with all or part of the requirements of this technical regulation is assumed to be acquired if the operator can demonstrate compliance with the relevant recommendations of this guide.
   The use of the guide of good practices is neither mandatory nor exclusive.

PART SIX: INTERIM AND FINAL PROVISIONS

Article 55 – Interim provisions
1. For space object launch operations, the following interim provisions are implemented:
   a) The authorization application files for launch operations using a launch system which was operated for the first time from French territory before 4th June 2008

can refer to the technical files already examined by the Centre national d'études spatiales, in particular within the framework of existing international agreements, especially those concluded with or through the European Space Agency.

In this case, the requirements of paragraph 6 of article 21 of this order do not apply. If it can be duly proven that the requirements of paragraph 5 of article 21 of this order cannot be implemented, the launch operator will do everything it can to approach the thresholds mentioned.

b) Concerning systems for which the first launch from French territory takes place between 4th June 2008 and 31st December 2011, the requirements of paragraph 6 of article 21 of this order do not apply;

c) Concerning systems for which the first launch from French territory takes place after 31st December 2011, the requirements of this order apply in full.

2. Concerning space object control and return operations, the following interim provisions apply:
   a) For space objects launched before 10th December 2010:
      - with regard to the provisions of articles 32 and 33, the studies will only concern the hazards and impacts associated with the procedures implemented subsequent to 10th December 2010;
      - the provisions of article 38, those of paragraphs 1, 2, 6 and 7 of article 40 and those of article 45 do not apply;
      - with regard to the provisions of paragraphs 3, 4 and 5 of article 40 and those of article 41, the operator must implement the best possible strategy considering the space object definition;
      - with regard to the provisions of article 44, the operator must implement the best possible strategy considering the space object definition and must perform a risk estimate.
   b) For space objects launched between 10th December 2010 and 31st December 2020:
      - the provisions of paragraphs 1 to 2 of article 40 and those of article 45 do not apply;
      - with regard to the provisions of paragraph 3 to 6 of article 40 and those of article 41, the operator must implement the best possible strategy considering the space object definition;
      - with regard to the provisions of article 44, the operator must implement the best possible strategy considering the space object definition and must perform a risk estimate.

Article 56
The President of the Centre national d'études spatiales (CNES), is responsible for the execution of this order, which shall be published in the Official Gazette of the French Republic.

ANNEX 2.7

Order of 9th December, 2010 regulating the operations on CSG facilities (REI)

Order of 9th December 2010 regulating the operation on CSG facilities (REI)

Preamble

The President of the Centre national d'études spatiales (CNES),

Having regard to:

the agreement of 16th December 2008 between the Government of the French Republic and the European Space Agency concerning the Guiana Space Centre and the associated services;

Act 2008-518 of 3rd June 2008 concerning space operations (hereinafter referred to as the "Space Operations Act");

decree 65-388 of 21st May 1965 and its amendment by decree of 25 July 1967 constituting the declaration of public utility and urgency for the performance by the CNES of the work to establish a satellite launch base in French Guiana, along with the relevant acquisition of land for said base;

decree 89-314 of 16th May 1989 as amended, concerning the coordination of safety measures during space launch operations in French Guiana;

the decree of 22nd January 2001 determining the extent of the areas and applicable auxiliary systems in the vicinity of the Kourou (French Guiana) radio centre n° 9730510314 for protection of radio reception against electromagnetic disturbances;

decree 2009-643 of 9th June 2009 concerning the authorisations issued pursuant to Act 2008-518 of 3rd June 2008 concerning space operations;

decree 84-510 of 28th June 1984 concerning the CNES, as amended, in particular by decree 2009-644 of 9th June 2009 (hereinafter referred to as the "CNES decree");

the order of 2nd June 1988 concerning the creation of a regulated area (air traffic) (Guiana Space Centre in Kourou);

the order of 2nd June 2006 setting the list of sectors of activity of vital importance and designating the ministers coordinating said sectors;

the order concerning the technical regulations pursuant to decree 2009-643 of 9th June 2009 concerning the authorisations issued pursuant to Act 2008-518 of 3rd June 2008 concerning space operations (hereinafter referred to as the "technical regulations");

the administrative act of 10th October 1971 concerning the "Îles du Salut" (Salvation Islands).

Orders the following:

PARTIE I – GENERAL REQUIREMENTS

CHAPITRE 1.1 PRELIMINARY REQUIREMENTS

Article 1 – Definitions
Allocation: in accordance with article 1 of the technical regulations, level of probability given to the occurrence of a critical or specified event, during the definition of the safety objectives.
Close-range zone: authorised envelope for launch vehicle movements during the first moments of flight. The close-range zone ends no later than the radio horizon or the range limit of the CNES/CSG TCN.
CNES/Guiana Space Centre (CNES/CSG): establishment or set of establishments belonging to the Centre national d'études spatiales and located within the perimeter of the CSG. It comprises all the facilities and personnel placed under the responsibility or direct authority of the Director of the CSG.
Confined atmosphere: atmosphere in which air renewal may be insufficient for a person to stay in place safely.
Controlled re-entry: in accordance with article 1 of the technical regulations, atmospheric re-entry of a space object with a predefined contact or ground impact zone for the object or fragments thereof.
Coordination instruction: step taken by the President of the CNES as part of his role to coordinate safety measures as laid down in articles 14-11 à 14-14 of the above-mentioned CNES decree.

Danger limit: geographical limit beyond which no danger zone liable to be created by a hazardous system or activity on the ground or in flight should exist. It is the boundary between the protected zone and the unprotected zone.

Danger zone: zone which could be the location of effects liable to cause damage, owing to the proximity of one or more hazardous systems.

Declaring party: any organisation, establishment, operator, client, prime contractor or agent of the above, which intends to build a new facility or modify an existing facility within the CSG perimeter.

Disabling: interruption of the continuity of the potential path of a critical event or a specific function in a hazardous system. Cancellation of disabling requires approval by the safety entity and is called "safety authorisation".

Disposal phase: in accordance with article 1 of the technical regulations, final phase of the space operation during which the space object is made safe in order to limit the risks related to space debris.

Establishment: facilities intended for production and operation activities under the responsibility of a given operator and generally located on the same site, including their equipment and related activities when at least one of the facilities is subject to legislation concerning facilities classified on environmental protection and pyrotechnic safety grounds. This definition is given without prejudice to the qualification given by other legislations (in particular the Labour Code, the Tax Code, the Defence Code, the Environment Code and the Code of Commerce).

Explosive atmosphere: atmosphere liable to become explosive owing to particular local conditions.

Fail Operational (FO): mission capable after a failure.

Fail Safe (FS): safe following a failure. Maintained safety following two independent failures is referred to as FS/FS.

Flight corridor: in accordance with article 1 of the technical regulations, volume within which the launch vehicle is liable to fly and outside of which it is neutralised.

Flight phase of a space object: the different flight phases of a space object are as follows:
- <u>Launch phase</u>: as defined in article 1 of the above-mentioned Space Operations Act;
- <u>Return phase or return</u>: in accordance with article 1 of the technical regulations, period which starts with re-entry of the space object into Earth's atmosphere and ends with its immobilisation on the Earth's surface, whether re-entry is controlled or otherwise.

Formal instruction: official decision taken by the President of the CNES or his representative pursuant to a specific requirement of this present order.

Guiana Space Centre (CSG): technical, industrial and operational complex, the perimeter of which is defined by order of the minister responsible for space, comprising establishments, companies, organisations of various statuses and all resources necessary for the preparation and performance of launch operations. These activities in particular concern the design, preparation, production, storage and transport of space objects and their components, as well as testing and the operations performed within or from this perimeter.

Hazard level: in accordance with article 1 of the technical regulations, probabilistic estimate characterising the "lack of safety" of a system with regard to a critical event, expressed by the probability of occurrence of this event.

Hazard: two-dimensional value associated with a precise circumstance in the life of the system and characterising a critical event according to the severity of its consequences and the probability of its occurrence.

Hazardous activities fall into two categories, depending on how the system status evolves during the course of said activities:
- dynamic phase hazardous activity: hazardous activity during which at least one hazardous element of the system undergoes a state change (in particular mechanical, electrical, pneumatic or chemical) whether intentional or inadvertent;
- static phase hazardous activity: hazardous activity during which no hazardous element of the system undergoes a state change.

Hazardous activity: activity involving one or more hazardous products or systems or taking place in a danger zone.

Hazardous element: component of a hazardous system or part of a system which is capable, in the event of material or human failure, to generate a critical event with catastrophic or severe consequences.

Hazardous product or fluid: product or fluid liable to cause damage owing to its intrinsic properties (mechanical, physical, chemical, biological, nuclear, thermal, etc.), or owing to a reaction with the surrounding environment. This notion in particular includes all hazardous substances and preparations as defined in the regulations in force, refrigerated liquefied neutral gases (nitrogen, helium, etc.) in their capacity as cryogenic fluids, as well as hot fluids.

Hazardous system: system which meets at least one of the following two criteria:
- contains one or more hazardous products or fluids;
- comprises one or more hazardous elements.

Independent: two devices, elements, functions, signals, systems, etc. are said to be independent if they have no common failure mode and if they generate no reciprocal action between each other.

Instantaneous safety factor (Js): ratio between the allowable rupture pressure and the relative pressure attained at the moment considered by the system in question.

Irreversible effects threshold (SEI): threshold defining the zone of significant danger for individuals. The SEI threshold values are defined by the legislation applicable to facilities classified on environmental protection grounds.

Jr: see rupture safety factor.

Js: see instantaneous safety factor.

Jt: see proof-pressure factor.

L.B.B. (Leak Before Burst): failure mode of a pressurised container whose design, for all types of structural faults, limits the risk by ruling out bursting. Only leakage of the fluid and its potential hazards are to be considered in this case.

Lag failure: non-performance of a wanted function.

Launch complex (EL): the facilities necessary for deploying and controlling a type of launcher with a view to its launch. Examples: ARIANE launch complex (ELA), SOYUZ launch complex (ELS), VEGA launch complex (ELV_{ega}).

Launch vehicle: in accordance with article 1 of the technical regulations, assembly comprising the launcher and the space objects intended to be placed in orbit.

Layout master plan: document specified in article 14-8 of the above-mentioned CNES decree concerning CSG land occupancy:
- summarising the regulatory constraints in terms of the safety of people and property, the protection of public health and the environment and the utilisation of equipment linked to the present use of the CSG land and its peripheral zone;
- characterising each zone (launch zone, industrial zone, natural zone);
- determining the potential of the free zones and their foreseeable future uses.

Lead failure: unwanted performance of a function.

Maximum expected service pressure (pms): maximum relative pressure that a container, device or component containing pressurised fluid is liable to experience during its operational life, in its operational environment.

Mean exposure limit value (VME): value of the concentration of a toxic substance in the atmosphere of a workplace, accepted for a maximum personnel exposure period equivalent to the duration of a working shift (8 hours) without health risk. This value is defined by the Labour Code.

Neutralisation chain: on-board equipment used to neutralise the launcher in flight.

Neutralisation system: set of remote-controlled ground systems and on-board neutralisation systems leading to neutralisation of the launch vehicle in flight.

Neutralisation: in accordance with article 1 of the technical regulations, intervention on the launcher designed to protect the safety of people and property and to protect public health and the environment. It can in particular be characterised by an action to destroy or halt the thrust of a launch vehicle, to terminate the flight of said vehicle or a stage which is no longer functioning correctly.

Nominal: corresponding to the specifications or the performance announced by the operator or designer of the space object, in accordance with article 1 of the technical regulations.

Passive safety barrier: safety barrier, the function of which entails no human intervention and no stored energy, in order to rule out any possible lead failure.

Payload contractor: company bound directly or indirectly by a contract to the launch operator and responsible for the preparation and deployment of a payload within the CSG perimeter with a view to its launch.

Payload: object (satellite, probe, etc.) designed to be carried on a launcher for launch into extra-atmospheric space.

Phlegmatisation: reduction of the sensitivity of a material or pyrotechnic device to a given type of external hazard.

Predictive intervention criteria: criteria for launch vehicle neutralisation before the end of the safety and intervention mission as specified in 0 of this order, based on the fact that it would be impossible for the space vehicle to reach a stable orbit in terms of the safety of people and property, taking account of the various failure cases modelled or taking account of the possibility of stages falling back on land.

Proof-pressure factor (Jt): ratio between the proof-pressure and the maximum pressure attained in the presence for a given fluid system.

Proof-pressure test: test involving pressurisation of a system to a specific pressure known as the proof-pressure.

Qualified staff: all qualified individuals, in the conditions stipulated in article 14-15 of the above-mentioned CNES decree, responsible for carrying out the checks required for performance of the duties specified in article L. 331-6 of the Research Code.

Reliability, Availability, Maintainability, Safety study: study which identifies all technical and functional risks, demonstrates that the desired safety objectives have been reached, enables the ranking of risks to be incorporated as of the design stage, along with a check on correct application of risk management measures.

Rupture safety factor (Jr): ratio between the allowable rupture limit of a parameter characterising a system or an element and its maximum expected value in normal operation. For any element of a pressurised fluid system, this is the ratio between the allowable rupture pressure (the allowable rupture pressure is the calculated rupture relative pressure, validated during qualification tests) and the maximum expected pressure in service (hereinafter referred to as "pms").

Safe-life: required duration and number of cycles during which it is proven by testing or analysis that a structure, even if comprising the largest crack that cannot be detected by the means of inspection, will not fail under the expected service load and environment.

Safety (general mission): in accordance with article 21 of the above-mentioned Space Operations Act and chapter I of part IV of the above-mentioned CNES decree, a set of requirements designed to manage the technical hazards relating to the preparation and performance of launches, to ensure the safety of people and property and to protect public health and the environment, on the ground and in flight.

Safety on the ground

Set of requirements:

- designed to manage technical hazards resulting from activities taking place on the ground and contributing to the flight of a launch vehicle;
- concerning supplements to the applicable safety regulations made necessary by the particular aspects of the site's activities.

<u>Safety in flight</u>

Requirements designed to manage technical hazards during the flight of a launch vehicle controlled from the CSG.

The purpose of these requirements is to ensure the safety of people and property and to protect public health and the environment on the surface of the Earth, concerning aircraft in flight or in atmospheric space, with regard to all damage that could arise from the movements of said vehicle.

Safety (measures): measures concerning the protection of people and facilities as specified by the applicable legislation and regulations and the implementation of which is coordinated by the President of the CNES, as stipulated in article 14-11 of the above-mentioned CNES decree.

Safety barrier: function, product, hardware, software or human intervention designed to prevent the appearance or propagation of an event prejudicial to safety.

This may in particular be:
- a physical property;
- an intrinsic characteristic of the product, hardware or software;
- a technological device.

Exceptionally, and if duly justified, this barrier may consist of a procedure.

The effectiveness of a safety barrier is evaluated on the basis of its reliability.

Safety coefficient: in accordance with article 1 of the technical regulations, the ratio between the allowable limit of a parameter characterising a system or an element and its maximum expected value in nominal operation. Its value includes the scattering specific to each field concerned.

Safety entity: entity within each establishment situated inside the CSG perimeter, which ensures compliance with the safety measures within its establishment and which is the specific point of contact for the qualified staff. This entity is independent of those responsible for production or operation, within this same establishment.

Short-term limit value (VLCT): value of the concentration of a toxic substance in the atmosphere of a workplace, accepted for a maximum personnel exposure period of fifteen minutes without health risk. This value is defined by the Labour Code.

Space object: in accordance with article 1 of the technical regulations, any man made object, functional or not, during launch time, its time spent in extra-atmospheric space or return, including the elements of a launcher placed into orbit.

Space system: in accordance with article 1 of the technical regulations, arrangement consisting of one or more space objects and the associated equipment and installations needed to perform a specified mission. With regard to a launch operation, the space system contains the launcher, the interfaced launch base, including the tracking stations, and the space object to be launched. With regard to a control operation, the space system consists of the space object and the interfaced ground segment.

TCN: remote-control and neutralisation station.

Technical event: any event, whether or not intentional, occurring on hardware or software and liable to create a planned deviation from the original definition, including with regard to de performance (modification), or an unplanned deviation (anomaly).

Technical hazard: in accordance with article 1 of the technical regulations, hazard of technological, industrial, operational, man-made or natural origin. Expression used to differentiate between a technical hazard and all other types of hazards, in particular financial or related to installations safety.

Technical regulations: order from the minister responsible for space, pursuant to article 4 of the above-mentioned Space Operations Act.

Toxic hazardous atmosphere: atmosphere liable to contain substances toxic to humans.

Tracking: remote determination of the variables characteristic of the relative movements of a space object.

Trajectory analysis: determination, recreation and display of the trajectory of a launch vehicle, based in particular on the launcher tracking systems.

Uncontrolled re-entry: in accordance with article 1 of the technical regulations, atmospheric re-entry of a space object for which it is not possible to predefine the ground impact zone by the object or fragments thereof.

Article 2 – Scope

This order is the special police regulations for operation of the Guiana Space Centre (CSG) facilities. It defines the administrative policing measures applicable to the activities conducted within or from the perimeter of the CSG, pursuant to I. of article L.331-6 of the Research Code and articles 14-7 to 14-10 plus 14-15 and 14-16 of the above-mentioned CNES decree, without prejudice to the legislation and regulations applicable elsewhere.

Article 3 – Control procedures

All persons mentioned in article 14-7 of the above-mentioned CNES decree appoint a special contact for the personnel qualified to carry out the controls necessary for performance of the special policing duties for operation of the CSG facilities, in compliance with article 14-15 of the same decree.

The qualified staff have access to the land and premises in the conditions laid down in III. of article L.331-6 of the Research Code.

Their presence is mandatory in the launch centres during the final launch countdown, in order to carry out real-time monitoring of how any particular and unforeseen events involving safety are handled, in close liaison with the representatives designated by the launch operator. The launch operator thus provides the qualified staff with the necessary technical and logistical resources and information.

CHAPITRE 1.2 ORGANISATIONAL AND PROFESSIONAL REQUIREMENTS

Article 4 – General obligations of the installation operators or owners
All persons covered by article 14-7 of the above-mentioned CNES decree are subject to the following obligations:
- manage the configuration of their installations and any changes to it;
- operate and maintain these installations in the required conditions of safety;
- set up a safety unit specific to their establishment, as defined in – Article 1 – of this order;
- immediately inform the President of the CNES of any modification to the equipment, system, configuration, operations plan, procedure, as well as of any technical event, incident or accident, liable, as defined in – Article 21 – and – Article 23 – of this order, to compromise the safety of people and property and the protection of public health and the environment, or generate new hazards.

Article 5 – Organisation, facilities and resources
All persons covered by article 14-7 of the above-mentioned CNES decree must have the expertise and resources necessary for preparing and carrying out the activities they perform, in particular:
- appropriate organisations and facilities concerning manufacture, integration, testing, launch vehicle preparation and performance of the launch operation;
- qualified industrial processes;
- adequate numbers of qualified personnel;
- equipment, tools, software and hardware appropriate to the activity envisaged;
- documentation concerning tasks, responsibilities and procedures;
- access to the data of use for preparation of the activity envisaged;
- recording, operation and archival of the technical data;
- processing of technical events.

Article 6 – Subcontractors, suppliers and customers
All persons covered by article 14-7 of the above-mentioned CNES decree must:
- inform their subcontractors and suppliers of application of this order within the perimeter of the CSG;
- under their responsibility, ensure that their subcontractors and suppliers intervening within the perimeter of their establishment apply the requirements of this order.

The launch operator must also, under its own responsibility, have the requirements of this order applied by its customer and, as applicable, the payload contractor.

PARTIE I. ACCESS AND TRAFFIC RULES

Article 7 – Interface with the facilities safety regulations
The access and traffic regulations stipulated in this order are without prejudice to application of the regulations concerning activities of vital importance, in particular the order of 2nd June 2006 designating space as a sector of activity of vital importance, and of safety measures linked to classification of the Guiana Space Centre as a Restricted Access Establishment by the General Secretariat for Defence and National Security, whereby the majority of the facilities within the CSG perimeter are also classified as Facilities of Vital Importance. These facilities are split up into protected sectors subject to the provisions of articles 413-7 and 413-8 of the Penal Code. The President of the CNES coordinates and ensures the implementation of these regulations in the facilities inside the CSG perimeter and in this respect issues all necessary coordination instructions, in accordance with the requirements of article 14-13 of the above-mentioned CNES decree.

Article 8 – Access rules for people and vehicles
1. Any individual entering a facility situated within the CSG perimeter must be officially identified and authorised.
   This identification and this authorisation take the form of issue of an individual access badge specific to the various access situations. The badge shows the organisation to which the person belongs and its validity period.
   This badge, which is the property of the CNES, is issued on behalf of the President of the CNES and is returned as specified at issue or at the request of the CNES.
   This access badge can only be obtained or renewed if the safety training specified in – Article 9 – has been followed.
   The specific conditions for access to the facilities by people and vehicles are specified by a formal instruction from the President of the CNES.
   For safety reasons, the personnel in charge of safety may, at any moment, search vehicles, in the presence of the driver, at the exits from and entrances to the fenced and monitored CSG zones. These searches may also be carried out within the establishments, with the agreement of the heads of establishment concerned.
   For the same reasons, these staff may have a vehicle towed or moved if incorrectly parked.
2. In the facilities, access to certain premises or areas is controlled by programming an electronic card, according to criteria relating to:
   - safety and security measures implemented in the premises or area concerned;

- the need to know with regard to the activity of the personnel concerned;
- the defence clearance required for access to certain premises or areas, or needed to take part in certain activities.

The need to access these premises or areas leads to a programming request from the head of establishment concerned to the President of the CNES.

3. In a hazardous area, a permanent means of communication is required between the safety entity concerned and the individual carrying out the activity in the area. In the case of work on a hazardous system, a minimum two-man team is required. Nonetheless, the number of persons authorised to be present simultaneously in the danger zones of a hazardous operation is as small as possible.

In the event of an activity in a hazardous area without intervention on a hazardous system, a single person may work. The permanent contact required with the safety entity concerned may in this case be replaced by a permanent link with the CSG fire department emergency centres.

Access to certain areas may depend on the nature of the hazards created by the activities and the use of appropriate collective or individual protection equipment.

Article 9 – "Safety" training

Any person liable to be moving around unaccompanied within the CSG perimeter must receive "safety" training, the content and conditions of which are specified by the formal instruction from the President of the CNES.

Safety training is a minimum prerequisite for any pyrotechnic qualification issued under the applicable legislation concerning pyrotechnic establishments.

Article 10 – Access control measures

Certain areas and premises are subject to access control measures using electronic and video surveillance systems. The President of the CNES therefore issues a formal instruction to specify the various security systems and how they are installed and used, to ensure overall consistency and technical compatibility with the existing systems and networks.

Article 11 – Traffic rules within the CSG perimeter

The highway code applies on all roads and tracks inside the CSG perimeter. The policing powers of the President of the CNES concerning traffic are exercised without prejudice to the general policing powers of the préfet of French Guiana with regard to public traffic. The President of the CNES may be required to close or restrict public traffic on all or part of the roads or tracks inside the CSG perimeter, for safety or security reasons linked to the performance of activities within the CSG.

Stopping and parking are prohibited for vehicles of all categories on the verges of the portion of the *route de l'Espace* between the Carapa section and the Orchidée guardhouse. Standard roadside signs indicate this prohibition.

Article 12 – Evacuation of a facility or area
In accordance with article 14-8 of the above-mentioned CNES decree, in the context of an activity presenting a serious danger for people or property or for the protection of the environment of public health, the President of the CNES may order the evacuation of any facility or any structure or natural area within the perimeter of the CSG.
The activities concerned in particular comprise operations linked to the transfer of payloads and launcher and to the launch count-down.

Article 13 – Access, traffic, time spent on and evacuation of the Salvation Islands
The conditions for access to, moving around and staying on the Salvation Islands, which comprise operational technical facilities related to space activities and hotel and tourism facilities, and which are in particular subject to a series of protective measures agreed with the coastline and lakesides conservation agency, are specified in a formal instruction from the President of the CNES.
The President of the CNES may ban access to these islands and order their evacuation in the conditions specified in0 – Article 12 – of this order.
In any case, persons not involved in the launch activity are evacuated from the islands during the launch count-down.

Article 14 – Access to and evacuation of the leisure area
The President of the CNES may ban access to the leisure area, which in particular comprises the CSG airfield and sports and association infrastructures, and may order evacuation in the conditions specified in – Article 12 – of this order.
In any case, the leisure area is evacuated during the launch countdown.

Article 15 – Transport of dangerous goods
The transport of dangerous goods inside the perimeter of the CSG is governed by the regulations applicable to the transport of dangerous goods by road (ADR).
If it is impossible to implement the regulation requirements of the ADR, owing to the specific nature of the space objects or their component parts, the transport of these objects or parts is the subject of specific safety and security measures, which are specified in a formal instruction and a coordination instruction from the President of the CNES.
Any plans to deliver class 1 objects inside the perimeter of the CSG, with the exception of class 1.4S objects in transport packaging, and class 7objects, as defined by the ADR, require

ANNEX 2.7

that a specific access request be sent to the President of the CNES no later than the 30 days preceding the planned date of their arrival.

PARTIE III – FACILITIES SITING RULES

Article 16 – Facility siting

It is recalled that ownership of the land on which the CSG is situated and the land of the Salvation Islands was transferred to the CNES by the State by virtue of the administrative transfer document of 20th October 1971. Part of this land is made available to the European Space Agency by the CNES, at the request of the State, under the Agreement between the French Government and the European Space Agency, concerning the CSG and the above-mentioned associated services.

Any creation or modification of an installation or structure inside the perimeter of the CSG and requiring a building permit, as well as any modification of a facility that is hazardous or situated within a danger zone or which could affect the roads and major networks of the CSG, must conform to the siting plan for facilities, roads and networks defined in the formal instruction from the President of the CNES, to the requirements of this 0, as well as those of 0 and 0 of this order.

Article 17 – Provision of land

The President of the CNES defines the perimeter of the land allocated to the intended facility, consistently with the studies carried out in compliance with the legislation applicable to facilities classified on environmental and pyrotechnic safety grounds.

The owner of the facility marks out the boundary of the land as of the construction phase, by means of a perimeter fence or appropriate signage.

The President of the CNES maintains an updated reference plan of the land made available.

Article 18 – Operation of facilities

Any owner or operator of a facility located on land allocated to it is required to maintain said land and maintain the fencing or signage around it.

Article 19 – Change of operator

Any plan to change the operator on a facility at the CSG is submitted to the President of the CNES who will in particular check that the new operator meets the requirements of 0 of this order.

Article 20 – Cessation of activity

Any owner or operator of a facility which is to cease operations must, at its own expense and before the activity ceases, restore it to a condition such that it cannot constitute a threat to the safety of people and property and the protection of public health and the environment and so that it is compatible with the CSG master plan. Before the cessation of activity, the President of the CNES may in this respect and without prejudice to application of the legislation applicable to facilities classified on environmental protection grounds, require that the owner or operator, at its own expense, carry out rehabilitation, dismantling or destruction of the facilities and return the allocated land to its initial condition.

PARTIE IV – GENERAL SAFETY RULES

CHAPITRE IV.1 – GENERAL SAFETY OBJECTIVES

Article 21 – Hazard classes for ground-based activities

Two hazard class categories are defined by this order, according to the severity of the damage:

Hazard class	definition of damage
Hazard with catastrophic consequences	– **Immediate or delayed loss of human life** – **Permanent invalidity** – **Irreversible harm to public health**

Hazard with severe consequences	– **Serious injury to individuals leading neither to loss of human life nor permanent invalidity**
	– **Reversible harm to public health**
	– **Significant property damage:**
	  – total or partial destruction of public or private property
	  – total or partial destruction of a facility critical to the launch operation
	– **Significant environmental damage**

It should be noted that catastrophic environmental hazards fall within the hazard class comprising catastrophic consequences for human life and public health, because they lead to one of the forms of damage defined for this class.

Article 22 – Requirements concerning ground-based activities
Principles:
Any hazardous system identified in the conditions specified in – Article 29 –, – Article 30 – and – Article 31 – of this order and utilised for ground-based activities must comply with a clearly identified reliability objective that is compatible with the qualitative and quantitative requirements below. This reliability objective must explicitly contribute to the safety of people and property and to the protection of public health and the environment.

ANNEX 2.7

The demonstration of compliance with the reliability objective must take account of aspects relating to the equipment and its utilisation and may use RAMS rules and methods recognised in the good practice guide specified in article 54 of the technical regulations.

Qualitative requirements:

1. For all hazardous activities carried out inside the perimeter of the CSG or from the CSG, the space systems, safety systems, integrated stages and associated ground systems must meet the following requirements:
   - **activity with a risk of severe consequences: single failure criterion**
     No failure (single failure or human error) must entail a risk of severe, let alone catastrophic consequences (known as "Fail Safe" (FS)).
     However, compliance with the single failure criterion is not required:
     - for a launch system as of the moment at which the launch operation becomes irreversible, and until such time as it is made safe in the event of an aborted launch attempt;
     - for the structural elements of a launch vehicle or payload if application of said criterion is unfeasible in economically acceptable conditions, based on current knowledge and practices and the vulnerability of the environment in which said launcher is liable to operate.
   - **activity with a risk of catastrophic consequences: double failure criterion**
     No combination of two failures (fault or human error) must present a risk of catastrophic consequences (FS/FS or FO/FS).
     The double failure criterion does not apply to the combination of two human errors.
2. The qualitative requirements mentioned in the 1st paragraph above do not apply to structural elements, which are designed in accordance with standards and using appropriate engineering methods, in order to ensure an equivalent level of safety. A formal instruction from the President of the CNES specifies these standards and methods.

Quantitative requirements:

For all activities with a risk of catastrophic consequences carried out within the perimeter of the CSG, the maximum allowable probability of causing at least one victim (collective hazard) included in the design of the launch systems, test benches and associated technical resources, is 10^{-6} per launch preparation or test campaign.

Article 23 – Hazard classes for in-flight activities

A single hazard class is defined by this order for in-flight events which could lead to damage on the surface of the Earth.

Hazard class	definition of damage
Hazard with catastrophic consequences	– **Immediate or delayed loss of human life** – **Serious injury** – **Irreversible harm to human health**

It should be noted that catastrophic environmental hazards fall within the hazard class comprising catastrophic consequences for human life and public health, because they lead to one of the forms of damage defined for this class.

Article 24 – Requirements concerning in-flight activities
Principles:
Any hazardous system identified in the conditions specified in – Article 32 – of this order and utilised in flight must meet a clearly identified reliability objective compatible with the qualitative and quantitative requirements below. This reliability objective must explicitly contribute to the safety of people and property and to the protection of public health and the environment.

The demonstration of compliance with the reliability objective must take account of aspects relating to the equipment and its utilisation and may use RAMS rules and methods recognised in the good practice guide specified in article 54 of the technical regulations.

Quantitative requirements
The flight requirements fall within the general framework set by the technical regulations.

Qualitative requirements
Activities with a risk of catastrophic consequences must meet the double failure criterion, defined as follows: No combination of two failures (fault or human error) must present a risk of catastrophic consequences (FS/FS or FO/FS).

The double failure criterion does not apply to the combination of two human errors.

Article 25 – Software
Software making a direct or indirect contribution to the safety of people and property and the protection of public health and the environment, in particular those constituting safety barriers, undergo criticality analyses to deduce the design, development and validation requirements as well as the risk mitigation measures appropriate to their criticality.

These elements are submitted to the President of the CNES in accordance with the requirements of 0 of this order.

ANNEX 2.7

CHAPITRE IV.2 SAFETY PROCEDURE

Article 26 – Safety submission process

An iterative, continuous safety file submission process ("safety submission") enables the President of the CNES to check compliance with the requirements of this order by all persons covered by article 14-7 of the above-mentioned CNES decree.

For each hazardous activity they intend to conduct, these persons:
- identify and assess the hazards defined in – Article 21 – and – Article 23 – of this order;
- as applicable, implement a hazard reduction programme.

As soon as possible, they send the President of the CNES a written file containing a demonstration of compliance with the requirements specific to each type of safety submission, as stipulated in the requirements of – Article 29 – to – Article 32 – of this order respectively.

Article 27 – Change processing

Any change to a launch vehicle, payload, ground facility and associated equipment, the use or implementation of which presents a risk of severe or catastrophic consequences as defined in 0 and 0 of this order, is the subject of a further safety submission, in accordance with the procedure specified in 0 of this order.

Article 28 – Disposition of non-conformities

If it is impossible to comply with one or more requirements of this order, all persons covered by article 14-7 of the above-mentioned CNES decree, send a written waiver request to the President of the CNES, accompanied by a backup file which must specify and give reasons for:
- in the particular case in question, the impossibility of taking all measures such as to establish, maintain or restore conformity with the requirements of this order;
- the steps taken to attempt to ensure conformity with the requirements of this order insofar as this is possible;
- the residual level of hazard arising from the non-conformity.

The President of the CNES may issue an express decision constituting an exceptional waiver, in particular linked to the operating environment conditions prevailing at that time.

Article 29 – Ground facilities

The declaring party is clearly identified. If there is no identification then the declaring party is the owner for a new facility or the operator concerned in the case of modification of an existing facility.

The declaring party submits to the President of the CNES the file as required in – Article 26 – of this order, which demonstrates compliance on the one hand with the requirements of this article and, on the other, with the rules applicable to the ground facilities stipulated in 0 and 0 of this order.

Phase 0 – Feasibility
The feasibility file must comprise a preliminary hazard analysis based on the following:
- the characteristics concerning:
  - the nature of and dangers involved in the envisaged products;
  - the maximum quantities of each of these products in the facility.
- the list of hazardous systems and their preliminary description;
- the description of the procedures and technical options envisaged, in particular:
  - the types of activities performed in the facility;
  - any associated hardware resources used;
  - the operational constraints relating to the activities, in particular evacuation of areas, incompatibility between activities or restrictions on the number of persons present;
  - the facility's interfaces with the existing roads and major networks.
- the reference trajectories for siting of a launch area.

This study must demonstrate:
- that the envisaged location of the facility is in conformity with 0 of this order;
- compliance with the legislative and regulatory requirements applicable to facilities classified on environmental protection and pyrotechnical safety grounds.

Phase 1 – Design
The declaring party supplies the definition files for the installation and its equipment, including the specifications and the comments made by the President of the CNES at the end of phase 0.

The procedures defined during this phase are detailed enough so that it is possible to check that the operational constraints defined in the feasibility phase have been taken into account. The declaring party carries out or has carried out the required studies necessary for obtaining the operating authorisations and permits as required by the legislation applicable to facilities classified on environmental protection and pyrotechnic safety grounds, in the conditions provided for in these legislations.

These studies are submitted to the President of the CNES, in the conditions specified by the instruction issued by himself as part of his safety measures coordination role, as defined in II. of article L. 331-6 of the Research Code.

Phase 1 is closed on receipt of the building permit.

ANNEX 2.7

Phase 2 – Construction
At any time during the facility construction phase and in the conditions specified in 0 of this order, the authorised personnel may:
- make site inspection visits;
- check and confirm the operability of the facility in accordance with the operational deployment plan and the planned procedures. For this, they attend the acceptance and the technical and operational qualification of systems for which a malfunction could be prejudicial to the safety of people and property and the protection of public health and the environment;
- check that the facilities have no negative impact on the reliability and safety of roads and major networks.

Phase 2 is closed at the end of the facility technical acceptance.

Phase 3 – Implementation
The declaring party submits a file to the President of the CNES confirming configuration management of all hazardous facilities and confirming that conformity with the requirements of this order are maintained on a long-term basis.

Opening file submission phase 3 is independent of closure of phases 0 to 2 mentioned above. It must begin as early as possible, as soon as the definition of the facility and its validation and operating procedures are sufficiently well known.

The file must comprise the following documents:
- the implementation specifications;
- the implementation procedures;
- the safety instructions linked to the site and to the activities taking place on it.

Article 30 – Payloads
Under the responsibility of the launch operator, the payload contractor submits to the President of the CNES the file specified in 0 of this order, which includes a demonstration of compliance with the requirements of this article and the rules applicable to payloads contained in 0 and 0 of this order.

When the system is designed on the basis of a system which has already been covered by a submission file, the new submission can be by comparing the differences. This type of "differential" submission can only be used twice over a three-year period. Over and above this number a further complete file submission is required.

Phases 1, 2, and 3 can be conducted in parallel, with opening of one phase not being dependent on closure of the previous one.

Phase 0 – Feasibility
The feasibility phase is optional, except for new platforms using innovative technologies. The feasibility file comprises at least:
- the list of hazardous systems and their preliminary description;
- a presentation of the technical choices envisaged;
- a list of the hazards related to the on-board system and associated specific ground equipment;
- as applicable, the list of legislations, regulations and standards applicable to the project.

Phase 1 – Design
The design file comprises at least:
- a detailed description of the hazardous systems, their control circuits and their associated ground equipment. This description also comprises the components of the systems and the reliability data used to evaluate the hazard level;
- the intended frequency plan for transmitters and receivers, plus the emissions characteristics (spectrum, power output, modulation, coding, etc.);
- the preliminary hazard analysis, even partial;
- the qualification plans for the important elements of hazardous systems.

Phase 2 - Qualification
The qualification file comprises at least:
- the results of the partial or total qualification tests on the hazardous systems;
- the plan of the partial or total acceptance tests for the hazardous systems;
- any particular study or design report for assessing the characteristics of the hazardous systems (in particular the fracture analysis);
- the document defining the interfaces between the payload and associated equipment and the various CSG installations;
- the preliminary hazard analysis to which the data from the phase in progress are added;
- as applicable, changes to the frequency plan and the emissions characteristics.

Phase 3 – Implementation
The implementation phase begins no later than six months before launch and is closed before the beginning of each of the hazardous activities. The corresponding file comprises:
- the activity control procedures, including procedures concerning activities to restore safety and emergency procedures in the event of an incident. These procedures must implement the following measures:
  - identify the hazardous activities;
  - take account of the specific aspects of the CSG (sites, means, job descriptions, etc.);

- for each step, specify the number and function of the persons who have to be in the danger zones;
- specify the list of means and products used;
- step by step, specify the procedure involved in restoring safety;
- give the activity durations, including those involved in restoring safety, as well as any interruptions.
- the analysis of conformity with the launcher on ground safety requirements for payload configuration and safety restoration activities in the launch zone;
- the results of the acceptance tests of certain components of the hazardous systems, in particular the proof-pressure test certificates for pressurised gas vessels. These documents can be supplied when the equipment arrives inside the perimeter of the CSG;
- the licences for the possession and use of equipment subject to administrative authorisation (example: object emitting ionising radiation);
- the medical certificates for personnel working on certain hazardous systems, in particular those emitting ionising radiation or containing toxic products. These documents may be supplied on arrival of said systems inside the perimeter of the CSG;
- the personnel qualification certificates for handling of pyrotechnic products;
- the final version of the satellite operations plan, in particular comprising the final list of procedures, the operations sheets and the operations schedule.

Article 31 – Launchers on the ground

The launch operator, or anyone responsible for the design or development of the launcher, in particular the owner, submits to the President of the CNES the file specified in 0 of this order, which comprises the demonstration of compliance with the requirements of this article and the rules applicable to launch vehicles stipulated in 0 and 0 of this order.

Phase 0 – Feasibility

The feasibility file comprises:
- the project specifications;
- the description of the technical choices and solutions envisaged for the project;
- the list of hazardous systems and their preliminary description;
- the allocation of safety objectives;
- an initial quantitative evaluation of the hazard levels of the various technical design options envisaged;
- the preliminary hazard analysis linked to the design and implementation of the project, identifying the hazards at system level, the circumstances and the events potentially at risk;
- identification of the critical aspects with regard to the safety of people and property and the protection of public health and the environment;

- the hazard prevention principles to be applied;
- the list of legislations, regulations, standards and specifications applicable.

Phase 1 – Design

The design file comprises:
- the evaluation of the design choices made;
- identification of the hazards and the preliminary studies demonstrating their mitigation;
- the qualification rules applicable to the hazardous systems and in particular the safety systems;

Phase 2 – Production / qualification

The production/qualification file comprises:
- an additional hazard analysis and assessment of the hazard level of the system and associated equipment, to demonstrate compliance with the safety objectives;
- the critical parameters management procedures;
- the qualification plans for systems classified as hazardous;
- evaluation of the qualification results of the systems classified as hazardous;
- the operations plan for implementation of the system and the resulting hazardous activities.

Phase 3 – Implementation

The implementation file comprises:
- the list of system control and implementation activities, which must cover all preparation and launch steps, or testing for the test specimens, from removal of the hazardous components from storage up until launch or until the end of testing, plus rehabilitation of the launch complex or the test bench;
- the operations plans;
- the implementation procedures covering nominal and degraded situations.

The President of the CNES may ask for the following documents:
- the implementation specifications for the launcher and its stages, or for the test specimen;
- the acceptance reports for all the equipment and the proof-pressure test certificates for the pressure vessels;
- the licences and permits for possession and use of equipment subject to administrative authorisation pursuant to the pertinent regulations (example: object emitting ionising radiation).

The launch operator submits to the President of the CNES the final document setting out the standard activity procedures and the standard operations plans.

Any change from a standard procedure to a specific procedure must be approved by the safety entity before it is submitted to the President of the CNES.

Article 32 – Flight safety

The launch operator, or any person responsible for the design or development of the launcher, in particular the owner:
- submits to the President of the CNES the file specified in – Article 26 – of this order, which comprises a demonstration of compliance with the requirements of this article as well as the rules applicable to launchers as stipulated in PARTIE VI of this order, in particular with regard to equipment contributing to safety, to the planned trajectory of the launch vehicle, the equipment settings and the algorithms contributing to safety;
- supplies information, data and technical information necessary for performance of its duties in accordance with this order, as defined in Article 63 and 0 of this order.

a) Feasibility, design and construction phases

The launch operator, or any person responsible for the design or development of the launcher, in particular the owner, submits to the President of the CNES a file comprising:
- the list of hazardous systems involved in the safety and intervention function defined in Article 63 of this order;
- its safety methods contributing to the safety of people and property and the protection of public health and the environment;
- the design and construction of the ground/on-board device, in accordance with the requirements of PARTIE VI of this order.

b) Flight preparation phase

The launch operator, or any person responsible for the design or development of the launcher, in particular the owner, submits to the President of the CNES a file comprising:
- the mission configuration (launcher version, type of mission, trajectory and associated ground resources) from the safety viewpoint;
- the information and data allowing implementation of the applicable safety rules and calculations;
- the information and data conforming correct operation of the intervention device (on-board/ground);
- the information and data used on behalf of air and sea users, to check the declaration of the nominal stage fall-back zones in anticipation of the launch.

c) Launch phase and disposal phase

The launch operator submits to the President of the CNES a file comprising:
- the information and data allowing use of the applicable safety rules and calculations;
- the information and data allowing management of the hazards created on the ground and in the atmosphere by the launch vehicle;
- the information and data used to produce and transmit information concerning the fall-back area for dangerous elements or products, as part of the emergency plan.

PARTIE V. – Safety rules applicable on the ground

CHAPITRE V.1 COMMON RULES

Article 33 – General rules for safety on the ground
The rules of this 0 apply to hazard management for the activities performed on the ground, to the ground installations, the launcher and the payloads, except for the activities conducted on the ground during the space vehicle's flight, which are covered by 0 of this order.
In order to ensure the safety of people and property and the protection of public health and the environment, the design, construction and implementation of ground and on-board systems classified as hazardous in accordance with 0of this order are based on:
- the reliability of said systems and compliance with the safety coefficients meeting the RAMS specifications and the safety requirements;
- the creation of safety and disabling barriers at the disposal of the safety entity on the facility concerned, a display of or reports giving the disabling status, used to check the configuration of the hazardous systems;
- the implementation of procedures, remote controls and automation enabling the number of exposed persons to be limited;
- the safeguarding of the exposed persons by means of individual protection appropriate to the risks incurred.

Article 34 – Organisation of activities
On each of the facilities situated inside the perimeter of the CSG, the organisation of the ground activities during the production phase, the launch campaign, or testing, must comprise a safety entity.
The safety function is performed permanently by the creation of a duty system and by constant monitoring of the safety alarms.
All persons covered by article 14-7 of the above-mentioned CNES decree send the President of the CNES the operational and safety organisation they are implementing.

On a site (building, platform, workstation, etc.) where a hazardous activity takes place, persons not involved in the activity are informed by means of clear and unambiguous signs.

The nature, place and beginning and end times of all activities generating a hazard that goes beyond the perimeter of the establishment are notified to the President of the CNES.

Article 35 – Activity control procedures

All actions or interventions linked to the safety of people and property and the protection of public health and the environment implemented by the persons mentioned in article 14-7 of the above-mentioned CNES decree are formally written up in the form of:
- procedures for nominal and degraded situations;
- safety instructions;
- documents determining how to respond in the event of an incident or accident.

The procedures are designed so that they are reversible, in other words, at a certain number of key points during the activity, it is possible to revert to a situation in which the system concerned is safe.

The hazardous activity control procedures are approved by the establishment's safety entity and submitted to the President of the CNES with respect to those activities generating hazards which go beyond the perimeter of the establishment.

Before a system enters a hazardous configuration, the safety entity is informed of the configuration check and the correct functioning of the system circuits.

Article 36 – Roles and resources of the safety entity

A hazardous activity can only begin after obtaining the approval of the safety entity of the establishment concerned. This entity therefore checks that the means and pre-conditions necessary for safe performance of the operation, such as fire protection, security guards, weather monitoring, pre-alerting of medical resources, the presence on the premises of a representative of the safety entity, evacuation of a particular area, or compatibility with other activities being carried out in parallel, are in place or met.

All safety entities must have the technical resources required for supervision of the hazardous activities, in particular:
- the video resources needed to monitor activities on the site;
- the means of communication for maintaining a link with the personnel concerned and for collecting and distributing information or alerts, in liaison with the President of the CNES.

All representatives of the safety entity may attend the activities in the field at his/her own initiative, in accordance with the safety studies defined according to the applicable regulations.

Article 37 – Anomalies, incidents or accidents

For all anomalies, incidents or accidents occurring on a hazardous system or element and all events with serious or catastrophic consequences which occurred during the courses of hazardous activities, in particular during the launch campaign or count-down, all persons covered by article 14-7 of the above-mentioned CNES decree:
- take the necessary emergency measures, such as alerting the emergency services and restoring the safety of the installations;
- ensure that these anomalies, incidents or accidents are immediately notified to their safety entity;
- immediately notify the President of the CNES of these anomalies, incidents or accidents;
- ensure that these anomalies are the subject of a technical instruction such as to identify the causes and define the remedial measures.

Subsequent to the technical instruction mentioned above, the safety lessons learned and the measures adopted are notified to the safety entity and the President of the CNES.

Article 38 – Safety barriers

Safety barriers are required for hazardous circuits or systems which could be inadvertently activated, either owing to hardware failure or through human error.
Their minimum number depends on the severity of the critical event:
- three barriers for an event with catastrophic consequences;
- two for an event with serious consequences.

For hazardous circuits or systems, the device located on said circuit or system, which controls the passage of the fluid or current, is considered to be a barrier.
The barriers countering a given critical event are independent and, if possible, of different types. They may be mechanical, electrical, software or procedural, when physical barriers are technologically impossible.
The procedures for implementation of the barriers are designed so that several barriers of a given circuit or system cannot be lifted simultaneously.

Article 39 – Disabling

For circuits or systems entailing hazards with catastrophic consequences as defined in 0 of this order, the safety entity of the establishment concerned must be able:
- on the one hand to control one of the barriers or inhibit its cancellation;
- on the other, to obtain the status report for the barrier concerned.

This barrier is known as a "disabling device". It must not be technically possible to override it.
A loss of power to the circuits of a disabling device must not change the status of the system or circuit.

After cancelling the disabling device and executing the order, re-application of this disabling must have no impact on the circuit or system in question.

Article 40 – Pyrotechnic systems

The components of pyrotechnic systems and the pyrotechnic materials, if bare during nominal activity or if the structure of the object containing them provides no protection, are chosen for their low sensitivity to external thermal (hot spot, fire), mechanical (fall, shock, impact, friction, vibration), electrical (static electricity, lightning, electromagnetic emissions) and chemical (chemical compatibility) hazards.

For performance of a function, the launch operator or payload contractor ensures that it has chosen the pyrotechnic object or material representing the least risk when subjected to an external hazard.

Any solid propellant motor making up the propulsion system of a launcher stage, is designed and implemented in such a way as to prevent all risk of uncontrolled ignition during all phases in the life of the motor: production, storage, transport, testing, integration on the launcher, up to and including the launch count-down.

The on-board and ground anti-flight systems, are preferably of the passive safety barrier type.

The electro-explosive initiators (squib, primer/detonator) must provide a level of safety at least equivalent to those of type 1 A, 1 W, 5 mn non-firing.

In addition to the particular design rules for the electrical systems defined in 0 of this order, the electrical circuits of the pyrotechnic systems are designed such as to limit the current induced on the firing circuit to at least 20 dB below the maximum non-firing current, when exposed to an electromagnetic field defined by the electromagnetic environment generated by the ground systems, the launcher and the payloads.

If a filter is added to the circuit, it is installed as close as possible to the initiator to be protected and the portion of the circuits situated between the filter and the initiator is shielded. The components are capable of supporting the following discharge without ignition or deterioration:

- 25,000 V supplied by a 470 to 500 pF capacitor, through a pure 5,000 Ω resistor, the voltage being applied to the terminals of the component;
- 25,000 V supplied by a 470 to 500 pF capacitor, without resistor, the voltage being applied across the short-circuited terminals of the component and its housing.

The electrical power supply source for the pyrotechnic systems is preferably a DC source. If not, the electrical power supply source must comply with the electromagnetic compatibility requirements as defined in 0 of this order.

The current output by the electro-explosive devices control equipment is such that inadvertent ignition or phlegmatisation of the initiator cannot occur. The control current is limited to at least 20 dB below the maximum non-firing current.

The establishment's safety entity ensures that the electrical control equipment is approved. It must not be possible for an electrostatic charge to build up in a firing circuit.

The electro-explosive elements are in a safe configuration during storage, handling and after assembly, in particular with respect to the possibility of external hazards. A no-voltage check is run prior to connection.

Radio silence periods are stipulated in the procedures.

The installation of electro-detonators and/or connection of hazard classified electro-explosive systems must take place as late as possible in the launcher or payload preparation sequence. Once connected, the establishment's safety entity must be able to monitor the status of the pyrotechnic systems.

In addition to the measures contained in the safety data sheets for pyrotechnic objects and materials, the following are specified:
- the occupational pyrotechnic hazard division classification;
- the results of the safety tests concerning mechanical (fall, shock, impact, friction, vibration), thermal (hot spot, fire), electrical (static electricity, lightning, electromagnetic emissions) and chemical (chemical compatibility) hazards to which the components of the pyrotechnic systems and pyrotechnic materials in question may be subjected during all their life phases in the CSG;
- the expected pyrotechnic effects in nominal operating mode and in degraded mode, when subjected to an external hazard.

Unused pyrotechnic objects, or those which have reached their use-by date, are recovered by their owner and then destroyed. The destruction procedure is submitted to the President of the CNES.

Article 41 – Electrical systems

Even if in compliance with French regulations, electrical systems are considered to be hazardous systems, without restriction with regard to voltage, current, or frequency, when one of the following conditions is met:
- the electrical system activates systems or devices containing one or more hazardous products;
- the electrical system may, in the event of a failure, output energy (electrical, thermal, etc.) or effluents liable to cause direct damage (effect of electrical origin) or indirect damage (effect on a hazardous system connected to the electrical system).

Hazardous electrical systems are protected against over-currents and voltage surges.

The equipment is designed so that the exterior metal parts and shieldings can be grounded.

The following rules apply to cables:

- cables must withstand and be protected against abrasion and twisting;
- the cables are chosen according to fire-resistance, smoke generation and compatibility with the surrounding fluids criteria;
- cable shielding must not be used as a grounding conductor nor as a signal line (except for coaxial cables in this latter case);
- the conductors in hazardous electrical circuits must not be routed through the same cableways or in the same passages as those used for other circuits;
- redundant links must be routed through different cables and passages;
- the structures must comprise no sharp edges in the cable installation areas, to avoid all risk of damage to the cables.

The following rules apply to hazardous system connectors:
- the connectors are designed so that there can be no ambiguity in their connection (mechanical fool-proofing of connectors). Colour coding may be used but cannot replace mechanical foolproofing;
- connectors are appropriately guided at insertion, so that the female and male contacts are subjected to no stresses during connection or separation;
- the connectors are guided and retained so that no stresses are transmitted to the contacts, such as to affect their correct operation;
- the connectors have female contacts on the power source side and male contacts on the operating side;
- deterioration of a connection (crushing of the connector or contact between two neighbouring pins) must not lead to any catastrophic or severe events;
- the connectors used for the hazardous circuits must be lockable;
- the positions of the pins must rule out all risk of short-circuit between two pins or between a pin and the plug;
- the conductors in hazardous circuits must have specific connectors and receptacles which can in no case be common with other circuits.

The following rules apply to batteries:
- the batteries must be easily disconnected;
- if the battery is not connected, the connection terminals are equipped with a means of protection to avoid all risk of short-circuit;
- in the event of a short-circuit, there can be no uncontrolled splashing of electrolyte.

Article 42 – Static electricity
Hazardous electrical systems as well as electrical systems contributing to or maintaining the safety of the installations are designed to be immune to electrostatic discharges.

A material is said to be a conductor in electrostatic terms when its volume resistivity is less than 10^8 Ωm.

Systems within which static electricity can constitute a risk of severe or catastrophic consequences as defined in 0of this order are designed and built such as to limit the creation and build-up of electrostatic charges through the use of conducting materials.

The fixed or mobile conducting elements (metal or non-metal) making up these systems are interconnected by equipotential links and are grounded. These links are electrically checked.

The various elements of the payload, the launch and their respective associated equipment, as well as the ground facilities, must not accumulate electrostatic charges during the integration activities or during transfer.

The installation of individual protective devices to prevent a build-up of electrostatic charges is mandatory when handling explosive objects or materials susceptible to electrostatic discharges. These protective devices may consist of conductive shoes or strips in the case of with a conductive floor, conductive bracelets, conductive working clothes.

They are produced, utilised, maintained and checked in accordance with the rules of professional good practice.

Article 43 – Electromagnetic compatibility (EMC)
The launchers, payloads, ground facilities and associated equipment are designed to ensure electromagnetic compatibility between the various electrical installations and equipment.
- The rules of professional good practice are adhered to, in particular those concerning:
- the creation of meshed networks or interconnected earth planes, which are grounded;
- equipotential links, with regard to high-frequency currents, electrical grounds, equipment grounds, shielding and screens;
- cabling and routing of high and low amperage cables;
- electrical continuity of cableways and metal ducts, between the various racks, at wall penetrations and with the equipment served;
- the separation of disruptive high-amperage devices and sensitive low-amperage devices;
- the electrical continuity and cable/connectors, connectors/receptacles and receptacles/connected equipment shielding.

The above requirements are implemented while taking account of environmental constraints (particularly corrosion) and are checked at implementation or, as applicable, after any structural modification, and then periodically.

Article 44 – Fluid systems
A circuit containing one or more hazardous fluids is considered to be a hazardous system.

A circuit containing one or more pressurised fluids and compliant with French regulations applicable to pressure equipment is considered to be a hazardous system if at least one of the fluids is a hazardous fluid.

Hazardous circuits are designed so that:
- mixing of incompatible fluids is impossible;
- connections are mechanically fool-proofed (connection, length) whenever there is a potential risk of assembly error or when the component is specific to a given fluid;
- the lubricants and materials used are compatible with the fluids concerned (chemical, thermal, mechanical, etc. hazard);
- any retention is impossible, except for those elements whose function entails retention (filters, steam traps, etc.).

Systems receiving hazardous fluids must systematically undergo a tightness test before filling, at least to the maximum pressure expected when personnel are present.

The elements or equipment of the fluid systems to be checked prior to each campaign must be given in a revalidation plan.

All metal, or non-metal, fixed or mobile conducting parts of the tanks, transfer circuits and associated devices (valves, filters, etc.) are interconnected by equipotential links and grounded before and during any transfer of fluid.

Article 45 – Mechanical and electromechanical systems
The mechanical and electromechanical systems used during the course of hazardous activities are the subject of a RAMS study.

Article 46 – Confined atmosphere
Confined atmosphere premises are signposted in compliance with labour legislation.

The personnel who are required to enter a confined atmosphere area must familiarise themselves with and apply the special safety instructions stipulating how to prevent the risk of anoxia, before they can access the area concerned, in the conditions defined in 0 of this order.

All the personnel must carry a breathable air mask or wear a sealed suit supplied with breathable air, when they enter an area from which evacuation is difficult. This area is permanently ventilated and an external supervisor is present for the duration of the activity.

Before the personnel enters a confined atmosphere area, the oxygen level is checked.

All work in a confined atmosphere with a risk of under-oxygenation requires the presence of at least two independent detectors, one of which is fixed, each fitted with a low-level alarm and permanently monitoring the atmosphere. The low-level alarm to be considered for detection is 19% oxygen (percentage by volume).

In the particular case of ground installations, any area with a risk of under-oxygenation is equipped with a fixed system to detect the oxygen level and is equipped with a remote alarm and a local visible and audible alarm.

When persons are required to enter confined atmosphere installations which are not normally accessible, the safety entity runs a safety analysis to take account of the above rules.

Article 47 – Breathable air circuits
Breathable air circuits are designed so that they cannot be polluted. The mobile connections and couplings are thus mechanically fool-proofed (connections, lengths).

Article 48 – Atmosphere with a toxic hazard
Areas or installations with an atmosphere comprising a toxic hazard are signposted.

The personnel required to enter an area with an atmosphere comprising a toxic hazard must familiarise themselves with and apply the particular safety instructions specifying how to prevent a risk of inhalation of toxic products before they can access the area concerned, in the conditions defined in 0 of this order.

All work in an atmosphere with a toxic hazard requires the presence of a detector permanently monitoring the atmosphere, equipped with an alarm.

In the particular case of ground installations, any area with an atmosphere comprising a toxic hazard is equipped with a fixed system to detect the toxic vapour/gas content, with an alarm designed in accordance with the requirements of 0 of this order, along with a local visible and audible alarm.

For all activities involving a toxic fluid, toxicity measurements are taken before, during and after the activity.

Detectors are set so that the alarm is tripped when the toxic substance concentration in the working place atmosphere is higher than 90% of the short-term exposure limit (STEL). If the STEL for a toxic substance is not defined, the alarm trigger threshold is set at 90% of its mean exposure limit.

All the personnel must have at their disposal a mask with filter cartridge appropriate to the various hazards in question, or a leaktight suit supplied with breathable air according to the hazards generated by the activity, in accordance with the following table:

Type of activity	*Individual protection equipment*
Presence in an area with an atmosphere comprising a toxic hazard or activity in an area in which toxic fluids are stored	Anti-acid suit and mask with filter cartridge on shoulder strap
Activities on networks polluted by a toxic fluid	Anti-acid suit and breathable air mask, possibly supplemented by protection against splashing
Transfer of propellants and filling, activities on systems containing pressurised toxic fluids	Leaktight suit able to withstand toxic fluid splashes, supplied with breathable air

Maintenance works or activities requiring venting of devices which have contained toxic fluids are preceded by drainage thereof and the participants are protected if the devices have not been decontaminated.
- Each intentional discharge of liquid or gaseous toxic effluents must obtain the approval of the establishment's safety entity, which checks that this discharge takes place in accordance with the legislation, in particular with regard to facilities classified on environmental protection grounds.
- Restrictions on personnel access to hazardous areas and the use of remote control systems are defined according to the hazardous nature of the hazardous fluids and the resulting risks.

Article 49 – Explosive atmosphere
In the case of systems containing flammable and toxic fluids, the facilities and equipment must not generate an explosive atmosphere outside the system, in normal operation.

Article 50 – Radionuclides

In addition to the dangerous goods transport requirements mentioned in 0 of this order, any party in possession of or using radionuclides as defined in the relevant provisions of the Public Health Code, in the form of a radioactive sources, or products or devices containing them, transmits a copy of the possession and utilisation authorisation files to the President of the CNES, along with the names and details of the persons with competence for radiation protection (PCR).

Article 51 – Laser radiation devices

Any party in possession of or using a laser radiation device entailing a risk of severe or catastrophic consequences as defined in 0 of this order transmits the file describing said device to the President of the CNES, including its classification and the associated hazards, as well as where it is to be used and its operating and storage configuration.

CHAPITRE V.2 SPECIFIC RULES CONCERNING GROUND FACILITIES AND ASSOCIATED EQUIPMENT

Article 52 – Alarm and safety systems

The alarm and safety systems are the subject of RAMS studies to demonstrate conformity with the requirements of 0 of this order.
Any failures are signalled by an alarm.
The alarms on the fixed fire and toxic vapour detectors are transmitted to the CSG's fire department emergency centres.

Article 53 – Electrical systems

All the electrical systems for the ground equipment associated with the launchers and payloads must have an emergency cut-off for the electrical power supplies, enabling the power to be interrupted to all active conductors. The emergency cut-offs are easily accessible and easily recognisable.
The safety systems are the subject of a detailed analysis in order to identify the systems which are to be kept active in the event of an emergency cut-off.
Inside an area in which a hazardous activity is taking place, emergency lighting is installed to ensure that the activity in progress can be conducted safely.
Battery storage and charging areas are sufficiently ventilated to guarantee that the concentration of emitted vapours is 25% below the lower explosive limit (LEL).

Article 54 – Electromagnetic compatibility (EMC)

Hazardous electrical systems and electrical systems contributing to safety or to maintaining the safety of the facilities, are immune to radiated electromagnetic emissions (radar, lightning, radio-communications, telephone) and to emissions conducted by the various high-amperage, low-amperage and other conducting networks (fluids for example).

Article 55 – Circuits containing hazardous fluids

In addition to the general requirements given in 0 the following rules apply.

The remote-controlled circuits containing hazardous fluids must comprise valves automatically setting them to a safe position (either open, or closed) in the event of a power loss (electrical, hydraulic, pneumatic, etc.).

Fluid circuits (cryogenic, corrosive, flammable) that could damage electrical equipment are designed so that a leak cannot damage the electrical control lines to the extent that it creates a risk of serious or catastrophic consequences as defined in 0of this order.

The storage tanks for hazardous fluids are fitted with distribution circuit isolation valves that can be operated in the maximum pressure and flow conditions that is allowed by the construction of the system.

For mobile devices (in particular carts), the vents on the valves and toxic or flammable fluid pressurisation devices are designed to be grouped and connected to the fixed installation vents.

Article 56 – Lightning protection

The provisions relating to lightning protection as required by the legislation on facilities classified on environmental protection grounds apply to the launch vehicle on the ground in all phases.

This protection against lightning preferably uses passive protection means and, failing which, active protection means. In this latter case, this protection is compatible with the weather forecasting and lightning protection capability of the CNES/CSG.

CHAPITRE V.3 Rules on the ground specific to launchers and payloads

Article 57 – On-board electrical systems

An on-board electrical system is considered to be hazardous if it can deliver a contact current capable of causing an electric shock and burns, with an intensity greater than or equal to:

- mA for DC and AC currents up to a frequency of 10 kHz;
- $350*f$ mA (f being the frequency expressed in MHz) for AC current with a frequency of from 10 kHz to 100 kHz;
- 35 mA for AC current with a frequency higher than 100 kHz.

Before any transfer of the launcher or the payload, the electrical circuits classified as hazardous are checked and kept safe for the duration of the transfer.

The umbilical connections for hazardous electrical circuits are checked before connection to the payload.

Article 58 – Hazard classification criteria for on-board fluid systems
On-board pressurised fluid systems are considered to be hazardous if the dimensions and operating pressures of each separate device (container or line) are as follows:

NATURE OF FLUID	CONTAINER (TANK)	LINE
GASES or liquids for which the vapour pressure at the maximum allowable temperature is 0.5 bar higher than the normal atmospheric pressure.	P > 0.5 bar And V > 1 litre And PxV > 50 bar x 1 Or P > 1000 bar	P > 0.5 bar And DN > 32 And PxDN > 1000 bar
LIQUIDS for which the vapour pressure at maximum allowable temperature is 0.5 bar or less above the normal atmospheric pressure.	P > 10 bar And PxV > 10000 bar x 1 Or P > 1000 bar	P > 10 bar And DN > 200 And PxDN > 5000 bar

V : internal volume of the container in litres
P : pressure in bar gauge
DN : nominal dimension in mm. – Numerical designation of the dimension common to all the elements of a line other than the elements referred to by their outside diameter or the thread size. This is a number rounded off for reference purposes and is not strictly related to the manufacturing dimensions. The nominal size is given by DN followed by a number.

It should be pointed out that the devices are considered to be separate, when failure of one cannot propagate to the other.

Article 59 – Pressurised, hazard classified, on-board fluid systems
The on-board pressurised, fluid systems classified as a hazard by 0 of this order are in conformity with a recognised standard or at least the requirements defined in 0 of this order and the following rules.
1. The pressure vessels of on-board fluid systems are designed for the pressure loads with a failure safety factor Jr of at least 2. In some particular cases, this factor can be reduced to 1.5 depending on the possible failure modes demonstrated by the studies and tests. An LBB type pressure vessel, used in the pressure domain required to obtain the LBB characterisation, only generates a danger zone owing to the possible leakage of the fluid contained. In this case, only the hazard related to this fluid is considered when determining the danger zone.
   The containers must undergo a test programme in order to confirm that they are of the correct size and check the quality of their construction.
2. On-board fluid systems and their components must have undergone proof-pressure testing as described below, before they arrive within the perimeter of the CSG:

A proof-pressure factor Jt is defined, such that the proof-pressure test is performed at Jt times the maximum presence reached in the presence of personnel.
If the failure safety factor Jr is 2 or higher, $Jt = 1.5$.
If the failure safety factor is less than 2,

$$Jt = \frac{1 + Jr}{2}$$

If the design renders this proof-pressure test impossible on the entire system, partial tests may be carried out. The final assembly of the entire system is subject to appropriate quality requirements to guarantee the overall mechanical strength at pressurisation. Any accepted deviation in relation to the applicable quality procedure is justified and the President of the CNES is notified accordingly.

3. The proof-pressure tested configuration should not undergo any change or technical incident liable to compromise its validity.
   After the system test, the maximum expected service pressure should never be exceeded. The pressure vessels in service must have been subjected to no hazard (mechanical, thermal, electrical, etc.) liable to affect their characteristics.
   In the event of repair or maintenance, a representative tightness test is required prior to any return to service. Furthermore, if the activity is not limited to disassembly/reassembly, but comprises more extensive work (welding, forming, etc.), the pressure vessel is inspected and proof-pressure tested.

4. The pressurisation and depressurisation rates must not lead to any uncontrollable hazardous situations (temperature gradient, pressure hammer, etc.).
   The relative pressure in millibars exerted on a device requiring manual intervention (disassembly, repair, tightening or loosening of couplings, etc.) is such that the product of this pressure by the flow section (expressed in cm^2) is less than 1000.
   All assembly of elements containing a pressurised fluid is of the "Safe-Life" type as defined in 0 of this order.
   In the particular case of a system assembled by welding, the welds between these various parts are checked after assembly using a non-destructive process recognised by the aerospace field. The President of the CNES is notified of any deviation observed during these checks.

5. During the dynamic pressurisation or depressurisation phases and during the static phase, the operational constraints are set with reference to the instantaneous safety factor Js defined as being the ratio between the allowable rupture pressure and the relative pressure reached at the moment considered by the system in question:
   Js = Allowable rupture pressure / Instantaneous relative pressure considered
   This variable factor Js is also such that Js is greater than or equal to Jr.

Access to the danger zones created by an on-board pressurised fluid system is governed by the following special rules:

Safety factor Js	Static phase access	Dynamic phase access (2)
$Js \geq 4$	No constraint	No constraint
$3 \leq Js < 4$	No constraint	Controlled access (1)
$2 \leq Js < 3$	Controlled access (1)	Limited access (3)
$Js < 2$	No access (4)	No access (4)

(1): Only those persons directly concerned by the activities and whose presence in the danger zone is essential, are admitted. These activities may concern any other launcher element than the container in question.

(2): The dynamic phase includes fluid movements and handling of pressurised containers, but excludes the hold periods required for temperature equalisation after pressurisation.

(3): Only those persons concerned by the pressurisation/depressurisation activity are admitted, provided that the activity cannot be carried out remotely.

(4):In the particular case of LBB type pressure vessels, access may be controlled in the conditions defined in note (1) up to $Js \geq 1.5$.

Article 60 – Pyrotechnic systems

The external conducting parts (metal or non-metal) and the shielding of the components of a pyrotechnic system, an initiator, a safety and arming unit, transmission and distribution components and functional devices (break-up strips, cutting fuses, igniters, valves, actuators, etc.) are equipotential and grounded.

For pyrotechnic systems entailing a risk of catastrophic consequences as defined in 0of this order, the barrier close to the hazard source must be mechanical (the safety and arming unit) which must prevent inadvertent firing of the system.

The safety and arming units are constructed such that:
- once set to "armed" or "disarmed", the barrier cannot leave this position without an order or under the effect of an external loading (shock, vibration, electrostatic phenomenon, etc.) in a normal or accident environment;
- the barrier is disabled in accordance with the requirements of 0of this order;
- the position status report is representative of the actual "armed" or "disarmed" status and can be transmitted;
- the "armed" or "disarmed" status is displayed by an indicator physically linked to the disabling device;
- they are remote controlled but manual disarming is always possible;
- it is physically impossible to install the detonator if the unit is not in the "disarmed" position.

ANNEX 2.7

The layout of the safety and arming units must allow easy access for installation and connection of the detonators and for manual disarming.

The safety and arming units are in the safe position in the presence of personnel. This safe position must be checkable to ensure that the system is in a safe state.

PARTIE VI. – IN-FLIGHT SAFETY RULES

CHAPITRE VI.1 GENERAL RULES IN-FLIGHT

Article 61 – Definition and marking out of zones and associated protection level
1. Three geographical zones are defined for the safety and intervention mission (MSI) defined in – Article 63 – of this order in the event of an in-flight accident situation.
   a) *Hazard area at launch (ZRL)*
      The hazard area at launch is defined as being the land and sea area for which the flight of a launch vehicle can, in a nominal or accident situation, create hazards as defined in 0 of this order, whether mechanical, thermal, or toxic.
      The land part of this area is therefore evacuated by the President of the CNES during the launch countdown, without prejudice to any measures that may be taken by the *Préfet*, particularly as stipulated in the above-mentioned decree 89-314 of 16th May 1989. However, certain buildings designed to withstand the critical effects may house the personnel strictly necessary for running the countdown.
   b) *Protected area (ZP)*
      The protected area is the land and sea complement to the hazard area at launch (ZRL).
      In the event of failure of the launcher, it is neutralised so that it cannot create any hazards in this area, as defined in 0 of this order, whether mechanical, thermal, or toxic.
   c) *Toxic hazard areas at launch (ZRTL)*
      A toxic hazard area at launch is a land area exposed to toxic hazards but protected from thermal and mechanical (heavy fragments) hazards as defined in 0 of this order, generated by a launcher accident. A ZRTL is specific to a type of mission by a given launcher. All the ZRTL are specified by formal instruction from the President of the CNES.
      In this area, human presence is dependent on the application of special measures designed in particular to provide protection against the potential toxic effects or against the fall-back of lightweight wind-borne fragments.
      In the event of a serious danger, the President of the CNES may however have this area evacuated in compliance with the requirements of 0 of this order.

Space Law in the European Context

2. The limits between the areas defined above are described below:
   a) ***Danger limit (LD)***
      The danger limit is the boundary between the ZP and the ZRL. Beyond this limit, the public in the ZP is not exposed to the hazards as defined in 0 of this order. The geographical coordinates of the points defining the danger limit are given in the appendix to this order.
   b) ***Impact limit (LI)***
      The impact limit is the boundary between the ZRL and the ZRTL.
      The following diagram illustrates these definitions.

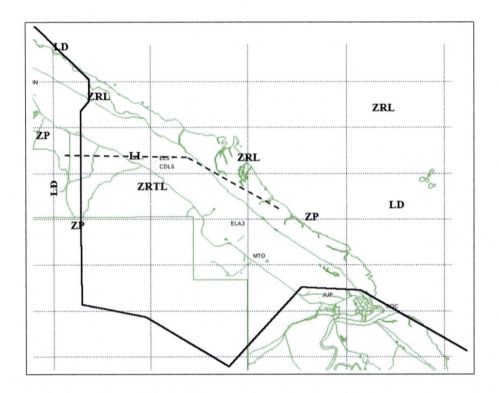

Article 62 – Flight corridor
The flight corridor is the volume within which the launch vehicle follows a trajectory compatible with its mission. Outside this volume, the launcher mission is considered to be lost and the President of the CNES may decide to order neutralisation of the launch vehicle.

The flight corridor, defined in accordance with article 17 of the technical regulations, and the method used to obtain it, are supplied to the President of the CNES by the launch operator.

Article 63 – Safety and intervention function (MSI)
As part of his safety duties related to launches, the President of the CNES performs a safety and intervention function (MSI) consisting in:
- at all times assessing the danger represented by the launch vehicle in-flight;
- intervening at any moment to neutralise the launch vehicle;
- checking the fall-back areas in nominal and degraded situations;
- evaluating the status of the resources used for this function.

The safety and intervention function begins at the moment the launcher leaves the ground and ends with the end of the ability to intervene from the CSG.

It must be possible for the flight of any launch vehicle to be intentionally interrupted from the ground by the President of the CNES during the safety and intervention function and before the flight conditions are such that the safety of people and property and the protection of public health and the environment can no longer be guaranteed.

For this purpose, the launch vehicle must comprise a means of neutralisation remote-controlled in the close-range zone from the ground. The neutralisation decision and process are the responsibility of the President of the CNES.

In the event of hazards with catastrophic consequences as defined in 0 of this order, the FS/FS criterion applies as follows: as the first failure is the failure of the launch vehicle, the failure of the neutralisation system must not therefore lead to a risk of catastrophic consequences. Therefore, all the ground and on-board systems contributing to implementation of neutralisation measures, must comply with the "Fail Operational" (FO) criterion. However, in the case of neutralisation based on predictive intervention criteria as defined in 0 of this order, the launch operator must whenever possible comply with the FO criterion.

Article 64 – Surveillance and alert function (MSA)
In addition to his safety function for launches, the President of the CNES also has a surveillance and alert function (MSA) consisting in:
- following the end of the MSI, monitoring the flight of the vehicle launched from the CSG in order to check that everything is running smoothly;
- in the event of failure of the launch vehicle, sending the competent authorities – in particular the Minister responsible for space – information concerning the fall-back

area, so that the authorities in the States concerned can be notified rapidly. This information is also sent to the launch operator.

The surveillance and alert function begins at the end of the safety and intervention function as defined in Article 63 of this order and finishes at the end of the disposal phase of the last stage of the launcher. When the disposal phase leads to immediate controlled re-entry, the surveillance and alert function continues until evaluation of the fall-back area.

Article 65 – Requirements common to the safety and intervention function (MSI) and the surveillance and alert function (MSA)
The launch operator makes available to the President of the CNES the resources and the data transmitted by the vehicle, needed for performance of the MSI and the MSA, so that he can analyse:
- the location of the launch vehicle;
- the behaviour of the launch vehicle as of lift-off;
- whether or not the flight constitutes a hazard;
- the status of the on-board intervention system;
- the reaction of the on-board intervention system when activated;
- the area affected following an in-flight accident or activation of the on-board intervention system.

Article 66 – Requirements specific to the MSI
In the close-range zone, the analysis of physically realistic diverted trajectories allows intentional neutralisation of the launcher in the interests of the safety of people and property and the protection of public health and the environment. At any time during the flight, the President of the CNES must, as part of his MSI function, be able to neutralise the launch vehicle so that it cannot constitute a hazard, as defined in 0 of this order in the protected area (ZP), whether mechanical, thermal or toxic.
For this purpose, the launch operator sends the President of the CNES all necessary data, in particular those specified in articles 16 to 19 of the technical regulations.
Predictive intervention criteria could be implemented by the President of the CNES from the ground, in particular according to the studies conducted under article 18 of the technical regulations, in order to neutralise the launcher before it overflies land. The launch operator therefore supplies the President of the CNES with all necessary information.

CHAPITRE VI.2 – neutralisation system

Article 67 – Objectives of the neutralisation system

The neutralisation systems consists of an on-board intervention device remote-controlled from the ground.

On-board automated systems may supplement this device but not replace it. Their exclusive use is only possible if the ground remote-control system is unable to guarantee an adequate link budget.

The launch operator must ensure that the on-board intervention device is compatible with the facilities of the CNES/CSG.

The launch operator ensures that the on-board elements of the neutralisation system under its responsibility are capable of neutralising the launch vehicle. Based on a single order from the ground, and for all stages, this neutralisation should be able:

- to ensure that the danger zone created by the neutralisation is compatible with the constraints relating to the various areas to be protected;
- to minimise the environmental impact;
- to shut down the thrust;
- to inhibit ignition of any stage capable of propulsion;
- to prevent any auto-propulsion by each stage;
- to ensure the direct or indirect dispersion of toxic propellants, with or without combustion;
- to prevent the detonation of solid or liquid propellants both at altitude and on any impact with the ground;
- to prevent the fall-back of fragments of a mass incompatible with the design of the ground facilities to be protected.

Article 68 – Functions of the neutralisation system

The launch operator ensures that the on-board intervention device can perform the various functions below:

- **controlled neutralisation**: a remote-control signal from the ground triggers the neutralisation function simultaneously on all the stages. When activated, no on-board functional process must be able to inhibit or delay performance of this function.
- **instantaneous automatic neutralisation**: an on-board automatic device instantaneously orders execution of the neutralisation of all stages, when non-nominal separation or rupture of a stage occurs, or in the event of drift with respect to specified conditions;
- **delayed automatic neutralisation**: an on-board automatic device orders execution of the function with a specified delay, to neutralise a stage after nominal separation, without inducing any risk for the upper stages, before impact on the ground, and ensuring dispersion of any remaining propellants;

- **inhibition of the on-board remote-control signal reception device**: this on-board remote-control signal reception device is inhibited at the end of the MSI.

Article 69 – Design of the neutralisation system
The launch operator ensures that the on-board elements making up the neutralisation system under its responsibility meet the following criteria:
- overall consistency in terms of reliability allocation, in particular between on-board and ground;
- redundancy and geographical segregation of the on-board safety systems, within the physical limits of the launch vehicle (FO criterion);
- mutually consistent levels of reliability for the inadvertent operation and lag failures. These levels must also be individually consistent with the safety objective and launcher mission success objective. The required reliability levels are specified in a formal instruction from the President of the CNES.
- the neutralisation safety functions are preferably independent of the on-board functions. Failing which, any link (dialogue bus, electrical ground, sequential order, etc.) between the equipment items performing neutralisation safety functions and the on-board functional equipment items must not delay or inhibit (regardless of the failure) the capability of the neutralisation functions.

Article 70 – On-board elements constituting the neutralisation system
The on-board elements constituting the neutralisation system mentioned below are the subject of a submission process as defined in 0 of this order:
- actuation devices affecting the launch vehicle (pyrotechnic safety system, valves, etc.);
- control devices which can be either an on-board receiver for a signal transmitted from the ground, or a specific on-board device;
- power supplies to these devices;
- power and communication circuits.

The on-board safety systems are redundant and segregated (FO criterion), in accordance with the requirements of Article 63 of this order. They are designed to withstand the hazards that could be encountered during the launch countdown and the launch phase.

If it is impossible to comply with the above segregation rule for certain existing systems as well as for new systems, a RAMS study must demonstrate compliance with the safety objectives as stipulated in 0 of this order.

When neutralisation is triggered, the operation of the devices on each stage of the launch vehicle is guaranteed with the required level of performance and the system must function in the harshest environmental conditions that could result from failure of the launch vehicle.

Article 71 – Implementation of the neutralisation systems

The launch operator provides the President of the CNES with the information necessary for taking account of and checking all the effects of in-flight explosion of the launch vehicle and those resulting from use of the neutralisation system.

The launch operator therefore supplies:
- the neutralisation scenarios (explosion, complete fall-back, rupture, etc.);
- the fragmentation and explosion data;
- the energy levels on impact;
- the aerodynamic data for all or part of the launcher falling back.

Article 72 – Orders sent from the ground

The ground elements of the neutralisation system must be able to send the following three orders:
- hold;
- neutralisation ordered;
- inhibition (or OFF).

The launch operator demonstrates that the on-board neutralisation systems are capable of performing the functions associated with each of these orders, as required in 0 of this order.

Article 73 – On-board remote-control receivers (RTC)

On-board, the orders are received simultaneously by two on-board receivers which each control two on-board safety systems.

The theoretical processing, reception and execution time by the on-board systems is sent to the President of the CNES during the design phase, as stipulated in 0 of this order.

For each flight, the launch operator measures the actual processing, reception and execution time by the on-board systems during the campaign activities and checks that it is consistent with the theoretical time. The launch operator sends this information to the President of the CNES as soon as possible and in any case no later than transfer to the launch area.

Article 74 – TCN visibility limit

The TCN link budget is defined by:
- the geometric limit of visibility, set at 2.5 degrees elevation, in order to protect against a rapid fall in automatic gain control observed at the end of radio visibility at the moment of passing below the horizon and any radio disturbances;
- the range limit, taking account of radio propagation losses and the margins defined by the formal instruction from the President of the CNES. It depends on the distance between the remote-control ground station and the launcher, as well as on the antenna used;

- actual reception by each RTC on the launch vehicle, within a range between -30 dBm and -90 dBm, along the nominal trajectory during the MSI.

The launch operator must define the launch vehicle trajectory to optimise the link budget.

Article 75 – Qualification and checks
As the launcher elements contribute to neutralisation, each subassembly and the complete device with its components (cabling, connectors, couplings, etc.) are qualified taking account of the ambient conditions representative of failure of the launch vehicle.
The launch operator must demonstrate this qualification by means of dedicated design tests.
The launch operator must also use testing to demonstrate the correct operation of the equipment after launcher integration.
The specifications concerning all of these tests are submitted to the President of the CNES in the conditions specified in 0 of this order.

CHAPITRE VI.3 – Positioning system

Article 76 – Elements of the positioning system
The ground and on-board elements of the system used to position the launch vehicle and determine the potential fall-back area are submitted to the President of the CNES in the conditions specified in 0 of this order during their design and construction phase. This submission in particular concerns:
- the frequency with which data are made available;
- the data precision;
- the various specified times and time-outs.

The on-board equipment contributing to the positioning function is compatible with the systems and procedures of the CNES/CSG. The launch operator provides the necessary elements to the President of the CNES enabling him to ensure this compatibility.
For performance of the MSI, the President of the CNES must at all times during powered flight have access to positioning data. These data are produced by at least two independent positioning systems. At least one of these systems must use resources outside the launch vehicle.
For performance of the MSA, the President of the CNES must have access to positioning data in the conditions specified in 0 and in 0 of this order.

Article 77 – Design of the positioning system
The launch operator ensures that the on-board elements of the positioning system under its responsibility meet the following criteria:

- overall consistency in terms of reliability allocation, in particular between on-board and ground;
- redundancy and geographical segregation of the positioning systems (FO criterion);
- mutually consistent levels of reliability for the inadvertent operation and lag failures. These levels must also be individually consistent with the safety objective and launcher mission success objective;
- the positioning function used for the MSI is independent of the active navigation function for the launch vehicle mission. All links (dialogue bus, electrical ground, sequential order, etc.) between equipment performing positioning functions and on-board functional equipment must not delay or inhibit (regardless of the failure) the capability of the positioning functions.

Article 78 – Visualisation of the launch vehicle

The launch operator must provide the President of the CNES with images allowing real-time observations of the behaviour of the launch vehicle. These images are compatible with the systems and procedures of the CNES/CSG and at least allow wide-field display in two orthogonal planes, covering the vertical space between 0 and 250 metres and a field width of about 600 metres.

Article 79 – Radar positioning

The launch vehicle is equipped with independent radar transponders compatible with the systems and procedures of the CNES/CSG. Any external positioning system is designed so that the kinematic conditions of the launch vehicle can be determined at any moment along the trajectory, in nominal or degraded situations.

Article 80 – Positioning using the on-board resources

The launch operator must ensure the precision and robustness of positioning using the launcher's internal resources in all possible failure situations. In accordance with the requirements of 0 of this order, the internal positioning data can only be taken into account when they do not take part in the navigation, guidance and control of the launch vehicle. The ground and on-board processing of these positioning data by the launch operator must not alter them (integrity guarantee).

Article 81 – Precision of positioning resources

The launch operator provides the President of the CNES with the elements necessary for determining positioning position and speed errors. These supplies are defined during the safety submission process as specified in 0 of this order.

Article 82 – Qualification and checks

As the launcher elements contribute to positioning, each subassembly as well as the complete system with its components (cabling, connectors, couplings, etc.) are qualified taking account of the ambient conditions representative of failure of the launch vehicle.

The launch operator must demonstrate this qualification by means of dedicated design tests.

The launch operator must also use testing to demonstrate the correct operation of the equipment after integration of the launcher.

The specifications concerning all these tests are submitted to the President of the CNES in the conditions specified in 0 of this order.

CHAPITRE VI.4 – Telemetry system

Article 83 – Objectives of the telemetry system

The launch operator sends the President of the CNES the telemetry data used to:
– characterise the status of the on-board/ground remote-control link, before lift-off and in-flight;
– assess the status of the on-board safety systems, before lift-off and in-flight;
– receive the remote-control orders on-board acquisition report;
– monitor the status of the on-board automated systems linked to the safety function, including the de-orbit and passivation functions;
– acquire the parameters needed for the use of predictive intervention criteria by the ground facilities;
– acquire the launcher's position;
– receive the launcher good operating status (propulsion, flight control, electrical equipment).

Article 84 – Use of telemetry for the MSI

At all times in powered flight, the President of the CNES must have real-time access to the following, for performance of the safety and intervention function as specified in Article 63 of this order:
– detailed positioning data;
– the status of the on-board intervention device;
– data on performance of the flight sequence;
– on-board data concerning the operation of the launch vehicle.

The detailed contents of the data necessary for the MSI as specified in a formal instruction from the President of the CNES for each launch system considered.

ANNEX 2.7

Article 85 – Use of telemetry for the MSA

During the powered phases, stage separation, de-orbiting and preparation for controlled re-entry of launch vehicle elements, the launch operator must provide the President of the CNES with the following real-time parameters, for performance of the surveillance and alert function as specified in 0 of this order:
- detailed positioning data;
- data on performance of the flight sequence;
- on-board data concerning the operation of the launch vehicle.

In the event of implementation problems arising from mission requirements, telemetry gaps in stabilised flight conditions (excluding ignition, shutdown or controlled speed change) can be accepted in the following conditions:
- justification of these difficulties by the launch operator, with associated proposals;
- implementation of on-board recording;
- osculating orbit with a perigee higher than 120 km for the duration of the telemetry gap;
- telemetry gap duration compatible with guaranteed acquisition by the next station in all non-nominal cases (excluding explosion during the telemetry gap phase).

Implementation of these measures is submitted by the launch operator to the President of the CNES.

The detailed contents of the data necessary for the MSA are the subject of a formal instruction from the President of the CNES for each launch system considered.

Article 86 – Use of telemetry for stage disposal

During the launch vehicle stage disposal phases, the President of the CNES must have real-time access to:
- data on performance of the flight sequence;
- on-board data concerning the correct operation of the launch vehicle.

In the event of implementation problems arising from mission requirements, a telemetry reception gap can be acceptable. It is submitted by the launch operator to the President of the CNES.

The detailed contents of the necessary data are the subject of a formal instruction from the President of the CNES for each launch system considered.

Article 87 – CSG telemetry system

The CSG has appropriate telemetry reception resources to be able to track the launch vehicle during standard eastwards GTO launch missions.

For other missions, the launch operator must provide the resources and input data necessary for creation of the specific network of stations. In this case, these resources are the subject of a safety submission as required in 0 of this order.

The resources deployed on-board during the launch are compatible with the systems and procedures of the CNES/CSG.

Article 88 – Qualifications and checks

The launcher elements contributing to telemetry, each subassembly and the complete device with its components (cabling, connectors, couplings, etc.) are qualified.

The launch operator must demonstrate this qualification by means of dedicated tests.

The launch operator must also use testing to demonstrate the correct operation of the equipment after integration of the launcher.

The specifications concerning all these tests are submitted to the President of the CNES in the conditions specified in 0 of this order.

Article 89 – Analysis of flight data

After the flight, the launch operator must systematically analyse the data transmitted by the launcher and concerning the systems contributing to the safety function.

A summary of these analyses is sent in writing to the President of the CNES. This summary at least comprises any anomalies encountered, which could have an impact on safety, and the planned disposition of these anomalies.

PARTIE VII – Conditions authorising final countdown

Article 90 – Pre-conditions for launch

Pursuant to article 14-8 of the above-mentioned CNES decree, the President of the CNES stops the launch countdown if one of the criteria defined in 0 and 0 of this order is not met.

Article 91 – Meteorological criteria
- **Wind at ground level**

The launch operator supplies the quantities and types of propellants used to define the close-range zone ground level wind criterion in order to ensure the safety of people and property and the protection of public health and the environment.

The ground level wind criterion is determined as being the maximum allowable wind for which it is possible to remain below the toxic effects threshold defined in the danger limit.
- **Wind at altitude**

The wind is measured on the day of the launch by means of a radiosonde.

For each launch, simulations using the winds measured by the latest radiosonde reading as close as possible to H0 are made by the President of the CNES to ensure compliance with the danger limit in accordance with 0 of this order.
- **Lightning**

The applicable criteria linked to the risk of lightning striking the launcher are as follows:
- C1: no lightning risk within a 10 km radius around the launcher.
- C2: no convective clouds more than 6500 m thick within a 10 km radius around the launch pad at H0.
- C3: no Cumulonimbus anvils vertically above the launch pad, if the storm cell is less than 20 km away.

Article 92 – Technical criteria
- **Flight safety function**

The launch is dependent on the status of the on-board safety systems, the correct working of the ground control systems and the status of any de-orbiting systems, in order to guarantee that the launcher is "positioning, telemetry and neutralisation" capable in the conditions stipulated in 0 of this order.

The last good operating check on the on-board neutralisation, positioning and telemetry system is carried out in a configuration as close as possible to the flight configuration and as late as possible in the launch countdown.

The final check on the on-board intervention system must be made in the configuration as close as possible to the flight configuration.
- **Authorisation and requirements from the Minister responsible for space**

The launch is dependent on the issue and continued validity of the launch authorisation from the Minister responsible for space, pursuant to the above-mentioned Space Operations Act.

Implementation of the requirements of this order is without prejudice to the application by the Minister or, by delegation, the President of the CNES, of the necessary instructions and measures in the interests of the safety of people and property and the protection of public health and the environment, as stipulated in article 8 of the above-mentioned Space Operations Act and article L. 331-7 of the Research Code.
- **Collision in orbit**

As part of his safety function as related to the performance of launches, the President of the CNES is responsible for protecting manned space objects.

To this end, the flight of the launch vehicle in the envisaged launch window is compatible with the position of manned space objects, for which the orbital parameters are precisely known and available.

- **Evacuation of areas at risk during launch**
In accordance with the requirements of 0 of this order, the ZRL is evacuated during the launch countdown. The only persons authorised to remain in certain reinforced buildings of the ZRL are those required for the launch and, in the ZRTL, those placed under the control of the President of the CNES.

Article 93 – CSG external protection
The President of the CNES may also stop the countdown at the request of the State's representative in charge of external protection, in the conditions stipulated in the above-mentioned decree of 16th May 1989.

PARTIE VIII – SANCTIONS

Article 94 – Administrative fine
In accordance with article 14-9 of the above-mentioned CNES decree, the President of the CNES may levy an administrative fine of an amount defined for category 5 breaches, on any individual or corporate body mentioned in article 14-7 of the same decree and carrying out an activity in breach of the requirements of this order.

PARTIE IX – Administrative provisions

Article 95 – Communication of information, data and files
All information, data and files to be transmitted or submitted to the President of the CNES for application of the requirements of this order are sent to the Director of the Guiana Space Centre.

Article 96 – Appeal
This order may be appealed to the competent administrative court by the applicant within a period of two months following its notification.
Within the same two-month period, the applicant may present an application for reconsideration. If the President of the CNES issues no response to the application for reconsideration for more than two months, then this application is implicitly rejected accordance with article R. 421-2 of the Administrative Justice Code.

Article 97 – Entry into force and publication
The provisions of this order take effect as of the date of its publication in the code of administrative procedures of the Préfecture of French Guiana.
This order may be freely consulted in the badge issue office of the Guiana Space Centre.

ANNEX 2.7

Issued in Paris, on 9th December 2010.

Appendix
Annex 1: Geographical coordinates of the points defining the Danger Limit

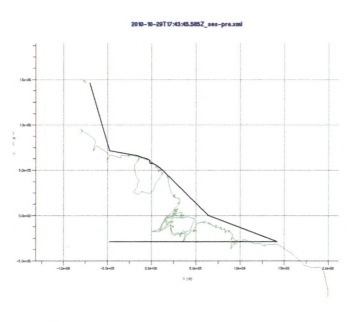

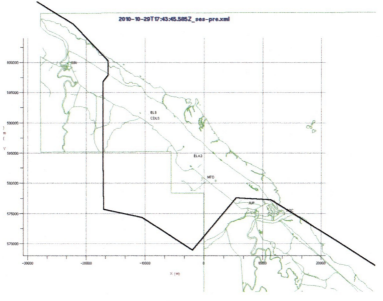

WGS84 coordinates of the points defining the Danger Limit (Longitude Latitude in decimal degrees)	
59.000000°W	13.0000000°N
57.000000°W	06.4000000°N
54.200000°W	05.9000000°N
53.120000°W	05.5400000°N
52.950000°W	05.4390000°N
52.896667°W	05.3850000°N
52.896667°W	05.3633333°N
52.904100°W	05.3539000°N
52.904167°W	05.2416667°N
52.903500°W	05.1650000°N
52.840400°W	05.1507000°N
52.768100°W	05.1043000°N
52.701400°W	05.1820000°N
52.647944°W	05.1788889°N
52.179300°W	04.8959000°N
51.847000°W	04.6691000°N
51.508900°W	04.4032000°N
47.000000°W	00.0000000°N
40.000000°W	02.6000000°S
57.000000°W	02.6000000°S

ANNEX III – COMPARISON LIST OF USUAL DEFINITIONS

Comparison list of usual definitions and associated acronyms between RT-FSOA and IADC, UNGA and ISO Space Debris Mitigation Instruments

Texts selected:
- **French Space Operation Act (FSOA)**: Act of 3rd June 2008.
- **Technical Regulation (RT)**: Order of 31St march 2011 as modified by Order of 11th July 2017.
- **IADC-SDMG (2007) or IADC:** Inter-Agency Space Debris Coordination Committee (IADC) Space Debris Mitigation <u>Guidelines</u> (SDMG), IADC-02-01-Revision 1, September 2007, action Item 22.4, issued by Steering Group and Working Group 4.
- **UNGA-COPUOS-SDMG 62/217 (2007) or UNGA 62/217:** United Nations General Assembly (UNGA), Resolution 62/217 adopted on 22 December 2007, based on the Report of the Scientific and Technical Subcommittee (STC) of the Committee of the Peaceful Uses of Outer Space (COPUOS) on Space Debris Mitigation Guidelines (SDMG), annexed in 62th session, official records, supplement N° 20 (A/62/20) of the First February 2008
- **ISO-SDMR 24113 (2011) or ISO:** International Standard Organization (ISO) 24113 of May 2011, second edition 2011-05-15, Space systems – Space Debris Mitigation <u>Requirements</u>
- **EU ICOC (2014):** European Union's **Draft** of International Code of Conduct for Outer Space Activities, version of 31st march 2014.

- Allocation (*Allocation*):
  - RT Art. 1: level of probability given to the occurrence of a critical or specified event, when determining the safety objectives.
  - No definition of "Allocation" in IADC, UNGA, ISO SDM measures ...
- Break-up (*Desintégration, rupture*):
  - RT: no specific definition of "break-up", but several uses of this term: Art. 16.3 (required proof on Launch operation requirements), 21.3 and 40.2 (Space debris limitation: probability of occurrence), 24 (wrecks and recovery of launched elements).

- IADC §3.4.4: any event that generates fragments, which are released into Earth orbit. This includes:
    - An explosion caused by the chemical or thermal energy from propellants, pyrotechnics and so on;
    - A rupture caused by an increase in internal pressure;
    - A break-up caused by energy from collision with other objects.

    However, the following events are excluded from this definition:
    - A break-up during the re-entry phase caused by aerodynamic forces;
    - The generation of fragments, such as paint flakes, resulting from the ageing and degradation of a spacecraft or orbital stage.

    ⇨ As to application, see IADC mitigation measure 5.2: "Minimize the Potential for On-Orbit Break-ups"
- ISO §3.2: same definition than IADC above.
    ⇨ As to application, see ISO Requirement 6.2: "Avoiding break-ups in Earth orbit"
- UNGA: no specific definition.
    ⇨ As to application, see Guideline 2: Minimize the potential for break-ups during operational phases. see ISO Requirement 6.2: "Avoiding break-ups in Earth orbit".
- Catastrophic damage *(dommage catastrophique)* and Casualty *(victime)*:
    - RT Art. 1: immediate or deferred loss of human life, or serious human injury (bodily injuries, other irreversible health impairments, occupational invalidity or illness, either permanent or temporary).
    - IADC: no specific definition and use.
    - UNGA Res. 62/217: no specific definition, term used in G. n°2 as to Break-ups failures;
    - ISO §3.3 - Casualty risk: probability that a person is killed or seriously injured. Used in §6.3.4 as to Re-entry requirements.
- Controlled re-entry *(Rentrée contrôlée)*:
    - RT Art. 1: atmospheric re-entry of a space object (SO below) with a predefined contact or ground impact zone for the object or fragments thereof.
    see R-E below.
- Damage *(Dommage)*:
    - FSOA only, Art. 1.1°: means damage to persons or property, and in particular to public health or to the environment, directly caused by a space object (SO below) as part of a "space operation", to the exclusion of the consequences arising from the use of the signal transmitted by this object for users.
- Flight corridor *(Couloir de vol)*:

COMPARISON LIST OF USUAL DEFINITIONS AND ASSOCIATED ACRONYMS BETWEEN RT-FSOA
AND IADC, UNGA AND ISO SPACE DEBRIS MITIGATION INSTRUMENTS

- RT Art. 1:
  - Original wording (2011): volume within which the launch vehicle (LV below) is liable to fly and outside of which it is **neutralized**.
    ⇨ see definition of "neutralization" below.
  - Updated wording (2017): volume within which the launch vehicle (LV below) is liable to fly **taking into account normal dispersions.**
    ⇨ no more reference to "neutralization" in 2017'version.
  - No definition of "flight corridor" in IADC, UNGA, ISO SDM measures...
- Hazard level *(Etude de dangers)*:
  - RT Art. 1: probabilistic estimate characterizing the lack of "safety" (see definition below) of a system with regard to a "critical event", expressed by the probability of occurrence of this event.
    ⇨ See RT's Articles 7 and 32 and others as referred to therein. Same definition in the REI-CSG.
  - No definition of "Hazard" in IADC, UNGA, ISO SDM measures. Term used in IADC §3.4.2 (de-orbit) 3.5.3 (disposal phase).
- Irreversible moment *(Instant irréversible)*:
  - RT Art. 1: for a launch operation, time at which the last order leading to launch vehicle lift-off is sent.
  See FSOA's definition for Launch Phase (LP) below.
- Disposal Phase *(Phase de retrait de service)* - DP:
  - RT Art. 1: final phase of the **space operation** during which the space object is made safe in order to limit the risks related to space debris (SD).
    ⇨ See FSOA's definition for "space operation" below.
  - IADC §3.5.3, under §3.5 (operational phases, see OP below): begins at the end of the mission phase for a spacecraft (S/C) or orbital stage (LVOS) and ends when the spacecraft or orbital stage has performed the actions to reduce the hazards it poses to other spacecraft and orbital stages.
    ⇨ See also IADC's definition for "Passivation" below.
  - ISO §3.5: interval during which a spacecraft (S/C below) or launch vehicle orbital stage (LVOS below) completes its disposal actions.
    ⇨ See EoL, EoM, OL and OP below.
- End of life *(Fin de vie)* - EoL:
  - RT Art. 1: end of the disposal phase (DP) of the space object (SO) or loss of control of it.
  - ISO §3.6: instant when a spacecraft or launch vehicle orbital stage is permanently turned off, nominally as it completes its disposal phase, or when it re-enters, or when the operator can no longer control it.

⇒ Equivalent to the end of the DP above or the OP below, nominally EoL is to occur after EoM below
- End of **Mission** *(Fin de mission)* - EoM:
  - RT: no definition of EoM see below "Operational Phase" (~) and "Space System".
  - ISO §3.7: instant when a spacecraft or launch vehicle orbital stage completes the **tasks or functions for which it has been designed**, or when it becomes **non-functional** or permanently halted because of a failure or because of a voluntary decision. To connect with c) of ISO introduction that prescribes "removing spacecraft and launch vehicle orbital stages from protected orbital regions **after end of mission.**
  ⇒ Ed. note: nominally EoM occurs before EoL above
- Launcher (vehicle) and its Components or its Elements" *(Lanceur et ses composants ou éléments)* - L&C:
  - No specific definition, terms used in RT (Part. II) only.
  ⇒ equivalent to the LV and LVOS's definitions below.
- Launch Phase *(Phase de lancement)* - LP:
  - Not defined as such in the RT (see below OP and SS regarding launch operation)
  - Defined by FSOA's Art. 1.4: "launching phase" means the period of time which, as part of a space operation, starts at the moment when the **launching operations become irreversible** and which, without prejudice to provisions contained, if necessary, in the authorization granted pursuant to the present act, ends when the object to be put in outer space is separated from its launch vehicle.
  - IADC §3.5.1, under §3.5 (operational phases, see OP below): LP begins when the launch vehicle is no longer in physical contact with equipment and ground installations that made its preparation and ignition possible (or when the launch vehicle is dropped from the carrier- aircraft, if any), and continues up to the end of the mission assigned to the launch vehicle.
  - Launch Phase safety is expressly excluded from ISO SDMR' scope (§1 last sentence).
- Launch Vehicle *(Véhicule de lancement)* - LV:
  - RT Art. 1: assembly comprising the launcher (LV) **and the Space Objects (SO)** intended to be placed into orbit.
  - IADC §3.2.2: any vehicle constructed for ascent to outer space, and for placing one or more objects (SO) in outer space, and any **sub-orbital rocket.**
  - No definition of "LV" in ISO 24113.
- Launch Vehicle Orbital Stage *(Etages et éléments du lanceur)* - LVOS:
  - RT: no specific definition of LVOS, mentioned in Art. 3 as to Part II' scope. See also Launcher's component or element (L&C above)
  - IADC §3.2.3: any stage of a Launch Vehicle (LV) left in Earth orbit.
  - ISO §3.9: stage of a Launch Vehicle (LV) that is designed to achieve orbit.

- Neutralization *(Neutralisation)*:
  - RT Art. 1: Action taken on the launcher in order to minimize damage to individuals and property. It can in particular be characterized by an action to destroy or stop the thrust of a launch vehicle, in order to terminate the flight of the considered vehicle or a stage which is no longer functioning correctly.
  - No definition of "Neutralization" in IADC, UNGA, ISO SDM measures…
- Nominal *(Nominal)*:
  - RT Art. 1: Corresponding to the specifications or performance levels announced by the operator or designer of the space object.
  - The term "nominal is not specifically defined but used in:
    - IADC (§5.3.2) as related to protection of region A: "nominal projection for solar activity".
    - ISO, systematically associated with mission (Nominal mission) in §3.6 (EoL) and Annex A as relates to the calculation of "Probability of successful disposal".
- Mission Phase *(Phase de mission)* - MP, M:
  - RT: no direct equivalent, see "Operational Phase" and "Space System" below.
  - IADC §3.5.2, under §3.5 (operational phases, see OP below): the phase where the spacecraft or orbital stage fulfils its **mission**. Begins at the end of the launch phase and ends at the beginning of the disposal phase.
  - ISO: see under §3.2.1 (for S/C): an orbiting object designed to perform a specific function **or mission (e.g. communications, navigation or Earth observation)** and under §3.7, see EoM above.
- On-board neutralisation device *(dispositif bord de neutralisation)*:
  - RT Art. 1: on-board means involved in neutralising the launch vehicle in flight;
  - No definition of "On-board neutralization device" in IADC, UNGA, ISO SDM measures
- Orbital Lifetime *(durée de vie en orbite)* - OL:
  - RT and IADC: no specific definition, corresponds to the one of the end of Disposal Phase (DP in §3.5.3) as indicated below.
  - ISO §3.12: period of time from when a Spacecraft (S/C) or Launch Vehicle Orbital Stage (LVOS) achieves Earth orbit to when it commences re-entry
- Operational Phase *(Phase opérationnelle)* - OP:
  - RT Art. 1: period of time which, during an operation involving **control** in extra-atmospheric space, begins at the moment the operator takes **control** of the space object (SO) and ends with the beginning of the disposal phase (DP).
    ⇒ no reference to any SO's "mission" (as to spacecraft payload) but to SO's "control" only.
  - IADC §3.5 "Operational Phases":

- 3.5.1 - **Launch phase** (see specific def. above): begins when the launch vehicle is no longer in physical contact with equipment and ground installations that made its preparation and ignition possible (or when the launch vehicle is dropped from the carrier- aircraft, if any), and continues up to the end of the mission assigned to the launch vehicle.
- 3.5.2 - **Mission phase** (see specific def. above): the phase where the spacecraft or orbital stage fulfils its mission. Begins at the end of the launch phase and ends at the beginning of the disposal phase.
- 3.5.3 - **Disposal phase** (see specific def. above): begins at the end of the mission phase for a spacecraft or orbital stage and ends when the spacecraft or orbital stage has performed the actions to reduce the hazards it poses to other spacecraft and orbital stages.

⇨ IADC also provides definitions in §3.4 for the following **operations as mitigations measures**:
- 3.4.1 **Passivation** (see specific def. above): the elimination of all stored energy on a spacecraft or orbital stages to reduce the chance of break-up. Typical passivation measures include venting or burning excess propellant, discharging batteries and relieving pressure vessels.
- 3.4.2 **De-orbit**: intentional changing of orbit for re-entry of a spacecraft or orbital stage into the Earth's atmosphere to eliminate the hazard it poses to other spacecraft and orbital stages, by applying a retarding force, usually via a propulsion system.
- 3.4.3 **Re-orbit**: intentional changing of a spacecraft or orbital stage's orbit.
- ISO: no specific definition of "Operational phase".

⇨ See also DP, EoM, EoL, LP, MP and OL below.
- Passivation *(Passivation)*:
  - RT and ISO: no specific definition.
    ⇨ corresponds to the one of the end of Disposal Phase, see DP above. Secondarily, see "Phase of Command" below as to FSOA's definition.
  - IADC §3.4.1: The elimination of all stored energy on a spacecraft or orbital stages to reduce the chance of break-up. Typical passivation measures include venting or burning excess propellant, discharging batteries and relieving pressure vessels.
  - UNGA: term associated to the mitigation measures of G. n°2 (Minimize the potential for break-ups during operational phases) and G. n° 5 (Minimize potential for post-mission break-ups resulting from stored energy).
- Phase of Command *(Phase de maîtrise)*:
  - Only defined in FSOA (Art. 1.5) as follows: means the period of time starting as part of a space operation at the moment when the object to be put in outer space

is separated from its launch vehicle (LV) and ending when the first of the following events occurs:
- when the final maneuvers for **de-orbiting** and the **passivation** activities have been completed (=> see DP above);
- when the operator has lost **control** over the space object (=> see EoL above);
- the return to Earth or the full disintegration of the space object into the atmosphere (=> see "Return" below).

- RT: no definition nor reference to the word "command" (as translation for *maîtrise*). This phase is indirectly covered in though the definition of the "operational phase" (see OP above) that involve "control" of the SO, and secondarily under the definition of Space System (SS below) with regard to "a control operation".
⇨ The terms "mastery" or "control" may be used as synonym of "command" in common language.
- IADC, UNGA, ISO SDM measures: no definition, nor any use of the term of "command" or "mastery". The terms "control" is however used regarding disposal (DP below), removal, re-entry (R-E below) from LEO (IADC §5.3.2 – UNGA G. n°6 – ISO §3.6, 6.2.2.3, 6.3.3) or GEO orbit (ISO §6.3.2), or prevention of on-orbit collision (IADC §5.4).
⇨ See also DP, EoM, EoL, LP, MP and OL above.

- Procedure *(Procédure)*:
  - RT Art. 1: Specified way of carrying out an activity or process.
  - No definition of "Procedure" in IADC, UNGA, ISO SDM measures.
- Process *(Processus)*:
  - RT Art. 1: Set of correlated or interactive activities which transform input elements into output elements;
  - No definition of "Process" in IADC, UNGA, ISO SDM measures.
- Protected Region A or B *(Regions protégées)* - PR:
  - RT Art. 1:
    - protected region A, low Earth orbit (LEO) – spherical region extending from the surface of the Earth up to an altitude (Z) of 2,000 km;
    - protected region B, geosynchronous region (GEO) – segment of the spherical envelope defined as follows: lower limit = geostationary altitude minus 200 km; upper limit = geostationary altitude plus 200 km ;15 degrees ≤ latitude ≤ +15 degrees; geostationary altitude " (Z GEO) = 35,786 km (altitude of geostationary terrestrial orbit;
  - IADC §3.2.2 => wording equivalent to that provided by RT.
  - UNGA: G. n° 6 & 7
  - ISO §3.14: region in space that is protected with regard to the generation of Space Debris (SD) to ensure its safe and sustainable use in the future.

- Return – Re-Entry *(Retour - Réentrée)* - R-E:
  - RT Art. 1:
    - **"Return"**: period which starts at re-entry of the space object into the Earth's atmosphere and ends when it is immobilized on the ground, as part of a controlled or uncontrolled re-entry.
    - **"Controlled re-entry"**: atmospheric re-entry of a space object (SO) with a predefined contact or ground impact zone for the object or fragments thereof
    - **"Uncontrolled re-entry"**: atmospheric re-entry of a space object (SO) for which it is not possible to predefine the ground impact zone by the object or fragments thereof.
  - IADC: no specific definition. => corresponds to "De-orbit" (§3.4.2) intentional changing of orbit for re-entry of a spacecraft (S/C) or orbital stage into the Earth's atmosphere to eliminate the hazard it poses to other spacecraft and orbital stages, by applying a retarding force, usually via a propulsion system.
  - ISO §3.15 (Re-entry): process in which atmospheric drag cascades deceleration of a spacecraft or launch vehicle orbital stage (or any part thereof), leading to its destruction or return to Earth (associated note: For operational purposes, this is when the period of the mean orbit is 89 min or less).
- Safety – Safeguard *(Sécurité, Sûreté – Sauvegarde (in RT, REI-CSG, FSOA)*, the word *"Sauvegarde"* may also being translated into "Safeguard"):
  - RT Art. 1: Set of arrangements intended to control risks in order to ensure protection of people, property and public health and the environment.
  - No definition of "Safety" nor of "Safeguard" in IADC, UNGA, ISO SDM measures.
- Safety coefficient *(coefficient de sécurité)*:
  - RT Art. 1: the ratio between the allowable limit of a parameter characterizing a system or an element and its maximum expected value in nominal operation. Its value includes the scattering specific to each field concerned.
  - No definition of "Safety coefficient" in IADC, UNGA, ISO SDM measures.
- Safety margin *(Marge de sécurité)*:
  - RT Art. 1: Margin between the allowable limit of a parameter characterizing a system or an element and its maximum value reached in normal operation, multiplied by the safety coefficient.
  - No definition of "Safety margin" in IADC, UNGA, ISO SDM measures.
- Space Object *(Objet spatial)* - SO:

COMPARISON LIST OF USUAL DEFINITIONS AND ASSOCIATED ACRONYMS BETWEEN RT-FSOA AND IADC, UNGA AND ISO SPACE DEBRIS MITIGATION INSTRUMENTS

- RT Art. 1: any human object made, **functional or not**, during its launch time, its time spent in extra-atmospheric space or its return, including the elements of a launcher placed into orbit.
  ⇒ this includes the LV during the Launch phase and LVOS. See also below the definition of Space system (SS) in RT Art. 1. No specific mention to any SO's **mission**. This term is also mainly used in FSOA but not defined therein as such.
- IADC and ISO: no specific definition nor any use (except on ISO's introduction d) on risk of collision)
  ⇒ see LVOS above and S/C, SS below.
- UNGA no specific definition, but mentioned in G. n°7 consistently with the terminology of the UN 1967's OST and 1972's Liability Convention. Basically, UNGA res. 62/217 uses the terms of "Spacecraft and launch vehicle orbital stages"
- Space Operation *(Opération spatiale)* – not associated here with an acronym:
  - FSOA only (Art. 1.3°): means any activity consisting in **launching or attempting to launch an object into outer space**, or of ensuring the **commanding** of a **space object (SO)** during its journey in outer space, including the Moon and other celestial bodies, and, if necessary, during its **return** to Earth.
  - No specific definition of "Space operation" in RT nor in IADC, UNGA, ISO SDM measures.
    ⇒ See also EoM, EoL, LP, MP, OL and OP above.
- Space Operator *(Opérateur spatial)* - not associated in this annex with an acronym:
  - FSOA only, Art. 1.2°: means any natural or juridical person carrying out a space operation under its responsibility and independently.
  - No specific definition of "Space Operator" in RT nor in IADC, UNGA, ISO SDM measures.
    ⇒ See also EoM, EoL, LP, MP, OL and OP above.
- Spacecraft *(Vaisseau spatial)* - S/C:
  - RT: no specific definition, see Space Object (SO) above or Space System (SS) below.
  - IADC-2007 §3.2.1: an orbiting object designed to perform a specific **function or mission (e.g. communications, navigation or Earth observation)**. A spacecraft that can no longer fulfil its intended mission is considered non-functional. (Spacecraft in reserve or standby modes awaiting possible reactivation are considered functional).
  - UNGA: no specific definition, but the words "Spacecraft and launch vehicle orbital stages" are used in §4 introduction (scope of mitigation guidelines) and guidelines n° 2, 4, 5, 6, 7.
  - ISO 24113 §3.18: system designed to perform specific **tasks or functions** in space (associated note: A spacecraft that can no longer fulfil its intended **mission** is con-

sidered non-functional. Spacecraft in reserve or standby modes awaiting possible reactivation are considered functional).
⇨ IADC and ISO's S/C definition equivalent to the SO's RT Definition except as to LV and LVOS.
- Space Debris *(Débris spatial ou spatiaux)* - SD :
  - RT Art. 1: any non-functional human made object, including fragments and elements thereof, in Earth orbit or re-entering the Earth's atmosphere.
  - IADC: §3.1: Space debris are all (hu)man-made objects including fragments and elements thereof, in Earth orbit or re-entering the atmosphere, that are non-functional.
  - ISO §3.17: orbital debris, (hu)man-made objects, including fragments and elements thereof, in Earth orbit or re-entering the atmosphere, that are non-functional.
- SDMG or SDMR: Space Debris Mitigation Guidelines (IADC 2007 and UNGA res; 62/217) or Requirements (ISO) – *Guide, Directives ou Exigences liées à la limitation des debris spatiaux.*
- Space system *(Système spatial)* – SS:
  - RT Art. 1: arrangement consisting of one or more space objects (SO) and the associated equipment and installations needed to perform a specified "**mission**" (ed. note: the term "mission" is used here instead of "function" as to RT's definition above of Space Object, SO). **With regard to a launch operation**, the space system contains the launcher, the interfaced launch base, including the tracking stations, and the space object to be launched. **With regard to a control operation**, the space system consists of the space object and the interfaced ground segment.
  - IADC and ISO: no specific definition, see EoM, LVOS, MP, OL, OP, S/C, SO above.
- Third party to a space operation *(Tiers à une operation spatiale)*:
  - FSOA only, Art. 1.6 (as to Art. 13 to 18 on damage and liability): means any natural or juridical person other than those taking part in the space operation or in the production of the space object(s) the launch or command of which is part of the operation. In particular, the space operator, its contractors, its subcontractors and its customers, as the contractors and subcontractors of its customers, are not regarded as third parties.

ANNEX IV – CONCORDANCE TABLE

Réglementation Technique (RT) de 2011 modifiée en 2017, LOS et Décret d'application (DA)	2011's Technical Regulation (RT) as modified in 2017, FSOA and Application Decree (DA)
Instruments internationaux de limitation des débris spatiaux (IADC, AGNU res.62/217, ISO…)	International instruments on Space Debris Mitigation measures (IADC, UNGA res.62/217, ISO…)
Tableau de concordance	Concordance table
Document d'information non opposable	Informative document not enforceable

N° (F) / N° (E)	Titres en français (F) / Heading in English (E)	Dispositions Communes / Common provisions (Part. I, II, IV, V & 6)	Lancement d'OS / Launch of a SO (Part II)	Maîtrise Et retour / Control and return of (Part. III)	Observations, references, links with other instruments. Included modification introduced by Order of 11th July 2017 on RT (see red wording below) English only
P. I	PREMIERE PARTIE - DISPOSITIONS PRELIMINAIRES / PART ONE - DEFINITIONS AND PRELIMINARY PROVISIONS				
1	Définitions (F) / Definitions (E)	1	1	1	- LOS-FSOA: Art. 1 - Changes made by Order of 11th July 2017 (Art. 2) on the definition of the "flight corridor" without any reference to "neutralization" outside this corridor. - IADC-SDMG (2007): § 3 (3.1 to 3.5.3) - UNGA-COPUOS-SDMG 62/217 (2007): no specific definitions see §1 to 3. - ISO-SDMR 24113 (2011): § 3 (§ 3.1 to 3.18). => For details on several definitions & acronyms, see Annex III the Comparison Table between RT-FSOA and IADC, UNGA and ISO Space Debris Mitigation Instruments.
2	Dispositions préliminaires (F) / Preliminary provisions (E)	2	2	2	- LOS-FSOA: Art 4 / Art. 2 & 3. Art. 4. 4°. Art. 13. Art. 7 on liability ↔ RT` Scope and exclusions (exclusion of manned mission) As to Space Debris (SD) instruments : - IADC-SDMG (2007): Introduction and § 1. - UNGA-COPUOS-SDMG 62/217 (2007): § 1 to 3. - ISO-SDMR 24113 (2011): Introduction and § 1. - EU ICOC (2014): I.1 – Purpose…(n°17 to n°22) – II. 4. - Measures on Outer space operations SDM (n°47 to 55).

N° (F)	Titres en français (F)	Dispositions Communes	Lancement d'OS	Maîtrise Et retour	Observations, references, links with other instruments
N° (E)	Heading in English (E)	Common provisions (Part. I, II, IV, V & 6)	Launch of a SO (Part II)	Control and return of (Part. III)	Included modification introduced by Order of 11th July 2017 on RT (see red wording below) English only:
P. II	DEUXIEME PARTIE - LANCEMENT D'UN OBJET SPATIAL PART TWO - LAUNCH OF A SPACE OBJECT		P. II	PIII	⇔ RT: Art. 3 to 27
T. I	Titre I – Champ d'application (F)		T. I	PIII-TI	Launch operations Launcher and its "components" (L&C) or "elements" or Launch vehicles (LV) included their Orbital Stage (LVOS) ⇔ RT: Unique article 3
S. I	Section I – Scope (E)		S. I	PIII-SI	
3	Champ d'application Scope		3	28	- LOS-FSOA: Art. 1. 4° (+ until end-of-life of stages and launcher elements): - IADC-SDMG (2007): 3.2.2 (LV), 3.2.3 (LVOS), 3.5.1 (L. Phase), 3.5.2 (Mission phase for LVOS), 3.5.3 (disposal of LVOS) - UNGA-COPUOS-SDMG 62/217 (2007): G.4 first para. - ISO-SDMR 24113 (2011): §1 (Scope) for unmanned systems with express exclusion of Launch phase safety. §3.9 on launch vehicle Orbital Stage (LVOS), for planned tasks and functions performed by a LVOS before its disposal. - EU ICOC (2014): I.1 (n° 20)
Launch safety phase, III S. II	Titre II : Dossier technique (F)		T. II	P. III – T. II	⇒ RT: Art. 4 to 27
	Section II : Technical File (E)		S. II	P. III – S. II	
C.I	Chapitre I – Documentation à fournir (F)		C. I	P. III – T. II CI	⇒ RT: Art. 4 to 10 ⇒ Document and mission planning as to SDM
	Chapter 1 – Required information (E)		C. I	P. III – S. II C.1	- IADC-SDMG (2007): § 4 (General guidance) - ISO-SDMR 24113 (2011): TR7 on SDM Plan

N° (F)	Titres en français (F)	Dispositions Communes / Common provisions (Part. I, II, IV, V & 6)	Lancement d'OS / Launch of a SO (Part II)	Maîtrise Et retour / Control and return of (Part. III)	Observations, references, links with other instruments
N° (E)	Heading in English (E)				Included modification introduced by Order of 11th July 2017 on RI (see red wording below) English only
4	Description... Description of the space operation and systems and procedures			29	- EU ICOC (2014) and UNGA-COPUOS-SDMG 62/217 (2007): no specific provision - DA 2009-643: Art. 1 II.1°
5	Notice Générale de conformité General notice of conformity			30	- DA 2009-643: Art. 1 II 2° a) - RT: Art. 6 to 10 - IADC-SDMG (2007): § 4.6 « compliance matrix » under General guidance (§ 4). - ISO-SDMR 24113 (2011): R 7.2.c) on "compliance matrix" and 7.3 as to "Approving Agent".
6	Normes internes et dispositions de gestion de qualité (F) Internal standards and quality management provisions			31	- FSOA Art. 4. first para - DA 2009-643: Art. 1 I. 2 and 1 II 2° b) - RT: articles 5 and 11 to 15 (Chapter 2 quality system requirements)
7	Etude de Danger (EDD) – évènements redoutés Hazard study (critical events, potential hazards)			32	- DA 2009-643: Art. 1 II 2° c) - RT: Articles 5, Art. 8 & 9, 16 & 17 on proof, mission analysis, and Art. 18 to 26 on requirements (Chap. 3) / Art. 9 - IADC-SDMG (2007): § 4 (General guidance) - ISO-SDMR 24113 (2011): TR 7 (SDM Plan)
8	Etude d'impact (environnement terrestre et spatial) Impact assessment (Terrestrial and Space environnement)			33	- DA 2009-643: Art. 1 II 2° d) - RT: Art. 5, Art. 7, Art. 21 - L161-1 Environment Code

N° (F)	Titres en français (F)	Dispositions Communes	Lancement d'OS	Maîtrise Et retour	Observations, references, links with other instruments
N° (E)	Heading in English (E)	Common provisions (Part. I, II, IV, V & 6)	Launch of a SO (Part II)	Control and return of (Part. III)	Included modification introduced by Order of 11th July 2017 on RT (see red wording below) English only
					- IADC SDMG 2007: MM 5, in particular 5.3.2 penultimate para. last sentence. - UNGA-COPUOS-SDMG 62/217 (2007): § 4, G 6 last sentence. - ISO-SDMR 24113 (2011): Introduction and § 1. TR 6 - EU ICOC (2014): § I 1 (n°17 to n°22).
9	Mesures de maîtrise des risques Hazard management measures		9	34	- DA 2009-643: Art. 1 II 2° e) - RT: Articles 5, 7, 8, 20 to 26 - IADC SDMG 2007: G4 - ISO-SDMR 24113 (2011): TR7
10	Mesures de secours Emergency measures		10	46.3 47 48.1 49.2	- LOS-FSOA: Art. 8, Art. 21-2° / L331-7 of CR on CNES on emergency measures - DA 2009-643: Art. 1 II 2 ° f) - RT: Art. 23 §3 - Minor drafting changes made by Order of 11th July 2017 (Art. 3).
C. II	Chapitre II – Exigences système qualité (F)		P. II - T. II C. II (F)	P. III - T. II C. II (F)	⇨ RT Art. 11 to 15 ⇨ no specific provision as to SD except as a consequence of mission planning
C. 2	Chapter 2 – Quality system requirements (E)		P. II - T. II C. 2 (E)	P. III - T. II C. 2 (E)	- IADC-SDMG (2007): § 4 (general guidance) - ISO-SDMR 24113 (2011): TR7 on SDM Plan
11	Assurance qualité		11	35	- LOS-FSOA: Art. 4 first paragraph (*alinea*) - DA 2009-643: Art. 1. I. 2°

N° (F)	Titres en français (F)	Dispositions Communes	Lancement d'OS	Maîtrise Et retour	Observations, references, links with other instruments
N° (E)	Heading in English (E)	Common provisions (Part. I, II, IV, V & 6)	Launch of a SO (Part II)	Control and return of (Part. III)	Included modification introduced by Order of 11th July 2017 on RT (see red wording below) English only
	Quality assurance		11		- RT Art. 16 (Required proof) §1 e) as to RAMS rules = Reliability, Availability, Maintainability, Safety study. This study which identifies all technical and functional risks, demonstrates that the desired safety objectives have been reached, enables the ranking of risks to be incorporated as of the design stage, along with a check on correct application of risk management measures (see REI-CSG's definitions in Art 1).
12	Compétences, moyens, organisation et installations Competence, resources, organisation and installation		12	36	- LOS-FSOA: Art. 4 al. 1 - DA 2009-643 : Art. 1.I. 2°
13	Visibilité technique Technical visibility		13	~36	- DA 2009-643: Art. 7 - RT: Art. 11.4. - Minor drafting changes made by Order of 11th July 2017 (Art. 4).
14	Revues techniques Technical reviews		14	37	- LOS-FSOA : Art. 7 - DA 2009-643 - Art. 19… (Tit./Sect. III on inspection)
15	Contractant, sous-traitants et clients Co-contractors, subcontractors and customers		15	38	- LOS-FSOA: Art. 1. 6°. 7. II. al. 1. Art ; 15. 2° al. 2, 19 & 20
C.III (F)	Chapitre III – Exigences spécifiques pour les opérations de lancement (F)		P. II T. II (F) Or S. II (E)	P. III T. II (F) or S. II (E)	⇨ RT Art. 16 to 26

N° (F) / N° (E)	Titres en français (F) / Heading in English (E)	Dispositions Communes / Common provisions (Part. I, II, IV, V & 6)	Lancement d'OS / Launch of a SO (Part II)	Maîtrise Et retour / Control and return of (Part. III)	Observations, references, links with other instruments Included modification introduced by Order of 11th July 2017 on RT (see red wording below) English only
C. 3 €	Chapter 3 – Specific requirements for the launch operations (E)		⇨ C. 3	C. 3 and C.4	
S. 1 (F)	Section 1 – Exigence techniques générales liées à l'opération de lancement (F).		P. II T. II (F) or S. II (E) C. 3	No specific S. (F) or S-S. (E) in P. III under C. 3 and C.4	
S-S. 1 (E)	Sub-section 1 – General technical requirements linked to the launch operation (E)		=>S.1 (F) =>S-S. 1 (E)		⇨ RT Art. 16 to 19
16	Justifications requises Required proof		16	-	- RT: Art. 7 (hazard study/critical events). Art. 8 (impact assessment) and associated references. =>Art. 11 on RAMS rules (Reliability. Availability. Maintainability. Safety study). On space objects (SO) see below Art. 35. - Minor drafting changes made by Order of 11th July 2017 (Art. 5).
17	Analyse spécifique de mission Specific mission analysis		17	48	- RT: Art. 7 (hazard study/critical events) & Art. 8 (impact assessment). - Art. 16. Art. 20. a and b. Art. 21 (§ 4, 5 & 7). - Minor drafting changes made by Order of 11th July 2017 (Art. 6).
18	Moyens embarqués de neutralisation On-board neutralisation systems		18	49	- RT: Art. 7 (hazard study/critical events) & Art. 8 (impact assessment). Art. 17. Art. 20. Art. 2&Art. 27 (/ launch site). - IADC SDMG 2007: MM 5.2 (3), 5.2.1 (4). 5.2.3.

N° (F)	Titres en français (F)	Dispositions Communes	Lancement d'OS	Maîtrise Et retour	Observations, references, links with other instruments
N° (E)	Heading in English (E)	Common provisions (Part. I, II, IV, V & 6)	Launch of a SO (Part II)	Control and return of (Part. III)	Included modification introduced by Order of 11th July 2017 on RT (see red wording below) English only
19	Suivi du volet retour d'expérience associé / Flight tracking and associated experience feedback		19	?	- UNGA-COPUOS-SDMG 62/217 (2007): G4. - ISO-SDMR 24113 (2011): no provision on launch phase safety - LOS-FSOA: Art. 4 Para. 1 & 2… for subsequent authorization application - RT: Art. 7 (/critical events) & 8.
S. 2	Section 2 – Objectifs quantitatifs pour la sécurité des personnes (F)		P. II T. II (F) or S. II (E) C. 3	No specific S. (F) or S-S. (E) in P. III under C. 3 and C. 4	⇨ RT: Art. 20 (unique) ⇨ dd ⇨ No « probability » rules set up by SDM instruments related to human safety: - IADC SDMG 2007: § 5.3.2 penultimate para. last sentence. - UNGA-COPUOS-SDMG 62/217 (2007): G6 last sentence. - ISO-SDMR 24113 (2011): R 6.3.4 the maximum acceptable risk shall be set up in accordance with norms issued by Approving Agents (3.1 and 3.16) - EU ICOC (2014): § I.1 (n°17 to n°22).
S-S. 2	Sub-section 2 – Quantitative objectives for human safety (E)		⇒ S.2 (F) ⇒ S-S. 2 (E)		
20	Objectifs quantitatifs pour la sécurité des personnes / Quantitative objectives for human safety		20	44	- RT: Art. 7 (hazard study/critical events) & Art. 8 (impact assessment), Art. 23. Art 21 - Minor drafting changes made by Order of 11th July 2017 (Art. 7). - ISO-SDMR 24113 (2011): TR 6.3.4
20.1	Probability of causing at least one casualty (cumulative risks - collective risk) a) lift-off risk - 2. 10⁻⁵ for the entire LP, included degraded launch and fall-back of non orbited components (boosters)		20.1	44.1	- As to Art. 20.1 a): ○ RT: Art. 23.1 on probability / fall-back zone - As to Art. 20.1 b): ○ RT: Art. 21.1 to 5 on limitation on debris (excluded Protected Region B interferences / Art. 21.6) ○ RT: Art. 23.1 on probability / fall-back zone - Minor drafting changes made by Order of 11th July 2017 (Art. 7).

N° (F) / N° (E)	Titres en français (F) / Heading in English (E)	Dispositions Communes / Common provisions (Part. I, II, IV, V & 6)	Lancement d'OS / Launch of a SO (Part II)	Maîtrise Et retour / Control and return of (Part. III)	Observations, references, links with other instruments. Included modification introduced by Order of 11th July 2017 on RI (see red wording below) English only
20.1	- 10^{-7} by nominal fall-back of those element designed to separate from LV without being placed in orbit. b) Re-entry risk - 2×10^{-5} for the "return phase" of each launcher element placed in orbit, in a controlled atmospheric re-entry; - including a specific allocation of 10^{-7} for nominal return of such element. - If a controlled atmospheric re-entry is impossible best efforts to meet a quantitative objective of 10^{-4} for the return phase of each launch element placed in orbit.		20.1		- ISO-SDMR 24113 (2011): • 3.3 definition of "casualty risk": probability that a person is killed or seriously injured. See TR 6.3.4 (Re-Entry). • No method of causality probability specified in the annex A, reference made to R 6.3.4's regime (/approving agent)
20.2	Calculation method of probability of casualty		20.2	44.2	Nota : The calculation, by the Operator, of probabilities of causality may use software or other tools formally recognized by CNES, in particular under the Guide of Good Practice below (Part V Art. 54), and made freely available under dedicated license. - Minor drafting changes made by Order of 11th July 2017 (Art. 7). - ISO-SDMR 24113 (2011): see observation under 20.1 above.

N° (F)	Titres en français (F)	Dispositions Communes	Lancement d'OS	Maîtrise Et retour	Observations, references, links with other instruments
N° (E)	Heading in English (E)	Common provisions (Part. I, II, IV, V & 6)	Launch of a SO (Part II)	Control and return of (Part. III)	Included modification introduced by Order of 11th July 2017 on RT (see red wording below) English only
20.3	"Specific" quantitative allocations for a risks of "particular" catastrophic damage		20.3	*Different wording in 44.3*	- DA 2009-643 - Art. 5 (License, preparation of the operation) mentioned on this article 20.3 - No "specific" allocation of risk provision in RT's Part III on SO. The corresponding article (44.3) just recalls that its probability objectives comprises nominal as well as non-nominal returns, without prejudice of articles 42 and 45 (nuclear safety, and uncontrolled re-entry of an End of life SO)... - Minor drafting changes made by Order of 11th July 2017 (Art. 7).
S. 3 S-S. 3	Section 3 - Limitation des débris spatiaux et prévention des collisions (F) Sub-section 3 - Space debris limitation and prevention of collisions risk (E)		P. II T. II (F) or S. II (E) C. 3 => S.3 (F) => S-S. 3 (E)	*No specific S. (F) or S-S. (E) in P. III under C. 3 and C. 4*	⇨ RT Art. 21 to 22 ⇨ The following RT's provisions are derived from best practices, guidelines or requirements set up by the international SDM instruments: IADC SDMG 2007, UNGA-COPUOS-SDMG 62/217 (2007), ISO-SDMR 24113 (2011), EU ICOC (2014)...
	=> *for information as to part III on SO* *Capacité de maîtrise de l'objet spatial (F)* Ability to control the space object (E)		-	*39 (PIII)*	⇨ *No direct equivalent to Art. 39 in this Part II (launching) regarding the operators' ability to control the Space Object (here the LVOS). See also on SO in Part Three, Sect. III below: Art. 32 (hazard study), 47 and 49 of regarding the performance of the Space operation.* ⇨ *Such objectives are in this part II expressed in terms of system design, mission planning, risk management, mitigation or probabilities (of risks tolerated): Art 10 / 23, Art. 20.1 a and b, the following Art.21*...
21	Limitation des débris spatiaux Space Debris (SD) limitation		21	*40 (Space debris limitation)*	- RT: Art. 7 (hazard study/critical events) & Art. 8 (impact assessment)

N° (F)	Titres en français (F)	Dispositions Communes	Lancement d'OS	Maîtrise Et retour	Observations, references, links with other instruments
N° (E)	Heading in English (E)	Common provisions (Part. I, II, IV, V & 6)	Launch of a SO (Part II)	Control and return of (Part. III)	Included modification introduced by Order of 11th July 2017 on RI (see red wording below) English only
				47 (nominal re-entries) 48 (status of the SO)	- Minor drafting changes made by Order of 11th July 2017 (Art. 8). - IADC SDMG 2007: § 4 - General guidance (GG), § 5 - Mitigation measures (MM). - UNGA-COPUOS-SDMG 62/217 (2007): § 4 – SDM Guidelines (G) - ISO-SDMR 24113 (2011): § 6 -Technical Requirements (TR) - EU ICOC (2014): II. 4 (Measures on Outer Space Operations and Space Debris Mitigation) n°49 to 55 included n°53 on Radio-frequency interference. => See also the definitions of End of Life (EoL), End of Mission (EoM), Nominal Operational phase (OP), Protected Regions, Phase of Command... in the Annex III's comparison list.

21.1	- Minimization of the production/release of SD during normal operation		21.1	40.1	- for launch of a single space object, a single launcher element (for example a stage) may be placed in orbit:
					- for launch of several space objects, a maximum of two launcher elements (for example a stage or the adapter structure) may be placed in orbit.
					- The above requirements do not apply:
					  - to pyrotechnic systems. The largest dimension of any products generated must be less than 1 mm;
					  - to solid propellant boosters. The size of any combustion debris generated in protected region B must be less than 1 mm. With regard to the design and operation of solid propellant boosters, the launch operator takes steps to avoid placing solid combustion products in long-term orbit which could contaminate protected region A.

N° (F)	Titres en français (F)	Dispositions Communes	Lancement d'OS	Maîtrise Et retour	Observations, references, links with other instruments
N° (E)	Heading in English (E)	Common provisions (Part. I, II, IV, V & 6)	Launch of a SO (Part II)	Control and return of (Part. III)	Included modification introduced by Order of 11th July 2017 on RI (see red wording below) English only
21.2	- Minimization of risks / SD returning to Earth (human safety, damage to property, environment…)		21.2	45.2 46, 47	- IADC SDMG 2007: MM 5.1 - UNGA-COPUOS-SDMG 62/217 (2007): G1 - ISO-SDMR 24113 (2011): TR 6.1.1 - EU ICOC (2014): II. 4…4.3 (n° 54 in routine mode) - RI: Art. 5 (General notice of conformity), Art. 7 (hazard study/critical events) & Art. 8 (impact assessment), Art 23 - IADC SDMG 2007: § 5.3.2 penultimate para. last sentence. - UNGA-COPUOS-SDMG 62/217 (2007): G6 last sentence. - ISO-SDMR 24113 (2011): R 6.3.4 - EU ICOC (2014): § I.1 (n°17 to n°22).
21.3	- Probability (10^{-3}) of accidental break-up. - prohibition of intentional fragmentation		21.3	40.2	- IADC SDMG 2007: G. n°5.2 without probability requirements. - UNGA-COPUOS-SDMG 62/217 (2007): G. n°2 without probability requirements. - ISO-SDMR 24113 (2011): TR. 6.2, 6.2.2.1&2 on probability (<10^{-3}) of accidental break-ups until end of life. - EU ICOC (2014): § II.4. (n°49 to 55) without probability requirements.
21.4	- Passivation following disposal phase (*retrait de service*)		21.4	40.3	=> Disposal Phase (DP), Passivation, as to stored energy, to avoid break-up. Between the End of Mission (EoM) and End of Life (after de-orbitation from the Protected Region): see relevant definitions in annex III.

N° (F)	Titres en français (F)	Dispositions Communes	Lancement d'OS	Maîtrise Et retour	Observations, references, links with other instruments
N° (E)	Heading in English (E)	Common provisions (Part. I, II, IV, V & 6)	Launch of a SO (Part II)	Control and return of (Part. III)	Included modification introduced by Order of 11th July 2017 on RI (see red wording below) English only
21.5	- Avoiding interference of Launcher and its Components (L&C) with **Protected Region A** (LEO) after the End of the Launch Phase (LP): ○ De-orbitation of L&C by controlled atmospheric re-entry after ELP; ○ If impossible: no presence 25 years after ELP, by uncontrolled atmospheric re-entry of L&C. Failing that: placing L&C to an orbit for which the perigee > Protected Region A for 100 years. - additional requirements since August 2017 regarding target orbit eccentricity with associated probability of success (new c and d)		21.5	40.4	- IADC SDMG 2007: G. n°5.2.1. - UNGA-COPUOS-SDMG 62/217 (2007): G. n°5. - ISO-SDMR 24113 (2011): TR 6.2.2.3 with probability requirements in Annex A. - EU ICOC (2014): § II.4. (n°51). => Avoiding interference of Launcher and its Components (L&C) with Protected Region A (LEO) after the End of the Launch Phase (LP): - Minor drafting changes made by Order of 11th July 2017 (Art. 8): ○ The first paragraph (alinea) on nominal controlled atmospheric re-entry to avoid interferences of L&C in Protected Region A was titled (a) without change of content ○ The second paragraph (alinea) on non-controlled atmospheric re-entry (25 years' rule…) was titled (b) without change of content - Completed by Order of 11th July 2017 as to Protected Region A (Art. 8) with additional requirements regarding the targeted disposal orbit eccentricity (+) of launchers components with associated probability of success: ○ A paragraph (c) is added as to following requirement: if the eccentricity (+) of the target orbit of L&C after disposal manoeuver is below 0.25 the probability of meeting requirements of a) and b) of this 21.5 shall be above 0.5 ○ Another paragraph (d) is added as to the following requirement: if the eccentricity of the target orbit of L&C after

N° (F)	Titres en français (F)	Dispositions Communes	Lancement d'OS	Maîtrise Et retour	Observations, references, links with other instruments
N° (E)	Heading in English (E)	Common provisions (Part. I, II, IV, V & 6)	Launch of a SO (Part II)	Control and return of (Part. III)	Included modification introduced by Order of 11th July 2017 on RI (see red wording below) English only
					disposal manoeuver is above 0.25 the probability of meeting requirements of a) and b) of this 21.5 shall be above 0.9 (*) Editor's note: The eccentricity measures how an orbit deviates from circular. A circular orbit has an eccentricity of zero; higher numbers indicate more elliptical orbits. - IADC SDMG 2007: G. n° 5.3.2. See also G. n°5.2.1 including specific provisions for self-destruct systems on (4) on radio frequency interference. - UNGA-COPUOS-SDMG 62/217 (2007): G. n°6. - ISO-SDMR 24113 (2011): TR. 6.3.3. - EU ICOC (2014): § II.4. (n°51 and n° 53 on harmful radio-frequency interference/ ITU regulations).
	Other orbits (MEO...)				- No protection requirements for other orbits (MEO...) in IADC SDMG 2007, UNGA-COPUOS-SDMG 62/217, EU ICOC and in FSOA's RT. - ISO-SDMR 24113: see § 5.3.3 Other orbits.
21.6	- Avoiding interference of Launcher and its Components (L&C) with Protected Region B (GEO) after the End of the Launch Phase (ELP) for more than one year, by placing in an graveyard orbit > Protected Region B.		21.6	40.5	- Minor drafting changes made by Order of 11th July 2017 (Art. 8): o The first paragraph (alinéa) in order to avoid interference of L&C with Protected Region B after the End of the Launch Phase (ELP) for more than one year has been titled (a) without any change of its content - Completed by Order of 11th July 2017 as to Protected Region A (Art. 8) with additional requirements regarding target orbit disposal eccentricity (•) with associated probability of success:

N° (F)	Titres en français (F)	Dispositions Communes	Lancement d'OS	Maîtrise Et retour	Observations, references, links with other instruments
N° (E)	Heading in English (E)	Common provisions (Part. I, II, IV, V & 6)	Launch of a SO (Part II)	Control and return of (Part. III)	Included modification introduced by Order of 11th July 2017 on RT (see red wording below) English only
					o A paragraph (b) is added regarding the following requirement: if the eccentricity (∗) of the target orbit of L&C after disposal manoeuver is above 0.25 the probability of meeting requirements of a) and b) of this 21.6 shall be above 0.9. (∗) *Editor's note*: the eccentricity measures how an orbit deviates from circular. A circular orbit has an eccentricity of zero; higher numbers indicate more elliptical orbits. - IADC SDMG 2007: G. n°5.3.1 (included a sub para. (2) on eccentricity requirement of GEO nominal orbit: less than or equal to 0.003). - UNGA-COPUOS-SDMG 62/217 (2007): G. n°7 - ISO-SDMR 24113 (2011): TR. 6.3.2 (general). § 3.8 (definition of GEO orbit). 6.3.2.2 (on disposal manoeuvres). On the eccentricity of GEO orbit see a) of § 6.3.2.2 (< or = to 0.003). - EU ICOC (2014): § II.4 (n°51, n° 53 on harmful radio-frequency interference/ ITU regulations and n°54 in nominal/routine operation).
21.7	- Probability of success of disposal maneuvers mentioned in 21. 4 to 6.		21.7	40.6	- Minor drafting changes made by Order of 11th July 2017 (Art. 8). - No specifications of probability in IADC SDMG 2007. UNGA-COPUOS-SDMG 62/217. EU ICOC. - ISO-SDMR 24113 (2011): - § 3.13. definition of probability of successful disposal. - § 6.3.1. Probability of successful disposal => at least 0.9 at the time disposal is executed.

N° (F) / N° (E)	Titres en français (F) / Heading in English (E)	Dispositions Communes / Common provisions (Part. I, II, IV, V & 6)	Lancement d'OS / Launch of a SO (Part II)	Maîtrise Et retour / Control and return of (Part. III)	Observations, references, links with other instruments Included modification introduced by: Order of 11th July 2017 on RT (see red wording below) English only
22	Prévention des risques de collision / Prevention of risks of collision		22	41	- Calculation methods / cases (3) in annex A. - RT: Art. 7 (hazard study/critical events) & Art. 8 (impact assessment) - Only risks of collision with manned Space Objects (≠ RT Art. 41 below / control of SO). - IADC SDMG 2007: § 5.4. - UNGA-COPUOS-SDMG 62/217 (2007): G. n°3. - ISO-SDMR 24113 (2011): only in d) of introduction. - EU ICOC (2014): § II.4. (n°52)
S. 4	Section 4 – Exigences liées à la retombée sur Terre (F)		P. II T. II (F) or S. II (E) C. 3	No specific S. (F) or S.-S. (E) in P. III under C. 3 and C. 4 => see:	
S-S. 4	Sub-section 4 – Requirements related to fall-back to Earth (E)		=> S.4 (F) => S.S. 4 (E)	- its C. 4 (under T/S II) - its T/S III	
23	Préventions des risques retombées (lanceurs et fragment => zone de retombée…) / Prevention of risks arising from fall-back by the launcher or fragments thereof		23	46 (controlled re-entry) 49 (intentional destruction)	- LOS-FSOA Art 8 & 21. 2° (/ CR L331-7) on emergency measures - RT: Art. 7 (hazard study/critical events), Art. 8 (impact assessment), Art. 10 (emergency measures) / this 23.3. Nota: The calculation, by the Operator, of probabilities as to fall-back zone determination may use software or other tools formally recognized by CNES, in particular under the Guide of Good

N° (F) / N° (E)	Titres en français (F) / Heading in English (E)	Dispositions Communes / Common provisions (Part. I, II, IV, V & 6)	Lancement d'OS / Launch of a SO (Part II)	Maîtrise Et retour / Control and return of (Part III)	Observations, references, links with other instruments Included modification introduced by Order of 11th July 2017 on RT (see red wording below) English only
	=> fall-back zone control with associated probability of determination (99.999 %)				**Practice below (Part V Art. 54), and made freely available under dedicated license.** International SDM instruments, without probability requirements: - IADC SDMG 2007: § 5.3.2 penultimate para. third sentence. - UNGA-COPUOS-SDMG 62/217 (2007): G. n°6 last sentence. - ISO-SDMR 24113 (2011): R. n° 6.3.3.2-b, 6.3.4 - EU ICOC (2014): on principles § I.1 (n°17 to n°22).
24	Épaves, récupération éléments lanceurs Wrecks and recovery of launcher elements		24	-	- LOS-FSOA: wrecks management appears to be basically out of scope of this space legislation (in particular as regards its extraordinary liability regime or Art. 13) since any space operation are completed. See definition of "Return" in RT's Art. 1, which ends when the space object is immobilized on the ground. - RT: Art. 7 (hazard study/critical events) & Art. 8 (impact assessment) and associated measures. - IADC SDMG 2007: § 5.3.2 penultimate para. (last sentence) and last para. - UNGA-COPUOS-SDMG 62/217 (2007): G. n°6 last sentence. - ISO-SDMR 24113 (2011): R. n° 6.3.3.2-b but not directly - EU ICOC (2014): on principles § I.1 (n°17 to n°22).
S. 5	Section 5 – Risques particuliers (F)		P. II I. II (F) or S. II (E) C. 3 =>S.5 (F)	*No specific S. (F) or S-S. (E) in P. III under C. 3 and C. 4*	⇐ RT Art. 25 and 26
S-S. 5	Sub-section 5 – Particular Hazards (E)		=>S-S. 5		

N° (F)	Titres en français (F)	Dispositions Communes	Lancement d'OS	Maîtrise Et retour	Observations, references, links with other instruments
N° (E)	Heading in English (E)	Common provisions (Part. I, II, IV, V & 6)	Launch of a SO (Part II)	Control and return of (Part. III)	Included modification introduced by Order of 11th July 2017 on RT (see red wording below) English only
			(E)	=> see its C.3 (under T/S. II)	
25	Sûreté nucléaire / Nuclear safety		25	42	- RT: Art. 7 (hazard study/critical events) & Art. 8 (impact assessment) and associated measures. - UNGA Resolution on Principe relevant to the Use of Nuclear Power Sources in Outer Space adopted on 14 September 1992 (Res. 47/68) + Safety framework for nuclear Power Source Applications in Outer Space as endorsed by UNGA (64/86/2010). - EU ICOC (2014): § I.3 (n°41) referring to UNGA Resolution 47/68 above. - No specific provisions on Nuclear propulsion in IADC° SDMG or ISO 24113.
26	Protection planétaire / Planetary protection		26	43	- RT: Art. 7 (hazard study/critical events) & Art. 8 (impact assessment) and associated measures. - Article IX of OST 1967 - "Planetary protection policy" standard published by Committee on Space Research (COSPAR). - Celestial bodies are not considered as protected region in IADC SDMG 2007, UNGA res. 62/217 and ISO 24113. - EU ICOC (2014) is applicable to any SO launched into Earth orbit or beyond
27	Exigences techniques liées au site de lancement / Technical requirements concerning the launch site		27	None	- REI-CSG (9 Dec. 2010) as issued by CNES' President - LOS-FSOA: Art. 4. §4 for other sites. - Out of scope of S IADC SDMG 2007, UNGA Res. 62/217, and ISO 24113 (§1 Scope).

N° (F)	Titres en français (F)	Dispositions Communes	Lancement d'OS	Maîtrise Et retour	Observations, references, links with other instruments
N° (E)	Heading in English (E)	Common provisions (Part. I, II, IV, V & 6)	Launch of a SO (Part II)	Control and return of (Part. III)	Included modification introduced by Order of 11th July 2017 on RI (see red wording below) English only
					- EU ICOC (2014): III 5; n° 79).

N° (F) / N° (E)	Titres en français (F) / Heading in English (E)	Dispositions Communes / Common provisions (Part. I, II, IV, V & 6)	Lancement d'OS / Launch of a SO (Part II)	Maîtrise Et retour / Control and return of (Part. III)	Observations, references, links with other instruments Included modification introduced by Order of 11th July 2017 on RT (see red wording below) English only
P.3	TROISIEME PARTIE – MAITRISE ET RETOUR SUR TERRE D'UN OBJET SPATIAL (F) PART THREE – COMMAND (OR CONTROL) AND RETURN TO EARTH OF A SPACE OBJECT (F)		P II	P III	⇨ RT Art. 28 to 49
T. I	Titre 1er – Champ d'application (F)		P. II T. I	P III => T. I (F)	⇨ RT. Art. 28 (unique) ⇨ Control and return to Earth of a Space object except S/C and LVOS covered by Part II above
S. I	Section I – Scope (E)		P. II S. I	P III => S. I (E)	
28	Champ d'application Scope		3	28	- Consistent with LOS-FSOA: Art. 1. 5° "phase of command but "the provision of this part do not apply to the control and return of stages and launchers elements". - IADC SDMG 2007: § 3.2.1 (S/C), § 3.5.2 (MP), § 3.5.3 (DP). - UNGA-COPUOS-SDMG 62/217 (2007): §4 (SDMG) first para. - ISO-SDMR 24113 (2011): § 1 (scope)– § 3.6 (EoL) § 3.7 (EoM) § 3.18 (S/C). - EU ICOC (2014): II 4.1 entitled "Measures on Outer Space Operations and Space Debris Mitigation (n°49 to 55 included n°53 on Radio-frequency interference).
T. II	Titre II – Dossier technique (F)		P. II T. II	P III => T. II (F)	⇨ RT Art. 29 to 46
S. II	Section II – Technical file (E)		P. II S. II	P III => S. II (E)	
C.I	Chapitre 1er – Document à fournir (F)		P. II T. II C. I	P III T. II => C. I (F)	⇨ RT. Art. 29 to 34

N° (F)	Titres en français (F)	Dispositions Communes	Lancement d'OS	Maîtrise Et retour	Observations, references, links with other instruments
N° (E)	Heading in English (E)	Common provisions (Part. I, II, IV, V & 6)	Launch of a SO (Part II)	Control and return of (Part. III)	Included modification introduced by Order of 11th July 2017 on RT (see red wording below) English only
	Chapter 1 – Document to be provided (E)		P. II S. II C. 1	P. III S. II => C. I (E)	
29	Description de l'opération… Description of the space operation and associated systems and procedures		4		- DA 2009-643: Art. 1 II 1° - RT: Art. 39 - Completed by Order of 11th July 2017 / RT (Art. 9) in or der to add the following requirement of providing information on the maximum duration of the operation foreseen initially
30	Notice générale de conformité General notice of conformity		5		- DA 2009-643: Art. 1 II. 2 ° a) - RT: Articles 31 to 34 (Chap. 1) and 47 and 48 (Part 3, Sect. III: Performance of the space operation). - IADC-SDMG (2007): § 4.6 on compliance matrix - ISO-SDMR 24113 (2011): R.7 (SDMP), included R 7.2.c) on compliance matrix and R 7.3 / Approving Agent.
31	Normes internes et dispositions de gestion de qualité Internal standards and quality management provisions		6		- FSOA Art. 4. first para - DA 2009-643: Art. 1 I. 2 and 1 II. 2 ° b) - RT: Articles 30 (conformity notice), Chapter 2: Quality system requirements (Art. 35 to 38).
32	Etudes de dangers – EDD ⇨ Sécurité des personnes Hazard study ⇨ Human safety		7		- DA 2009-643: Art. 1 II. 2 ° c) - RT: Articles 30 (conformity notice) + Art. 39 to 43 (Chap. 3 / common requirements on control on-orbit and return to Earth) + Art. 44 to 46 (Chap. 4 / requirements specific to return to Earth) - IADC SDMG 2007: G. N° 4 - UNGA-COPUOS-SDMG 62/217 (2007): no specific provision. - ISO-SDMR 24113 (2011): § 7

N° (F)	Titres en français (F)	Dispositions Communes	Lancement d'OS	Maîtrise Et retour	Observations, references, links with other instruments
N° (E)	Heading in English (E)	Common provisions (Part. I, II, IV, V & 6)	Launch of a SO (Part II)	Control and return of (Part. III)	Included modification introduced by: Order of 11th July 2017 on RT (see red wording below) English only
33	Etudes d'impact - EI ⇨ Environnement terrestre et spatial Impact Assessment - IA ⇨ Terrestrial and Space Environment		8	33	- DA 2009-643: Art. 1 II 2° d) - RT: Art. 30 (conformity notice). Art. 40 (Space debris limitation) To be linked with following international SDM measures: - IADC SDMG 2007: MM 5, in particular 5.3.2 penultimate para. last sentence. - UNGA-COPUOS-SDMG 62/217 (2007): § 4, G. 6 last sentence. - ISO-SDMR 24113 (2011): Introduction and § 1. TR 6... - EU ICOC (2014): § 1.1 (n°17 to n°22).
34	Mesures de maîtrise des risques Risk management measures		9	34	- DA 2009-643: Art. 1 II 2° e) - RT: Articles 30 (conformity notice), 32 (hazard study), 33, 40 to 46 - Minor drafting changes made by Order of 11th July 2017 (Art. 10). - IADC SDMG 2007: G. n°4. - UNGA-COPUOS-SDMG 62/217 (2007): No specific prov. - ISO-SDMR 24113 (2011): § 7.
	Mesures de secours *Emergency measures (on Part II)*		10	46.3 47 48.1 49.2 *Below*	*See Art. 46.3, 47, 48.1 (last para.),49.2 below*
C.II	Chapitre II – Exigence système qualité (F)		*P. II – T. II C. II*	P. III – T. II C. II (F)	⇒ RT Art. 35 to 38
	Chapter 2 – Quality System requirements (E)		*P. II – S. II C. 2*	P. III – T II C. 2 (E)	⇒ No specific quality system measures in SDM instruments of IADC, UNGA, ISO and EU.

N° (F)	Titres en français (F)	Dispositions Communes	Lancement d'OS	Maîtrise Et retour	Observations, references, links with other instruments
N° (E)	Heading in English (E)	Common provisions (Part. I, II, IV, V & 6)	Launch of a SO (Part II)	Control and return of (Part. III)	Included modification introduced by Order of 11th July 2017 on RT (see red wording below) English only
	Assurance qualité *Quality Assurance on Part II*		*11*	*31*	*See Art. 31 below on Part III*
35	Compétence, moyens, organisation et installations Competence, resources, organisation and installations		12	35	- LOS-FSOA: Art. 8, Art. 21-2° / L331-7 of CR on CNES - DA 2009-643: Art. 1 I. 2° and 1 II. 2° f) - RT: Art. 31 (quality management) ⇨ RAMS rules = Reliability. Availability. Maintenance. Liability. Safety.(art 11 and 16 above)
36	Faits techniques et d'organisation Technical and organisational events		13	36	- DA 2009-643: Art. 7 (Technical event) - RT: Art. 31 (quality management)
37	Revues techniques Technical reviews		14	37	- RT: Art. 31 (quality management)
38	Contractant et sous-traitants Co-contractors and subcontractors		15	38	- RT: Art. 31 (quality management)
C.III	Chapitre III- Exigences techniques spécifiques communes à la « maîtrise » en orbite et au retour (NDLR nominal ou non) sur Terre d'un objet spatial (F) Chapter 3 – Specific technical requirements common to "command" (or control) on-orbit and return (E.N. nominal or not) to Earth of a Space object. (E)		P. II – T. II C. III P. II – S. II C. 3	P. III – T. II C. III (F) P. III – T. II C. 3 (E)	⇨ Common requirements to command (control) on-orbit and return to Earth. ⇨ RT. Art. 39 to 43 ⇨ This Chapter 3 is to be completed by Chapter 4 below (Art. 44 to 46) on specific requirements for return to Earth ⇨ No direct concordance with sub-sections (Section in F.) n° 1 to 5 of Chapter 3 of Part II - S. II/T.II above. ⇨ This Chapter 3 is closely associated with SDM measures required by IADC, UNGA, ISO and EU relevant instruments, especially as to the End of Mission (EoM) and the related Disposal Phase (DP).
	PII-TII-CIII- Section 1 – Exigences techniques générales liées à l'opération de lancement		16 to 19	39	For recall: no corresponding Sub-section (Section) 's heading as to "General technical requirements" in this Part III on "command" (or control) and return to Earth of a space object (SO) contrary to what is put forward above in Part II on Launch of a SO

N° (F)	Titres en français (F)	Dispositions Communes	Lancement d'OS	Maîtrise Et retour	Observations, references, links with other instruments
N° (E)	Heading in English (E)	Common provisions (Part. I, II, IV, V & 6)	Launch of a SO (Part II)	Control and return of (Part. III)	Included modification introduced by Order of 11th July 2017 on RT (see red wording below) English only
	PII-SII-C3-Sub-section 1 – General technical requirements linked to the launch operation				
39	Capacité de maîtrise de l'objet spatial Ability to "command" (control) the Space Object		16 to 19 SS.1	39	- RT: Art. 32 (hazard study), 47 and 49 (this Part Three. Sect. III below: Performance of the Space operation). - To be considered as to cubesat or nano satellites constellation - Equivalent provision in Part II as to the "ability to control (or command) a SO" for a LV or a LVOS are set in its Section (*Titre*) II, Chap. 3, Sub-section (*Section*) 1. Art. 16 to 19.
	PII-TII-CIII- Section 3 – Limitation des débris spatiaux et prévention des risques de collision *PII-SII-C3-Sub-section 3 – Space debris limitation and prevention of collision risks*		21 to 22 SS. 3	40	- *For recall: no corresponding Sub-section (Section)'s heading as to "space debris limitation" in this Part III on "command" (or control) and return to Earth of a space object (SO) contrary to what is put forward above in Part II on Launch of a SO.*
40	Limitation des débris spatiaux (original heading of 2011) ⇨ Re-named in 2017 : «Protection de l'environnement spatial» Space debris limitation (original heading of 2011) ⇨ Re-named in 2017 : « Space Environnement protection »		21 SS. 3	40	- RT: Art. 32 (hazard study). - Protection of Space environment - Completed and/or redrafted by Order of 11th July 2017 / RT (Art. 11). - IADC SDMG 2007: § 4 - General guidance (GG), § 5 – Mitigation measures (MM). - UNGA-COPUOS-SDMG 62/217 (2007): § 4 – SDM Guidelines (G) - ISO-SDMR 24113 (2011): § 6 -Technical Requirements (TR) - EU ICOC (2014): II. 4 (Measures on Outer Space Operations and Space Debris Mitigation) n°49 to 55 included n°53 on Radio-frequency interference.

N° (F) / N° (E)	Titres en français (F) / Heading in English (E)	Dispositions Communes / Common provisions (Part. I, II, IV, V & 6)	Lancement d'OS / Launch of a SO (Part II)	Maîtrise Et retour / Control and return of (Part. III)	Observations, references, links with other instruments. Included modification introduced by Order of 11th July 2017 on RT (see red wording below) — English only
					⇨ See also the definitions of End of Life (EoL), End of Mission (EoM), Nominal Operational phase (OP), Protected Regions, Phase of Command… in the Annex III's comparison list.
40.1	- Nominal operations: no generation of debris		21.1 SS. 3	40.1	- Completed by Order of 11th July 2017 / RT (Art. 11) in order to allow the release in-orbit of one additional propulsion module, without prejudice of complying to S. III below (Art. 47 to 49). - IADC SDMG 2007: § 5.1 - UNGA-COPUOS-SDMG 62/217 (2007): G. n°1 - ISO-SDMR 24113 (2011): TR § 6.1. - EU ICOC (2014): II. 4.1 (n°49 to 55)
	- Minimizing excessive risks for individuals, property, … environmental pollution by hazardous substances		21.2	45.2	See Art. 45.2 below for concordance with Art. 21.2 of Part II
40.2	- Accidental break up probability < 10-3 until the SO's End-Of- Life (EOL)		21.3 SS. 3	40.2	- IADC SDMG 2007: G. n°5.2 without probability requirements. - UNGA-COPUOS-SDMG 62/217 (2007): G. n°2 without probability requirements. - ISO-SDMR 24113 (2011): TR. 6.2, 6.2.2.1&2 on probability (<10⁻³) of accidental break-ups until end of life. - EU ICOC (2014): § II.4. (n°49 to 55) without probability requirements.
40.3	- Passivation following Disposal phase (*retrait de service*)		21.4 SS. 3	40.3	⇒ **Disposal Phase (DP)**, Passivation, as to stored energy, to avoid break-up. Between the End of Mission (EoM) and End of Life (after de-orbitation from the Protected Region): see relevant definitions in annex III. - Completed by Order of 11th July 2017 / RT (Art. 11). In order t introduce the requirement to put an end, after disposal manoeuvres,

N° (F)	Titres en français (F)	Dispositions Communes	Lancement d'OS	Maîtrise Et retour	Observations, references, links with other instruments
N° (E)	Heading in English (E)	Common provisions (Part. I, II, IV, V & 6)	Launch of a SO (Part II)	Control and return of (Part. III)	Included modification introduced by Order of 11th July 2017 on RT (see red wording below) English only
					to any emission of radio frequency from the SO's platform or payload. - IADC SDMG 2007: G. n°5.2.1 including specific provisions for self-destruct systems on (4) on radio frequency interference. - UNGA-COPUOS-SDMG 62/217 (2007): G. n°5. - ISO-SDMR 24113 (2011): R 6.2.2.3 with probability requirements in Annex A + reference, in the ISO Introduction to the *ITU Recommendation on GEO Disposal*, ITU-RS.1003, January 2004 - EU ICOC (2014): § II.4. (n°51 and n° 53 on harmful radio-frequency interference/ ITU regulations).
40.4	- Avoiding interference of Launcher and its Components (L&C) with Protected Region A (LEO) after the End of the Operational phase: ○ De-orbitation of L&C by controlled atmospheric re-entry after ELP. ○ If impossible: no presence 25 years after ELP, by uncontrolled atmospheric re-entry of L&C. Failing that: placing L&C to an orbit for which the perigee > Protected Region A for 100 years - additional requirements since August 2017 regarding:		21.5 SS.3	40.4	=> After SO's operational phase to protect Low Earth Orbit (Region A): - Redrafted by Order of 11th July 2017 (Art. 11), in particular to take into account cubesat (as non-controlled Space object) as regard to Protected Region A: ○ The previous first paragraph (alinéa) related to controlled re-entry in order to meet the 25 years' duration rule of presence in this Protected Region A (LEO) is henceforth titled (a) and concerns only "controllable SO" (i.e. equipped with appropriate propulsion system). ○ The second previous paragraph (*alinéa*) is henceforth titled (b). It (just) privileges the controlled atmospheric re-entry as a mean to meet the objective above (25 years' rule…) or, failing that, requires to place the SO in a stable orbit for which the perigee remains above protected Protected Region A, for one hundred years following the end of the SO soperational phase . ○ A new paragraph (c) is added as to take into account Space Objects NOT equipped with appropriate propulsion system

N° (F) / N° (E)	Titres en français (F) / Heading in English (E)	Dispositions Communes / Common provisions (Part. I, II, IV, V & 6)	Lancement d'OS / Launch of a SO (Part II)	Maîtrise Et retour / Control and return of (Part. III)	Observations, references, links with other instruments / Included modification introduced by Order of 11th July 2017 on RI (see red wording below) — English only:
40.4	○ Space Objects NOT equipped with appropriate propulsion system ○ target orbit eccentricity with associated probability of success (new d and e)				(i.e. non controllable SO: CubeSat…). For this SO, the event for which the limit 25 years is calculated is the "injection", i.e. at the end of the launch phase (/ FSOA Art. 1.4), instead of the SO's end-of-life (or end-of-mission or end-of-operational phase) as stated elsewhere in this RI. ○ Another new paragraph, titled d) is added to introduce the following requirement: if the eccentricity (E) of the target orbit of L&C after disposal manoeuver is below 0.25 the probability of meeting requirements of a), b and c) of this 40.4 shall be above 0.5 ○ Another new paragraph (e) is added to set up the following requirement: if the eccentricity (E) of the target orbit of L&C after disposal manoeuver is above 0.25 the probability of meeting requirements of a), b) and c) of this 40.4 shall be higher than 0.9 - IADC SDMG 2007: G. 5.3.2. See also G. 5.2.1 including specific provisions for self-destruct systems on (4) on radio frequency interference. - UNGA-COPUOS-SDMG 62/217 (2007): G. n°6. - ISO-SDMR 24113 (2011): TR 6.3.3. - EU ICOC (2014): § II.4. (n°51, n° 53 on harmful radio-frequency interference/ ITU regulations, n°54 in nominal/routine operation)
	Protected Region A (LEO)				
	Other orbits (MEO…)		21.6 SS.3		- No protection requirements for other orbits (MEO…) in IADC SDMG 2007, UNGA-COPUOS-SDMG 62/217, EU ICOC and in FSOA's RI. - ISO-SDMR 24113: see § 5.3.3 Other orbits.
40.5	- Design for placing the SO in a "graveyard" orbit after its end-			40.5	=> Redrafted by Order of 11th July 2017 (Art. 11) as follows, regarding Protected Region B:

N° (F)	Titres en français (F)	Dispositions Communes	Lancement d'OS	Maîtrise Et retour	Observations, references, links with other instruments
N° (E)	Heading in English (E)	Common provisions (Part. I, II, IV, V & 6)	Launch of a SO (Part II)	Control and return of (Part. III)	Included modification introduced by Order of 11th July 2017 on RI (see red wording below) English only
	of-mission to avoid interference with Protected Region B (GEO)				○ A new paragraph (a) titles, without any change of content, the previous single paragraph requiring to avoid the presence of the SO in Protected Region B after the end of its operational phase for more than one year. ○ Additional paragraph b) et c) are introduced regarding targeted disposal orbit eccentricity with associated probability of success: - Paragraph (b) provides that if the eccentricity (E) of the target orbit of the SO after disposal manoeuver is above 0.25 the probability of meeting requirements of paragraph a) of this 40.6 shall be above 0.9. - Paragraph (c) provides that if the eccentricity (E) of the target orbit of L&C after disposal manoeuver is below 0.1; this orbit shall respect requirements of paragraph a) of this 40.5 above. - IADC SDMG 2007: G. n°5.3.1 (included a sub para. (2) on eccentricity requirement of GEO nominal orbit: less than or equal to 0.003. - UNGA-COPUOS-SDMG 62/217 (2007): G. n°7 - ISO-SDMR 24113 (2011): TR. 6.3.2 (general). § 3.8 (definition of GEO orbit), 6.3.2.2 (on disposal manoeuvres). On the eccentricity of GEO orbit see: a) of § 6.3.2.2 (< or = to 0.003). - EU ICOC (2014): § II.4. (n°51, n° 53 on harmful radio-frequency interference/ ITU regulations and n°54 in nominal/routine operation).

N° (F)	Titres en français (F)	Dispositions Communes	Lancement d'OS	Maîtrise Et retour	Observations, references, links with other instruments
N° (E)	Heading in English (E)	Common provisions (Part. I, II, IV, V & 6)	Launch of a SO (Part II)	Control and return of (Part. III)	Included modification introduced by Order of 11th July 2017 on RT (see red wording below) English only
40.6	- Probability to have sufficient energy for disposal manoeuvres		21.7 SS.3	40.6	=> Redrafted by Order of 11th July 2017 (Art. 11). The probability of being able to successfully carry out the disposal maneuvers mentioned in paragraphs 3, 4 and 5 above is duly specified in this 40.6 (instead of 40.7 in the original RT of 2011) at least at 0.85 (against 0.9 before). But this probability does not include the availability of energy resources, that must be calculated by the operator before the launch for the total duration of the operation as foreseen initially and take account of all systems, subsystems and equipment usable for these maneuvers, their level of redundancy, if any, and their reliability. - No equivalent requirement "on sufficient energy for DP manoeuvres" in part II (Art. 21.7) as to Launcher design... - No specifications of probability in IADC SDMG 2007. UNGA-COPUOS-SDMG 62/217, ISO-SDMR 24113, EU ICOC. - ISO-SDMR 24113 (2011): see probability of "successful disposal "below.
40.7	- Probability of success of disposal manoeuvres		21.7 SS.3	40.7	=> Redrafted by Order of 11th July 2017 (Art. 11). New § 7. The probability, calculated before the launch and at any time during SO's mission, of having sufficient energy resources to successfully carry out the disposal maneuvers mentioned in paragraphs 3, 4 and 5 above must be at least 0.99 (instead of 0.9 before). - No specifications of probability in IADC SDMG 2007. UNGA-COPUOS-SDMG 62/217, EU ICOC.

N° (F)	Titres en français (F)	Dispositions Communes	Lancement d'OS	Maîtrise Et retour	Observations, references, links with other instruments
N° (E)	Heading in English (E)	Common provisions (Part. I, II, IV, V & 6)	Launch of a SO (Part II)	Control and return of (Part. III)	Included modification introduced by Order of 11th July 2017 on RT (see red wording below) English only
					- ISO-SDMR 24113 (2011): - § 3.13. definition of probability of "successful disposal" - § 6.3.1. Probability of successful disposal => at least 0.9 at the time disposal is executed. - Calculation methods / cases (3) in annex A.
	PII-TII-CIII- Section 3 – Limitation des débris spatiaux et prévention des risques de collision PII-SII-C3- Sub-section 3 – Space debris limitation and prevention of collision risks		21 to 22 SS.3	41	For recall: no corresponding Sub-section (Section)'s heading as to "Space debris limitation and prevention of collision risks" in this Part III on "command" (or control) and return to Earth of a space object (SO) contrary to what is put forward above in Part II on Launch of a SO
41	Prévention des risques de collision Prevention of risks of collision		22 SS.3	41	- RT: Art. 32 (hazard study) - Risks of collision with manned Space Objects + Geostationary orbit (# RT Art. 22 above / launch of SO). - IADC SDMG 2007: § 5.4. - UNGA-COPUOS-SDMG 62/217 (2007): G. n°3. - ISO-SDMR 24113 (2011): only in d) of introduction. - EU ICOC (2014): § II.4. (n°52)
	PII-TII-CIII-Section 5 – Risques particuliers PII-SII-C3-Sub-section 5 – Particular hazards		25 to 26 SS.5	42 to 43	For recall: no corresponding Sub-section (Section)'s heading as to "Particular hazards" in this Part III on "command" (or control) and return to Earth of a space object (SO) contrary to what is put forward above in Part II on Launch of a SO.
42	Sûreté nucléaire Nuclear safety		25 SS.5	42	- RT: Art. 32 (hazard study). - UNGA Resolution on Principe relevant to the Use of Nuclear Power Sources in Outer Space adopted on 14 September 1992 (Resolution 47/68) - EU ICOC (2014): § I.3 (n°41) referring to UNGA Resolution 47/68 above.

N° (F)	Titres en français (F) / Heading in English (E)	Dispositions Communes / Common provisions (Part. I, II, IV, V & 6)	Lancement d'OS / Launch of a SO (Part II)	Maîtrise Et retour / Control and return of (Part. III)	Observations, references, links with other instruments / Included modification introduced by Order of 11th July 2017 on RI (see red wording below) English only
43	Protection planétaire / Planetary protection		26 SS.5	43	- No specific provisions on Nuclear propulsion in IADC' SDMG or ISO 24113 - RT: Art. 32 (hazard study). - Article IX of OST 1967 - "Planetary protection policy" standard published by Committee on Space Research (COSPAR). - Celestial bodies are not considered as protected region in IADC SDMG 2007, UNGA res. 62/217 and ISO 24113. - EU ICOC (2014) is applicable to any SO launched into Earth orbit or beyond.
C. IV	Chapitre IV – Exigences techniques spécifiques pour le retour (nominal ou non) d'un objet spatial. (F) Chapter 4 – Specific technical requirements for the return of a Space object (I.e. nominal or not). (E)		P II –TII- CIII	P III – TII C. IV (F)	⇨ Specific requirements for return to Earth ⇨ Art. 44 to 46 ⇨ No direct concordance with sub-sections (Section in F.) n° 1 to 5 of Chapter 3 of Part II - S. II/T II above ⇨ This Chapter 3 is closely associated with SDM measures required by IADC, UNGA, ISO and EU relevant instruments, especially as to the End of Mission (EoM) and the related Disposal Phase (DP). ⇨ This Part III's Chapter 4 for" the return of a Space object "has no relation with its corresponding Part II's chapter 4, the latter relating to "technical requirements concerning the launch site.
			P II –TII- CIII	P III – S II C. 4 (E)	
	PII-TII-CIII- Section 2 – Objectifs quantitatifs pour la sécurité des personnes		20 S.2	C. IV (F) 44	For recall: no corresponding Sub-section (Section)'s heading as to "Quantitative objectives for human safety" in this Part III on "command" (or control) and return to Earth of a space object (SO) contrary to what is put forward above in Part II on Launch of a SO.
	PII-SII-C3- Sub-section 2 – Quantitative objectives for human safety		20 SS. 2	C. 4 (E) 44	

N° (F)	Titres en français (F)	Dispositions Communes	Lancement d'OS	Maîtrise Et retour	Observations, references, links with other instruments
N° (E)	Heading in English (E)	Common provisions (Part. I, II, IV, V & 6)	Launch of a SO (Part II)	Control and return of (Part. III)	Included modification introduced by Order of 11th July 2017 on RI (see red wording below) English only
44	Objectifs quantitatifs (/ personnes) / retour sur Terre d'OS Quantitative human safety objectives for return of a SO to the Earth		20 SS.2	44	- RT: Art. 32 (hazard Study), 42 to 45 - Redrafted by Order of 11th July (Art. 12). ⇨ No "probability" specifications set up by international SDM instruments related to "human safety": - IADC SDMG 2007: § 5.3.2 penultimate para. last sentence. - UNGA-COPUOS-SDMG 62/217 (2007): G6 last sentence. - ISO-SDMR 24113 (2011): TR 6.3.4 the maximum acceptable risk shall be set up in accordance with norms issued by Approving Agents (3.1 and 3.16) - EU ICOC (2014): § I.1 (n°17 to n°22).
44.1	Probability of causing at least one casualty (i.e. probability that a person is killed or seriously injured). (collective risks) =>original requirements of 2011: - 2.10^{-5} for return of an integral SO - 2.10^{-5} for controlled atmospheric reentry with destruction of the SO - Best efforts to meet a quantitative objective of 10^{-4} if a controlled atmospheric re-entry with destruction is impossible ⇨ brought back to a unique objective of 10^{-4} for any return to Earth		20.1 (a) and (b) SS.2	44.1	- no prejudice / Art. 42 (nuclear safety) and Art. 45 (uncontrolled reentry of an end-of-life SO) ⇒ Redrafted by Order of 11th July 2017 (Art. 12): As refers to the return of a SO, the "quantitative objective of safety", expressed in maximum probability of causing at least one casualty is of 10^{-4} (instead of 2.10^{-5} / 2011 as recalled aside). - ISO-SDMR 24113 (2011): - 3.3 definition of "casualty risk": probability that a person is killed or seriously injured. See TR 6.3.4 (Re-Entry). - No method of causality probability specified in the annex A, reference made to TR 6.3.4's regime (approving agent)

N° (F)	Titres en français (F)	Dispositions Communes	Lancement d'OS	Maîtrise Et retour	Observations, references, links with other instruments
N° (E)	Heading in English (E)	Common provisions (Part. I, II, IV, V & 6)	Launch of a SO (Part II)	Control and return of (Part. III)	Included modification introduced by Order of 11th July 2017 on RT (see red wording below) English only
44.2	Calculation method of probability. =>original requirements of 2011: • Consideration of all phenomena leading to a risk of catastrophic damage; • Consideration of the trajectories before fragmentation; • Modelling of the fragmentation and debris generation scenarios corresponding to re-entry; • Dispersion of the debris on the ground and evaluation of their effects; • Consideration of the reliability of the space object.		20.2 SS.2	44.2	=> Completed by Order of 11th July 2017 (Art. 12) with the introduction of two additional considerations (as to original requirements of 2011 aside): • Strategy of atmospheric reentry (controlled or not) • Population at the date of foreseen re-entry • + five bullets on the left (original requirements of 2011) Nota : The calculation, by the Operator, of probabilities of causality may use software or other tools formally recognized by CNES, in particular under the Guide of Good Practice below (Part V Art. 54), and made freely available under dedicated license - ISO-SDMR 24113 (2011): - 3.3 definition of "casualty risk": probability that a person is killed or seriously injured. See TR 6.3.4 (Re-Entry). - No method of causality probability specified in the annex A, reference made to TR 6.3.4's regime (approving agent)
44.3	=> nominal and non-nominal re-entry of SO, no prejudice (Art. 42 and Art. 45)		Different wording in 20.3	44.3	The corresponding article 20.3 applicable to launch operations has a different wording, the latest: - Provides for "Specific" quantitative allocations for a risks of "particular" catastrophic damage; - Refers to the application of DA's Art. 5 on (License, preparation of the operation) - does not refers to any other RT's articles This Art. 44.3 on SO just recalls that its probability objectives comprises nominal as well as non-nominal returns, without prejudice of RT's articles 42 and 45 (nuclear safety, and un-controlled re-entry of an End of life SO). No reference to any DA's Article here ....

N° (F)	Titres en français (F)	Dispositions Communes	Lancement d'OS	Maîtrise Et retour	Observations, references, links with other instruments
N° (E)	Heading in English (E)	Common provisions (Part. I, II, IV, V & 6)	Launch of a SO (Part II)	Control and return of (Part. III)	Included modification introduced by Order of 11th July 2017 on RT (see red wording below) English only
	PII-TIII-CIII- Section 4 - Exigences liées au retour sur Terre		23 to 24 SS.4	45 to 47	*For recall: no corresponding Sub-section (Section)'s heading as to "Requirements related to fall-back to Earth" in this Part III on "command" (or control) and return to Earth of a space object (SO) contrary to what is put forward above in Part II on Launch of a SO.*
	PII-SIII-C3- Sub-section 4 - Requirements related to fall-back to Earth				
45	Rentrée non-contrôlée de l'OS en fin de vie. **Requirements concerning uncontrolled re-entry of an end-of-life SO** (not expressed in a form of probability of risk)		21.1 *16 and 17 as to justifications about Critical Events*	45.1	⇨ Choice of architecture and materials of the SO to limit the number and energy (kinetic or explosive) of fragments liable to reach the ground. - To be connected in this RT's Part III with : Art. 30 (General notice of conformity), Art. 32 (hazard study/critical events), Art. 33 (impact assessment), Art. 46 & 47. - The corresponding specifications of RT's article 21.1 applicable to launcher design (Part. II) are more detailed and specify explicitly the number of space debris allowed (one stage, or one stage + the adapter structure...).

N° (F)	Titres en français (F)	Dispositions Communes	Lancement d'OS	Maîtrise Et retour	Observations, references, links with other instruments
N° (E)	Heading in English (E)	Common provisions (Part. I, II, IV, V & 6)	Launch of a SO (Part II)	Control and return of (Part. III)	Included modification introduced by Order of 11th July 2017 on RI (see red wording below) English only
			21.2	45.2	⇨ Design and operation of the SO as to avoid "**unacceptable**" risk (instead of "excessive" in Art. 20.2 above on LV) for individuals, property, public health or the environment, as to "**elements**" liable to reach the ground. - IADC SDMG 2007: § 5.3.2 penultimate para. third sentence. - UNGA-COPUOS-SDMG 62/217 (2007): G. n°6 last sentence. - ISO-SDMR 24113 (2011): R. n° 6.3.3.2-b, 6.3.4 - EU ICOC (2014): on principles § I.1 (n°17 to n°22).
46	Prévention risques retombées (OS et fragments) en <u>rentrée contrôlée</u> Prevention of risks arising from fall-back of the SO or fragments thereof during <u>controlled</u> re-entry With associated probabilities of determination		23. 1&2 & SS. 4 16 and 17 as to justifications about Critical Events Others: 20 b §2 & 3	46. 1&2	⇨ Control of the fall-back zone of the SO and its fragments with an associated probability of success (Design and operation of the SO in order to avoid "**unacceptable**" risk (instead of "excessive" in Art. 20.2 above on LV) for individuals, property, public health or the environment, as to "**elements**" liable to reach the ground. ⇨ Associated with probabilities of fall-back zone determination of 99 % for a SO and 99.999 % for a fragments thereof (to compare with the unique probability of 99.999 % for launcher and elements as set up in Art 23.1 above) ⇨ Nota: The calculation, by the Operator, of probabilities of causality may use software or other tools formally recognized by CNES, in particular under the Guide of Good Practice below (Part V Art. 54), and made freely available under dedicated licenses

Nº (F)	Titres en français (F)	Dispositions Communes	Lancement d'OS	Maîtrise Et retour	Observations, references, links with other instruments
Nº (E)	Heading in English (E)	Common provisions (Part. I, II, IV, V & 6)	Launch of a SO (Part II)	Control and return of (Part. III)	Included modification introduced by Order of 11th July 2017 on RT (see red wording below) English only
					- To be connected in this RT's Part III with : Art. 30 (General notice of conformity), Art. 32 (hazard study/critical events), Art. 33 (impact assessment), Art. 46 & 47.
			23.3 as to 10	46.3	⇨ Information of competent authorities (/CNES…) in nominal, or non-nominal situations (emergency) of re-entry of SO and/or elements thereof - LOS-FSOA Art 8 & 21. 2° (/ CR L331-7) on emergency measures (/ this RT Art. 46.3) - DA 2009-643: Art. 1 II. 2° f) - IADC SDMG 2007: § 5.3.2 penultimate para. third sentence. - UNGA-COPUOS-SDMG 62/217 (2007): G. n°6 last sentence. - ISO-SDMR 24113 (2011): R. n° 6.3.3.3.2-b, 6.3.4 - EU ICOC (2014): on principles § I.1 (n°17 to n°22).
T. III	Titre III – Obligations liées à la conduite de l'opération spatiale (F)		No T. III.	Part III T III	⇨ This Section III (Titre III in F.) on obligations related to performance of the Space operation has no equivalent Section's heading in Part. II above as to launch operations. The latest encompasses in its corresponding requirements design, production and implementation of LV.
S. III	Section III – Obligations related to performance of the Space operation (E) => as to non-nominal situation		No S. III In Part II	Part III S III	⇨ Can be referred to provisions of Part II – S. II (or T II in F) – Chap 1 (Art. 10) and Chap 3 - SS (S) 1 to 4 (Art. 16 to 24). ⇨ No probability determination => determinist requirements ⇨ No Chapter's subdivision in this Section.

N° (F)	Titres en français (F) / Heading in English (E)	Dispositions Communes / Common provisions (Part. I, II, IV, V & 6)	Lancement d'OS / Launch of a SO (Part II)	Maîtrise Et retour / Control and return of (Part. III)	Observations, references, links with other instruments — Included modification introduced by Order of 11th July 2017 on RI (see red wording below) — English only
N° (E)					
47	Rentrées Non-nominales d'OS ⇨ Priorité à la limitation de risque au sol Non-nominal (premature or accidental) re-entries of SO ⇨ Priority on ground limitation risks		21.2 23.1 first sentence SS. 3 & 4 10/23.3 (emergency) Others: 20.1 b)	47	⇨ Art. 47 to 49 ⇨ Priority implementation of ground risk limitation measures - LOS-FSOA Art 8 & 21.2° (/ CR L331-7) on emergency measures (/RT Art. 46.3). - DA. Art. 1.II.2 (technical file), Art. 7 (technical events) - To be connected in this RT's Part III with: Art. 30 (General notice of conformity). Art. 32 (hazard study/critical events), Art. 33 (impact assessment), Art. 46 & 47. - IADC SDMG 2007: § 5.3.2 penultimate para. third sentence. - UNGA-COPUOS-SDMG 62/217 (2007): G. n°6 last sentence. - ISO-SDMR 24113 (2011): R. n° 6.3.3.2-b, 6.3.4 - EU ICOC (2014): on principles § I.1 (n°17 to n°22).
48	Etat de l'O.S ⇨ Capacité de réaliser les manœuvres de retrait de service Status of the SO ⇨ 1) Ability to perform disposal manœuvres (DP) ⇨ 2) Information to CNES		21 C.3, SS. 1 (16 to 18)	48	PII-SII-C3-Sub-section 3 – Space debris limitation and prevention of collision risks - LOS-FSOA Art 8 & 21.2° (/ CR L331-7) on emergency measures (/RT Art. 46.3). - DA. Art. 1.II.2 (technical file), Art. 7 (technical events) - To be connected in this RT's Part III with : Art. 30 (General notice of conformity). Art. 32 (hazard study/critical events), Art. 33 (impact assessment), Art. 40 (disposal manœuvres), Art. 44 (probability of casualty). Art. 46 & 47 above. - Explicit references made to RT's Articles 30 (conformity notice) and 40.3 to 5 (disposal manœuvres).

N° (F)	Titres en français (F)	Dispositions Communes	Lancement d'OS	Maîtrise Et retour	Observations, references, links with other instruments
N° (E)	Heading in English (E)	Common provisions (Part. I, II, IV, V & 6)	Launch of a SO (Part II)	Control and return of (Part. III)	Included modification introduced by Order of 11th July 2017 on RT (see red wording below) English only
					- IADC SDMG 2007: § 1.3, § 3.5.3, § 4.4 para. 1, MM. 5.2.1 on passivation, MM. 5.3.1, MM. 5.3.2 para. 1, MM. 5.4 last sentence - UNGA-COPUOS-SDMG 62/217 (2007): G. n°4, 5 (on passivation), G: n° 6 and 7. - ISO-SDMR 24113 (2011): § 1, § 3.4, §3.5, 3.11, 3.13, TR 6.3.2 and 6.3.3. - EU ICOC (2014): II. 4.1.
					PII-SII-C3-Sub-section 3 – Space debris limitation and prevention of collision risks
49	Destruction intentionnelle (d'OS) Intentional destruction (of SO)		21 C.3, SS. 3 18 neutralisation 10 / 23.3	49	- LOS-FSOA Art 8 & 21, 2° (/ CR L331-7) on emergency measures - Equivalent to REI-CSG' provisions on MSI-MSA (Art. 63 to 66 and 83 to 89) - RT 21.3 last sentence (Part II: on LV) on prohibition of "intentional fragmentation of launcher elements". - IADC SDMG 2007: MM. 5.2 Intro. (3), 5.2.3. - UNGA-COPUOS-SDMG 62/217 (2007): G. 4 - ISO-SDMR 24113 (2011). Intro. (a). TR. 6.2.1 - EU ICOC (2014): II. 4.1 n°51.

| P. IV | QUATRIEME PARTIE – CONFORMITE PRELIMINARE (CP) A LA REGLEMENTATION TECHNIQUE (F)

PART FOUR- PRELIMINARY CONFORMITY (PC) WITH THE TECHNICAL REGULATION | | | | ⇨ RT Art. 50 to 53 |

N° (F)	Titres en français (F)	Dispositions Communes	Lancement d'OS	Maîtrise Et retour	Observations, references, links with other instruments
N° (E)	Heading in English (E)	Common provisions (Part. I, II, IV, V & 6)	Launch of a SO (Part II)	Control and return of (Part. III)	Included modification introduced by Order of 11th July 2017 on RT (see red wording below) English only
	(E)				
T. I	Titre 1ᵉʳ – Champ d'application (F)				
S. I	Section I – Scope (E)				⇨ Applicable to all RT's requirements
50		50	all	All	⇨ Definition of critical systems and sub-systems: SS, SO, SO's platform associated with a monitoring and controlling system as applicable. Lauch Installation (Art. 27) - DA 2009-643: Art. 11 (on Preliminary Conformity- PC)
51		51	all	All	⇨ Design and development steps (or phases) of critical systems and sub-systems: Preliminary Design , Detailed Design, Production and Ground Testing , Qualification. - DA 2009-643: Art. 11 (on Preliminary Conformity- PC).
T. II	Titre II – Procédure de délivrance du document attestant conformié (F)				
S. II	Section II – Procedure for issue of the document certifying conformity (E)				
52	Pièces à fournir Documents to be provided	52	4 to 10	29 to 34	- DA 2009-643: Art 1. II. 2° (technical file). Art. 11 (on Preliminary Conformity- PC above) - RT: Art. 4 to 10 (Part II. S(T). I. Chapter 1) for launch system: Art. 29 to 34 (Part III. Sect. I. Chapter 2) for space system other than launch systems
53	Contrôle, essais et analyses Checks, tests and analyses	53	53	53	- DA 2009-643: Art. 11 (on Preliminary Conformity- PC) - RT: Art. 52 above

N° (F)	Titres en français (F)	Dispositions Communes	Lancement d'OS	Maîtrise Et retour	Observations, references, links with other instruments
N° (E)	Heading in English (E)	Common provisions (Part. I, II, IV, V & 6)	Launch of a SO (Part II)	Control and return of (Part. III)	Included modification introduced by: Order of 11th July 2017 on RT (see red wording below) English only
P. V	CINQUIEME PARTIE – GUIDE DES BONNES PRATIQUES (GBP) PART FIVE – GUIDE OF GOOD PRACTICES				⇨ RT: Art. 54 (Unique)
T. I	Titre unique Single Section				
54	Guide des bonnes pratiques Guide of good practices	54	54	54	⇨ Set up and defined by this RT's Art. 54 only

N° (F) / N° (E)	Titres en français (F) / Heading in English (E)	Dispositions Communes / Common provisions (Part. I, II, IV, V & 6)	Lancement d'OS / Launch of a SO (Part II)	Maîtrise Et retour / Control and return of (Part. III)	Observations, references, links with other instruments / Included modification introduced by Order of 11th July 2017 on RI (see red wording below) English only
P. V	SIXIEME PARTIE – DISPOSITIONS TRANSITOIRES ET FINALES (F) / PART SIX – INTERIM AND FINAL PROVISIONS (E)				⇨ RT: Art. 55 and 56
55	Dispositions transitoires / Interim provisions	55	55	55	- Minor drafting changes made by Order of 11th July 2017 (Art. 13) - To be considered as regards to relevant SD mitigation guidelines of IADC, UNGA and ISO associated with the named RT's articles.
55.1.	Opérations de lancement d'O.S. / S.O. Launch operations				
55.1 a)			For exempt. of 21.6 For cond. exempt. of 21.5		Launch system operated for the first time from French territory before 4th June 2008 (date of publication of FSOA): - Recognition of technical files already examined by CNES (Ariane & CSG) - Full exemption of RT's Art. 21. 6 (interference / Protected Region B-GEO after the end of the launch phase) - Conditional exemption of RT's Art. 21. 5 (best effort as to interference / Protected Region A after the end of the launch phase). ⇨ Ex: Ariane 5
55.1 b)			For exempt. of 21.6		Launch system operated for the first time from French territory between 4th June 2008 and 31st December 2011 (end of the year of the RT's publication): - Full exemption of RT's Art. 21. 6 (interference / Protected Region B-GEO) (but no conditional exemption of RT's Art. 21. 5 / Protected Region A-LEO)

N° (F)	Titres en français (F)	Dispositions Communes	Lancement d'OS	Maîtrise Et retour	Observations, references, links with other instruments
N° (E)	Heading in English (E)	Common provisions (Part. I, II, IV, V & 6)	Launch of a SO (Part II)	Control and return of (Part. III)	Included modification introduced by Order of 11th July 2017 on RT (see red wording below) English only
55.1 c)					⇨ Ex: Soyuz in Guyana (first launch on 21th October 2011 Launch system operated for the first time from French territory after 31st December 2011: - Full application of this RT ⇨ Ex :Vega (February 2012) , future Ariane 6 (> 2020)
55.2.	Operations de maitrise et de retour sur Terre d'O.S. S.O Control and return to Earth				
55.2 a)				-Partial application of 32,33 -Exempt of 38, 40.1, 40.2, 40.6, 40.7 and 45 - Best strategy for 40.3, 40.4, 40.5, and 41 - Best strategy + risk estimation for 44	SO launched before 10th December 2010 (date of entry into force of FSOA): - Application of RT's articles: o 32 (hazard studies) and 33 (impact assessment) limited to hazards and impacts associated with activities on the SO carried out after the 10th December 2010. - Full exemption of RT's articles: o 38: co-contractors and sub-contractors RT's compliance; o 40.1, 40.2, 40.6 and 40.7 for space debris limitation as to nominal operations (40.1), accidental break up (40.2), probability to have energy for disposal manoeuvres (40.6) and probability of success of disposal manoeuvres (40.7); o 45: Requirements / uncontrolled re-entry of an end-of-life SO.
55.2 a) (contd)					

N° (F)	Titres en français (F)	Dispositions Communes	Lancement d'OS	Maîtrise Et retour	Observations, references, links with other instruments
N° (E)	Heading in English (E)	Common provisions (Part. I, II, IV, V & 6)	Launch of a SO (Part II)	Control and return of (Part. III)	Included modification introduced by Order of 11th July 2017 on RT (see red wording below) English only

					- Best strategy to be implemented on the SO definition as to article:
					  ○ 40.3, 40.4 and 40.5 for Space debris limitation: on design for disposal energy passivation (40.3), on design for controlled re-entry of the SO's after its end-of-mission to avoid interference with Protected Region A (40.4) and on design for placing the SO in a graveyard orbit after its end-of-mission to avoid interference with Protected Region B (40.5);
					  ○ 41: Risk of collision (Manned SO →GEOSAT).
					- Best strategy on SO definition + performance of a risk estimation as to article:
					  ○ 44: Human safety objectives for return of a Space object to Earth.

55.2 b)				-Exemption of 40.1, 40.2 and 45
				- Best strategy for 40.3 to 40.6 and 41
				- Best strategy+ risk estimation for 44
					Launch system operated for the first time from French territory between 10th December 2010 (date of entry into force of FSOA) and 31st December 2020 (end of the first 10 years' period of FSOA's application):
					- Full exemption of RT's articles:
					  ○ 40.1 and 40.2: Space debris limitation on nominal operations (40.1) and accidental break up (40.2);
					  ○ 45: Requirements / uncontrolled re-entry of an end-of-life SO.
					- Best strategy to be implemented on the SO definition as to articles:
					  ○ 40.3, 40.4, 40.5 and 40.6 for Space debris limitation: on design for disposal energy passivation

N° (F)	Titres en français (F)	Dispositions Communes	Lancement d'OS	Maîtrise Et retour	Observations, references, links with other instruments
N° (E)	Heading in English (E)	Common provisions (Part. I, II, IV, V & 6)	Launch of a SO (Part II)	Control and return of (Part. III)	Included modification introduced by Order of 11th July 2017 on RI (see red wording below) English only

					(40.3). on design for controlled re-entry of the SO after its end-of-mission to avoid interference with Protected Region A (40.4), on design for placing the SO in a graveyard orbit after its end-of-mission to avoid interference with Protected Region B (40.5). and on probability to have energy for the SO disposal manoeuvres (40.6);
					   ○ 41: Risk of collision (Manned SO +GEOSAT).
					- Best strategy on SO definition + performance of a risk estimation as to article:
					   ○ 44: Human safety objectives for return of a SO to Earth.

56	Dispositions finales Final provisions	56	56	56	Execution by CNES' President LOS- FSOA's Article 28 *and 21*, CR *L.331-2. g) and L.331-6 to 8*

ANNEXE V – Line Ministry for the Centre National d'Études Spatiales

Line Ministry for the Centre National d'Études Spatiales

Decree	Prime Minister	Minister	Line Ministry
December 1961 - March 1962	Michel Debré	Pierre Guillaumat	Prime Minister Minister Delegate to the Prime Minister
27 April 1962	Georges Pompidou	Gaston Palewski	Prime Minister Minister of State responsible for Scientific Research and Atomic and Space Questions
12 March 1965		Yvon Bourges	Prime Minister Secretary of State to the Prime Minister responsible for Scientific Research and Atomic and Space Questions
8 January 1966		Alain Pierrefitte	Minister Delegate responsible for Scientific Research and Atomic and Space Questions
7 April 1967		Maurice Schumann	Prime Minister Minister of State responsible for Scientific Research and Atomic and Space Questions
4 June 1968		Christian de la Malène	Prime Minister Minister of State responsible for Scientific Research and Atomic and Space Questions
26 July 1968	Maurice Couve de Murville	Robert Galley	Prime Minister Minister to the Prime Minister responsible for Scientific Research and Atomic and Space Questions
18 July 1969 Constitutional Council, Decision n° 69-56 L du 9 July 1969	Jacques Chaban Delmas	François Ortoli	Minister for Industrial and Scientific Development
19 July 1972	Pierre Messmer	Jean Charbonnel	Minister for Industrial and Scientific Development
7 March 1974		Yves Guéna	Minister for Industry, Commerce and Crafts
14 June 1974	Jacques Chirac	Michel d'Ornano	Minister for Industry and Research

Decree	Prime Minister	Minister	Line Ministry
25 August 1976	Raymond Barre	Michel d'Ornano	Minister for Industry and Research
29 April 1977		Jacques Sourdille	Prime Minister Secretary of State to the Prime Minister responsible for Research
16 May 1978		André Giraud	Minister for Industry
28 July 1981	Pierre Mauroy	Jean-Pierre Chevènement	Minister of State, Minister for Research and Technology
30 March 1983		Laurent Fabius	Minister for Industry and Research
2 August 1984	Laurent Fabius	Edith Cresson Hubert Curien	Minister for Industrial Redeployment and Foreign Trade Minister for Research and Technology
17 April 1986	Jacques Chirac (cohabitation)	René Monory Alain Madelin	Minister of Higher Education and Research Minister for Industry, Post and Telecommunications, and Tourism
24 April 1986		René Monory Alain Madelin Alain Devaquet	Minister of Education Minister for Industry, Post and Telecommunications and Tourism Minister Delegate to the Minister for National Education responsible for Research and Higher Education
19 February 1987		René Monory Alain Madelin Jacques Valade	Minister of National Education Minister for Industry, Post and Telecommunications and Tourism Minister Delegate to the Minister for National Education responsible for Research and Higher Education
28 May 1988	Michel Rocard	Lionel Jospin Paul Quilès Jean-Pierre Chevènement	Minister of State, Minister of National Education, Research and Sports Minister of Post, Telecommunications and Space Minister for Defence

Decree	Prime Minister	Minister	Line Ministry
20 July 1988	Michel Rocard	Paul Quilès Hubert Curien Jean-Pierre Chevènement	Minister of Post, Telecommunications and Space Minister for Research and Technology Minister for Defence
18 June 1991	Edith Cresson	Paul Quilès Hubert Curien Pierre Joxe	Minister for Infrastructure, Housing, Transport and Space Minister for Research and Technology Minister for Defence
15 April 1992	Pierre Beregovoy	Hubert Curien Pierre Joxe	Minister for Research and Space Minister for Defence
8 April 1993-May 1995	Edouard Balladur (cohabitation)	François Léotard Gérard Longuet François Fillon	State Minister, Minister for Defence Minister of Industry, Post and Telecommunications and Export Trade Minister of Higher Education and Research Space Counsellor : Jérome Paolini
May to November 1995	Alain Juppé	François Bayrou Elisabeth Dufourcq François Fillon Charles Millon	Minister of National Education, Higher Education and Research Secretary of State for Research Minister for Information Technology and the Post Office Minister for Defence
November 1995 to June 1997		François Bayrou François d'Aubert François Fillon Charles Millon	Minister of National Education, Higher Education and Research Secretary of State for Research Minister Delegate responsible for the Post Office, Telecommunications and Space Minister for Defence
4 June 1997 to March 2000	Lionel Jospin (cohabitation)	Claude Allègre Alain Richard	Minister of National Education, Research and Technology Space Counsellor: Didier KecheMayr Minister for Defence
27 March 2000 to May 2002		Roger-Gérard Schwartzenberg Alain Richard	Minister for Research Space Counsellor: Philippe Duval Minister for Defence

Decree	Prime Minister	Minister	Line Ministry
May-June 2002	Jean-Pierre Raffarin	François Loos Michelle Alliot-Marie	Minister Delegate for Higher Education and Research Minister for Defence
June 2002 to March 2004		Claudie Haigneré Michelle Alliot-Marie	Minister Delegate for Research and New Technologies Space Counsellor: Eva Portier Minister for Defence
March 2004 to May 2005		François d'Aubert Michelle Alliot-Marie	Minister Delegate for Research Space Counsellor: Eva Portier Minister for Defence
May 2005 to May 2007	Dominique de Villepin	François Goulard Michelle Alliot-Marie	Minister of Higher Education and Research Space Counsellor: Cyrill Condé Minister for Defence
May 2007 to 14 November 2010	François Fillon I	Valérie Pécresse Hervé Morin	Minister of Higher Education and Research Space Counsellor: Edouard de Pirey from May 2007 to September 2009, then Nicolas Sennequier from October 2009 to November 2010 Minister for Defence
14 November 2010 to 27 February 2011	François Fillon II	Valérie Pécresse Alain Juppé	Minister of Higher Education and Research Space Counsellor: François Alter Minister for Defence
27 February 2011 to 10 May 2012	François Fillon III	Laurent Wauquiez Gérard Longuet	Minister of Higher Education and Research Space Counsellor: Emmanuel Terrasse Minister for Defence
May 2012 to August 2014	Jean-Marc Ayrault	Geneviève Fioraso Jean-Yves Le Drian	Minister of Higher Education and Research Space Counsellor: Riadh Cammoun Minister for Defence
August 2014-May 2017	Manuel Valls	Najat Vallaud-Belkacem Geneviève Fioraso Thierry Mandon Jean-Yves Le Drian	Minister of Higher Education and Research on August 26th 2014 Secretary of State for Research Space Counsellor: David Phiipona from 2014 to 2015 Secretary of State for Research on June 17th 2015 Space Counsellor: Gilles Rabin from 2015 to 2017 Minister for Defence

Line Ministry for the Centre National d'Études Spatiales

Decree	Prime Minister	Minister	Line Ministry
17 May 2017 to June 2017	Edouard Philippe (I)	Frédérique Vidal Sylvie Goulard	Minister of Higher Education, Research and Innovation Space Counsellor: David Cavaillolès – Order 30 May 2017 Minister for the Armed Forces
21 June 2017	Edouard Philippe (II)	Frédérique Vidal Florence Parly	Minister of Higher Education, Research and Innovation Space Counsellor: David Cavaillolès – Order 30 May 2017 Minister for the Armed Forces

Bibliography

1. CNES Law and French Space policy

CNES Constitutive Act (1961) official preliminary works:
National Assembly (Assemblée nationale):
- Minutes in *Documents de l'Assemblée Nationale 1961.*
- Act Draft n° 1429 and report n° 1460 by Michel Sy.
- First session 12 September 1961.
- Session of 13 October 1961, p. 569.
- Final discussion and adoption on 18 October 1961 session.

Senate (Sénat):
- Minutes in the 1961-1962 *Session Senate Journal.*
- Act Draft n° 29 and Report n° 97 by Jacques Baumel.
- First session 24 October.
- Session of 30 November 1961.
- Final discussion and adoption on 7 December 1961's session.

History:
CNES, *La Recherche spatiale*, bimestrial edited between 1962 and 1978.
A. Lebeau and R. Aubinière, *Le général Robert Aubinière, propos d'un des pères de la conquêtes spatiale française* (The General Robert Aubinière, words from one of funding fathers of the French Space conquest, l'Harmathattan, 5-7, rue de l'Ecole polytechnique, 75005 Paris, 2008 2008, ISBN: 978-2-296-05193-5.
C. Carlier, *The First Thirty Years at CNES – The French Space Agency*, para. 1, CNES from its origin to 1992, p. 3-57, la Documentation Française/CNES Paris 1994, English edition, 1995. ISBN: 2-11-003368-1.
IFHE – Institut Français d'Histoire de l'Espace, Hervé Moulin and Nathalie Tinjod. *la France et l'Europe Spatiale (1957-1972)* (France and the European space), Third meeting, Paris 30-31 October 2003, published on 2004, ISBN: 2-9518920-1-2
P. Lelong, *De Gaulle et son siècle* (F) (De Gaulle in his Century), Tome III, *Moderniser la France – La recherche scientifique et technique* (*Modernize France – Scientific and Technical Research*), Proceedings of the International days held in UNESCO, Paris, in 19-24 November 1990, organized by Charles de Gaulle's Institute, in La Documentation Française – Plon Collection Espoir. *See* contributions of P. Lelong under "le General de Gaulle et la recherche en France," p. 643 and "de l'action concertée Espace à la création

du CNES," p. 677-681; H. Curien under "Introduction," p. 735-737 and A. Lebeau under "Recherche spatiale," p. 742-744.

P. Varnoteaux, (F), *L'aventure spatiale française de 1945 à la naissance d'Ariane* (the French Space Adventure from 1945 to the birth of Ariane), Nouveau Monde Editions, 2015, p. 21, Square Etienne Saint-Charles, 75012 Paris ISBN: 978-2-36942-157-3.

CNES' Publication *'Témoignages'* or 'Testimonials', 1968-1998, *Le Centre spatial de Toulouse a 30 ans* or the Toulouse Space Center is 30 years old: deals with the CST establishment and history - October 1998.

IFHE – CNES 3A, *Proceedings of the Colloquium on the 50 years of CNES* hold on 9 February 2012 at CNES, Paris, 2 place Maurice Quentin. Published in December 2013.

Official and high level experts' reports on CNES and on French and European space policy (listed in chronological order):
CNES' Annual Reports from 1962 to nowadays. Published by CNES Communication Directorate, cnes.fr.

J.-P. Causse, rapport du directeur du Comité consultatif des programmes de la Conférence spatiale européenne (CSE), Janvier 1968.

P. Aigrain, *La politique spatiale française* – Rapport au ministre du développement industriel et scientifique (*the French Space Policy* – Report for the minister of scientific and industrial development), March 1970.

J.-P. Capron, *la politique spatiale française* – Report for the French Minister of industry, commerce and small businesses, October 1977.

P. Sahut d'Izarn, *L'Espace* – Rapport au ministre des postes et télécommunications et du tourisme, (Space, report for the Minister), November 1986.

F. Lepatre, *l'espace industriel européen* (the European Space Sector) rapport présenté au nom du Conseil Economique et Social (CES). JORF avis et rapport du CES, session 1988, séances des 28 et 29 juin 1988, – n° 11 NOR CES X 8800 112 V – Samedi 30 juillet 1988.

P. Loridant, Sénateur et rapporteur du "rapport sur les orientations de la politique spatiale française et européenne" (Orientation of the French and European Space Policy) au nom de l'Office parlementaire d'évaluation des choix scientifiques et technologiques (OPECST), enregistré à la Présidence de l'Assemblée nationale le 18.12.1991.

CNER, Rapport sur l'Evaluation du programme spatial français (Assessment report on the French space program). Experts: Gérad Megie, Jean Voge, Jean Carpentier, Noel Mignot, Jean-Loup Burgaud. Paris, 10 septembre 1992.

A. Paecht, *Une nouvelle donne pour l'espace militaire* – Rapport d'information à la Commission des finances de l'Assemblée Nationale (A new deal for military space, report to the National Assembly's Finance Commission…), n° 1892, 10 January 1995.

M. Carpentier, *la politique spatiale de la France dans le contexte européen et mondial* (The French space policy in the European and worlwide context). Rapport et avis adopté par le Conseil économique et social (CES), séance du 10 Juin 1997.

H. Revol, Senateur Sénateur et rapporteur du rapport *L'espace: une ambition politique et stratégique pour l'Europe* ('Space: a political and strategic ambition for Europe) au nom de l'Office parlementaire d'évaluation des choix scientifiques et technologiques (OPECST), enregistré à la Présidence de l'Assemblée nationale 3 mai 2001, n° 3033 (Sénat n° 293, 2 mai 2001).

X. Pintat, Sénateur, *coopération spatiale Franco-russe* (Space cooperation France-Russia), commission des affaires étrangères du Sénat, n° 283, session 2000-2001. Annexe au PV de la séance du 26 avril 2001, au titre du projet de loi ayant pour objet de ratifier le protocole du 19 janvier 1999 à l'accord franco-russe du 26 novembre 1996, dans le domaine de l'exploration et de l'utilisation de l'espace à des fins pacifiques.

R.-M. Bonnet, *rapport de la commission de réflexion sur la politique spatiale (CRPS) – sans un CNES fort, pas d'Europe spatiale* (or "report of the appraisal commission on space policy – without a strong CNES, no Space Europe"), draft on 15 January 2003. Commission set up by letter of mission on 12 November 2002 at the request of both supervising ministers of the CNES, Michelle-Alliot Marie, Minister of Defence, Claudie Haigneré, minister delegate on the research and the new technologies, in charge of space policy

A. Pompidou, avis et rapport du conseil économique et social (CES) *la politique spatiale de recherche et de développement industriel* (Space policy on industrial research and development); JORF "avis et rapport du CES, séance des 22 et 23 juin 2004," n° 19/2004, NOR: CES X000030419V. Mercredi 30 Juin 2004.

J.-L. Pujet (edited by), report from the Academy of Science to the Ministry ot Research, 'French Space Research'. EDP sciences, mars 2006. ISBN 2-86883-887-1, www.edp-sciences.org.

M. Alliot-Marie, Minister of Defence, *Donnons plus d'espace à notre défense – orientations d'une politique spatiale de défense pour la France et l'Europe* (Let us make more space for our defence – strategic guidelines for a space defense policy in France and Europe). In *Analyse et références*, February 2007, DICOD (délégation à l'information et à la communication de la defense). ISBN: 2-11-096440-5, www.defense.gouv.fr.

B. Bigot (Administrateur Général du CEA), Y. d'Escatha (Président Directeur Général du CNES) et L. Collet-Billon (Délégué Général pour l'Armement) *L'enjeu d'une politique spatiale : assurer durablement à l'Europe un accès autonome à l'espace* (A stake for space policy: ensuring an autonomous and sustainable access to space for the Europe), report submitted to the Prime Minister on 18 May 2009, and disclosed for public on 25 mai 2009. Can be downloaded from www.ladocumentationfrancaise.fr/rapports-publics.

J.-L. Pujet (sous la direction de), rapport de l'Académie des sciences au ministre de la recherche, *Les sciences spatiales – adapter la recherche française aux enjeux de l'espace*

(Space sciences – adapting French research to space issues). EDP sciences, October 2010. ISBN: 978-2-7598-0575-4, www.edpsciences.org.

Comité d'études pour la défense nationale (committee for national defence studies), Les cahiers de la défense nationale, *l'espace au service des opérations* (Space for operations). Paris, France 2nd Quarter 2011.

E. Sartorius, rapport pour le Centre d'analyse Stategique (CAP) auprès du Premier ministre *Une ambition spatiale pour l'Europe* (A space ambition for Europe); October 2011 www.strategie.gouv.

L. Wauquiez, Ministre de l'enseignement supérieur et de la recherche, *Stratégie spatiale française* (French Space Strategy) rapport de synthèse publié en 2012 en réponse à une demande faite en Conseil des Ministres le 23 mars 2011, dans la lignée du discours du Président de la République de février 2008 à Kourou en Guyane: http://www.enseignementsup-recherche.gouv.fr/strategie-spatiale-francaise.

D. Lucas, Directeur de l'Institut Choiseul, *Quelle politique spatiale pour la France? Donner plus d'espace à l'industrie* (Which space policy for France – Let us give more space to the industry) Juillet 2012, in *les notes stratégiques de l'institut Choiseul*, www.choiseul.info. ISBN: 979-10-91525-00-8.

AERES, Rapport d'auto évaluation 2010 du CNES à l'AERES (self-evaluation report of 2010 from CNES to AERES), Paris, le 15 Juillet 2012.

HCERES, Rapport d'évaluation du Centre National d'Études Spatiales – (Assessment report on CNES by the High committee of assessment of research and high education), April 2015.

G. Fioraso, former minister for higher education and research, V. Dedieu and L. Menetrier (rapporteurs), *Rapport au Premier ministre « Open Space - L'ouverture comme réponse aux défis de la filière spatiale »* (report to the Prime minister – "Open Space – openess as a response to the challenges of space sector"), published on 26 July 2016, can be downloaded from www.ladocumentationfrancaise.fr › Rapports publics

Other publications on CNES Law and French Space Policy:
R. Bensaid (CNES's Head of the documentation division), C. Van-Zandt (CNES' librarian) in partnership with H. Moulin (HMI/IFHE), *Histoire du CNES à travers le journal officiel 1961-2002* or *CNES history through the French official gazette 1961-2002*. Six books edited by CNES-Paris on 30 November 2002: Tome I – Ministers, Attributions, Central Administration (ISBN: 2-11-088534-1; 380 pages); Tome II – Organization and Functioning of CNES (ISBN: 2-11-088534-3; 384 pages); Tome III – Guyana – CNES' Subsidiary and Shareholdings ... (ISBN: 2-11-088534-X; 354 pages); Tome IV – International and Multilateral Treaties and Agreements (ISBN: 2-11-088535-2; 316 pages); Tome – V European Treaties and Agreements (ISBN: 2-11-088536-X; 374 pages); Tome VI – International Bilateral Agreements (ISBN: 2-11-088535-1; 370 pages).

C. Paquin (CNES's Head of the documentation division), C. Van-Zandt (CNES' librarian) in partnership with H. Moulin (HMI/IFHE) *Histoire du CNES à travers le journal officiel 2002-2009* or *CNES history through the French official gazette 2002-2009*. One consolidated book edited by CNES-Paris on 2010 (ISBN: 978-2-85440-019-9, 558 pages);

P. Clerc, *Le cadre institutionnel des activités spatiales en France : le CNES* (The institutional Framework of Space activities in France – CNES'statute and missions), in *le cadre institutionnel des activités spatiales des Etats*, under the direction of Simone Courteix – 1997, A. Pedone Editor, Paris, p. 64-89.

"Partnership between CNES and Industry: a New Market Oriented Approach," in *"New Space Market"* – Proceedings of International Symposium 26-28 May 1997, Strasbourg, France. Edited by G. Haskell and M. Rycroft – Edition International Space University – Kluwer Academic Publisher. *Les moyens juridiques et contractuels d'action des agences spatiales* (legal and contracting tools to support Space Agencies missions), under the direction of Prof. Philippe Achilleas, in *Pratiques juridiques dans l'industrie aéronautique et spatiale* 2014, éditions A. PEDONE, p. 157-197.

S. Courteix, France – *Législation et participation aux accords internationaux dans le domaine spatial*, (legislation and participation on international agreement in the space domain) *Annales de Droit aérien et spatial*, 1968/69.

B. Schmidt Tedd (DLR) "IV Modell CNES: Offendtlich-rechtliche Agentur mit industriell-Kommerziel Charakter" in *Staatliches Engagement bei partiell marktfähigen Raumfahrtanwendungen* published in Liber Amicorum, edited by K.-H. Böckstiegel, M. Benkö, W. Kröll, Köln 2001, p. 437-461.

2. French Space Operation Law

FSOA official preliminary works:
Ministry for Research and new technology in charge of Space affairs, Technology Directorate Space and Aeronautics Department: Study report "Evolution of Space Law in France" (synthesis available in English), edited on February 2003 by the Ministry documentation service, 1, rue Decartes 75231 Paris Cedex 05, www.recherche.gouv.fr.

State Council (Conseil d'Etat): Appraisal Studies, 6 April 2006, "A Legal Policy for Space Activities" (Pour une politique juridique des activités spatiales), edited by La Documentation Française, Paris 2006.

Senate: Mr. Henri Revol's report, on behalf of the Economics Affairs Commission, 15 January 2008, n° 161 et n° 328 (2007-2008).

National Assembly (Assemblée nationale): Mr. Pierre Lasbordes's report, on behalf of the Economics Affairs Commission, 2 April 2008, n° 775.

Books and publications with regard to French Law on space activities:

P. Clerc: "La prévention des contentieux: l'apport de la loi française relative aux opérations spatiales" (Prevention of Dispute: contribution of the French Space Operation Act), in *le règlement des différends dans l'industrie spatiale*, Conference proceedings of 9-10 October 2015 in Dijon (France), 2016, edited by L. Ravillon, Credimi-CNRS UMR 6295 – LexisNexis Editor EAN, 13, ISBN: 9782711025206, p. 41-65.

"The French Space Operation Act – one year of implementation," contribution au 6th Eilene "M. Galloway Symposium on Critical Issues in Space Law: A Comparative Look at National Space Laws and Their International Implications." *Proceedings of the International Institute of Space Law* 2011 (Eleven International Publishing, 2012), p. 543-554, ISBN: 978-94-90947-69-9.

"Consequences of the French Space Law on Space Operation on CNES' mission as a contracting space agency" in *Contracting for Space, Contract practice in the European Space Sector*, edited by L.J. Smith and I. Baumann, Ashgate Publishing Limited, September 2011.

"Consequences of the French Space Law on Space Operation (FSOA)" on CNES' mission as a space agency – IAC-IISL Prague September 2010.

A. Pedone, "La gestion et le partage des risques sous l'angle de la puissance publique et les solutions envisagées par la future loi spatiale française" (Risk management and haring from governmental views and future national space legislation solutions) – Air and Space Law Association (SFDAS) for its 2007' Studies Days, Dijon 2007 Editor, Paris.

The Institute of Air and Space Law of the University of Cologne and DLR, "French current plans for a national space legal framework" in "Project 2001" – Legal Framework for the Commercial Use of Outer Space, *Proceedings of an International Colloquium*, Cologne 29-31 May 2001, edited by K.-H. Böckstiegel. Carl Heymanns Verlag KG. Köln, p. 591-599.

"Plans of National Space Law," Proceedings of the "project 2001" – *Workshop on National Space Legislation*, 5-6 December 2000, Munich, Germany.

M. Couston, "l'avenement du droit spatial français (editorial) – commentaires sur la loi française relative aux opérations spatiales" (the advent of the French space law – Comments on the French law on space operations), in *Revue Française de Droit Aérien et Spatial*, vol. 247, July, August, September 2008, p. 325-332.

Droit spatial (space law), collection *mise au point*, Ellipse, Paris France, 2014, ISBN: 978-2-7298-8669-1, www.edition-ellipse.fr.

Droit spatial économique – régimes applicables à l'exploitation de l'Espace, Sides, Paris 1992, ISBN 2 86861 084 6.

L. Rapp, "Une loi spatiale française" (A French Space law), in *AJDA – Actualité Juridique Droit Administratif* – 29 September 2008, p. 1755-1763.

L. Ravillon, *Droit des activités spatiales, adaptation aux phénomènes de commercialisation et de privatisation* (Law on Space Activities – Adaptation to the Commercialisation and Privatisation Phenomenon). Litec 2004.

B. Schmidt Tedd and I. Arnold (DLR), "The French Act relating to space activities – From international law idealism to national industrial pragmatism", in *ESPI (European Space Policy Institute) Perspectives* No 11, August 2008. Available for free downloading from the ESPI website www.espi.or.at.

About the Author

Philippe Clerc is an internationally recognized expert and in-house practitioner in the field of space law and policy in France and Europe. He has a unique knowledge of the law-making process of the French Space Act: Being privileged to have initiated the first preliminary studies in this respect already in the early 2000s, he was monitoring the development of French Space Law in the Council of State's study group, in the government and parliamentary process in all related consultations between the stakeholders involved. Then, he was involved continuously until the end of 2017 in the implementation of French Space Legislation with regard to CNES responsibilities in this process.

His broad vision and understanding in matters of space law and policy are based *interalia* on experience gathered by occupying since 1989 a number of positions and responsibilities in the French Space Agency (CNES), the French Ministry of Research and Arianespace, the private European launch operator, where he could serve in a number of major space projects under international cooperation or under the aegis of the European Space Agency and the European Union.

Philippe Clerc is the Compliance and Ethics Senior Officer at CNES. He has been the Head of CNES' Legal Department from 2007 to 2017. He has also been member of the French delegation at the Legal Subcommittee of the United Nations Committee on the Peaceful Uses of Outer Space (UNCOPUOS), actively involved in the elaboration of all legal instruments which had been adopted and negotiated in that forum during the last decade. In the framework of his academic work, Philippe Clerc is guest lecturer on Space Law, Policy, and Strategy at technical universities for engineering: (ISAE, ENAC, ENPC in Toulouse) as well as at the International Space University (Strasbourg), the University of Burgundy, and at Paris-Saclay University. As a scholar and practitioner, Philippe Clerc holds the award of appreciation for his work, especially on French space legislation by the Board of Directors of the International Institute of Space Law (IISL). He is corresponding member at the International Academy of Astronautics (IAA) and alumni of the French Institute of High Studies of National Defense (IHEDN, 53°SN).

Essential Air and Space Law (Series Editor: Marietta Benkö)

Volume 1: Natalino Ronzitti & Gabriella Venturini (eds.), The Law of Air Warfare – Contemporary Issues, ISBN 978-90-77596-14-2

Volume 2: Marietta Benkö & Kai-Uwe Schrogl (eds.), Space Law: Current Problems and Perspectives for Future Regulations, ISBN 978-90-77596-11-1

Volume 3: Tare Brisibe, Aeronautical Public Correspondence by Satellite, ISBN 978-90-77596-10-4

Volume 4: Michael Milde, International Air Law and ICAO, ISBN 978-90-77596-54-8

Volume 5: Markus Geisler & Marius Boewe, The German Civil Aviation Act, ISBN 978-90-77596-72-2

Volume 6: Ulrich Steppler & Angela Klingmüller, EU Emissions Trading Scheme and Aviation, ISBN 978-90-77596-79-1

Volume 7: Heiko van Schyndel (ed.), Aviation Code of the Russian Federation, ISBN 978-90-77596-80-7

Volume 8: Zang Hongliang & Meng Qingfen, Civil Aviation Law in the People's Republic of China, ISBN 978-90-77596-91-3

Volume 9: Ronald M. Schnitker & Dick van het Kaar, Aviation Accident and Incident Investigation. Concurrence of Technical, ISBN 978-94-90947-01-9

Volume 10: Michael Milde, International Air Law and ICAO, second edition, ISBN 978-90-90947-35-4

Volume 11: Ronald Schnitker & Dick van het Kaar, Safety Assessment of Foreign Aircraft Programme. A European Approach to Enhance Global Aviation Safety, ISBN 978-94-9094-793-4

Volume 12: Marietta Benkö & Engelbert Plescher, Space Law: Reconsidering the Definition/Delimitation Question and the Passage of Spacecraft through Foreign Airspace, ISBN 978-94-6236-076-1

Volume 13: Heiko van Schyndel (ed.), Aviation Code of the Russian Federation, second edition, ISBN 978-94-6236-433-2

Volume 14: Alejandro Piera Valdés, Greenhouse Gas Emissions from International Aviation: Legal and Policy Challenges, ISBN 978-94-6236-467-7

Volume 15: Peter Paul Fitzgerald, A Level Playing Field for "Open Skies": The Need for Consistent Aviation Regulation, ISBN 978-94-6236-625-1

Volume 16: Jae Woon Lee, Regional Liberalization in International Air Transport: Towards Northeast Asian Open Skies, ISBN 978-94-6236-688-6

Volume 17: Tanveer Ahmad, Climate Change Governance in International Civil Aviation: Toward Regulating Emissions Relevant to Climate Change and Global Warming, ISBN 978-94-6236-692-3

Volume 18: Michael Milde, International Air Law and ICAO, third edition, ISBN 978-94-6236-619-0

Volume 19: Nataliia Malysheva, Space Law and Policy in the Post-Soviet States, ISBN 978-94-6236-847-7

Volume 20: Philippe Clerc, Space Law in the European Context, ISBN 978-94-6236-797-5